THE PAPERS OF

THOMAS JEFFERSON

JAMES P. McCLURE
GENERAL EDITOR

THE PAPERS OF

Thomas Jefferson

Volume 42
16 November 1803 to 10 March 1804

JAMES P. McCLURE, EDITOR

ELAINE WEBER PASCU, SENIOR ASSOCIATE EDITOR

TOM DOWNEY, MARTHA J. KING, AND
W. BLAND WHITLEY, ASSOCIATE EDITORS

ANDREW J. B. FAGAL AND MERRY ELLEN SCOFIELD,
ASSISTANT EDITORS

LINDA MONACO, EDITORIAL ASSISTANT

JOHN E. LITTLE, RESEARCH ASSOCIATE

PRINCETON AND OXFORD
PRINCETON UNIVERSITY PRESS

2016

Copyright © 2016 by Princeton University Press

Published by Princeton University Press, 41 William Street,
Princeton, New Jersey 08540

In The United Kingdom:
Princeton University Press, 6 Oxford Street,
Woodstock, Oxfordshire OX20 1TR

ISBN 978-0-691-17046-6

Library of Congress Number: 50-7486

This book has been composed in Monticello

Princeton University Press books are printed on
acid-free paper and meet the guidelines for permanence
and durability of the Committee on Production
Guidelines for Book Longevity of the
Council on Library Resources

Printed in the United States of America

SUPPORTERS

THIS EDITION was made possible by an initial grant of $200,000 from The New York Times Company to Princeton University. Contributions from many foundations and individuals have sustained the endeavor since then. Among these are the Ford Foundation, the Lyn and Norman Lear Foundation, the Lucius N. Littauer Foundation, the Charlotte Palmer Phillips Foundation, the L. J. Skaggs and Mary C. Skaggs Foundation, the John Ben Snow Memorial Trust, Time, Inc., Robert C. Baron, B. Batmanghelidj, David K. E. Bruce, and James Russell Wiggins. In recent years generous ongoing support has come from The New York Times Company Foundation, the Dyson Foundation, the National Trust for the Humanities, the Florence Gould Foundation, the "Cinco Hermanos Fund," the Andrew W. Mellon Foundation, the Pew Charitable Trusts, and the Packard Humanities Institute (through Founding Fathers Papers, Inc.). Benefactions from a greatly expanded roster of dedicated individuals have underwritten this volume and those still to come: Sara and James Adler, Helen and Peter Bing, Diane and John Cooke, Judy and Carl Ferenbach III, Mary-Love and William Harman, Frederick P. and Mary Buford Hitz, Governor Thomas H. Kean, Ruth and Sidney Lapidus, Lisa and Willem Mesdag, Tim and Lisa Robertson, Ann and Andrew C. Rose, Sara Lee and Axel Schupf, the Sulzberger family through the Hillandale Foundation, Richard W. Thaler, Tad and Sue Thompson, The Wendt Family Charitable Foundation, and Susan and John O. Wynne. For their vision and extraordinary efforts to provide for the future of this edition, we owe special thanks to John S. Dyson, Governor Kean, H. L. Lenfest and the Lenfest Foundation, Rebecca Rimel and the Pew Charitable Trusts, and Jack Rosenthal. In partnership with these individuals and foundations, both the National Historical Publications and Records Commission and the National Endowment for the Humanities have been crucial to the editing and publication of *The Papers of Thomas Jefferson*. For their unprecedented generous support we are also indebted to the Princeton University History Department and Christopher L. Eisgruber, president of the university.

FOREWORD

HE NAMED IT Orleans Territory. In November 1803, taking up his own pen when John Breckinridge seemed reluctant to frame a territorial government for the lands the United States was acquiring from France, Jefferson drafted a bill to make the more settled and agriculturally developed southern portion of the region "a territory of the US. under the name of the territory of Orleans." He sent the bill to Breckinridge, who would introduce it in the Senate without revealing the president's role in creating it. Jefferson had pulled the draft together "with more boldness than wisdom," he confided, creating something like an artist's canvas that contained only "a few daubs of outline." It became the basis for the enabling act for the territory that Congress passed in March 1804. In accordance with the plan that he had developed during the summer, upper Louisiana (that is, what we know as Arkansas and everything within the purchase to the north and west of it) would not be organized under territorial government or opened to new settlement, but would instead come under the jurisdiction of Indiana Territory.

He and his supporters saw the purchase as a harbinger of prosperity. "I look to this duplication of area for the extending a government so free and economical as ours," Jefferson wrote to Joseph Priestley, "as a great achievement to the mass of happiness which is to ensue." The legislature of Mississippi Territory declared that nothing since the achievement of American independence "has been more joyfully or more thankfully received" by the people. "I am happy and proud of my Government," proclaimed John Langdon of New Hampshire. Fully engaging for the first time the theories of Thomas Malthus, Jefferson argued that the addition of the vast tract west of the Mississippi River ensured that the United States was safe from any crisis of population growth outstripping the nation's ability to produce food.

The optimism overlooked complicating issues that demanded resolution. Jefferson ignored slavery in his bill for territorial government, but the day after he sent the draft to Breckinridge, he asked the Kentucky senator to insert a clause prohibiting the direct importation of slaves into the territory from outside the United States. Protracted debate in the Senate, largely unnoticed in Jefferson's correspondence, produced a different clause, but to the same effect, in the act of Congress. It did not include Jefferson's provision that would have freed the grandchildren of any slaves brought into the territory. The trade in enslaved persons required the administration's attention in other ways as well. With the passage of a South Carolina act allowing the importation of slaves, Secretary of the Treasury Albert Gallatin and Attorney General Levi Lincoln considered whether a $12\frac{1}{2}\%$ duty on merchandise could be applied (a discussion that soon shifted to Congress). A petition from ship captain Nathaniel Ingraham for a remission of his sentence caused Jefferson to review papers from the slave-trading case against Ingraham and Rhode Island merchant James D'Wolf. The president also delved into the details of Henry Putnam's case, in which a revenue cutter was complicit in slave trading in Georgia.

Another complication was dissonance between what Governor William C. C. Claiborne in New Orleans characterized as "serious doubts as to the capacity of the people to govern themselves" and the inhabitants' expectations. Jefferson predicted to DeWitt Clinton that the creation of territorial government for Louisiana "will encounter great difficulty," for "altho' it is acknoleged that our new fellow citizens are as yet as incapable of self-government as children, yet some cannot bring themselves to suspend it's principles for a single moment." The mayor of New Orleans, Jean Étienne Boré, spoke for many of the region's inhabitants when he reminded the president that "nos pères ont découvert, peuplé, dèfrichè ce pays: il est arrosé de notre Sang et de nos Sueurs"—*our fathers discovered, settled, and cleared this land; it is watered with our blood and sweat.*

News of the acquisition of Louisiana prompted inquiries from prospective candidates seeking any government employment that might develop. For example, "I contemplate removing to Louisiana, in March or April next," Virginian Peachy R. Gilmer wrote in February: "my pecuniary affairs will render any appointment of sufficient emolument to support me, very acceptable." Even apart from fielding applications for offices in the new territory that did not actually exist yet, managing appointments to office continued to demand much of the president's attention. There was a "prevailing Itch for Office" and a "numerous & sordid Tribe of Office Hunters," George Clinton observed. Moreover, Republicans continued to push for the removal of Federalists from government offices. The clamor from Rhode Island was particularly strong in the winter of 1803-1804. There, as two politicians from the state reminded the president, several "Federal Characters" could still be found in office, "and a major part of them as Bitter as wormwood."

Yet Jefferson believed the extreme Federalists were finished everywhere except in Congress, where they clung on and would, he thought, destroy themselves by their resistance on issues relating to Louisiana. He and others now routinely employed the labels Repub-

lican and Federalist, and used the term "party" for themselves as well
as their opponents. They sometimes called the opposition party simply the "Feds." Jefferson knew that he was "the single object" of the
"accumulated hatred" of his fiercest opponents and anyone he had
removed from office. They sought any occasion to come after him
with "bloody teeth & fangs." As he wrote to Thomas Cooper, "you
know that if I write as a text that two and two are four, it serves to
make volumes of sermons of slander and abuse." The 1804 presidential election must be a referendum, and he could not yet, as he wrote
to Elbridge Gerry, retire to "a life of tranquility." His opponents
"force my continuance," he explained.

He was particularly suspicious of the political leanings and influence
of the Bank of the United States and the merchant community. To
Gallatin in December, Jefferson cast the bank as a threat to legitimate
political authority, declaring that "I deem no government safe which
is under the vassalage of any self-constituted authorities." It was "the
greatest duty we owe to the safety of our constitution, to bring this
powerful enemy to a perfect subordination." To William Short, he
decried the "mass of anti-civism which remains in our great trading
towns," and he asked Littleton Tazewell at Norfolk if merchants in
port cities seemed ready to go along with the course set by his administration. Gallatin argued for the establishment of a branch of the
B.U.S. at New Orleans, assuring the president that bank directors
were not a threat. They would "vote as they please" and read newspapers that suited them, "but they are formidable only as individuals
and as Merchants, and not as Bankers." Tazewell reported that the
"whole attention" of the commercial sector in Virginia "is absorbed
by calculations of pecuniary profit and loss, and reflections of any
other kind are rarely permitted to disturb this chain of arithmetical
reasoning." Jefferson's concerns about "anti-civism" would not be
assuaged by Tazewell's observation that merchants "extolled to the
skies" any action by government that was to their benefit, "but when
a burden is imposed on them in common with their fellow Citizens,
they murmur and complain." Near the end of 1803, Jacob Crowninshield asserted that the country had at least $100 million in trading
capital at its command: "We shall be a great commercial nation almost against our inclination."

Above all, Jefferson sought harmony. "I wish to consolidate the
nation," he wrote Short, hoping to see the hardened opponents of his
political cause "disarmed either of the wish or the power to injure
their country." Recognition and acceptance of the correct course of action by everyone would avert costly conflict and promote the general

good. As he told a visiting delegation of Choctaw leaders, "by living in peace, we can help & prosper one another." To praise from the legislative council of the Mississippi Territory for the acquisition of the new lands by "the true American Policy, which prefers pacific Negotiation to rash and sanguinary measures," he replied: "By obtaining the exclusive navigation of the Missisipi we prevent the National dissensions which rival interests there would have been ever producing, & destroy the germ of future and inevitable wars." He continued: "That nations should, in friendship & harmony, take liberal & dispassionate views of their interfering interests, and settle them by timely arrangements, of advantage to both undiminished by injuries to either, is certainly wiser than to yield to short-sighted passions." He sought agreement, unity, and harmony on the personal level as well. To congressional leader John Randolph, he declared that he had no inclination to influence the political opinions even of his sons-in-law. Regarding interactions of the cabinet, he affirmed to Gallatin on 22 February that "there never has arisen a case and I am persuaded never will, where the respect we mutually entertain for the opinions of one another will not produce an accomodation of opinion." When Benjamin Henry Latrobe came into bitter conflict with William Thornton over designs for the Capitol building, Jefferson tried to soothe him with flattery: "it is to overcome difficulties that we employ men of genius." (Latrobe, unpersuaded, avowed: "I am prepared for open war.")

Similarly, he counseled unity and concord against any fissuring of Republican ranks. Republicans in Congress must be "aware of the necessity of accomodation & mutual sacrifice of opinion," he wrote to DeWitt Clinton. To Joseph T. Scott, who had written to him about accusations of the formation of a third party in Philadelphia, Jefferson conceded that someday splits might arise among the Republicans. He hoped it would not happen until "federalism is compleatly eradicated." Until then, "I think it the duty of every republican to make great sacrifices of opinion to put off the evil day." Yet privately, he made notes of political intelligence about Aaron Burr that Matthew Lyon and Benjamin Hichborn reported to him (see 31 December and 2 January). Burr himself called on Jefferson on 26 January, pledging his fealty and his wish to avoid "a disadvantageous schism" in the party. After Burr left, Jefferson made extensive notes of the conversation, confiding in them that he had never trusted the New Yorker.

Harmonious relations in the capital encountered a setback in December, when the British minister to the United States, Anthony Merry, and his wife, Elizabeth Leathes Merry, took umbrage at what they considered to be insults suffered at dinners at the president's and the Madisons' residences. The presumed offenses involved the failure to seat guests at the table by rank, Jefferson's failing to honor Elizabeth Merry by escorting her to the table, and the presence of French chargé Louis André Pichon at the same dinners. Jefferson refused to change the "pele-mele practice" that was based on a principle that in "social circles all are equal, whether in, or out, of office, foreign or domestic." In this case, harmony had its foundation in equality. Although he did not change the custom of his administration, he reluctantly saw that the "canons" of his republican administration's official etiquette were circulated and publicized. A collision of politics and polite society also disrupted harmony in New Orleans, where the dispute centered on whether to favor the new regime's Anglo-American style of dancing or Creole society's French dances at balls.

Early in 1804, Jefferson began his engagement with two material objects that came to be closely identified with him. In February, he used a double-penned writing machine—a polygraph—borrowed from Latrobe to make a duplicate of a message to Congress. He also tried writing letters using the device. He encountered frustrations, but set Latrobe and Charles Willson Peale to work to get him a polygraph of his own, modified to meet his specifications. And in January, from his supplier of books in Philadelphia, N. G. Dufief, he ordered two identical copies of the New Testament in Greek and Latin and two identical copies in English. These he would cut up, following a technique learned from Joseph Priestley, so that he could bring together each of the "morsels of morality" of Jesus. Although the English-language compilation he produced during his presidency has not been found, the multilingual scissors-and-paste edition he later compiled became known as the Jefferson Bible.

He spent the winter in Washington, but as was his custom, he ordered building materials and issued instructions by letter in an effort to keep renovation work on Monticello moving forward in his absence. He was also anxious to see work begun at Pantops to make it a residence for his daughter Mary and her family close to his own home. Mary was expecting a child, and as the time for the birth drew near, her father's and the family's anxiety grew. Mary's medical history, and her mother's death from a breast infection following Mary's birth, gave rise to the apprehension. The alarm subsided after the baby's birth in mid-February, until word reached Jefferson on 3 March that Mary was seriously ill. He was needed in Washington to sign bills passed by Congress as the first session of the Eighth Congress came to a close, and although he was wracked by "terrible anxiety," he could not leave. He would get away as soon as he could, he pledged in a hasty letter to Mary, and in the meantime, "god bless you my ever dear daughter and preserve you safe to be the blessing of us all."

This editorial team had the good fortune and great pleasure to be guided by Barbara Oberg from 1999 to early 2014. She came to the edition with a profound understanding of Jefferson's era based on deep engagement with the papers of his contemporaries Benjamin Franklin, Albert Gallatin, and Philip Mazzei. She led by example and fostered a warm collaborative spirit. She enlarged the staff, strengthened the project's utilization of modern tools and methods, and increased the edition's pace of production without compromising our commitment to the highest standards of scholarship. She oversaw the most significant revision of editorial policy since the project began and took the leading role in establishing procedures for handling the papers of Jefferson's vice presidency and presidency. With her rare combination of resolution and grace, she worked with Princeton University and other sponsors to establish a firm foundation of support for the editorial project. She gave us the benefit of her generosity, her warmth, and her erudition. Although her name no longer appears on our masthead, her influence is woven into the fabric of this edition.

ACKNOWLEDGMENTS

MANY individuals have given the Editors the benefit of their aid in the preparation of this volume, and we offer them our thanks. Those who helped us use manuscript collections, answered research queries, assisted with translations, or advised in other ways are William C. Jordan, Princeton University; Valeria Escauriaza-Lopez Fadul for Spanish translations; in the libraries at Princeton, Karin A. Trainer, University Librarian, and Elizabeth Z. Bennett, Colleen M. Burlingham, Stephen Ferguson, Daniel J. Linke, Deborah T. Paparone, AnnaLee Pauls, Ben Primer, and Don C. Skemer; James H. Hutson, Julie Miller, and the staff at the Manuscript Division of the Library of Congress, especially Jeffrey Flannery and Patrick Kerwin; Peter Drummey, Anna Clutterbuck-Cook, Elaine Heavey, and Laura Wulf of the Massachusetts Historical Society, especially Nancy Heywood for providing digital scans; Kathleen Williams, Lucy Barber, and Darrell Meadows of the NHPRC; Alan Degutis of the American Antiquarian Society; Robert C. Ritchie, Sara N. Ash Georgi, Juan Gomez, and Olga Tsapina at the Huntington Library; Anna Berkes, Endrina Tay, and Gaye Wilson of the Thomas Jefferson Foundation at Monticello; Paige Newman of the Virginia Historical Society; Nicole Bouché, Regina Rush, and the staff of Special Collections at the University of Virginia Library, especially the multispectral scans provided by Christina Deane and Taylor Krystowiak; Beatriz Hardy and Susan A. Riggs, Swem Library, the College of William and Mary; Brent Tarter, Library of Virginia; Molly Kodner of the Missouri History Museum Library and Research Center; Martin Levitt, Roy Goodman, Charles B. Greifenstein, Earl E. Spamer, and Keith S. Thomson of the American Philosophical Society; the Gilder Lehrman Institute of American History and Jean W. Ashton and Edward O'Reilly of the New-York Historical Society; Charles M. Harris of the Papers of William Thornton, and our fellow editors at the Thomas Jefferson Retirement Series at Monticello, the Adams Papers at the Massachusetts Historical Society, the Papers of George Washington and the Papers of James Madison at the University of Virginia, the James Monroe Papers at the University of Mary Washington, and the Papers of Benjamin Franklin at Yale University. For sharing her wisdom and knowledge about Monticello and its peoples, we are grateful to Lucia C. Stanton. For assistance with illustrations we are indebted to Alfred L. Bush of Princeton; Bonnie Coles of the Library of Congress; Natalia Martín Hernando, Museo Lázaro Galdiano; Lynn Parker of the Royal Botanic Gardens, Kew; and Diana Sykes of the Clements Library at the University of Michigan. Jason Bush, Helen Langone, and Paul Hayslett of IDM provided essential technical support. At Princeton, our thanks to Judith Hanson, Debora Macy, and Barbara Leavey at the Department of History and to Barbara Zlotnik, Ann Halliday, Janet Upperco, Steven Semenuk, Thomas Roddenbery, and Rand Mirante. For smoothing the editorial project's relocation to temporary office space we are grateful for the aid of Peggy Kehrer of the Firestone Library renovation team; Mary Ferlise at Princeton; Maria DiFalco-Orofino, Tracy Mincher Hall, Eugene Kaganovich, Larry Woods, and Jeffrey Rowlands at the library; Stacy Snyder of Richard L. Hoffman & Associates, Inc.; and Chris Dugan of Bohren's Moving and Storage. We thank Gretchen Oberfranc for careful reading. We appreciate especially the support and leadership of Peter J. Dougherty, director of Princeton University Press. We welcome Lauren Lepow as our volumes' guide through the publication process and give our most heartfelt thanks and good wishes to Linny Schenck. Others at the Press who never fail to give these volumes the benefit of their expertise are Adam Fortgang, Dimitri Karetnikov, Neil Litt, Elizabeth Litz, Erin Suydam, Meghan Kanabay, and Brigitta van Rheinberg.

This is the last of many volumes of this edition, including several of the Second Series and Retirement Series, to have the benefit of the incomparable eye and expertise of Jan Lilly. As she steps aside, she takes with her our warmest thanks. Early in her career, she worked as an apprentice and assistant under P. J. Conkwright, who gave the books their original design. A distinguished designer, Jan has preserved the volumes' graceful look and effortless utility as the edition has moved through different eras of Jefferson's life in documents, and as technologies of typography and book production have undergone significant changes. The volumes stand in tribute to her great contributions of—to borrow an image from Jefferson—both head and heart.

Two eminent members of the Advisory Committee, John Murrin and Robert Darnton, recently retired from their service with that group. They have our deepest appreciation for the intellectual support and practical counsel they have given this edition over the course of many volumes. With this volume, we welcome two members of the Princeton University faculty, David Bell and Sarah Rivett, to the project's advisory group.

EDITORIAL METHOD
AND APPARATUS

1. RENDERING THE TEXT

Julian P. Boyd eloquently set forth a comprehensive editorial policy in Volume 1 of *The Papers of Thomas Jefferson*. Adopting what he described as a "middle course" for rendering eighteenth-century handwritten materials into print, Boyd set the standards for modern historical editing. His successors, Charles T. Cullen and John Catanzariti, reaffirmed Boyd's high standards. At the same time, they made changes in textual policy and editorial apparatus as they deemed appropriate. For Boyd's policy and subsequent modifications to it, readers are encouraged to consult Vol. 1:xxix-xxxviii; Vol. 22:vii-xi; and Vol. 24:vii-viii.

The revised, more literal textual method, which appeared for the first time in Volume 30, adheres to the following guidelines: Abbreviations will be retained as written. Where the meaning is sufficiently unclear to require editorial intervention, the expansion will be given in the explanatory annotation. Capitalization will follow the usage of the writer. Because the line between uppercase and lowercase letters can be a very fine and fluctuating one, when it is impossible to make an absolute determination of the author's intention, we will adopt modern usage. Jefferson rarely began his sentences with an uppercase letter, and we conform to his usage. Punctuation will be retained as written and double marks of punctuation, such as a period followed by a dash, will be allowed to stand. Misspellings or so-called slips of the pen will be allowed to stand or will be recorded in a subjoined textual note.

English translations or translation summaries will be supplied for foreign-language documents. In some instances, when documents are lengthy and not especially pertinent to Jefferson's concerns or if our edition's typography cannot adequately represent the script of a language, we will provide only a summary in English. In most cases we will print in full the text in its original language and also provide a full English translation. If a contemporary translation that Jefferson made or would have used is extant, we may print it in lieu of a modern translation. Our own translations are designed to provide a basic readable English text for the modern user rather than to preserve all aspects of the original diction and language.

2. TEXTUAL DEVICES

The following devices are employed throughout the work to clarify the presentation of the text.

[. . .]   Text missing and not conjecturable.
[   ]   Number or part of a number missing or illegible.
[roman]   Conjectural reading for missing or illegible matter. A question mark follows when the reading is doubtful.
[*italic*]   Editorial comment inserted in the text.
<*italic*>   Matter deleted in the MS but restored in our text.

3. DESCRIPTIVE SYMBOLS

The following symbols are employed throughout the work to describe the various kinds of manuscript originals. When a series of versions is recorded, the first to be recorded is the version used for the printed text.

Dft   draft (usually a composition or rough draft; later drafts, when identifiable as such, are designated "2d Dft," &c.)
Dupl   duplicate
MS   manuscript (arbitrarily applied to most documents other than letters)
N   note, notes (memoranda, fragments, &c.)
PoC   polygraph copy
PrC   press copy
RC   recipient's copy
SC   stylograph copy
Tripl   triplicate

All manuscripts of the above types are assumed to be in the hand of the author of the document to which the descriptive symbol pertains. If not, that fact is stated. On the other hand, the following types of manuscripts are assumed *not* to be in the hand of the author, and exceptions will be noted:

FC   file copy (applied to all contemporary copies retained by the author or his agents)
Lb   letterbook (ordinarily used with FC and Tr to denote texts copied into bound volumes)
Tr   transcript (applied to all contemporary and later copies except file copies; period of transcription, unless clear by implication, will be given when known)

4. LOCATION SYMBOLS

The locations of documents printed in this edition from originals in private hands and from printed sources are recorded in self-explanatory form in the descriptive note following each document. The locations of documents printed from originals held by public and private institutions in the United States are recorded by means of the symbols used in the National Union Catalog in the Library of Congress; an explanation of how these symbols are formed is given in Vol. 1:xl. The symbols DLC and MHi by themselves stand for the collections of Jefferson Papers proper in these repositories; when texts are drawn from other collections held by these two institutions, the names of those collections will be added. Location symbols for documents held by institutions outside the United States are given in a subjoined list.

CLjC	James S. Copley Library, La Jolla, California
CSmH	The Huntington Library, San Marino, California
CtHC	Hartford Seminary Foundation, Connecticut
CtNhHi	New Haven Colony Historical Society, Connecticut
CtY	Yale University, New Haven, Connecticut
DLC	Library of Congress
De-Ar	Delaware Hall of Records, Dover
DeGH	Hagley Museum, Greenville, Delaware
IHi	Illinois State Historical Library, Springfield
KAbE	Dwight David Eisenhower Library, Abilene, Kansas
LU-Ar	Louisiana State University, Dept. of Archives and Manuscripts, Baton Rouge
MH	Harvard University Library, Cambridge
MHi	Massachusetts Historical Society, Boston
MdAA	Hall of Records Commission, Annapolis, Maryland
MdBJ-G	Johns Hopkins University, John Work Garret Library, Baltimore
MdHi	Maryland Historical Society, Baltimore
MoSHi	Missouri History Museum Library and Research Center, St. Louis
Ms-Ar	Mississippi Department of Archives and History, Jackson
NCooHi	New York State Historical Association, Cooperstown
NHi	New-York Historical Society, New York City
NN	New York Public Library
NNC	Columbia University Library, New York City

NNFoM	Forbes Magazine, New York City
NNMus	Museum of the City of New York
NNPM	Pierpont Morgan Library, New York City
NcU	University of North Carolina, Chapel Hill
NhHi	New Hampshire Historical Society, Concord
NhPoS	Strawbery Banke, Portsmouth, New Hampshire
NjMoHP	Morristown National Historical Park, New Jersey
NjP	Princeton University
PHarH	Pennsylvania Historical and Museum Commission, Harrisburg
PHi	Historical Society of Pennsylvania, Philadelphia
PPAmP	American Philosophical Society, Philadelphia
PU	University of Pennsylvania Library
PWacD	David Library of the American Revolution, Washington Crossing, Pennsylvania
TxU	University of Texas, Austin
R-Ar	Rhode Island State Archives, Providence
Vi	Library of Virginia, Richmond
ViHi	Virginia Historical Society, Richmond
ViU	University of Virginia, Charlottesville
ViW	College of William and Mary, Williamsburg, Virginia
VtMS	Archives of Secretary of State, Montpelier, Vermont

The following symbol represents a repository located outside of the United States:

GyLeU	Universität Leipzig Universitätsbibliothek, Germany

5. NATIONAL ARCHIVES DESIGNATIONS

Documents in the National Archives have the location symbol DNA, with identifications of record groups and series as follows:

RG 11	General Records of the United States Government	
	RA	Ratified Amendments of the United States Constitution
RG 26	Records of the United States Coast Guard	
	LL	Lighthouse Letters
	MLR	Misc. Letters Received
RG 28	Records of the Post Office Department	
	LPG	Letters Sent by the Postmaster General

RG 29   Records of the Bureau of Census

RG 42   Records of the Public Buildings and Public Parks of the National Capital

         LRDLS   Letters Received and Drafts of Letters Sent

         PC   Proceedings of the Board of Commissioners for the District of Columbia

RG 45   Naval Records Collection of the Office of Naval Records and Library

         LSO   Letters Sent to Officers

         LSP   Letters Sent to the President

RG 46   Records of the United States Senate

         EPEN   Executive Proceedings, Executive Nominations

         EPFR   Executive Proceedings, Foreign Relations

         LPPM   Legislative Proceedings, President's Messages

         LPPMRSL   Legislative Proceedings, Petitions, Memorials, Resolutions of the State Legislature

RG 53   Records of the Bureau of Public Debt

         RES   Registers, Estimates, and Statements

RG 56   General Records of the Department of the Treasury

         PFLP   Papers Relating to the Financing of the Louisiana Purchase

RG 58   Letters of the Internal Revenue Service

         LSCR   Letters Sent to the Commissioner of Revenue

RG 59   General Records of the Department of State

         CD   Consular Dispatches

         DL   Domestic Letters

         GPR   General Pardon Records

         LAR   Letters of Application and Recommendation

         MLR   Misc. Letters Received

         MPTPC   Misc. Permanent and Temporary Presidential Commissions

         RD   Resignations and Declinations

         TP   Territorial Papers

RG 75   Records of the Bureau of Indian Affairs
      LSIA   Letters Sent by the Secretary of War Relating to Indian Affairs

RG 76   Records of Boundary and Claims Commissions and Arbitrations

RG 84   Records of the Foreign Service Posts of the Department of State
      CR   Consular Records

RG 104   Records of the Mint
      DL   Domestic Letters

RG 107   Records of the Office of the Secretary of War
      LSMA   Letters Sent by the Secretary of War Relating to Military Affairs
      LSP   Letters Sent to the President
      MLS   Misc. Letters Sent
      RLRMS   Register of Letters Received, Main Series

RG 233   Records of the United States House of Representatives
      PM   President's Messages

RG 360   Records of the Continental Congress
      PCC   Papers of the Continental Congress

6. OTHER SYMBOLS AND ABBREVIATIONS

The following symbols and abbreviations are commonly employed in the annotation throughout the work.

Second Series   The topical series to be published as part of this edition, comprising those materials which are best suited to a topical rather than a chronological arrangement (see Vol. 1:xv-xvi)

TJ   Thomas Jefferson

TJ Editorial Files   Photoduplicates and other editorial materials in the office of The Papers of Thomas Jefferson, Princeton University Library

TJ Papers   Jefferson Papers (applied to a collection of manuscripts when the precise location of an undated, misdated, or otherwise problematic document must be furnished, and always preceded by the symbol for the institutional repository; thus "DLC: TJ Papers, 4:628-9" represents a document in the Library of Congress, Jefferson Papers, volume 4, pages 628 and 629. Citations to volumes and folio numbers of the Jefferson Papers at the Library of Congress refer to the collection as it was arranged at the time the first microfilm edition was made in 1944-45. Access to the microfilm edition of the collection as it was rearranged under the Library's Presidential Papers Program is provided by the Index to the Thomas Jefferson Papers [Washington, D.C., 1976])

RG   Record Group (used in designating the location of documents in the National Archives)

SJL   Jefferson's "Summary Journal of Letters" written and received for the period 11 Nov. 1783 to 25 June 1826 (in DLC: TJ Papers). This register, kept in Jefferson's hand, has been checked against the TJ Editorial Files. It is to be assumed that all outgoing letters are recorded in SJL unless there is a note to the contrary. When the date of receipt of an incoming letter is recorded in SJL, it is incorporated in the notes. Information and discrepancies revealed in SJL but not found in the letter itself are also noted. Missing letters recorded in SJL are, where possible, accounted for in the notes to documents mentioning them or in related documents. A more detailed discussion of this register and its use in this edition appears in Vol. 6:vii-x

SJPL   "Summary Journal of Public Letters," an incomplete list of letters and documents written by TJ from 16 Apr. 1784 to 31 Dec. 1793, with brief summaries, in an amanuensis's hand. This is supplemented by six pages in TJ's hand, compiled at a later date, listing private and confidential memorandums and notes as well as official reports and communications by and to him as Secretary of State, 11 Oct. 1789 to 31 Dec. 1793 (in DLC: TJ Papers, Epistolary Record, 514-59 and 209-11, respectively; see Vol. 22:ix-x). Since nearly all documents in the amanuensis's list are registered in SJL, while few in TJ's list are so recorded, it is to be assumed that all references to SJPL are to the list in TJ's hand unless there is a statement to the contrary

V   Ecu

f Florin

£   Pound sterling or livre, depending upon context (in doubtful cases, a clarifying note will be given)

s   Shilling or sou (also expressed as /)

d   Penny or denier

₶   Livre Tournois

℘   Per (occasionally used for pro, pre)

7. SHORT TITLES

The following list includes short titles of works cited frequently in this edition. Since it is impossible to anticipate all the works to be cited in abbreviated form, the list is revised from volume to volume.

ANB   John A. Garraty and Mark C. Carnes, eds., *American National Biography*, New York and Oxford, 1999, 24 vols.

Allen, *History of the United States Capitol*   William C. Allen, *History of the United States Capitol: A Chronicle of Design, Construction, and Politics*, Washington, D.C., 2001

Annals   *Annals of the Congress of the United States: The Debates and Proceedings in the Congress of the United States . . . Compiled from Authentic Materials*, Washington, D.C., Gales & Seaton, 1834-56, 42 vols. All editions are undependable and pagination varies from one printing to another. The first two volumes of the set cited here have "Compiled . . . by Joseph Gales, Senior" on the title page and bear the caption "Gales & Seatons History" on verso and "of Debates in Congress" on recto pages. The remaining volumes bear the caption "History of Congress" on both recto and verso pages. Those using the first two volumes with the latter caption will need to employ the date of the debate or the indexes of debates and speakers.

APS   American Philosophical Society

ASP   *American State Papers: Documents, Legislative and Executive, of the Congress of the United States*, Washington, D.C., 1832-61, 38 vols.

Bear, *Family Letters*   Edwin M. Betts and James A. Bear, Jr., eds., *Family Letters of Thomas Jefferson*, Columbia, Mo., 1966

Bedini, *Jefferson and His Copying Machines*   Silvio A. Bedini, *Thomas Jefferson and His Copying Machines*, Charlottesville, 1984

Betts, *Farm Book*   Edwin M. Betts, ed., *Thomas Jefferson's Farm Book*, Princeton, 1953

Betts, *Garden Book*   Edwin M. Betts, ed., *Thomas Jefferson's Garden Book, 1766-1824*, Philadelphia, 1944

Biog. Dir. Cong.   *Biographical Directory of the United States Congress, 1774-1989*, Washington, D.C., 1989

Brigham, *American Newspapers*   Clarence S. Brigham, *History and Bibliography of American Newspapers, 1690-1820*, Worcester, Mass., 1947, 2 vols.

Bush, *Life Portraits*   Alfred L. Bush, *The Life Portraits of Thomas Jefferson*, rev. ed., Charlottesville, 1987

CVSP   William P. Palmer and others, eds., *Calendar of Virginia State Papers . . . Preserved in the Capitol at Richmond*, Richmond, 1875-93, 11 vols.

DAB   Allen Johnson and Dumas Malone, eds., *Dictionary of American Biography*, New York, 1928-36, 20 vols.

Dexter, *Yale*   Franklin Bowditch Dexter, *Biographical Sketches of the Graduates of Yale College with Annals of the College History*, New York, 1885-1912, 6 vols.

DHSC   Maeva Marcus and others, eds., *The Documentary History of the Supreme Court of the United States, 1789-1800*, New York, 1985-2007, 8 vols.

Dictionnaire   *Dictionnaire de biographie française*, Paris, 1933- , 19 vols.

DNB   H. C. G. Matthew and Brian Harrison, eds., *Oxford Dictionary of National Biography, In Association with The British Academy, From the Earliest Times to the Year 2000*, Oxford, 2004, 60 vols.

DSB   Charles C. Gillispie, ed., *Dictionary of Scientific Biography*, New York, 1970-80, 16 vols.

DVB   John T. Kneebone and others, eds., *Dictionary of Virginia Biography*, Richmond, 1998- , 3 vols.

EG   Dickinson W. Adams and Ruth W. Lester, eds., *Jefferson's Extracts from the Gospels*, Princeton, 1983, *The Papers of Thomas Jefferson*, Second Series

Evans   Charles Evans, Clifford K. Shipton, and Roger P. Bristol, comps., *American Bibliography: A Chronological Dictionary of All Books, Pamphlets and Periodical Publications Printed in the United States of America from . . . 1639 . . . to . . . 1820*, Chicago and Worcester, Mass., 1903-59, 14 vols.

Ford   Paul Leicester Ford, ed., *The Writings of Thomas Jefferson*, Letterpress Edition, New York, 1892-99, 10 vols.

Gallatin, *Papers*   Carl E. Prince and Helene E. Fineman, eds., *The Papers of Albert Gallatin*, microfilm edition in 46 reels, Philadelphia, 1969, and Supplement, Barbara B. Oberg, ed., reels 47-51, Wilmington, Del., 1985

HAW   Henry A. Washington, ed., *The Writings of Thomas Jefferson*, New York, 1853-54, 9 vols.

Heitman, *Dictionary*   Francis B. Heitman, comp., *Historical Register and Dictionary of the United States Army*, Washington, D.C., 1903, 2 vols.

Heitman, *Register*   Francis B. Heitman, *Historical Register of Officers of the Continental Army during the War of the Revolution,*

April, 1775, to December, 1793, new ed., Washington, D.C., 1914

Higginbotham, *Pennsylvania Politics*   Sanford W. Higginbotham, *The Keystone in the Democratic Arch: Pennsylvania Politics 1800-1816*, Harrisburg, 1952

Jackson, *Lewis and Clark*   Donald Jackson, ed., *The Letters of the Lewis and Clark Expedition, with Related Documents, 1783-1854*, 2d ed., Urbana, Ill., 1978

JEP   *Journal of the Executive Proceedings of the Senate of the United States . . . to the Termination of the Nineteenth Congress*, Washington, D.C., 1828, 3 vols.

JHR   *Journal of the House of Representatives of the United States*, Washington, D.C., 1826, 9 vols.

JS   *Journal of the Senate of the United States*, Washington, D.C., 1820-21, 5 vols.

Kline, *Burr*   Mary-Jo Kline, ed., *Political Correspondence and Public Papers of Aaron Burr*, Princeton, 1983, 2 vols.

Kuroda, *Origins of the Twelfth Amendment*   Tadahisa Kuroda, *The Origins of the Twelfth Amendment: The Electoral College in the Early Republic, 1787-1804*, Westport, Conn., 1994

L & B   Andrew A. Lipscomb and Albert E. Bergh, eds., *The Writings of Thomas Jefferson*, Washington, D.C., 1903-04, 20 vols.

LCB   Douglas L. Wilson, ed., *Jefferson's Literary Commonplace Book*, Princeton, 1989, *The Papers of Thomas Jefferson*, Second Series

Latrobe, *Correspondence*   John C. Van Horne and Lee W. Formwalt, eds., *The Correspondence and Miscellaneous Papers of Benjamin Henry Latrobe*, New Haven, 1984-88, 3 vols.

Leonard, *General Assembly*   Cynthia Miller Leonard, comp., *The General Assembly of Virginia, July 30, 1619-January 11, 1978: A Bicentennial Register of Members*, Richmond, 1978

List of Patents   *A List of Patents Granted by the United States from April 10, 1790, to December 31, 1836*, Washington, D.C., 1872

Madison, *Papers*   William T. Hutchinson, Robert A. Rutland, J. C. A. Stagg, and others, eds., *The Papers of James Madison*, Chicago and Charlottesville, 1962-   , 37 vols.
    Sec. of State Ser., 1986-   , 10 vols.
    Pres. Ser., 1984-   , 8 vols.
    Ret. Ser., 2009-   , 2 vols.

Malone, *Jefferson*   Dumas Malone, *Jefferson and His Time*, Boston, 1948-81, 6 vols.

MB   James A. Bear, Jr., and Lucia C. Stanton, eds., *Jefferson's Memorandum Books: Accounts, with Legal Records and Miscellany, 1767-1826*, Princeton, 1997, *The Papers of Thomas Jefferson*, Second Series

Miller, *Alexandria Artisans*   T. Michael Miller, comp., *Artisans and Merchants of Alexandria, Virginia, 1780-1820*, Bowie, Md., 1991-92, 2 vols.

Miller, *Treaties*   Hunter Miller, ed., *Treaties and Other International Acts of the United States of America*, Washington, D.C., 1931-48, 8 vols.

Moulton, *Journals of the Lewis & Clark Expedition*   Gary E. Moulton, ed., *Journals of the Lewis & Clark Expedition*, Lincoln, Neb., 1983-2001, 13 vols.

NDBW   Dudley W. Knox, ed., *Naval Documents Related to the United States Wars with the Barbary Powers*, Washington, D.C., 1939-44, 6 vols. and *Register of Officer Personnel and Ships' Data, 1801-1807*, Washington, D.C., 1945

NDQW   Dudley W. Knox, ed., *Naval Documents Related to the Quasi-War between the United States and France, Naval Operations*, Washington, D.C., 1935-38, 7 vols. (cited by years)

Notes, ed. Peden   *Thomas Jefferson, Notes on the State of Virginia*, ed. William Peden, Chapel Hill, 1955

OED   J. A. Simpson and E. S. C. Weiner, eds., *The Oxford English Dictionary*, Oxford, 1989, 20 vols.

Papenfuse, *Maryland Legislature*   Edward C. Papenfuse, Alan F. Day, David W. Jordan, and Gregory A. Stiverson, eds., *A Biographical Dictionary of the Maryland Legislature, 1635-1789*, Baltimore, 1979-85, 2 vols.

Parry, *Consolidated Treaty Series*   Clive Parry, ed., *The Consolidated Treaty Series*, Dobbs Ferry, N.Y., 1969-81, 231 vols.

Peale, *Papers*   Lillian B. Miller and others, eds., *The Selected Papers of Charles Willson Peale and His Family*, New Haven, 1983-2000, 5 vols. in 6

PMHB   *Pennsylvania Magazine of History and Biography*, 1877-

PW   Wilbur S. Howell, ed., *Jefferson's Parliamentary Writings*, Princeton, 1988, *The Papers of Thomas Jefferson*, Second Series

RCHS   *Records of the Columbia Historical Society*, 1895-1989

Rowland, *Claiborne Letter Books*   Dunbar Rowland, ed., *The Official Letter Books of W. C. C. Claiborne, 1801-1816*, Jackson, Miss., 1917, 6 vols.

RS   J. Jefferson Looney and others, eds., *The Papers of Thomas Jefferson: Retirement Series*, Princeton, 2004-   , 11 vols.

S.C. Biographical Directory, House of Representatives   J. S. R. Faunt, Walter B. Edgar, N. Louise Bailey, and others, eds., *Biographical Directory of the South Carolina House of Representatives*, Columbia, S.C., 1974-92, 5 vols.

Shaw-Shoemaker   Ralph R. Shaw and Richard H. Shoemaker, comps., *American Bibliography: A Preliminary Checklist for 1801-1819*, New York, 1958-63, 22 vols.

Sowerby   E. Millicent Sowerby, comp., *Catalogue of the Library of Thomas Jefferson*, Washington, D.C., 1952-59, 5 vols.

Stanton, *Free Some Day*   Lucia Stanton, *Free Some Day: The African-American Families of Monticello*, Charlottesville, 2000

Stets, *Postmasters*   Robert J. Stets, *Postmasters & Postoffices of the United States 1782-1811*, Lake Oswego, Ore., 1994

Sturtevant, *Handbook*   William C. Sturtevant, *Handbook of North American Indians*, Washington, 1978- , 15 vols.

Syrett, *Hamilton*   Harold C. Syrett and others, eds., *The Papers of Alexander Hamilton*, New York, 1961-87, 27 vols.

Terr. Papers   Clarence E. Carter and John Porter Bloom, eds., *The Territorial Papers of the United States*, Washington, D.C., 1934-75, 28 vols.

TJR   Thomas Jefferson Randolph, ed., *Memoir, Correspondence, and Miscellanies, from the Papers of Thomas Jefferson*, Charlottesville, 1829, 4 vols.

Tulard, *Dictionnaire Napoléon*   Jean Tulard, *Dictionnaire Napoléon*, Paris, 1987

U.S. Statutes at Large   Richard Peters, ed., *The Public Statutes at Large of the United States . . . 1789 to March 3, 1845*, Boston, 1855-56, 8 vols.

VMHB   *Virginia Magazine of History and Biography*, 1893-

Washington, *Papers*   W. W. Abbot, Dorothy Twohig, Philander D. Chase, Theodore J. Crackel, Edward C. Lengel, and others, eds., *The Papers of George Washington*, Charlottesville, 1983- , 60 vols.

    Confed. Ser., 1992-97, 6 vols.

    Pres. Ser., 1987- , 18 vols.

    Ret. Ser., 1998-99, 4 vols.

    Rev. War Ser., 1985- , 22 vols.

WMQ   *William and Mary Quarterly*, 1892-

Woods, *Albemarle*   Edgar Woods, *Albemarle County in Virginia*, Charlottesville, 1901

CONTENTS

CONTENTS

CONTENTS

CONTENTS

CONTENTS

CONTENTS

1804

CONTENTS

CONTENTS

CONTENTS

CONTENTS

CONTENTS

CONTENTS

CONTENTS

CONTENTS

CONTENTS

APPENDICES

ILLUSTRATIONS

Following page 276

DIONAEA MUSCIPULA

Jefferson had long been interested in the Venus flytrap, an insectivorous plant found in marshy areas of the American southeast. Known by its Latin binomial (*Dionaea muscipula*) as well as by the common "tipitiwitchet," the plant was a curiosity for amateur gardeners and trained botanists alike on both sides of the Atlantic and seemed to defy simple categorization as flora or fauna. In 1760, North Carolina governor Arthur Dobbs described the "great wonder of the vegetable kingdom." Naturalists helped to popularize it. William Bartram characterized the plant as a "carnivorous vegetable." A botanical description written by John Ellis, published in London in 1770, circulated widely and was frequently accompanied by an illustrated plate depicting "A sensitive Plant from the Swamps of North America with a spike of white blossoms like the English Ladysmock. Each leaf is a miniature figure of a Rat trap with teeth; closing on every fly or other insect, that creeps between its lobes, and squeezing it to Death" (William Bartram, *Travels Through North & South Carolina, Georgia, East & West Florida* [Philadelphia, 1791], xx; E. Charles Nelson, *Aphrodite's Mousetrap: A Biography of Venus's Flytrap with Facsimiles of an Original Pamphlet and the Manuscripts of John Ellis, F.R.S.* [Aberystwyth, Wales, 1990], 5, 6, 11, 17, 28-9, 30, 45, 49, 118).

From 1786 to 1789, Jefferson enlisted the assistance of David Ramsay of South Carolina and Benjamin Hawkins of North Carolina in trying to secure seeds of the plant, some of which he hoped to send to Madame de Tessé for her gardens outside Paris. He again asked Hawkins for seeds in 1796 and made the same request of William Hamilton of the Woodlands in 1800. On Christmas Day 1803, Jefferson finally received seeds from Timothy Bloodworth, customs collector at Wilmington, North Carolina. On the following day, the president gave some of them to Elizabeth Merry, the wife of the new British minister to the United States, who had an avid interest in horticulture (Vol. 9:238; Vol. 10:240, 513-14; Vol. 11:187, 201, 206, 260, 279, 413; Vol. 15:506-7; Vol. 29:43; Vol. 31:535; Timothy Bloodworth to TJ, 12 Dec. 1803; TJ to Elizabeth Merry, 26 Dec. 1803; Elizabeth Merry to TJ, 26 Dec. 1803; TJ to Timothy Bloodworth, 29 Jan. 1804).

This hand-colored engraving of *Dionaea muscipula*, illustrated by the Welsh botanical artist Sydenham Edwards, appeared in 1804 in Volume 20 of *Curtis's Botanical Magazine; or, Flower-Garden Displayed: In Which the Most Ornamental Foreign Plants, Cultivated in the Open Ground, the Green-House, and the Stove, are Accurately Represented in their Natural Colours.* The London magazine, founded as an octavo in 1787 by William Curtis, was renowned for its color illustrations of plants. The Venus flytrap appears here with a fly and earwig within its clasp. This copper-etched engraving by Francis Sansom, tinted with watercolor, was accompanied by a two-page textual account of the class and order, generic character, specific character, and synonyms of the plant, as well as a description of its roots, leaves, seeds, places of growth, and time of flowering. Plate No. 785, published on 1 Oct. 1804, measures $9\frac{1}{8}$ inches by $5\frac{1}{4}$ inches.

Courtesy of the Board of Trustees of the Royal Botanic Gardens, Kew.

PRESIDENT'S HOUSE FLOOR PLAN

In 1803, Congress appropriated $50,000 for repairs to Washington's public buildings and the road adjoining them. The president was to oversee the project with the assistance of a newly appointed surveyor of public buildings, meant to replace the existing board of commissioners. Jefferson chose Benjamin Henry Latrobe, to whom he explained that most of the congressional funding was designated for the Capitol building, particularly for construction of the south wing. The President's House would realize only enough money to cover rudimentary construction and repairs. Of immediate concern were the sinking of a well, repairs to the pump and chimneys, new roofing, and general plastering of the interior (abstract of expenditures for the President's House during 1803, in DNA: RG 233, Reports and Communications from the Secretary of the Treasury, 10th Cong., 2d sess.). Over the next four years, Congress continued to divert funding primarily to the Capitol building, but in 1807, it appropriated $15,000 specifically toward repairs to the President's House. With that, Latrobe drew up two floor plans: an elegantly rendered "Plan of the principal story, as proposed to be altered," and the retrospective "Plan of the Principal Story in 1803," illustrated in this volume. The purpose of the 1803 floor plan, according to the editors of Latrobe's papers, was to serve both as a striking contrast to Latrobe's ideas for improvement and as a visual reminder of the structural problems that the architect had faced after his appointment as surveyor. The plans, though, lay dormant for a year. Because Latrobe had recently caused an uproar with his design changes to the Capitol, he chose to defer presenting his ideas for the President's House (U.S. Statutes at Large, 2:235-6; ASP, *Miscellaneous*, 1:722; Jeffrey A. Cohen and Charles E. Brownell, eds., *The Architectural Drawings of Benjamin Henry Latrobe*, 2 vols. [New Haven, 1994], 2:499, 501; Latrobe, *Correspondence*, 2:228, 686-7; Vol. 40:16-8).

The ink, watercolor, and graphite "Plan of the Principal Story in 1803," of which this illustration is a detail, was drawn on paper measuring approximately 19 inches by 15 inches. The interior inscriptions read clockwise from upper left: "Public Dining room"; "Porters Lodge" and "Pr. Stairs"; "Hall"; "Staircase"; "Public audience Chamber" and "entirely unfinished, the cieling has given way"; "Common Dining room"; "Drawing room"; "Presidents' Antechamber"; "Library & Cabinet"; "This Staircase is not yet put up. (1803)." Below the plan Latrobe noted: "During the short residence of President Adams at Washington, the wooden stairs & platform were the usual entrance to the house, and the present drawing-room, was a mere Vestibule." The architect signed his drawing, "B Henry Latrobe S.P.B.U.S. 1807."

Courtesy of the Library of Congress.

ELIZABETH MERRY

Gilbert Stuart painted about 40 portraits in Washington, D.C., over a period of a year and a half beginning in December 1803. His subjects included

James and Dolley Madison; Spanish minister Carlos Martínez de Irujo and his wife, the former Sally McKean of Philadelphia; the mercurial Virginia congressman John Randolph; Jerome and Elizabeth Patterson Bonaparte; and President Thomas Jefferson. Stuart painted this portrait of Elizabeth Merry just before he left the capital city in July 1805.

As he did with the Madisons and other couples, Stuart may have painted a pair of complementary portraits, one of Anthony Merry, the British minister to the United States, and this one of his wife. Anthony Merry paid Stuart $200 in July 1805, which, according to the artist's rate for his work in Washington, would have purchased two portraits. If the artist captured the likenesses of both Merrys, however, the pictures became separated, for there appears to be no extant portrait of the husband by Stuart. Moreover, when Merry made the payment, he said nothing about a portrait of himself, acknowledging only "the valuable portrait of Mrs. Merry, on which Mr. Stuart has had the goodness to exert his known talents with so much success."

Following Elizabeth Merry's death, this portrait was incorrectly attributed to Sir William Beechey, an English painter patronized by King George III and the royal family. Beechey probably did paint her, in a full-length portrait that in 1907 was at Herringfleet Hall in Suffolk, where Elizabeth Merry was buried. Another portrait was by Richard Cosway, which Anthony Cardon reproduced as a stipple engraving of an idealized portrait that presented its subject standing in classical garb and setting.

In the twentieth century, José Lázaro Galdiano of Madrid, where Anthony Merry was British consul from 1789 to 1790, acquired this portrait, which is in oil on canvas, approximately 29 inches high by 24 inches wide (Robert Upstone, "Retrato de la Esposa de Anthony Merry," in Letizia Arbeteta Mira and others, *Obras Maestras de la Colección Lázaro Galdiano: Sala de Exposiciones de la Fundación Santander Central Hispano, 16 Diciembre 2002 - 9 Febrero de 2003* [Madrid, 2002], 282-3; Carrie Rebora Barratt and Ellen G. Miles, *Gilbert Stuart* [New York, 2004], 239-42, 272; Lawrence Park, *Gilbert Stuart: An Illustrated Descriptive List of his Works*, 4 vols. [New York, 1926], 2:522-3; Charles Merrill Mount, "Gilbert Stuart in Washington: With a Catalogue of His Portraits Painted between December 1803 and July 1805," RCHS, 71/72 [1971-72], 123, 126; William Roberts, *Sir William Beechey, R.A.* [London, 1907], facing 182, 208-9; DNB, s.v. "Beechey, Sir William"; stipple engraving by Cardon after Cosway, National Portrait Gallery, London).
Courtesy of Fundación Lázaro Galdiano, Madrid.

THOMAS JEFFERSON BY AMOS B. DOOLITTLE

In October 1803, New Haven profilist and miniaturist Amos B. Doolittle (d. 1809) advertised to draw profiles with his "accurate physiognotrace," for which he charged $3 for "a likeness done in gold and set in a gilt frame." A son of Amos Doolittle (1754-1832), the Connecticut engraver famous for his four plates of the battles of Lexington and Concord, he had samples of his own work on view at his father's house. In addition to artistic training acquired in his father's shop, the younger Doolittle may have assisted John Wesley Jarvis and Joseph Wood with their physiognotrace in New York. Sometime in late 1803, Doolittle traveled to Washington, where he took the likenesses of the president and all the heads of departments "in a stile superiour to any ever yet attempted." From 23 Dec. 1803 to 10 Feb. 1804, Jefferson recorded total payments to Doolittle of $35 for profiles. In late February, Doolittle spent two or three weeks in Philadelphia, where he promoted his skill with a "Physiognotrace on a new construction" and advertised that he would "execute Profiles in Gold, at a moderate price." Doolittle was in Hartford by late May and advertising for sale profiles "enamel'd on Glass, in gold or in black," as well as copies "of the most distinguished characters in the United States" recently made in the nation's capital. Before his death at the age of 23, Doolittle branched out into jewelry and watchmaking.

This small portrait of Jefferson on glass, likely executed by Doolittle in late 1803 or early 1804 using an artistic technique known as *verre églomisé,* is 3 inches by 3½ inches. The process, popular in Europe in the 14th and 15th centuries, consisted of sketching a medallion design through gold leaf on one side of a glass background and rapidly blacking the back. Doolittle did not sign this portrait, but it is similar in technique and style to a signed profile of John Adams, owned by William Bentley of Salem, Massachusetts. In a diary entry for the Fourth of July 1804, Bentley recorded seeing an engraving of Jefferson in glass on gold on display at the town meeting house (Bush, *Life Portraits,* 48-9; William Bentley, *Diary of William Bentley, D.D.: Pastor of the East Church, Salem, Massachusetts,* 4 vols. [Salem, Mass., 1905–14], 3:96; Donald C. O'Brien, *Amos Doolittle: Engraver of the New Republic* [New Castle, Del., 2008], 1, 4, 71, 90-2; Harold E. Dickson, *John Wesley Jarvis: American Painter 1780-1840 with a Checklist of His Works* [New York, 1949], 65-6; Colin Eisler, "Verre Églomisé and Paolo di Giovanni Fei," *Journal of Glass Studies,* 3 [1961], 30-7; New Haven *Visitor,* 25 Oct. 1803; *United States Gazette,* 29 Feb. 1804; New Haven *Connecticut Journal,* 16 Jan. 1806, 28 July 1808, 1 June 1809; MB, 2:1114, 1118, 1119; Appendix IV).

Courtesy of the Thomas Jefferson Foundation at Monticello.

ORDER ON JOHN BARNES

This 12 Dec. 1803 order on John Barnes, written and signed by Jefferson on paper approximately 5 inches tall by 7 inches wide, settled the account of maître d'hotel Étienne Lemaire for domestic expenses accrued at the President's House from 4 to 10 Dec. Lemaire signed the order as receipt of payment, and Barnes endorsed the transaction on verso as paid on 12 Dec. From 1801 through September 1804, Jefferson settled accounts with Lemaire each week that he was in residence; after that, he settled monthly. The physical look of the orders, whether weekly or monthly, varied little. Because such expenditures were a private expense, they received detailed consideration in Jefferson's financial memoranda. Between 4 and 10 Dec., Lemaire spent $94.87 on food, wood, furniture, contingencies, and miscellaneous servant expenses, reduced to $80.87 because of a $14 credit from the previous week's accounting. Lemaire had purchased 194 pounds of meat, 21 dozen eggs, 36½ pounds of butter, and $7.06 worth of vegetables, four staples that Jefferson tracked faithfully for the rest of his presidency. Staff wages were settled with Lemaire monthly when the president was available, or soon thereafter upon his return from Monticello. In 1803, wages normally totaled $143 each month for eleven servants, ranging downward from Lemaire's $30 salary to enslaved cook Edith Fossett's $2 gratuity. Lemaire's responsibilities did not extend to expenses connected to the stables or the icehouse. Coachman Joseph Dougherty handled those, settling his accounts with Jefferson as needed (Appendix IV; Stanton, *Free Some Day*, 129-30; MB, 2:1100, 1114; Vol. 37:332n, 442n).

The payments to Dougherty, as well as those to Lemaire, represent a portion of the orders, invoices, bills, and receipts left to history by Jefferson. Separately, the items shed light on Jefferson's everyday world, whether it was feeding his presidential household, paying his barber, or buying a cage for his mockingbird. Together, these monetary odds and ends not only help solve the puzzle of Jefferson's finances but also provide insight into the economic times in which he lived (MB, 2:1112; Appendix IV).

Courtesy of the Massachusetts Historical Society.

A PHILADELPHIA BAPTISM

On 20 Jan. 1804, Jefferson acknowledged receiving a memorial from the Baptist Society of Portsmouth, Virginia, one of many similar exchanges between him and local religious bodies during the course of his presidency. Despite Jefferson's unorthodox religious beliefs and Federalist-spread rumors that he was an atheist, evangelical groups became some of his staunchest supporters, attracted to his opposition to state support of religion and to the democratic rhetoric of his political movement, which corresponded with the populist orientation of their own denominations. Just as Jeffersonian Republicans swept aside their Federalist rivals, evangelical denominations surged during the first decades of the nineteenth century.

A *Philadelphia Anabaptist Immersion during a Storm*, made about 1812, after Jefferson's presidency, captures the combination of fascination and disdain that evangelical groups engendered in the early republic. In this scene, a Baptist minister stands in a shallow part of a large body of water, probably the Delaware River, as he performs the rite of baptism on an adult woman. Above them, a crowd of onlookers has gathered on a jetty. The range of clothing styles and colors indicates a mix of social types and contrasts with the uniform band of converts, all clothed in grayish-white cloaks or dresses and waiting in the shallows for their turn with the minister. Countenances of the onlookers display curiosity, bewilderment, delight, and, in the case of a scowling workman hanging his leg over the jetty wall, borderline hostility. The penitents ignore the onlookers above them, and the minister looks up toward the heavens as a storm cloud frames the upper-left corner.

In watercolor and black ink on white wove paper and approximately $9\frac{5}{8}$ inches wide by 7 inches high, the picture has been attributed to Pavel Petrovich Svin'in, secretary to the Russian consul general in Philadelphia from 1811 to 1813. From a minor aristocratic family, Svin'in was educated at the boarding school attached to Moscow University and at the Imperial Academy for Fine Arts in St. Petersburg. During his stint in America, he collected a portfolio of pictures from various sources, including his own work, as potential illustrations for a book on the United States that he published in St. Petersburg in 1815. The baptism picture has also been attributed to John Lewis Krimmel, a Philadelphia genre painter who supplied or inspired some of the watercolors in Svin'in's portfolio. Eight of the 52 watercolors in Svin'in's collection have been reattributed to Krimmel, and several others, including the baptism picture, resemble Krimmel's work. Certainty is prevented by the variety of styles that Svin'in employed and by the existence of several unacknowledged copies of the works of other artists in his portfolio (Kevin J. Avery, *American Drawings and Watercolors in the Metropolitan Museum of Art: Volume 1, A Catalogue of Works by Artists Born before 1835* [New Haven, 2002], 15, 130-4, 322-3, 347-50; Marina Swoboda and William Benton Whisenhunt, eds., *A Russian Paints America: The Travels of Pavel P. Svin'in, 1811-1813* [Montreal and Kingston, 2008], 24-33, 77-9; Anneliese Harding, *John Lewis Krimmel: Genre Artist of the Early Republic* [Winterthur, Del., 1994], 23, 25-6, 235-51; Vol. 36:250-4).

Courtesy of the Metropolitan Museum of Art, New York.

THE LOSS OF THE FRIGATE PHILADELPHIA

On the morning of 31 Oct. 1803, the frigate *Philadelphia*, commanded by Captain William Bainbridge, began pursuit of a Tripolitan vessel off the North African coast. After a chase lasting more than two hours, the *Philadelphia* ran aground on uncharted rocks four to five miles from the city of Tripoli. Because of the listing of the vessel, the crew of the *Philadelphia* was unable to bring any guns to bear on approaching Tripolitan gunboats. For a period of four hours the crew attempted to refloat the vessel by throwing overboard the forward anchors, cannon, and other naval stores, all while under the attack of enemy vessels. This engraving highlighted with watercolor, titled *A Perspective View of the Loss of the U.S. Frigate Philadelphia*, depicts Bainbridge's "last resort" when he ordered the foremast cut away in a final attempt to free the vessel before Tripolitan reinforcements arrived. In the face of these unsuccessful efforts and an increasing enemy force, Bainbridge surrendered the *Philadelphia* and its 307 crewmembers. While the officers of the *Philadelphia* were lodged in the American consul's house for the duration of the war, the enlisted crewmen were imprisoned and suffered from "hunger, cold, hard labour, and the lash of the whip." Their ordeal ended when the United States agreed to a $60,000 ransom as part of an 1805 peace treaty with Tripoli. *A Perspective View of the Loss of the U.S. Frigate Philadelphia* was the first in a two-part series of prints illustrating the eyewitness account of Charles Denoon, a seaman captured on board the frigate and who later observed Commodore Edward Preble's attack on the city. Upon his repatriation to the United States, Denoon, working with the editor of the Richmond *Enquirer*, advertised his prints in newspapers. Denoon hoped to attract the attention of the public by appealing to their sense of charity for his "miserable existence in perpetual slavery." Despite a minor delay in the engraving process in Philadelphia, the engraver Frederick Bossler conveyed the plates to Richmond for printing in late February 1806.

The image is 20 inches wide and 14 inches high, with a caption reading "A perspective View of the loss of the U.S. Frigate Philadelphia in which is represented her relative position to the Tripolitan Gun-boats when during their furious attack upon her she was unable to get a single gun to bear upon them" (*Message from the President of the United States; Communicating to Congress, A Letter Received from Capt. Bainbridge, Commander of the Philadelphia Frigate, Giving Information of the Wreck of that Vessel, On the Coast of Tripoli; and that Himself, his Officers, and Men, had Fallen into the Hands*

of the Tripolitans [Washington, D.C., 1804; Lawrence A. Peskin, *Captives and Countrymen: Barbary Slavery and the American Public, 1785-1816* [Baltimore, 2009], 153-5; NDBW, 3:187; Richmond *Enquirer*, 5 Nov. 1805; Boston *New-England Palladium*, 19 Nov. 1805; Richmond *Virginia Gazette*, 22 Feb. 1806).
Courtesy of the William L. Clements Library, University of Michigan.

AN IRON FOUNDER

During the time covered by this volume, Jefferson placed numerous orders for iron. He continued to supply his nailery with nailrod from the Philadelphia firm Jones & Howell, obtained sheet iron for Monticello's roof and gutters from the rolling mill established by Benjamin H. Latrobe, ordered some specialized files and spindles for the use of his blacksmith William Stewart, and had a Washington manufacturer contrive a thin piece of cast iron to help stabilize a polygraph writing machine with which he was experimenting. In addition, Latrobe's plans for the President's House called for the slate roof to be replaced with sheet iron (TJ to Jones & Howell, 22 Nov. and 22 Dec.; Latrobe to TJ, 30 Nov.; Jones & Howell to TJ, 27 Dec.; enclosure to Latrobe to TJ, 20 Feb.; TJ to Latrobe, 26 Feb.).

This image of an iron foundry worker appeared as a plate in the 1807 Pennsylvania publication *The Book of Trades, or Library of the Useful Arts*. Intended for children, the work fit into a longstanding publishing genre that combined illustrations with brief, often moralizing descriptions of various social types. Such works gained prominence through the work of sixteenth-century German printers and could be arranged hierarchically and with a strong dose of pietism or conceived more as a practical instruction in the working lives of tradespeople. A related sub-genre showcased urban "cries," that is, the calls of merchants and peddlers plying their wares through city streets and markets. The first American publication of this sort, *The Book of Trades* took its text and illustrations from an edition of the same name published in London in 1804 and 1805. Spread over three *trigesimo-secundo* volumes (with covers approximately $5\frac{1}{2}$ inches by $3\frac{1}{2}$ inches) were 67 profiles of professions, almost all accompanied by an image taken from a copper engraving. Like most of the plates, the engraving of the iron worker was signed "WR," indicating that it was likely the work of William Ralph, an engraver active in New York and Philadelphia during this period. Ralph copied plates from the London edition, although in the case of the iron worker, he engraved a mirror image of the original. In the picture, the worker fills his ladle with melted ore to be poured into a mold. He wears a loose-fitting shirt with the sleeves rolled up and what appears to be a protective cloth over his head. Evident from the picture, the job required "great strength, and a constitution that will bear a vast degree of heat" (Helmut Lehman-Haupt, *The Book of Trades in the Iconography of Social Typology* [Boston, 1976], 2-9; *The New-York Directory and Register, for the Year 1794* [New York, 1794], 151; David McNeely Stauffer and Mantle Fielding, *American Engravers upon Copper and Steel*, 3 vols. [New York, 1907-17; v. 3 repr. 1964], 1:217; 2:434; 3:219-20).
Courtesy of Princeton University Library.

Volume 42

16 November 1803 to 10 March 1804

JEFFERSON CHRONOLOGY

1743 · 1826

1743	Born at Shadwell, 13 April (New Style).
1760	Entered the College of William and Mary.
1762	"quitted college."
1762-1767	Self-education and preparation for law.
1769-1774	Albemarle delegate to House of Burgesses.
1772	Married Martha Wayles Skelton, 1 Jan.
1775-1776	In Continental Congress.
1776	Drafted Declaration of Independence.
1776-1779	In Virginia House of Delegates.
1779	Submitted Bill for Establishing Religious Freedom.
1779-1781	Governor of Virginia.
1782	His wife died, 6 Sep.
1783-1784	In Continental Congress.
1784-1789	In France as Minister Plenipotentiary to negotiate commercial treaties and as Minister Plenipotentiary resident at Versailles.
1790-1793	Secretary of State of the United States.
1797-1801	Vice President of the United States.
1801-1809	President of the United States.
1814-1826	Established the University of Virginia.
1826	Died at Monticello, 4 July.

VOLUME 42

16 November 1803 to 10 March 1804

24 Nov.	Sends draft bill for organization of Orleans Territory to John Breckinridge.
2 Dec.	British minister Anthony Merry and his wife, Elizabeth, dine at the President's House.
13 Dec.	Begins to transmit copies of the Twelfth Amendment to the states for ratification.
13 Dec.	Meets with Choctaw delegation in Washington.
20 Dec.	United States takes formal possession of Louisiana.
25 Dec.	Receives Venus flytrap seeds from Timothy Bloodworth.
4 Jan.	Articles of impeachment against Judge John Pickering presented to the Senate.
26 Jan.	Meets with Aaron Burr to discuss their strained political relationship.
27 Jan.	Attends dinner at Stelle's Hotel celebrating the acquisition of Louisiana.
6 Feb.	Joseph Priestley dies at home in Northumberland, Pennsylvania.
15 Feb.	Maria Jefferson Eppes, TJ's granddaughter, born at Edgehill.
16 Feb.	Sailors under the command of Lieutenant Stephen Decatur, Jr., burn the frigate *Philadelphia* in Tripoli harbor.
22 Feb.	Fire destroys more than 260 buildings in Norfolk, Virginia.
22 Feb.	Commences use of polygraph writing machine.
25 Feb.	Republican congressional caucus nominates TJ for president and George Clinton for vice president.
27 Feb.	Calculates tobacco crop for 1803 at Poplar Forest to be 36,509 pounds.
3 Mch.	Learns that his daughter Mary is seriously ill.

THE PAPERS OF
THOMAS JEFFERSON

·《══════════》·

From Johann Abraham Albers

SIR   Bremen th. 16 Novbr 1803.

By this I have the Honour to send Your Excellency the third Volume of my American Annals, and as a proof of my profound respect, have taken the liberty of dedicating it to You.

At same time allow me to assure You of the sincere esteem, which the German Nation feels for the United States of America, and that the publication of my Annals, whose principal aim is the extension of one part of their Literature, has been received here in the most flattering manner.

I have the Honour to be Sir Your most obedient servant

J. A. ALBERS Dr.

RC (DLC); endorsed by TJ as received 9 July 1804 and so recorded in SJL. Enclosure: J. A. Albers, *Americanische Annalen der Arzneykunde, Naturgeschichte, Chemie und Physik*, vol. 3 (Bremen, 1803; Sowerby, No. 4728).

German physician Johann Abraham Albers (1772-1821) studied medicine at Jena, Vienna, London, and Edinburgh before returning to his hometown of Bremen in 1798, where he established a large and successful practice. Although an accomplished researcher in his own right, his primary contribution to medical science came from translating foreign research into German. His most ambitious work in this realm was his *Americanische Annalen*, a short-lived serial published from 1802 to 1803 that included translations of writings by a number of prominent American physicians and scientists. Albers dedicated the third and final volume to "Seiner Excellenz dem Herrn Thomas Jefferson, Präsidenten der vereinigten Staaten von Amerika" (that is, to "His Excellency the Honorable Thomas Jefferson, President of the United States of America") with deepest respect (William F. Bynum, "Johann Abraham Albers [1772-1821] and American Medicine," *Journal of the History of Medicine and Allied Sciences*, 23 [1968], 50-62).

From Louis Alexis Hocquet de Caritat

Sir,   New York Nov. 16th. 1803

The important subject of Lousiana which has engaged your attention for sometime past, and the succes with which it has been crowned gives me hope that the enclosed prospectus relative to the Voyage of General Collot through that Country will appear to you worthy of some examen. My Partner in France has been induced by Mr Livingston and all the Americans in Paris to purchase the copy-right of the original work from the author, and he has devoted a large proportion of his fortune to the suitable expence for its appearance before the public of the United States. He has even done more, he left his family and all other business to come over and attend in person to that interesting object.

Its favourable reception and the number of subscribers depends entirely on your approbation, and the copies will be struck off in exact proportion to the encouragement obtained. We intend to offer the Original Charts Maps &c to Congress; Their Size (some being 12 & 13 feet long) and the elegance of their Style making them fit for the Archives of the United States as well as for those of France, where they should have been placed had that Republic remained in Possession of Lousiana. This offer will be without any condition and we shall be happy if accepted to feel consious of having done some thing useful to our adopted Country.

The favour of a word of answer will be received with the utmost gratefulness by

Sir Your most Obedient Servant   H. Caritat
                                              Book-seller

The translation of the Prospectus was not finished, or otherwise I should have sent it in English.

RC (DLC); at foot of first page: "Thomas Jefferson President of the United States"; endorsed by TJ as received 19 Nov. and so recorded in SJL. Enclosure not found, but see below.

Louis Alexis Hocquet de Caritat (b. 1752) emigrated to the United States in 1792, settling in New York City. There, he ran afoul of the Washington administration when he outfitted a French privateer, one of the incidents that led the administration to formalize its neutrality stance in 1793. After federal charges against him were quashed, he returned to France, where he was declared an émigré, resulting in the revocation of his citizenship. He again moved to New York in 1797 and took over the operation of a circulating library and bookstore. He augmented its collection, which at one time numbered some 25,000 volumes, and also published books. In 1805, Caritat moved back to France, where he published a periodical devoted to the United States. He returned to the United States in 1816 but moved back to France the following year (New York *Diary, or Loudon's Register,*

1 May 1797; New York *Republican Watch-Tower*, 26 June 1805; *Poulson's American Daily Advertiser*, 2 Apr. 1806; New York *National Advocate*, 15 Oct. 1816; *New-York Columbian*, 23 June 1817; George Gates Raddin, Jr., *Caritat and the Genet Episode* [Dover, N.J., 1953], 10, 16-17, 41-6; George Gates Raddin, Jr., *Hocquet Caritat and the Early New York Literary Scene* [Dover, N.J., 1953], 30; Vol. 26:259-60, 282n).

A translation of the enclosed PROSPECTUS appeared in newspapers, describing the proposed work as an account of the "travels through Louisiana" undertaken in 1796 by Victor COLLOT. It would consist of two volumes in quarto with 30 engraved plates and maps and encompass observations on the climate, topography, rivers, population, commerce, and natural productions of the North American interior. Caritat explained that the French government had been prepared to publish the work, but the sale of Louisiana to the United States suspended that plan, and now the work enjoyed the patronage of Robert R. Livingston, James Monroe, and Joel Barlow, among other prominent Americans in Paris. Collot's journey had been a reconnaissance mission seeking information on a region that France expected to regain and, if necessary, to fortify against American and British encroachments. Although Caritat filed for copyright under the title *Journey of Gen. Victor Collot*, he apparently did not attract enough subscribers. An English translation of the work was printed in 1826 in Paris as *A Journey in North America* (New York *Evening Post*, 2, 5 Dec. 1803; George W. Kyte, "A Spy on the Western Waters: The Military Intelligence Mission of General Collot in 1796," *Mississippi Valley Historical Review*, 34 [1947], 427-42; Durand Echevarria, "General Collot's Plan for a Reconnaissance of the Ohio and Mississippi Valleys, 1796," WMQ, 3d ser., 9 [1952], 512-20; Vol. 33:406n).

PARTNER IN FRANCE: during a visit to Paris in the winter of 1801 and 1802, Caritat joined the English Press, a publishing consortium. Other principals included John Hurford Stone, Helen Maria Williams, and the Levrault brothers, who were printers (Raddin, *Hocquet Caritat and the Early New York Literary Scene*, 96-101, 137-8; Vol. 40:98n; Vol. 41:397, 398n).

From Henry Dearborn

War Department 16. Nov. 1803.—

The Secretary of War has the honor to propose to the President of the United States, that,

Robert Richie and Richard Smith both of the State of Maryland, be appointed 2d. Lieutenants respectively in the Regiment of Artillerists.

That, Alpha Kingsley and Gideon Warner, both of the State of Vermont, be appointed Ensigns respectively, in the 1st. Regiment of Infantry.

That, Samuel Williamson of the State of Pennsylvania, be appointed an Ensign in the 2d. Regiment of Infantry.[1]

That, John Watson of the State of New York and John Griffen of the State of North Carolina, be respectively appointed Surgeons[2] Mates in the Army of the United States; and,

That Morris Jones of the State of North Carolina be appointed a Cadet in the Regt. of Artillerists, and Prentiss Willard be appointed a Cadet in the Regiment of Artillerists.

RC (DLC); in a clerk's hand, with an addition by TJ (see note 1 below); endorsed by TJ as received from the War Department on 17 Nov. and "Nominations Military" and so recorded in SJL. FC (Lb in DNA: RG 107, LSP).

TJ included the names listed above in his military nominations sent to the Sen-ate on 18 Nov. 1803, except for MORRIS JONES and PRENTISS WILLARD, whose appointments as cadets did not require Senate approval.

[1] Below this paragraph TJ interlined in pencil "Gilbert C Russel" (see Dearborn to TJ, [17 Nov.]).
[2] MS: "Sugeons."

From John Goulding

SIR   Georgetown 16 Novr. 1803

I have heretofore had the honor & the pleasure to know your gentle & amiable handwriting; of course I must feel on the present sudden occasion, the sensations of delight & surprize at once, upon seeing my name written by you, on any occasion: This being for some flour from Mr. Thomas, I have promptly pointed out to the bearer how the matter stood. It is not in words to express how much I wish for opportunity to shew, in any measure, the sincerity, the respect and the esteem, with which,

I have the honor to be, Sir, Your most Obedient And most Hume. Servt.   JOHN GOULDING

RC (MHi); endorsed by TJ as received 16 Nov. and so recorded in SJL.

John Goulding was a notary public, broker, and commission merchant in Georgetown (*Washington Federalist*, 27 Jan. and 20 Mch. 1802; Washington *Federal Republican*, 10 Nov. 1815; Gallatin, *Papers*, 47:337).

To Meriwether Lewis

DEAR SIR   Washington Nov. 16. 1803.

I have not written to you since the 11th. & 15th. of July, since which yours of July 15. 22. 25. Sep. 8. 13. & Oct. 3. have been recieved. the present has been long delayed by an expectation daily of getting the inclosed 'account of Louisiana' through the press. the materials are recieved from different persons, of good authority. I inclose you also copies of the Treaties for Louisiana, the act for taking possession, a letter from Dr. Wistar, & some information collected by myself from Truteau's journal in MS. all of which may be useful to you. the act for taking possession passes with only some small verbal variations from that inclosed, of no consequence. orders went from hence, signed by the king of Spain & the first Consul of France, so as to arrive at Natchez yesterday evening, and we expect the delivery of the province at New Orleans will take place about the close of the ensuing week, say about the 26th. inst. Govr. Claiborne is appointed to execute the powers of Commandant & Intendant, until a regular government shall be organised here. at the moment of delivering over the posts in the vicinity of N. Orleans, orders will be dispatched from thence to those in Upper Louisiana to evacuate & deliver them immediately. you can judge better than I can when they may be expected to arrive at these posts. considering how much you have been detained by the low waters, how late it will be before you can leave Cahokia, how little progress up the Missouri you can make before the freezing of the river; that your winter might be passed in gaining much information by making Cahokia or Kaskaskia your head quarters, & going to St. Louis & the other Spanish forts, that your stores &c. would thereby be spared for the winter as your men would draw their military rations,[1] all danger of Spanish opposition avoided, we are strongly of opinion here that you had better not enter the Missouri till the spring. but as you have a view of all circumstances on the spot, we do not pretend to enjoin it, but leave it to your own judgment in which we have entire confidence. one thing however we are decided in: that you must not undertake the winter excursion which you propose in yours of Oct. 3. such an excursion will be more dangerous than the main expedition up the Missouri, & would, by an accident to you, hazard our main object, which, since the acquisition of Louisiana, interests every body in the highest degree. The object of your mission is single, the direct water communication from sea to sea formed by the bed of the Missouri & perhaps the Oregan: by having mr Clarke with you we consider the expedition as double manned, & therefore the less liable to failure: for which reason neither of you should be exposed to risques by going off of your line. I have proposed in conversation, & it seems generally to be assented to, that Congress shall appropriate 10. or 12.000 D. for exploring the principal waters of the Missipi & Missouri. in that case I should send a party up the Red river to it's head, then to cross over to the head of the Arcansa, & come down that. a 2d party for the Pani & Padouca rivers, & a 3d perhaps for the Moingona & St. Peters. as the boundaries of interior[2] Louisiana are *the high lands inclosing all the waters which run into the Misipi or Missouri directly or indirectly,* with a greater breadth on the gulph of Mexico, it becomes interesting to fix with precision by celestial observations the longitude & latitude of the sources of these rivers, as furnishing points in the contour of our new limits. this will be attempted distinctly from your mission, which we consider as of major importance, & therefore not to be delayed or hazarded by any episodes whatever.

The votes of both houses on ratifying & carrying the treaties into execution have been precisely party votes, except that Genl. Dayton has separated from his friends on these questions & voted for the treaties. I will direct the Aurora & National Intelligencer to be forwarded to you for 6. months at Cahokia or Kaskaskia, on the presumption you will be there. your friends & acquaintances here & in Albemarle are all well as far as I have heard: and I recollect no other small news worth communicating; present my friendly salutations to mr Clarke, & accept them affectionately yourself.

TH: JEFFERSON

PrC (DLC); at foot of first page: "Capt Lewis." Enclosures: (1) *An Account of Louisiana, Being an Abstract of Documents, in the Offices of the Departments of State, and of the Treasury* (see Vol. 41:721). (2) Treaty and conventions between the United States and France, 30 Apr., for the sale of Louisiana. (3) "An Act to enable the President of the United States to take possession of the territories ceded by France to the United States, by the treaty concluded at Paris, on the thirtieth of April last; and for the temporary government thereof" (see Vol. 41:583-4). (4) Caspar Wistar's communication to Lewis not found, but see Wistar to TJ, 18 July.

YOURS OF JULY: TJ recorded Lewis's letter of 26 July as one of 25 July.

PANI & PADOUCA RIVERS: TJ probably derived his names for rivers from the map of North America executed by John Mitchell in 1755. On that map, the river labeled Pani corresponds with the Platte River, and the river labeled the Padoucas corresponds with the Kansas River, both major tributaries of the Missouri. The map also included the MOINGONA River, which corresponds with the Des Moines River, and the ST. PETERS, now known as the Minnesota River (John Mitchell, *A Map of the British and French Dominions in North America* [London, 1755]; Michael Dickey, *The People of the River's Mouth: In Search of the Missouria Indians* [Columbia, Mo., 2011], 46; *Congressional Globe*, 32d Cong., 1st sess., 1852, 24, pt. 2:1376).

In the Senate on 20 Oct., Jonathan DAYTON voted with the majority to ratify the treaty and conventions for the purchase of Louisiana. The votes against ratification were cast by James Hillhouse, Simeon Olcott, Timothy Pickering, William Plumer, Uriah Tracy, William H. Wells, and Samuel White (JEP, 1:450).

[1] Preceding eight words interlined.
[2] Word interlined.

Extracts from Accounts of Indians and the Fur Trade along the Missouri River

Extracts from the Journal of M. Truteau, Agent for the Illinois trading company, residing at the village of Ricara, up the Missouri.

This company was confirmed in 1796. with the exclusive right for 10. years to trade with all the nations above the Poncas, as well to the South, & the West, as to the North of the Missouri with a premium of 3000. pes. for the discovery of the South Sea: and a gratification of 10,000. pes. which the King of Spain is to pay for the support of a milice. The company however have[1]

In the Missouri river there is depth sufficient to carry a frigate as far up as it is known. it has no cataracts, no portages. the winds on it are so violent that the periagues are sometimes obliged to lie by one, two, three, or four days, & sometimes take as long time to descend as to ascend the river. the Canadians employed in the trading voyages on it have 250.tt to 300.tt for 18. months, & take it often in goods, on which the merchant gains half. the soil of the Missouri is the most fertile in the universe. the rivers falling into it are all navigable more or less from 50. or 100. to 200 or 300. leagues.

The Ricaras, are a branch of the Panis, residing up the Missouri, about 430. leagues from the Illinois. there are 2. villages of them, half a league apart, the one 800. yds from the river, the other 100. yards. they are a mild people, having about 500. warriors. there is no timber on the Missouri for 50. leagues above or below them.

The Crow nation inhabit near the Rock mountain.

The Sioux inhabit the Northern part of the Missisipi, and are hostile to the Ricaras, Mendannes, big bellies & others. others of them live on the river St. Pierre. they have from 30. to 40,000. men, and abound in fire-arms. they are the greatest beaver hunters; and could furnish more beavers than all the nations besides, and could bring them to a depot on the Missouri, rather than to St. Pierre, or any other place. their beaver is worth the double of the Canadian for the fineness of it's down & parchment.

The Chaquiennes, Panis Mahas, Mendannes, Big bellies are in the neighborhood of the Ricaras.

The Pados are 80. leagues from the Ricaras, South, on a branch of the river.

The Cayoguas, Caminanbeihes & Pitapahatos are to the South & S.W. of the Ricaras, on a branch of the Missouri. they have had no communication with the Whites. this river is broad but too shallow for a periague.

The Grand Osages are from 7. to 800. men. they furnish 20,000. skins of the small deer, and take 14. to 15. M pes de Mes. [qu. whether these characters *pes de Mes* mean *pieces de Marchandise* or *piastres de Mexique*?]

The Petits Osages are 250. to 300. men. furnish 7. to 8000. fine deerskins & take 4. to 5 M pes. des Mes.

The Kansas, 250 to 300. men. furnish & take the same as the Petits Osages.

With the three last nations the hunt continues to Oct. Nov. & even the middle of Dec. the hunters then meet, fix their prices, which are a blanket of $2\frac{1}{2}$ points for 6. 7. or 8. deerskins. in 2 days the whole are sold, & if the ice did not hinder, the traders could be returned by Christmas, whereas they do not return till April or May. these nations are very certain of the arrival of traders among them, but those above are often disappointed; because the merchants of St. Louis recieve their goods from Mackinac, or Montreal, & they do not arrive at St. Louis early enough to reach the upper nations in time for the season. through the Ohio the goods might be brought in time to reach the uppermost nations.

The Otoctatas take 2 M̃ to 2500. pes. marchse. & furnish 3500. to 4000 fine peltries of Deer, & $\frac{1}{4}$ of that of beaver.

The Mahas are from 4. to 500. men. the Poncas 200. to 250. men. these two nations furnish and take each about the same as the Otoctatas, but more beaver. the English however draw them off by land to the river Moingona.

The Panis of the 2. villages are from 4. to 500. men. take 2000. to 2500. pes. Marche. & furnish 4000. skins, robes & Castor of the 1st. quality. those of the Republic are from 400 to 500. men, take & furnish about half as much as the last. they are 50. or 100 leagues apart.

The Loups, which are Panis also are from 200. to 250. men.

PrC (DLC); entirely in TJ's hand, including bracket.

Jean Baptiste TRUTEAU, sometimes spelled Trudeau, was a French Canadian who settled in St. Louis and who led an expedition organized by the Spanish-commissioned Missouri Company (ILLINOIS TRADING COMPANY). From 1794 to 1796, he explored the Missouri River, with the ultimate purpose of establishing Spanish influence over the Mandan villages in present-day Montana and expelling British and Canadian traders. Truteau failed to reach the Mandans but did spend a winter with the Arikaras (RICARA), who occupied two villages near the confluence of the Cheyenne and Missouri Rivers. He sent an account of his experiences to his superiors in St. Louis filled with careful observations of the Indians he encountered and with whom he attempted to trade. It is unclear when TJ obtained a copy of a portion of the journal, although there has been some speculation that it was among the "modern Manuscripts" enclosed by James Wilkinson in a letter of 1 Sep. 1800 (DNA: RG 59, TP, Orleans, 46 p., in French, endorsed in English: "Journal of a Voyage on the Missouri"; endorsed in French: "Journal tenu par J Bte Truteau agent de la Compagnie du haut du Missouris addressé à Mrs Clamorgan et Reihle directeurs de la Compagnie Commencé Le 1er juin *1795*" and "Seconde partie"; DAB, s.v., "Truteau,

Jean Baptiste"; Jean-Baptiste Trudeau, *Voyage sur le Haut-Missouri, 1794-1796,* ed. Fernand Grenier [Quebec, 2006]; A. P. Nasatir, ed., *Before Lewis and Clark: Documents Illustrating the History of the Missouri, 1785-1804,* 2 vols. [St. Louis, 1952], 1:217-28, 243-53, 294-311; John Logan Allen, *Passage through the Garden: Lewis and Clark and the Image of the American Northwest* [Urbana, Ill., 1975], 67-8; Vol. 32:119-20). TJ conflated his copy of Truteau's journal with a different manuscript that also derived from the efforts of the Missouri Company. Endorsed "Account of Indian trade by C___[n]," the document may have been composed by Jacques Clamorgan, the company's director. References to the company's royal charter in 1796 and to the commission merchant Andrew Todd, who became that year Clamorgan's principal supplier of goods, indicate that it was written sometime near the end of or after that year (DNA: RG 59, TP, Orleans, 12 p., in French, undated; Nasatir, *Before Lewis and Clark,* 2:419, 464-7). Before compiling the extracts for Lewis, TJ took notes from the documents, first drawing from Truteau demographic and geographical information on Indian nations living up the Missouri, and next drawing information on the fur trade from the "Account." For his enclosure to Lewis, TJ scrambled this organization, interspersing lines derived from the two sources, with the majority coming from the fur trade document. The information contained in TJ's notes and in the enclosure to Lewis was substantively identical (MS in DLC: TJ Papers, 137:23685; entirely in TJ's hand; undated; endorsed "Louisiana"; consisting of notes headed "1795. Journal of Truteau the Agent of the Company of the haut Missouri, establd at <St Louis> Illinois" followed on same sheet by notes headed "Account of the commerce").

MILICE: militia.

The Arikaras were closely related to the Pawnees (PANIS). Both were members of the Caddoan language group and derived from common ancestors. The Pawnees were divided into four distinct bands that did not include the Arikaras, although Truteau seems to have believed otherwise. The Gros Ventres (BIG BELLIES) at this time lived north of the Missouri River in Canada, so it is likely that Truteau was confusing them with the Hidatsas, who lived in close proximity to the Mandans (Sturtevant, *Handbook*, 13:365-6, 515, 517-19, 693).

CHAQUIENNES: that is, the Cheyennes. Truteau used the name PANIS MAHAS for the Skiri band of the Pawnees, also known as the Loups. The PADOS were the Comanches. The CAYOGUAS were the Kiowas, and the CAMINANBEIHES were the Arapahos. The PITAPAHATOS were a band of the Kiowas (same, 13:517-19, 860, 880, 970).

PIECES DE MARCHANDISE OR PIASTRES DE MEXIQUE: TJ transcribed the abbreviation "pes de Mes" directly from the fur trade document. It likely represented the monetary value of the merchandise intended for the Indians in exchange for furs. In a report of 8 July 1795, for example, Jacques Clamorgan indicated that the Missouri Company had allocated for Truteau's expedition merchandise worth 20,000 of an unidentified denomination, probably pesos, possibly French livres. In his notes on the "Account of the commerce," TJ wrote his query as: "qu. if the characters pes. de Mes [here called pieces or bales of merchandise] do not every where mean 'piastres de Mexique'?" The author of the fur trade account evidently had an intimate knowledge of the Spanish-sanctioned Missouri River trade as it stood in the mid-1790s, as well as of the obstacles to and opportunities for drawing the lucrative Sioux trade from the Mississippi River and Great Lakes to the Missouri. The sequence of tribes that TJ extracted follows the Missouri upriver and is similar to a 1794 allocation of trade concessions to St. Louis merchants. That allocation listed all but one of the same tribes: the two divisions of the OSAGES, the Kansas, the Otoes (OTOCTATAS), the Omahas (MAHAS), and the different bands of the Pawnees. The document indicated, therefore, a trade that did not extend farther north than present-day Nebraska. Individual traders from St. Louis had ventured farther upriver but not in the organized fashion that the Missouri Company was attempting (Nasatir, *Before Lewis and Clark*, 1:209-11, 339; W. Raymond Wood, *Prologue to Lewis and Clark: The Mackay and Evans Expedition* [Norman, Okla., 2003], 27-31).

In his notes on the "Account of the commerce" cited above, TJ wrote of the Pawnees of the two villages, the REPUBLIC Indians, and the LOUPS: "these hunt little, take few blankets & cloths, cloathing themselves in skins."

[1] In TJ's notes cited above, he continued "mostly withdrawn, the business has been a losing one, & now almost discontinued."

From John Page

MY DEAR SIR   Richmond Novr. 16th. 1803

I beg your pardon, for delaying so long, my acknowledgments of the favor conferred on me, by your transmitting to me your Address or Message to the Congress. It afforded me high Satisfaction, not only as communicating most interesting information respecting your Treaty with France; & the friendly disposition of the great Powers in Europe towards the United States; but as containing the most flattering prospect of the flourishing Condition of their Revenue; & as inculcating on the minds of the members of Congress, & their Constituents, Sentiments of the soundest policy, & the purest Philanthropy.

You will oblige me Sir, by informing me what has been the result of your Enquiries on the subject of the secret Correspondence between you & Governor Monroe, respecting the Transportation of Slaves in certain Cases; as some information on that Subject, may be expected by our Legislature in the course of their next Session.

I return with many thanks your Letter to Dr. R.—I wish I had leisure to give you my thoughts on the interesting Subject it contains. I am happy to find that I was not mistaken in my opinion that the difference between us was not so great, as many have supposed. I send it now because in our Friend Mr. Short, I find a more safe conveyance than I may meet with again: I am with the highest Respect & Esteem Your obedient Servant   JOHN PAGE

RC (DLC); endorsed by TJ as received 26 Nov. and so recorded in SJL. Enclosure: TJ to Benjamin Rush, 21 Apr., and enclosure.

From Caspar Wistar

DEAR SIR,   [on or before 16 Nov. 1803]

It has happened to me more than once, to feel great pain & regret while I was writing to you, on account of the trouble I occasioned you, & the liberty I was taking, in soliciting promotion &ca., for the persons in question. I assure you those sensations occur with unusual force on the present occasion, which is this—Dr. Bache has nearly concluded his tour [of] attendance on the Missisippi Boat[-men], for this year, & I should suppose with great success, as he has lost but [7] out of 400 Patients he has however been sick twice, & is so much discouraged, by the smallness of the Compensation, & the severity of the duty, that he has requested my Sister to solicit for him the place of Land-Officer, which he supposes to be vacant.

Your Knowledge of the Gentleman, & of the business, makes you really a better Judge than any other person, & I therefore will only add my sincere request & wish that you would forgive the [libe]rty taken by Your affectionate friend   C. WISTAR J[UNR.]

RC (DNA: RG 59, LAR); undated; torn; at foot of text: "His Excellency [the President] [. . .]"; endorsed by TJ as received 16 Nov. and "Bache Wm to be land officer N.O." and so recorded in SJL.

MY SISTER: Catharine Wistar Bache.

From Henry Dearborn

SIR,   [17 Nov. 1803]

I take the liberty of proposing the above named Gilbert C. Russell as an Ensign in the 2d. Regt. of Infantry and that his name be added to the list I had the honour of submitting this morning.

Your Huml. Servt   H. DEARBORN

RC (DLC); undated; endorsed by TJ: "Cocke Wm. Washn. Nov. 16. 03. recd. Nov. 17. to Genl Dearborne" (see below) and "Russell Gilbert C. to be ensign." Recorded in SJL as a letter of 17 Nov. received that day with notation "military nominns."

ABOVE NAMED: the letter printed above was written at the foot of a brief letter to Dearborn from Senator William Cocke of Tennessee, dated Washington, 16 Nov. 1803, in which he recommended Gilbert C. Russell as possessing "good moral character" and "a liberal education." TJ sent Russell's nomination to the Senate on 18 Nov. 1803.

For the LIST submitted THIS MORNING, see Dearborn to TJ, 16 Nov.

From Henry Dearborn

                                                        War Department
SIR,   November 17th. 1803

It does not appear on a strict examination of the papers in this Office, that any documents remain, which will enable me to give any information on the subject of the Arrest of Zachariah Coxe—If there ever were any documents in this Office relative to that subject, they were probably consumed with the War Office in November 1800—

With respectfull Consideration I am, Sir, Your Obedt. Servt.

                                                        H. DEARBORN

RC (DLC); in a clerk's hand, signed by Dearborn; at foot of text: "The President of the United States"; endorsed by TJ as received from the War Department on 17 Nov. and "Coxe's case" and so recorded in SJL. FC (Lb in DNA: RG 107, LSP).

On 15 Nov., the House of Representatives issued a resolution requesting that the president submit any documents in his possession regarding the case of Zachariah Cox (COXE). Cox gained notoriety during the 1790s for his controversial western settlement schemes. On 2 Nov. 1803, he submitted a memorial to the House, protesting his arrest and confinement in 1798 at Natchez by the U.S. army while he was ostensibly on a mercantile voyage to New Orleans. Cox fled to New Orleans, where he learned from the Spanish governor that he had been accused of being the leader of a "lawless banditti" and that federal and territorial officials were demanding his extradition. Returning to the United States, Cox was arrested in Nashville and incarcerated for almost three months "without any charge, crime, or offence being alleged against him." In addition, he claimed that federal officers had seized some $9,000 worth of property from him at Natchez (Isaac Joslin Cox and Reginald C. McGrane, eds., "Documents Relating to Zachariah Cox," *Quarterly Publication of the Historical and Philosophical Society of Ohio*, 8 [1913], 31-114; ASP, *Miscellaneous*, 1:361-2; JHR, 4:434-5, 444-5; Vol. 22:29-30).

From Nathaniel Macon

SIR   17 Novr. 1803

Mr. Finley coming in this morning, prevented my informing you, that John Hay & Robert Cochran both live in or very near to Fayetteville, and that Robert Troy lives in the county of Anson, about 40 miles distant from Fayetteville

I am Sir Yr. most obt sert—   NATHL MACON

RC (DNA: RG 59, LAR); endorsed by TJ as received 17 Nov. and "Lyne, Roberts & Hunt. Commrs. bkrptcy" and so recorded in SJL.

FINLEY: William Findley.

For the recommendation of JOHN HAY and ROBERT COCHRAN as bankruptcy commissioners to hear a case in Anson County, North Carolina, see Samuel D. Purviance to TJ, 24 Oct.

Macon had received correspondence calling for the appointment of commissioners to hear the case against Joshua Wynne, a merchant from Granville County. James Lyne was one of those recommended to hear this "Business of the Highest Consequence." Macon wrote three names in the corner of an address sheet: Lyne, William Roberts, and Washington Norwood, to which TJ added a fourth, William Hunt, in pencil. On 18 Nov., TJ named Lyne, Roberts, and Hunt as commissioners for Williamsboro, a post town in Granville County. This was the last set of bankruptcy commissioners appointed by TJ (Joseph M. Myers to Macon, 19 Oct., and Kemp Plummer to Macon, 7 Nov., in DNA: RG 59, LAR, 7:0447-51 [James Lyne]; list of commissions in Lb in DNA: RG 59, MPTPC; Jedidiah Morse, *The American Gazetteer*, 2d ed. [Charlestown, Mass., 1804], s.v. "Williamsborough"; Vol. 37:711).

To the Senate

TO THE SENATE OF THE US.

During the last recess of the Senate I have granted commissions for promotion and appointment in the military corps of the US. for the following persons & commands, which commissions will expire at the end of the present session of the Senate. I therefore now nominate the same persons for reappointment to the same commands, to wit.

Regiment of Artillerists

Capt. Richard S. Blackburn to be Major, vice Danl. Jackson resigned Apr. 30. 1803.

1st. Lieutt. John Saunders to be Captain vice Blackburn promoted Apr. 30. 1803.

1st. Lieutt. Howell Cobb to be Captain vice   Izard resigned June 1. 1803.

John Livingston to be 2d. Lieutt. appointed April 25. 1803. of Virginia.

Charles M. Taylor of Pensylva: to be 2d. Lieutt. appointed July 18. 1803.

William L. Brent of Maryland to be 2d. Lieutt. appointed July 18. 1803.

First regiment of Infantry.

Lt. Col. Thomas Hunt to be Colonel, vice Hamtramck died Apr. 11. 1803.

Majr. Jacob Kingsbury of the 2d. regimt of infantry to be Lt. Col. of the 1st. regimt vice Hunt promoted Apr. 11. 1803.

1st. Lieutt. John Whipple to be Capt. vice Pasteur promoted Apr. 11. 1803.

2d. Lieutt. Horatio Stark to be 1st. Lieutt. vice Whipple promoted Apr. 11. 1803.

Ensign William Richardson to be 2d. Lieutt. vice McComb transferred to the Corps of engineers Oct. 12. 1803.

Ensign Anthony Campbell to be 2d. Lieutt. vice Stark promoted Apr. 11. 1803.

Ensign Thomas B. Steele to be 2d. Lieutt. vice Brownson resigned Nov. 15. 1803.

Neal Duffee of New York to be Ensign. appointed July 18. 1803.

Jonathan Eastman of Vermont to be Ensign. appointed July 18. 1803.

Second regiment of Infantry.

Capt. Thomas Pasteur of the 1st. regimt of Infantry to Majr. of the 2d. regimt. vice Kingsbury promoted Apr. 11. 1803.

1st. Lieutt: George Salmon to be Capt. vice Butler died May 6. 1803.

1st. Lieutt. John Campbell to be Capt. vice Purdy resigned Sep. 30. 1803.

2d. Lieutt. William Wooldridge to be 1st. Lieutt. vice Salmon promoted May 6. 1803.

2d. Lieutt. James Wilkinson to be 1st. Lieutt. vice Campbell promoted Sep. 30. 1803.

Ensign Wm. Simmons to be 2d. Lieutt. vice B. Wilkinson promoted Jan. 15. 1803.

Ensign Joseph Doyle to be 2d. Lieutt. vice Wooldridge promoted May 6. 1803.

Ensign John Miller to be 2d. Lieutt. vice J. Wilkinson promoted Sep. 30. 1803.

Samuel W. Sayre of Pensylvania to be[1] Ensign appointed Apr. 14. 1803.

William P. Clyma of Virginia to be Ensign. appointed Apr. 14. 1803.

Reuben Chamberlin of New Hampshire to be Ensign. appointed July 19. 1803.

Richard Chew of Maryland to be Surgeon's mate. appointed May 2. 1803.

Calvin Taylor of Vermont to be Surgeon's mate. appointed July 16. 1803.

I also nominate the following persons for the appointments now proposed

Robert Richie of Maryland to be 2d. Lieutt. in the regiment of Artillerists.

Richard Smith of Maryland to be 2d. Lieutt. in the regiment of Artillerists.

Alpha Kingsley of Vermont to be Ensign in the 1st. regiment of Infantry.

Gideon Warner of Vermont to be Ensign in the 1st. regiment of Infantry.

Samuel Williamson of Pensylvania to be Ensign in the 2d. regiment of Infantry.

Gilbert C. Russell of Tennessee to be Ensign in the 2d. regiment of Infantry.

John Watson of New York to be Surgeon's mate in the army of the US.

John Griffin of North Carolina to be Surgeon's mate in the army of the US.[2]

TH: JEFFERSON
Nov. 18. 1803.

RC (DNA: RG 46, EPEN, 8th Cong., 1st sess.); endorsed by a clerk. PrC (DLC); TJ later added "apprd." in ink in the left margin next to the first name on the list and placed check marks beside all the names. Recorded in SJL with notation "military re-nominations."

Henry Dearborn forwarded this list of recess PROMOTION AND APPOINTMENT, from Richard S. Blackburn through Calvin Taylor, to TJ in his letter of 9 Nov. Dearborn supplied the remaining names to the president on 16 and 17 Nov. The Senate consented to all of the nominations on the 22d (JEP, 1:458-9).

[1] Preceding four words interlined in place of "appointed."

[2] TJ here canceled two appointments: "Morris Jones of North Carolina to be Cadet in the regimt of Artillerists" and "Prentiss Willard of   to be a Cadet in the regimt of Artillerists."

From Jones & Howell

RESPECTED FRIEND   Phila. 19th Novr. 1803

Your Obliging favors of 6th & 8th Inst are both reced. the first requesting us to send Two Tons of rod Iron the last Inclosing Check for 45\frac{31}{100}$ which is to your Credit. we should have reply'd sooner, but waited for an opportunity to send you the rod Iron. we Can now Inform You, we have Shippd. on Board the Schooner Jane Ephraim Pearson Master.

80 Bundles rod Iron assorted
wt 2.0.0-0 at $124 $248 —
      porterage   1.33
                       $249.33

And have Consigned them to Gibson & Jefferson Richmond. Agreeable to Your orders

with Sentiments of respect we are Your Friends

JONES & HOWELL

RC (MHi); at head of text: "Thomas Jefferson Esqr"; endorsed by TJ as received 23 Nov. and so recorded in SJL with notation "80. b. rod. 249.33."

From the Mississippi Territory Legislative Council

SIR   Novemr. 19th 1803

We the Legislative Council of the Mississippi Territory possessing in Common with our fellow Citizens the livliest Sentiments of Gratitude towards the general Government for the unremitted Attention it has discovered to the Interests of this Country, are desirous of expressing to you, Sir, our great satisfaction and Joy at the interesting Event, which has lately resulted from executive and diplomatic management in the Concerns of the Mississippi. It will be faithfully representing the Feelings of our Constituents as well as those of our own, to declare, that the Knowledge of no Occurrence except the Establishment of American Independence, has been more joyfully or more thankfully received, than the important Cession of Louisiana.

By this great acquisition our Commerce, Peace and Prosperity are secured; and the true American Policy, which prefers pacific Negotiation to rash and sanguinary measures is preserved justified and admired.

Receive, Sir, our cordial congratulations on this Occasion, accompanied by our sincere Wishes, that you may long live to enjoy the Confidence, and promote the prosperity of your Countrymen.

JOHN ELLIS President
of the Legislative Council

Attest
  Felix Hughes Secy
  to the Legislative Council

RC (DLC); in Hughes's hand, signed by Ellis; endorsed by TJ as received 19 Dec. and so recorded in SJL.

The above address was submitted to the LEGISLATIVE COUNCIL on 11 Nov. 1803 by member David Lattimore. It was intended originally to have been a joint communication from both houses of the territorial assembly, but when the House of Representatives failed to report on it, the council approved the address on its own on 19 Nov. and requested that the governor forward it to the president (*Journal of the Legislative Council, of the Second General Assembly of the Mississippi Territory at Their Second Session* [Natchez, 1804], 21-2, 33).

To Louis Alexis Hocquet de Caritat

SIR   Washington Nov. 20. 1803.

I recieved last night your favor of the 16th. instant, with the Prospectus for the publication of General Collot's travels through Louisiana & his account of that country. I willingly subscribe for a copy of it, and now return you the Prospectus which I presume will be published in the gazettes. although every thing respecting that country is interesting to the US. yet I suspect that the expansiveness of this edition will circumscribe the benefit of the publication to a narrow circle, and that one on a more economical scale by extending it's sale, might have increased it's usefulness to the public & it's profit to you. but this is matter of opinion only, and your own judgment formed on experience is more to be relied on. should any new views of the subject induce you to vary the plan, you will still be pleased to consider me as a subscriber, on whatever scale it shall be published. Accept my salutations & good wishes.

TH: JEFFERSON

P.S. the French edition will be preferred.

PrC (DLC); at foot of text: "M. Carritat"; endorsed by TJ in ink on verso.

To Stephen Cathalan, Jr.

DEAR SIR   Washington Nov. 20. 1803.

My friend Mr. Butler, a Senator of the US. from South Carolina
having a desire to get some White Hermitage wine, I take the liberty
of addressing him to you and of mentioning at the same time that I
recieved from your friend at Cette what you were so kind as to order
for me. there were two qualities, the one of the crop of de Loche
which made up nearly the whole of what was sent, which is not at all
to our taste. but there were 3. bottles of what was called in the invoice
White Hermitage Virgin 179[5] of the crop of Jourdan. the quality of
this was delicious, and it is of this quality [which] mr Butler wishes
the supply he writes for. I shall soon renew my application to you for
the same quantity I asked the last year, all of this quality: but on this
subject you will hear from me particularly as soon as the last parcel of
fruits arrive which you mentioned would be soon dispatched. your
attention to mr Butler's order will be considered as a favor to myself.
Accept my friendly & respectful salutations   TH: JEFFERSON

PrC (MHi); faint, with text in brackets
supplied from Dupl; at foot of text: "M.
Cathalan. Commercial Agent of the US.
at Marseilles"; endorsed by TJ in ink on
verso. Dupl (Archives municipales, Marseilles, France); in a clerk's hand, signed
by TJ; at head of text: "Copy." Recorded
in SJL with notation "for Majr. Butler."

From John Francis Renault

                                     Blandfort près Petersburg en Virginie
MONSIEUR LE PRÉSIDENT,   le 20 novembre 1803.

Depuis 3 ans entiers je travaille au crayon fin un tableau historique
et allégorique qui aura pour titre,

Les Anglais rendant les Armes au Général Washington Commandant en Chef L'armée Américaine et Française, après leur défaite à
york &a.

Il ne m'appartient point de faire à votre Caractère l'éloge de cet
ouvrage, un Auteur a pour soi de l'indulgence, mais si des Personnes
de gout et de distinction m'honorent de leur visite, et me disent toutes
que la Dédicace n'en convienne qu'à vous seul, c'est qu'elles ont plus
de confiance en la générosité avec laquelle vous encouragez les Arts
et les Sciences, que dans le mérite de mes talents.

Les Grands hommes effectivement, Monsieur, se plurent dans tous
les tems à donner leur protection aux Sçavans et aux Artistes habiles:

Les Amphictyons portèrent un décret solemnel qui obligeait la Gréce en général à défrayer Polygnote célébre peintre de ses dépenses hospitalieres partout où il passerait; Les fameux Auteurs de L'Enéïde, et des Métamorphoses s'acquirent l'estime D'Auguste et de Mécene; L Empereur Charles V, disait à le Titien (qui avait laissé tomber un pinceau en peignant ce prince et que celui ci lui ramassa) qu'il était digne d'etre servi par César; Pierre le Grand Czar de Moscovie, Louis XIV &a. se rendirent magnanimes par la fondation d'illustres Académies et Institutions et par l'accueil favorable qu'ils firent aux Etrangers éclairés.

Conséquemment il serait d'un heureux augure pour moi de vous offrir la dédicace de mon ouvage, s'il avait quelque rapport à la sublimité de leurs travaux admirables, puisque s'il obtenait votre approbation, ce serait le mettre sous la bienveillance d'un homme dont le Génie profond et l'amour de la Sagesse l'ont élevé à la plus haute dignité; mais cette production est médiocre, et ne peut vous étant présentée me laisser d'autre espoir qu'elle vous sera agréable, que dans votre bonté et affection pour les artistes inférieurs.

Ce sera donc, Monsieur le Président à vos Vertus, si vous voulez bien le permettre que je dédierai ce faible tribut de mon respectueux hommage, qui paraissant en public sous vos Auspices acquerra le titre le plus recommandable, et si mes vœux s'accomplissent la main des Parques, pour le bonheur de l'humanité, enchainera si bien vos jours d'un tissu de roses, qu'ils seront toujours à leur printems.

Je Suis très profondément, Monsieur le Président, Votre très humble Et très obéissant Serviteur   JN. FIS. RENAULT

P.S. J'aurai l'honneur incessamment de vous présenter ce tableau dont le prospectus est ci inclus; pour cet effet j'attends, Monsieur le Président la faveur de votre Réponse afin de le terminer et le mettre sous verre.

EDITORS' TRANSLATION

                                        Blandford, near Petersburg, Virginia
MR. PRESIDENT,   20 Nov. 1803
    For three full years I have been drawing a historical and allegorical tableau entitled *The British Surrendering to General Washington, Commander in Chief of the French and American Army, After their Defeat at Yorktown,* etc.
    It is not my role to praise this work to you, since a creator is always biased. If people of taste and distinction honor me with their visits and tell me that you are the only person to whom the work can rightfully be dedicated, their words speak less about my talent than about their confidence in the generosity with which you encourage the arts and sciences.

[20]

In all eras, Sir, great men have taken pleasure in protecting talented scholars and artists. The Amphictyons solemnly decreed that everyone in Greece should defray the expenses of the famous painter Polygnotus wherever he traveled. The famous authors of the *Aeneid* and the *Metamorphoses* earned the esteem of Augustus and Maecenas. When Titian dropped a brush while painting a portrait of Charles V, the emperor himself picked it up, telling him that Titian was worthy of being served by Caesar. Peter the Great, czar of Russia, Louis XIV, and others showed magnanimity in founding famous academies and institutions and welcoming enlightened foreigners.

If my tableau were in the same league with these artists' sublime works, I would happily dedicate it to you, for the approval of a man of profound genius and love of wisdom would give it prestige. But since my work is mediocre, I can only hope that in your generosity and affection toward inferior artists, you will look kindly on it.

For this reason, Mr. President, if you permit, I will dedicate this modest tribute of my respectful homage to your moral qualities. When it appears in public under your auspices, it will become worthy. And if my wishes are fulfilled, the fates will envelop your days in a net of roses so you will have an eternal springtime, for the happiness of humanity.

I am, Mr. President, most sincerely, your very humble and obedient servant. Jn. Fis. Renault

P.S. Very soon I shall have the honor of presenting the tableau to you. The prospectus is attached. I await the favor of your reply to finish it and install the glass.

RC (DLC); endorsed by TJ as received 25 Nov. and so recorded in SJL. Enclosure: "Prospectus d'un Tableau historique et Allégorique," a work that will depict on one side the Goddess of Liberty crushed by a chariot driven by tyrants and enemies of the people; on the other side will be a monument to American heroes who shed their blood to defend their country; in the center will be an urn holding the ashes of illustrious men such as Montgomery, Franklin, Warren, Mercer, Greene, Laurens, Hancock, and others; around the grave, three deities, representing the ideals of justice, peace, and prosperity that Americans fought for, will trample on symbols such as crowns, scepters, crosses, and spears; the image will also depict prominent leaders and officers and will show Lord Cornwallis surrendering his sword to George Washington; the subscription price is $12 for the unframed picture, with $1 as a down payment and the remainder due upon delivery; under the title Renault wrote "Dedié à" (dedicated to), followed by a blank (MS in same; in French; in Renault's hand, signed).

John Francis Renault had been a secretary and engineer with the Comte de Grasse's fleet at Yorktown and performed similar roles with other French squadrons before that. He also at one time held a staff position with French military forces in Saint-Domingue. His best-known artistic work was "The Triumph of Liberty," an engraved print, published in New York, of an allegorical scene that honored the American Revolution. He sold that work by subscription beginning in 1796. In 1804, Renault filed for copyright and printed a prospectus (in English) of his picture of the Yorktown surrender, which he intended to call "The Siege of York." In 1815 and 1816, he published notices in newspapers to explain to subscribers why the plate for the printing was still unfinished. When the print did appear in 1819, it had the title "The British Surrendering their Arms to Gen: Washington after their defeat at York Town in Virginia October 1781." In 1825, Renault published a copy of a 1782 map of the Yorktown siege by Sebastian Bauman and dedicated it to Lafayette (George C. Groce and David H. Wallace, *The New-York Historical Society's Dictionary of Artists in America, 1564-1860* [New Haven, 1957], 531; Newburyport *Impartial Herald*, 15 Jan. 1796; New York *Argus*, 15 Apr., 6 Dec. 1796; *National Intelligencer*, 11 Apr. 1804; *Baltimore Patriot*, 20, 23 Dec. 1816; *Prospectus of an Historical and Allegorical Picture, Entitled, The Siege of York; or, The British Surrendering Their Arms to General Washington, After their Defeat at York-Town, in Virginia, in the* *Month of October, 1781* [n.p., 1804], Shaw-Shoemaker, No. 7168; *Plan of York Town in Virginia and Adjacent Country* [Philadelphia, 1825]; E. McClung Fleming, "From Indian Princess to Greek Goddess: The American Image, 1783-1815," *Winterthur Portfolio*, 3 [1967], 55-6; Bernard F. Reilly, Jr., *American Political Prints, 1766-1876: A Catalog of the Collections in the Library of Congress* [Boston, 1991], 7-8).

From John Richman, with Jefferson's Note

MAY IT PLEASE YOUR EXCELLENCY   New York Novr. 21. 1803

To permit me to State to your Honour That last Jany, I wrote to the Honble the Secretary Of the Treasury for A patent, for An Invention To the Bedstead line; which Instead of the present Mode of Chords Attached to Studs & Flat holes In the Sacking bottom; my Plan is with Rolers And Cogg wheels Under the Sacking with A Clock And Spring; which has mett with the approbation Of Gentlemen; and Cabbinett makers here; I duly received An Answer, requireing the Usual documents and Small remittance Usual

Permit me Sir Notwithstanding my Sure Interest in the business Oweing to A large Sum of mony that is due me Since last Feby. which to gett my due I shall be Obliged to proceed in Our Court of Chancery To Obtain; and Our late misfortunate Sickness Of the fever prevents me on my return to this Afflicted City, and the very Great Scarceity of Cash To Send on the Small Sum requisite; And I am Sorry to Say Stops me from proceeding with Some Bedsteads bespoke as my Humble hope is just now, Knowing the Excellence of your private Charracter to promote merrit and Industry—On this hope I am Emboldend to pray Your Excellencys pleasure To be pleased to Assist in this difficulty A man Who for the Sake of the thirty $ has been Idle in A manner Since the Middle of Augt. as the fever Obliged me to retreat. The want of the patent has Cost me many wakeing midnight Hours And I see little prosspect this winter of Spareing the Cash To send; necessity Oh necessity Please Your Excellency Has Embolden me in Hope of Your Goodness Sir To Raise Up A man, brought Up A, Artist and Mechanic, I shall have; bespoke work Immeadiately to go About, I have Sent A Good deal to different Vendues for Sale but purchasers so little it would not pay my Journeymens wages in the Common run of work I have for Sale

I remain with the profoundest Respect in duty will be bound to Bless Your Excellencys Goodness to Your Obedient Humble Servt

JOHN RICHMAN

Carver, Cabbinet maker &c

[*Note by TJ in margin:*]

Nov. 26. Returned him his papers with an assurance that there was a patent in 1792. for exactly the same bedstead.

RC (DLC); below signature: "No 5 Burling Slip N.Y"; at foot of text: "To His Excellency Thomas Jefferson President of the United States of America Whom may the Great Creator long preserve Has been my Publick wish; and private prayer this 32. m. Past"; endorsed by TJ as received 25 Nov. and so recorded in SJL. Enclosures not found.

John Richman trained in London and had been employed for over 30 years in the furniture trade. He became a U.S. citizen in 1795 and worked as a cabinetmaker, carver, and gilder in Philadelphia. In 1805, he sought work in TJ's household. In 1832, a John Richman of Lancaster, Ohio, received a patent for bedstead fastening (Cornelius William Stafford, *Philadelphia Directory, for 1801* [Philadelphia, 1801], 61; James Robinson, *Philadelphia*

Directory, City and County Register, for 1802 [Philadelphia, 1801], 204; John Adams Paxton, *Philadelphia Directory and Register for 1818* [Philadelphia, 1818]; Edmund Burke, *List of Patents for Inventions and Designs, Issued by the United States, from 1790 to 1847* [Washington, D.C., 1847], 308; Richman to TJ, 22 July 1805).

RETURNED HIM HIS PAPERS: no letter from TJ to Richman of 26 Nov. has been found or is recorded in SJL.

A PATENT IN 1792: a British patent of 1792 incorporated pulleys, ropes, and hinges into the design of a bed. Ludwig C. Kuhn of Philadelphia received a U.S. patent for an "improved bedstead" in 1791 (*Patents for Inventions. Abridgments of Specifications Relating to Furniture and Upholstery* [London, 1869], 13; ASP, *Miscellaneous*, 1:423).

To the Senate

TO THE SENATE OF THE UNITED STATES

I nominate Nicholas Fitzhugh of the county of Fairfax in Virginia to be an Assistant judge of the Circuit court of the district of Columbia, vice James Marshall resigned.

William S. Pennington of New Jersey to be Attorney for the US. in the district of New Jersey vice George Maxwell resigned.

George Hay of Virginia to be Attorney for the US. in the district of Virginia vice Thomas Nelson deceased.   TH: JEFFERSON

Nov. 21. 1803.

RC (DNA: RG 46, EPEN, 8th Cong., 1st sess.); endorsed by a Senate clerk. PrC

(DLC). Recorded in SJL with notation "nomns. Fitzhugh. Pennington. Hay."

Lewis Harvie delivered these nominations to the Senate on 21 Nov. The next day, the Senate read the message and ordered it to lie for consideration. The senators considered and consented to the nominations on 25 Nov., the same date entered on the three commissions issued by the State Department (FCs in Lb in DNA: RG 59, MPTPC; JEP, 1:458, 459).

From John Vaughan

DEAR SIR   Philad: Nov. 21. 1803

Capt Merewether Lewis having been chosen a Member of our Society, I take the liberty of enclosing to you his Certificate of Election, & the letter advising of his Election, as the only Certain channel, by which the information can be Conveyed to him.

Our friend D Priestley has been very Ill, D Wistar saw him previous to the Serious attack & found him much Broken—since D W. left him, he was incapable of Swallowing any food; the last intelligence however States, that he was much relieved, the most alarming symptoms having disappeare'd.

Our Volume which could not be commenced on acct. of the fever, is now in the press—The Communications from M Dunbar which came thro' your hands are in part printed & the whole will be—Your late Valuable Communication to Congress of the Political &c State of Louisiana is highly interesting—It is possible that in Collecting the materials from which it was digested, That many important circumstances relative to the Natural History, Climate &c may have come to hand, should this be the Case, & no other disposition of them be intended, our Society would recieve them with the highest Interest.

D Priestley notwithstanding his feeble State of body still retains a Vigorous mind, he has made a Communication to the Society, in reply to D Darwin on Equivocal Generation, & is now dictating a reply to Mr Linns last pamphlet on the Socratic dispute, in which he has forgotten to treat the Dr. P. with *Courteousness* & indeed treats him with great harshness—

The Socy. now receives regularly the Philos. Journals of France & England, & One from Germany—By this means our professors and men of Science will know early, what has been Done in Europe, & can direct their attention more readily to discoveries, or to the perfectioning of Discoveries already announced. Knowing the attention you ever pay to the attempts to make Science progress in this Country—I make no Apology for troubling you—

Mr Poyntell & Mr Bradford, are on the point of embarking in a scheme to print on a Very large Scale—All the Greek & Latin Classicks, it is intended to supersede the future importation of them from Europe—They have been led to the plan, from the very great & increased Demand for these Works latterly—It is proposed to invest not less than 100,000. Ds. in the Scheme

I remain with the Greatest respect Dear sir Your friend & servt

Jn Vaughan

We have just reced. Michaux—Am: flor: Bor: in 2 Elegant 4to Vol with 51. Plates

RC (DLC); addressed: "Thomas Jefferson President of the United States"; endorsed by TJ as received 24 Nov. and so recorded in SJL. Enclosures not found.

The American Philosophical SOCIETY elected Meriwether Lewis to membership on 21 Oct. (APS, *Proceedings*, 22, pt. 3 [1884], 343).

OUR VOLUME: in the spring of 1802, the APS appointed a committee to assemble papers for a sixth volume of the society's *Transactions*. That summer, Vaughan thought that the work would soon be ready for typesetting. Yellow FEVER intervened, forcing the cancellation of the society's meetings in the fall. The society granted the committee more time, and in the spring of 1803 agreed to a publication plan offered by Jane Aitken (APS, *Proceedings*, 22, pt. 3 [1884], 324, 326-7, 337; Vol. 38:115-16; Vol. 40:515-16n).

The volume would include five papers on various subjects that TJ received from William DUNBAR in 1800 and 1801 and an abstract of information from Martin Duralde that Dunbar sent to TJ early in 1803 (APS, *Transactions*, 6 [1809], 1-23, 25, 40-58; Vol. 32:35-7, 54-5, 262, 311, 448-9; Vol. 35:121-4; Vol. 39:269-70).

Joseph Priestley conducted experiments with algae to refute theories expressed in a posthumously published work by Erasmus DARWIN, *The Temple of Nature*. On 18 Nov., the APS received Priestley's paper, "Observations and Experiments relating to equivocal, or spontaneous, Generation" (APS, *Proceedings*, 22, pt. 3 [1884], 344; APS, *Transactions*, 6 [1809], 119-29; F. W. Gibbs, *Joseph Priestley: Adventurer in Science and Champion of Truth* [London, 1965], 245-6).

REPLY TO MR LINNS LAST PAMPHLET: in September, John Blair Linn responded to Priestley's *Letter to the Reverend John Blair Linn* with *A Letter to Joseph Priestley, L.L.D. F.R.S. In Answer to his Letter, in Defence of his Pamphlet, Entitled Socrates and Jesus Compared* (Philadelphia, 1803; Shaw-Shoemaker, No. 4528; see Priestley to TJ, 25 June). On 12 Dec., Priestley sent TJ a copy of his rejoinder, *A Second Letter to the Revd. John Blair Linn*.

William POYNTELL sold the inventory of his stationery and fancy-goods store in Philadelphia to Samuel F. BRADFORD and established what he called the Classic Press to reprint works in Latin and Greek that he hoped to sell in wholesale lots at rates below the prices of imported books (*Gazette of the United States*, 2 Apr. 1802; *Port Folio*, 3 Dec. 1803; *Library; or, Philadelphia Literary Reporter*, 1 Dec. 1804; Horace L. Hotchkiss, Jr., "Wallpaper from the Shop of William Poyntell," *Winterthur Portfolio*, 4 [1968], 25-33).

The American Philosophical Society paid $15 for the work by André MICHAUX, *Flora Boreali-Americana: Sistens Caracteres Plantarum Quas in America Septentrionali*, recently published in Paris (APS, *Proceedings*, 22, pt. 3 [1884], 345).

From John Beckley

SIR,   Washington, 22d: November 1803.

Permit me, on behalf of my brother in law, Mr: Isaac Prince, now residing in the Island of Saint Bartholomew, and carrying on business there as a Merchant, to present to your consideration, his application & pretensions for the appointment of Consul or Commercial Agent for the Swedish Island of Saint Bartholomew, and the three Danish Islands of Santa Cruz, Saint Thomas, and Saint Johns.

This application, Sir, is offered, equally, on the ground of the well known wish of Merchants and others of those Islands having Commercial intercourse with the United States, and of the approbation and consent of the respective Consul and 'Charge des affairs' of Sweden and Denmark, now residing here, who are not only desirous of such an Arrangement, but have assured me, that your Authorization to whomsoever given, will be promptly recognized by the Authorities of those Islands, and that *they* will respectively apply to their Courts for Exequators to confirm the same. In respect to Mr: Prince, it is within my own knowledge to say that to much intelligence and Capacity in Commercial affairs, he unites an unblemished reputation and well established Credit, and is the Son of an old and Meritorious Revolutionary Whig, now no more, who, to the most excellent of private Characters, added an integrity of adherence to his public principles, which produced to him a deprivation by the Enemy, of all his property, and a painful imprisonment of Eight Months, on board of a loathsome prison ship at New York, by which he was prevented from leaving to his Children, other inheritance than his own pure integrity of Character.

Perhaps, Sir, it may not be improper to add that I have communicated to the Secretary of State, on behalf of Mr: Prince, the inducements to this application as herein stated.

With great personal attachment and esteem, I am, Sir, Your most obedt: Servt: JOHN BECKLEY

RC (DNA: RG 59, LAR); endorsed by TJ as received 22 Nov. and "Prince Isaac to be Consul St. Bartholomew, Santa Cruz &c" and so recorded in SJL.

On 9 Dec., TJ nominated ISAAC PRINCE to be the American consul in St. Barthélemy (BARTHOLOMEW). The Senate approved the nomination six days later (JEP, 1:459-60; TJ to the Senate, 9 Dec.).

CONSUL AND 'CHARGE DES AFFAIRS': Richard Söderström and Peder Pedersen (Vol. 39:495n; Vol. 40:493-4; Albert Gallatin to TJ, 8 Sep. 1808).

REVOLUTIONARY WHIG: James Prince, Sr., Beckley's father-in-law (Edmund Berkeley and Dorothy Smith Berkeley, *John Beckley: Zealous Partisan in a Nation Divided* [Philadelphia, 1973], 52-3).

From Justus Erich Bollmann

SIR,   Philada. November 22d. 1803

Several of my Friends, being of Opinion that the Island of St. Domingo, as soon as evacuated by the French, will become a Theatre of important commercial as well as political Occurrences, have expressed a Wish that I might go there, and I confess that I feel myself considerably tempted by the Prospect of an extensive and beneficial Activity. This Temptation would be the greater if I could hope to have an Opportunity on that Station of rendering Services to Your Excellency personally or to the Government of the United States.

I therefore take the Liberty of inquiring whether I may flatter myself so far to possess Your Excellency's Confidence as to indulge an Expectation that I should enjoy the Preference for Your Comands in that Quarter?

I remain with great Respect Your Excellency's obt. humble St.

J. ERICH BOLLMANN

RC (DNA: RG 59, LAR); at foot of text: "The President of the United States"; endorsed by TJ as received 25 Nov. and "to be Consul St. Domingo" and so recorded in SJL.

To John Breckinridge

Nov. 22. 03.

Extract of a letter from a judicious & well informed American who has for some time been at the settlement of Natchitoches.

'What kind of government would at first be most suitable & proper god only knows. it would be farcical to see a lawyer in a court of justice addressing a jury of them at present. with a few exceptions they have no other idea of any kind of government than a Commandant with both civil & military jurisdiction. they have been accustomed to such ill luck in any attempt to obtain justice, they seldom apply, & submit to any thing that happens quietly'

Th: Jefferson with his salutations to mr Breckenridge sends him the above extract, as also a separate paper from an American on the same subject. this last being an office paper he desires to have returned after mr Breckenridge shall have made what use of it he thinks best.

RC (DLC: Breckinridge Family Papers); addressed: "The honble John Breckinridge." Not recorded in SJL. Enclosure not found, but perhaps Daniel Clark's answers to TJ's queries on Louisiana (see *Terr. Papers*, 9:38).

TJ made the EXTRACT from the 10 Oct. letter of John Sibley enclosed by William C. C. Claiborne on 28 Oct. (same, 9:78).

From Henry Dearborn

War Department
SIR, Novr. 22d. 1803

I have the honor to propose Edmund Hayward of Maryland & James Lanier of Kentucky for Surgeons Mates, and Reuben Smith & Thomas A. Smith of Georgia for 2d. Lieutenants in the Corps of Artillerists and James Logan of Kentucky for an Ensign of the 2d. Regiment of Infantry—
With respectfull consideration I am your Obedt. Servt.

H. DEARBORN

RC (DLC); in a clerk's hand, signed by Dearborn; at foot of text: "The President of the United States"; endorsed by TJ as received from the War Department on 24 Nov. and "Nominations" and so recorded in SJL. FC (Lb in DNA: RG 107, LSP).

HONOR TO PROPOSE: TJ sent these nominations to the Senate on 9 Dec. The Senate approved the commissions on 15 Dec. (JEP, 1:459-60).

To Jones & Howell

GENTLEMEN Washington Nov. 22. 03.

William Stewart, a smith who has lived with me at Monticello some years, is now in Philadelphia, and wishes to have some files and bars of iron and some steel[1] of his own choice, sent on for me to Richmond. I will therefore pray you to ship for that place such as he may chuse, consigning them to Gibson & Jefferson. I must also trespass on your benevolence with respect to this man. he is one of the first workmen in America, but within these 6. months has taken to drink, which seems to have deranged his mind at times. in one of those[2] alienations of mind he abandoned his family, consisting of a very excellent wife & several children, with a declared purpose of never returning to them, & they are consequently in the most distressed situation, taken care of at present indeed on charitable motives, but with a dreary prospect before them. he writes me word he will return, & desires me to send him 20. D. to bear his expences back. were I to put them into his own hands, they would only enable him to continue his dissipations. I therefore take the liberty of inclosing that sum to you,

& on the ground of charity for his family of asking the favor of you to encourage him to return to them, to pay his passage to this place in the stage, & give him in money his reasonable expences on the road, which for three days would not be more than 2. or 3. dollars a day. if he has more it will only enable him to drink & stop by the way. when he arrives here I shall take other measures to forward him. he is become so unfit for any purposes of mine, that my only anxiety now is on account of his family, and it is for them I wish to interest your humanity so far as to take the trouble I have proposed to you. Accept my salutations and good wishes.   TH: JEFFERSON

PrC (MHi); at foot of text: "Messrs. Jones & Howell"; endorsed by TJ in ink on verso. Recorded in SJL with notation "Stewart."

A letter of 15 Nov. from WILLIAM STEWART, recorded in SJL as received from Philadelphia on 20 Nov., has not been found. TJ recorded sending Stewart a letter, also not found, at 22 Nov.

Stewart's WIFE, Mary Stewart, sent TJ an undated letter, recorded in SJL as received from Monticello on 20 Nov. but not found. TJ recorded sending a reply on 21 Nov., but that letter has also not been found.

[1] Preceding three words interlined.
[2] TJ here canceled "[fits of]."

To John Milledge

DEAR SIR   Washington Nov. 22. 03.

Altho' I am so late in answering your favor of Aug. 5. yet it was not unattended to; and has, in execution, had it's effect. while we were negociating with the Creeks for the extension of your Oakmulgee boundary, we thought it unadvisable to press any other topic which would be disagreeable to them. as soon as the unfavorable turn which that negociation took, was known, I desired the Secretary at War to take the proper measures for effecting the object of your letter of Aug. 5.

The Cherokees have at length ceded to us the road from Knoxville to the Savanna, under some cautions & restrictions which it is believed they will soon retire from in practice. we have now to press on the Creeks a direct road from this place to New Orleans, passing always below the mountains. it will probably brush the Currahee mountain, pass through Tuckabatchee & Fort Stoddart. we hope to bring N. Orleans to within 1000. miles of this place, and that the post will pass it in 10. days. the acquisition of Louisiana will it is hoped put in our power the means of inducing all the Indians on this side to transplant themselves to the other side the Missisipi, before many years get about.

I thank you for the seeds & stones you have been so kind as to send me. I hope Congress will rise early enough to let me pass the month of March at home to superintend the planting them and some other things which may be growing & preparing enjoiment for me there when I retire from hence. Be so good as to present my respectful compliments to mrs Milledge, & to accept yourself my friendly salutations & assurances of great esteem & consideration.

TH: JEFFERSON

RC (Neal Auction Company, New Orleans, 2006); at foot of text: "Govr. Milledge." PrC (DLC).

TO TAKE THE PROPER MEASURES: in a letter dated 14 Oct., Dearborn instructed Benjamin Hawkins to assist agents from the state of Georgia in finding and recovering any "prisoners or negroes" held by the Creek Indians (DNA: RG 75, LSIA).

In the spring of 1803, Dearborn declared to Return Jonathan Meigs that the CHEROKEES "must be brought to reason" on the subject of a road running through their lands to connect Tennessee and Georgia. Dearborn advised the agent that "it may be proper to offer an inducement" to a few influential individuals to achieve the desired result. Meigs obtained an agreement for the road in October, but most Cherokee chiefs did not sign. Those who did, along with an allied group of entrepreneurs who were members of the Cherokee nation by marriage, received advantages in the selection of the route, other concessions, and gifts. Dearborn overruled a provision for a small army outpost at the Cherokees' border with Georgia. He wrote to Milledge and John Sevier on 21 Nov., informing the gover-nors that the president, having no U.S. funds available for surveying and opening the road, suggested that their states take the necessary action (Dearborn to Meigs, 30 May, and to Milledge, Meigs, and Sevier, 21 Nov., in same; William G. McLoughlin, *Cherokee Renascence in the New Republic* [Princeton, 1986], 77-8, 88-91).

FROM THIS PLACE TO NEW ORLEANS: the president "has it in contemplation to establish a communication between the Seat of Government and New Orleans, in as direct a line as circumstances will admit," Dearborn informed Hawkins. TJ "therefore requests," Dearborn continued, that "you will give him all the information in your power relative to the practicability of finding a road from the Southwestern frontier of North Carolina near the Northwestern corner of South Carolina to your residence & from thence to the Mouth of the Alabama" (Dearborn to Hawkins, 22 Nov., in DNA: RG 75, LSIA).

In April 1804, TJ had SEEDS of the Cherokee rose (*Rosa laevigata* Michx.) that he had received from Milledge planted in the nursery at Monticello (Betts, *Garden Book*, 291, 293).

From John Rhea and Thomas Moore

Washington
November 22d, 1803

William Martin of Smith County in the state of Tennessee, who also is a member of the General Assembly of that State, requested that he might be named to the President of the United States for an appointment to the office of a Surveyor in the Louisiana territory, if such an office should be created—

We therefore agreeably to his request have taken the liberty to name him to You *for* that purpose. We believe him qualifyed to discharge the duties of such office—and with pleasure we can also say that we believe him to be an honest man, and firmly attached to the Principles of Republicanism

With consideration of respect and esteem—Your Obedt Servts

JOHN RHEA
of Tennessee
THO MOORE
of So. Carolina

RC (DNA: RG 59, LAR); in Rhea's hand, signed by Rhea and Moore; at foot of text: "The President of the United States"; endorsed by TJ as received 23 Nov. and "Martin Wm. of Tennissee to be Survr. Louisiana" and so recorded in SJL.

John Rhea (ca. 1753-1832), a native of Ireland, represented Sullivan County in the Tennessee General Assembly before his election to Congress, where he served nine terms in the House of Representatives between 1803 and 1823 (ANB; *Biog. Dir. Cong.*). Thomas Moore (1759-1822) was a planter from Spartanburg District, South Carolina. He served three terms in the state legislature during the 1790s and

seven terms in Congress from 1801 to 1817. As was Rhea, Moore was a solid Republican and supporter of TJ's administration (*Biog. Dir. Cong.*; *S.C. Biographical Directory, House of Representatives*, 4:411-12).

WILLIAM MARTIN, a son of Indian agent Joseph Martin and a former resident of upstate South Carolina, did not receive an appointment, but he did serve as a presidential elector for TJ in 1804 and for James Madison in 1808 (Robert M. McBride and Dan M. Robison, *Biographical Directory of the Tennessee General Assembly*, 2 vols. [Nashville, 1975-79], 1:502-3; *S.C. Biographical Directory, House of Representatives*, 4:382-3, 411-12).

Bill for the Organization of Orleans Territory

[23 Nov. 1803]

Be it enacted &ca. that all that portion of country ceded by France to the US. under the name of the province of Louisiana, which lies south of the Missipi territory & of an East & West line passing from the Missipi 10. miles North of the town of Natchitoches to the Western boundary of the said cession, shall constitute a territory of the US. under the name of the territory of Orleans the government whereof shall be organised & administered as follows.

The Executive power shall be vested in a Governor who shall hold his office during the term of 4. years unless sooner removed by the Pres. of the US. who shall be commander in chief of the militia of the said territory, shall have the power to grant pardons for offences against the sd territory & reprieves for those against the US. until the decision of the President of the US. thereon shall be made known, to appoint and commission all officers civil & of the militia whose appointments are not herein otherwise provided for & which shall be established by law. but the legislature of the territory may, by law, vest the appointment of such inferior offices as they think proper in other persons. he may on extraordinary occasions convene the legislature & shall take care that the laws be faithfully executed.

A Secretary of the territory shall also be appointed who shall hold his office during the term of 4. years unless sooner removed by the Pres. of the US. and whose duty it shall be under the direction of the Governr[1] to record & preserve all the proceedings & papers of the Executive and all the acts of the legislature. in case of the vacancy of the office of Governor, or of his absence[2] from the territory, the government thereof shall devolve on the Secretary.

The Judicial power shall be vested in a Superior court, & in such county courts and justices of the peace as the legislature of the territory may from time to time establish. the judges of the Superior court and the justices of peace shall hold their offices for the term of 4. years.

The Superior court shall consist of 3. judges who shall have jurisdiction in all criminal cases, and exclusive jurisdiction in those[3] which are capital; and original and appellate jurisdiction in all civil cases of the value of 100. D. it's sessions shall commence on the first Monday of every month, and continue till all the business depending before them in a state to be acted on, shall be gone through. they shall appoint their own clerk.[4] the county courts shall consist of such quorum of[5] the justices of the peace of the county as the legislature shall establish, shall have jurisdiction in all criminal cases not capital, and in all civil cases of the value of 50. D. and shall hold it's sessions monthly:[6] and the justices of the peace shall individually be conservators of the peace, and have jurisdiction in civil cases under 20. D. value.[7]

In all criminal prosecutions which are capital, the trial shall be by a jury of 12. good & lawful men of the vicinage; in all other cases criminal & civil, it shall be the duty of the legislature to introduce the trial by jury so soon, and under such modifications as to number & other circumstances, as the habits & state of the people of the territory will admit.

The legislative powers shall be vested in 24. of the most notable[8] fit & discreet persons of the territory to be selected annually by the Governor from among those holding real estate therein who shall have resided one year at least in the said territory[9] and hold no office of profit under the territory or the US.: they shall keep and publish a journal of their proceedings, shall chuse their Speaker & other officers: shall meet on their own adjournments, as well as on the summons of the Governor; shall determine the rules of their own proceedings, save only that every law shall be passed at 3 several readings on three several days, & by a majority of those present at each respective reading: and before it become a law, shall be presented to the Governor, & if approved by him, he shall sign it, but if not approved, it shall be no law.

Their power shall extend to all the rightful[10] subjects of legislation; but no law shall be valid which is inconsistent with the constitution of the US. with the laws of Congress, or which shall lay any person under restraint, burthen, or disability on account of his religious opinions, declarations or worship; in all of which he shall be free to maintain his own, & not burthened for those of another.

The laws in force in the territory at the commencement of this act, and not inconsistent with the preceding restrictions, shall continue in force, unless repealed, altered or modified by the legislature.

The Governor, Secretary, Judges, Attorney for the US in the Superior court, Marshal of the same court, and all General officers of the militia shall be appointed by the President of the US.[11] in the recess of the Senate, but shall be nominated at their next meeting for their advice and consent.

The Governor shall recieve a salary of 5000. D.
the Secretary   of 2000. D.
the Judges each   of 2500. D.
the Attorney for the US   of   500. D.
to be paid out of the revenues of impost & tonnage accruing within the territory[12]

The members of the legislature, justices of the peace, and officers of the militia shall recieve no compensation.

§ Slaves may be admitted into the sd. territory of Orleans from any of the US. or of their territories which prohibit their importation from abroad, on condition that their grandchildren shall be free: but they shall be admitted from no other state, territory or country.[13]

The residue of the province of Louisiana so ceded to the US. shall remain under the same name & form of government as heretofore: save only that the paramount powers exercised by the former governors of the province shall now be transferred to a Governor to be appointed by[14] the President of the US. and that the powers exercised by the Commandant of a post or district shall be hereafter vested in a civil officer to be appointed by the President in the recess of the Senate, but to be nominated at the next meeting thereof for their advice & consent: under the orders of which commandant the officers, troops, & militia of his station shall be: who, in cases where the military have been used under the laws heretofore existing, shall act by written orders, & not in person: and who shall recieve as a full compensation the pay, rations & emoluments allowed to a Colonel in the army of the US. acting at a separate station. the Governor shall recieve an annual Salary of   D. to be paid from out of the impost & tonnage of N. Orleans.[15]

It shall moreover be lawful for the President of the US. to unite the districts of two or more commandants of posts into one, where their proximity, or ease of intercourse will permit without injury to the inhabitants thereof.

Dft (DLC: TJ Papers, 137:23695); undated, but see TJ to John Breckinridge, 24 Nov.; entirely in TJ's hand. Enclosed in TJ to Breckinridge, 24 Nov., and in Breckinridge to TJ, 26 Nov.

BE IT ENACTED: in the Senate on 28 Nov., Robert Wright introduced a motion calling for the appointment of a committee "to prepare a form or forms of government for the territory of Louisiana." The Senate tabled the motion, then took it up on 5 Dec. and named Breckinridge, Wright, James Jackson, Abraham Baldwin, and John Quincy Adams as the committee. When Breckinridge, as chairman, convened the committee on 9 Dec., he "had a form of Government ready prepared," as Adams recorded in his diary. In a long meeting on the 17th, a majority approved "several principles, on which the chairman is to draw up his bill." At their next meeting a week later, however, Jackson and Wright also brought frameworks for a bill. Opposed to the formation of the committee "on the ground that we ought to make no form of Government for them without consulting the people, and without knowing something more of them," Adams decided early on that his "ideas are so different from those entertained by the Committee, that I have nothing to do but to make fruitless opposition." As a result, Adams did not record details of Breckinridge's original "form" or of any of the proposals presented on the 24th. The group made no decision on that day, but on the 26th Breckinridge was able once again to get approval of "principles" that would be "drawn into form" by him. On the 30th, the committee passed a draft bill prepared by Breckinridge and he introduced it in the Senate. The bill, for "erecting Louisiana into two Territories" and providing for its temporary government, preserved most of the contents of TJ's draft printed above. In modified form and with significant additions, the bill became law after it passed both houses of Congress and TJ signed it on 26 Mch. 1804. It was to become effective on 1 Oct. 1804 and be in force for a year after that, and then to the end of the next session of Congress. Until this new law took effect, the 31 Oct. 1803 act to enable the president to take possession of Louisiana remained in force (JS, 3:316, 320-1, 331; Adams, diary 27 [1 Jan. 1803 to 4 Aug. 1809], 54-9, in MHi: Adams Family Papers; MS bill in DNA: RG 46, Original Senate Bills, 8th Cong., 1st sess., in Breckinridge's hand; U.S. Statutes at Large, 2:283-9; Vol. 41:583-4).

Breckinridge's bill followed TJ's draft by placing the line that would set off Orleans Territory ten miles north of NATCHITOCHES. As passed, the act put the new territory's boundary farther north, at 33 degrees north latitude, which later became the northern boundary of the state of Louisiana west of the Mississippi River.

In the bill and subsequently in the act, the GOVERNOR was to be a resident of the territory and have a term of three years. The bill as introduced did not give the territorial legislature the power to VEST THE APPOINTMENT of any offices. Late in the process of forming the bill, Breckinridge deleted the power of the governor to CONVENE THE LEGISLATURE in extraordinary circumstances. Breckinridge transposed the section on JUDICIAL POWER to follow the section on the legislature. The bill left blank the terms of service of judges and justices of the peace. In the act, those terms were four years. Breckinridge struck from the bill specifications for COUNTY COURTS, and the act contained no provision for county or township courts. The bill granted inhabitants of the territory the protection of the writ of habeas corpus, gave them the right to obtain bail, and barred cruel and unusual punishment.

In the section on LEGISLATIVE POWERS, the bill omitted the word "notable" from the qualifications for members of the legislature. In final form, the act reduced the legislature to a legislative council of 13 members appointed by the president. Late in the process of formulating the bill, the committee excised the specific requirements for approval of laws, including the provision for readings on three separate days. The bill, and subsequently the act, called for the governor to publish the laws and report them to the president to be laid before Congress. The statute as passed named 21 federal laws that were to be IN FORCE in the territory.

SHALL RECIEVE A SALARY: the bill left blanks for the officers' salaries, and added a requirement that officeholders take an oath to the Constitution.

SLAVES MAY BE ADMITTED: the draft bill as TJ sent it to Breckinridge did not include this paragraph; see TJ to Breckinridge, 25 Nov. The act as approved by Congress prohibited importation of slaves from outside the United States or of any slave imported to the U.S. after 1 May 1798. Slaves could be introduced into the territory only by owners who were U.S. citizens "removing into said territory for actual settlement" (U.S. Statutes at Large, 2:286).

In the act of 26 Mch. 1804, THE RESIDUE OF THE PROVINCE became the district of Louisiana. The governor of Indiana Territory was to exercise executive authority there, and the territory's judges were to hold courts. In 1805, Congress made the district of Louisiana a territory (*Terr. Papers*, 7:188-9n).

WITHOUT INJURY TO THE INHABITANTS THEREOF: Breckinridge's bill added a section authorizing the president to arrange land exchanges with Indian tribes east of the Mississippi to relocate them to the west side of the river. Tribes that took advantage of that arrangement would have to acknowledge that they were under the protection of the United States, affirm that they could not make treaties, and agree that they could sell or dispose of their new land in the west only to the United States. Congress retained that section of the bill in the final act. The law also contained a section that nullified land titles from Spain, with an exception for tracts up to one mile square occupied by bona fide settlers (see Resolution on Land Titles in Louisiana, [ca. 29 Feb.-14 Mch. 1804]). That section of the act also specified a fine of up to $1,000 and imprisonment for up to 12 months for anyone who settled on, surveyed, or marked lands belonging to the United States within Louisiana (U.S. Statutes at Large, 2:287-9).

[1] Preceding six words interlined.

[2] TJ first wrote "in case of the removal of the Governor from office, or of his death, resignation, or absence" before altering the passage to read as above.

[3] TJ first wrote "shall have exclusive jurisdiction in all criminal cases" before altering the passage to read as above.

[4] Preceding two sentences interlined and continued in margin.

[5] Preceding three words interlined.

[6] Preceding six words interlined.

[7] TJ here canceled "with [a] right of appeal."

[8] Word interlined, as is "annually" later in the sentence.

[9] Remainder of clause interlined.

[10] Word interlined.

[11] Remainder of sentence interlined in place of "to continue in office to the end of the next session of Congress, & no longer

unless renewed with the advice & consent of the Senate."
[12] Clause interlined.

[13] Paragraph interlined.
[14] Preceding six words interlined.
[15] Sentence interlined.

From Christopher Ellery

Senate Chamber
Novr. 23d. 1803.

C. Ellery begs leave to present his highest respects to the President of the United States—and to mention that application has been made to him, by an old friend, of great worth, to aid Mr. Henry Wilson in the obtainment of a Consular appointment, for which he will ask through other friends—and further to mention that from the knowledge C. Ellery has of the character of his friend, he cannot doubt but that Mr. Wilson is well qualified for such an appointment and highly worthy of the confidence of the Executive—

RC (DNA: RG 59, LAR); endorsed by TJ as received 24 Nov. and "Wilson Henry to be Consul" and so recorded in SJL.

TJ nominated Baltimore merchant HENRY WILSON to be commercial agent at Ostend on 9 Dec. and the Senate confirmed the nomination on 15 Dec. Wilson later received consular appointments for posts at L'Orient in 1816 and Nantes in 1817 (Papenfuse, *Maryland Legislature*, 2:898; JEP, 1:459, 460; 3:38, 39, 73, 74; TJ to the Senate, 9 Dec.).

From Edward Johnston

SIR   Norfolk, Novr. 23d. 1803

Above I now inclose Capt. Butler's Receipt for a Case which Messrs. Gibson & Jefferson of Richmond lately forwarded with a request that it might be sent on to you—Wishing it safe to hand I remain very respectfuly, Sir,

Your Obed: Servt.   EDWARD JOHNSTON

RC (DLC); at head of text: "Thomas Jefferson Esquire"; subjoined to receipt signed by Tristram Butler, Norfolk, 23 Nov., for a box "in good order" to be conveyed to Alexandria and delivered to the President's House; at foot of text in TJ's hand: "Besides the above there are 2. hampers of wine"; endorsed by TJ. Recorded in SJL as received 2 Dec.

Edward Johnston established a mercantile partnership in Norfolk in 1799 and three years later was operating solely on his own credit. He may have moved to Richmond about 1806 (Richmond *Virginia Argus*, 20 Aug. 1799, 31 July 1802, 22 Aug. 1807; *Norfolk Gazette and Publick Ledger*, 19 Feb. 1806).

The wine that TJ also received with the shipment was 100 bottles of burgundy from Chambertin, which had been shipped from Le Havre to Norfolk. In his financial memoranda, TJ recorded paying $86 for the wine, including freight and customs duties (MB, 2:1116; Vol. 41:612).

To John Breckinridge

DEAR SIR   Washington Nov. 24. 03.

I thought I percieved in you the other day a dread of the job of preparing a constitution for the new acquisition. with more boldness than wisdom I therefore determined to prepare a canvass, give it a few daubs of outline, and send it to you to fill up. I yesterday morning took up the subject, & scribbled off the inclosed. in communicating it to you I must do it in confidence that you will never let any person know that I have put pen to paper on the subject, & that if you think the inclosed can be of any aid to you, you will take the trouble to copy it & return me the original. I am thus particular, because you know with what bloody teeth & fangs the federalists will attack any sentiment or principle known to come from me, & what blackguardisms & personalities they make it the occasion of vomiting forth.   my time does not permit me to go into explanations of the inclosed by letter. I will only observe therefore as to a single feature of it, the legislature, that the idea of an Assembly of Notables came into my head while writing, as a thing more familiar & pleasing to the French, than a legislature of judges. true it removes their dependance from the judges to the Executive: but this is what they are used to & would prefer. should Congress reject the nomination of judges for 4. years & make them during good behavior, as is probable, then, should the judges take a kink in their heads in favor of leaving the present laws of Louisiana unaltered, that evil will continue for their lives, unamendable by us, & become so inveterate, that we may never be able to introduce the uniformity of law so desireable. the making the same persons so directly judges & legislators is more against principle, than to make the same person Executive, and the elector of the legislative members. the former too are placed above all responsibility, the latter is under a perpetual controul if he goes wrong. the judges have to act on 9. out of 10. of the laws which are made; the Governor not on one in ten. but strike it out & insert the judges if you think it better, as it was a sudden conceit to which I am not attached; and make what alterations you please, as I had never before time to think on the subject, or form the outlines of any plan, & probably shall not again. accept my friendly salutations   TH: JEFFERSON

RC (DLC: Breckinridge Family Papers); at foot of text: "Mr. Breckenridge." PrC (DLC). Enclosure: Bill for the Organization of Orleans Territory, [23 Nov. 1803].

To the House of Representatives

To the House of Representatives
of the United States.

In conformity with the desire expressed in the resolution of the House of Representatives of the 15th. instant, I now lay before them copies of such documents as are in possession of the Executive relative to the arrest & confinement of Zachariah Cox by officers in the service of the US. in the year 1798. from the nature of the transaction, some documents relative to it might have been expected from the war office. but if any ever existed there, they were probably lost when the office and it's papers were consumed by fire.   Th: Jefferson
                                                                          Nov. 24. 1803.

RC (DNA: RG 233, PM, 8th Cong., 1st sess.); endorsed by a clerk. PrC (DLC). Recorded in SJL with notation "Zachariah Cox." Enclosures: (1) Extract of a letter from Governor Winthrop Sargent to Secretary of State Timothy Pickering, Mississippi Territory, 20 Aug. 1798, stating that an armed party under the command of Zachariah Cox was planning to assume control of the territory for the state of Georgia; Sargent arrested and confined Cox and requests instructions from the president on how to proceed; in support of his actions, Sargent encloses copies of six documents: a letter from James Wilkinson to Sargent, Massac, 2 Aug. 1798, informing the governor that boats carrying Zachariah Cox and 35 men have passed the post by river, but that Cox had also landed an armed force to pass overland below the post in violation of the act regulating trade with the Indians, also warning that Cox is a "usurper" at the head of an "extensive confederacy" and urging his arrest before passing Natchez; R. Buntin to Wilkinson, Fort Massac, 1 Aug. 1798, in response to Wilkinson's command to investigate the town of Smithland, Kentucky, on the Ohio River between the mouths of the Tennessee and Cumberland, found that six militia companies had been formed there under Kentucky law and were fortifying the place in expectation of an attempt by the United States to dislodge them under the pretext that the town is on Indian territory, that Cox was determined to force his way past Massac if necessary, that set-tlers have been promised a town lot in Smithland and 1,000 acres at Muscle Shoals; Major Thomas Gist to the commandant at New Madrid, from Smithland, 30 May 1798, stating that he is in command at Smithland, which was founded by Cox in February and which now contains 350 inhabitants who plan to pursue agriculture and commerce and to establish friendly intercourse with all their neighbors; Colonel Moses Shelby to Captain William Compton, 5 July 1798, authorizing Compton to muster his company when he thinks proper to maintain good order, and in all cases of insurrection or invasion to hold himself in readiness "to pursue the enemies of the regiment," but also to remain accountable to Kentucky law and Shelby's immediate orders; warrant signed by M. Mitchell, Smithland, 1 June 1798, appointing Jeremiah Wheeler a sergeant in Mitchell's "company of emigrants" at Smithland and allowing him 500 acres of land in addition to the "common allowance" of land granted on the great bend of the Tennessee River; Sargent to Captain Isaac Guion, Concord House near Natchez, 18 Aug. 1798, requesting that he immediately apprehend and confine Cox and hold him at Natchez until he receives further instructions. (2) Sargent to Governor Manuel Gayoso de Lemos, Natchez, 28 Sep. 1798, informing Gayoso that Cox, who had been arrested at Natchez "for the most atrocious misdemeanors, some of them tending to involve the United States in a war with Spain," escaped his confinement on 26 Sep. and is said to have fled to New Orleans; Sargent requests that Gayoso arrest Cox if found in Spanish territory and return him to the United States. (3) Proclamation by Sargent, Natchez, 7 Nov. 1798, offering a $300 reward for the apprehension and return of Cox, who had been arrested and confined "for high crimes and misdemeanors against the United States." (4) Extract of a letter from Pickering to Sargent, 10 Dec. 1798, stating that Cox's actions, as described by Sargent, appear to be infringements on Indian lands in violation of law, and Cox and his followers may be arrested in any state or territory in which they are found; the "only question that occurs is, whether the warrant of arrest was issued on adequate *proof* of the offence," asks Pickering, adding that such proof, "it is hoped, will be timely found" (Trs in DNA: RG 233, PM, 8th Cong., 1st sess.; printed in ASP, *Miscellaneous*, 1:358-61).

For the House RESOLUTION of 15 Nov., see Dearborn to TJ, 17 Nov. (second letter). After receiving TJ's message and accompanying papers, which Lewis Harvie delivered on the 24th, the House referred them to the committee appointed on 2 Nov. to consider Cox's memorial. Presenting its report on 28 Nov., the committee agreed that Cox's arrest and detention had been "irregular and oppressive," but did not deem the U.S. government bound to compensate him for his losses. Any redress, the committee concluded, "must be from a court of justice" (JHR, 4:456, 460; ASP, *Miscellaneous*, 1:361).

From James Sullivan

SIR   Boston 24th November 1803

Some time ago the Secretary of State, Mr Madison, requested of me information in regard to the method of ascertaining the boundary between the United States, on their northern angle, and the British dominions. He was lead to this by my having been the agent of our nation in the settlement of the St. croix line. I readily complied with his wishes; and now observe in the Presidents communication to Congress, that a convention is formed by the two nations to describe the boundaries, as yet unsettled, by demarkation. There can, as I beleive, be no need of an agent in this business, unless the convention renders it necessary. There are no state papers to examine, or old charters and grants to revise, a familiar knowledge of the country is all that is wanting, and therefore the commissioners can settle the matter—

I do not know that I should be thought of as a commissioner, nor have I any thing to say in my own favour on that score; I do not know of any reason which would induce me to decline the appointment. But as, in this day, misrepresentations spring up in every soil and climate and grow in every season I take the liberty to intrude this letter upon the President to let him be assured that I am ready to obey his commands.

May I be indulged to say, that the public opinion in favour of the present administration gains so fast, that the inveterate enemies to republicanism are obliged to call upon silence to shield them from public contempt.

I am Sir with those feelings and sentiments, which are due from an american citizen to his countrys best friend, your very humble Servant

JA SULLIVAN

RC (DLC); at foot of text: "The President of The United States"; endorsed by TJ as received 4 Dec. and "to be Comr. N.E. boundary" and so recorded in SJL.

SOME TIME AGO: Madison had written Sullivan on 10 May 1802, requesting that he supply "whatever information and observations" he thought proper to assist the United States in its negotiations with Great Britain to fix jurisdiction over the islands in Passamaquoddy Bay and to establish regulations for navigating the channels between them. Sullivan had served as agent for the United States in

the St. Croix commission authorized by Article 5 of the Jay Treaty. Sullivan made a lengthy reply to Madison on 20 May 1802 (Madison, *Papers, Sec. of State Ser.*, 3:203-4, 237-42).

CONVENTION IS FORMED: see TJ to the Senate, 24 Oct. 1803.

Also on 24 Nov., Sullivan wrote a similar, albeit briefer, letter to Madison, reminding the secretary of state of their previous correspondence and declaring his willingness to serve as a commissioner (RC in DLC; endorsed by TJ: "Sullivan Jas. to be Commr. N.E. boundary").

To John Breckinridge

TH:J. TO MR BRECKENRIDGE   Nov. 25. 1803.

Insert in some part of the paper of yesterday 'Slaves shall be admitted into the territory of Orleans from such of the United States or of their territories[1] as prohibit their importation from abroad, but from no other state, territory or country.' salutations.

RC (DLC: Breckinridge Family Papers); addressed: "The honble Mr. Breckenridge." Not recorded in SJL.

[1] Preceding four words interlined.

From Richard Cutts

SIR—   Washington Novr. 25th. 1803

Agreeable to your wish—I have made every enquiry respecting the situation[1] of Joseph Tucker Collector of the district of York &c in Maine & feel no hesitation in saying that the Public good requires his removal from office, *for continued intoxication*—

At the same time I will take the liberty to name Samuel Derby of York—as a suitable person to be appointed successor to Mr Tucker, being an old revolutionary Officer—at present holding the most responsible Offices in the gift of his fellow Townsmen & the best recommended—gives him the preference to all other candidates in my humble opinion—

I am Sir, with sentiments of high respect & esteem—yr Humbe. Sert.   RICHD CUTTS

RC (DNA: RG 59, LAR); torn at endorsement; at head of text: "The President of the United States"; endorsed by TJ as received 25 Nov. and "Saml. Derby to be Collectr. of York vice Tucker. a [sot]" and so recorded in SJL.

AGREEABLE TO YOUR WISH: for TJ's request that Cutts inquire into the facts relating to the collectorship at York, see Vol. 39:358. In January 1803, TJ had received a memorial from the town committee at York in favor of retaining JOSEPH TUCKER (same, 358-60). On 30 Sep., Tucker wrote the Treasury secretary that he understood that complaints against him had been made to Cutts. He assured Gallatin that the accusations were "entirely groundless, and false" and were made to obtain his office. Tucker requested "a fair investigation" before the president took any action (RC in DNA: RG 59, LAR; endorsed by TJ: "Tucker

Joseph. Collectr. of York. Sep. 30. 03. to mr Gallatin").

REVOLUTIONARY OFFICER: Samuel Derby was promoted to major of the 7th Massachusetts Regiment in 1778, the rank he held when he left the army in 1783 (Washington, *Papers, Rev. War Ser.*, 3:293). MOST RESPONSIBLE OFFICES: in 1801, Derby began representing York in the Massachusetts General Court. TJ sent Derby's nomination as collector and inspector of the revenue at York to the Senate on 9 Dec. Derby held the office until his death in January 1807 (Charles Edward Banks, *History of York Maine*, 2 vols. [Baltimore, 1967], 2:359-60; Newburyport *American Intelligencer, and General Advertiser*, 11 June 1801; Boston *Republican Gazetteer*, 9 June 1802; *Newburyport Herald*, 7 June 1803; Portsmouth *New-Hampshire Gazette*, 13 Jan. 1807; TJ to the Senate, 9 Dec.).

[1] MS: "situation."

From Jones & Howell

RESPECTED FRIEND   Phila. 25th Novr. 1803

Your favor of 22nd inst. reach'd us this day, and agreeable to your request, went immediately in quest of Mr Stewart, who had been with us some days before and had told us he wanted some Iron for You, but as you had not mentioned any thing of it to us, and his appearance being rather unfavorable, we evaded his request. this day in our search for him we found his son, who informs us, he had prevail'd on him to start for home three days ago, and by this time we hope he is with you. and we wish you may be able, by your influence, to render him more worthy of that family, whom he had deserted. he is an excelent mechanic, and has abilities to provide well for them, if under proper direction. any Iron or steel that you may wish sent on shall be promptly attended to, as soon as we are informed what kinds they are.

with Respect we Remain Your Friends   JONES & HOWELL

PS The 20 Dollar note Inclosed awaits your orders

RC (MHi); at head of text: "Thomas Jefferson"; endorsed by TJ as received 28 Nov. and so recorded in SJL.

Earlier in the year, TJ had sent funds to William Stewart's SON, William G. Stewart, but the younger Stewart at this time was likely aboard the *Argus*, a naval brig beginning a lengthy tour in the Mediterranean. Jones & Howell may have been referring to another son, Alexander Stewart, who handled some transactions for TJ in 1804 and 1805 (NDBW, *Register*, 68; MB, 2:1101, 1158; Vol. 38:63n; TJ to Jones & Howell, 28 Nov. 1804, 12 July 1805).

To John Page

MY DEAR FRIEND   Washington Nov. 25. 1803.

Supposing that your curiosity would make an Account of Louisiana acceptable, I inclose to you one of those which contains a digest of the most interesting information we have been able to collect in so short a time. the information we recieve weekly from N. Orleans confirms our belief that quiet possession will be delivered to us; that there has never there been a thought of opposition, & that all the letters & extracts we have seen in the papers from Cadiz & New Orleans were fabricated here & at Philadelphia to excite war if possible, & alarm at any rate. I expect that our troops are arriving about this day at New Orleans to recieve the possession, and that we shall hear of it's delivery in three weeks from this time. this transaction being once peaceably closed this great work will be crowned, and tho' we shall be only the 2d of the civilized nations in [mere][1] *extent* of territory, we shall be the first in that which is cultivable.

The Syllabus I put into your hands was borrowed of my daughter. it has no value but that which she sets upon it, and which alone induces me to recall it to your memory. it will come to me by post with perfect safety. present my friendly respects to mrs Page, & accept yourself my affectionate salutations, and assurances of constant esteem & respect.   TH: JEFFERSON

PrC (DLC); blurred; at foot of text: "Governor Page." Enclosure: *An Account of Louisiana, Being an Abstract of Documents, in the Offices of the Departments of State, and of the Treasury* (see Vol. 41:721).

Appearing first in the *Philadelphia Gazette* and reprinted widely, a letter from a correspondent in CADIZ reported that Spain, upset by the "conduct of Bonaparte" in selling Louisiana to the United States, was preparing for war with France. The correspondent also speculated that the "small fleet arming here" was destined for Havana, with the ultimate goal of blockading the Mississippi in the event of ratification of the purchase treaty. A separate letter from NEW ORLEANS reported the arrival of a Spanish schooner from Havana "with orders to the Governor not to give up the possession of Louisiana, to either France or the United States: but to wait for farther instructions from the Court of Spain" (New York *Commercial Advertiser*, 24 Oct.; New York *Evening Post*, 24 Oct.; *Alexandria Daily Advertiser*, 25 Oct.; Philadelphia *Gazette of the United States*, 25 Oct.; *New-York Herald*, 26 Oct.; Philadelphia *Aurora*, 28 Oct.).

Page enclosed TJ's SYLLABUS on the philosophy of Jesus in his letter of 16 Nov.

[1] Word interlined.

To the Senate and the House of Representatives

TO THE SENATE &
HOUSE OF REPRESENTATIVES OF THE US.

The treaty with the Kaskaskia Indians being ratified with the advice and consent of the Senate, it is now laid before both houses in their legislative capacity. it will inform them of the obligations which the US. thereby contract, and particularly that of taking the tribe under their future protection; and that the ceded country is submitted to their immediate possession and disposal.

TH: JEFFERSON
Nov. 25. 1803.

RC (DNA: RG 233, PM, 8th Cong., 1st sess.); endorsed by clerks. PrC (DLC). RC (DNA: RG 46, LPPM, 8th Cong., 1st sess.); endorsed by a clerk. Recorded in SJL with notation "Kaskaskia treaty." Enclosure: treaty of 13 Aug. between the United States and the Kaskaskia tribe (Tr in DNA: RG 233, PM, certified as a true copy by Joshua Wingate, Jr., 15 Oct.); see Enclosure No. 1 at TJ to the Senate, 31 Oct.

POSSESSION AND DISPOSAL: Lewis Harvie delivered the message to the House and the Senate on the 25th (JHR, 4:458; JS, 3:315). By an act that TJ signed on 26 Mch. 1804, Congress provided for the survey and sale of public lands north of the Ohio River and east of the Mississippi River "to which the Indian title has been or shall hereafter be extinguished" (U.S. Statutes at Large, 2:277-83).

To Jesse Simms

SIR   Washington Nov. 25. 03.

I have learned with real regret that my bill for the Canvasbacks you were so obliging as to furnish me the last year, had been suffered to remain unpaid. I took it for granted my Steward had taken care to pay it in time. immediately on finding it had not been done I desired mr Barnes of Georgetown to remit you 57. D. the amount which I hope has been done. Colo. Brent had promised he would intercede to obtain the same favor from you for the present year also, which will

be very acceptable to me, if convenient for yourself. I pray you to recieve my thanks for the past, and my salutations & good wishes.

TH: JEFFERSON

PrC (MHi); at foot of text: "Mr. Jesse
Sims"; endorsed by TJ in ink on verso.

Jesse Simms had lived in Alexandria
since at least 1792, when he added his
name to a petition favoring the incorporation of a bank in the town. An investor
in the Potomac River Company, he advertised at different times as a merchant,
shipowner, cash broker and stockbroker,
attorney, and manager of the postal stage
connecting Alexandria with Baltimore.
For several years, he ran the coffeehouse
at the tavern of John Gadsby (Miller,

Alexandria Artisans, 1:152; 2:9, 146, 236;
*Columbian Mirror and Alexandria Ga-
zette*, 1 July and 19 Aug. 1797; *Centinel
of Liberty, and George-Town and Washington Advertiser*, 16 July 1799; "Petition of Merchants of Alexandria, 1792,"
WMQ, 2d ser., 3 [1923], 206-7; Washington, *Papers, Ret. Ser.*, 2:6-7).

On the preceding day, TJ endorsed an
account between Simms and Gadsby for
38 pairs of ducks, dated 7 Jan. 1803, with
the note, "desired mr Barnes to remit 57.
D." (MS in MHi).

From John Breckinridge

Saturday Morning 26. Novr. 1803.

J Breckinridge returns the inclosed with his thanks to the President, for the trouble he has been so obliging as to take on this interesting subject. A copy has been taken, & the caution ('tho unnecessary) shall be borne in sacred recollection.—The scheme, so far as JB
has been able to consider it, appears well adapted to the object & will
be submitted to such as appear disposed to take any Interest in the
subject, without delay.

RC (DLC); addressed: "Mr. Jefferson"; endorsed by TJ as received 26 Nov. and so
recorded in SJL. Enclosure: Bill for the Organization of Orleans Territory, [23 Nov.
1803].

From DeWitt Clinton

SIR   New York 26 Novr. 1803.

I take the liberty of recalling to your mind the appointing Pierre C.
Van Wyck a Commissioner of Bankruptcy vice Mr. Sandford District Atty. who has or will resign

The enclosed papers were put into my hands by a friend for perusal—
and as they disclose some extraordinary proceedings I have thought
it a duty I owe to you to transmit them for your perusal at a leisure
moment—In doing this I do not mean to enter into the merits of the
subject or to interfere in any other shape than to solicit your applica-

tion of a corrective to an evil if any should be found to exist—Mr Wolstonecraft is a Citizen of this state.

A certain gentleman was to leave this place yesterday Morning—He has been very active in procuring information as to his probable success for Governor at the next election—This I believe is his intention at present altho' it is certain that if the present Govr. will consent to be a candidate he will prevail by an immense majority. Upon this subject I am sorry to inform you that I recd. a confidential letter from him mentioning his intention to decline: as this is known to nobody but one or two intimate friends[1] and as it is of great consequence that he should not persist in this determination, I am in hopes that he may be prevailed upon to change it. Perhaps a letter from you may be of singular service

I am most respectfully Your most obedt servt.

DeWitt Clinton

RC (DLC); at foot of text: "The President of the U.S."; endorsed by TJ as received 30 Nov. and so recorded in SJL. Enclosures not found.

RECALLING TO YOUR MIND: see Clinton to TJ, 7 Sep.

Evidently the ENCLOSED PAPERS concerned charges brought against Lieutenant Charles Wollstonecraft, the younger brother of Mary Wollstonecraft, who was stationed at Fort Jay on Governor's Island in New York harbor. Major George Ingersoll, the commander at Fort Jay, charged Wollstonecraft with disobedience of orders and neglect of duty, citing, along with other examples, his failure to act as judge advocate to a general court-martial. Ingersoll also charged Wollstonecraft with "scandalous & infamous conduct," including attempts to undermine the confidence and authority of his commanding officer by addressing embarrassing notes to Ingersoll and defaming his character in front of visiting officers. The lieutenant was also charged with entertaining prostitutes while acting as commanding officer at the garrison, "living in common with one of them for some time." Wollstonecraft brought countercharges, accusing Ingersoll of profiting by selling milk in the garrison. In September, Dearborn directed Thomas H. Cushing, adjutant general and inspector of the army, to bring both men to trial by court-martial. The court found Wollstonecraft guilty and reprimanded him for disrespect to his commanding officer. Wollstonecraft was promoted to captain in 1806 and to major in 1813. Ingersoll submitted his resignation in late 1804 instead of accepting a transfer to New Orleans (*Memoirs of Gen. Joseph Gardner Swift, LL.D., U.S.A., First Graduate of the United States Military Academy, West Point, Chief Engineer U.S.A. from 1812 to 1818. 1800-1865* [Worcester, Mass., 1890], 41-4; Jacob Kingsbury, Orderly Book, 16 Mch. 1804, NHi: Jacob Kingsbury Papers; JEP, 1:411, 414, 415, 434, 479; 2:23, 27, 480, 508; Dearborn to Cushing, 14 Sep., 13 Oct.; Dearborn to Wollstonecraft, 24 Dec. 1803, all in Lb in DNA: RG 107: MLS; *Washington Federalist*, 28 Dec. 1803; Boston *Columbian Centinel*, 7 Jan. 1804).

CERTAIN GENTLEMAN: Aaron Burr. The CONFIDENTIAL LETTER from George Clinton to his nephew was dated 26 Nov. The governor declared that the factors that had previously influenced his decision to run for office no longer existed. Because the "Cause of Republicanism" was so well established "as not to require any new sacrifice," he intended to decline a bid for reelection (Craig Hanyan, *De Witt Clinton: Years of Molding, 1769-1807* [New York, 1988], 278-9, 314n).

[1] Preceding six words interlined.

From William Henry Harrison

Vincennes 26th. Novr. 1803.

The Governor of the Indiana Territory presents his respectful Compliments to the President of the United States and requests his acceptance of the enclosed map which is a Copy of the manuscript map of Mr. Evans who ascended the Missouri River by order of the Spanish Government much further than any other person—

RC (DLC); in Harrison's hand; endorsed by TJ as received 20 Dec. and so recorded in SJL. Enclosure not found, but see below.

TJ forwarded the MAP to Meriwether Lewis on 13 Jan. 1804. By that time Lewis and William Clark obtained from other sources, including directly from Harrison to Clark, copies of maps based on information collected by John Thomas EVANS on a trip up the Missouri River beginning in 1796 on instructions from James Mackay, a trader affiliated with the Missouri Company (Moulton, *Journals of the Lewis & Clark Expedition*, 1:6, maps 5, 7-12, 30; 2:2-3; Jackson, *Lewis and Clark*, 1:135-6).

From Volney

MONSIEUR LE PRESIDENT   paris 26 novembre 1803

j'eûs l'honneur au mois d'avril dernier de Vous adresser un Exemplaire de la Nouvelle traduction des *Ruines*, dont je vous dois à tant de titres L'hommage: Le paquet fut confié aux soins de Mr *Curwen* de philadelphie, et la reponse que j'ai deja obtenue de diverses personnes ne me laisse pas doutes que le Votre Ne Vous ait été rendu: aujourdhui je Vous envoye par Mr Lee, Voye de Bordeaux, mon ouvrage intitulé *Tableau du climat et du Sol des Etats-unis*. Le jugement que Vous en porterez Sera pour moi le type de l'opinion qu'en prendra le public éclairé; j'ai eu pour but, non de flatter et de plaire, mais de dire la Verité; et il est possible que cette methode ne Soit pas plus agréable audelá qu'elle n'est endeça de l'atlantique. j'attache un grand prix a connaitre Votre opinion dont je connais l'impartialité. peu s'en est fallu que je ne perisse en fructidor, par les effets de ma cruelle maladie; mais la fievre qui a failli de me tuer parait avoir operé une crise heureuse: pour la consolider je pars et me rends à Marseille et à Montpellier où les Medecins m'ordonnent de passer L'hyver. j'attends avec desir quelque lettre de Votre amitié au primptems prochain. Vous connaissez trop Mes Sentimens de respect et d'attachement pour que j'aye besoin de Vous en renouveller L'assurance

C VOLNEY

MR. PRESIDENT,   Paris, 26 Nov. 1803

Last April I had the honor of sending you a copy of the new translation of *Ruines*, for which am indebted to you in so many ways. The package was entrusted to Mr. Curwen of Philadelphia and the responses I received from several people make me confident that you received yours. Today I am sending you through Mr. Lee, by way of Bordeaux, my work entitled *Tableau du Climat et du Sol des États-Unis*. I consider your judgment to represent that of the enlightened public. My goal was not to flatter and please but to tell the truth. It may be that this method is no more pleasant on your side of the Atlantic than on ours. I give great weight to knowing your opinion, since I know that you are impartial.

I almost died in September because of my cruel illness, but the fever that almost killed me seems to have produced salutary results. To continue my recovery, I am leaving for Marseilles and Montpellier, where the doctors have ordered me to spend the winter. I hope you will be kind enough to send me a letter in the spring. You know all too well my feelings of respect and attachment for me to have to repeat them here.   C VOLNEY

RC (DLC); alongside signature: "rue de la Rochefoucault No. 7. a paris"; endorsed by TJ as received 14 May 1804 and so recorded in SJL.

AU MOIS D'AVRIL: in a letter dated 21 Mch., Volney informed TJ that he was sending a copy of the *New Translation of Volney's Ruins*.

TABLEAU: see Volney's letter of 10 May for his *Tableau du climat et du sol des États-Unis d'Amérique*.

To Mary Jefferson Eppes

Washington Nov. 27. 03.

It is rare, my ever dear Maria, during a session of Congress, that I can get time to write any thing but letters of business: and this, tho' a day of rest to others, is not at all so to me. we are all well here, and hope the post of this evening will bring us information of the health of all at Edgehill and particularly that Martha and the new bantling are both well: and that her example gives you good spirits. when Congress will rise no mortal can tell: not from the quantity but the dilatoriness of business. mr Lillie having finished the mill, is now I suppose engaged in the road which we have been so long wanting, & that done, the next job will be the levelling of Pantops. I anxiously long to see under way the works necessary to fix you there, that we may one day be all together. mr Stewart is now here on his way back to his family, whom he will probably join on Thursday or Friday. will you tell your sister that the pair of stockings she sent me by mr Randolph are quite large enough and also have fur enough in them. I inclose some papers for Anne; and must continue in debt to Jefferson a letter for a while longer. take care of yourself my dearest Maria, have good spirits and know that courage is as essential to triumph in your case as in that of the Souldier. keep us all therefore in heart by being so yourself: give my tender affections to your sister, and recieve them for yourself also, with assurances that I live in your love only & that of your Sister. Adieu my dear daughter.   TH: JEFFERSON

RC (DLC); addressed: "Mrs. Eppes Edgehill near Milton"; franked; postmarked 28 Nov. Enclosures not identified.

DAY OF REST: 27 Nov. was a Sunday.

MARTHA AND THE NEW BANTLING: TJ had written John Wayles Eppes on 19 June about "Patsy fattening for an autumn exhibition." Martha Jefferson Randolph delivered a daughter on 2 Nov. and named her Mary Jefferson Randolph after

the baby's aunt (*Thomas Jefferson's Prayer Book*, ed. John Cook Wyllie [Charlottesville, 1952], plate 7; Vol. 40:576).

Gabriel Lilly (LILLIE) was likely overseeing work on the construction of the road that went from the east front of Monticello to the ford at Shadwell (Bear, *Family Letters*, 250n).

IN DEBT TO JEFFERSON: TJ had not yet replied to the 30 Oct. letter from his grandson, Thomas Jefferson Randolph.

From William Eustis

Sunday 27th Novr. 1803.

Dr. Eustis will with great pleasure take charge of the five dollars enclosed by the President for Mr Lillie Editor of the Telegraph.

RC (DLC); endorsed by TJ as received 28 Nov.

Under this date, TJ recorded a payment of $4.50 to Eustis for John S. LILLIE "for one year" (MB, 2:1112). Lillie sent TJ a receipt, dated 14 Dec., for the money re-

ceived "by the hand of Jacob Eustis," William Eustis's brother, being "payment in full for the Constitutional Telegraphe" for a year and a half, but stipulating from 1 Oct. 1800 to 1 Apr. 1801 (MS in MHi, in Lillie's hand and signed by him; Vol. 39:368n).

To Craven Peyton

DEAR SIR   Washington Nov. 27. 03.

If my note for 558.14 D paiable the 15th. of Dec. is still in your own hands, I should be very glad if it could be either postponed awhile or paid by monthly portions, as I find I shall be very hard pushed, during the next month. if however it is gone out of your hands I shall endeavor to make provision for it if possible. accept my friendly salutations and best wishes.   TH: JEFFERSON

RC (ViU); addressed: "Mr. Craven Peyton Stumpisland near Milton"; franked;

postmarked 28 Nov. PrC (same); endorsed by TJ in ink on verso.

MY NOTE: in his financial memoranda, TJ recorded under 11 Aug., "on settlement with Craven Peyton on account of Henderson's land, there is due to him 558.14 for which sum I gave him my note payable Dec. 15 at Gibson & Jefferson's counting house" (MB, 2:1106).

VERY HARD PUSHED: see TJ to George Jefferson, 20 Dec. Also, during December, TJ made several sizable payments in addition to his customary expenses for household contingencies and provisions, books and bookbinding, and charity. These included roofing material, frieze ornaments, and carpentry and masonry work for Monticello, as well as a $100 donation to Greenville College in Tennessee (MB, 2:1113-14).

For a promotional campaign in the 1930s, a Virginia bank produced thousands of facsimile copies of the manuscript of this letter. Some of the reproductions have been mistaken for the original (Leonard Rapport, "Fakes and Facsimiles: Problems of Identification," *American Archivist*, 42 [1979], 19, 21, 38-9; Bank of Virginia, *Credits and Debits*, October 1961, 7-8).

From John Conrad & Co.

SIR   Philada Novemb 28th 1803

We beg you will excuse the freedom we have used of transmitting to you by this days mail stage, The first number of an American Magazine Review—We are sensible that from the situation you hold in society & more from the high character you bear as a man of science & a friend to the Litterature of our country, that you must frequently be troubled with parcels & letters of the same kind, we have not therefore in any instance heretofore intruded them upon you and are now only induced to do it from a supposition that an American publication, in the conducting of which every effort will be made to render it a usefull means of conveying information on Politics, Agriculture[1] Commerce &c will not be entirely unacceptable to you—

With the highest Respect We are sir Your Obed Humb serts

JOHN CONRAD & CO

RC (MHi); at foot of text: "His Excellency Thomas Jefferson President of the Utd States"; endorsed by TJ as received 1 Dec. and so recorded in SJL. Enclosure: see below.

The FIRST NUMBER of the *Literary Magazine, and American Register*, published by Conrad in Philadelphia, appeared on 1 Oct. Charles Brockden Brown, its editor and primary contributor, had advertised proposals for an octavo periodical to include reviews of American publications as well as "such portions of information of a scientific, commercial and agricultural nature, as shall be deemed most remarkable and most deserving of notice." The magazine continued under his editorship until 1807 (H. Glenn Brown and Maude O. Brown, *A Directory of the Book-Arts and Book Trade in Philadelphia to 1820 Including Painters and Engravers* [New York, 1950], 34; Frank Luther Mott, *A History of American Magazines: 1741-1850* [Cambridge, Mass., 1957], 218-22; *Poulson's American Daily Advertiser,* 9 Sep. 1803; Vol. 32:93).

[1]MS: "Agricuture."

To James Oldham

Sir   Washington Nov. 28. 1803

I recieved last night your letter of the 26th. I am afraid from the account you give of the sheet iron there will not be enough to finish. however let it be put on the part where long sheets are wanting, so that whatever supply may be necessary may be of common sheet iron, and let me know as soon as done, how much will be wanting. I am in hopes you have recieved the screws. mr Stewart set out from here this morning on his return to Monticello where he will be about Friday. be so good as to inform mrs Stewart of this. accept my best wishes.

Th: Jefferson

RC (PWacD: Feinstone Collection, on deposit PPAmP); at foot of text: "Mr. Oldam."

Oldham's LETTER of 26 Nov., recorded in SJL as received from Monticello on 27 Nov., has not been found. A letter of 12 Nov. from Oldham, recorded in SJL as

received 20 Nov., and a reply from TJ, recorded at 21 Nov., have also not been found.

TJ received a shipment of SHEET IRON for Monticello's roof from Benjamin H. Latrobe in October (Latrobe to TJ, 2 Oct. and 30 Nov.).

From Robert Smith

Sir,   [28 Nov. 1803]

The names of the Officers I introduced to you are

Mr Jenks Lieut

Mr Ludlow Lieut, Nephew of Mr Ludlow of New-York Navy Agent—

Mr Perry Midshipman who served as acting Lieut—

Mr Ellery is his friend—

I am sorry to see such an account of the Midshipman. He was strongly recommended by Mr Thompson of Virginia Member of Congress and from the great interest he took in procuring him the Station on board the Schooner I concluded he was safe on the score of politicks—

Respectfully   Rt Smith

RC (DLC); undated; endorsed by TJ as received from the Navy Department on 28 Nov. and "Thom" and so recorded in SJL.

William C. Jenckes (JENKS), Charles LUDLOW, and Oliver Hazard PERRY had all returned from the Mediterranean in the frigate *Adams*. On 21 Nov., following the

ship's arrival at Washington, Smith ordered the *Adams* dismantled and its crew paid off "without delay" (NDBW, 2:101, 436; 3:96, 233; *Register*, 28, 32, 42, 67-8).

THE MIDSHIPMAN: possibly William H. Thom, a midshipman from the frigate *Chesapeake*. On 8 Nov., Smith granted Thom permission to make a voyage to

Europe. He sailed on the schooner *Citizen*, the private vessel chartered to carry the ratified Louisiana treaty to France and gun carriages to Morocco (Smith to Thom, 8 Nov., DNA: RG 45, LSO; NDBW, 3:401, 452, 460, 464; *Register*, 55). On 26 Nov., TJ received an undated letter from John Strode, which has not been found but is recorded in SJL with notation "Hedgeman Thom."

From Park Woodward

SIR   New London 28 November 1803

After congratulating you as the first Majestrate of the United States of America, upon the many happy and promising events that has occured and taken place to us as a Nation, within the limits of your Administration; and having great confidence in your Wisdom, and the simplicity of your mind, in conjunction with the great Council of our Nation, under the auspicious Goverment of the good providence of God; that every exertion shall yet be made, to make us as happy People. From which confidence, and to answer my own mind, with submission, have presented you with the following lines; wishing, if it could be consistent, it might be read before both Houses of Congress. As it is obviously evident that the United States of America are under a great Calamity as a Nation, and more especially some of our Cities and Capitals, in many parts of the Union; by reason of the Epidemical disease generally called the yellow Fever. And as I put no confidence in chance, as that any thing can take place, without the limits of true Philosophy; there must be a special or natural cause for every thing that does exist; and finding that no natural cause can be assigned by our most skilfull Physicians, and much less on Philosophical principles, of the origin, of the aforesaid calamity brought on us by the yellow Fever. From which my mind was lead to search for the special cause of the aforesaid calamity; and fully believing that all civil and moral goverment in every Department, from a private Family, to that of a Nation, was constituted by the Wisdom of Heaven; to contribute mutual happiness and tranquility to the whole mass of man kind. As every moral precept carries this signiture, do to all men as you would be done by; from which constituted goverment, and from the righteous Administration of every Department, the Citizens of the United States have a right to contemplate The greatest blessing. But a departure from the above signiture of moral goverment, special calamities must await us as a Nation; as well as in all other communitive bodies. For the righteous Judge of Heaven and Earth shall give to everyone as his works shall be. In my aforesaid search I find the Constitution of the United States in its Articles a sure foundation for such Laws and goverment as will protect all good morals; and the equal rights, liberties, freedom, and property to all its subjects, without any discrimination. I have no doubt this would be admitted by nine tenths of the freemen of our Nation; and so the special cause of the aforesaid calamity is not found in our National Constitution. But when I conptemplate of the many Thousands of our fellow men, within the limits of the United States, captivated to perpetual slavery, from generation to generation; either by Law, or without Law; all having from the God of our existence an equal right to liberty and freedom with all the rest of mankind. I am not at a loss for the special cause of the aforesaid calamity; when so many Thousands of our fellow men are deprived of their natural rights, and the just protection of Law; this truth being obviously witnessed from attended Circumstances to the rational mind. firstly. As I have had personal knowledge of several of our Eastern States for more than Fifty years, and I never heard of the Yellow Fevers being in this Country, untill since our Independence took place; tho' there is no doubt, but that the subjugation of the Negroes to slavery took place in the very early settlements of America; but the sin of ignorance we read is winked at. But since the founding of our present Constitution upon its true Republican principles, constituting equal good to all its subjects, which has been almost universally approbated and acknowledged, and in many Instances sworn to protect. We can no longer plead Ignorance in suffering so many of our fellow men to be Subjected in slavery. For he that knoweth his masters will, and commiteth things worthy of stripes, shall be beaten with many. Secondly. It obviously appears that the righteous Judge of Heaven and Earth, has marked out our great capitals and marritime Towns, and Cities, as the greatest offenders, and the just victims of his displeasure, as the judge of all the Earth will do right. Showing us that these maratime Towns and Cities were in the first transgression, in subjecting these unhappy People. Thirdly. It is obviously witnessed before our eyes, that God,[1] in his providence has made a discrimination, as in Egypt, between the oppressor, and the oppressed; for this Ethiopean Nation, by Gods power, in almost every Instance are protected from this destroying pestilence that wasteth at noon Day. From which circumstantial evidence, I feel justified in myself, and from the love I feel for my fellow men, to solicit our chief Majestrate, with the advise of our National Council, to see if these People now in slavery within the United States, cannot be liberated; least as was once said in a simular case, we be all Dead men. I would not wish to feel prejudiced against the private Interest of any of our fellow Citizens, that any one should wrongfully suffer a single Cent. For which end I should wish, (except something better can be devised) that Congress would appoint a Committee or constitute a Court, to hear and determine on a primeval of Right, whether those Negro slaves in the United States alluded to, are an honest acquired Property to the Possessor, or was subjected by fraud and held by power. If found in the former case, I could wish there might be ways appointed to have them all appraised at their just value, and paid for out of our Public Chest; and let them all be Emancipated and made free according to the true Spirit of our National constitution. But if found in the latter case, that they might by Law be made free and Emancipated from Slavery. Which would redound to the honor of our National constitution. Were this to take place in Either case, the same Country & Land that now is cultivated by the Labor of Negroes, would want their Labor, and no doubt they might be contracted with by the white planters at a moderate price. And as our territorial Dominion of the United States by a late contract and cession by France, is extended to a vast extent in the Southern Climate, and when I review the probable events that may take place in future times, if those Negroes could be liberated and made free on principles of Righteousness, and some means provided for their Education, and subjection to the Laws of the Land & Millitary Discipline, what a vast number of the hardy sons of freedom might be cultivated, that nature has adapted to a hot Climate, and would be as a Bulwark of Strength to our Nation in case of a Southern invasion, as it would not be likely any temptation would bias them to desert our cause. But Wisdom is profitable to direct the temptations that those People are now under. I should always wish we might never have a man reside in our National Councils that had a greater value for private Interest than for perfect Justice, and the honor of our present Constitution—

I have the honor to be Your most Obdt. & very Hbl. Servt.

PARK WOODWARD

RC (MoSHi: Jefferson Papers); in a clerk's hand, signed by Woodward; at foot of text: "Thomas Jefferson President of the United States"; endorsed by TJ as received 8 Dec. and so recorded in SJL.

Park Woodward (1726-1808) spent most of his life in the area of New London, Connecticut, where he advertised as a merchant and brewer. In the last years of his life, he became a Universalist preacher and published two pamphlets, both in New London in 1805, *A Guide to Faith,* *or Christian Monitor; in Which Is Represented, the Great Contest between Good and Evil* and *The Triumph of Faith, or Anti-Christian Policy Detected, in the Field of High Places . . . Being Displayed in the Form of a Dialogue between Christian and Calvin* (Mabel Thacher Rosemary Washburn, "From Puritan, Hugenot, and Patroon: An American Lineage in the Families of Van Rennselaer, Van Cortlandt, Floyd, Holland, Boudinot, Evertsen, Teller, Woodward, Nicolls, Bailey, Park, and Redfyne, with Allied Descents,"

Journal of American History, 12 [1918], 436; New London *Connecticut Gazette,* 28 July 1769, 3 Feb. 1786, 30 Oct. 1808).

WE BE ALL DEAD MEN: Exodus 12:33.

[1] MS: "Good."

From John Bradford

SIR   Lexington (Kentucky) Novr. 29th. 1803

I was favored (by a French gentleman from St. Louis) about 4 years ago, with a piece of the rock Salt of Louisiana; and judging from your communication to congress, in which mention is made of that Salt mountain, that you had never seen a specimen of the Salt, have taken the liberty of forwarding to you a piece thereof; it is inclosed in a small tin cannister, soldered at both ends (to prevent damage,) and inclosed in white leather, and accompanies this letter by mail.

from sr Yr. Obedt. servt   JOHN BRADFORD

RC (DLC); endorsed by TJ as received 13 Dec. and so recorded in SJL.

A native of Virginia, John Bradford (1749-1830) first came to Kentucky as a surveyor in 1779 and settled there permanently in the mid-1780s. He became the state's pioneer printer, establishing the *Kentucky Gazette* in Lexington in 1787 and the *Guardian of Freedom* in Frankfort in 1798. Acting on recommendations from Kentucky senators John Brown and John Breckinridge, TJ appointed Bradford a commissioner of bankruptcy in 1802 (ANB; Brigham, *American Newspapers,* 1:152-3, 163; Vol. 37:402, 706, 710).

SALT MOUNTAIN: the digest of information on Louisiana that TJ sent to Congress on 14 Nov. included an "extraordinary fact relative to salt" in upper Louisiana: "There exists about 1000 miles up the Missouri, and not far from that river, *a Salt Mountain!* The existence of such a mountain might well be questioned, were it not for the testimony of several respectable and enterprising traders, who have visited it, and who have exhibited several bushels of the salt to the curiosity of the people of St. Louis, where some of it still remains." The account described this natural wonder as 180 miles long and 45 miles wide and consisting of solid rock salt, "without any trees, or even shrubs on it." Numerous

salt springs allegedly ran underneath the mountain and flowed "through the fissures and cavities of it" (*An Account of Louisiana, Being an Abstract of Documents, in the Offices of the Departments of State, and of the Treasury* [Washington, D.C., 1803; Shaw-Shoemaker, No. 5196], 10). Federalist newspapers were quick to ridicule the remarkable claim. The *New-York Evening Post* pondered why TJ's account of Louisiana did not also cite the existence of "an immense lake of molasses" near the salt mountain, with "an extensive vale of hasty pudding" located in between. In a similar vein, the *Gazette of the United States* proffered several additional natural wonders waiting to be discovered in Louisiana, including a "vast river of *golden eagles* ready coined," an "immense mountain of *solid refined sugar,*" and a "considerable lake of pure Whiskey." Other newspapers suggested that TJ preserve the salt mountain by constructing a dry dock over it, or that he appoint a "committee of wise ones" to investigate whether the mountain "may not be *Lot's wife,* magnified by the process of time." Observing the sheer quantity of such remarks, one Federalist editor opined that TJ's salt mountain "has called forth more queer remarks, puns and epigrams, than any thing which has come to light, under the present 'enlightened government'" (*New-York Evening Post,*

28 Nov. 1803; *Gazette of the United States*, 21, 23, 25 Nov. 1803; *Albany Centinel*, 13 Dec. 1803; *New-York Gazette & General Advertiser*, 25 Nov. 1803; Hudson, N.Y., *Balance, and Columbian Repository*, 13 Dec. 1803). The source of the administration's information regarding the salt mountain is uncertain. Thomas T. Davis reported the existence of "a Salt Rock of immense size" in his letter to TJ of 5 Oct., and William Henry Harrison forwarded a sample of rock salt from the Missouri River in his 29 Oct. letter to the president. A report on Louisiana prepared in August 1803 at Kaskaskia by Zebulon M. Pike and forwarded to Samuel L. Mitchill included accounts of a "mountain of salt" on the Missouri. Citing French sources, Pike estimated the salt mountain to measure "60 leagues by 15." Writing to Benjamin Waterhouse in 1813, TJ asserted that the salt mountain claim originated in a paper written by Captain Amos Stoddard, "an officer, a federalist and an honest man," abridged by Jacob Wagner of the State Department "and put by him into the bundle of documents made up at that office for Congress, & passed through me without ever having been seen or read by me." TJ claimed that he had no knowledge of the salt mountain reference "till the federal writers drew forth the morsel so delicious for the exercise of their wit. I thought it as innocent a tub for the whale as could be given them, & said nothing" (*Medical Repository*, 7 [1804], 410; Donald Jackson, ed., *The Journals of Zebulon Montgomery Pike, with Letters and Related Documents*, 2 vols. [Norman, Okla.,

1966], 1:227, 228n; RS, 5:682; Vol. 41:675-6). The probable inspiration for the salt mountain account was the Big Salt Plain, a massive salt plain located next to an escarpment on the Cimarron River, a tributary of the Arkansas River in western Oklahoma. Its vast rock and crystalline salt deposits have attracted the interest of Indians, explorers, traders, and scientists for centuries (Thomas D. Isern, "Jefferson's Salt Mountain: The Big Salt Plain of the Cimarron River," *Chronicles of Oklahoma*, 58 [1980], 160-75).

About the time Bradford wrote the letter printed above, his son and fellow newspaper publisher, James M. Bradford, was attempting to secure an appointment in Louisiana. Writing Senator John Brown for assistance on 19 Dec. 1803, the younger Bradford explained his frustration at not becoming public printer of Kentucky and weariness over his rivalry with opposition printer William Hunter. Bradford hoped to secure the office of territorial secretary for Louisiana. He suggested that the salary would allow him to establish a newspaper in the remote territory, "and thereby diffuse those political principles which are the glory of the present administration" (RC in DNA: RG 59, LAR, endorsed by TJ: "Bradford James M. to John Brown. for Louisiana. mr Brown says he is honest, industrious, republican, and of good strong understanding. brought up a printer"). Although Bradford did not receive the appointment, he moved to New Orleans and established the *Orleans Gazette* in December 1804 (Brigham, *American Newspapers*, 1:152-3, 190-1).

From Frank Nash

[29 Nov. 1803]

I now take this Oppertunity to inform you that I am well and that I am going to London as I wrote to you before

I have agreed to gow to london buy the run for four guines and a half If it will be agreeable for you to send for me home or give me a passage from london you may expect that the ammerican consul at London will have information of where I shall be at the time that I should expect that I may have time from this to hear from you FRANK NASH

Perhaps it may be agreeable for you and your Ceuntary to find me with imploy to be in some place of office if it should be mothing mour than what I could with the Navy of the united states perhaps I could contrive some way or other without makeing many words about your busine or mine as the ways of the world ar so wise I would not say that the ways of the world ar so foolis that I dont car wha I due nor what I is that I would and so I have wrote this letter to you as I might due this twenty Ninth day of November from Dublin to London

FRANK NASH

RC (DLC); dateline supplied; endorsed by TJ as received 27 Apr. 1804 and so recorded in SJL with notation "probably an idiot."

AS I WROTE TO YOU BEFORE: Nash to TJ, 12 Sep.

From Joseph H. Nicholson

SIR   Novr. 29. 1803

I beg Leave to introduce Mr. Cutler of the Eastern Shore of Maryland, who has a Letter which he wishes to deliver you—He has brought with him a Petition signed by a Number of respectable Men in his quarter praying for the Removal of a Collector, at the Port of Snow Hill—It is address'd to Mr. Gallatin and has been delivered to him—I am extremely well acquainted with several of the Subscribers, and should feel entire Confidence in the Propriety and Rectitude of their Wishes—Snow Hill is in Mr. Dennis's District, and the Collector is stated to have been guilty of some vexatious Conduct, which is one of the Grounds on which his Removal is asked for—

I have the Honor to be, Sir with perfect Respect yr. Ob. Servt.

JOSEPH H. NICHOLSON

RC (DNA: RG 59, LAR); endorsed by TJ as received 29 Nov. and "Cutler John. to be Collector Snowhill" and so recorded in SJL, where it is connected by a brace with William Polk to TJ, 15 Nov.

SJL indicates that John CUTLER delivered the 15 Nov. LETTER from William Polk to TJ, which discussed an address to the Treasury secretary signed by 13 residents of Snow Hill, Maryland, concerning the COLLECTOR, William Selby. For Cutler's appointment, see TJ to the Senate, 9 Dec.

DENNIS'S DISTRICT: elected to the Fifth Congress as a Federalist, John Dennis continued to represent Maryland's Eighth District until March 1805 (Biog. Dir. Cong.; Manning J. Dauer, The Adams Federalists [Baltimore, 1953], 299).

From Mary Osborne

SIR   City of Washington Dec [i.e. Nov.] 29 [1803]

you who have studied your peopels happiness and so generaly bestowed it will no dought be suprised to be individually asked for assistance and from an intire stranger

the motives which induce me to so an action as appling to one in the station Mr Jefferson holds if I was to relate particularly would plead my pardon for so bold an intersession

a daughter beges for a widowed mother whose misfortuns have bean many and who has long suferd bodly and mentily with a tender family whose sex will not permit them to seak a livly hood from under her protection—my Mother keeping a shop of Ladys goods and as the summer being very dull and this faul unhealthy in canciquence my Mother could not intirely pay her Merchant and as this is the only seson of year which bisness can be done with the help of som friend my Mother cauld free her self from all incombrence and doe very well at her imployment

the many libral bestowments Mr Jefferson has give in incoragin arts and industry and his munificence to the unfortunate has made me hope and dare [. . .] him to be my mothers friend and if Mr j—n can put so much confidence [. . .] word and honesty of a femail and Lend my mother five hundred dollers [. . .] Mounths for with in that time it shall be returnd it will inabel my [mother] with industry and the incom of a small property establish her self in her bisness and free her self from all det

if Mr Jefferson can make it convenint and find satisfaction in granting my requst and make a mother and family comfortible and happy he will never have cause to repent a bounty and charity which will never be for got and ever greatfull for and punctually returnt

I am sencibel I have broke throw thos ruls prescrib to my sex and actied undutifull with out my Mothers knowledg and unnone to any person solisited Mr J—ns friendship and for fear of miscarage asked it in a fictitious name if ancred[1] shall be knawn

if Mr Jefferson is so Beneficent as to grant the above favour he will please to anceret this week and derect it to

SUSANA P ROBOSON
City of Washington

PS Mr jefferson will blame but if he new my unhappy resons for so bold a solisitation which principels and sentiment makes shuder at he would pity pardon and grant and with the hope he will I conclude a

[57]

letter which I am sencibel the manar is not proper but the motives great

    with Obd. & Rrct.   S P Roboson

RC (MHi); partially dated; torn; addressed: "Mr Jefferson"; endorsed by TJ as a letter of 29 Dec. corrected to November, received 2 Dec., and so recorded in SJL.

Mary Osborne wrote to TJ from Havre de Grace, Maryland, in 1808, revealing that she had written the letter printed above, "concealing my real name." She stated that her mother had died in the interval since her first letter. Her mother was perhaps Susanna or Susannah Osborne, a resident of Washington who owed taxes on property in the city and who died in the spring of 1806. Mary Osborne may have been of a young age when she made her first appeal to TJ, for a notice of Susanna Osborne's death declared that "her children have suffered an irreparable loss." In 1808, Mary was living with a married sister, and "in the space of 12 Months from this I shall inherit a small portion from the wreck of my Mothers estate." She asked the president for a loan of $50 to enable her sister and brother-in-law to move to Ohio (*Washington Federalist*, 2 Apr. 1806; *National Intelligencer*, 7 May 1806; Mary Osborne to TJ, 12 Oct. 1808, in MHi).

[1] That is, "answered."

To the Senate and the House of Representatives

To the Senate and
House of Representatives of the US.

I now communicate an Appendix to the information heretofore given on the subject of Louisiana. you will be sensible from the face of these papers, as well as of those to which they are a sequel, that they are not, and could not be, official, but are furnished by different individuals as the result of the best enquiries they had been able to make, and now given, as recieved from them,[1] only digested under heads to prevent repetitions.   Th: Jefferson
                                Nov. 29. 1803.

RC (DNA: RG 233, PM, 8th Cong., 1st sess.); endorsed by a House clerk. RC (DNA: RG 46, LPPM, 8th Cong., 1st sess.); endorsed by a Senate clerk. PrC (DLC). Recorded in SJL with notation "Louisiana Appendix." Enclosure: see below. Message and enclosure printed as "Digest of the Laws of Louisiana" in ASP, *Miscellaneous*, 1:362-84.

Lewis Harvie delivered TJ's message and the APPENDIX to the Senate and the House on 29 Nov. After the papers were read, the Senate ordered both to lie for consideration and the House referred them to the select committee, composed of John Randolph, John Rhea, William Hoge, Gaylord Griswold, and George M. Bedinger, that was appointed earlier to provide arrangements for the governance of Louisiana (JS, 3:316-17; JHR, 4:463; Vol. 41:584n). INFORMATION HERETOFORE GIVEN: see TJ to the Senate and the House of Representatives, 14 Nov., for the *Account of Louisiana* previously submitted by TJ.

TJ sent printed copies of the *Appendix* to Congress, but the edition has not been identified. Perhaps it was the separate *Appendix to an Account of Louisiana, Being an Abstract of Documents in the Offices of the Departments of State, and of the Treasury* printed in Philadelphia in 1803 (see Shaw-Shoemaker, No. 3622). The *Appendix* was also published with its own title page as an addition to the *Account of Louisiana* (see Shaw-Shoemaker, Nos. 5197, 5199). One appendix included a translation of the laws of Spain promulgated by authorities for the governance of the province and "the ordinances formed expressly for the colony." The five remaining appendices included the census of Louisiana in 1785 and other population tables, which were summarized in William Duane's newspaper on 21 Nov. and reproduced as tables on the 29th, the same day TJ transmitted the *Appendix* to Congress (*Account of Louisiana* [Washington, 1803; Shaw-Shoemaker, No. 5199], 30, i-xc; *Aurora*, 21, 29 Nov.).

[1] In RC in RG 233, TJ first wrote "as we recieved them" before altering the text to read as above.

From Albert Gallatin

SIR   Treasury Department 30th Nover. 1803

I have the honour to enclose a letter from the Commissioner of the revenue informing me of the resignation of the Supervisor of Maryland.

It seems that the office may be discontinued; and the propriety of annexing its duties to the office of Surveyor of the district of Baltimore with the salary of two hundred & fifty dollars a year and a reasonable allowance for clerk hire is respectfully submitted.

I have the honour to be with great respect Sir Your obedt. Servt.

ALBERT GALLATIN

RC (DLC); at foot of text: "The President of the United States"; endorsed by TJ as received from the Treasury Department on 30 Nov. and "Superintt. Maryld" and so recorded in SJL, where TJ altered "Superintendt." to "Supervisor." Enclosure: William Miller to Gallatin, Revenue Office, Treasury Department, 30 Nov., noting that on 28 Nov. John Kilty resigned as supervisor of Maryland to become the state's register of the land office for the Western Shore; Kilty recommends Daniel Delozier, surveyor at Baltimore, as the public officer "who is already perfectly acquainted with the business and Accounts of the Office" and could complete the work with "much promptitude" if he has a "suitable provision for Clerk hire"; Kilty assures Miller that he will "give all the aid towards completing the business, that his new engagement will permit" (FC in Lb in DNA: RG 58, LSCR; Gallatin, *Papers*, 47:947-8).

For the procedure followed when a revenue office was DISCONTINUED, see Gallatin to TJ, 30 June 1803.

From Albert Gallatin

Dear Sir   [30 Nov. 1803]

I enclose my intended[1] answer to the Comee. of W. & Means, respecting the intended suppression of the offices of Comrs. of loans. Will you have the goodness to examine it & communicate your remarks?

There is but one observation, not inserted in the answer, which may deserve consideration. There are near 5000 Stockholders in Massachussets, and a considerable number in some other States. As the suppression of the loan offices will lay them under the necessity of having transfers effected only at Washington; although the inconvenience may not substantially be great, it is difficult to calculate how far it may be magnified by party & used as an engine to enlist under its banners the whole of that body. It is indeed possible that, by raising a clamour, *stockjobbers* should produce an artificial depression in the price of stock.

With sincere respect & attachment Your obedt. Servt.

ALBERT GALLATIN

RC (DLC); undated; addressed: "The President of the United States"; endorsed by TJ as received from the Treasury Department on 30 Nov. and "Commrs. of loans" and so recorded in SJL. Enclosure: Gallatin to John Randolph, chairman of the Committee of Ways and Means, 28 Nov. 1803, submitting "facts and observations respecting the practicability and expediency of discontinuing the Office of Commissioner of Loans in the different states, and of transferring the duties" to the Treasury Department; Gallatin reviews the procedures established by the 4 Aug. 1790 "Act making provision for the debt of the United States" that calls for the appointment of a commissioner of loans in each of the 13 states to oversee the payment of the domestic debt owned by stockholders; the register of the Treasury and the commissioners keep the books and dispense quarterly payments; Gallatin notes that if the state offices were closed, arrangements would be made to ensure that stockholders continue to receive dividends at a branch of the Bank of the United States, in banks incorporated by the states, or, in the case of New Jersey and North Carolina, through a designated federal officer in the state; transfer and sale of stock, however, would necessarily take place at the Treasury Department, with the stockholder giving a person in Washington the power of attorney to execute the sale; Gallatin gives assurances that the transfer could be done by a public officer "without any expence to the parties"; except for that inconvenience, Gallatin informs the committee, the "proposed arrangement is practicable"; by concentrating all the transfers, accounts, and payments relative to the public debt in the Treasury Department, there will be less "danger of fraud or delinquency" and the suppression of offices will save $20,000 per year; two annexed statements, signed by Joseph Nourse, Register's Office, 30 Nov., indicate the amount of domestic debt on the books of the loan commissioners and at the Treasury as of 30 June and the amount of the debt owned by "foreigners, by states, by banks and other incorporations," and by individuals residing in the United States (*Report of the Committee of Ways and Means, to Whom was Referred, on the Seventeenth Ultimo, a Motion, Relative to the Expediency of Discontinuing the Office of Commissioner of Loans* [Washington, D.C., 1803], 6-14; *National Intelligencer*, 16 Dec. 1803).

SUPPRESSION OF THE OFFICES: on 17 Nov., John Wayles Eppes introduced a resolution in the House "to discontinue the office of Commissioner of loans in the different states, and to transfer the duties of that officer to the Secretary of the Treasury," with an allowance for additional clerks. The motion was immediately referred to the Committee of Ways and Means, and on 19 Nov., John Randolph requested that Gallatin lay before the committee "such information, touching the practicability and expediency" of car-rying the resolution into effect. On 8 Dec., the committee submitted its report with a resolution that it was "inexpedient" to discontinue the office. The committee argued that under the act of 4 Aug. 1790, the office of commissioner of loans "may be considered as a part of the contract between the public and its creditors." On 14 Dec., the House agreed with the committee by a 58 to 53 vote (JHR, 4:448, 481, 486-8; *Annals*, 13:562).

[1] Word interlined.

To Jones & Howell

GENTLEMEN   Washington Nov. 30. 03.

Your favor of the 25th. has been recieved. Stewart passed through this place on his way back to Monticello. the 20. D. may be passed with you to my general credit. he informed me his son could make as good a choice of the iron & files as himself. I will pray you therefore to send a quarter ton of such bar iron as he shall chuse, making it include 2. mill spindles; and to forward also such files as he shall select, and till the arrival of which Stewart informed me he could not do the work wanting. Accept my salutations & best wishes.

TH: JEFFERSON

PrC (MHi); at foot of text: "Messrs. Jones & Howell"; endorsed by TJ in ink on verso.

William STEWART was likely expected to fashion some of the works for TJ's recently constructed MILL at Shadwell. On 27 Nov., TJ sent an order on John Barnes to pay Stewart $15, likely to cover Stewart's traveling expenses and because Stewart had not collected the $20 intended for him in Philadelphia (MS in ViU, endorsed by Barnes; MB, 2:1099n, 1113; TJ to Mary Jefferson Eppes, 27 Nov.).

From Benjamin H. Latrobe

DEAR SIR,   Philadelphia, Novr. 30th. 1803.

The difficulties I have met with in my surveys & levellings for the Canal which is to unite the Bays of Chesapeake & Delaware, have *forced* me to pay much less attention, otherwise than by correspondence to the duties with which you have intrusted me, than I could have wished.—I am now here solely for the purpose of urging the progress of those works which must be performed *here*, and find that much Iron has been sent on to Washington for the roofs,—& that the stoves are ready to go by the next Vessel.—I will not take up your time now with the details; I am exerting myself to be at Washington in a fortnight at most,—and hope eventually, not to disgrace the confidence you have placed in me.—

All the Iron specified in the enclosed bill having been forwarded to Monticello,—Mr. Mifflin, the principal partner of the Rolling Company, has requested me to solicit,—that, whenever convenient You would please to pay the amount of the enclosed bill, to Mr. Jo. Lenthall to whom an order is endorsed upon it,—& who will forward the amount, as it is impossible to dispose here of a bill on Richmond.—Mr. Mifflin hopes this arrangement may not be inconvenient to you.—

Fully sensible of the great obligations I owe to you, & regretting exceedingly that the duties of my engagement to the Ches. & Del. Canal Company has prevented that constant personal attention to my business at Washington which I so much desire to bestow upon it,—I hope to receive the assurances of your indulgence, when, in the course of a very short time, I shall wait upon you.

I am with true respect Your faithfull hble Servt

B HENRY LATROBE

RC (DLC); endorsed by TJ as received 4 Dec. and so recorded in SJL. Enclosure: not found, but see below.

Over the course of 1803, TJ received six boxes of sheet iron, totaling 1,733 feet, from the mill Latrobe ran with Samuel MIFFLIN. In his financial memoranda, TJ recorded at 8 Dec. an order on John Barnes to pay John LENTHALL $330 for 17.33 squares of sheet iron (MB, 2:1113; Statement of account with Mifflin and Latrobe, 24 May 1803-12 Dec. 1805, in MHi).

From John Randolph

SIR   House of Representatives 30 Nov: 1803

Certain expressions of mine, used in debate on friday last, having been interpreted by some as conveying an allusion to the executive, I have no hesitation most explicitly to disavow every intention of such a nature. To this step I am induced not by any impression that you, Sir, might be disposed to give such a construction to the terms in question, because a consciousness of your own worth &, I flatter myself, a knowledge of my character would forbid the suspicion of the slightest intention on my part to attack, in any shape, much less *indirectly*, a character for which I have uniformly felt & professed the highest esteem & veneration. I have hastened to give you this assurance as soon as it could be done with propriety, & I pray you to accept my heartfelt wishes for your private & public prosperity.

JOHN RANDOLPH JR.

RC (DLC); at foot of text: "Thomas Jefferson esqr."; endorsed by TJ as received 30 Nov. and so recorded in SJL.

On 25 Nov., FRIDAY LAST, John Wayles Eppes introduced a resolution instructing the Committee of Ways and Means to see what reductions could be made "in the expenses of the different Departments of the Government" and to report "such arrangements as they may think calculated to promote economy." As chair of the committee, Randolph immediately declared that the resolution was unnecessary because those duties already devolved on the committee by the standing rules of the House. He moved to postpone consideration of the resolution until January 1804. In the ensuing exchange between the two Republicans, Eppes demanded that the House immediately adopt or reject the resolution. ALLUSION TO THE EXECUTIVE: Randolph responded to the president's son-in-law, noting that the House had the power to dispose of the resolution as it saw fit, but he would always exercise his freedom "without any consideration of

the quarter from which a motion comes." He continued: "I shall use that degree of understanding with which it has pleased God to invest me, in forming a judgment of the course proper to be pursued on this as well as on every other occasion." Randolph also made reference to Eppes's earlier resolution to discontinue the office of commissioner of loans, which the Ways and Means Committee had under consideration (see Gallatin to TJ, 30 Nov., second letter). Joseph H. Nicholson, another member of the committee, declared that although he did not believe Eppes meant to censure the committee, he thought the resolution was "useless" and would vote immediately to reject it. Caesar A. Rodney, a new committee member, assured all of his "independent judgment on any proposition submitted to the House, without regard to the quarter from which it may come." He thought the resolution should be postponed. In the end, the House voted to consider the resolution on the first Monday in December (*Annals*, 13:625-31). The debate appeared in the 28 Nov. issue of the *National Intelligencer*.

From Adam Seybert

SIR Philadelphia November 30th. 1803

I lately received a Letter from Professor Blumenbach of Göttingen— Wherein he mentions his never having received a Certificate as a Member of the American Philosophical Society—After a diligent search I could not find one with your signature & therefore hope that you will excuse the liberty I have taken in forwarding the enclosed— May I beg the favour of your early attention to this business—The Professor is very urgent on the occasion and feels himself highly flattered by his election.

Please to accept of my particular esteem and believe me with sentiments of high consideration your sincere friend & very humble Servant ADAM SEYBERT

RC (DLC); at foot of text: "Thomas Jefferson President of the United States"; endorsed by TJ as received 2 Dec. and so recorded in SJL.

Adam Seybert (1773-1825) studied medicine under Caspar Wistar and received an M.D. degree from the University of Pennsylvania in 1793. He continued his studies in London, Edinburgh, Göttingen, and Paris, building particular expertise in chemistry and mineralogy. In Philadelphia he operated a pharmacy and chemical laboratory. Elected to membership in the American Philosophical Society in 1797, he served as one of the society's secretaries from 1799 to 1808 and as a counselor, 1810-11. Seybert was a member of the U.S. House of Representatives, 1809-15, 1817-19 (DAB).

Johann Friedrich BLUMENBACH, a professor of medicine and the curator of the natural history collection at the University of Göttingen, wrote influential works on anthropology and comparative anatomy.

The APS received an English translation (from Latin) of his textbook on physiology in 1795 and elected him to membership in April 1798. From Philippe Reibelt in 1805 TJ purchased a French translation of a natural history textbook by Blumenbach. Later, Wistar's copy of an English translation of a study of comparative anatomy by the Göttingen scientist came into TJ's library. Both of those works appeared originally in German. TJ, who studied Blumenbach's system of classification of species along with those of Linneaus and Georges Cuvier, considered Blumenbach's to be too heavily based on anatomy (DSB; APS, *Proceedings*, 22, pt. 3 [1884], 232, 270; Sowerby, Nos. 1000, 1019; RS, 7:208-10; TJ to Reibelt, 23 Jan. 1805; Reibelt to TJ, 25 Jan. 1805).

To Marten Wanscher

SIR   Washington Nov. 30. 03.

I have recieved a letter for you, which appearing to have come from Germany I do not hazard to send, till I know where you are, as the late fever in Alexandria obliged many to leave it.

Mr. Dinsmore was here lately. the Parlour & Hall at Monticello are ready for plaistering. the Domeroom will be so before the spring; and probably some of the bedrooms above: so that the plaistering for the next season will be a job of length: and renders it proper for me to attend to the circumstance of price, which I always thought too high at the rate I paid you before. I can get the best hands for plain plaistering at a dollar a day, but I would give you the preference at that price as you have been employed already in the business. I shall be glad to learn from you whether you wish the job at that price, and I shall govern myself accordingly. Accept my best wishes.

TH: JEFFERSON

PrC (MHi); at foot of text: "Mr. Martin Wanscher"; endorsed by TJ in ink on verso.

The LETTER from Germany has not been identified.

DINSMORE WAS HERE: see TJ to John Barnes, 3 Nov. 1803.

WHETHER YOU WISH THE JOB: Wanscher returned to TJ's employment in 1804, arriving at Monticello on 8 May and receiving his final payment on 6 Oct. (MB, 2:1126, 1137; TJ to Wanscher, 10 Apr. 1804). For his earlier work at Monticello, see Wanscher to TJ, 10 Dec. 1802.

From Andrew Ellicott

Dear Sir   Lancaster December 1st. 1803.

For some time past Mr. William Barton, and myself, have been objects of abuse in Mr. Duane's paper; but this abuse would be disregarded on our part, was it not from an opinion generally prevailing in this state, and probably in some others that, that paper is the organ of the will, and wishes, of the administration of the general government; because, it is this opinion alone which gives any weight to the charges. —

It was insinuated a few days ago in the paper above alluded to, that I am an applicant for office under the government of the United States. For the incorrectness of this insinuation, I have only to appeal to yourself, and then ask if there is not a probability of the other charges being equally groundless?—This insinuation if not contradicted, might lead Govr. Mc.Kean to suppose that I felt myself uneasy under his administration, and wished to leave my present situation; — which is the reverse of truth.

Mr. Duane has been for some months past indirectly attacking the Governor,—his allusions are too plain not to be understood. In this however, he has shewn more caution than his friend Mr. Binns (a British subject), and editor of a paper in Northumberland called the republican Argus, in which he has in direct terms accused the inhabitants of this State, of want of wisdom, in choosing such a *man* as Govr. Mc.Kean for their *ruler*! —

The republican interest in this State has been much injured by the denunciations of some of our best, and most influential friends, by Mr. Duane, which has created an unnecessary jealousy, and in some cases a determined enmity.—Whether this is the effect of his own imprudence, or a premeditated design in himself, and those by whom he is backed, to destroy all government, all law, and throw the nation into confusion, for the purpose of rendering republicanism contemptible is difficult to determine: but at present, it appears that the United States are to take their tone from three foreign printers, (viz), Messrs. Duane, Cheetham, and Binns; the latter, as has been already observed, is a British subject.—These men with as little ceremony, and remorse, as a wolf devours his prey, are constantly employed in adding fuel to the flames of discord among our native born citizens, and so far, as it is within the compass of their power, destroying the character of every person in this country, whose conduct is not in perfect unison with their views.—What may eventually be the consequence of this influence of foreigners, (if not foreign influence), time alone must determine: And whatever other native-born citizens may think, and feel on this subject, it appears to me, that the conduct of those men is calculated to depress the american character, and carries with it an evidence, that we have decreased in vigour of mind, and independence of sentiment, since we were lopped off from the original stock.—

If republicanism consists in supporting the constitution of the United States, and those of the individual states, both Mr. Barton, and myself may lay claim to the title of republicans; but if it consists in introducing into this country either *anarchy*, or the strong arm of a consular government, we have been mistaken, for our conduct, and sentiments, have ever been hostile to both.—But it has been stated in some of the prints well known to be under the influence of the Aurora, that, we are adverse to the administration of the United States, as well as to that of this State.—How does this appear?—It is a fact, as certain as any ever deduced from the most rigid experiment, that we were denounced for supporting the republican administration of Govr. Mc.Kean,—and the charge is equally false as it relates to the administration of the general government.—No information has ever been withheld by me from the latter when asked, and the materials which formed the basis of the report of the committee last winter relating to the Floridas, were certainly those which I had some time before sent to the Treasury department.—And I am confident was Mr. Lewis now here, he would admit that he had every assistance from me which I could give him, to render his undertaking both useful, and important. In short, I have been uniform in my wishes, and would have rendered more services had they been required.—It is stated by Mr. Duane in a number of his papers, that Mr. Barton, and myself, are in a league with Mr. Charles Smith, a leading federalist of this place, and one of our 13 senators who so streniously opposed your election to the presidency.—To point out the inaccuracy of this statement, I shall observe *first*, that Mr. Charles Smith of this place was never one of our senators! Mr. Richard Smith from one of our western counties was a senator at time alluded to, but with him we have no acquaintance. *Secondly* so far from being in a league with Mr. Charles Smith of this place as stated by Mr. Duane our ticket for representatives to the ensuing legislature of this state was publickly opposed by him under his own signature in both the republican and federal papers of this borough.—These are facts of which Mr. Duane cannot be ignorant:—he nevertheless continues to give publicity to those falshoods!—

If Mr. Duane is in the confidence of the administration of the general government, and been informed by any of the departments, that

I am an applicant for office, it is certainly incorrect, and ought to be corrected for the reasons already stated; and if he is not in that confidence, we who have been the objects of his abuse, and denunciations, ought in some degree to be aware of it, least, in defending ourselves (if it should become necessary) we might take ground, which would have a tendency to hasten the maturity of discord, the seeds of which are beginning to vegetate in consequence of the denunciations that have already taken place; for it cannot be expected, that all the individuals of the republican party, whose characters have been traduced by those foreign printers, will calmly submit to so much degrading abuse without making a single exertion to vindicate their characters, or repel their assailants; but in making this defense, the administration for very obvious reasons ought to be kept out of sight, which cannot be done if Mr. Duane is to be considered as being in the confidence of Government, because it is that opinion alone which gives weight to his charges.—

I have the honour to be with great esteem and regard your friend and Hble. Servt.

ANDW. ELLICOTT

RC (DLC); at foot of text: "Thos. Jefferson President of the United States"; endorsed by TJ as a letter of 5 Dec. and so recorded in SJL, where it was entered as received the same day.

On 18 Nov., William DUANE'S PAPER, the *Aurora*, published a piece charging that Ellicott, William Barton, brother of Benjamin Smith Barton, and Charles Smith, an attorney and Lancaster's leading Federalist, had joined forces to create a third party in support of Governor Thomas McKean, whom Duane and others criticized for vetoing bills passed by the state legislature. APPLICANT FOR OFFICE: the writer noted that two of the triumvirate were "longing for places under the federal government." In fact, only Barton had sought a federal office, his most recent application being for comptroller of the Treasury in November 1802. Ellicott twice declined TJ's offer to become surveyor general (Higginbotham, *Pennsylvania Politics*, 51-3, 64; Andrew Shankman, *Crucible of American Democracy: The Struggle to Fuse Egalitarianism & Capitalism in Jeffersonian Pennsylvania* [Lawrence, Kan., 2004], 99-100; Vol. 35:164-5, 424n; Vol. 36:448, 535, 579-80, 629; Vol. 37:45; Vol. 38:625-6). PRES-ENT SITUATION: Ellicott became secretary of the Pennsylvania Land Office in 1801 (Vol. 35:424n).

John BINNS, a United Irishman who had been imprisoned many times by the British authorities before his departure for the United States in 1802, settled in Northumberland, Pennsylvania, to be near fellow exiles Thomas Cooper and Joseph Priestley. Through the *Republican Argus*, he reportedly turned Northumberland from a Federalist to a Republican stronghold (Jeffrey L. Pasley, *"The Tyranny of Printers": Newspaper Politics in the Early American Republic* [Charlottesville, 2001], 222-3; Binns to TJ, 13 Apr. 1804). As for the two other FOREIGN PRINTERS, Duane was born near Lake Champlain in 1760, but his widowed mother took him to Ireland when he was a child, and he did not return to the United States until 1796. James Cheetham emigrated from Britain in 1798 (Vol. 31:453-4n; Vol. 34:224n).

In a 7 Aug. 1803 letter to the Treasury secretary, Ellicott expressed his belief that possession of the FLORIDAS was of "more importance to the United States than that of Louisiana." He supported the opinion in the preface to his recently published *Journal*, and was criticized for it in the *Aurora*. The newspaper's commentator "wished that the astronomer & geographer had not absorbed the *journalist* and the *politician*, for the absurdities (speaking mildly) of the two latter characters have thrown a *dark cloud* over the two former" (*Aurora*, 10 Nov. 1803; Gallatin, *Papers*, 8:585; Ellicott, *The Journal of Andrew Ellicott, Late Commissioner on Behalf of the United States . . . for Determining the Boundary between the United States and the Possessions of His Catholic Majesty in America* [Philadelphia, 1803], v-vii).

OPPOSED YOUR ELECTION: in 1800, Federalists in the Pennsylvania Senate were determined to limit the Republican impact in the choice of presidential electors by calling for a concurrent vote, rather than a joint vote with the Republican-dominated House of Representatives (see Vol. 32:307-10). Abraham Carpenter, who represented Lancaster County, and RICHARD SMITH, who represented Bedford, Huntingdon, and Somerset, were members of that Federalist opposition (*Journal of the Senate of the Commonwealth of Pennsylvania*, Dec. 1797-Apr. 1798 [Philadelphia, 1798], 3; *Journal of the Senate of the Commonwealth of Pennsylvania*, Dec. 1798-Apr. 1799 [Philadelphia, 1799], 3; *Gazette of the United States*, 14, 17 Nov. 1800).

For a defense of the TICKET for the state assembly submitted by Lancaster citizens who called themselves "old, tried and respectable *Republicans*" and friends of McKean, see *To the Electors of the Borough and County of Lancaster*, dated 16 Sep. 1803 (Shaw-Shoemaker, No. 5168; Higginbotham, *Pennsylvania Politics*, 64).

To William Eustis

Dec. 1. 03.

Th: Jefferson presents his friendly salutations to Doctr. Eustis and his thanks for the fish which he has been so kind as to send him. it is a very fine article, when it can be got of the good kind, which is rare & difficult to those not of the country where produced.

RC (R. M. Smythe, New York City, 1995); addressed: "The honble Doctr. Eustis"; endorsed by Eustis. Not recorded in SJL.

To Albert Gallatin

DEAR SIR   Washington Dec. 1. 03.

I return you the letter of mr Miller notifying the resignation of the Supervisor of Maryland, & I approve your proposition of suppressing the office, annexing it's duties to that of Surveyor of the district of Baltimore with the salary of 250. D. a year & a reasonable allowance for Clerk hire.

I return you also your proposed report on the suppression of the Commissionrs. of loans, with an entire approbation of it.

The letter inclosed is for your perusal and will merit our consideration. the man who rights[1] it is honest & zealous. Affectionate salutations   TH: JEFFERSON

RC (NHi: Gallatin Papers); at foot of text: "The Secretary of the Treasury"; endorsed. PrC (DLC). Recorded in SJL with notation "Supervisr Maryld. Commrs. loans. Morse." Enclosure: Samuel Morse to TJ, 13 Nov., recorded in SJL as received 30 Nov. from Savannah, but not found; see Notes on Henry Putnam's Case, at 13 Feb. 1804.

For the letter of William MILLER, see Gallatin to TJ, 30 Nov. (first letter).

PROPOSED REPORT: see Gallatin to TJ, 30 Nov. (second letter).

[1] Thus in MS; TJ interlined "writes" in ink above this word on PrC.

Petition of Jesse Page and Wife

[on or before 1 Dec. 1803]

The Petition of Jesse Page, and Wife, of Ann Arundel County, in the State of Maryland; respectfully sheweth, that they are the Parents of a Profligate Son, who now lies, in Confinement, for Desertion, at the military Corps, in Frederick Town;

Your Petitioners would beg Leave, to represent, that they have always sustained a fair and reputable Character, in Society—that their Son, Shadrach Page, from Habits of Intemperance and Intoxication, after having enlisted in the Army, has deserted twice, and is now under Tryal, or Sentence for the Offence:—That they have nothing to plead, in his Behalf: but his Youth and Infirmities:—but confiding in the well known Humanity of the President, they pray, that Mercy may be extended, to their unfortunate Son, and thereby their Afflictions will be lessened: and they, in Duty bound—will &c:

RC (PHi); undated; at head of text: "To Thomas Jefferson, Esquire, President of the United States"; endorsed by a clerk; with subjoined affidavit by Richard Ridgely and ten others describing the petitioners as "fair and honest" and recommending clemency; attestation by Gabriel Duvall, dated Washington, 1 Dec. 1803, stating that "I do not know the petitioner" but those who have advised clemency "are respectable."

To John Randolph

DEAR SIR   Washington Dec. 1. 03.

The explanation in your letter of yesterday was quite unnecessary to me. I have had too satisfactory proofs of your friendly regard, to be disposed to suspect any thing of a contrary aspect. I understood perfectly the expressions stated in the newspaper, to which you allude, to mean that 'tho' the proposition came from the *republican quarter* of the house, yet you should not concur with it.'   I am aware that in parts of the union, & even with persons, to whom mr Eppes & mr Randolph are unknown, & myself little known, it will be presumed from their connection[1] that what comes from them comes from me. no men on earth are more independent in their sentiments than they are, nor any one less disposed than I am to influence the opinions of others. we rarely speak of politics, or of the proceedings of the house but merely historically, and I carefully avoid expressing an opinion on them, in their presence, that we may all be at our ease. with other members I have believed that more unreserved communications would be advantageous to the public. this has been perhaps prevented by mutual delicacy. I have been afraid to express opinions unasked, lest I should be suspected of wishing to direct the legislative action of members. they have avoided asking communications from me, probably lest they should be suspected of wishing to fish out executive secrets.   I see too many proofs of the imperfection of human reason to entertain wonder or intolerance at any difference of opinion on any subject; and acquiesce in that difference as easily as on a difference of feature or form: experience having taught me the reasonableness of mutual sacrifices of opinion among those who are to act together, for any common object, and the expediency of doing what good we can, when we cannot do all we would wish. Accept my friendly salutations and assurances of great esteem & respect

TH: JEFFERSON

PrC (DLC); at foot of text: "John Randolph esq."   [1] Preceding three words interlined.

To DeWitt Clinton

DEAR SIR   Washington Dec. 2. 03.

Your favor of the 26th. ult. has been recieved. mr Van Wyck's appointment as Commr. of bankruptcy only awaits mr Sandford's resignation. the papers in the case of Lt. Wolstencroft shall be recommended to the enquiries & attentions of the Secretary at War. I should think it indeed a serious misfortune should a change in the administration of your government be hazarded before it's present principles be well established through all it's parts. yet, on reflection, you will be sensible that the delicacy of my situation, considering who may be competitors, forbids my intermedling, even so far as to write the letter you suggest. I can therefore only brood in silence over my secret wishes.

I am less able to give you the proceedings of Congress than your correspondents who are of that body. more difference of opinion seems to exist, as to the manner of disposing of Louisiana, than I had imagined possible: and our leading friends are not yet sufficiently aware of the necessity of accomodation & mutual sacrifice of opinion for conducting a numerous assembly, where the opposition too is drilled to act in phalanx on every question. altho' it is acknoleged that our new fellow citizens are as yet as incapable of self-government as children, yet some cannot bring themselves to suspend it's principles for a single moment. the temporary or territorial government of that country therefore will encounter great difficulty. the question too whether the settlement of upper Louisiana shall be prohibited occasions a great division of our friends. some are for prohibiting it till another amendment of the constn shall permit it; others for prohibiting by authority of the legislature only; a third set for permitting immediate settlement. those of the first opinion apprehend that if the legislature may open a land office there, it will become the ruling principle of elections, & end in a Yazoo scheme: those of the 2d opinion fear they may never get an amendment of the constitution permitting the settlement. Accept my friendly salutations & assurances of great esteem & respect. TH: JEFFERSON

RC (NNC); addressed: "Dewitt Clinton esq. Mayor of New York"; franked; postmarked 4 Dec.; endorsed by Clinton. PrC (DLC).

Pierre C. Van Wyck did not receive an APPOINTMENT as bankruptcy commissioner (see list of commissions in Lb in DNA: RG 59, MPTPC, where the last entries were dated 18 Nov.). In an undated note on a torn scrap of paper, TJ wrote: "Smith Caleb to be Commr. bkrptcy [. . .] Sands Van Wyck having been [. . .] to Ryker in the duel with Swartwout. appmt would be unpopular" (MS

in DNA: RG 59, MCL; entirely in TJ's hand). It is unclear who recommended Caleb Smith for the office or when TJ learned of the duel. On 15 Nov., the *New-York Gazette* reported on an "affair of honor" between Clintonian Republican Richard Riker and Robert Swartwout, a Burrite. Van Wyck evidently served as Riker's second (*New-York Gazette & General Advertiser*, 15 Nov. 1803; Kline, *Burr*, 2:709, 731, 836, 1146). For the 1802 duel between DeWitt Clinton and John Swartwout, Robert's brother, at which Riker served as Clinton's second, see Kline, *Burr*, 2:734-6.

To John Conrad & Co.

Washington Dec. 2. 03.

Th: Jefferson presents his compliments to Messrs. John Conrad & co. & thanks them for the first No. inclosed him of their American magazine & willingly becomes a subscriber for a copy.

PrC (MHi); endorsed by TJ in ink on verso.

BECOMES A SUBSCRIBER: scholars have not located a subscription list for the *Lit-* *erary Magazine* (Michael Cody, *Charles Brockden Brown and the* Literary Magazine: *Cultural Journalism in the Early American Republic* [Jefferson, N.C., 2004], 162).

From Albert Gallatin

[on or before 2 Dec. 1803]

Is it proper to permit this man to take a couple of guns on board?
Respectfully submitted ALBERT GALLATIN

RC (DLC: TJ Papers, 136:23474); undated, but see below; at foot of text: "The President of the United States." Enclosure: Richard Howard to Caesar A. Rodney, New Castle, Delaware, on board the revenue cutter belonging to the district of Philadelphia, 31 Oct. 1803, requesting permission to arm the cutter with four three-pounders, four howitzers, and a musket and cutlass for each man on board, as there is great danger of "loosing My men by the British Cruisers"; arms would also compel "Ower Vessels" to re-spect the flag; Howard continues, "hoisting my Cullers, as the Law Directes is of No use, unless I had Sumthing to Compell them" (RC in same).

It is not clear when Rodney enclosed Howard's 31 Oct. letter to the Treasury secretary. On 2 Dec., Gallatin responded: "Is not the object of Captn. Howard's application, to fight foreign vessels or boats rather than to bring to our own? I have sent his letter to the President" (Gallatin, *Papers*, 9:18).

To William Prentis

SIR   Washington Dec. 2. 1803.

Your favor of Nov. 14. was recieved some days ago. however sincerely I wish well to the work of mr Burke which you propose to print, yet it is utterly out of my power to undertake any previous examination of it. the labors of my office are so incessant, and all the moments which can be given to reading are so filled with something to be read which relates to it, that I am obliged to abandon all attention to literary matters. but the competence of mr Burke to the work in question, and that of the other gentlemen you name, & still others who may be found, to supply any little oversights which might escape him, will render my inability to attend to it of little consequence. I pray you to consider me as a subscriber to the work whenever printed, & to accept my salutations & best wishes.   TH: JEFFERSON

PrC (DLC); at foot of text: "Mr. William Prentis."

WORK OF MR BURKE: for the *History of Virginia* by John Daly Burk, see Vol. 34:388n.

GENTLEMEN YOU NAME: John Page and Bishop James Madison (Vol. 41: 718).

TJ first asked to become a SUBSCRIBER to the history in his letter to Burk of 21 Feb. 1803 (Vol. 39:559).

From Thomas Rodney

DEAR SIR   Natchez December 2d. 1803.

It is with great Pleasure that I imbrace This Early Opurtunity by the First Mail after My Arrival To Communicate To you My arrival here in good health yesterday at 5 oClock P.M. and that my brother Commissioner Mr. Williams arrived the day before and that we Met yesterday Evening With Mr. Turner the Register and formed the Board Agreably To Law at the Town of Washington and Tomorrow Shall proceed To business—But from the Information we have Acquired since our arrival We find that it would be More Convenient & agreable To us as well as To the People for to Sit in this Place in preference To Washington at least Till April Next if we Can Obtain your Permission To do so—We find on forming the Board that the Law Under which we are to Act is defective in some respects which we Mean to Communicate by the Next Mail that the Legislature if they Think proper May remedy by a supplementary Law—Please To permit me to Congratulate you on the general approbation I have heard expressed of Your Conduct through My Travels, and please To Accept Assurance of a Continuance of my very high respect and Esteem and shall I take the Liberty To beg you to present my love To my Son C. A. R.

Your Most Obedient   THOMAS RODNEY

RC (DLC); endorsed by TJ as received 19 Dec. and so recorded in SJL.

TJ had appointed Rodney and Robert WILLIAMS claims commissioners for the land office in Adams County, Mississippi Territory. Edward TURNER was register of the office. TJ had also appointed Rodney a territorial judge (commission, 18 Nov. 1803, Lb in DNA: RG 59, MPTPC; Vol. 40:3n; Vol. 41:41, 698, 702, 733).

LAW UNDER WHICH WE ARE TO ACT: "An Act regulating the grants of land, and providing for the disposal of lands of the United States, south of the state of Tennessee" (U.S. Statutes at Large, 2:229-35).

C.A.R.: Caesar A. Rodney.

From Jesse Simms

SIR, Alexandria 2nd December 1803

your favour came duly to hand and the Contents noted. I considered your bill for the Canvas[1] back Ducks settled long since through Col. Brent who I had an acct. with and he requested me to charge it to him. Col Brent informs me he handed the bill in to know of the Steward how many pairs he had Recvd. for you, and Mr. Barnes informs me that the Steward Received thirty pair for you which amounts to 45 Dollars and I have wrote Mr. Barnes to day to settle that amount with Col. Brent. the others Col. Brent Received for him self and friends—I will use my Interest this Season to procure Ducks for you with pleasure and will take care to have them more Regularly Delivered to Mr. Barnes or the Steward

From Sir yr. Obt Hbe Servt JESSE SIMMS

RC (MHi); at foot of text: "President of the U States"; endorsed by TJ. Recorded in SJL as received 4 Dec.

YOUR FAVOUR: TJ to Simms, 25 Nov.

[1] MS: "Cavas."

From James Madison

[4 Dec. 1803]

A few alterations are suggested on the supposition that it may be best to present the transaction, as a disavowal of war &[1] a conformation of peace, rather than as a pacification which might involve the necessary idea of Treaty—I take for granted that Mr Smith will have an oppy. of expressing his opinion as to the graduation of praise to the Officers—

As so many names are mentioned, & it is known that Lear was concerned in the affair, & may not be known that he was unofficially there—might it not be well to throw in a clause alluding to his presence, & the aid of his Zealous & judicious counsels—This however for consideration.

RC (DLC); undated; in Madison's hand; addressed: "The President"; endorsed by TJ as a letter of 4 Dec. 1803 received from the State Department on the same day and "Marocco message of Dec. 5. 03." Recorded in SJL as an undated letter received from the State Department on 4 Dec. 1803 with notation "Marocco message."

ALTERATIONS ARE SUGGESTED: Madison's suggestions related to a draft version, no longer extant, of TJ's message to both houses of Congress of 5 Dec.; see also Robert Smith's comments, below at 4 Dec.

CONFORMATION OF PEACE: Captain John Rodgers of the frigate *New York* arrived in Washington on 2 Dec., bringing news of the restoration of peace between the United States and Morocco (Baltimore *Federal Gazette*, 5 Dec. 1803; *National Intelligencer*, 5 Dec. 1803). The papers he carried presumably included Mawlay Sulayman's letter to TJ of 11 Oct. and dispatches to James Madison from James Simpson of 15 and 17 Oct., Edward Preble of 15 Oct., and Tobias Lear of 18 Oct. (Madison, *Papers, Sec. of State Ser.*, 5:532-4, 536-9, 540-9). In addition, Rodgers probably carried Preble's lengthy report to Robert Smith, dated 5 to 17 Oct., providing a comprehensive account of the negotiations with Sulayman as well as U.S. naval activities at Tangier, Gibraltar, and along the Moroccan coast (RC in DLC; NDBW, 3:139-43). For details on the negotiations and reaffirmation of peace, see Vol. 41:509-10n. TJ's papers also contain a list captioned "Naval force of Tunis furnished by Capt Rogers. 1803." As captain of the *John Adams*, Rodgers had visited Tunis in late February 1803 as part of an unsuccessful negotiation with the bey. At the principal Tunisian naval base at Porto Farina, Rodgers

identified a new 32-gun frigate "about the size of the John Adams"; six xebecs of 18 to 24 guns; two polacre-rigged ships of 16 guns; six galleys armed with two guns in the bow and swivels; two gunboats; and one "Frigate built ship pierced for 30. guns, but not capable of being made seaworthy." At La Goulette, he counted 20 to 25 gunboats. In addition, Rodgers noted that Tunis also had three xebecs and two galleys at sea (MS in DLC: TJ Papers, 232:41537, undated, entirely in TJ's hand; John H. Schroeder, *Commodore John Rodgers: Paragon of the Early American Navy* [Gainesville, Fla., 2006], 32; Kenneth J. Perkins, *Historical Dictionary of Tunisia* [Metuchen, N.J., 1989], 55).

Tobias LEAR, the recently appointed American consul general at Algiers, participated only UNOFFICIALLY in the Morocco negotiations, since his supervisory authority over American consuls in North Africa extended only to those at Tunis and Tripoli (Vol. 41:50, 508-10).

[1] Preceding four words and ampersand interlined.

From Samuel Latham Mitchill

Stelle's hotel, Decr. 4, 1803.

I beg leave to offer to the President, for his amusement, the inclosed Speculations on a *Geographical* name for the country which enjoys so much political happiness under his administration. The project has been noticed in a number of the Newspapers of the States. The Song was written for a Company of Militia, who have assumed the name of "Fredonian" volunteers. Now that *Louisiana* is about to be annexed to "Fredonia," there will be a good Opportunity for the "Fredes" to extend their proper national Name over the territory occupied by the "Fredish" People. I am with great Respect, yours very sincerely

SAML L MITCHILL

It may be derived from φρην virtus sapientia & δος the imperative of the verb διδωμι.

RC (DLC); addressed: "Thomas Jefferson. President of the U.S."; endorsed by TJ as received 4 Dec. and so recorded in SJL. Enclosure: see below.

Mitchill had been an ardent advocate for the creation of a new NAME FOR THE COUNTRY. Believing the term "United States" was too political, he proposed

"Fredon," or for rhetorical or poetical purposes, "Fredonia." He coined other descriptive derivatives for common use. Despite pitching the idea to giants of lexicography and geography Noah Webster and Jedidiah Morse to no avail, he continued his naming campaign. Mitchill was the likely author of an unsigned essay, "Generic Names for the Country and People of the United States of America," appearing in several NEWSPAPERS beginning in April and widely reprinted throughout the summer. An undated one-sheet broadside by the same title, probably printed in New York, may have been what Mitchill enclosed in his letter to TJ (Shaw-Shoemaker, No. 4267). In a December issue of his journal, the *Medical Repository*, Mitchill again promoted adoption of the terminology ("New National Distinctions," *Medical Repository*, 6 [1803], 449-50; New York *Morning Chronicle*, 28 April 1803; *National Intelligencer*, 22 June 1803; Hudson, N.Y.,

Balance, and Columbian Repository, 19 July 1803; Joseph Jones, "Hail, Fredonia!" *American Speech*, 9 [1934], 12-17; Alan David Aberbach, *In Search of an American Identity: Samuel Latham Mitchill, Jeffersonian Nationalist* [New York, 1988], 154-6).

SONG: "The Blessings of Fredon," 16 verses written for the Fourth of July, sung to the tune "Yankee Doodle" (New York *American Citizen*, 4 July 1803; see also Mitchill to Catharine Mitchill, 19 Nov. 1803, in NNMus).

In June 1803, Captain Benjamin Egbert of New York established an infantry company called the Fredonian VOLUNTEERS (New York *Chronicle Express*, 20 June 1803).

MAY BE DERIVED: Mitchill connected the proposed name to Greek terms (and noted the Latin equivalent of one of them) to indicate that the nation of Fredon imperatively bestowed life-power and wisdom.

From Robert Smith

[4 Dec. 1803]

*The temperate and Correct[1] Course pursued by our Consul Mr Simpson, the promptitude of Commodore Preble, the effecacious Co-Operation of Commodore Rodgers of the returning Squadron, the judicious conduct of Capt Bainbridge and the general zeal of the other Officers and Men are

It is proper to state to you that Rodgers being the Oldest Officer was the person that formed the plan of attack and had established the Code of Signals for the same—His feelings are to be Consulted—I will do myself the honor of calling upon you before I go to my Office in the morng—

RS

RC (DLC); undated, but entered in SJL as a letter of 4 Dec.; endorsed by TJ as received from the Navy Department on 4 Dec. and "Marocco message" and so recorded in SJL.

TEMPERATE AND CORRECT COURSE: in the first paragraph, Smith suggested alterations for TJ's 5 Dec. message to Congress on Morocco.

On 22 June, as senior officer of the squadron blockading the coast of Tripoli, John RODGERS and the frigate *John Adams* led the successful ATTACK that destroyed a 22-gun Tripolitan warship, which Rodgers asserted was "the Bashaw of Tripoli's largest cruiser" (NDBW, 2:459-60, 465-6; *National Intelligencer*, 7 Dec.).

[1] Smith here canceled "Conduct."

From Robert Daniel

Louisiana post of Oppelousos

SIR   Decr. 5th. 1803

The present Anxiety which I feel for the population of my country together with a wish to render my fellow cittizens every service in my power will I hope be a sufficient apoligy for addressing you on the following subject—permit me sir to represent to you the situation of some hundreds of our countrymen who have In the Inexperience of youth Deserted from the American Service to the spanish Territories, as they supposed an assalum from oppression the Majority of which have now their little family around them and without a pardon must be benished from their country for ever—Should they be obliged to fly to Mexico they will draw a number of their connections with them which will to a certain Degree Depopolate our country and Deprive us of many Good Industrious Cittizens and I assure you Sir situated as we are I had rather see ten Industrious Americans come in to our country than to see one go out of it—

Therefore your petitioner doth most Humbly pray that your Sympathy may be so far reciprocal as to grant your proclamation Declaring all Deserters that was in this province Twelve months previous to the cession of the french to the United States free from The Service; and penelties anexed to Desertion It will be bringing to life so many of our brethren which In gratitude will be for ever bound to their country—

I have the honour to be with Every Sentiment of Esteam your Most Obt Servt   ROBT DANIEL

RC (DLC); addressed: "His Excellency Thomas Jefferson President of the United States Washington City"; franked; postmarked Natchez, 17 Dec.; endorsed by TJ as received 1 Jan. 1804 and so recorded in SJL.

From Isaac Hammer

Washington County
State of Tennessee,

HOND. & MUCH RESPD. FRIEND,   12th. Month 5th. Day 1803

it is from that Respectable Carecture that we hear of thee that Encourages Me to believe that thee wishes well to all the Citesons of the United States, And as there are a few of the Inhabitants of this State who are Called Dunkers who would wish to be at peace with all mankind; and at this time we are thretened to be Drafted to go a Campaign toward the mouth of the Missisippy; and as we Cannot hear that Any of the other States are Drafted; it Causes the Inhabittants of this State to fly to the other States for Shelter and has Caused great Distress alreadry; in many famelies; and as I understand by some that the Coppy of the Express from thee was read in the Court Martial in Jonesborough and that the army was to be raised by Volluntary inlistment; I Desire that thee would write to me and let me know whether it is thy Express orders that the State of Tennessee Should be Drafted or not; and if it is thy orders that this State Should be Drafted let me know why it Should be Drafted more then any of the rest of the States; Seeing that Drafting is Very Distresing on the poor of whome there are many in this State—

So much at present from me thy Friend ISAAC HAMMER

RC (DLC); at foot of text: "Thomas Jefferson President of the United States"; endorsed by TJ as received 19 Dec. and so recorded in SJL.

Isaac Hammer (1769-1835) was born in Philadelphia and migrated with his family to Tennessee about 1783. Initially a Methodist, he became one of the first preachers for the Church of the Brethren, or Dunkers, in Tennessee. He subsequently joined the Society of Friends around 1808, becoming a respected minister and traveling widely in the United States and Europe (Roger E. Sappington, *The Brethren in Tennessee and Alabama* [Dandridge, Tenn., 1988], 36-8; Stephen B. Weeks, *Southern Quakers and Slavery: A Study in Institutional History* [Baltimore, 1896], 136-7).

CAMPAIGN TOWARD THE MOUTH OF THE MISSISIPPY: for the arrangements to utilize militia from the western states if necessary to assist with the occupation of Louisiana, see Vol. 41:632-5. According to a Tennessee militia law passed on 5 Nov., members of religious denominations that opposed bearing arms would not be fined for refusing to attend musters, but they would nevertheless "be classed, drafted and ordered on duty as other privates in all other cases" and subject to penalty if they failed to comply (*Acts Passed at the First Session of the Fifth General Assembly of the State of Tennessee, Begun and Held at Knoxville, on Monday the Nineteenth Day of September, One Thousand Eight Hundred and Three* [Knoxville, 1803], 23).

From James Mease

SIR   Philadelphia Deceb. 5, 1803

Permit me to draw your attention from the great concerns of the union, to view the inclosed plate of your plough, which I have had engraved for the 4th Vol of the Domestic Encya, now nearly printed. I deemed it necessary to have two views of the Mould board, taken, to give an idea of the thing to those who might not be able fully to Comprehend your truly plain and excellent demonstration of the progress of the work.—I have corrected two mistakes which are to be found in the impression of the Phil: trans: from which I copied, viz the omission of K. and the insertion of an e for an l.—

I also inclose a view of the famous English plough,—called the Beverstone plough.—

If you could procure me any facts upon the subject of Tobacco, in the course of two weeks, I should be much indebted to you. Mr Leiper mentioned to me, that you once traced the line or district of the Country in which the first quality of that article grew;—but he could not recollect it. This fact alone would be important, and is connected with the plan of the work. I suppose the detail of the mode of Cultivating and Curing the plant, would be too tedious: however a few general observations not commonly known or attended to, would be proper, and highly acceptable.—

I hope you will excuse the liberty I take in thus freely asking the use of your valuable pen.—

Accept my Very Sincere respects.   JAMES MEASE

P.S. Your remarks on my errors or deficiencies in the additions to the Dom: Encya. will always be thankfully Received.—

RC (DLC); at foot of text: "The President U: States"; endorsed by TJ as received 8 Dec. and so recorded in SJL. Enclosures not found, but see below.

PLATE OF YOUR PLOUGH: for the inclusion of TJ's moldboard plow in Mease's American edition of the *Domestic Encyclopædia*, see Mease to TJ, 9 Aug., and TJ to Mease, 19 Aug. The plate included a reprinting of eight sections drawn by TJ that originally appeared in the American Philosophical Society's *Transactions*, as well as two original engravings providing an inside and outside view of the moldboard (APS, *Transactions*, 4 [1799],

313-22, with diagrams at end of volume; *Domestic Encyclopædia; or, A Dictionary of Facts, and Useful Knowledge*, 5 vols. [Philadelphia, 1803-04], 4: plate facing 289; Vol. 30:202-5).

The BEVERSTONE plow was a well-regarded English wheel plow attributed to Lewin Tugwell of Beverstone, Gloucestershire. Mease included a plate and other remarks on the device reproduced from the *Annals of Agriculture* (*Domestic Encyclopædia*, 4:295-6, plate facing 295; Arthur Young, *Annals of Agriculture, and Other Useful Arts*, 32 [1799], 191-2, plate facing 191).

From John Page

DEAR SIR   Richmond Decr. 5th. 1803

I return you many thanks for your favor of the 25th. ultmo. The Account of Louisiana is highly interesting; & the information you are pleased to communicate respecting your prospect of getting quiet possession of New Orleans, is truely agreable; & the more acceptable after reading the malignant Tales fabricated by the Enemies of our peace.

I had hoped that Mr. Short, to whom I had confided a Letter to you in which was inclosed the Syllabus which you had permitted me to copy, had delivered it before the date of your Letter, in which you desire it may be sent by post.

I trust however that he did deliver it soon after.

I am sorry to trouble you with Applications for Offices, especially when I know you must be so much beset by Applicants. I will therefore only mention the Names of the Persons who have desired me to make a tender of their Services to you in such department as you may be pleased to place them, & as they, I think are known by you & will by themselves, or some other Friends explain their Views. They are both employed here, & are valuable officers, & firm Friends to our Constitution & the present Administration of the Government of the United States. I mean Major Saml. Coleman; & Captn. Alexr. Quarrier of the public Guards.

Our Assembly met to-day, about 150 Members of the House of Delegates took their Oaths of Office before Noon.

Mrs. Page returns her best thanks for your friendly attention to her & unites with me in presenting assurances of high Respect & Esteem.

I am most sincerely yours   JOHN PAGE

RC (DLC); endorsed by TJ as received 10 Dec. and so recorded in SJL.

A letter of 3 Sep. from Samuel COLEMAN, recorded in SJL as received from Richmond on 5 Sep., has not been found.

To the Senate

TO THE SENATE OF THE UNITED STATES.

In compliance with the desire of the Senate, expressed in their resolution of the 22d. of November, on the impressment of seamen in the service of the United States by the agents of foreign nations, I now lay before the Senate a letter from the Secretary of state, with a specification of the cases of which information has been recieved.

TH: JEFFERSON
Dec. 5. 1803.

RC (DNA: RG 46, LPPM, 8th Cong., 1st sess.). PrC (DLC). Recorded in SJL with notation "impressed seamen."

Lewis Harvie delivered this message to the Senate on 5 Dec. The Senate's RESOLUTION of 22 Nov. is recorded in SJL as

received that day with the notation "resoln respecting impressed seamen," but has not been found. It was part of the Senate's broader consideration of a House bill regarding "the further protection of the seamen and commerce of the United States" (JS, 3:312-14, 320).

ENCLOSURE

From James Madison

SIR,   Department of State, December 2, 1803.

Agreeably to a Resolution of the Senate, passed on the 22d of last month, requesting the President of the United States to cause to be laid before them such information as may have been received, relative to the violation of the flag of the United States, or to the Impressment of any seamen in the service of the United States, by the Agents of any foreign Nation, I do myself the Honor to transmit to you the enclosed abstract of Impressments of persons belonging to American vessels, which, with the annexed extracts from the letters of some of our Agents abroad, comprises all the information on the subject that has been received by this Department since the report to Congress, at its last session, relative to Seamen. To the first mentioned Document I have added a summary, shewing the number of Citizens of the United States impressed, and distinguishing those who had protections as Citizens; those who are stated to be Natives of the British Dominions, and not stated to be naturalized as Citizens; and those of all other Countries, who are equally not stated to have been naturalized in the United States.

Another source of injury to our neutral navigation has taken place in the blockade of Guadeloupe and Martinique, as notified in the annexed letter from Mr Barclay, Consul General of His Britannic Majesty for the Eastern States.

Beside the above, I have received no official information of any material violations of our flag during the present European war, except in the recent aggressions of the Emperor of Morocco.

With very High Respect, I have the Honor to be, sir, Your mo: Obedt servant,   JAMES MADISON

RC (DNA: RG 46, LPPM, 8th Cong., 1st sess.); in a clerk's hand, signed by Madison; at foot of text: "The President of the United States"; endorsed by a Senate clerk. PrC (DNA: RG 59, LMP, 1796-1814). Enclosures: (1) "Abstract of Impressments of Seamen belonging to American Vessels by the Agents of foreign Nations," 2 Dec., containing a list of 77 persons impressed from American vessels from approximately March to October 1803, with individual entries including the following information (if known): name of the seaman, his place of birth, the date and place of his impressment, the name of the American vessel from which he was taken, the name of the foreign vessel that impressed him, his citizenship, and whether or not he carried a protection; three of the individuals on the list are identified as "Black men"; summaries at the conclusion of the abstract state that the British impressed 43 U.S. citizens, including 12 carrying protections, as well as 10 British natives and 17 seamen from other countries who were not naturalized citizens of the U.S. at the time of their impressment; the summary also notes that two men on the list had been impressed by France and one by the Batavian Republic. (2) Extract of James Maury, U.S. consul at Liverpool, to secretary of state, 24 Mch., warning that the threat of war between Great Britain and France "has occasioned a great press for Seamen"; he adds that many American mariners, confident in the continuation of peace, had not taken the precaution of furnishing themselves with proof of citizenship, "which exposes them to impressment." (3) Extract of Robert W. Fox (misidentified as John W. Fox), U.S. consul at Falmouth, England, to secretary of state, 14 May, stating that "The Impress is very severe," but that U.S. citizens have not been molested except for "two or three without protections," who were taken while on board British ships; Fox had applied for their release and warns that U.S. seamen should carry their certificates of citizenship, "otherwise they will run great risk of being impressed." (4) Extract of William Savage, agent for the relief and protection of American seamen at Kingston, Jamaica, to secretary of state, 25 June, reporting that a "hot press throughout this Island" has taken about 60 sailors from American vessels at his port; Savage has secured the release of those who are American citizens; several vessels on the north side of the island have found themselves in distress due to the loss of men; Savage has compiled a list of impressed seamen and will apply for their discharge once the British frigates carrying them arrive. (5) Thomas Barclay, British consul general for the eastern states of the U.S., to secretary of state, 20 Oct., enclosing a letter from Commodore Samuel Hood, 25 July, informing the U.S. government that the Royal Navy has blockaded Martinique and Guadeloupe since 17 June and warning that merchant vessels "may have no plea for attempting to enter the ports of those Islands" (Trs all in DNA: RG 46, LPPM, 8th Cong., 1st sess., in a clerk's hand; printed in ASP,

Foreign Relations, 2:593-5. See also Madison, *Papers, Sec. of State Ser.*, 4:451, 615-16; 5:124, 557).

REPORT TO CONGRESS, AT ITS LAST SESSION: in December 1802, Madison sent the Senate abstracts of returns from customs collectors and communications from U.S. agents abroad regarding the impressment of American seamen and efforts to secure their relief and protection (Madison, *Papers, Sec. of State Ser.*, 4:214-15; JS, 3:248; ASP, *Foreign Relations*, 2:471-4; *Commerce and Navigation*, 1:500-2).

For the RECENT AGGRESSIONS OF THE EMPEROR OF MOROCCO, see TJ to the Senate and House of Representatives, 4 Nov.

After reading TJ's message and its accompanying papers, the Senate ordered them to lie for consideration (JS, 3:320). William Duane printed them by order of the Senate as *Message From the President of the United States, Enclosing a Report of the Secretary of State, on the Violation of the Flag of the United States, the Impressment of American Seamen and Others, on Board American Vessels, Conformable to a Resolution of the Senate of the United States of the 22d November, 1803* (Washington, D.C., 1803).

To the Senate and the House of Representatives

To THE SENATE AND
HOUSE OF REPRESENTATIVES OF THE US.

I have the satisfaction to inform you that the act of hostility, mentioned in my message of the 4th. of November to have been committed by a cruiser of the Emperor of Marocco on a vessel of the United States, has been disavowed by the Emperor. all differences in consequence thereof have been amicably adjusted, and the treaty of 1786. between this country and that has been recognised and confirmed by the emperor, each party restoring to the other what had been detained or taken. I inclose the emperor's orders given on this occasion.

[82]

The conduct of our officers generally, who have had a part in these transactions, has merited entire approbation. the temperate & correct course pursued by our Consul, mr Simpson, the promptitude & energy of Commodore Preble, the efficacious cooperation of Captains Rodgers and Campbell of the returning squadron, the proper decision of Capt. Bainbridge that a vessel which had committed an open hostility was of right to be detained for enquiry and consideration, & the general zeal of the other officers & men, are honourable facts, which I make known with pleasure. And to these I add, what was indeed transacted in another quarter, the gallant enterprize of Capt. Rodgers in destroying, on the coast of Tripoli, a Corvette of that power of 22. guns.

I recommend to the consideration of Congress a just indemnification for the interests of the Captors[1] of the Mishouda & Mirboha, yielded by them for the public accomodation.   TH: JEFFERSON
Dec. 5. 1803.

RC (DNA: RG 233, PM, 8th Cong., 1st sess.); endorsed by a House clerk. PrC (DLC). RC (DNA: RG 46, LPPM, 8th Cong., 1st sess.); endorsed by a Senate clerk. Recorded in SJL with notation "peace with Marocco." Enclosures: (1) English translation of decree of Mawlay Sulayman, 9 Oct. 1803, proclaiming peace between Morocco and the United States; see Mawlay Sulayman, Sultan of Morocco, to TJ, 11 Oct. (Tr in DNA: RG 46, LPPM, in a clerk's hand; PrC in DNA: RG 233, PM). (2) Mawlay Sulayman, order to the governor and all officers at Mogador, 11 Oct., informing them of the restoration of peace and warning them to "Take care—Take care that none of you do any thing against" American vessels or merchants, "for they are as they were in friendship and in Peace"; attested by James Simpson at Tangier, 17 Oct., as translated from Arabic into Spanish by Manuel de Baccas, and from Spanish into English by Simpson (Tr in DNA: RG 46, LPPM, in a clerk's hand; PrC in DNA: RG 233, PM).

ACT OF HOSTILITY: the capture of the American brig *Celia* by the Moroccan cruiser *Mirboka*. The cruiser was subsequently captured, and the brig liberated, by William Bainbridge and the frigate *Philadelphia* (Vol. 41:490, 491n, 672-3).

EACH PARTY RESTORING TO THE OTHER: as part of the reaffirmation of peace, Sulayman ordered the release of the American brig *Hannah* with its cargo and crew, which had been detained at Mogador since early September 1803. In return, the United States gave up possession of the Moroccan cruisers *Mirboka* and *Meshouda* (NDBW, 3:21, 63, 117, 140; Vol. 41:282-3, 508-10).

TEMPERATE & CORRECT COURSE: in framing this passage, TJ drew on the suggestions sent by Robert Smith on 4 Dec.

RETURNING SQUADRON: in October, Commodore Edward Preble ordered home the frigates *New York* and *John Adams* from the Mediterranean. The vessels arrived at Washington on 2 and 3 Dec., respectively (*National Intelligencer*, 5 Dec. 1803; NDBW, 3:154, 160).

GALLANT ENTERPRIZE OF CAPT. RODGERS: see Smith to TJ, [4 Dec.].

A JUST INDEMNIFICATION: after Lewis Harvie delivered TJ's message on 5 Dec., the Senate took no action, but the House of Representatives referred it to a special committee, which offered a pair of resolutions that were approved by the full House on 22 Dec. The first declared further hostilities against Morocco to be inexpedient, unless made necessary "by future aggressions." The second recommended that the captors of the Moroccan cruisers be indemnified for the prize money to which they were entitled. An act passed later in the session awarded $8,594.50 in prize money and $738.25 in expenses to the captors of the *Meshouda*, and $5,000 in prize money to the captors of the *Mirboka*

(JS, 3:320; JHR, 4:467, 490, 497; U.S. Statutes at Large, 6:54).

[1] RC in RG 46: "interests acquired by the Captors."

From Robert Simons

DEAR SIR,   Mount Republic Decr 5 1803

As an old Soldier; who has met with severe Losses in the Mercantile line; I Request Your Friendship in nominating me as Collector for the Port of New Orleans.

Major P. Butler and Genl Sumter can Inform you of my Character, as to Family I am an Elder Brother of the Collector of the Port of Charleston; and I am of Opinion that after holding the Office applied for as long as he has held his, that I Will give you equal Satisfaction.

I am Dear Sir with Sentiments of Respect and Esteem Your most Obt Hble Servt   ROBT SIMONS

RC (DNA: RG 59, LAR); at foot of text: "Thomas Jefferson Esqr. President of the United States"; endorsed by TJ as received 30 Dec. and "to be Collector N.O." and so recorded in SJL.

Robert Simons (1758-1807) was an elder brother of Charleston collector James Simons. A veteran of the American Revolution and former merchant at Georgetown, South Carolina, Simons dabbled in politics in the 1790s and early 1800s as an unsuccessful candidate for Congress and vocal foe of John Jay's mission to Great Britain and the resultant Jay Treaty. In public letters written in 1794, he declared

Jay's appointment as special envoy to be "both unconstitutional and tyrannical" and urged the election of Republicans to Congress. Two years later, he sent petitions to James Madison in the House of Representatives calling for the impeachment of George Washington and the 20 members of the Senate who supported the treaty (*South Carolina Historical and Genealogical Magazine*, 37 [1936], 145, 150; *State Gazette of South-Carolina*, 12 Dec. 1785; Charleston *City Gazette and Daily Advertiser*, 14 June, 29 Aug. 1794, 12 Oct. 1796, 20 Sep., 20 Oct. 1800; Madison, *Papers*, 16:210-11, 220, 237-8).

From Peter Kuhn, Sr.

SIR   Philadelphia 6 Dec 1803

Being charged to forward the enclosed Letter by my old Correspondent Mr Cathalan at Marseilles, I beg leave to avail myself of the opportunity in addressing, a few lines to your Excellency—Mr Cathalan informs me that from certain circumstances, with which your Excellency has been in this acquainted, a change in the Consulate at Genoa will probably be made—

Permit me to take the liberty of making known, that my Son Peter Kuhn Junr. is now a resident at that Place, to conduct a branch establishment of his Gibraltar House, in conjunction with Mr. Thos. H. Storm, Son of Thos Storm Esqr. late Speaker of the House of Representatives in the State of New York—I have just receivd Letters from my Son, in which he expresses his wish of that appointment, if your Excellency should think proper to honor him with that confidence, he flatters himself, that the Letters & recommendations he had the honor personaly to deliver, on a former occasion, may be considered in this instance—

My Sons residence at Genoa, is formed on a permanent establishment, and the business at Gibraltar is now solely conducted by his Partner my Son in Law Mr. H. Green, a young Gentleman of respectable connexions in this City, whose character & establishment, I believe is generaly known, to such of the Americans, that have visited that Port since his residence there—

Being without the honor of a personal acquaintance with your Excellency, or any introduction further than what may have been made known, through my Sons Letters & recommendations, I trust you will pardon the liberty of thus addressing you, the exalted station, in which I have the happyness to see you, promts me the more to this freedom, not only as being the Father of the American People in that station, but also from an impression, that your fostering cares are extended to its Sons in foreign Countries, when compatible with the general interests of the Nation—

With the highest esteem Your very obd h Svt.

PETER KUHN

RC (DNA: RG 59, LAR); addressed: "The Honbe. Thos. Jefferson Esqr. President United States Washington"; franked and postmarked; endorsed by TJ as received 9 Dec. and "Kuhn Peter junr. to be Consul at Genoa" and so recorded in SJL. Enclosure: see below.

Peter Kuhn (1751-1826) was a merchant in Philadelphia. His brother Adam Kuhn was a prominent physician in that city and an officer of the American Philosophical Society. Peter Kuhn frequently advertised shipments to and from Virginia and also imported goods from Malaga, Spain. He eventually took over a Philadelphia auction house, but after the economic collapse of 1819 he sought bankruptcy protection (R. Winder Johnson, comp., *The Ancestry of Rosalie Morris Johnson, Daughter of George Calvert Morris and Elizabeth Kuhn, his Wife* [Philadelphia, 1905], 120; APS, *Transactions*, 2 [1786], xxiv; Philadelphia *Dunlap's American Daily Advertiser*, 26 July 1791, 6 Mch. 1792; Philadelphia *Federal Gazette*, 12 Nov. 1792, 19 Dec. 1794; Philadelphia *Gazette of the United States*, 28 Mch. 1798; Philadelphia *Poulson's American Daily Advertiser*, 24 Mch. 1809; Philadelphia *Franklin Gazette*, 26 Oct. 1820; *Charleston Courier*, 28 Nov. 1826).

Kuhn was likely referring to the letter of 18 Aug. from Stephen CATHALAN to TJ. Cathalan also enclosed the letter in a message to James Madison (Madison, *Papers, Sec. of State Ser.*, 5:325).

ON A FORMER OCCASION: see Vol. 38:640-1n.

From Joseph Léonard Poirey

EXCELLENCE.   Paris ce 6 decembre 1803.

Mr. Bureaux de Pusy en arrivant en france m'a communiqué la Lettre que vous lui avez ecrite pour lui annoncer la récéption du Mémoire que J'ai adressé au Congrès et des Certificats qui y etoient joint

Vous eutes la bonté de L'assurer de votre intérés à ma demande

Permettez moi de le reclamer de Nouveau: J'ai été honoré de votre estime en France et vous m'avez vu à Richemond; à cette epoque j'etois heureux de servir la Cause de l'indépendance américaine et je n'ai rien Epargné pour me rendre digne de l'aveu et de l'estime de mes chefs

Le Général Washington a exprimé cette verité dans une lettre que vous avez entre les mains: il m'a placé au rang des officiers de l'armée et admis aux Cincinnati; Ces marques de sa bienveillance suffisoient à mon bonheur, j'etois jeune alors et croyois pouvoir obtenir un jour par mon Travail, les moyens honorables nécéssaires à l'Existence, les evenements ont tous boulversé, la captivité du General La Fayette et ses malheurs m'ont eloigné des Emploit.

Actuellement, Monsieur, je n'ai que votre Protection pour appui, Veuillez me l'accorder et obtenir pour moi la premiere recompense de mes services en Amérique. Serois-je le seul francois qui n'auroit point eu de part à ses bienfaits

J'ai l'honneur d'être avec un tres profond Respect, de Votre Excellence, Le tres Humble et tres obeissant serviteur   POIREY

E D I T O R S '   T R A N S L A T I O N

YOUR EXCELLENCY,   Paris, 6 Dec. 1803

On his arrival in France, Mr. Bureaux de Pusy gave me your letter announcing that you had received the report I sent to Congress and the certificates that accompanied it.

You were kind enough to assure him of your interest in my request.

Allow me to renew that request. You honored me with your esteem in France and met with me in Richmond. At that time I was gladly serving the cause of American independence and spared nothing to merit the confidence and admiration of my leaders.

General Washington said as much in a letter you have. He awarded me the rank of officer in the army and admitted me to the Society of the Cincinnati.

I was very pleased by these kind gestures. I was young and believed that by working hard I could earn the honorable means of ensuring my livelihood. Events have upset all of that. General Lafayette's captivity and misfortunes have prevented me from being employed.

Now, Sir, your protection is my only support. Please provide it by obtaining the compensation I earned for my services in America. Should I be the only Frenchman not to be rewarded for his good deeds?

With very deep respect, I have the honor of being your excellency's very humble and obedient servant.   POIREY

Dupl (DLC); at head of text: "A Son Excellence Jefferson President des Etats unis d'Amerique" and "Duplicata"; at foot of text: "Rue Mézieres No 4 près le Luxembourg" (4 Rue Mézières, near the Luxembourg Palace).

In 1801, Jean Xavier BUREAUX DE PUSY, who was then in New York, transmitted to TJ a request from Poirey for compensation for his service as the Marquis de Lafayette's secretary during the Revolutionary War. In a reply to Bureaux de Pusy on 3 Sep. 1801, TJ indicated that he had given the papers, which included a letter written by George WASHINGTON to Lafayette's wife in 1790, to a member of Congress (Vol. 33:594-5; Vol. 35:68-9, 201).

To the Senate and the House of Representatives

TO THE SENATE AND
HOUSE OF REPRESENTATIVES OF THE US.

Since the last communication made to Congress of the laws of the Indiana Territory, I have recieved those of which a copy is now inclosed for the information of both houses.   TH: JEFFERSON
                                                                              Dec. 7. 1803.

RC (DNA: RG 233, PM, 8th Cong., 1st sess.); endorsed by a House clerk. PrC (DLC). RC (DNA: RG 46, LPPM, 8th Cong., 1st sess.); endorsed by a Senate clerk. Both letters recorded in SJL and connected with a brace to notation "Indiana laws." Enclosures: copies of one law and two resolutions passed by the governor and judges of the Indiana Territory from 16 Feb. to 24 Mch. 1803 (Trs in DNA: RG 233, PM; PrCs in DNA: RG 46, LPPM).

LAST COMMUNICATION: TJ to the Senate and the House of Representatives, 14 Feb. 1803 (Vol. 39:525).

TJ's message and its accompanying papers were received by the House of Representatives on 7 Dec. and by the Senate on 8 Dec. Both houses ordered them to lie on the table (JHR, 4:472, 481; JS, 3:321-2). They were subsequently printed as *Message from the President of the United States, Transmitting Certain Laws of the Indiana Territory of the United States* (Washington, D.C., 1803).

From David Stone

Senate Chamber 7th. Decr. 1803.

David Stone asks leave to present to Mr Jefferson the two enclosed Letters and to observe of the Writers that James Read was formerly Collector of the port of Wilmington North Carolina and removed by Mr Adams He was afterwards appointed a Col in the[1] Army, for the Regiment raised in North Carolina. John Sibley is a Physician (of some respectability) he formerly lived, and edited a paper, at Fayette-Ville in North Carolina, and has been uniformly I believe a Republican.

RC (DNA: RG 59, LAR); endorsed by TJ as received 7 Dec. and so recorded in SJL with notation "Sibley & James Read to be employed in Louisiana"; also endorsed by TJ: "Sibley Dr. John. emploimt. Louisiana. perhaps Surgeon. Natchitoches." Enclosures: (1) James Read to Stone, Wilmington, North Carolina, 8 Nov., noting that after he pays his debts, he will have "little Property left"; he plans to go to Louisiana and requests that Stone "procure for me an elligable appointment to that place" (RC in same; endorsed by TJ: "Read James to David Stone. to be empld. in Louisiana"). (2) John Sibley to Stone, Natchitoches, "250 Miles up red River in Louisiana," 8 Oct., noting that he was in Louisiana when news of the cession arrived; he fears that "some efforts might be made to exchange the Floridas for that part of Louissiana west of the Missisippi," but if that happens it will be from "a want of proper information"; he is anxious to convey "Historical & Geographical Sketches of this country" to Stone, Senator Jesse Franklin, and others in Congress, but "Jealousey" of the government renders "communications somewhat difficult"; he plans to send Governor Claiborne information useful to the government; he sent a detailed account to Fayetteville and requested that his son, George C. Sibley, transmit a copy of it to Stone, who may share it with the president or secretary of state, if he thinks proper; Sibley wishes to settle at Natchi-

toches and seeks an office under the new government; Stone and Franklin can vouch for his "republican Principles and attachment to the Present administration"; his knowledge of the French language will give him a great advantage; he thinks a small military force will be necessary at first in the territory "or they will not respect the government," not because there is opposition to the cession, but because the "Government has always been a Military One" (RC in same; endorsed by TJ: "Sibley Dr John").

In 1801, Nathaniel Macon and others sought the reappointment of JAMES READ as collector at Wilmington, but Gallatin argued against it, noting that Read was removed for "remissness in official duties," not for his political views. He owed the Treasury Department $7,000 in 1801 (Vol. 35:467, 468-9n).

William C. C. Claiborne considered JOHN SIBLEY an "ingenious correspondent." In late October, the governor sent TJ a long letter and map from the Natchitoches resident (Claiborne to TJ, 24 Aug., 28 Oct. 1803; Sibley to TJ, 20 Mch. 1804). EDITED A PAPER: the weekly *Fayetteville Gazette* (1789-94) was titled the *North-Carolina Chronicle, or, Fayetteville Gazette* from 1790 to 1791 (Brigham, *American Newspapers*, 2:762-3).

[1] Stone here canceled "provisional."

From William C. C. Claiborne

Dear Sir,   Fort-Adams December 8th. 1803.

Before my departure from this Post, I cannot deny myself the pleasure of addressing to you a private and inofficial Letter.—Information of the Mission to New-Orleans, with which you honored me, I received on the evening of the 17'th Ultimo, and the measures which I have taken since that period, have been faithfully detailed to you by my Communications to the Department of State.—The incessant rains which fell during the latter part of the last Month, the necessary attention of the Planters to their Cotton Crops, and the general opinion which prevailed thro' this Country, that no serious resistance would be made to the surrender of Louisiana to the U.S, prevented me from raising as many Volunteers as I *at first* expected: But this circumstance ceases to be a matter of regret, since force is not now necessary to support our Claims, as Louisiana has been peaceably delivered to the French *Prefect*, and that officer has already officially communicated to the American Commissioners his solicitude for their arrival, in order that he might resign to them the care of the Province.—Thus Sir, the most anxious wish of my heart, the speedy consummation of the Negociation for Louisiana, is likely to be accomplished without the effusion of Blood, or the further expenditure of public Treasure.—

I reached Fort-Adams on the evening of the 4th. Instant, and met *General Wilkinson*, who had arrived here on the morning of the same Day: every possible exertion for a speedy embarkation seems to have been made by *that officer*. But we have been thus long necessarily delayed, the means of transport not being completed.—It is expected however that we shall be enabled to make a movement by Tomorrow evening, or the Morning following at furthest, and I presume that in less than ten Days thereafter, we shall be in Orleans. The Militia Volunteers of the Territory who rende'voused at this Post, were mustered this Afternoon and are about 200 strong;—These, in addition to the Regular Troops at this Garrison, will make a force of between 450 and 500 Men.—The Volunteers from Tennessee have not arrived; But I understand (altho' not officially) that they will certainly be in Natchez in six or seven Days; the ordering into service, this patriotic Corps, I shall always consider a wise measure, and I am confidently of opinion, that the energetic preparations directed by the Government for the taking possession of Louisiana, tended to hasten the surrender of the Province to the French Commissioner.

General Wilkinson has been so entirely engaged in Military arrangements, that we have had little conversation on the subject of our Mission; But I do sincerely hope, that the utmost *harmony* in opinion and action will exist between us; I consider *it* as so essential to the Interest of our Country, that a fervent spirit of accommodation will uniformly be manifested on my part.

From the superior Military pretensions of the General, I was apprehensive that the Rank attach'ing to the station, in which I am now placed, might excite some Jealousy—I have therefore studied to avoid every appearance of command, *even of the Militia*, since I arrived at Fort-Adams; nor do I contemplate interference of any kind in the Military Arrangements: If therefore I do not succeed in conciliating the Confidence of the General in this particular, I shall only have to regret, that my best efforts towards that object, have been fruitless.— In the Diplomatic proceedings, I shall not hesitate to act in my place with energy; But shall at the same time, pay all due respect to the opinions and advice of my Colleague.

The Mississippi Territory is now perfectly tranquil, and I have the satisfaction to add, that I leave the people much more harmonised in political sentiment than I found them, and better reconciled to the principles of our Government—When therefore my Duties in Louisiana may be closed, I shall return to my Post, with a pleasing expectation, that the *attachment* of my fellow Citizens to correct principles will continue to encrease.—

I pray you Sir, to accept Assurances of my great Respect and sincere Esteem! WILLIAM C. C. CLAIBORNE

RC (DLC); at foot of text: "The President of the U. States"; endorsed by TJ as received 27 Dec. and so recorded in SJL.

INFORMATION OF THE MISSION TO NEW-ORLEANS: see Notes on Preparations to Occupy Louisiana at 30 Oct. and Draft of a Proclamation for the Temporary Government of Louisiana at 31 Oct.

In New Orleans on 30 Nov., Spanish commissioners PEACEABLY DELIVERED possession of Louisiana to Pierre Clément Laussat, who issued a proclamation stating that French authority would be very brief—"d'un instant." A week earlier, replying to a letter from Claiborne of 18 Nov., Laussat pledged his full and friendly cooperation in transferring control to the United States. When he wrote Claiborne on the 23d, the prefect was still waiting for official papers from his government to empower him to make the transfer, but he urged Claiborne to hurry to New Orleans (*Terr. Papers*, 9:110-12, 125-32; Madison, *Papers, Sec. of State Ser.*, 6:136-7).

James WILKINSON traveled to Fort Adams from Mobile Bay, stopping for a day in New Orleans along the way. He conferred with Laussat, who had received the papers he needed late on the 25th but had not yet taken possession of Louisiana from the Spanish. Wilkinson and Laussat made plans for the transfers of authority, and the general concluded that the United States would not have to wrest control of Louisiana from the Spanish by force (*Terr. Papers*, 9:113, 115).

ENABLED TO MAKE A MOVEMENT: Wilkinson left Fort Adams with the troops on 10 Dec. and arrived in New Orleans on the 16th. The Spanish had already withdrawn their soldiers from the garrison in the city. Claiborne, who encountered a delay coming down the river, arrived in New Orleans on the evening of the 17th.

Laussat ceded the province to the U.S. commissioners on 20 Dec. (same, 138-9; Dearborn to Wilkinson, 6 Jan. 1804, in DNA: RG 107, LSMA; Madison, *Papers, Sec. of State Ser.*, 6:181, 188-9).

From Andrew Marschalk

Natchez Decr. 8—

SIR   9. O'Clock—P.M—

I do myself the honor to inform Your Excellency, that a Gentleman this moment arrived from New-Orleans—(and who left it since the Post) informs me, that the Province was officially delivered to M. Laussat—and the Flag of the French Republic displayed on the 29th. Ult.—

Very respectfully Your Excellencys Most-Obt. H Sert

                     ANDW. MARSCHALK
                     Editor of the
                     Mississippi Herald

RC (ViW: Tucker-Coleman Collection); at foot of text: "His Excellency Thomas Jefferson"; endorsed by TJ as received 27 Dec. and so recorded in SJL.

Andrew Marschalk (1767-1838) entered the army as an ensign in 1791, and military service took him to the Mississippi Valley by 1797. While still in the army, he set up a press and began to print a variety of items, including the laws of Mississippi Territory. In 1802, he left the army and started a weekly newspaper in Natchez, the *Mississippi Herald*, which became the *Natchez Gazette* shortly before it folded in 1808. He later established the *Washington Republican* in Washington, Mississippi, and, in 1818, the *Mississippi State Gazette*. Marschalk served as a staff officer of the territorial militia and was, in 1803, a Natchez alderman (New York *Mercantile Advertiser*, 18 July 1803; *Norfolk Gazette and Publick Ledger*, 9 Nov. 1810; New Orleans *Daily Picayune*, 17 Aug. 1838; Charles S. Sydnor, "The Beginning of Printing in Mississippi," *Journal of Southern History*, 1 [1935], 49-55; [Isaac M. Patridge], "The Press of Mississippi—Historical Sketch," *DeBow's Review*, new ser., 4 [1860], 500-9; Dunbar Rowland, *Encyclopedia of Mississippi History*, 2 vols. [Madison, Wis., 1907], 2:169-70; Brigham, *American Newspapers*, 1:423, 426, 428, 430; *Terr. Papers*, 5:253, 260, 560-1; Heitman, *Dictionary*, 1:690; Vol. 39:xlv).

ON THE 29TH. ULT.: the transfer from Spanish to French authority took place on 30 Nov.; see preceding letter.

From Craven Peyton

DEAR SIR   Stump Island 8 Dcr. 1803

I waited on the Sheriff Yancy to whom the Note was negotiated with an Accompt. of a debt due from Colo. Lewis to Gamble in Richmd. on Judgement. Yancy informed me he had Just enclosed it to M. Kenny in stanton the Attorney for the plantiff. coud I of seen M. Kenny I think I coud. of made some arangement with him so as to of made the paymt. in apl. in a formar lettar I named. to you I thought Henderson had done nothing in Kentuckey, but a short time aftar convinced. me he had he began & has compleated a very excellent canal & was still going on but at last court I presented a bill in consequence of which the court stoped his proceeding: which woud of been done at a formar Court but M. Barbar thought from the right which I had Obtained he coud not possibly cut them Out & Observd. the More work he did the bettar for the real proprietor, but Henderson considers him self in a very desperate situation & conducts him self Accordingly. Fantress has not returned. with the deed from Kentuckey. he is expected every day.

I Am with great Respt. Yr. Mst. Obt.   C PEYTON

RC (ViU); endorsed by TJ as received 19 Dec. and so recorded in SJL.

For THE NOTE of $558.14 in settlement for the Henderson lands, see TJ to Craven Peyton, 27 Nov.

THE DEED FROM KENTUCKEY: see Vol. 38:578 and Vol. 41:349.

List of Nominations from Albert Gallatin

[before 9 Dec. 1803]

Dudley Broadstreet Hobart—Collector of Bath, Massachusetts, vice William Webb—
  The Same—Inspector of the Revenue for same place—
Samuel Derby, Collector of York, Massachusetts, vice Joseph Tucker—
  The Same—Inspector of the Revenue, for same place—
George Wolcott—Surveyor of Saybrook, district of Middletown[1] Connecticut—vice Richard Dickenson—
  The Same, Inspector of the Revenue, for same place—
Aaron Hassert, Surveyor of New-Brunswick, district of Perth Amboy[2] N. Jersey, vice Andrew Lyle
  The Same—Inspector of the Revenue for same place—

John Cutler, Collr. of Snow-Hill, Maryland, vice William Selby

The Same, Inspector of the Revenue, for the same place

Martin Tapscott, Collr. of Yeocomeco River, Virginia, vice James A. Thompson

The Same—Inspector of the Revenue for the same place

Peterson Gurley, Surveyor of Winton district of Edenton[3] N. Carolina, vice Laurence Mooney

The Same, Inspector of the Revenue for same place—

Thomas C. Ferebee, Surveyor of Indian Town district of Camden[4] N. Carolina—vice Thomas Williams—

The Same, Inspector of the Revenue for same place[5]

Add if approved by the President

Erastus Granger Surveyor of Buffaloe Creek, district of Niagara, New York vice Callendar Irvine resigned

The same Inspector of the revenue for the same

MS (DNA: RG 59, MCL); undated, but see TJ to the Senate, 9 Dec.; in a clerk's hand, with emendations and last entry in Gallatin's hand (see notes below); endorsed by Gallatin: "Nominations"; endorsed by TJ: "Designations of office."

COLLECTOR OF BATH: for the resignation of William Webb and the decision to appoint Dudley B. Hobart, see Vol. 41:511-12, 571-2.

In early 1803, Ephraim Kirby and other Connecticut Republicans urged TJ to appoint GEORGE WOLCOTT in place of Richard Dickinson (Vol. 39:581; Vol. 40:61-2, 85-7).

On 18 Nov., New Jersey senator John Condit wrote to Gallatin, recommending the appointment of AARON HASSERT to the vacancy at New Brunswick (RC in DNA: RG 59, LAR, endorsed by TJ: "Hassert Aaron. to be Surveyor of customs at New Brunswick & Inspector of revenue at do. in the district of Perth Amboy"). ANDREW LYLE, appointed by TJ in March 1802, submitted his resignation to the secretary of state on 19 Aug., citing "ill health" and "the pressure of domestic avocations" (RC in DNA: RG 59, RD, endorsed by TJ: "Lyle Andrew to mr Madison. resigns office of Surveyor of New Brunswick. enquire Doctr. Condit"; Vol. 37:23, 53).

MARTIN TAPSCOTT: see Gallatin to TJ, 8 Nov.

SURVEYOR OF WINTON: on 16 Nov., Samuel Tredwell, collector at Edenton, North Carolina, informed the Treasury secretary that three Winton residents, including Peterson Gurley and Thomas N. Brickell, a former applicant, had applied for the surveyorship upon learning of Laurence Mooney's death. He noted that all were known to Congressman Thomas Wynns and Senator David Stone (RC in DNA: RG 59, LAR, endorsed by TJ: "Mooney Laurence. Surveyor of Winton. dead"; Biog. Dir. Cong.; Vol. 37:314n, 341, 343n). According to SJL, on 26 Nov. TJ received a letter from North Carolina congressman Willis Alston recommending Gurley as surveyor, but it has not been found.

[1] Preceding three words interlined by Gallatin.

[2] Preceding four words interlined by Gallatin.

[3] Preceding three words interlined by Gallatin.

[4] Preceding three words interlined by Gallatin.

[5] Remainder of text in Gallatin's hand.

List of Nominations from
Jacob Wagner

[before 9 Dec. 1803]

Jacob Ridgway of Pennsylvania— Antwerp. Note a blank commission for this port was sent to Mr. Livingston at Paris with authority to fill it up. This happened many months ago: and lately the offer has been made to Mr. Barnet to take his choice of it and Havre.

Francis Coffin (a Frenchman) of Dunkirk was formerly our Consul there. Quer. is he intended?

Henry Wilson of Maryland— Ostend.

Wm. Foster jr. Morlaix

John Leonard of New Jersey— Barcelona

Lawson Alexander of Maryland— Rotterdam

John M. Forbes of New York to be Consul for such parts of the Circle of Lower Saxony as may be nearer to Hamburg than to the Residence of any other Consul or Vice Consul of the U. States. Note this limitation may be necessary to prevent him from superseding the Consul at Bremen &c.

MS (DNA: RG 59, MCL); undated, but see TJ to the Senate, 9 Dec.; entirely in Wagner's hand; endorsed by TJ: "Consuls. list of Dec. 1803."

Isaac Cox Barnet recommended Jacob Ridgway as commercial agent at ANTWERP when Barnet decided to accept the position at Le Havre (see Vol. 40:719n).

For Fulwar Skipwith's recommendation of Francis Coffyn, who had long cared for U.S. commercial interests at DUNKIRK, see Vol. 41:159, 160n.

For the earlier appointment of William Foster, Jr., as commercial agent at MORLAIX, see Vol. 36:400. In 1803, Foster sought the consulship at Nantes. TJ did not submit his nomination to the Senate

at this time (Madison, *Papers, Sec. of State Ser.*, 4:275; TJ to the Senate, 9 Dec.).

For the appointment of John Leonard as vice consul at BARCELONA, see Vol. 41:698, 700n, 702.

When Joseph Forman submitted his resignation in December 1802, he recommended Lawson Alexander as commercial agent at ROTTERDAM in his place and appointed Alexander to act as consular agent (Madison, *Papers, Sec. of State Ser.*, 4:209). In a letter written at Amsterdam on 29 Dec. 1803 to an unnamed recipient, Sylvanus Bourne advised that Alexander was suffering from health issues, "his mind being in disorder." Unaware that TJ had appointed William Clark of Massachusetts to another position, Bourne recommended Clark to take over at Rotterdam (DNA: RG 59, LAR, possibly intended as a duplicate of Bourne to Madison, 29 Dec., endorsed by TJ: "Clarke Wm to be consul Rotterdam"; Madison, *Papers, Sec. of State Ser.*, 6:244-5; TJ to the Senate, 9 Dec.).

For the appointment of John M. Forbes as consul at HAMBURG, see Vol. 36:608-9. CONSUL AT BREMEN: Frederick Jacob Wichelhausen (Madison, *Papers, Sec. of State Ser.*, 5:506-7; Vol. 35:407).

To the Senate

To THE SENATE OF THE UNITED STATES.

I nominate the following persons to the offices affixed to their respective names. to wit.

Francis Coffyn of Dunkirk in France to be Commercial agent of the US. at Dunkirk vice Charles D. Coxe declined.

Jacob Ridgway of Pensylvania to be Commercial agent of the US. at Antwerp. vacant.

John Mitchell of Pensylvania to be Vice-commercial Agent at Havre in France vice the Sieur de la Motte declined.

Henry Wilson of Maryland to be Commercial Agent of the US. at Ostend. vacant.

Lawson Alexander of Maryland to be Commercial Agent at Rotterdam v. Joseph Forman resignd.

John Forbes of New York now Consul at Hamburg to be Consul also for such parts of the circle of Lower Saxony as may be nearer to Hamburg than to the residence of any other Consul of the US.

William Clarke of Massachusets to be Consul at Embden, vacant.

John Leonard of New Jersey now Vice Consul of the US. at Barcelona, to be Consul at the same place vice William Willis resigned.

John F. Brown of Massachusets to be Consul at the island of St. Thomas. vacant

Isaac Prince of New York to be Consul for the island of St. Bartholomew, vacant.

It is to be noted to the Senate that the commission appointing a Consul to any port generally extends his powers to 'such places within the same allegiance as are nearer thereto than to the residence of any other Consul of the US. within the same allegiance.'

John Childress junr of West Tennissee to be marshal of West Tennissee vice Robert Hays removed[1]

Thomas G. Thornton of Massachusets to be Marshal of the district of Maine, vice Isaac Parker whose commission is near expiring.

Dudley Broadstreet Hobart of Massachusets to be Collector and Inspector of revenue of Bath in Massachusets vice William Webb resigned.

Samuel Derby of Massachusets to be Collector of York in Massachusets and Inspector of revenue for the same vice Joseph Tucker removed.[2]

George Wolcott of Connecticut to be Surveyor and Inspector of the revenue for Saybrook in the district of Middletown in Connecticut, vice Richard Dickenson.[3]

Erastus Granger of New York to be Surveyor and Inspector of the revenue of the port of Buffalo creek in the district of Niagara vice Callender Irvine who declines.

Aaron Hassert of New Jersey to be Surveyor & Inspector of the revenue for New-Brunswick in New Jersey vice Andrew Lyle resigned

John Cutler of Maryland to be Collector & Inspector of the revenue for Snowhill in Maryland vice William Selby.[4]

Martin Tapscott of Virginia to be Collector & Inspector of the revenue for Yeocomico river in Virginia vice A. Thompson decd.

Peterson Gurley of N. Carolina to be Surveyor & Inspector of revenue for Winton in the district of Edenton in N. Carolina vice Lawrence Mooney decd.

Thomas T. Ferebee of N. Carolina to be Surveyor & Inspector of revenue for Indian town in the district of Cambden in N. Carolina vice Thomas Williams decd.

Reuben Smith of Georgia to be a 2d. Lieutenant in the Corps of Artillerists.

Thomas A. Smith of Georgia to be a 2d Lieutenant in the corps of Artillerists.

James Logan of Kentuckey to be an Ensign in the 2d. regiment of infantry.

Edmund Hayward of Maryland to be Surgeon's mate in the corps of artillerists

James Lanier of Kentucky to be Surgeon's mate in the corps of Artillerists.   Th: Jefferson
                                                      Dec. 9. 1803.

RC (DNA: RG 46, EPEN, 8th Cong., 1st sess.); endorsed by a Senate clerk. PrC (DLC); in ink in left margin, TJ added comments at four entries (see notes below) and check marks at the other entries. Recorded in SJL with notation "original Nominations."

On 10 Oct., John F. brown applied to William Eustis, seeking an appointment as commercial agent at St. Thomas. Brown described the importance of having an American official on the Danish island. Merchants in New York and at St. Thomas had encouraged him to apply for the position, predicting that "from the present appearance of affairs, there will be considerable trade to that Island from America" (RC in DNA: RG 59, LAR; endorsed by TJ: "Brown John F. to Dr. Eustis. to be consul at St. Thomas").

For the Treasury secretary's effort to have Robert HAYS replaced, see Vol. 40:587-8, 589n, and John Childress, Jr., remained marshal for the district of West Tennessee until his death in 1819 (*Nashville Gazette*, 11 Sep. 1819). MARSHAL OF THE DISTRICT OF MAINE: see John Langdon to TJ, 1 Oct. 1803. Thomas G. Thornton remained in office until his death at Saco, Maine, in 1824, at age 54 (*Portland Advertiser*, 6 Mch. 1824). Both Childress and Thornton received com-

missions for four-year terms, dated 21 Dec. 1803 (FCs in Lb in DNA: RG 59, MPTPC).

THOMAS T. FEREBEE: that is, Thomas C. Ferebee.

Lewis Harvie delivered TJ's message to the Senate on 9 Dec., where it was read and ordered to lie for consideration. The Senate confirmed 16 of TJ's nominations on 15 Dec. and approved the other 10 on 21 Dec. (JEP, 1:459-61).

[1] In margin on PrC: "drunkenness."
[2] In margin on PrC: "drunkenness."
[3] In margin on PrC: "extortion from his under officers."
[4] In margin on PrC: "for active opposition."

From Littleton W. Tazewell

DEAR SIR;   Norfolk. December 9th. 1803.

Anxious to close all the transactions which I have with the representatives of the late house of Robert Cary & Co. of London, and to put a period to the little business of theirs yet remaining under my direction, I have taken the liberty of calling your attention to the balance due from yourself to that firm, and to solicit that you will make arrangements as early as your convenience will permit for the satisfaction of this claim—In making this application it is proper I should say to you, that your Creditor feels perfect satisfaction as to the present situation of his debt, and I believe has no particular anxiety as to its very speedy collection—It is my own situation alone which prompts this request of payment—You will therefore submit yourself to no sacrifice on this account, but in your arrangements will consult only your own convenience—I feel disposed to terminate my agency, which cannot be done with propriety while any debts remain uncollected, & hence I have a wish to make these collections quickly—Let me repeat however, that it is far from being my desire, that you should consult my convenience at the expense of your own—.

Permit me sir to close this letter of business by tendering you the assurance of my very high respect, and to offer my best wishes for a long continuation of the happiness of a life, so valuable to our Country—.

I am your obdt. servt.   LITTN: W TAZEWELL

RC (MHi); endorsed by TJ as received 17 Dec. and so recorded in SJL.

TJ had last made a payment of $1,000 on the outstanding debt of the Wayles estate to ROBERT CARY & CO. in January 1801. He also owed money to the firm on his own account. YOUR CREDITOR: Wakelin Welch, Jr., the firm's surviving partner (MB, 1:395n-96n, 616n-17n; 2:1034; Vol. 29:173).

From J. P. G. Muhlenberg and Others

[before 12 Dec. 1803]

Understanding that Major John Mifflin Irwin of the City of Philadelphia intends to apply to the President of the United States for the appointment of Naval Officer, or Surveyor of the Port at New Orleans—We the subscribers recommend him as a Gentleman of Honor and integrity and well qualifyed to fill either of the said Offices.—

P. MUHLENBERG
TENCH COXE
JNO. SHEE
JNO PORTER
JOHN BARKER
ISRAEL ISRAEL
BLAIR MCCLENACHAN
THOMS. PROCTER
JAMES GAMBLE
NATHAN DORSEY L.P.

RC (DNA: RG 59, LAR); undated; in Muhlenberg's hand, signed by all; endorsed by TJ as received 12 Dec. and "Irwin John Mifflin to be Naval officer N. Orleans."

From Timothy Bloodworth

DEAR SIR   Wilmington December 12th 1803

Enclos'd is a few of the seeds of the Venus fly Trap, which som time past I remember to hear You express a desire to obtain.

will You pleas to Indulge me with a few observations on the state of Pollitics in this place, which in times past has been the seat of Federalism. in my last Address I mentioned the Change that was likely to take place, the Justness of this opinion has been verifyed by the event of the last Election, where the principle, & not the Charecter, crown'd the Triuph. since that period the rapid progress of Republican Interest has been more Appearant. the Wisdom, & success, of Youre Measures, has smote with Silent Astonishment Youre inveterate Enemies. their Loud, & popular Clamors, is reduc'd to silent whispers. som of their leading Charecters have Ventured to express encomiams on Youre Administration. General Benjamin Smith declar'd as his opinion, that if You supported the Credit of the public, Youre Measures would prove a Blessing to the United States. & the late Judge Haywood, declar'd in this place, that the purchase of Louissiana was worth sixty Million to the Nation, & applauded the wisdom of the Measure, & Reprobated the opposition in Congress, by the party who last Sessions Urgd the Necessity of war, to acquire the possession. this purchase is generally popular in this place, & few attempts to say any thing Against the Measure.

I am Sanguine in my expectation of Electing a Republican Elector, at the Insuing Election, & I flatter my self that You will carry the Election by a respectable Majority, let Youre antagonist be who he May.

Permit me to acquaint You that they second, & third Lieutenant of the Cutter Dilligence, have resign'd, & withdrew from the Service. the Captain has taken into Service from Necessity, a Man by the Name of Charls Betts, a person of Reputable Charecter, & said to be the Ablest Pilot on the river. should it be Youre pleasure to favor him with a Commission of second Lieutenant, it would afford satisfaction to the other officers. & if it should appear Advisable to appoint a third, I beg leave to Mention Robert Brown, Son of the Captains, who is a promising sober Youth, & I make no doubt would in a short time, do Honor to the Appointment. At the request of Coll: James Reed, I take the liberty to acquaint You that he has discharg'd the public Debt, & is Moving to Loiusiana, & is willing to except any appointment, the President May pleas to bestow, in the Army, or otherways. the like request is made by my Nephew, James Bloodworth, who sets out for that Country in a few weaks, his Charecter stands Unimpeach'd by friend, or foe, he is an Active, Industreeous, Sober Youth, in the Bloom of Life.

My Heart flows with Gratitude for the favours You have bestow'd, & I can not too often express my obligation to my Benefactor. pleas to Except the Sincearity of this declaration, & my earnest Desire that you may long continue a Blessing to Youre Country, in the Station that you now fill with so much Dignity, & advantage to youre fellow Citisens. From Dear Sir

Youre Most Obedient Humble Servant.

TIMOTHY BLOODWORTH

RC (DNA: RG 59, LAR); endorsed by TJ as received 25 Dec. and so recorded in SJL; also endorsed by TJ: "Bloodworth James" and " Reed Colo. James," connected by a brace to notation "for Louisiana."

VENUS FLY TRAP: TJ's interest in the Venus flytrap (*Dionaea muscipula*) dated back several years, but the seeds from Bloodworth were the first he ever acquired. It does not appear that he attempted to cultivate them until after his presidency. In April 1809, shortly after his retirement to Monticello, TJ recorded in his garden book that he "sowed seeds of Dionaea muscipula in a pot. they were several years old" (Betts, *Garden Book*, 385; Vol. 9:238; TJ to Elizabeth Leathes Merry, 26 Dec. 1803; TJ to Bloodworth, 29 Jan. 1804).

In his LAST ADDRESS to TJ, dated 14 Dec. 1802, Bloodworth expressed his belief that TJ's election had provided the "Blinded multitude" in North Carolina with "a ray of light" (Vol. 39:155).

LAST ELECTION: for the Republicans' success in the recent North Carolina congressional elections, see Vol. 41:311-12.

Benjamin SMITH of Brunswick County lost his seat in the North Carolina legislature to a Republican in 1801 (Vol. 35:390). John HAYWOOD was a member of the state superior court from 1793 until his resignation in 1800 (William S. Powell, ed., *Dictionary of North Carolina Biography*, 6 vols. [Chapel Hill, 1979-96], 3:87).

TJ appointed JAMES BLOODWORTH an ensign in the army in March 1804. He resigned the following year, settled in Natchitoches, changed the spelling of his name to Bludworth, and became a colonel in the Louisiana militia during the War of 1812 (Marie Norris Wise, *Norris-Jones-Crockett-Payne-Blanchard: The Heritage of Marie Norris Wise*, rev. ed. [Sulphur, La., 1998], 126-8; Heitman, *Dictionary*, 1:226; TJ to the Senate, 24 Mch. 1804).

From Paul Dalrimple

DEAR SIR   Philadelphia Decemr. 12th. 1803

The old Toryes are Murdering of me, and no one Takes my part, I wass beatten Thre times in N. York by them Parsecuted to Philadelphia have allso been beatten five Different time, thease beatings Generally Consist of forty or fifty People thowing brik bats & the lik—till I wuld Start frrom my bed at three in the morning—Rushing into my Hous and beating the breath out of my body Stealing the things out of my hous & leaving me half dead—This Has been dun unto me and no one to tak my part, one passeth by on the Rite hand and the other on the left & Phitty me with insolence as they pas and now they theten me with with a nother beating & that they will beat me from time to to time untill the kill me—I take no rest Day nor night & I am threttened with another beatting which will put an end to my existance—I perceveired in your Electon and thos under you throughout the continent and haveing Succeded all the old torye are killine me My Beloved President it is in thy power to take me out of this place of torment—Dath will bee the unvilable Consiquence of my remaning hear—worse than the Turke for I have no Money nor friends and thetened my Life every moment by a Sett of Ruffins—O Pitty my

Distrissed Situation and grant me relief as Soon as Possible, that I may See you and be at Rest is the Ardent prayer of your Humble Sarvt— PAUL DALRIMPLE

P.S. I have rote a Letter to the Attorney General Levi Lincoln with whome I am acquainted I am so weake from the Abuse I have Received that I can scarsely rite

I have heard a number of them say that they would give tean Dollars a peas to have me Rid Skimington or to have me beaten—this is the truth

RC (DLC); addressed: "Thomas Jefferson President of the United States City of Washington"; franked and postmarked; endorsed by TJ as received 21 Dec. and so recorded in SJL; also endorsed by TJ: "lunatic certainly."

In 1791, a Paul Dalrimple, recently returned from South Carolina, advertised his shoe and boot manufactory in Leicester, Massachusetts, in a Worcester newspaper. LEVI LINCOLN, with whom Dalrimple claimed acquaintance, was also a resident of Worcester. In New York in 1800, Dalrimple advertised for the return of a runaway apprentice. Dalrimple moved to Lexington, Kentucky, and wrote again to TJ from there on 19 Feb. 1805 (Worcester *Massachusetts Spy*, 9 June 1791; New York *Mercantile Advertiser*, 11 Aug. 1800).

RID SKIMINGTON: a skimmington was a rowdy parade or procession with "rough music," including the banging of pots and pans to mock someone or run them out of town (OED; William Pencak and others, eds., *Riot and Revelry in Early America* [University Park, Pa., 2002], 5-6).

From Joseph Priestley

DEAR SIR   Northumberland Decbr. 12. 1803

I take the liberty to send you *a second defence of my pamphlet about Socrates*, in the 16th page of which you will find, that I have undertaken the task you were pleased to recommend to me. On giving more attention to it, I found, as the fox did with respect to the lion, that my apprehensions entirely vanished. Indeed, I have already accomplished a considerable part of the work, and in about a year from this time I hope to finish the whole, provided my health, which is very precarious, be continued in the state in which it now is.

I directed a copy of the *tract on phlogiston* to be sent to you from Philadelphia, and I shall order another, which, together with the inclosed papers, I shall be much obliged to you if you will convey to Mr Livingston. Please also to cast an eye over them yourself; and if you can with propriety promote my interest by any representation of yours, I am confident you will do it:

When you wrote to me at the commencement of your administration, you said "the only dark speck in our horison is in Louisiana." By your excellent conduct it is now the brightest we have to look to.

Mr Vaughan having applied to me for a copy of my Harmony of the Evangelists, which was not to be had in Philadelphia, and intimated that it was for you, my son, whose copy is more perfect than mine, begs the honour of your acceptance of it, as a mark of his high esteem, in which he has the hearty concurrence of

Dear Sir, Yours sincerely   J PRIESTLEY

RC (DLC); endorsed by TJ as received 19 Dec. and so recorded in SJL. Enclosures: see below.

For Priestley's contentious exchange with Presbyterian minister John Blair Linn over Priestley's PAMPHLET *Socrates and Jesus Compared*, see John Vaughan to TJ, 21 Nov. After reading the pamphlet, TJ composed an outline for a work that would compare Jesus to a larger array of ancient philosophers, a TASK that he hoped Priestley would perform (Vol. 40:157-9, 253-5).

Although Priestley indicated that he was enclosing his latest rejoinder, published in Northumberland as *A Second Letter to the Revd. John Blair Linn, D. D. Pastor of the First Presbyterian Congregation in the City of Philadelphia, in Reply*

to *His Defence of the Doctrines of the Divinity of Christ and Atonement*, it is likely that TJ received it from John Vaughan, along with two copies of a second edition of Priestley's work on PHLOGISTON. Priestley may have here enclosed a letter intended for Robert R. LIVINGSTON, which was to accompany the second copy of the phlogiston pamphlet (see Vaughan to TJ, 20 Dec.; TJ to Priestley, 29 Jan. 1804).

WHEN YOU WROTE: see Vol. 39:85-7.

In August, Vaughan reported obtaining Priestley's personal copy of the Greek and English versions of *A Harmony of the Evangelists*, but TJ was worried about depriving Priestley of it. It is likely that Priestley was here enclosing his son's copy (Sowerby, No. 1492; Vol. 41:136, 201-2).

From Benjamin Rush

DEAR SIR,   Philadelphia Decemr. 12. 1803

The bearer Dr: Chapman—formerly one of my private pupils, wishes for the honor of your acquaintance. He has just returned from Europe, where he has spent his time profitably in improving himself in every kind of knowledge as well as in medicine. During his residence in Scotland he was not only entertained; but patronized by your friend the Earl of Buchan. He will repay you by his anecdotes for your civilities to him.

With great respect, I am Dear Sir yours sincerely

BENJN: RUSH

PS: Your reasons for not writing the letter of condolence to &c—are perfectly satisfactory.

RC (NjP: Rush Family Papers); endorsed by TJ as received 19 Jan. 1804 and so recorded in SJL.

In October 1801, Rush wrote a letter of introduction for his former student Nathaniel CHAPMAN to the EARL OF BUCHAN

(L. H. Butterfield, ed., *Letters of Benjamin Rush*, 2 vols. [Princeton, 1951], 2:838-9).

LETTER OF CONDOLENCE: see TJ to Rush, 4 Oct.

From John Smith of Ohio

SIR   Monday Morn. [12 Dec. 1803]

I beg leave to inform you that

Mr. Breckinridge

Mr Wright

Mr Jackson

Mr Baldwin &

Mr. Adams compose the Committee, to prepare & report a bill for the Government of the Ceded Territories. I learn they have met two or three times, but Cannot agree on the principles of a bill. Butlers proposed amendment to the Constitution is rejected. Those who voted in the affirmative are

Mr Anderson

Mr Butler

Mr Dayton &

Mr Jackson

The residue who were present voted in the negative. The House have sent up their agreement to the proposed Constitutional amendment of the Senate—And also a Joint Resolution requesting the Executive to transmitt copies of it to the several States.

I am Sir very respectfully your Humble Servt.

JOHN SMITH

RC (DLC); partially dated; endorsed by TJ as received 12 Dec. and so recorded in SJL.

The Senate COMMITTEE called to prepare for the governance of Louisiana was named on 5 Dec. (*Annals*, 13:211).

The PROPOSED AMENDMENT of Pierce Butler, who as a member of the Constitutional Convention in 1787 had played a key role in developing the electoral college and who opposed current efforts to alter the rules for electing presidents, would have limited presidents to three terms, with a minimum of four years separating the second and third terms (*Annals*, 13:213-14; ANB). For the JOINT RESOLUTION, which concerned what became the Twelfth Amendment to the Constitution, see the following document.

To Albert Gallatin

The Attorney Genl. having considered and decided that the pre-
scription, in the law for establishing a bank, that the officers in the
subordinate offices of discount & deposit shall be appointed 'on the
same terms and in the same manner practised in the principal bank'
does not extend to them the principle of rotation established by the
legislature in the body of Directors in the principal bank, it follows
that the extension of that principle has been merely a voluntary &
prudential act of the principal bank, from which they are free to depart. I think the extension was wise & proper[1] on their part; because
the legislature having deemed rotation useful in the principal bank
constituted by them, there would be the same reason for it in the subordinate banks to be established by the principal. it breaks in upon the
esprit de corps so apt to prevail in permanent bodies, it gives a chance
for the public eye[2] penetrating into the sanctuary of those proceedings & practices which the avarice of the directors may introduce for
their personal emolument, & which the resentments of excluded directors, or the honesty of those newly admitted might betray to the
public; and it gives an opportunity at the end of a year, or at other
periods, of correcting a choice which on trial proves to have been
unfortunate; an evil of which themselves complain in their distant
institutions. whether however they have a power to alter this, or not,
the Executive has no right to decide; & their consultation with you[3]
has been merely an act of complaisance, or a desire to shield so important an innovation under the cover of Executive sanction. but ought
we to volunteer our sanction in such a case? ought we to disarm ourselves of any fair right of animadversion whenever that institution
shall be a legitimate subject of consideration? I own I think the most
proper answer would be that we do not think ourselves authorised to
give an opinion on the question.

From a passage in the letter of the President, I observe an idea of
establishing a branch bank of the US. in New Orleans. this institution is one, of the most deadly hostility existing, against the principles & form of our constitution. the nation is at this time so strong &
united in it's sentiments that it cannot be shaken at this moment. but
suppose a series of untoward events should occur sufficient to bring
into doubt the competency of a republican government to meet a crisis
of great danger, or to unhinge the confidence of the people in the public functionaries, an institution like this, penetrating by it's branches
every part of the Union, acting by command & in phalanx may in a

critical moment[4] upset the government. I deem no government safe which is under the vassalage of any self-constituted authorities, or any other authority than that of the nation or it's regular functionaries. what an obstruction could not this bank of the US. with all it's branch banks, be, in time of war? it might dictate to us the peace we should accept, or withdraw it's aids. ought we then to give further growth to an institution so powerful, so hostile? that it is so hostile we know 1. from a knolege of the principles of the persons composing the body of Directors in every bank, principal or branch and those of most of the stockholders:[5] 2. from their activity in opposition to the measures & principles of the government, & to the election of those friendly to them: & 3. from the sentiments of the newspapers they support. now, while we are strong,[6] it is the greatest duty we owe to the safety of our constitution, to bring this powerful enemy to a perfect subordination under it's authorities. the first measure would be to reduce them to an equal footing only with other banks as to the favors of the government. but, in order to be able to meet a general combination of the banks against us, in a critical emergency, could we not make a beginning towards an independant use of our own money, towards holding our own bank,[7] in all the deposits where it is recieved, and letting the Treasurer give his draught or note, for paiment at any particular place, which in a well conducted government, ought to have as much credit as any private draught or bank note or bill; and would give us the same facilities which we derive from the banks? I pray you to turn this subject in your mind, and to give it the benefit of your knowlege of details, whereas I have only very general views of the subject. affectionate salutations.

RC (NHi: Gallatin Papers); endorsed. PrC (DLC).

The 1791 LAW FOR ESTABLISHING the Bank of the United States outlined the process for organizing branches for discount and deposit. Under a PRINCIPLE OF ROTATION, not more than three-fourths of the 25 directors, excluding the president, were eligible for reelection the next year (U.S. Statutes at Large, 1:191-5). The bank found it difficult to obtain qualified candidates to serve as directors at the smaller branches, even though only 13 were required for each branch. In the case of the branch at Washington, it was decided to decrease the number to nine. The directors of the Bank of the United States elected the directors of each branch annually. By 1804, the bank had decided "to abandon the principle of partial rotation in the appointment of branch directors" (James O. Wettereau, "The Branches of the First Bank of the United States," *Journal of Economic History*, 2 [1942], supplement, 74-6, 78-83, 89-92; Vol. 35:132, 133-4n, 136n, 190-1; Vol. 39:531).

LETTER OF THE PRESIDENT: the letter from Thomas Willing, president of the Bank of the United States, to Gallatin has not been found (see also the following document). In March 1804, Congress passed an act authorizing the bank to establish branches "in any part of the territories or dependencies of the United States, in the manner, and on the terms prescribed" by the 1791 act (U.S. Statutes at Large, 2:274).

From Albert Gallatin

DEAR SIR   [13 Dec. 1803]

Wherever our monies may be deposited, the Treasurer's draught for the same has the same credit as any bank note, and the circulation of those draughts would be more extensive than now, if they were, like bank notes, payable to bearer. Unless, however, we wanted; which we do not; to issue exchequer bills or paper money of some description or another, it never will happen that our draughts shall be issued except in payment of a demand and made payable to the person whose demand is thus discharged. The great advantages we derive from Banks & especially from the Bank of the United States are 1st. a safe place of deposit for the public monies—2dly. the instantaneous transmission of such monies from any one part of the continent to another, the Bank giving us immediately credit, at New York if we want it, for any sum we may have at Savannah or at any other of their offices & vice versa—3dly. the great facility which an encreased circulation and discounts give to the collection of the revenue.

For these reasons I am extremely anxious to see a Bank at New Orleans; considering the distance of that place, our own security & even that of the collector will be eminently promoted, and the transmission of monies arising both from the import & sales of lands in the Mississippi territory would without it be a very difficult, & Sometimes dangerous operation.

Against this there are none but political objections; and these will lose much of their force when the little injury they can do us & the dependence in which they are on Govt. are duly estimated. They may vote as they please & take their own papers; but they are formidable only as individuals and as Merchants, and not as Bankers. Whenever they shall appear to be really dangerous, they are completely in our power and may be crushed.

As to the answer to the letter I agree fully with you & intended only to give a civil answer without committing us on the question of expediency. It shall be altered so as to *answer* that object. What must be done with the New Orleans hospital and Doctor Bache's indirect application for encrease of salary? One thd. dollars is fully sufficient; we give no more any where else.

With sincere respect and attachment Your obedt. Servt.

ALBERT GALLATIN

<table>
<tr><td>

RC (DLC); undated; at foot of text: "The President of the United States"; endorsed by TJ as received from the Treasury Department on 13 Dec. and "Banks. Bache" and so recorded in SJL.

</td><td>

Gallatin's ANSWER to Thomas Willing's letter has not been found (see preceding document).

BACHE'S INDIRECT APPLICATION: see Caspar Wistar to TJ, printed at 16 Nov.

</td></tr>
</table>

To the Governors of the States

SIR   Washington Dec. 13. 1803

At the request of the Senate and H. of Rep. of the US. I transmit to you a copy of an article of amendment proposed by Congress to be added to the constitution of the US.[1] respecting the election of President and Vice president to be laid before the legislature of the State over which you preside: and I tender you assurances of my high respect and consideration.   TH: JEFFERSON

RC (NjMoHP); in Lewis Harvie's hand, signed by TJ; endorsed by Joseph Bloomfield as received 17 Dec. and answered. RC (De-Ar); in Harvie's hand, signed by TJ. RC (R-Ar); in Harvie's hand, signed by TJ. RC (NNFoM); in Harvie's hand, signed by TJ; added later at foot of text: "Gov'r of North Carolina." RC (MdAA); in Harvie's hand, signed by TJ. RC (Vi); in Harvie's hand, signed by TJ; endorsed. RC (DLC: TJ Papers, Ser. 9); in Harvie's hand, signed by TJ; endorsed. Dupl (facsimile in *Chattanooga Times*, 14 Apr. 1963); in Harvie's hand, signed by TJ; at head of text: "Duplicate"; addressed: "His Excellency The Governor of the State of Georgia Louisville"; franked and postmarked; endorsed. Enclosure: see below.

The proposed Twelfth AMENDMENT to the Constitution passed the Senate on 2 Dec. by a vote of 22-10, and the House of Representatives concurred on 9 Dec. by a vote of 84-32. Three days later a joint resolution of Congress called on the president to send copies to the governors of the states. The amendment altered the process for electing the president and vice president, requiring electors to designate their votes specifically for president and vice president (JS, 3:319-20, 322-3; JHR, 4:482-4; John Smith to TJ, 12 Dec.).

A State Department memorandum dated 13 Dec. records that the department that day sent TJ's letter with certified copies of the amendment to the governors of Georgia, South Carolina, North Carolina, Pennsylvania, Ohio, Virginia, New Jersey, Rhode Island, and New Hampshire, and by express to the governor of Kentucky. The letter and amendment were sent to the governors of Massachusetts, Connecticut, Maryland, Delaware, New York, Vermont, and Tennessee on 14 Dec., and duplicates to the governors of Ohio, Tennessee, and Georgia on 21 Dec. (DNA: RG 59, DL).

[1] RC in R-Ar: "United States."

Notes on a Conversation with Charles Coffin

1803. Dec. 13. the revd mr Coffin of New England who is now here solliciting donations for a college in Greene county in Tennessee tells me that when he first determined to engage in this enterprize, he wrote a paper recommendatory of the enterprize, which he meant to get signed by clergymen, and a similar one for persons in a civil character, at the head of which he wished mr Adams to put his name, he being then President, & the application going only for his name & not for a donation. mr Adams after reading the paper & considering, said 'he saw no possibility of continuing the union of the states, that their dissolution must necessarily take place, that he therefore saw no propriety in recommending to New England men to promote a literary institution in the South, that it was in fact giving strength to those were to be their enemies, & therefore he would have nothing to do with it.'

MS (DLC: TJ Papers, 113:19521); entirely in TJ's hand; follows, on same sheet, Notes on a Conversation with Andrew Ellicott, 23 June 1801.

A native of Newburyport, Massachusetts, Charles Coffin (1775-1853) graduated from Harvard and became a Presbyterian minister. After visiting eastern Tennessee, he decided to help operate a school there, serving as financial agent of Greenville College until 1810, when he became the school's president. In 1827, he started a six-year tenure as president of East Tennessee College, forerunner of the University of Tennessee (*Christian Observer*, new ser., 32 [1853], 109; Leroy P. Graf and Ralph W. Haskins, eds., *The Papers of Andrew Johnson*, 16 vols. [Knoxville, 1967-2000], 1:147n; *Quinquennial Catalogue of the Officers and Graduates of Harvard University, 1636-1910* [Cambridge, Mass., 1910], 164).

On 18 Dec., TJ addressed an order on John Barnes to pay Coffin $100 "for the use of the college of Tennissee for which he acts" (MS in ViU, in TJ's hand and signed by him, signed by Coffin acknowledging payment, endorsed by Barnes as paid 22 Dec.; MB, 2:1114).

Notes on Speeches of Homastubbee and Puckshunubbee

1803. Dec. 13. Mingo Omah Stebbé
We are the fathers of red men
    has come far to state affrs his nation
    hopes will listen
does not go into old talks
    to begin anew

supposes has heard his business
he is red, people poor, no slaves no money
game destroyed. in debt.
called on for paimt. no means but land
not secret. public, not ashamd of poverty
Indians who are decd. gave lands to British.
this laid over till we desired line which was run
the land he wishes to sell is joining on Tombigby
this he supposes we have heard before.
the land he offers is by the voice of his nation
    this settled at mr Dinsmore's
      he is going to move to other side of nation
    is that by our orders?
he sent a talk from Ft. Adams askg. a factory on Tombigby. they were
    sent accdly.
when they were sent with annuity asked for a bit of land to fix on.
the annuity he thot a present not to be paid for in land.
agent wanted a place higher up river or he would move to Chicka-
    sawhay or six towns or send them back
the land they now offer is the last they can spare
    must now turn in to work.
    begs we will not incroach on land, but protect it
this is what he has long wished to say, face to face
    little land many people hunting done, must work
    individuals want to buy land.
will be reduced to poverty without assistce & protection
has often heard of big white house, never saw it
his house is also called White house, house of peace
has heard of 3. fathers. 1st. decd. 3d here
hopes will be always peace between reds & wh.
he is willing to go on & see country as soon as talks are done, & to
    return back
when he returns back to this place wishes to go back partly by water,
    but rather by land thro' the Creek nation. he is a heavy man. yet was
    no more than a leaf on board ship. hopes to be sent back by land.
the interpreter old as himself, agent has moved him to Chickasawhay.
    this part of nation was this our order.
white people who read & write never forget
    not so with reds, nothing but memory.
    he is sent here by the young not the old.
    does not speak for the opposition party.

Puckshanubbé

his part of nation considd as one fire
he never before spoke to the great men
has come contrary to his expectn
they have always been friends to whites
never warred agt whites. never shed their blood
poor red men
people to whom old talks sent, all decd
his part of nation without a great man
what now says is from warriors of his part of nation
there are crazy red people, young & foolish tho' long acqd with whites.
the elder decd. & gone
he sent a talk by Genl Wilkinson Ft. Adams
in that he proposed to come. he rejoices
tho' the day is cloudy he expresses what his heart thinks.
his wishes always for peace
white path from him to Chickasaws
their talk all one tho a little way apart
from them informn of whites
his thoughts are only for to make provn
glad to see me in my own house
if I was young would invite to his house
consider them as poor & love them.
are red, surrounded by whites.
has no thought of turng eyes but to us.
hopes we will extricate from poverty
white path is open. a long one.
the mischief done by whites as well as reds
white man always notes on paper.
wishes what they now say may be committed to paper & sent to his
     red men that they may know what he said.
it was to the English not to us they gave lands
has been lately re-marked to us.
the old who are decd sold it.
but never heard they recieved anything for it.
yet he does not ask pay, is too late.
he cannot trace it down. can only repeat hearsay.
when the English bot, their talks were in their country. promd shd.
     be the last line
hopes it will be the last line that will be run between them & whites.
Wilkinson's line is come on paper.
     nobody to live on the line, a little way off.

people settling on the line. disputes.

poor. red. make nothing but children. make many
   lands scarce of game. great debt. cant pay

their mercht. calls for money.

if they had property to pay, would not beg.

no money no slaves.

has given land to pay debt if we will take it

the place sold us is his favorite place.

   it is to be the last.

   remr will be soon filled with red people

a man loves his chdr. hopes we will love & assist them

   little land, many people. willing to work, no means

if any thing occurs will speak another day.

[on verso:]

land begins on bank of Talahatche Yazoo opposite where, Genl:
   Wilkinson begun his

running on a direct line across to Missipi

their boundary with Chickasaws on the Mispi is Little prairies, a
   little below mouth of St. Francis

about 34–30

MS (DLC: TJ Papers, 137:23620); entirely in TJ's hand; endorsed: "Choctaws. notes of their speeches."

Homastubbee (d. ca. 1809) was the principal chief of one of the three geographical divisions of the Choctaws. In an address to U.S. commissioners in 1801, he asked that the United States carry through with an intention to provide the Choctaws with instruction in spinning and weaving and with tools and agricultural implements. He participated in other treaty negotiations in 1802 and 1805. Homastubbee's name often appears in conjunction with the title "Mingo," which in his case acknowledged his position as a leader of one of the major tribal divisions. As shown by TJ's writing it "Omah Stebbé" in the notes printed above, the name appears with various spellings (ASP, *Indian Affairs*, 1:662; Charles J. Kappler, comp. and ed., *Indian Affairs: Laws and Treaties*, 5 vols. [Washington, D.C., 1975], 2:57, 64, 88; Greg O'Brien, *Choctaws in a Revolutionary Age, 1750-1830* [Lincoln, Neb., 2002], 102-3; Clara Sue Kidwell, *Choctaws and Missionaries in Mississippi, 1818-1918* [Norman, Okla., 1995], 17; Valerie Lambert, *Choctaw Nation: A Story of American Indian Resurgence* [Lincoln, Neb., 2007], 27; Grayson Noley, "1540: The First European Contact" and "The Early 1700s: Education, Economics, and Politics," in Carolyn Keller Reeves, ed., *The Choctaw Before Removal* [Jackson, Miss., 1985], 56-7, 96).

HAS COME FAR TO STATE AFFRS HIS NATION: in September, Puckshunubbee headed a group of leaders who proposed a cession of land to clear the Choctaws' debts to traders. Forwarding that petition, U.S. agent Silas Dinsmoor advised Dearborn that a Choctaw delegation would be traveling to Washington. In addition to Homastubbee and Puckshunubbee, the group included three other men. Dearborn referred to all of them as chiefs. The notes printed above are TJ's record of what Homastubbee and Puckshunubbee said in conference with him on 13 Dec. Homastubbee opened his address by identifying the delegation as leaders, "fathers," of their nation. The meeting with TJ appears to have followed the protocols of a Choctaw council meeting, with speakers going in turn by seniority. It was common for orators in council meetings to pause after each sentence to allow hearers to express their approval. From TJ's notes, it seems likely that in this meeting an interpreter translated each sentence into English during that pause (Dinsmoor to Dearborn, 30 Sep., 2 Oct., recorded in DNA: RG 107, RLRMS; Dearborn to Dinsmoor, 9 Jan. 1804, in DNA: RG 75, LSIA; Sturtevant, *Handbook*, 14:508; Vol. 41:401-3).

SENT A TALK FROM FT. ADAMS ASKG. A FACTORY ON TOMBIGBY: in an address to commissioners James Wilkinson, Benjamin Hawkins, and Andrew Pickens in a treaty conference at Fort Adams in December 1801, Homastubbee directed a portion of his remarks to the president of the United States. The mingo asked for a trading store at Fort Stoddert, which was on the Mobile River downstream from the confluence of the Tombigbee and the Alabama, or at Fort St. Stephens, which was on the Tombigbee. The government established a trading factory at St. Stephens in 1802 (ASP, *Indian Affairs*, 1:662; Kidwell, *Choctaws and Missionaries*, 22; Vol. 39:277n).

Choctaws called the division of their nation located in the watershed of the CHICKASAWHAY River the SIX TOWNS people (Kidwell, *Choctaws and Missionaries*, 3-4).

HEARD OF 3. FATHERS. 1ST. DECD. 3D HERE: that is, three presidents of the United States, the first of whom was deceased. Some of the Choctaws at the treaty negotiation with the federal commissioners in 1801 had met George Washington in Philadelphia (ASP, *Indian Affairs*, 1:662).

For what lay behind Homastubbee's request to return home BY LAND, see TJ's reply of 17 Dec.

Speakers at the conference at Fort Adams in 1801 pointed out the limitations of having only one INTERPRETER for the three divisions of the Choctaws (ASP, *Indian Affairs*, 1:661-2).

THEIR TALK ALL ONE THO A LITTLE WAY APART: the Choctaw and Chickasaw languages, although not identical, were closely related (Sturtevant, *Handbook*, 14:71; 17:109).

LAND BEGINS ON BANK OF TALA-HATCHE YAZOO: the Tallahatchie River is an upper tributary of the Yazoo. Little Prairie, located on the Arkansas River a few miles above where that river enters the Mississippi, had been the site of a French trading outpost beginning in the seventeenth century. Before and during the American Revolution, a British post on the eastern bank of the Mississippi marked the vicinity of Little Prairie to the west (Jeannie M. Whayne, Thomas A. DeBlack, George Sabo III, and Morris S. Arnold, *Arkansas: A Narrative History*, 2d ed. [Fayetteville, Ark., 2013], 43, 68).

From William Rue

SIR,   Dec. 13th 1803
I Pray the in thy mercy full tenderness to hear me with patience and generously grante me my Request if agreable to they will—Whear as I have spent my time in the servis of my Land and Nation untill old Age has overtaken me that I am not Capeble of heard Laber with severrel other Deficoltes that Lies in my way which Renders it not Convinent for me to undertake the Buisness of a planter I have undertaken a smawl Bisness of Retalen goods in this and some other states as Bisness seems to Cawl me—as a Law Can not Be made to sute Every Capasite there fore the Nesesary tax thakes from my small

store the Proffets that mite help to suporte me as my Begining is small—Therfore my Request to the grate Representiv or President of the united states is, if it is not Contrary to our Rites and Liberty that He would grant me Lesons for selling Drey goods or grosrys in any State or County with out further Expence if it is Consistent with His Good Pleasur and if not Pray Excues my Ignorance—

Sir I am obeden subject   Wm. Rue

RC (ViW: Tucker-Coleman Collection); addressed: "Mr. Thomas Jefferson President of the united States"; endorsed by TJ as received 15 Dec. and so recorded in SJL.

From Mountjoy Bayly

Sir   George Town Decr. 14th 1803

From your well known disposition to attend to what ever may promote the interests of the community whose concerns are committed to you, I am incouraged to solicit your attention to the application I had the Honor to make to you on the 13th. respecting the Sulphur Spring in the Genessee Country. I have some time since delivered to the Secretary at War a discription of that spring which I suppose has been laid before you.

When this property was about to be sold to a subject of Great Britain my first wish was to secure to my own Country what I deemed an Object of Great importance. with this View I made the effort I had the Honor to explain to you. In persuing this Object I have been put to both trouble and expence. It is now in the power of the United States to Obtain this spring at what I think a very Low price, and in doing so I trust its agents will not deem the small profit I hope for, illy bestowed upon a man who possessing every wish to serve his Country, is not in circumstances to justify his diverting any part of his time or money from a large family, who have no dependance but upon his personal exertions.

I have the Honor to be with High respect & Esteem your Hum. Servt.   Mountjoy Bayly

NB I will have the Honor to call on you on Saturday at noon. MB

RC (DLC); at foot of text: "To the President"; endorsed by TJ as received 15 Dec. and so recorded in SJL.

Mountjoy Bayly (1755-1836) of Frederick County, Maryland, served as a Continental officer during the American Revolution, as a representative in the Maryland legislature in the 1780s and 1790s, and as a general in the state militia. A Federalist, he made a failed bid for a seat in Congress in 1800 and declared himself insolvent in 1805. From 1811 to 1833, he was sergeant at arms of the U.S. Senate

(Papenfuse, *Maryland Legislature*, 1:119; *Maryland Herald and Elizabeth-Town Advertiser*, 21 Nov. 1799, 2 Oct. 1800; New York *Republican Watch-Tower*, 29 Oct. 1800; *Maryland Gazette*, 2 Jan. 1806).

The SULPHUR SPRING to which Bayly refers was probably the mineral spring that later spawned the town of Clifton Springs in Ontario County, New York.

Like Bayly, several of the initial explorers and settlers of the area were from Frederick County, Maryland (O. Turner, *History of the Pioneer Settlement of Phelps & Gorham's Purchase, and Morris' Reserve* [Rochester, N.Y., 1852], 228-9, 258n; Frederick Loren Gifford, *The Early History of the Village of Clifton Springs* [Canandaigua, N.Y., 1984], 9).

From Christopher Ellery
and Nehemiah Knight

Washington Decr. 14th. 1803—

C. Ellery & N. Knight present their highest respects to the President of the United States—

And beg to be permitted to observe, that having perused a letter of this date from General Stanton to the President, recommending Peleg S. Thompson for the place of surveyor, they find no difficulty in joining in the recommendation; convinced from the circumstance of his having been brought up under the immediate care of General Stanton, that his acquirements and character must be well known to the General, and that the representation made is perfectly just.

CHRIST. ELLERY
N. KNIGHT

RC (DNA: RG 59, LAR); in Ellery's hand, signed by both; at foot of text: "The President of the United States"; endorsed by TJ "Thompson Peleg S. to be Surveyor N. Orleans" and so recorded in SJL as received 14 Dec., joined by a brace with Joseph Stanton, Jr., and Samuel J. Potter to TJ, 14 Dec.

Nehemiah Knight (1746-1808), a native of Cranston, Rhode Island, who long served as its town clerk, was elected to the Rhode Island General Assembly in 1783 and 1787 and served in Congress as a Republican representative from March 1803 until his death in June 1808 (*Biog. Dir. Cong.*; Providence *Columbian Phenix*, 18 June 1808).

From John Godbold

SIR   Boston 14 December 1803.

An Address from a distant and private Individual, for an Appointment under the Government of the United States in its newly acquired Territory of Louisiana; may from the nature of the Request and the manner of the Application seem presumptuous or arrogant:

yet from your Excellency I hope excuse if compliance should be inconvenient or improper.

When Arrangements shall have been made for the effective operation of a Civil Code; the Commercial Interests of that portion of the United States will doubtless next engage the attention of Government: to aid the Treasury Department in the collection of the Revenue resulting from Mercantile enterprize, the establishment of a Collector, Naval Officer, and Surveyor will probably be necessary either at New Orleans or some other Port in that territory: to obtain an Appointment to either of these Offices is the object of the present Address if that be not already prevented by a more fortunate Applicant—humbly circumstanced as I am, and unknown as I must be, respect to your Excellency, and justice to myself require the recital of some facts to evince that I am not altogether unsuitable for either of the solicited Employments.

By recommendation of Judge Wendell in August 1790, I was employed as a Clerk in the Custom House of this District by General Lincoln the then and present Collector, in which I continued until March 1794: in this Department of Public Utility, my deportment was such as to afford general satisfaction to the Merchants of the District, and to obtain the Approbation of my Principal, and of his Official Colleagues: in March 1794, I retired to the service of a Merchant of Boston, on an offer of a hundred Dollars a year more than I received from the Collector: after an absence of five years, I was, in April 1799, again employed by the Collector, and continued in the Public Service until the 31 January 1801, at which time I was discharged, because my Constitution, not naturally robust, compelled me to be occasionally absent; an inconvenience[1] which care and attention have removed.

The opportunity afforded to understand the nature and the practice of the Revenue Statutes by an Employment of more than five years; I hope will acquit me in your Excellency's opinion of presumption, or arrogance in soliciting Appointment to a Service, I am not qualified to perform.

To a successful Application, commendation of some kind is proper, perhaps is necessary: on that Principle, I am persuaded that any Declaration in the case, which might be requisite, either from the Collector or the Associate Officers, would not be withholden: to their testimony, I flatter myself I could add the favourable opinions of many among the most eminent Mercantile men in this Metropolis; for whom I have done Business while engaged in the Public Service.

When the Government of that territory shall have been so far organized as to make these Appointments necessary: if, among the numerous Applicants for them, there should be no one better qualified than myself, I wish to be remembered by your Excellency: a love of Employment and a wish to be useful, have occasioned and I hope will excuse the freedom of this Address.

Wishing every felicity may attend your Excellency, I am most respectfully yours JOHN GODBOLD.

RC (DNA: RG 59, LAR); at foot of text: "His Excellency Thomas Jefferson, Esquire"; endorsed by TJ as received 24 Dec. and "emploimt in customs N.O." and so recorded in SJL.

John Godbold was listed as a clerk in the Boston custom house in 1800 and continued to appear as a resident of Boston in subsequent directories (*The Boston Directory. Containing the Names of the Inhabitants, Their Occupations, Places of Business, and Dwelling-Houses* [Boston, 1800], 43; *Boston Directory* [Boston, 1816], 37).

[1] MS: "incovenience."

Memorial from Great Egg Harbor, New Jersey

To THOMAS JEFFERSON ESQR.
PRESIDENT OF THE
UNITED STATES OF AMERICA

State of New Jersey
Great-Egg-Harbour.
Gloucester County
December 14th. 1803

Whereas the Collector of the Port of Great-Egg-Harbour, Namely Alexander Freeland Esqr., has become so dilatory and Negligent in Performing his Official duty as a proper Officer, that we deem it absolutely Necessary to lay before your Excellency, a statement of his Conduct, praying he may be dismissed from his office, being well assured that it will be highly conducive to the Welfare of the public in particular.

He has for several months back taken to excessive hard drink & still remains so[1] and is frequently intoxicated, so that oftentimes he is by no means Capable of performing his official duty when its required of him, and we regret that we have not made Application, for redress at an earlier period, but we hope that your Excellency will take our Grievances into Consideration, and by his Removal from office we shall conceive ourselves abundantly Retrieved.

JOHN HOLMES.—Cptn.
CLEMENT IRELAND Capt.
JONAS ADAMS

[116]

ENOCH INGRESOL
JOB IRELAND Capt.
JESSE STRATTAN
JOHN DOUGHTY
ADRIAL CLARK—
OBEDIAH READ—
JOHNATHAN REED
FELIX SMITH—
RICHARD MORRIS RISLEY Capt.

RC (DNA: RG 59, LAR, 4:0366-7); in David Mason's hand (see Great Egg Harbor petition at 15 Dec.), signed by all, Job Ireland with his mark; addressed: "To His Excellency Thomas Jefferson Esqr. President of the United States of America"; endorsed by TJ: "Freeland Alexr. Collector to be removed for sottishness. Winner Joseph to be appd." Enclosure: Certificate signed by Peter Steelman, master of the sloop *Rover*, and Holmes, captain of the schooner *Rebecca*, with same dateline as the petition above but with a blank for the day of the month, testifying that "we the Subscribers have actualy received ill treatment and sustained considerable Damage by the Wilfull and Obstinate Neglect of Alexander Freeland Esqr. Collector of the Port of Great Egg-Harbour" and "We have frequently been Disappointed and imposed on by his illegal Conduct and unfaithfullness in the Discharge of his office as Witness our Hands" (MS in same, 4:0368).

TJ's endorsement indicates that he received this call for the removal of ALEXANDER FREELAND at the same time he received the petition from Great Egg Harbor, dated 15 Dec., recommending the appointment of Joseph Winner. TJ entered both petitions as a single entry in SJL as received on 7 Feb. 1804 (see Petition from Great Egg Harbor, New Jersey, 15 Dec.).

APPLICATION, FOR REDRESS: Benjamin B. Cooper had informed TJ of problems at the custom house at Great Egg Harbor in his letter of 7 Sep.

[1] Preceding three words and ampersand interlined.

From Ephraim Kirby

Natchez, Mississippi Territory
SIR   Decemr 14th. 1803

I avail myself of the first moment to announce my arrival, with my associate (Mr Nicholas) at this place. It is not from any defect in reasonable calculation, or want of proper exertion, that has prevented our being at the place assigned for the discharge of our official duty on the first of the present month. I commenced my journey in the month of Septemr and have been twelve weeks pursuing it with indefatigable industry. Advers winds, and the uncommon lowness of the waters, which presented impediments unforeseen and almost insurmountable retarded our progress beyond all calculation. More time must necessarily be consumed before we can reach Fort Stodard. Should it be deemed necessary that a legislative act be passed, extending the time for claimants to make entry at the Registers Office in the county of Washington, I hope this communication will reach the seat of Government in season for that purpose.

I have the honor to be, with great respect Your Obedt Servt

EPHM KIRBY

RC (DLC); at foot of text: "The President of the U. States"; endorsed by TJ as received 1 Jan. 1804 and so recorded in SJL.

TIME FOR CLAIMANTS TO MAKE ENTRY: according to the act of 3 Mch.

1803, the commissioners were to meet from 1 Dec. 1803 to 1 Apr. 1804 "and until they shall have completed the business of their appointment" (U.S. Statutes at Large, 2:229, 231; Vol. 40:557).

From Benjamin H. Latrobe

DEAR SIR   Philadelphia, Decr. 14h. 1803

I have for some days hoped that every day of my stay here would be the last. But I am so dependent of the exertions of others, and so unwilling to leave any thing to their neglect after I shall be gone, that I am still detained. Every however draws to a conclusion. In the mean time, on referring to the date of my letter to the Vice president on the subject of the means of warming the Senate Chamber, to which I have never received an answer, I think it possible that it may have reached Charleston after his departure from that city, & that he may never have received it. I have therefore again written to him both with a view to excuse the delay that has occurred in the completion of the work, and to suggest the idea of charging the whole expense of the furnaces to the contingent fund of the Senate: an idea which I before have had the honor to mention to you, and which, if adopted, would aid the building fund very materially, as so great a quantity of Ironwork as has been required cannot but amount to a very considerable Sum—

One of the principal causes of the extreme coldness of the Senate Chamber has certainly been the want of a cieling to the Cellar. The air of the Chamber above being rarified has been replaced by the external cold atmosphere rising through the joints of the flooring. The communication with the external air was formerly circuitous, tho' not less operative, than it at present is, through the Cellar windows.—I have therefore directed Mr. Lenthall to prepare immediately to ciel that cellar. This will also produce better security against fire.—The idea was raised in my mind, by my having been unable to warm or inhabit a parlor at New castle untill the Cellar was cieled. One coat trowelled on will be sufficient.—I am astonished & vexed that this so well known fact should not have occurred to me long ago.—

I am with the truest respect Your much obliged hble Servant,

B HENRY LATROBE

RC (DLC); addressed: "The President of the United States; city of Washington"; franked; postmarked 17 Dec.; endorsed by TJ as received 19 Dec. and so recorded in SJL.

Shortly after becoming supervisor of the public buildings, Latrobe sent a LETTER to Aaron Burr, then visiting his daughter in Charleston. Not having received an answer, Latrobe wrote Burr on 13 Dec., this time apologizing for the slow progress in devising a solution for the chilly conditions of the SENATE CHAMBER (Latrobe, *Correspondence*, 1:390-2).

From Mary Coles Payne

Jefferson County 14th. Decr.

It is with great diffidence I address the President of the United States—but the feelings of a Mother will I hope plead an excuse for the freedom, thy kind attention to my children in general emboldens me to solicit still further thy kindness to my Son, who is now my only surviving one; his health is very much impair'd by the inactive life his present business imposes on him, I shall feel myself forever indebted to thy generosity, and goodness of heart, if among the many establishments in thy gift, thee would favor me, by promoting my poor Son to some more active employment—Collo. Madisons extreme delicasy in regard to his own relations has discouraged me from attempting to get him to intercede for me; It is my particular wish that this letter may not be seen by any eye except thy own and should it be thy pleasure to oblige me let it appear as a free and unsolicited[1] act of thy own in so doing the will add greatly to the obligations I already owe thee

With much respect I subscribe myself thy friend

MARY PAYNE

PS—

My Daughter Washington, who is my only confidant in this request, begs leave to present her respectful Compliments—   MP—

RC (DNA: RG 59, LAR); endorsed by TJ as received 19 Dec. and "Payne for emploimt" and so recorded in SJL.

Mary Coles Payne (ca. 1745-1808) was a Quaker relation of Patrick Henry and the wife of John Payne, with whom she had eight children, including Dolley Madison. Her family moved repeatedly in Virginia and North Carolina, and after her husband's failed business attempts and the manumission of slaves who worked their farm, they settled in Philadelphia in 1783. Faced with ongoing financial difficulties, she had converted her home by

1791 into a boardinghouse for members of the federal government, including Aaron Burr. After her husband's death, Payne moved with her two youngest children to Harewood, near Berkeley Springs, Virginia, to live with her daughter Lucy (Conover Hunt-Jones, *Dolley and the "Great Little Madison"* [Washington, D.C., 1977], 1; David B. Mattern and Holly C. Shulman, eds., *The Selected Letters of Dolley Payne Madison* [Charlottesville, 2003], 10-14, 16-17, 409).

MY SON: John Coles Payne was the profligate youngest son of Mary Coles Payne. Unable to find steady employment, he was sent to Tripoli as an aide to the American consul there in 1806, but returned to the United States in 1811 in worse physical and financial shape than when he left. He later supervised arranging and copying the papers of his brother-in-law James Madison at Montpelier (Mattern and Shulman, *Dolley Madison*, 221; Madison, *Papers*, 1:xviii).

MY DAUGHTER WASHINGTON: Lucy Payne Washington, who eloped at the age of 15 in 1793 with George Steptoe Washington, George Washington's nephew (Mattern and Shulman, *Dolley Madison*, 409, 414).

[1] MS: "usolicited."

From Stephen Perkins

SIR, Lancaster Ky 14th. Dec. 1803

Altho I've never had the Honour of being Personally Acquainted With Your Excellency, I flatter myself that you will Condisend to hear the Petition of any One of your Subjects as soon as that of another And not having the Smallest doubt in my mind But What all Stand on the Same footing as to Preferment, With Your Excellency; being Equal in Merit. Under those Impressions, I am Induced to Make Known to Your Excellency that Provided You think me Worthy of the Trust, I Shou'd be happy to meet With the Appointment of Register for the Mississippi Territory. It is an Office Which wou'd Suit me Exceedingly Well, Being, for a Considerable time Past, Conversant With Business of that Nature, But as my Bair Word, or family Connection (Some of Which I have Reasons to believe You have been acquainted With in the State of Virginia) is not a Sufficient Recommendation, I trust You Will Condesend so fair as to make enquery of the Members of Congress from this State as to my Abilities, but more especially Mr. Jno. Boyle Who is much better Acquainted With my Qualifications than Any Other Person that You Can Converse With. And Shou'd I be So fortunate as to meet With the Appointment from Your Excellency, No Attention that Can Possibly be Rendered Shall be Wanting to make the Office Respectable on the part of

Sir Your Mo. Ob Sert. STEPHEN PERKINS

RC (DNA: RG 59, LAR); endorsed by TJ as received 29 Dec. and so recorded in SJL, where TJ connected it by a brace with entries for letters received the same day from William Stark of 19 Dec. and William Hardy of 26 Dec. with notation "emploimt. Louisiana"; also endorsed by TJ: "to be Register of New Orleans."

Stephen Perkins of Garrard County was a justice of the peace and member of the Kentucky legislature (*Kentucky Gazette*, 16 Aug. 1803; Lewis Collins, *Collins' Historical Sketches of Kentucky. History of Kentucky*, rev. and enlarged by Richard H. Collins, 2 vols. [Covington, Ky., 1878], 2:288).

John BOYLE served Kentucky in the U.S. House of Representatives from 1803 to 1809. He was one of the House managers for the impeachment trials of federal judges John Pickering and Samuel Chase (ANB).

From John Smith of Ohio

SIR   Wednesday Morn—[14 Dec. 1803]

Col. McKee has not been able to give any information on the Subject of enquiry this Morn. but states as his opinion, that the boundary of the Chocktaw Tribe, does not extend so far South as the Mouth of Pearl River.

I am Sir very respectfully your most obedient Servt.

JOHN SMITH

RC (DLC); partially dated; at foot of text: "The President of the United States"; endorsed by TJ as received 14 Dec. and so recorded in SJL.

From Joseph Stanton, Jr., and Samuel J. Potter

SIR/   City Washington Decr. 14th 1803

The Important & desirable aquisition of Louisiana makes It Necessary to Create a Number of Revenue Officers for the Security & Collection of the Same. Permit us to Recomend to your Patronage Peleg S Thompson of Charlestown & State of R Island; He is a young man of 22 years of Age of an Irreproachable Character—His Education & Talents are, We presume, Sufficient to quallify him to perform with Propriety the duty Attached to the Office of Naval Officer or Surveyor of the port of New Orleans; If he Should Be So Auspicious as to be Honored with a nomination from the President & the Constitutional Sanction of the Senate We make No doubt, But, that he will give perfect Satisfaction by a faithfull discharge of his Official duty In a manner Acceptable to his patrons as well as honor to himself; His Conciliating manners & Strict adherence to the Principals of Justice has Gained him the Love and Esteem of all who Know him: With Sintements of high Esteem we are Very Truly your Obedt. Huml Servants

JOS: STANTON
SAML. J. POTTER

NB Let it be Remembered that in the State of R Island the district Judge & Attorney Commissioner of Loans all the Collectors of the Revenue Six Surveyors out Nine all Federal Characters and a major part of them as Bitter as wormwood—

RC (DNA: RG 59, LAR); in Stanton's hand, signed by both; at head of text: "His Excellency the President United States of America"; endorsed by TJ "Thompson Peleg S. to be Surveyor Customs N.O." and so recorded in SJL at 14 Dec., joined by a brace with Christopher Ellery and Nehemiah Knight to TJ, 14 Dec.

Samuel J. Potter (1753-1804) served as deputy governor of Rhode Island from 1790 until 1803, when he was elected to the U.S. Senate. A Republican, he attended only one session of Congress before his death at South Kingston on 26 Sep. 1804 (*Biog. Dir. Cong.*; *Newport Mercury*, 29 Sep. 1804; *Providence Phoenix*, 6, 13 Oct. 1804).

To Abraham Bishop

Th: Jefferson requests the favour of *mr Abraham Bishop* to dine with him *on Saturday the 17th. inst.* at half after three.

Dec. 15. 03.

The favour of an answer is asked.

RC (CtNhHi: New Haven Custom House Papers); printed form, with blanks filled by TJ reproduced in italics; addressed by TJ: "Mr. Abraham Bishop"; endorsed by Bishop.

SATURDAY THE 17TH: the next day, 18 Dec., Bishop attended a dinner hosted by the vice president at Tunnicliff's Washington City Hotel. New York congressmen Samuel L. Mitchill and Daniel C. Verplanck also attended the event, but it was the New Haven collector's presence in Washington that was noted in James Cheetham's newspaper, where he was associated with Burr's friends "from New-York and other places" who were zealously planning to restore Burr's influence (Kline, *Burr*, 2:814n; New York *American Citizen*, 27 Jan. 1804; MB, 2:1033n).

From Silvanus Ewer

SIR   Nantucket Decr. 15th 1803

Enclosed, is a detale of the Illegal and unjust Capture and dention, of the Sloops Union, & Dolphin and Schooner Mary, by the French National Schooner Telegraph, and the cruel proceeding of the Government Officers at Jacomel

I was the Princaple owner of the Two Sloops and have suffered a verry heavy loss. being fully satisfied that compensation was due me for the damage I had suffered but ignorant & unacquanted with the proper mode of procedure added to my loss having rendered me ill able to be at any considerable expence to pursue the property I thought the most proper step for me to take would be to lay the business before the Secretary of State accordingly I addressed him on the subject as early as the 16th of Augt. 1803. copy of my letter of that date I now enclose you. not having any answer to it I addressed him again on the 15th & 17th of October but have not as yet received any answer to either letter. I beg you to consider this as a sufficient apoligy for my now addressing you, and if consistant beg you to point out to me how & in what manner I may proceed to get redress. as an Individual my loss is great, but I must leave it to some other, more capable to point out the consequence it will be to the Inhabitants of this Town if they are to be debared whaling in the West India seas

With all due respect & esteem I am Sir your Obedient Humble Servant   SILVANUS EWER

RC (DLC); at foot of text: "To Thomas Jefferson Esqr President of the United States"; endorsed by TJ as received 31 Dec. and so recorded in SJL. Enclosures: (1) Ewer's account of the seizure of the three vessels, dated Nantucket, 15 Dec.; the *Mary*, commanded by David Folger and owned by Jeremiah Lawrence and David Worth, cleared Nantucket in July 1802, outfitted for a whaling voyage with a crew of 13; the *Union*, commanded by William Clisby, and the *Dolphin*, commanded by Silvanus Smith, were both owned by Ewer and others; the two sloops cleared Nantucket in November 1802, and were likewise fitted for a whaling voyage with crews of 13 men each; the *Mary* proceeded to Cape Verde, where it took on about 80 barrels of oil, then sailed to the West Indies; the *Union* and *Dolphin* sailed directly to the West Indies, where all three vessels met and cruised together off the southern coast of Hispaniola; they were taken by the *Télégraphe*, commanded by Anthony St. Quint, about five to six leagues offshore and carried to Jacmel; the French captain was under orders to bring in all vessels found near the island, but believed that the three whalers would not be detained for long; shortly after their arrival at Jacmel, however, the ships' crews were charged with being taken at anchor near the shore and told that they could not be released without orders from the Vicomte de Rochambeau; the crews remained in confinement until more than half were dead, including several officers, and only six have returned home; Ewer refers the president to depositions and protests forwarded to the secretary of state confirming his account of the cruel treatment; no trial appears to have taken place; Folger obtained his freedom and traveled to Port-au-Prince in an unsuccessful attempt to secure a trial, which left him "without money cloths or Friends" and "under the necessity to get away as well as he could"; Ewer has since learned that the cargoes were landed and the vessels employed in evacuating people from the island, which he believes was the true cause of their detention; he reiterates that the intent of the voyages was whaling and not to engage in trade, and that the vessels were all taken at least five leagues from land; he estimates the loss in vessels, cargo, and damages at $11,833 for the *Union*, $9,466 for the *Dolphin*, and $16,000 for the *Mary* (MS in same; in Ewer's hand and signed by him). (2) Ewer to Madison, dated Nantucket, 16 Aug. 1803, detailing the captures on 7 Apr. 1803 and the detention of the crews and condemnation of the vessels "*without Trial*" under the pretense that they were trading with rebels on the coast; Folger returned to Nantucket on 12 Aug. and made a protest before a notary "against the illegal procedure of the Officers" of the French government, copies of which and other documents will be forwarded to Madison; Ewer encloses certificates from the collector and selectmen at Nantucket confirming the property and the citizenship of the crews; he asks Madison to advise him on how to obtain redress and secure the release of those members of the crew still remaining "in loathsome imprisonment in the Unhealthy port of Jacomel" (Dupl in same; in Ewer's hand; at head of text: "Copy"; Madison, *Papers, Sec. of State Ser.*, 5:313-14).

Silvanus Ewer (1767-1836) trained as a ship carpenter in Massachusetts before moving to Nantucket, where he became a successful whale merchant and manufacturer of oil and candles (*Memorial Biographies of the New England Historic Genealogical Society*, 9 vols. [Boston, 1880-1908], 2:319-20).

LAY THE BUSINESS BEFORE THE SECRETARY OF STATE: Madison received another account of the capture of the three American whaling vessels from a co-owner of the *Mary*, Jeremiah Lawrence, in a letter from Nantucket dated 15 Aug. It does not appear that the State Department took any action on the matter. The owners' protests were rejected by the French Council of Prizes in 1810. Not until after the signing of a convention between the United States and France in 1831 would the claims be settled. The claimants for the *Dolphin* received $4,850, those for the *Mary* received $9,050, and those for the *Union* received $5,650 (Madison, *Papers, Sec. of State Ser.*, 5:309-10, 370; Ulane Bonnel, *La France, les États-Unis, et la Guerre de Course*, [Paris, 1961], 182-3; Miller, *Treaties*, 3:641-51; *Message from the President of the United States, Transmitting Reports from the Secretary of State and Secretary of the Treasury*, 24th Cong., 1st sess., 1836, H. Ex. Doc. 117, 25, 53, 77).

Memorial from Great Egg Harbor, New Jersey

To THOMAS JEFFERSON ESQR.
PRESIDENT OF THE
UNITED STATES OF AMERICA

State of New-Jersey
Great-Egg-Harbour
Gloucester County
December 15th. 1803

We the Inhabitants of Great Egg Harbour in the County & state aforesaid do beg leave to Recommend to your Excellency Joseph Winner as a Suitable person to be appointed Collector of the port of Great Egg-Harbour in the Room of Alexander Freeland Esqr the present Collector

He the said Joseph Winner is Competent in his Literary Capacity to perform all the Duties of the office that may legally be required of him. We have been personally acquainted with him a number of years and we have never Knew him guilty of any Mal-conduct, fraudulent or deceptive practices whatever but he has allways Maintained and supported a firm and Respectable Character. & &c

DAVID MASON—
JAMES STEELMAN Capt.
JOHN HOLMES—Cptn.
ABNER DOUGHTY
JOHN PRICE—Cptn.

OBEDIAH REED—Senior Capt.

LEVI ROGERS Esqr.

JONAS ADAMS

CLEMENT IRELAND Captn.

JOS. SHARP

WILLIAM READ

RC (DNA: RG 59, LAR, 12:0492); in Mason's hand, signed by all; addressed: "Thomas Jefferson Esqr. President of the United states." Recorded in SJL as received 7 Feb. 1804 with notation "Petn to remove Freeland Collectr. appt Winner."

For an earlier call to appoint JOSEPH WINNER in place of Alexander Freeland, see Benjamin Brown Cooper to TJ, 7 Sep. 1803. See also the petition from Great Egg Harbor at 14 Dec.

Petition of Nathaniel Ingraham

RESPECTFULLY SHEWETH

Nathaniel Ingraham of Bristol in the County of Bristol and District of Rhode Island mariner, That on a former occasion, he presented a petition, to the President setting forth, that a Judgement of the circuit Court in this district at the November term 1801 was rendered against your petitioner on the suit of one John W. Leonard, who sued for the United States as well as for himself for a sum exceeding $14,000 Doll.

That execution was sued out on said judgement when your petitioner was committed to Goal, where he now remains a prisoner; that your petitioner is advanced in life, that he has a wife & a helpless family of Children, that he is destitute of property & they dependent entirely on him for support, that he and they are reduced to the necessity of begging their daily Bread, having no resource for subsistence but the bounty of the humane & Charitable, & praying that the President in his humanity, would interpose, & be pleased to remit that part of said Judgement which belongs to the United states; since the presentation of said petition your petitioner has learned that the President has been graciously pleased to intimate in a letter to the Honor. Christopher Ellery Senator of the United States, that after a Confinement of two years, the prayer of said Petitioner might be attended to, cheered by this ray of hope, & grateful to the Author of it, your petitioner is encouraged to renew his Application; He begs leave now to represent that he still remains destitute of all means of subsistence; but the charity of those, who know his distress & are disposed to relieve it. That the failure of this Charity, must leave him to die of hunger

That his Innocent Wife & Children and aged mother are in the same deplorable state, of dependency & wretchedness. That they are compelled to suffer in his sufferings. That he is informed that the laws of the United States have made no provision for a Prisoner in his situation, & that if he cannot subsist himself or receive charities to Subsist on he must starve and perish, and there is no legal help for him. If contrition for his offence & the most cutting self reproaches for having been instrumental in depriving others of their liberty, by which he him self has suffered so much, or the most thorough purpose of never so offending in future, are proper considerations to plead, he can plead them most sincerely, he can only say that he is the most wretched of human beings, & prays that his demerrits may not be thought, too great for the speedy interposition of Executive mercy agreeably to the prayer of his former petition, to which he now begs leave to refer, together the accompanying papers. And your petitioner as in duty bound will ever pray.—

Bristol Rho Isld. Decem. 15th. 1803

NATHANIEL INGRAHAM

RC (DNA: RG 59, GPR); in an unidentified hand, signed by Ingraham; at head of text: "Thomas Jefferson President of the United States"; endorsed by TJ as received 26 Dec. and so recorded in SJL; with order by TJ subjoined (see 21 Feb. 1804). Enclosed in Ingraham to Christopher Ellery, dated Bristol, 16 Dec., asking that Ellery present his petition to the president and "interpose your good offices in my behalf; that I may be relieved from a loathsome imprisonment, and restored again to an innocent and helpless family" (RC in DLC; in an unidentified hand; signed by Ingraham; endorsed by TJ). Enclosed in TJ to David Leonard Barnes, 31 Dec. 1803, and in Barnes to TJ, 10 Feb. 1804.

ON A FORMER OCCASION: for previous attempts by convicted slave trader Nathaniel Ingraham to procure a pardon, see Vol. 37:199-200, 648, Vol. 38:606, Vol. 39:398-401, and Vol. 40:279.

LETTER TO THE HONOR. CHRISTOPHER ELLERY: TJ to Ellery, 9 May 1803 (Vol. 40:337-8).

From Ephraim Kirby

Natchez, Mississippi Territory

Decemr. 16th. 1803

SIR

Being necessarily detained in this place a few days to prepare for the remaining part of my journey, I have availed myself of the opportunity which it presented to designate some suitable character for the office of Register in The County of Washington.—I have heard but of one person who would do justice to the appointment. Among all the respectable characters, with whom I have conversed, there seems to be a concurrence of opinion in favour of this Gentleman. The information was spontaneously afforded, under an impression that he had been previously appointed. Upon this evidence I have discharged the trust with which you was pleased to honor me, by filling the Registers Commission for the County of Washington with the name of Joseph Chambers.[1]—He resides near Fort Stodard, and of course I have had no communication with him, but have no doubt of his acceptance

With great respect I am sir Your Obedt. Servt

EPHM KIRBY

RC (DNA: RG 59, LAR); at foot of text: "The President of the United States"; endorsed by TJ as received 1 Jan. 1804 and so recorded in SJL; also endorsed by TJ: "Chambers Joseph. Register Ld. office. Tombigbee."

DISCHARGED THE TRUST: see TJ to Kirby, 15 July. Highly recommended by James Wilkinson, JOSEPH CHAMBERS was serving as U.S. factor to the Choctaws and learning their language (*Terr. Papers*, 5:176n, 238).

On this date, Kirby also wrote to his friend Gideon Granger. After describing his long journey to Natchez, during which he was "many times in the most eminent danger," Kirby informed the postmaster general that he had made up his mind "to become an inhabitant of this part of the United States." He wrote: "I leave to my friend to designate for me the service which he thinks me most competent to Perform.—In the organization of the government of Louisiana I hope I shall not be forgotten" (RC in DNA: RG 59, LAR; endorsed by TJ: "Kirby Ephraim. for employment N.O. his lre to mr Granger").

[1] Kirby first left a blank, into which he inserted Chambers's name.

To Homastubbee and Puckshunubbee

BROTHERS OF THE CHOCTAW NATION.   Dec. 17. 1803.

We have long heard of your nation, as a numerous, peaceable & friendly people; but this is the first visit we have had from it's great men, at the seat of our government. I welcome you here; am glad to take you by the hand; & to assure you, for your nation, that we are their friends. born in the same land, we ought to live as brothers, doing to each other all the good we can, and not listening to wicked men who may endeavor to make us enemies. by living in peace, we can help & prosper one another; by waging war, we can kill and destroy many on both sides: but those who survive will not be the happier for that. then, brothers, let it forever be peace & good neighborhood between us. our seventeen states compose a great and growing nation. their children are as the leaves of the trees, which the winds are spreading over the forest. but we are just also. we take from no nation what belongs to it. our growing numbers make us always willing to buy lands from our red brethren, when they are willing to sell.

but be assured we never mean to disturb them in their possessions. on the contrary, the lines established between us by mutual consent, shall be sacredly preserved: and we will protect your lands from all encroachment, by our own people or any others. we will give you a copy of the law, made by our great council, for punishing our people who may encroach on your lands, or injure you otherwise. carry it with you to your homes, and preserve it, as the shield, which we spread over you, to protect your land, your property & persons.

It is at the request which you sent me in September, signed by Puckshanubbee, & other chiefs, and which you now repeat, that I listen to your proposition to sell us lands. you say you owe a great debt to your merchants, that you have nothing to pay it with but lands, and you pray us to take lands, & pay your debt. the sum you have occasion for, brothers, is a very great one. we have never yet paid as much to any of our red brethren for the purchase of lands. you propose to us some on the Tombigby, & some on the Missisipi. those on the Missisipi suit us well. we wish to have establishments on that river, as resting places for our boats, to furnish them provisions, and to recieve our people who fall sick on the way to or from New Orleans, which is now ours. in that quarter therefore we are willing to purchase as much as you will spare. but as to the manner in which the line shall be run, we are not judges of it here, nor qualified to make any bargain. but we will appoint persons hereafter to treat with you on the spot, who knowing the country & quality of the lands, will be better able to agree with you on a line which will give us a just equivalent for the sum of money you want paid.

You have spoken, brothers, of the lands which your fathers formerly sold and marked off to the English, and which they ceded to us with the rest of the country they held here, & you say that, tho' you do not know whether your fathers were paid for them, you have marked the line over again for us, & do not ask repaiment. it has always been the custom, brothers, when lands were bought of the red men, to pay for them immediately, and none of us have ever seen an example of such a debt remaining unpaid. it is to satisfy their immediate wants that the red men have usually sold lands; & in such a case, they would not let the debt be unpaid. the presumption from custom then is strong: as it is also from the great length of time since your fathers sold these lands. but we have moreover been informed, by persons now living, & who assisted the English in making the purchase, that the price was paid at the time. were it otherwise, as it was their contract, it would be their debt, not ours.

I rejoice, brothers, to hear you propose to become cultivators of the earth for the maintenance of your families. be assured you will support them better & with less labour, by raising stock & bread, and by spinning & weaving clothes, than by hunting. a little land cultivated, & a little labour, will procure more provisions than the most successful hunt: and a woman will clothe more by spinning & weaving, than a man by hunting. compared with you, we are but as of yesterday in this land. yet see how much more we have multiplied by industry, and the exercise of that reason which you possess in common with us. follow then our example, brethren, and we will aid you with great pleasure.

The clothes & other necessaries which we sent you the last year, were, as you supposed, a present from us. we never meant to ask land, or any other paiment for them: and the store which we sent on, was at your request also & to accomodate you with necessaries at a reasonable price. you wished of course to have it placed on your land; but the land would continue yours, not ours.

As to the removal of the store, the Interpreter, & the Agent, and any other matters you may wish to speak about, the Secretary at war will enter into explanations with you; and whatever he says, you may consider as said by myself; and what he promises you, will be faithfully performed.

I am glad, brothers, you are willing to go & visit some other parts of our country. carriages shall be ready to convey you, & you shall be taken care of on your journey; and when you shall have returned here & rested yourselves to your own mind, you shall be sent home by land. we had provided for your coming by land, and we are sorry for the mistake which carried you to Savanna instead of Augusta, and exposed you to the risks of a voyage by sea. had any accident happened to you, tho' we could not help it, it would have been a cause of great mourning to us. but we thank the great spirit who took care of you on the ocean, & brought you safe and in good health to the seat of our great council. and we hope his care will accompany & protect you on your journey & return home; and that he will preserve & prosper your nation in all it's just pursuits.   Th: Jefferson

PrC (DLC). FC (Lb in DNA: RG 75, LSIA); dated January 1804; at head of text: "A talk delivered by the President of the United States to a Deputation of Chiefs from the Choctaw Nation of Indians" and "Talk with the Choctaw Deputation."

to assure you, for your nation, that we are their friends: following well-established protocols, Dearborn prepared a document that the Choctaw deputation could take with them when they returned home. Using language that he had employed as early as the spring of

1801, he began: "The President of the United States takes you by the hand, and invites you and all the Nations of Red people within the territory of the United States to look up to him as their father and friend; and to rely, in full confidence, upon his unvarying disposition to lead and protect them in the paths of peace and harmony, and to cultivate friendship with their Brothers of the same colour, and with the Citizens of the United States." The document, following the pattern of "assurances, written on parchment" that Dearborn gave to some earlier Native American delegations, bore his signature and an official seal. Again echoing his language from 1801, Dearborn declared a wish that "So long as the mountains in our land shall endure, and our Rivers flow, so long may the Red and White People dwelling in it, live in the bonds of brotherhood and friendship!" The document, which the War Department labeled as a "Deed to the Choctaw Nation of Indians," affirmed "by the authority of the United States, that all lands belonging to you, lying within the Territory of the United States, shall be and remain the property of your Nation forever, unless you shall voluntarily relinquish or dispose of the same. And all persons Citizens of the United States, are hereby strictly forbidden to disturb you or your Nation in the quiet possession of said Lands." Accompanying the written assurances, as had also been the case with the written assurances given to some other delegations, was a chain "made of pure Gold, which will never rust," sent by the president to the Choctaws as "an emblem" of the links of friendship that bound their nations together and must always be kept bright (Dearborn to chiefs and warriors of the Choctaw nation, 20 Dec., Lb in DNA: RG 75, LSIA; Dearborn to chiefs and warriors of the Cherokees, the Chickasaws, and the Choctaws, 18 June 1801, and to Little Turkey, 7 July 1801, in same; Thomas Foster, ed., *The Collected Works of Benjamin Hawkins, 1796-1810* [Tuscaloosa, Ala., 2003], 359-60; Vol. 34:506; Vol. 36:526).

GIVE YOU A COPY OF THE LAW: the March 1802 "Act to regulate trade and intercourse with the Indian tribes" imposed fines or imprisonment for citizens or residents of the United States who hunted game or drove livestock on lands secured to Indian tribes, entered into Indians' territory without authorization, committed robbery, larceny, or trespass against Indians, or settled or surveyed Indians' land. The law authorized the president to use military force to remove encroaching settlements, called on the military to apprehend violators of the law, and prescribed the death penalty for the crime of murdering an Indian (U.S. Statutes at Large, 2:141-2, 144-5).

REQUEST WHICH YOU SENT ME IN SEPTEMBER: Petition of Puckshunubbee and Others, 20 Sep.

THOSE ON THE MISSISIPI SUIT US WELL: Dearborn wrote to Silas Dinsmoor in January that any cession of land by the Choctaws to retire their debts to the Panton and Leslie trading firm "must be defered until we have more leisure." When the time did come to pursue the matter, Dearborn indicated, the "land most desirable is a tract bounded on the Mississippi from the Yazoo to the Chickasaw Boundary, extending easterly so as to include the lands between the Yazoo and the Big Black" (Dearborn to Dinsmoor, 7 Jan. 1804, in DNA: RG 75, LSIA).

CULTIVATORS OF THE EARTH: at the Fort Adams treaty conference in December 1801, Homastubbee and Puckshunubbee asked for blacksmithing equipment and farm implements. Dearborn intended to send plow irons, axes, hoes, and bar iron and steel to the Choctaws in 1803, but drought conditions thwarted shipment of the items by river. In February 1804, in response to a complaint from Dinsmoor that no plows had come, Dearborn ordered supplies of those items and two sets of blacksmithing tools to be sent. "Every effort ought to be made to attach the Chocktaws to our Country and Government," Dearborn advised the agent, "and to induce them to attend to some of the Arts of Civilization, such as agriculture and domestic manufactures" (ASP, *Indian Affairs*, 1:661-2; Dinsmoor to Dearborn, 24 Jan. 1804, recorded in DNA: RG 107, RLRMS; Dearborn to Dinsmoor, 27 Feb., in DNA: RG 75, LSIA).

SECRETARY AT WAR WILL ENTER INTO EXPLANATIONS: Dearborn had "a long conversation with the Chiefs" about allowing the establishment of way stations along the road that was to run across the Choctaws' lands. The visiting Choctaw leaders agreed with Dearborn "as individuals" on guidelines for those "Houses of entertainment" and agreed to "use their influence in favor of the measure" (Dearborn to Dinsmoor, 7 Jan. 1804, in DNA: RG 75, LSIA).

From Matthew Lyon

SIR—   Washington Decem. 17th. 1803

Some weeks since I took the liberty of mentioning to you the Situation of the Alexandria Expositor and the low & discourageing state of the means of its support, since that time the hope of Aid from the government has kept the paper from fainting & drooping under the Terrors & effects of poverty—Since I have been here I have I believe done every thing in my power to encourage Mr Dinmore to keep the thing along, I have advanced him 50 Dollrs out of my own pocket; notwithstanding which I am convinced the Expositor will certainly expire within a week or two without some efficacious encouragement, possess'd of the knoledge of this circumstance which will be cause of Exultation to its enemies & the enemies of the present Administration, I have thought it my duty to communicate this information to you.

I will not pretend to Judge of the importance of that paper to the Government, or to say any thing on a subject that the members of the Administration liveing here must know much more about than I can, but I think it possible that after the event I have been makeing mention of shall have taken place there are those who may mourn & say, that had they known it soon enough relief should have been afforded—

The Sickness at Alexandria haveing much deranged Mr Dinmores business & Impeded his collections He entertain'd hopes by a change of the Secretary of the Senate to have obtained the printing for that house, which would have abundantly enabled him to proceed with his paper; but in this he fail'd, the Secy keeps his place & our friend Duane has got the printing. Mr Dinmore next fixed his Eye on the Contract for printing the proposed edition of the Laws of the US; he has as he fancied received some slight encouragement from the Secretary of State on this Subject—he has since been informed that the Contract is to be otherwise disposed of, that the encouragement he received was mere courtly smiles, & he is now in despair. I know not how he received this information & am led to believe it is groundless, I have only to sugest the posibility of Mr Madisons removeing those doubts & this Despair by a single line, I have no acquaintance with

Mr Madison & have before mentioned the subject to you. I hope to be pardoned for troubleing you when I assure you that if I was not moved more by attachment to what I consider the public intrest, than by good Will to any individual I should have been silent—

Mr Dinmore is a very honest as well as a very deserveing man, he has friends and can have what credit he pleases whenever he can see a sure source of future payment. As to his manageing the Contract creditably & Honourably as it respects the public he is able to give the best Security; as to his manageing it advantageously to himself, I who do know as much as any person on that subject can assure you that he can do it as well as any person

I am with great respect your Obedt Servt.   M LYON

RC (DLC); addressed: "The President of the United States"; endorsed by TJ as received 19 Dec. and so recorded in SJL.

In November 1802, Richard DINMORE and James Lyon, the son of Matthew Lyon, began the tri-weekly newspaper, *The Alexandria Expositor, and the Columbian Advertiser*. The paper became a daily in December 1803. TJ subscribed to the *Expositor*, which changed format and moved to Washington before being discontinued in 1809 (Brigham, *American Newspapers*, 2:1108-9; MB, 2:1123).

SICKNESS AT ALEXANDRIA: for concerns over the spread of yellow fever, see Robert Smith to TJ, 10 Sep. and TJ to Samuel Snowden, 29 Sep.

THE SECY KEEPS HIS PLACE: for Samuel A. Otis, see Vol. 38:29n and Vol. 40:7-8.

Dinmore and James Lyon wrote Madison on 21 Apr. 1802 with a proposal for the publication of LAWS in their newspaper, the *American Literary Advertiser*. On 29 Oct. 1803, the House of Representatives appointed a committee to investigate the expediency of reprinting all House documents since the sitting of the first Congress. The House resolved, on 26 Dec., that the secretary of state should order a complete edition of the laws of the United States, to consist of 10,000 copies. In March 1804, after Congress passed an act for the more extensive distribution of the statutes, Dinmore again sought Madison's permission to publish the laws in his newspapers (Madison, *Papers, Sec. of State Ser.*, 3:150, 6:68n; *Annals*, 13:789; U.S. Statutes at Large, 2:302-3).

To the Vermont General Assembly

TO THE GENERAL ASSEMBLY
OF THE STATE OF VERMONT

I join you, fellow citizens, in grateful acknolegements to the Ruler of the universe, for the prosperous situation of our common country, it's rapid increase in wealth & population, & our secure & uninterrupted enjoiment of life, liberty & property. he conducted our fathers to this chosen land, he has maintained us in it in prosperity & safety, & has opened the hearts of the nations, civilized & savage, to yield to us enlargement of territory, as we have encreased[1] in numbers to fill it with the blessings of peace[2] freedom & self-government. it must be a great solace to every virtuous mind that the countries lately acquired are for equivalents honestly paid, & come to us unstained with blood.

Sensible, as we are, of the superior advantages of civilized life, of the nourishment which industry provides for the body, & science for the mind, & morals, it is our duty to associate our Indian neighbors in these blessings, & to teach them to become fit members of organised society.

The spirit which manifested itself on the suspension of our right of deposit at New-Orleans, the cool & collected firmness with which our citizens awaited the operations of their government for it's peaceable restoration, their present approbation of a conduct strictly neutral & just between the powers of Europe now in contention, evince dispositions which ought to secure their peace, to protect their industry from new burthens, their citizens from violence, and their commerce from spoliation.

The falsehoods and indecencies you allude to, in which certain presses indulge themselves habitually, defeat their own object before a just and enlightened public. this unenviable and only resource, be it our endeavor to leave them, by an honest and earnest pursuit of the public prosperity.

I thank you, fellow-citizens, for the affectionate expressions of your concern for my happiness, present and future: and I pray heaven to have yourselves, as well as our common country, in it's holy keeping.

Th: Jefferson
Dec. 18. 1803.

RC (VtMS). PrC (DLC).

I JOIN YOU: see Abel Spencer to TJ, 14 Nov., and enclosure (Vol. 41:721-3).

[1] TJ first wrote "expanded" before overwriting on the RC to change the word. PrC: "expanded."

[2] Word interlined. TJ made this change before he made the PrC.

From Andrew Ellicott

Dear Sir   Lancaster December 19th. 1803.

A few days ago I received a letter from Mr. Livingston our Minister at Paris, which contains some ideas that are new to me. If he has not written to you on the same subject, I presume the extract which is enclosed will afford you some amusement. —The fall of stones from the sky, as Mr. Livingston expresses it, is at war with my theory of the falling stars, as they are termed, to which subject I have lately been paying some attention.

In my journal which is published, I have given a new theory of the gulf stream, the principles of which I should be glad to see discussed.—This part of the work cannot be considered as political, the public has nevertheless been informed by the republican printer of this borough, that the whole is an attack upon you! If this is the case, it certainly was not intended.—Truth has ever been my object, and I trust no circumstance will ever make me change it for a less valuable one.

I have the honour to be with great esteem your friend and Hbl. Serv.

ANDW. ELLICOTT

RC (DLC); at foot of text: "T. Jefferson President of the U.S."; endorsed by TJ as received 22 Dec. and so recorded in SJL. PrC (DLC: Ellicott Papers).

STONES FROM THE SKY: regarding meteorites that fell around L'Aigle, France, in April 1803, see John Wheatcroft, Sr., to TJ, at 29 Sep. AT WAR WITH MY THEORY: on a vessel near Key Largo in 1799, Ellicott witnessed a spectacular meteor shower. He favored a hypothesis by Antoine Lavoisier that meteors were bursts of burning gas ignited by friction between layers of the atmosphere (Ellicott, *The Journal of Andrew Ellicott, Late Commissioner on Behalf of the United States . . . for Determining the Boundary between the United States and the Possessions of His Catholic Majesty in America* [Philadelphia, 1803], 248-9; APS, *Transactions*, 6 [1809], 28-9).

In his recently published journal from the survey of the southern boundary of the United States, Ellicott discussed the GULF STREAM and theories advanced to explain it. He made no direct reference to TJ, but did cautiously contradict statements of Benjamin Franklin about the Gulf Stream (*Journal of Andrew Ellicott*, 260-6).

REPUBLICAN PRINTER OF THIS BOROUGH: William Dickson, the publisher of the *Intelligencer* of Lancaster, like William Duane of the *Aurora*, attacked Ellicott in his newspaper. Ellicott responded with a libel suit. Dickson, along with Duane, became one of Thomas McKean's leading opponents in the press (*Aurora*, 20 Oct., 10 Nov.; G. S. Rowe, *Thomas McKean, The Shaping of an American Republicanism* [Boulder, Colo., 1978], 363, 367; James Hedley Peeling, "Governor McKean and the Pennsylvania Jacobins, [1799-1808]," PMHB, 54 [1930], 343-4).

E N C L O S U R E

Extract of Robert R. Livingston to Andrew Ellicott

"The fact of the fall of stones from the sky, having been put, by some late inquiries almost beyond a doubt the philosophers are now disputing whether they are generated in the atmosphere or whether we owe them to volcanic eruptions in the moon, as much remains to be said on both sides; prudent men have not yet thought proper to pronounce judgment.—But it may be new to you to learn that while the moon is pelting us with red hot pebbles, the fixed Stars are counteracting her measures, and raying down cold upon us.—This I assure you upon the authority of Count Rumford who has made a number of very new and very important discoveries on the transmission of heat and cold, for cold it seems is not a negative quality, but as much a body as heat, and may like it be reflected from a polished surface.—If two polished brass balls are heated to the same degree and one of them is covered with linnen or varnish it will cool much quicker than that which is uncovered:— if covered with a black animal substance; still quicker; because black absorbs the rays of cold &c.—

This work is not yet published, but he tells me he means to go to England as soon as possible for the purpose of publishing it.—If Doctr. Priestley should fall in your way I will pray you to present my compliments to him, and to mention this subject to him, his ingenious researches will probably add much to them—I am sorry he has not executed the resolution that he told me he had formed of paying a visit to the arts and sciences in this country that I might have had the pleasure of seeing him while I remain here."

PrC (DLC); in Ellicott's hand.

In the autumn of 1803, the French government granted Benjamin Thompson, COUNT RUMFORD, who had left England in 1802 and resided for a time in Munich, permission to live in Paris. A foreign associate of the National Institute, he presented several papers to the mathematical and physical sciences division of that body, including reports of experiments with HEAT. The Royal Society of London published an English-language version of one of those papers, titled "An Enquiry concerning the Nature of Heat, and the Mode of its Communication" (Sanborn C. Brown, *Benjamin Thompson, Count Rumford* [Cambridge, Mass., 1979], 254, 262-8; Royal Society, *Philosophical Transactions*, 94 [1804], 77-182; Rumford and others, *Mémoires sur la chaleur* [Paris, 1804]).

From Albert Gallatin

DEAR SIR   19th Decer. 1803

Before I shall make a formal report on Gen. Dearborn's application, I enclose the papers for your information. The facts he had stated & on which his claim is grounded, vizt. that Shell castle Island was not a real Island, but a shoal left bare only at low water; and that he was detained both there & at Cape Hatteras, by the non attendance of the Superintendent, Collector Treadwell, appear to be sufficiently substantiated. The Comissr. of the revenue, however, objects, that the saving made by Gen. Dearborn, in not being obliged to dig as deep and to build to that depth a solid stone foundation, as had been contemplated by the contract, is a sufficient compensation for the additional expense incurred by Gen. Dearborn on the other accounts. This Mr Dearborn denies, and insists that there was no comparison between the saving of the foundation to the contemplated, and the unforeseen expense actually incurred. Of this I am not a competent judge; but feel satisfied that the representation of Gen. Dearborn is correct, as he states facts, and Mr Miller merely draws an inference from conjectural estimates.

With me the great objection to the claim is the introduction of a new principle that of Govt. making, in case of contracts, an additional allowance; and that objection is stronger in the present instance, because Gen. Dearborn had originally made conditional propositions which were rejected by the President for the very reason, that nothing should, in Government contracts, be left uncertain.

If you shall agree that an allowance shall be made, the power of making the contract having originally been vested by law in the President, it will be necessary that you should give your official sanction to such allowance; and, the appropriation being exhausted, it will be also necessary to bring the subject before Congress, for the purpose of obtaining an appropriation.

With respectful & sincere attachment Your obedt. Servt.

ALBERT GALLATIN

RC (DLC); addressed: "The President of the United States"; endorsed by TJ as received from the Treasury Department on 20 Dec. and "Genl. Dearborne's case" and so recorded in SJL. Enclosures not found.

For Henry Dearborn's APPLICATION requesting additional compensation for constructing a lighthouse and beacon in North Carolina, as well as Gallatin's efforts at OBTAINING AN APPROPRIATION from Congress for the purpose, see Vol. 39:452-6.

From Albert Gallatin

DEAR SIR   Decer. 19th 1803

Will you have the goodness to examine the enclosed sketch of the order to be given by you to the Secretary of the Treasury for the delivery of the Louisiana Stock, and to return it, with such remarks as you may think fit, in order that a fair copy may be prepared for your signature, whenever you shall think it proper to issue the order.

Respectfully Your obedient Servt.   ALBERT GALLATIN

RC (DLC); at foot of text: "The President of the United States"; endorsed by TJ as received from the Treasury Department on 19 Dec. and "French stock" and so recorded in SJL. Enclosure: see below.

The SKETCH OF THE ORDER has not been found, but for the order as issued by the president, see TJ to Gallatin, 16 Jan. 1804.

From Meriwether Lewis

DEAR SIR.   Cahokia, December 19th 1803

On my arrival at Kaskaskias, I made a selection of a sufficient number of men from the troops of that place to complete my party, and made a requisition on the Contractor to cause immediately an adequate deposit of provisions to be made at Cahokia subject to further orders or other destination should circumstances render it necessary— This done, it became important to learn as early as possible the ultimate decision of Colo. Charles Deheau de Lassuse, (the Governor of Upper Louisiana) relative to my ascending the Missouri; it became the more necessary to learn his determination on this subject, as from the advanced state of the season it must in a good measure govern my arrangements for the present winter, and seeing also from the usual course of things, that the period was near at hand, when it was expected that the navigation of both the Mississippi & Missouri would be obstructed by the ice, and of course some disposition necessarily made to protect my party from the inclemency of the season, I determined to loose no time in making this application: with a view therefore to greater expedition, I thought it best to travel by land to St Louis (the residence of the Govr) and accordingly set out from Kaskaskias in the evening of the 5th Inst. on horse-back, Capt Clark having proceeded with the party by water the preceeding day, I arrived at Cahokia on the 7th and immediately took occasion to make myself acquainted with Mr. John Hay (the Post Master of this place) and a Mr Jarrot, in whom from previous information I had every confidence; both these Gentleman are well acquainted with the English & French Languages, a necessary qualification to enable them to be serviceable on the present occasion, as the Spanish Commandant cannot speak the English Language, and I am unfortunately equally ignorant of that of the French—these gentlemen readily consented to accompany me, and the next day (the 8th) I set out in company with them to visit Colo. Lasuse; on our arrival at his quarters we were received with much politeness by him, and after a friendly interchange of the usual salutations, I proceeded to make him acquainted with the objects of my visit, handed him the passports which I had received from the French & English Ministers, and your letter to Monsr Peyroux, at the same time in a summary manner adding a few observations relative to those papers, the views of my government in[1] fitting out this expedition, and my own wishes to proceed on my voyage: after perusing the papers he returned me an answer nearly to this effect, that he was sensible the objects of the Government of the U States as well as

[137]

my own were no other than those stated in my passports or such as had been expressed by myself; that these in their execution, would not be injurious to his royal master, the King of Spain, nor would they in his opinion prove in any manner detrimental to his Majesty's subjects with whose interests he was at that moment particularly charged, that as an individual he viewed it as a hazardous enterprize, but wished it every success, nor would he from his personal inclinations obstruct its[2] progress a single moment; he then concluded by observing that whatever might be his feelings as a man, his duty as an Officer, and his orders as such, strengthened also by the undeviating policy of the Spanish Government, with the regard to the nonadmission of foreigners into the interior of their provinces, equally forbad his granting me permission at this time to asscend the Missouri river; however he would if permitted by me take a transcript of my passports, and send them immediately by an express to New Orleans to the Govr Genl of the Province, and that he would with cheerfulness give the aid of his influence with that officer, to promote my wishes; and finally as a friend advised my remaining at Cahokia untill the next spring, alledging that by that time he had no doubt the Govrs. consent would be obtained, and that then all obstructions would be removed to my asscending the Missouri.

In return for this abundant politeness of the Colo. I granted him permission to take a transcript of the papers I had presented him, alledging that it was not the object of my Government to conceal any views which it entertained relative to my mission and that his goverment had already been advised of it through their minister resident in the U. States, that I did not doubt the sincerity of his good wishes for the success of the enterprize, and thanked him for the willingness he displayed in procuring from the Govr. Genl. the permission I had asked. I further observed, that it was not my intention at that time, to question either the policy or the right of the Spanish Government to prohibit my passage up the Missouri, that the reasons he had given for his refusal of my application, were considered by me, as furnishing an ample apology on his part as an Officer for his refusal, and that I should not attempt to asscend the Missouri this season—I concurred with him in the opinion, that by the ensuing spring, *all obstructions would be removed to my asscending the Missouri*: this effect however I anticipated as eminating from a very different cause, than that which seemed to govern the predictions of the Commandant.—I concluded by thanking him for the personal friendship he had evinced, in recommending to me a winter residence, which certainly in point of society or individual comfort must be considered as the most eligible of any in this quarter of the country, but that other considerations of more importance had induced me to assign myself a different position that I had selected for this purpose (provided it answered the description I had received of it) the mouth of a small river called Dubois on the E. side of the Mississippi opposite to the mouth of the Missouri.—Thus defeated in my application, tho' not much disappointed nor at all diverted from my future views, I spent the evening with the Commandant, and returned the next day to join Capt Clark who had just arrived at Cahokia—On the evening of the 10th Inst. we left Cahokia, and continued our route up the Mississippi four miles, opposite to St. Louis where we remained for the night, early the next morning Capt Clark continued his route with the party to the river Dubois (distant from St Louis 18 Miles) in order to erect Cabins for our winter residence at that place (provided it answered the description we had received of it) or otherwise to establish himself on a more eligible one as near it as possible—I passed over to St. Louis with a view to obtain from the inhabitants such information as I might consider usefull to the Government, or such as might be usefull to me in my further prosecution of my voyage—

I have the honor to be with much respect Your Obt Servt

MERIWETHER LEWIS Capt
1st US Regt. Infty.

Tr (PHi); in an unidentified hand; at foot of text: "The President of the U States." Recorded in SJL as received 27 Feb. 1804.

For Lewis's PASSPORTS from French and British diplomatic representatives and TJ's letter to Henri PEYROUX de la Coudrèniere, see Vol. 40:8-9, 653-4. Charles Dehault Delassus sent copies of those papers along with a report of his meeting with Lewis to Manuel de Salcedo and the Marqués de Casa Calvo (A. P. Nasatir, ed., *Before Lewis and Clark: Documents Illustrating the History of the Missouri, 1785-1804*, 2 vols. [St. Louis, 1952], 2:719-21.)

[1] MS: "it."
[2] MS: "it."

To Thomas Mann Randolph

DEAR SIR   Washington Dec. 19. 03.

The post of last night brings us agreeable information from New Orleans & Natchez. Genl. Wilkinson arrived at N. Orleans from Mobille Nov. 25. settled immediately with Laussat all the circumstances of the delivery, & proceeded next day to Fort Adams, where he would arrive on the 30th. & expect to meet Claiborne there ready for embarcation. on the 29th. Laussat demanded possession of the Spanish officers, who instantly agreed to deliver the place[1] on the next day (30th.)

at Noon, & every thing was arranged for that purpose. Laussat meant to garrison the forts with militia, & to appoint a person to every office civil & military to take the place of the Spanish incumbents. in all this he acted in concert with Clarke, mixing many Americans in the offices, & giving the command of the militia to a friend of Clarke's. Claiborne embarked 100. militia Dec. 1 from Natchez[2] for Fort Adams, & set out Dec. 2. by land for the same place, expecting to fall in with & carry on to that place 80. militia more. he would find Wilkinson there with all the regulars ready for embarcation, which probably took place on the 3d. or 4th. & they would arrive at N. Orleans the 6th. or 7th. if on the 6th. we shall hear of it Christmas night; if not till the 7th. we shall not hear it till the night of New year's day. the Marquis of Casa Calva had ordered the barracks to be got ready to recieve & accomodate our troops, and proposed to embark all his own, the moment he had delivered the place, on board an armed vessel then lying ready to recieve them: so that they will be gone before the arrival of our troops. Laussat would hold the government about a week. this is for yourself & mr Eppes. my tender love to my dear Martha & Maria, and all the young ones, & affectionate salutations to yourself & mr Eppes.   TH: JEFFERSON

RC (DLC); at foot of text: "T M Randolph." PrC (MHi); endorsed by TJ in ink on verso.

POST OF LAST NIGHT: the State Department evidently received communications of 28 and 29 Nov. from Daniel Clark and of 2 Dec. from William C. C. Claiborne. In the first of two letters of the 29th, Clark, who distrusted the intentions of French prefect Pierre Clément LAUSSAT, indicated his disapproval of the replacement of officers in New Orleans but also Laussat's willingness to allow Clark to substitute candidates for those Laussat had previously chosen. In addi-

tion to naming Joseph Deville de Goutin Bellechasse, Clark's FRIEND, head of the local militia, Laussat created a temporary municipal government consisting of a mayor, two mayor-adjuncts, a secretary general, and a 12-member council (Pierre Clément Laussat, *Arreté pour l'établissement de l'autorité municipale a la Nouvelle-Orléans* [New Orleans, 1803]; *Terr. Papers*, 9:112-14, 123-5; Madison, *Papers, Sec. of State Ser.*, 6:106-7, 111-13, 127).

[1] Preceding two words interlined in place of "it."
[2] Preceding two words interlined.

From William Stark

VENERABLE SIR,   Youngstown Decr. 19th 1803

To you I tender my service in any office, which you may think proper, to confer on me in Louisiana or New Orleans. & would prefer the Military or Judiciary as I think I have some tast for Tactics &

tolerable Knowledg of Law, having had a regular education in that profession.

I am 28 years of age have received the honors of Dartmouth University, & am now practising law at Youngstown County of Trumbull State of Ohio.

I am with due respect Your devoted servant

WILLIAM STARK

RC (DNA: RG 59, LAR); at foot of text: "His Excellency Thomas Jefferson President U.S.A."; endorsed by TJ as received 29 Dec. and so recorded in SJL, connected by a brace with entries for letters received the same day from Stephen Perkins of 14 Dec. and William Hardy of 26 Dec. with notation "emploimt. Louisiana"; also endorsed by TJ: "Military or Judiciary. Louisiana."

A native of New Hampshire, William Stark (1775-1808) was a 1799 graduate of Dartmouth College and a nephew of General John Stark. He later emigrated to Canada (George T. Chapman, *Sketches of the Alumni of Dartmouth College* [Cambridge, Mass., 1867], 99).

From Albert Gallatin

DEAR SIR   Decer. 20th 1803

When Doctr. Bache went to New Orleans we allowed him a salary at the rate of 1000 dollars commencing on the 16th Nover. when he left Virginia. Of that he received a quarter in advance, & has received three other quarters from D. Clarke in New Orleans. On the 16th Nov'er. when he left that city, he obtained another draft for 250 dollars on the Treasury from Mr Clark. As he has received his whole year's salary, if this draft shall be paid, it will be a further advance towards services which may not be rendered. Under those circumstances, do you think I ought to pay it? I submit the case to you not only on general grounds because the hospital money is particularly under your direction, and is disbursed only in conformity with the general regulation established by the President; but also because you are perhaps informed of the probability of Doctr. Bache returning to New Orleans. You may have perceived from Mr Clarke's letter which I had sent the other day that he must have contemplated an increase of salary; and as that is not expedient, he may perhaps decline returning, in which case the 250 dollars advance would not be easily recovered.

With great respect Your obedt. Servt.   ALBERT GALLATIN

Enclosed is a letter just received from a Rhode Island member; which, though not very civil, shows the spirit of the times—

RC (DLC); addressed: "The President of the United States"; endorsed by TJ as received from the Treasury Department on 20 Dec. and "Bache" and so recorded in SJL. Enclosure not found.

PARTICULARLY UNDER YOUR DIRECTION: see Vol. 36:632n.

Daniel Clark's LETTER has not been found.

To George Jefferson

DEAR SIR   Washington Dec. 20. 03.

I gave a note last August or September to Craven Peyton for 558. D 14 c payable at your counting house some time this month. the session of Congress & the season occasioning accumulated demands on me, I wrote to ask him if the note was still in his own hands, to let it lie over according to his convenience, but whenever necessary for him, it should be paid. he writes me he had just sent it to Staunton to mr Kinney on account of Colo. Gamble. the object of the present is to mention that whenever the note comes to hand, on giving me notice, I will remit the money immediately.

If you could send me by the stage[1] a copy of the laws of Virginia lately published by one of the printers in Richmond I should be obliged to you. among the packages lodged with you for me last fall were some boxes of window glass and table China. I desired them to lie till they could be sent by water. yet hearing that Peyton's waggon had been sent for things of mine with you, I have feared these also might have been sent, and as they were packed for water carriage only, that they may have suffered greatly if sent by land. will you be so good as to inform me whether they went by the waggon, or are still with you, & in the latter case to retain them still for water carriage. Accept my affectionate salutations   TH: JEFFERSON

PrC (MHi); at foot of text: "Mr. George Jefferson"; endorsed by TJ in ink on verso.

For the transaction with CRAVEN PEYTON, see TJ to Peyton, 27 Nov., and Peyton's response of 8 Dec.

TJ was requesting an updated version of the LAWS OF VIRGINIA that reflected changes made as recently as the 1801-02 session of the General Assembly. The PRINTERS were Samuel Pleasants and Henry Pace (*A Collection of All Such Acts of the General Assembly of Virginia, of a Public and Permanent Nature, As Are Now in Force; with a New and Complete Index* [Richmond, Va., 1803]; Sowerby, No. 1868).

[1] Preceding three words interlined.

From Rufus King

Dear Sir   New york december 20. 1803

While abroad I took some pains to collect the Publications that have been made respecting the discovery and settlement of America; among the Reports and Letters of the Early Settlers, I have a manuscript account of Bacon's Rebellion in 1675, written by a member of your assembly for the County of Northumberland, and addressed to Sr. Robert Harley.

As this account is more particular than any other of the same transaction that I have seen, and differs from that of our historians in some important Circumstances, I have thought that you might be gratified in reading it: should it be in your power, I shall be obliged to you to give me the name of the author, whose initials only are subscribed to the Dedication—

With great Respect I have the honour to be your obt. & faithful Servt.   RUFUS KING

RC (DLC); at foot of first page: "Mr. Jefferson"; endorsed by TJ as received 23 Dec. and so recorded in SJL. FC (NHi: Rufus King Papers). Enclosure: "The Beginning, Progress and Conclusion of Bacons Rebellion in Virginia in the Years 1675 & 1676" (MS in DLC: TJ Papers, ser. 8, no. 1).

At the time the enclosed MANUSCRIPT was written, ROBERT HARLEY, later prime minister and Earl of Oxford, was speaker of the House of Commons and a key adviser to Queen Anne (DNB).

In the cover letter to Harley, dated 13 July 1705, the AUTHOR of the account signed as "T. M." Although TJ does not appear to have made the connection himself, the initials stood for Thomas Mathew, a planter and merchant who lived in Northumberland County for a couple of decades. Mathew also owned land in Stafford County and represented that county, not Northumberland, in the General Assembly that met in 1676 in the midst of the rebellion led by Nathaniel Bacon. His account emphasized his own efforts to avoid taking sides in the conflict, while indicating the unsteady and often harsh leadership of Governor William Berkeley and portraying Bacon as a rash, honorable youth who had been influenced by some of the governor's more experienced opponents. When asked by Harley to write his narrative, Mathew had been living in England for about 25 years (Charles M. Andrews, ed., *Narratives of the Insurrections, 1675-1690* [New York, 1915], 11-41; Warren M. Billings, ed., *The Papers of Sir William Berkeley, 1605-1677* [Richmond, Va., 2007], 213n).

From John Page

Sir,   Richmond December 20th. 1803.

I have this day sent to the General Assembly your letter and the copy of an Article of Amendment proposed by Congress to be added to the Constitution of the United States respecting the election of President and Vice President inclosed therein. They would have been earlier communicated to the Legislature could I have done it in my official Character. They were received when I was only a private Citizen.

I am with high respect & Esteem Sir Your most obedt. Servt.

JOHN PAGE

RC (DNA: RG 11, RA); endorsed by TJ as received 27 Dec. and so recorded in SJL. FC (Vi: Executive Letterbook); in a clerk's hand; at head of text: "The President of the United States."

YOUR LETTER: TJ to the Governors of the States, 13 Dec. On 19 Dec., the state legislature reelected Page to a one-year term as governor (Richmond *Virginia Argus*, 21 Dec. 1803).

To Mawlay Sulayman, Sultan of Morocco

GREAT & GOOD FRIEND   Dec. 20. 1803

I learnt with great concern the acts of violence which took place between some vessels of your Majesty and of the United States, and with equal pleasure that you had promptly interposed & arrested the progress of the misunderstanding. this proof of your dispositions to remain in friendship with the US. is duly estimated on my part, and will be reciprocated on all occasions, by corresponding endeavors to preserve the peace & good understanding so happily subsisting between us.

Separated by a wide ocean from the nations of Europe, & under circumstances peculiar to ourselves, our practices & principles of intercourse are not always the same with theirs. all religions are[1] equally free[2] and independent here. our laws know no distinctions of country or of classes among individuals, and with nations our rule is justice and reciprocity. in these principles of justice & reciprocity was founded the treaty of peace & friendship concluded with your Imperial father, and recently recognised by your Majesty. in this recognition I willingly concur; promising that the stipulations of that treaty shall be faithfully observed on our part. We shall moreover avail ourselves of every occasion of performing good offices to your people, and of manifesting the cordial friendship and respect we bear to the person and character of your Imperial Majesty; and I pray god to have you, great & good friend, in his safe & holy keeping.

Done at Washington in the United States of America &c.

PrC (DLC); dated in ink; at foot of text: "The Emperor of Marocco." Enclosed in Madison to James Simpson, 26 Dec. 1803 (Madison, *Papers, Sec. of State Ser.*, 6:217-18).

CORRESPONDING ENDEAVORS TO PRESERVE THE PEACE & GOOD UNDERSTANDING: see Sulayman to TJ, 11 Oct., and TJ to the Senate and the House of Representatives, 5 Dec.

[1] TJ here canceled "by [law] equals."

[2] TJ interlined the remainder of this sentence and the sentence that follows in place of "here, and the honors and offices of government are equally open to all in them. from all nations justice & reciprocity, and [. . .] to them."

From John Vaughan

DEAR SIR   Philad: 20 Dec 1803

By desire of Dr Priestley I have sent per Post for your acceptance, the New Edition of his pamphlet on Phlogiston, & his last answer to Lynn—The Dr. requests you will permit him to trouble you to cause one to be forwarded to M Levingston at Paris—I have taken the liberty of forwarding one to you for that purpose.—

D Priestley has been very ill, he is now somewhat better but I fear we shall not long have him with us—

Vaccination has been renewed here both from the Scab. 7. months Old in the hands of Dr Hewson, & by matter from England sent to Dr Coxe

I remain with the greatest respect Your frend &c

JN VAUGHAN

RC (DLC); at foot of text: "Thos. Jefferson Prest. of US"; endorsed by TJ as received 24 Dec. and so recorded in SJL. Enclosures: (1) Two copies of Joseph Priestley, *The Doctrine of Phlogiston Established, and that of the Composition of Water refuted, the second edition with additions* (Northumberland, Pa., 1803; Sowerby, No. 836). (2) Priestley, *A Second Letter to the Revd. John Blair Linn, D.D. Pastor of the First Presbyterian Congregation in the City of Philadelphia, in Reply to His Defence of the Doctrines of the Divinity of Christ and Atonement* (Northumberland, Pa., 1803; Sowerby, No. 1663).

From Benjamin B. Carter

MAY IT PLEASE YOUR EXCELLENCY,   New York Dec. 21, 1803.

Among the numerous applicants who trespass upon your time, the writer of this craves leave to draw your attention, for a few moments to an object of some importance. Your Excellency's profound knowledge of the sciences and your known good will towards the cultivators of them, embolden me to make the advances. The U.S. of America now flourishing under the happy auspices of your Excellency's administration, are justly esteemed, as one of the first commercial countries. But the Charts hitherto published of our extensive sea coast, being done by Foreigners, who had but an imperfect knowledge of the subject are, as you well know, very inaccurate. To suggest to your Excellency, the expediency of supplying their defects by making a reformed set of Charts, is the object of this letter.

Not having the honour of a personal acquaintance with your Excellency, you will perhaps ask the qualifications of the person addressing. This information might with more propriety come from another; but I have declined introductory or recommendatory letters, (which might be obtained from those respectable for knowledge & virtue,) preferring the imputation of egotism to the premature disclosure of a plan of this nature. But as it may be deemed requisite to say something, the writer of this with due respect begs leave to observe, that he is a native of Providence in Rhode Island, was educated at the College in that town, graduated A.D. 1786, and proceeded A.M. in 1789, Learning being ever a primary object with him, he hopes he has not been wanting in application, during his attendance on the Lectures of the most eminent professors of Philadelphia, London & Utretch; also the mathematical & Astronomical Lectures of Prof. Calcoen and others of the University of Leyden. He has made three voyages to China and New Holland, one to the Friendly Islands, to Batavia, St Helena and many of the capital cities of Europe, and now lately returned from St Petersburg in Russia. Having been accustomed from early youth to mathematical pursuits, and having had many years practice in Astronomical observations and calculations at Sea; observing moreover that the charts published in Europe of the Sea Coast of the U.S. of America, are much distorted as to the Situation of places and replete with Errors, the Long. of most places being laid down rather from the uncertain deductions of the Seamans log, than from Cœlestial observations which alone can assign their true relative Situation; he has had it long in contemplation, to reform the numerous errors by making a more correct set of Marine Charts upon Mercators principles, ascertaining from actual observation of the ⊕ & \☽'s dist, the eclipses of Jupiters Satellites, or a well regulated Chronometer, the precise Long. of a sufficient number of points. The requisite observations might be made, at the remarkable Capes and head lands of the Coast, together with a survey of the harbours, at the same time the dip & variation of the needle might be observed. The result of the observations might be published in a general Chart, accompanied by separate Charts of each maritime State on a larger scale, or otherwise as might be judged best.

This Undertaking your excellency will immediately perceive, to be beyond the reach of a private man, as the advances must be considerable; and it is probable that a remuneration of the Charges by the Sales would be slow and uncertain. Other arguments indeed might be adduced, to prove it rather a national, than an individual enterprize. It would moreover be a work of labour, requiring time and application; but being free from avocations at present, the writer of this would be happy to devote himself solely to the undertaking, provided it meets with your approbation and patronage. The great number of shipwrecks annually on our coast, is owing in a measure to want of knowledge in Mariners, of the Situation of dangers by reason of the imperfection of Charts, which thus deceive the unwary and are productive of indefinite mischief. Among the many great actions performed by your Excellency for the good of our Country, that of giving to the nautical world more permanent ease and security, by enabling mariners to navigate the deceitful billows with security, would not be deemed the most inconsiderable. Such a work would prove your Excellency's regard for the Commercial interests of our country, as well as for the lives & safety of mariners. The U.S. of America have been reproached with inattention to the Sciences; but as no one has done more to obviate such a charge than your Excellency, so from no one is there more expected, and to no one could a proposition of the nature above mentioned be with more propriety addressed. Should you be favourably disposed towards this undertaking, proper steps might be taken to carry it into effect and you will find me ready with heart & hand to lend my assistance. A Letter may be directed to me at New York (where I shall remain this fortnight) or at Providence; or if necessary, I can wait on your Excellency at Washington. I have one request to make, which is that if this proposition should not meet your approbation; or that you have not time to attend to it, the nature of the business as propounded by me may not be disclosed, further that you would pardon the freedom of my letter, to one of your Excellencys eminent rank & merit.

I am with the greatest respect, Your Excellencys most obedt. Servt.

BENJAMIN B. CARTER

RC (DNA: RG 59, LAR); endorsed by TJ as received 25 Dec. and so recorded in SJL with notation "to be empld in chart of sea coast."

Benjamin Bowen Carter (1771-1831) grew up in Providence and graduated from the College of Rhode Island in 1786. He studied medicine in Philadelphia under Benjamin Rush and spent part of the 1790s in South Carolina and Georgia. After returning to Providence, he may have taught school for a short time but in 1798 signed on as surgeon of the *Ann*

and Hope, which pursued the China trade. Carter went on four voyages with the ship and enjoyed much success speculating in Chinese and Russian goods. From 1804 to 1806, Carter worked as a doctor and merchant in Canton. Increasingly unhappy with Jeffersonian governance, Carter lived in England for about 12 years before settling in New York in 1819 (Robert W. Kenny, "Benjamin B. Carter, Physician Extraordinary," *Rhode Island History*, 16 [1957], 97-113; *Providence Gazette*, 13 Mch. 1798).

To the Senate

To the Senate of the United States

On the 11th. of January last I laid before the Senate for their consideration and advice, a Convention with Spain on the subject of indemnities for spoliations on our commerce committed by her subjects during the late war; which Convention is still before the Senate. as this instrument did not embrace French seisures & condemnations of our vessels in the ports of Spain, for which we deemed the latter power responsible, our Minister at that court was instructed to press for an additional article, comprehending that branch of wrongs. I now communicate what has since passed on that subject. the Senate will judge whether the prospect it offers will justify a longer suspension of that portion of indemnities conceded by Spain, should she now take no advantage of the lapse of the period for ratification.

As the settlement of the boundaries of Louisiana will call for new negociations,[1] on our recieving possession of that province, the claims not obtained by the Convention now before the Senate, may be incorporated into those discussions.

Th: Jefferson
Dec. 21. 1803.

RC (DNA: RG 46, EPFR, 8th Cong., 1st sess.). PrC (DLC). Tr (Edward Lamb, Toledo, Ohio, 1945); entirely in TJ's hand, with notation at foot of text, "The above is truly copied from the press-copy retained of the original sent to the Senate," which he signed and dated 1 Jan. 1824; enclosed in TJ to John Hollins, 1 Jan. 1824. Enclosures (all Trs in DNA: RG 46, EPFR, in clerks' hands): (1) Secretary of state to Charles Pinckney, 8 Mch. 1803, extract, asking for modification of the 11 Aug. 1802 convention between Spain and the United States so that it will cover seizures and condemnations by the French within Spain's jurisdiction; letter printed in Madison, *Papers, Sec. of State Ser.*, 4:398-401. (2) Secretary of state to Pinckney, 22 Mch., extract, suggesting alterations of wording of the convention; see same, 442-3. (3) Pinckney to secretary of state, 12 May, extract, asking if inclusion of the French condemnations is "indispensable"; see same, 595-8. (4) Pinckney to secretary of state, 2 Aug. continued 30 Aug., reporting progress of negotiations; see same, 5:260-70. (5) Pinckney to Pedro Cevallos, 23 May,

discussing the points at issue and enclosing the text in Spanish and English of a proposed substitute convention. (6) Pinckney to Cevallos, no date. (7) Pinckney to Cevallos, 15 July. (8) Cevallos to Pinckney, 23 Aug., in Spanish with English translation, rejecting the notion that Spain can have any responsibility for seizures by French privateers, in particular because the United States, having renounced the settlement of claims in its convention with France in 1800, cannot make Spain accountable for claims against France; enclosing answers of the prominent American lawyers Jared Ingersoll, William Rawle, Joseph B. McKean, Pierre S. Du Ponceau, and Edward Livingston in November 1802 to an "Abstract Question" related to this issue. (9) Pinckney to Cevallos, 28 Aug., countering those arguments. Message and enclosures printed in asp, *Foreign Relations*, 2:596-606.

After the Senate, at the close of the 7th Congress, postponed the question of ratification of the CONVENTION WITH SPAIN, Madison instructed Pinckney to "avail yourself of the opportunity" to persuade the Spanish government of "the reasonableness and the sound policy of remodelling the Convention in such a manner as to do full justice" by allowing claims for condemnations by French consuls in Spain's ports. The Senate turned to the convention again on 25 Nov. with the appointment of Stephen R. Bradley, Abraham Baldwin, and James Jackson as a committee to inquire if further action was needed. Lewis Harvie delivered TJ's message and the accompanying papers to the Senate on 21 Dec. In executive session on 9 Jan. 1804, the Senate ratified the convention by a vote of 21 to 7 (Madison, *Papers, Sec. of State Ser.*, 4:400; JEP, 1:459, 461-2; Vol. 39:316-17).

NOW COMMUNICATE WHAT HAS SINCE PASSED: John Quincy Adams noted in his diary that the Senate clerks' reading aloud of the papers that came with TJ's message of 21 Dec. "took more than two hours." On the 22d, Bradley reported for his committee that the president's message "gave the Senate all the information within their power to obtain," and the Senate discharged the committee. Bradley then presented a resolution to refer the message and documents to a select committee that would report on whether "further proceedings ought to be had by the Senate" in regard to "disclosures" in the papers. According to William Plumer, in his journal of the Senate's proceedings, and to Adams in his diary, it was clear that the purpose of Bradley's resolution was to initiate prosecution under the Logan Act of the attorneys who had answered the "Abstract Question" posed to them by the Spanish government. Bradley, Plumer asserted, considered Rawle to be the author of the Logan Act and wanted to see him held accountable under his own law (although Plumer understood from Roger Griswold that the act had been Griswold's creation, not Rawle's). Following the vote to ratify the convention on 9 Jan., the Senate agreed to Bradley's resolution and named him, Baldwin, and Jackson as the select committee. In a report presented on 24 Feb., the committee found that "certain unauthorised acts and doings of individuals contrary to law, and highly prejudicial to the rights and sovereignty of the United States, tending to defeat the measures of the government thereof," had occurred—that Ingersoll, Rawle, McKean, Du Ponceau, and Livingston, by corresponding with agents of the government of Spain about a matter in dispute between that country and the United States, had gone against the Logan Act. Declaring that those violations would go unpunished "without the aid of the executive," the committee proposed a resolution that would ask the president to obtain an opinion from the attorney general, and if Lincoln found that the law had been broken, the president should order "the proper law officer" to undertake prosecution. The Senate ordered a limited printing of the report under injunction of secrecy. Not until the evening of 27 Mch. did the Senate return to the committee's report. Samuel White proposed a resolution that the body "take no further order" on the report, senators "not considering it within the province of their duty to do so," and that the injunction of secrecy be lifted. The Senate postponed action on the resolution until Congress reconvened in the fall. Madison expressed the administration's view of the matter in a letter to Pinckney on 6 Feb.: "It was probably unknown to the Spanish Government that the lawyers in giving the opinion to which it attaches so much value, violated a positive statute of their own Country forbidding communications of any sort with foreign Governments or Agents on subjects to which their own Government is a party; that one of them being in a public trust under his own Government"—Edward Livingston, who when the American lawyers gave their opinion was a U.S. district attorney—"violated his official duty, and that another being allied by affinity to the Minister of His Catholic Majesty here"—Joseph B. McKean, brother-in-law of Carlos Martínez de Irujo—"would have consulted his personal delicacy more by withholding, than by adding his name to the rescript" (Adams, diary 27 [1 Jan. 1803 to 4 Aug. 1809], 57, 61, in MHi: Adams Family Papers; Everett Somerville Brown, ed., *William Plumer's Memorandum of Proceedings in the United States Senate, 1803-1807* [London, 1923], 94-5; *Report of the Select Committee of the Senate of the United States, Appointed on the*

9th January, 1804, to Consider & Report Whether Any, and What Further Proceedings Ought to be had by the Senate, in Relation to the Message and Documents Communicated by the President of the United States, on the 21st December Last [Washington, D.C., 1804; MS of report in DNA: RG 46, EPFR, filed with the message of 21 Dec.; Madison, *Papers, Sec. of State Ser.*, 6:440, 441n; JEP, 1:461, 463, 464-5, 468-70).

[1] TJ here canceled "with Spain."

From George Clinton

DEAR SIR   Albany 22d. December 1803

I have lately read in a scurilous Pamphlet entitled "an examination of the various charges exhibited against Aaron Burr Esquire" &c, a Paragraph charging me with having expressed at a meeting held at his House in the Spring of 1800 Sentiments highly derogatory to your political Character and inconsistent with private Friendship—I am sensible of the impropriety of troubling you with Matters of a private Nature at a Time when your whole Attention must be employed in the important Duties of your Station; but the Object of that publication is such that I cannot reconcile it to my Feelings to delay declaring to you as I now do that it is a base and dishonorable Misrepresentation I shall however defer communicating a circumstantial detail of every Thing that passed at that Meeting 'till an Opportunity of more leisure—Considering that some of the Facts stated in the paragraph referred to are in direct Opposition to others advanced with equal boldness in the same Pamphlet, and that the whole of them stand contradicted by the uniform Tenor of my conduct—It might have been thought unnecessary to take this Notice of them, if a referrence had not been made for their Truth to a person whom I have mentioned to you since that Time in favourable Terms and as a Man of Integrity—Whether he has authorized this referrence I know not; but he has not yet disavowed it to me which if innocent I had a right to expect.

I have indeed to regret that my Zeal for the public Interest led me on that Occasion into bad Company without suspecting that I was under the Roof of a corrupt Intriguer surrounded by his worthless Minions

With unabated Esteem & Respect I am yours sincerely

GEO: CLINTON

RC (DLC); at foot of text: "Thomas Jefferson Esquire"; endorsed by TJ as received 30 Dec. and so recorded in SJL.

Signing as "Aristides," William P. Van Ness authored the PAMPHLET in consultation with the vice president. Published in New York in early December, it was a response to James Cheetham's *A View of the Political Conduct of Aaron Burr, Esq. Vice-President of the United States.* At a meeting at Burr's HOUSE, Clinton reportedly "declared, *that he had long entertained an unfavorable opinion of Mr. Jefferson's talents as a statesman and his firmness as a republican.*" He thought that TJ was "*an accommodating trimmer, who would change with times and bend to circumstances for the purposes of personal promotion.*" Clinton reportedly said he could not "*acquiesce in the elevation of a man destitute of the qualifications essential to the good administration of the government,*" but if Burr were the candidate, he "*would act with pleasure and with vigor.*" Van Ness noted that David Gelston, John Mills, John Swartwout, and Matthew L. Davis were present at the meeting and could verify the account ([William P. Van Ness], *An Examination of the Various Charges Exhibited Against Aaron Burr, Esq. Vice-President of the United States: And a Developement of the Characters and Views of His Political Opponents* [New York, 1803; Sowerby, No. 3446], 35-6; Kline, *Burr,* 2:726, 812n; Vol. 38:94n).

To Hugh Holmes

Washington Dec. 22. 03.

Th: Jefferson presents his friendly salutations to mr Holmes, & his congratulations on his appointment to the chair of the H. of Representatives of Virginia, and prays his acceptance of the small volume inclosed.

RC (Mr. and Mrs. James J. White, Charlotte, North Carolina, 1981); pasted by Holmes, or later, into a copy of TJ's *A Manual of Parliamentary Practice. For the Use of the Senate of the United States* (Washington, D.C., 1801); signed by Holmes and with corrections to the text by TJ. Not recorded in SJL.

To Jones & Howell

MESSRS. JONES & HOWELL.   Washington Dec. 22. 03.

I inclose you a letter from Gibson & Jefferson in Richmond which will inform you of the reciept of only 70. instead of 80. bundles of nail-rod, which you will doubtless have rectified wherever the error has happened. when you forward on the 10. bundles deficient, I shall be glad if you will send at the same time 3. sheets of sheet-iron 5 f. 9 I. long, and of whatever width above 16. I. they may happen to be. it is wanting at Monticello for a particular purpose.

Your house, under some one of it's former firms, (say about the year 1794.) furnished me with some sheets of iron, between 8. & 9. feet long, made up, each, of two sheets put together at the end in the manner of the paper herein inclosed, and as perfectly consolidated at the joint as if they had originally been rolled together. perhaps they were cemented while hot, & in the rolling press. how it was done I know not. I should have occasion for a good deal, next summer, if they could be got, of still greater length than this, say 10.$\frac{1}{2}$. feet, & 16. I. wide. not knowing in what way the edges are annealed together, nor whether several sheets can be put together to the extent above mentioned, I ask your information on the subject, that I may be enabled to take my measures accordingly. Accept my friendly salutations & good wishes.   TH: JEFFERSON

PrC (MHi); endorsed by TJ in ink on verso. Enclosures not found.

TJ did not record receiving a letter from GIBSON & JEFFERSON around this time, and the letter has not been found.

FORMER FIRMS: on several occasions during the 1790s, TJ ordered iron, most identified as nailrod, from Samuel Howell, Jr., the father of Samuel E. Howell of Jones & Howell. He also ordered sheet iron from Caleb Lowndes in 1794 (MB, 2:910, 940, 942, 948; Vol. 29:89n; Vol. 39:172n).

To John Langdon

MY DEAR SIR   Washington Dec. 22. 03.

The inclosed commission was made out immediately on the reciept of your recommendation as it's date will shew: but as I wished to accompany it with a line to you, it has laid by me ever since waiting a moment of leisure to drop you one. in the mean time the law is repealed: but this commission will still do for existing cases.

I have the happiness to assure you that we shall recieve Louisiana without opposition, or rather that we have recieved it, as we know that our troops embarked from Natchez the 1st. & 2d. inst. and would arrive at N. Orleans on the 7th. where possession would be instantly delivered according to arrangements agreed to between Genl. Wilkinson & the French prefect. this matter quietly finished, & peace made with the emperor of Marocco dictated by ourselves, leaves nothing in our horison but the little speck of Tripoli, where the substitution of Preble for Morris will probably soon enforce peace also. from both the contending powers of Europe we have equal proofs of friendship; but most especially Gr. Britain. we shall therefore I hope be able to maintain an impartial & honourable neutrality. at home we learn from all quarters that these measures have brought over to us nearly the whole of our candid opponents, except in three of the New England states, & in Delaware. these we trust will in time be convinced also. this, my friend, is a rapid view of our affairs, and is as much as incessant interruption & business will permit me to put on paper. Accept my affectionate salutations and assurances of constant esteem.

TH: JEFFERSON

RC (NhPoS: John Langdon Papers); at foot of text: "John Langdon esq."; endorsed by Langdon. PrC (DLC). Enclosure: Commission, dated 16 Nov., to Richard Cutts Shannon as a commissioner of bankruptcy for New Hampshire (FC in Lb in DNA: RG 59, MPTPC).

YOUR RECOMMENDATION: Langdon to TJ, 29 Oct. 1803.

Congress REPEALED the Bankruptcy Act of 1800 on 19 Dec., but stipulated that bankruptcy commissions issued prior to the repeal "may and shall be proceeded on and fully executed" (U.S. Statutes at Large, 2:248).

From James Turner

SIR   Raleigh 22nd. December 1803

I have the honor of transmitting to you, an Authenticated copy of an Act of the General Assembly of the state of North Carolina, passed at their late Session, Ratifying on the part of this state, the amendment proposed by Congress to be made in the Constitution of the United States, respecting the Election of President & Vice President: For the purpose of Your Communicating the same to Congress—

I have the honor to be With high consideration and respect Your obdt. Servt   J. TURNER

RC (DNA: RG 11, RA); at foot of text: "The President of the United States"; endorsed by TJ as received 30 Dec. and so recorded in SJL with notation "ratificn"; also endorsed by TJ: "Ratifn of Amdmt to Constn for N.C." Enclosure: North Carolina General Assembly, "An Act to ratify an Amendment to the Constitution of the United States," enacted 22 Dec. (MS in same; printed in *Laws of North Carolina. At a General Assembly, Begun and Held at Raleigh, on the 21st Day of November, in the Year of our Lord One Thousand Eight Hundred and Three* [Raleigh, 1803], 4).

North Carolina was the first state to ratify the proposed Twelfth AMENDMENT to the U.S. Constitution. Turner submit-

ted it to the General Assembly on 20 Dec., and a bill to ratify was presented the same day. It passed both houses the following day, succeeding in the House of Commons by a vote of 91 to 18 (*Journal of the House of Commons of the State of North-Carolina. At a General Assembly, Begun and Held at the City of Raleigh, on Monday the Twenty-First Day of November, in the Year of our Lord One Thousand Eight Hundred and Three* [Raleigh, 1803], 57-9; *Journal of the Senate of the State of North-Carolina. At a General Assembly, Begun and Held at the City of Raleigh, on Monday the Twenty-First Day of November, in the Year of our Lord One Thousand Eight Hundred and Three* [Raleigh, 1803], 52, 55).

Canons of Official Etiquette

I. NOTES ON DIPLOMATIC ETIQUETTE IN ENGLAND,
[AFTER 22 DEC. 1803]
II. CANONS OF ETIQUETTE, [BEFORE 12 JAN. 1804?]
III. MEMORANDUM ON OFFICIAL ETIQUETTE, [BEFORE 12 JAN. 1804?]
IV. RESPONSE TO THE *WASHINGTON FEDERALIST,*
[BEFORE 13 FEB. 1804]

E D I T O R I A L   N O T E

After Jefferson hosted the newly arrived British Minister Anthony Merry and his wife, Elizabeth, for dinner at the President's House on 2 Dec., a debate over diplomatic protocol ensued. The British consul took umbrage when the widowed president did not accompany his wife to the dining room, but instead escorted Dolley Madison, whom he seated at his side. Secretary of State James Madison accompanied Elizabeth Merry to dinner, while Anthony Merry had to find his own place at the table. Among the other guests were William Short, French chargé d'affaires Louis Pichon and his wife, and Spanish minister Carlos Martínez de Irujo and his wife. Jefferson's informal seating style insulted Merry as a breach of etiquette and an affront to his position. When Madison hosted the Merrys for dinner four days later, the secretary of state escorted to table Hannah Gallatin, the wife of the Treasury secretary, and not Elizabeth Merry. Madison did so, as he reported to Monroe, because the president's "example could not with propriety be violated" (Madison, *Papers, Sec. of State Ser.,* 6:361; TJ to Short, 23 Jan. 1804).

As a widower without a spouse to look after his female guests, Jefferson relied on his cabinet members' wives to fulfill this social role at formal dinners. The Merrys assumed the dinner at the President's House to have been given in their honor. They were shocked to discover that Pichon and his wife were also guests. Merry interpreted the etiquette lapses as a coordinated, premeditated design of administrative shunning. The agitated British minister reported his version of events to his superiors in England, decrying the "absolute Omission of all Distinction." He claimed that his arrival in Washington society became the occasion "to establish Alterations in the Respect and Distinctions—which Foreign Ministers enjoyed here during the Administrations of General Washington and Mr Adams." Upon learning that his usage at social dinners could be misconstrued, Jefferson "from that moment changed it." He decided to discontinue the practice of escorting the wife of one of his secretaries to table and adopted a disorderly mingling of guests without any attention to rank or title, a custom known as "pell-mell" (Merry to Hawkesbury, 6 Dec. 1803, PRO: FO 5/41; Merry to Hawkesbury, 7 Dec. 1803, PRO: FO 5/41; Madison *Papers, Sec. of State Ser.,* 6:361-6, 484-6; TJ to James Monroe, 8 Jan. 1804; TJ to William Short, 23 Jan. 1804).

Madison informed Monroe that although it had been Jefferson's custom "to hand to his table a wife of one of the Secretaries, & not of a foreign Minister, when both were present," the president had done so "without inquiring into the usage of his predecessors, or perhaps under the presumption that it was the same." Madison noted that "the practice of Mr Jefferson had gone on for near three years without a whisper or a suspicion that it was disrelished." With the assistance of Madison, Jefferson began to gather information on precedence during the Washington and Adams administrations. They inquired of Timothy Pickering and John Quincy Adams on past practices. Madison also consulted on the custom in the European courts and queried Rufus King, who had recently returned from his mission in England. The secretary of state shared with the president King's letter of 22 Dec. in response to these queries. Written sometime after this date, Document I reflects Jefferson's abstract of King's response (Madison, *Papers, Sec. of State Ser.*, 6:186-7, 197-9, 361; PMHB, 44 [1920], 331-3).

Merry "wished that the President's decision might be obtained & made known." Merry also enlisted Irujo, who urged Madison to inform the entire diplomatic corps in Washington of current American protocol. Despite his "distaste for such a subject," Jefferson decided to lay out on paper the customs for diplomatic purposes. Also through Madison, Jefferson advised Monroe "to apply an antidote to this poison" and to "lose no opportunity and to spare no pains" to appease the British administration. According to Madison, the president wanted to keep "open for cordial civilities whatever channels the scruples of Master Merry might not have closed" (Madison, *Papers, Sec. of State Ser.*, 6:362, 485).

Documents II and III below are the president's compilations of what he called "Canons of Etiquette." He reduced the issues to two categories, one concerning etiquette of social calls and "first visits," the other relating to "perfect equality" at events such as dinners. He applied this classification to Document II by labeling the items in that list as "a" or "b." He organized Document III on the basis of "these two principles," which hints that he may have written Document III after Document II. His notation "by President Jefferson" at the top of Document II and his endorsement on Document III that "this rough paper contains what was agreed on" indicate that these two undated manuscripts were part of an attempt to codify the administration's official practice. Madison communicated the substance of Jefferson's views on the matter to Merry in a meeting on 12 Jan. 1804 and also informed Irujo, but there is no indication that he handed them a written exposition of protocol (same, 6:362, 461; Merry to Hawkesbury, 30 Jan., PRO: FO 5/41).

As much as Jefferson may have thought that setting the administration's practice down on paper and informing the diplomatic corps would put the matter to rest, newspapers gave it continued life. The *New-York Herald* of 7 Jan. reported that "Mr. Jefferson and his ministers had been closetted nine hours without intermission" prior to the release of this statement of etiquette. The *Gazette of the United States,* on 13 Jan., ran an "Extract of a letter from a gentleman at Washington," mocking Jefferson's and Madison's treatment of the Merrys. Accompanied by a brief header, which asserted that U.S. citizens had "an *unalienable right* to be informed of the etiquette of our court," it queried "what can be Mr. Jefferson's motives for these outrageous insults?" On the following day, the *Aurora* countered with a brief piece that jabbed: "the stupid etiquette of the English monarchy is not pursued in a republic." Writing to William Short on 23 Jan., Jefferson acknowledged, "you will have seen by the newspapers that there is something of etiquette between the diplomatic gentry & us. that there exists such a subject of disagreement is true. but every particular fact respecting it which I have yet seen in any newspaper is false" (Newburyport, Mass., *New-England Repertory*, 14 Jan. 1804; Worcester *Massachusetts Spy*, 18 Jan.; *New-York Herald*, 21 Jan.; *Portsmouth Oracle*, 21 Jan.; *New Haven Visitor*, 26 Jan.; Fredericktown, Md., *Hornet*, 31 Jan.).

Then the *Washington Federalist*, which reprinted the item from the *Gazette of the United States* on 30 Jan., ran an unattributed two-paragraph statement on 1 Feb.:

Etiquette of the Court of the U. States

The President waits on no person. The Vice President only on the President.—Senators of the United States, only on the President and Vice President.—All the officers of government, all public and private characters, natives, or foreigners call on them first, and the President is exempt from the ceremony of returning visits.—their ladies take precedence of all others in the same order. Since the arrival of the British minister and his lady, a difficulty has occurred as to the etiquette proper to be observed in visits of ceremony between foreign ministers and the heads of departments; and as to the right of precedency among their ladies. Each party, especially the ladies, have resisted with no small pertinacity the pretensions of the other, and yet hold out, so as in a great measure to have destroyed all intercourse between them; but it seems now to be settled by order of the President, and by the custom of his table, that the heads of departments and their ladies, shall take rank of all diplomatic characters and their ladies. During the Administrations of Washington and Adams the etiquette that prevailed, and which seems to have been dictated by both necessity and politeness, was that all foreign Ministers should wait on the Secretary of State first, because to him they had to present their credentials, before which they could not be officially known to the government, and by him they were to be presented to the President; but the other Heads of Departments, viz. the Secretary of the Treasury, of the Navy, and of War, without any previous regulation on the subject, governed perhaps by the respect they might think due to the representative of a foreign nation, and from a sentiment of politeness to strangers of the first distinction, were in the habit of visiting foreign ministers first—among their ladies there was certainly never any right of precedency claimed or exercised, the only rivalship when they met, was, which should treat the other with the most respectful and lady-like politeness, not which should take, but which should yield precedency. The Members of the House of Representatives wait on Foreign Ministers, and the Heads of Departments first.

In order to settle forever the point of etiquette that now disturbs our Court, it is recommended that hereafter at all official dinners, the Ladies shall be led into the dining-room according to *seniority, the oldest first*; Maiden Ladies, above seven and twenty to have the privilege, nevertheless of going in when they please, without any questions being asked.

This article piqued Jefferson to offer an uncustomary rebuttal in print (see Document IV). How the president transmitted his corrective to William Duane of the *Aurora* is unknown, but Duane printed the anonymous piece in his paper on 13 Feb. with slight modifications. Although not identified with him by name, this rejoinder to the *Washington Federalist* would be Jefferson's published statement of policy and practice. The sparring in newspapers went on, with Federalist papers widely reprinting the "Etiquette of the Court" and Republican papers circulating Jefferson's anonymous rebuttal (Philadelphia *Aurora*, 13 Feb. 1804; Boston *Repertory*, 14 Feb.; *Albany Centinel*, 17 Feb.; Wilmington *Mirror of the Times*, 18 Feb.; Richmond *Virginia Argus*, 22 Feb.; *Columbian Museum and Savannah Advertiser*, 25 Feb.; Providence *United States Chronicle*, 1 Mch.; Bennington *Vermont Gazette*, 6 Mch.; Charleston *City Gazette*, 9 Mch.; Malone, *Jefferson*, 4:499-500).

Although Elizabeth Merry refused to attend the annual New Year's visitation at the President's House, Jefferson again attempted to reach out to Anthony Merry by inviting him to a private dinner party "en famille" in early February. The British minister sent his regrets to the secretary of state on 9 Feb. rather than to the president directly. Merry explained that he could not accept an invitation in his private capacity without sacrificing his duty to the king in "Consideration of his public Character." He would decline further invitations until he received instructions from his government on what diplomatic distinctions were his due. Jefferson extended no further invitations to the British couple, who entered a self-imposed social exile. Even when Merry received a dispatch instructing him to conform to local practice in Jefferson's company, he held out for an apology, which was not forthcoming, and never dined at the President's House again for the remainder of his residence in the United States (Madison, *Papers, Sec. of State Ser.*, 6:460-2; Joel Larus, "Pell-Mell Along the Potomac," wmq, 3d ser., 17 [1960], 355-7; Merry to Hawkesbury, 31 Dec. 1803, PRO: FO 5/41).

For more about the Merry affair and its significance, see, in addition to the sources cited above, Henry Adams, *History of the United States of America During the First Administration of Thomas Jefferson*, 2 vols. (New York, 1889), 2:367-76; Catherine Allgor, *Parlor Politics: In which the Ladies of Washington Help Build a City and a Government* (Charlottesville, 2000), 35-40; Irving Brant, *James Madison*, 6 vols. (Indianapolis, 1941-61), 4:162-8; Cynthia D. Earman, "Remembering the Ladies: Women, Etiquette, and Diversions in Washington City, 1800-1814," *Washington History*, 12 (2000), 109-11; Malcolm Lester, *Anthony Merry Redivivus: A Reappraisal of the British Minister to the United States, 1803-6* (Charlottesville, 1978).

I. Notes on Diplomatic Etiquette in England

[after 22 Dec. 1803]

Mr. King to mr Madison. N.Y. Dec. 22. 1803.

1. all foreign ministers pay the 1st. visit to the ministers of Engld. by going in their carriage & leaving a card without asking[1] for them. this visit is rarely if ever returned.
2. foreign ministers nor their wives never invited to Queen's balls, concerts, parties. the king gives none.

at king's levee forn. & domest. ministers, dignifd clergy, Ld. Chancr. Judges assemble in a room adjact to K's bedroom. others in outer room. when his door opens, for. min. go in first, & are spoke to first. the residue enter pell-mell.

for. min. have little intercourse with other ministers except of forn. affrs.

Min. for. affrs. gives 2. diplom. dinners a year, viz. on K's and Q's birthdays. corps diplomat. without thr wives, & the secrets.[2] of hs deptmt invitd. no other persons invited. dinner servd. at 6. P.M. ends between 8. & 9. by the Min. for. affrs. retirg to his cabinet.

for. min. and domest. min. having family society, their intercourse on same footing as among people of fashn. of the country

in the house of a forn. min. precedce. given to the Eng. Min. & vice versâ in house of Eng. min. subject however in the houses of the English to a preference given to hereditary titles, national or foreign.

3. Wives of for. Min. have no precedence of the women of the country at the Queen's drawing room.

but they are placed with their husbands in the K's chapel on a marriage of one of the Royal family

they recieve the first visit from the wives of the Eng. min. as from all others, & as all other strangers forn. or domest. do.

in society persons of title, English or forn. take precedce. of wives of for. min. who are without title

e.g. at the dinners of the Ld. Chamberlain, at dinners of Min. of forn affrs. but where no lady of title is present the wife of a forn. min. wd from the courtesy shewn to strangers, recieve precedce.

on the continent, the gentlemen conduct the ladies from the drawg room to the Ding. room.

not so in higher English circles. there the ladies all go first, the highest taking lead. gentlemen follow

the English value etiquette little, only as a guard to keep off impertinence, conciet, & rudeness.

they live very little with the corps diplomatique, few foreigners travel, & none reside there.

MS (DLC: TJ Papers, 136:23651); entirely in TJ's hand; endorsed by TJ.

On 18 Dec., Madison wrote to Rufus KING with three questions on "usage abroad, particularly in England." Morti-
fied that he had to trouble King on a subject "unworthy the attention of either of us," Madison made three queries: "1. On the arrival of a foreign Minister, is the first visit paid by him or the Ministers of the Country? 2. To which is the prece-

dence given in scenes of a more public ceremony, and of ordinary hospitalities? 3. Is the order of attention precisely the same in the case of ladies, as of their husbands?" Madison concluded that "our wish would be to unfetter social intercourse as well as public business, as much as possible from ceremonious clogs, by substituting the pell mell." He believed it "proper" that the United States not lag behind other nations in civility or self-respect and that it be aware of "the manner in which other nations respect both us & themselves." King lost no time in writing on 22 Dec., which Madison passed along to the president. King enumerated responses to each of Madison's questions. He added a postscript: "The wives of foreign Ministers receive the first visit from the wives of the Eng. ministers: differing in this from the Course observed by their husbands." The document printed above is TJ's abstract of King's answers. TJ did not transcribe the postscript, but incorporated it into his notes on the third question (King to Madison, 22 Dec., in DLC; Madison, *Papers, Sec. of State Ser.,* 6:186-7, 197-9).

[1] Word interlined in place of "calling."
[2] That is, "secretaries."

II. Canons of Etiquette

[before 12 Jan. 1804?]

Canons of Etiquette to be observed by the Executive.

1. Foreign ministers arriving at the seat of government pay the first visit to the ministers of the nation, which is returned: and so likewise on subsequent occasions of reassembling after a recess.

2. The families of foreign ministers recieve the 1st. visit from those of the National ministers, as from all other residents and as all strangers, foreign or domestic, do from all residents of the place.

3. after the 1st. visit the character of Stranger ceases.[1]

4. Among the members of the Diplomatic corps, the Executive government on it's own principles of personal & national equality, considers every minister as the representative of his nation, and equal to every other, without distinction of grade.

5. No titles being admitted here, those of foreigners give no precedence.

6. Our ministers to foreign nations are as private citizens while here.

7. At any public ceremony to which the government invites the presence of foreign ministers and their families,[2] no precedence or privilege will be given them, other than the provision of a convenient seat or station, with any other strangers invited, and with the families of the national ministers.

8. At dinners in public or private, and on all other occasions of social intercourse, a perfect equality exists between the persons composing the company, whether foreign or domestic, titled or untitled, in or out of office.

9. To give force to the principle of equality, or pêle mêle, & prevent the growth of precedence out of courtesy, the members of the Executive, at their own houses, will adhere to the antient[3] usage of their nation,[4] gentlemen in mass giving precedence to the ladies in mass.

10. The President of the US. recieves visits, but does not return them.[5]

11. The family of the President recieves the 1st. visit and returns it.

12. The Presidents family in public or private

13. The President, when in any state, recieves the 1st. visit of the Governor and returns it.

14. The Governor of a state, in his state recieves the 1st. visit from foreign ministers

The Legislative and Judiciary branches being co-ordinate with the Executive, this last does not assume to lay down rules for them, but expressly declares the preceding not to affect them in any wise.[6]

MS (DLC: TJ Papers, 137:23714); undated; entirely in TJ's hand; at head of text added later by TJ (and not on PrC): "by President Jefferson"; endorsed by TJ: "Etiquette." PrC (same, 233:41636); with additions in ink by TJ, including diagonal strokes through items 1-5, 7-9, and the unnumbered final sentence of the document; he also added in ink an "a" in the margin alongside each item 1-3 and a "b" alongside each item 4-5 and 7-9; for his other additions in ink, see notes 5 and 6 below.

[1] TJ interlined this sentence, which required him to renumber the next four items in the list. He then continued writing with item 8. He made these changes before he made the PrC.

[2] Preceding three words interlined.

[3] Word interlined.

[4] Above this word TJ interlined "ancestors" without canceling the original word.

[5] In ink on PrC TJ added a comma and "except to the Vice President and a governor of a state."

[6] In ink on PrC TJ added: "independant of their offices, the usage of the country entitles them as strangers to the first visit from residents."

III. Memorandum on Official Etiquette

[before 12 Jan. 1804?]

In order to bring the members of society together in the first instance the custom of the country has established that the residents[1] shall pay the 1st. visit to strangers, & among strangers first comers to[2] later comers, foreign & domestic;[3]

When brought together in society all[4] are perfectly equal, whether foreign or domestic, titled or untitled, in or out of office.

To the 1st. rule there is a single exception. foreign ministers,[5] pay the first visit to the ministers of the nation: which is returned.[6]

All other observances are but exemplifications of these two principles.[7] e.g.

1. The families of foreign ministers arriving at the seat of government[8] recieve the first visit from those of the National ministers, as from all other residents.

3. No titles being admitted here, those of foreigners give no precedence.

4. Difference of grade among the diplomatic members[9] gives no precedence.

2. Members of the Legislature & of the Judiciary, independant of their offices, have a right as strangers to recieve the first visit.

5. At public ceremonies to which the government invites the presence of foreign ministers & their families, a convenient seat or station, will be provided for them with any other strangers invited, & the families of the national ministers, each taking place as they arrive, & without any precedence.

6. To maintain[10] the principle of equality, or pêle mêle, and prevent the growth of precedence out of courtesy, the members of the Executive will practise at their own houses & recommend, an adherence to the antient usage of the country, of gentlemen in mass giving precedence to the ladies in mass in passing from one apartment where they are assembled, into another.

Dft (DLC: TJ Papers, 233:41634); undated; entirely in TJ's hand; TJ drew diagonal strokes through the "observances" that he numbered 4, 2, and 6; endorsed: "Etiquette. this rough paper contains what was agreed on."

[1] TJ here canceled "or first comers."
[2] Preceding ampersand and five words interlined in place of "or."
[3] TJ here canceled "the character of stranger ceasing after the first visits."
[4] TJ first wrote "When brought together, it is a principle that all the members making part of a company" before altering the clause to read as above.

[5] TJ first wrote, "There is one exception to 1st. rule. in the case of foreign ministers, who, from the necessity of making themselves known, and from the usage of all nations" before altering the passage to read as above.
[6] TJ first wrote "which visit, here, is returned."
[7] TJ first wrote "principal rules" before altering the text to read as above.
[8] Preceding six words interlined.
[9] TJ first wrote "among the members of the diplomatic corps."
[10] Word interlined in place of "give force to."

IV. Response to the *Washington Federalist*

[before 13 Feb. 1804]

The Washington Federalist[1] of the 1st. inst. has published what he calls the 'Etiquette of the court of the US.' in his facts, as usual, truth is set at nought, & in his principles little correct to be found. the Editor having seen a great deal of unfounded stuff on this subject, in that & other papers of a party whose first wish it is to excite misunderstandings with other nations, (even with England, if they cannot with Spain or France), has taken pains to inform himself of the rules of social intercourse at Washington, and he assures his readers that they may rely on the correctness of the following statement[2] of them.

In the first place there is no 'court of the US' since the 4th. of Mar. 1801. that day buried levees, birthdays, royal parades,[3] and the arrogation of precedence in society by certain self-stiled friends of order, but truly stiled friends of privileged orders.

The President recieves but does not return visits, except to the Vice-President.

The Vice-President pays the 1st. visit to the President, but recieves it from all others, and returns it.

Foreign ministers pay the 1st. visit here, as in all other countries, to all the Secretaries, heads of department.

The Secretaries return visits of the members of the legislature & foreign ministers, but not of others; not from any principle of inequality, but from the pressure of their official duties, which do not admit such a disposal of their time.

No distinction is admitted between Senators & Representatives. that pretension of certain would-be Nobles was buried in the grave of federalism, on the same 4th. of March. the members of both houses & the domestic ministers interchange visits according to convenience, without claims of priority.

Members of both houses & foreign ministers also interchange visits, according to convenience & inclination; no intercourse between them being considered as necessary or due. were it necessary, the former, as newcomers, might claim the 1st. visit from the latter as residents, according to the American & English principle.

In social circles all are equal, whether in, or out, of office, foreign or domestic; & the same equality exists among ladies as among gentlemen. no precedence therefore, of any one over another, exists either in right or practice, at dinners, assemblies, or on any other occasions. 'pell-mell' and 'next the door' form the basis of etiquette in the societies of this country. it is this last principle, maintained by the administration, which has produced some dissatisfaction with some of the diplomatic gentlemen. not that they question the right of every nation to establish, or alter, it's own rules of intercourse, nor consequently our right to obliterate any germs of a distinction of ranks, forbidden by our constitution: but that it is a part of their duty to be watchful for the relative standing of their nation, and to acquiesce only so soon as they see that nothing derogatory of that is contemplated.

MS (DLC: TJ Papers, 111:19124); entirely in TJ's hand; undated. PrC (same, 233:41635). Printed with minor alterations in Philadelphia *Aurora*, 13 Feb. 1804.

[1] In the *Aurora* the sentence begins "*Etiquette*—The conductor of the Washington Federalist."

[2] TJ first wrote "state," then interlined "-ment."

[3] *Aurora* adds: "processions with white wands."

To Andrew Ellicott

DEAR SIR   Washington Dec. 23. 03.

I recieved last night your favor of Dec. 17. as I had before done that of Dec. 5. I find nothing surprising in the raining of stones in France, nor yet had they been mill-stones. there are in France more real philosophers than in any country on earth: but there are also a greater proportion of pseudo-philosophers there. the reason is that the exuberant imagination of a Frenchman gives him a greater facility of writing, & runs away with his judgment unless he has a good stock of it. it even creates facts for him which never happened, and he tells them with good faith. Count Rumford after discovering cold to be a positive body will doubtless find out that darkness is so too. as many as two or three times during my seven years residence in France, new discoveries were made which overset the whole Newtonian philosophy; two or three examples happened of spontaneous combustion of the living human body, of houses &c. in all these cases the evidence of nature, derived from experience, must be put into one scale, and in the other the testimony of man, his ignorance, the deception of his senses, his lying disposition &c. and we must see which preponderates.

I expect to be authorised by Congress to explore and ascertain accurately the geography of the great rivers running into the Missisipi & Missouri, in order to fix their course & their sources, because their sources are the points which give the contour of what will now be the US. and having these & the whole course of the great rivers taken astronomically we have an accurate outline & skeleton which can be filled up with details hereafter. I should think of one party to go up the red river, & from the source of that to the source of the Arkansa, & down that. another up the Padoucas & down the Panis &c. I should consequently want 2 or 3. such men as Capt. Lewis at about 4. or 5. D. a day: perfectly equal to take the observations of longitude & latitude, & otherwise well qualified. if in your travels you have had experience of such characters, I will thank you to inform me of them. Accept my friendly salutations & assurances of esteem.

TH: JEFFERSON

RC (DLC: Ellicott Papers); addressed: "Andrew Ellicott esq. Lancaster"; franked; postmarked 22 Dec. PrC (DLC).

FAVOR OF DEC. 17: that is, Ellicott to TJ, 19 Dec.

THAT OF DEC. 5: Ellicott to TJ, 1 Dec.

To John Page

DEAR SIR   Washington Dec. 23. 03.

Your favor of Nov. 16. recieved Nov. 26. is now before me and I inclose you a letter of mr Gore, which I presume we may consider as the final result of our endeavor to procure an asylum in the colony of Sierra Leone for such persons of the description composing that colony as we might find it expedient to send there.

Since the date of the resolution which has been the subject of this correspondence, the aspect of affairs in St. Domingo has undergone important changes. you can judge of the probability of their settling down in a form which may furnish that opening which the resolution desired. as yet however direct propositions for that purpose would be premature.

The acquisition of Louisiana, may also procure the opportunity desired. this will depend on the manner in which the legislature of the Union will dispose of that country. an expectation of some decision as to this had induced me to delay answering your letter earlier: but no progress being yet made in it, and a fear that the legislature of Virginia might rise before definitive arrangements are taken here, I do not venture on a further delay.

On the whole it appears probable that St. Domingo or Louisiana may open to the legislature of Virginia the recourse which their resolution contemplates.

Accept my affectionate salutations and assurances of great consideration and respect.

TH: JEFFERSON

PrC (DLC); at foot of text: "Governor Page." Enclosure: see below.

TJ was enclosing a letter of 10 Oct. 1802 from Christopher GORE, who, as acting chargé d'affaires to Great Britain, fielded TJ's query about the possibility of settling freed and rebellious American slaves in Sierra Leone. TJ had been prompted by a RESOLUTION of the Virginia General Assembly calling for such an asylum (Vol. 38:54-7, 473-6).

ST. DOMINGO HAS UNDERGONE IMPORTANT CHANGES: revolutionary forces in Saint-Domingue, under the overall leadership of Jean Jacques Dessalines, forced the final evacuation of French troops from the colony in early December 1803. On 1 Jan. 1804, Dessalines and his generals formally proclaimed their independence from France, naming their new country Haiti. The French, however, maintained nominal authority over the eastern, formerly Spanish, portion of Hispaniola, where they continued to occupy the port city of Santo Domingo (Gordon S. Brown, *Toussaint's Clause: The Founding Fathers and the Haitian Revolution* [Jackson, Miss., 2005], 227-31; Philippe R. Girard, *The Slaves Who Defeated Napoléon: Toussaint Louverture and the Haitian War of Independence, 1801-1804* [Tuscaloosa, Ala., 2011], 307-16; Boisrond Tonnerre, *Mémoires pour servir à l'histoire d'Haïti* [Port-au-Prince, Haiti, 1981], 1-8; Vol. 40:598-9n).

To John Bradford

Washington Dec. 24. 03.

Th: Jefferson presents his salutations to mr Bradford and returns him thanks for the specimen of rock-salt from the Missouri which he has been so kind as to send him, and which came safely to hand.

PrC (DLC); endorsed by TJ in ink on verso.

SPECIMEN OF ROCK-SALT: see Bradford to TJ, 29 Nov.

From Arthur Fenner

SIR   Providence Decmr 24th 1803

The bearer of this Mr Robert Sterry a Native of Providence decended from two respectable Families in this State He has received a Clasical Education and been regularly trained to the Bar—Literature has ever been his Amusement and the Days of his Youth in its pursuits among Books

History has been his favorit studies—He is twenty one Years of Age has tallents and Perseverance and I think will make a Respectable figure in his Profession—Not confined to no spot or place his Mind imbrace the Interest of his Country and Mankind—

His Talents may be useful to his Country He has chosen[1] New Orleans for his place of Professional residence—He is now on his way there Any aid that is given will be considered by me as giving aid to Tallents which I believe may be useful to his Country

I am with great esteem and Friendship Your Coleague in Abuse

A FENNER

RC (DNA: RG 59, LAR); at foot of text: "President United States"; endorsed by TJ as received 27 Feb. 1804 and so recorded in SJL with notation "Sterry"; also endorsed by TJ: "Sterry Robt. emploimt N.O." Enclosed in Christopher Ellery to TJ, 27 Feb. 1804.

ROBERT STERRY graduated from the College of Rhode Island and was admit-ted to the Rhode Island bar before moving to New Orleans. In 1805, he mortally wounded the brother-in-law of William C. C. Claiborne in a duel (Boston *New-England Palladium*, 18 Oct. 1803; *Poulson's American Daily Advertiser*, 25 Mch. 1805; *Boston Daily Advertiser*, 31 Jan. 1820).

[1] MS: "cohesen."

From Kuhn, Green & Co.

RESPECTED SIR, Genoa 24th Decr. 1803

We were commissioned by our esteemed friend, Stephen Caithalan Junr. Esqr. of Marseilles, to procure for your Excellency 50 ℔s. *Naples Maccaroni*, and 50 ℔s. *Pates de Genes*—which gains us the honor to inform you, of their being shipped on board the American Schooner Aurora Capt. Hammond, bound for New York, in the best possible order, and of the very first quality—to the address and care of Thomas Storm Esqr., Father of our T. H. Storm, of that place—who will use every exertion, on their arrival to have them, forwarded with first opportunity to Washington, or where, your Excellency may please direct.—

We shall allways feel highly honor'd by your direct commands for any articles of Italian growth or Manufacture, and as at Genoa, they are to be procured with the greatest facility, and of prime qualities, we beg you will make use of us, when occasions offer.

We also beg leave to assure you of our frequent prayers, for your long continuance, in the high office you now hold and fill with such Wisdom Utility & Honor—

We are with due respect Yr Excellencys Most Obt He Servts for Kuhn Green & Compy, T H STORM

RC (DLC); at head of text: "His Excellency Thomas Jefferson, Presdt. of the U.S. America"; endorsed by TJ as received 9 Apr. 1804 and so recorded in SJL.

Kuhn, Green & Co., was the partnership formed early in 1803 by three young American merchants: Peter Kuhn, Jr., Hugh Green, and Thomas H. Storm, who in addition to their commercial connec-tion were bound together through marriages to respective siblings. Green ran the firm's Gibraltar house, while Kuhn and Storm worked mostly in Genoa (New York *Mercantile Advertiser*, 13 Jan. 1803; New York *Commercial Advertiser*, 6 Apr. 1803; Vol. 38:641n; Peter Kuhn, Sr., to TJ, 6 Dec.; Thomas Storm to TJ, 12 Nov. 1804).

For TJ's order from Stephen Cathalan, see Vol. 39:470 and Vol. 40:457.

To William Marshall

Washington Dec. 24. 03.

Th: Jefferson presents his respectful salutations to mr Marshall and his thanks for the Chart of the coast of Florida, & mouth of the Missisipi which he has been so good as to send him. at a time when we are endeavoring to acquire exact knolege of that country, in order to make our first arrangements understandingly, so accurate a chart whose existence was not before known here, is doubly precious, and may render mr Marshall's kind attention really useful to the public

PrC (DLC); endorsed by TJ in ink on verso. THANKS FOR THE CHART: see Marshall to TJ, 29 Oct.

To J. P. G. Muhlenberg

DEAR SIR   Washington Dec. 24. 03.

Having reason to believe that a butt of Sherry wine sent to me from Cadiz by the Eliza Capt Bisell, has been, or will be landed, at Philadelphia, to your care, I ask the favor of you to reship it to Richmond to the address of messrs. Gibson & Jefferson of that place. all duties & charges shall be paid as soon as you will be so good as to make them known to me. the uncertainty to what port persons in foreign parts may find a conveyance for articles sent me, has obliged me to ask the favor of the Collectors generally to recieve & forward them for me. it is this circumstance which has repeated and may still repeat this kind of trouble to you & which demands my apology. Accept my friendly salutations & assurances of great esteem.

TH: JEFFERSON

RC (facsimile in Remember When Auctions, Inc., Wells, Maine, catalog for sale of 12 Mch. 1998, lot 1280); addressed: "Genl. Muhlenberg"; franked and postmarked. PrC (MHi); endorsed by TJ in ink on verso. HAVING REASON TO BELIEVE: TJ received a communication from Joseph Yznardi, Sr., about his sherry order on 22 Dec. (Vol. 41:596-7).

From Thomas Mann Randolph

DEAR SIR,   Edgehill Dec. 24. 1803.

I have been today to see your Mill & Canal. The river being uncommonly full afforded an opportunity to judge what work is yet wanting for the complete introduction of its water to the Wheel at all times. What I saw and judged I cannot refrain from communicating as I mentioned rather inconsiderately[1] the report of the neighbourhood in my last, as unfavorable as it was, and as likely to be incorrect. The current does not enter the Canal at all, for the first water which goes in receiving a check immediately from the narrowness & curvature of the channell and the unevenness of the sides becomes still and the current afterwards passes wholly by, not inclining in the least towards the Canals mouth. It is manifest that this must be completely remedied by the extension of the little jettee at the mouth and the throwing out another on the opposite side above: the main current must then get directly in the Canal. By the accounts of some, the Canal begins to have water in it when the river has risen about six inches above the state next to the lowest, which was its condition three days since. The water does not till it has continued to rise a short time perhaps till it has risen one foot higher, get well down to the mill. There are two places in its bottom too high; they are both between the middle point and the bridge and both in the part where the earth has been thrown from the greatest depth; where the long job of blowing last fall was done: some say neither of these elevations extends farther than four or five yards: Lillie believes not more than 10 or 12 feet. From the last of these there is a rapid current down to the mill at which the present state of the river would give a head as high as the eaves, all admitt, if the bank had not given way 300 yards above. The wheel begins to be completely submerged about the time the last rock in the ford from Shadwell to Monticello is covered. It is believed that it would turn with rapidity sufficient to grind well when covered 12 inches. The Jettees, a mere trifle of blowing and the increase of the bank about the forebay and at one place above, seem to be all the work wanting to make it the best Mill in the County. At present the water runs back into the river when it falls from the obstructions I mention & shews no current from the bend near the entrance to that place. The Wheel has been set in motion today & moved with great velocity when 4 inches covered. Lillie was determined to grind some grain before night—The N. orleans news Mr Eppes and myself return thanks for. The Ladies and all the children are perfectly well.

With sincere attachment   Th: M. Randolph

RC (ViU: Edgehill-Randolph Papers); addressed: "Thomas Jefferson President U.S. Washington"; endorsed by TJ as received 29 Dec. and so recorded in SJL.

MY LAST: Randolph to TJ, 17 Dec., recorded in SJL as received 19 Dec. but not found. TJ conveyed New Orleans NEWS in his letter of 19 Dec.

[1] Preceding two words interlined.

From Philip Spencer, Jr., and Joseph C. Field

SIR   Washington 24th. Decr. 1803

Having made choice of New Orleans as the place of our future residence, And being desirous of appointments to Office in that City,—We have taken the liberty of submitting our names and pretensions to your consideration, and with that view enclose a certificate from the Gentlemen representing the State of New York in the Senate of the United States   The offices we more particularly sollicit are those of Surveyor of the Port, and Marshall of the District Court.—the former for the underwritten P. Spencer jr.—the latter for J. C. Field.

With the highest consideration, We are Sir, Your most Obedt. Servants   PHILIP SPENCER JR

                                          JOSEPH C. FIELD

RC (DNA: RG 59, LAR); in Spencer's hand, signed by Spencer and Field; at foot of text: "the President"; endorsed by TJ as received 2 Jan. 1804 and so recorded in SJL; also endorsed by TJ: "Field Joseph C. to be Marshal of Louisiana Spencer Philip jr. to be Surveyor N.O." Enclosure: Certificate of John Armstrong and Theodorus Bailey, Washington, 23 Dec., stating that they have known Spencer and Field for "some years" and identifying Spencer as an attorney and Field as a farmer and justice of the peace; Armstrong and Bailey believe them to be "men of good standing, useful talents and sound political principles" (same).

Philip Spencer, Jr. (1763-1817), and Joseph C. Field (1768-1813) were brothers-in-law from Dutchess County, New York. Spencer was also the older brother of New York jurist and future congressman Ambrose Spencer. In their public careers, both served in the state legislature and held several local offices, with Spencer appointed county clerk three times and Field serving as county sheriff twice and as a local postmaster. Spencer went on to acquire a highly unsavory reputation. In 1814, he was accused of arson, and his reappointment as county clerk the following year was so unpopular that he was forced to resign. In October 1816, it was reported that he had secured ownership of some 70 convict slaves from the state prison and shipped them to Louisiana, where he died of typhus the following year (Frank Hasbrouck, ed., *The History of Dutchess County, New York* [Poughkeepsie, 1909], 73, 78; Frederick Clifton Pierce, *Field Genealogy*, 2 vols. [Chicago, 1901], 1:378-9; Nathaniel Goodwin, *Genealogical Notes, or Contributions to the Family History of Some of the First Settlers of Connecticut and Massachusetts* [Hartford, Conn., 1856], 318, 321; *Biog. Dir. Cong.*; Stets, *Postmasters*, 189; New York *Evening Post*, 2 Sep. 1814, 20, 21 Mch. 1815, 21 Oct. 1816, 9 Mch. 1821; *Albany Register*, 7 July 1815; *Boston Daily Advertiser*, 4 Jan. 1817; *Albany Gazette*, 22 Dec. 1817; Vol. 38:502n).

To the Tennessee General Assembly

Admist the anxieties which are felt for the favorable issue of measures adopted for promoting the public good, it is a consolation to meet the approbation of those on whose behalf they are instituted. I shall certainly endeavor to merit a continuance of the good opinion which the legislature of Tennessee have been pleased to express, in their address of the 8th of November, by a zealous attention to the interests of my constituents: and shall count on a candid indulgence whenever untoward events may happen to disappoint well founded expectations.

In availing our Western brethren of those circumstances which occur for promoting their interests, we only perform that duty which we owe to every portion of the Union, under occurrences equally favorable. and, impressed with the inconveniencies to which the citizens of Tenissee are subjected by a want of contiguity in the portions composing their state, I shall be ready to do for their relief, whatever the General legislature may authorise, & justice to our neighbors permit.

The acquisition of Louisiana, altho' more immediately beneficial to the Western states, by securing for their produce a certain market, not subject to interruption by officers over whom we have no controul, yet is also deeply interesting to the Maritime portion of our country, inasmuch as by giving the exclusive navigation of the Missisipi, it avoids the burthens & sufferings of a war, which conflicting interests on that river would inevitably have produced, at no distant period. it opens too a fertile region for the future establishment of their descendants in the progress of that multiplication so rapidly taking place in all parts.

I have seen with great satisfaction the promptitude with which the first portions of your militia repaired to the standard of their country. it was deemed best to provide a force equal to any event which might arise out of the transaction, & especially to the preservation of order, among our newly associated brethren in the first moments of their transition from one authority to another.

I tender to the legislature of Tenissee assurances of my high respect & consideration.   TH: JEFFERSON
                                                     December 24. 1803.

PrC (DLC).

To Mary Jefferson Eppes

Washington Dec. 26. 03.

I now return you, my dearest Maria, the paper which you lent me for mr Page, and which he has returned some days since. I have prevailed on Doctr. Priestly to undertake the work of which this is only the syllabus or plan. he says he can accomplish it in the course of a year. but in truth his health is so much impaired, and his body become so feeble, that there is reason to fear he will not live out even the short term he has asked for it. you may inform mr Eppes and mr Randolph that no mail arrived the last night from the Natchez. I presume the great rains which have fallen have rendered some of the watercourses impassable. on New year's day however we shall hear of the delivery of New Orleans to us. till then the legislature seem disposed to do nothing but meet & adjourn. mrs Livingston, formerly the younger miss Allen, made kind enquiries after you the other day. she said she was at school with you at mrs Pine's.   Not knowing the time destined for your expected indisposition, I am anxious on your account. you are prepared to meet it with courage I hope. some female friend of your Mama's (I forget who) used to say it was no more than a knock of the elbow. the material thing is to have scientific aid in readiness, that if any thing uncommon takes place, it may be redressed on the spot, and not be made serious by delay. it is a case which least of all will wait for Doctors *to be sent for*. therefore, with this single precaution, nothing is ever to be feared. I was in hopes to have heard from Edgehill last night, but I suppose your post has failed. I shall expect to see the gentlemen here next Sunday night, to take part in the Gala of Monday. give my tenderest love to your sister of whom I have not heard for a fortnight; and my affectionate salutations to the Gentlemen & young ones. continue to love me yourself and to be assured of my warmest affections.

RC (DLC); addressed: "Mrs. Eppes Edgehill near Milton"; franked. Enclosure: see below.

THE PAPER WHICH YOU LENT ME: TJ originally sent a copy of his SYLLABUS on the philosophy of Jesus to his daughter on 25 Apr. 1803. He borrowed it from her to lend to John Page, who returned it in his letter to TJ of 16 Nov.

Mary Masters Allen LIVINGSTON, the youngest of the three daughters of James and Elizabeth Allen of Philadelphia, was the wife of New York congressman

Henry W. Livingston. She and her husband were dinner guests at the President's House on 23 Dec. (PMHB, 9 [1885], 179; Anne Hollingsworth Wharton, *Social Life in the Early Republic* [Philadelphia, 1902], 30-1; Vol. 41:545, 550n).

In 1791-92, Mary Jefferson attended a boarding SCHOOL in Philadelphia run by Mary Pine, widow of artist Robert Edge Pine (Vol. 22:233n, 294).

Because New Year's Day fell on a Sunday, the annual GALA at the President's House occurred on MONDAY, 2 Jan. 1804. Samuel L. Mitchill described the event as "neither so numerous and splendid as on last new years day." Cabinet secretaries and their wives, members of Congress, some foreign envoys, military and naval officers, and local residents gathered to "make the congratulations of the day at Mr. Jefferson's" and celebrated with a "fine band of Musick" and a sideboard laden with cake and punch (Samuel L. Mitchill to Catharine Mitchill, 3 Jan. 1804, in NNMus; *National Intelligencer*, 4 Jan. 1804).

From William Hardy

Sir   New York Decr. 26. 1803

Urged by the calls of pressing necessity I am induced (tho reluctantly) to address your Excellency; Having Spent the best years and prime of life, and my Son having Spent his youth in the service of our common Country during the Season of Revolution, and being now fast declining in the vale of years, reduced from easy circumstances to financs too limited to afford (me & an amiable beloved Daughter, who is Still depending on me & Son for Support) a suitable Subsistance

I take the liberty of Soliciting a situation under the Goverment of the Union in New orleans. In the organization of our newly acquired Territory, a considerable number of Offices will necessarily be created, in the distribution of which Should your Excellency think proper to confer one on me, and one on my Son we Should with everlasting gratitude accept of them, and we would I flatter myself, Render full Satisfaction, in the fulfilment of the duties required, beg leave to refer your Excellency to Dor. Mitchell of this City in Congress, who will inform you of our pretensions to the patronage of a Country in the toils of Emancipating we have borne our full Share; But who am I addressing on this momentous accasion; (oh happy land that is bless'd with a ruler disposed to promote individual happiness when consistant with the public good)

Let my partiality (my good Sir), apologise for saying friend of the people, the protector of the rights of man, the promoter of just merit, the Rewarder of Revolutionary claims & the true friend of republicanism

Hoping your Excellency will pardon this Effusion of my sentiments, and receive them as expressive of my principles, as also of the confidence with which, I rely on your excellency's goodnes, to whome I submit, and most courtiouly crave the listning eare, and notice of your excellency to our Pretensions, and hope, & beleive, I will not ask, and solicit your Excellencys patronage in vain

with sentiments of the highest esteem & respect I remain your excellencys, most, Obidient & most Humble Servant   Wm Hardy

RC (DNA: RG 59, LAR); at head of text: "His Excellency Thomas Jefferson Esqr"; endorsed by TJ as received 29 Dec. and so recorded in SJL and connected by a brace with entries for letters received the same day from Stephen Perkins of 14 Dec. and William Stark of 19 Dec. with notation "emploimt. Louisiana"; also endorsed by TJ: "emploimt. in Louisa. for himself & son."

A merchant and veteran of the American Revolution originally from Philadelphia, William Hardy (ca. 1725-1810) was wounded at the battle of Princeton and later served as a regimental paymaster. His son, Joseph, served as a captain of marines during the war. During the 1780s, William acted briefly as a commissioner to destroy old Continental currency, but failed in later attempts to secure a federal position. Both William and Joseph applied to TJ for employment in 1801 without success, nor would either man receive a Louisiana appointment (*Longworth's American Almanac, New-York Register, and City-Directory, for the Twenty-Eighth Year of American Independence* [New York, 1803], 164; petition of William and Joseph Hardy, undated, received 11 Sep. 1781, in DNA: RG 360, PCC; Washington, *Papers, Pres. Ser.*, 2:438-9; 3:220; Syrett, *Hamilton*, 16:76-7; memorial of William Hardy, 10 Jan. 1809, in DNA: RG 46, LPPMRSL; JHR, 6:495; New York *Columbian*, 16 Apr. 1810; Vol. 33:95-6, 320-1).

From Hugh Holmes

Richmond Decr. 26th. 1803

Hh. Holmes returns his respects to President Jefferson and acknowledges with gratitude the reciept of the Parliamentary Manual which the Presdt. was so good as to enclose to him p. post. for his friendly salutations Hh H begs the Prest. to accept his sincere thanks & the compliments of Season

RC (DLC); endorsed by TJ as received 31 Dec. and so recorded in SJL.

MANUAL: see TJ to Holmes, 22 Dec.

From George Jefferson

DEAR SIR   Richmond 26th. Decr. 1803

The note alluded to in your favor of the 20th. was presented to me for payment on the 16th. instant when it became due; as I concluded it had for the moment escaped your recollection, and that you would place funds in our hands in the course of a few days to retire it, I took it up.

You may however consult your own convenience in reimbursing us, as we have no occasion whatever at this time for money.—these I assure you are not mere words of course, & written with the view to your accommodation only—but are literally true; for we do not wish during the present portentous state of affairs in Europe, which may produce we know not what changes here, to risk more than we already have at stake: preferring total idleness of our time & funds, to doing business which may turn out to be even worse than none.

I find that eleven boxes of yours, with some other things were forwarded by Mr. Peytons waggon on the 20th. of October—amongst these I conclude were the window glass & table-china, and which *I suppose* were forwarded without your former letter upon the subject being adverted to.

I am Dear Sir Your Very humble servt.   GEO. JEFFERSON

RC (MHi); at foot of text: "Thos. Jefferson esqr."; endorsed by TJ as received 30 Dec. and so recorded in SJL.

To Elizabeth Leathes Merry

Washington Dec. 26. 03.

Th Jefferson presents his respects to Mrs. Merry, and sends her a few seeds of the Dionaea muscipula, or Flytrap, so much celebrated as holding the middle ground between the animal & vegetable orders. tho' a native of Carolina, this is the first he has been able to recieve after a course of six years efforts & all the interest he could make there. he recieved it the last night by post & sends mrs Merry the half of what he recieved. the plant will be best in pots because it will need some shelter in winter.

RC (C. N. McLean, Binghamton, New York, 1947). Not recorded in SJL.

Elizabeth Death Leathes Merry (d. 1824), a wealthy widow, became the wife of career diplomat Anthony Merry on 21 Jan. 1803. Soon thereafter, her husband learned of his appointment as British minister to the United States. In late November, the couple arrived in Washington with a large retinue of servants and luggage and resided at the three-story brick British legation on the south side of K Street. Aaron Burr remarked that the intelligent Englishwoman, who had lived in Paris and whose acquaintance he wished his daughter to make, was "tall, fair, fat," but full of grace, dignity, and sprightliness. Margaret Bayard Smith described her as "so entirely the talker and actor in all companies that her good husband passes quite unnoticed." She had "at times overbearing spirits," commented Augus-tus John Foster, the secretary to the British legation: "Think of a fine woman accustomed to adulation." Manasseh Cutler reported that Elizabeth Merry was "quite a botanist" who maintained a fine collection of books and specimens and had an interest in American plants. Foster, however, declared that she "lives on conversations and would never look into a book if she had any body to talk to." Critical of her new surroundings, she lamented Washington's "uncultivated state" and lack of gardens as well as an undeveloped horticultural appreciation among American women. Although Anthony Merry was recalled in late 1806, Elizabeth's ill health delayed her return to England until June 1807 (Malcolm Lester, *Anthony Merry Redivivus: A Reappraisal of the British Minister to the United States, 1803-6* [Charlottesville, 1978], 10, 22, 119; William P. Cutler and Julia P. Cutler, *Life, Journals, and Correspondence of Rev. Manasseh Cut-*

ler, *LL.D.*, 2 vols. [Cincinnati, 1888; repr. Athens, Ohio, 1987], 2:190; Marilyn K. Parr, "Chronicle of a British Diplomat: The First Year in the 'Washington Wilderness,'" *Washington History*, 12 [2000], 85; Margaret Bayard Smith, *The First Forty Years of Washington Society*, ed. Gaillard Hunt [New York, 1906], 46; Charles O. Paullin, "Early British Diplomats in Washington," RCHS, 44-45 [1942-43], 245-8; Matthew L. Davis, *Memoirs of Aaron Burr: With Miscellaneous Selections from His Correspondence*, 2 vols. [New York, 1836-37], 2:269; Vol. 41:387-8).

For TJ's receipt of SEEDS of the Venus FLYTRAP, see the letter from Timothy Bloodworth of 12 Dec.

From Elizabeth Leathes Merry

Washington Monday 26th: 1803

Mrs: Merry presents her respects to Mr: Jefferson and returns him her best thanks for the very Valuable, and scarce seeds he has had the goodness to send her.

Mrs: M: has with her seeds, wch. She presumes may be of use in the Country, and begs leave to offer any part of them to Mr Jefferson.

RC (MHi); endorsed by TJ as received 26 Dec.

From Vandreville Larivière

à Boston 26 Xbre 1803

Jai l'honneur d'exposer a Son exélance qu'etant, Infortunée, pére de famille, jai perdus ce quil me restoient pour dé Bris de mes Mal'heur, tant a Saint domingue, qu'a la guadloupe—ce toit le fruit de mes painibles travaux dapres quarente ans que j'ai habité ces deux Colonies—jai été misérablement dé porté de la guadloupe par la haine particuliere de Mes opresseurs—je suis actuelment a Boston ou jai une existance Des plus affligeante—

je Supplie humblement de Votre humanitée ordinaire, espérant par elle, de vos Bien fait une concession de terre Sous Votre obeissance Des Contrees de la louizianne je Suis agriculteur de proffession—& en ce genre lobtantion de ma demande peut me me Mettre a méme de meritter au pres de Votre exélance—

Veuilles sil Vous plait M'honnorer de Votre reponce et agréer Mes Voeux pour la prospéritée de vos jours—je reste & suis de votre exélance avec le plus proffond respect & subordonné

VANDREVILLE LARIVIERE

je suis natif de lyon rhone & loire—

[175]

EDITORS' TRANSLATION

Boston, 26 Dec. 1803

I have the honor of informing your excellency of my situation. I am an unfortunate family man, overwhelmed by misfortunes after losing everything I had in Saint-Domingue and Guadeloupe. I lost the home that was the fruit of forty years of hard work in those two colonies. I was despicably deported from Guadeloupe by the targeted hatred of my oppressors and am now in Boston, leading a miserable existence.

I humbly appeal to your basic humanity in hopes that you will intervene to obtain a land concession for me in the Louisiana territories you control. Since I am a farmer, granting my request would give me the means of becoming worthy of your excellency.

Please do me the honor of responding, and accept my wishes for your well-being. I am and remain devoted to your excellency with the deepest respect.

VANDREVILLE LARIVIERE

I am a native of the Lyon-Rhône region and the Loire.

RC (DLC); at head of text: "a Monsieur Le president des etats unis—de la merique Septemtrionnale"; endorsed by TJ as received 2 Jan. 1804 and so recorded in SJL.

To Benjamin Smith Barton

DEAR SIR   Washington Dec. 27. 03.

Some propositions having been made to the public on the subject of a natural bed of Sulphur in Genesee, we wished to obtain information respecting it. Capt Williamson tells me you passed some time in examining it, and I am sure therefore you can give me better information respecting it than any other person, & on which I shall more rely. I pray you therefore to do it without delay, as we are pressed to conclude. the quality of the matter, the quantity existing, and the progress of the reproductive powers, & what kind of an operation suffices to give it due purity for common uses, are the most interesting objects of our enquiry. Accept my affectionate salutations & assurances of esteem & respect.   TH: JEFFERSON

RC (PHi); addressed: "Dr. Benjamin S. Barton Philadelphia"; franked and postmarked; endorsed by Barton. PrC (DLC).

PROPOSITIONS HAVING BEEN MADE: Mountjoy Bayly to TJ, 14 Dec.

From Jonathan Dayton

Brookes's at 7 buildings

SIR. Decr. 27th. 1803

I take the liberty of presenting to you the usual compliments & best wishes of this season of festivity & joy, and particularly of expressing my congratulations upon the happy event of the peaceable delivery of possession of one of the Forts in the city of New Orleans at the demand of the Prefect, to a company of our countrymen embodied under Mr. Clark. This may be regarded as a sure pledge for the surrender of the whole Province, agreeably to our Convention with France. As it is possible that a copy of Mr. Laussat's proclamation consequent thereupon, may not have been enclosed in your dispatches, I have the honor Sir, to send you one which I have received, with a request that you would do me the favor to keep it, if it be the only one in your possession.

Instead of taking the liberty of writing to you Sir, I should have called to pay you my respects & compliments in person upon this occasion, if I had not been afflicted by a painful swelling on my hand, which has confined me to my room for three days, & even now, (altho' better) prevents me from drawing a coat over it.

I have the honor to be Sir with the highest respect Your very hum. servt. JONA: DAYTON

RC (DLC); at foot of text: "The President of the U. States"; endorsed by TJ as received 27 Dec. and so recorded in SJL. Enclosure: Proclamation by Pierre Clément Laussat, New Orleans, 30 Nov., in French, to the people of Louisiana announcing that he has accepted the transfer of the province from the commissioners of Spain and will soon transfer it to commissioners of the United States; he emphasizes the benefits the inhabitants will receive by joining a populous and powerful nation known for its industriousness and progress; they will have the rights and privileges of citizens of the United States, access to justice and a government responsive to their needs, and a place in the commerce of the Nile of America ("le Nil de Amérique, ce Mississipi"); the French Republic is voluntarily giving up the colony, but will always have a bond to its people (*Proclamation. Au Nom de la République Française. Pierre Clément Laussat, Préfet Colonial, Commissaire du Gouvernement Français, Aux Louisianais* [New Orleans, 1803]; printed in *Terr. Papers*, 9:126-32, with translation).

From Rufus Easton

SIR, Washington Decemr. 27th. 1803

Permit me under the enclosed Recommendation to solicit the appointment of Attorney to the United States for the District of *Orleans*.

If a strong Attachment to the cause of Republicanism; if useful services rendered and personal sacrifices made in support of the principles by which it is mainted[1] have any claim for the place, I trust my application will be duly considered.—

I have the honor to be, with great consideration Your Excellencys Most Obedt. and most humble Servt. RUFUS EASTON

RC (DNA: RG 59, LAR); at foot of text: "His Excelly. President Jefferson"; endorsed by TJ as received 30 Dec. and "to be Atty Genl N.O." and so recorded in SJL. FC (MoSHi: Rufus Easton Papers). Enclosure not found.

Rufus Easton (1774-1834), a native of Connecticut and former law student of Ephraim Kirby, was a politically well-connected attorney from Rome, New York. He spent the winter of 1803-4 in Washington lobbying for an appointment, then headed west and settled in St. Louis, where he quickly became an influential and controversial figure. He was appointed postmaster at St. Louis in 1804, and TJ awarded him a recess appointment as one of the judges for the Louisiana Territory in March 1805. But unfavorable reports of Easton's conduct and character filtered back to Washington, and by the end of 1805, TJ decided not to reappoint him. Despite the loss of TJ's favor, Easton went on to a successful career, serving as the Missouri Territory's delegate to Congress and as attorney general for the state of Missouri (*Biog. Dir. Cong.*; Kline, *Burr*, 2:850, 918-19; *Terr. Papers*, 13:74, 105, 249, 272, 307, 319-25, 368-9, 380; William E. Foley, *The Genesis of Missouri: From Wilderness Outpost to Statehood* [Columbia, Mo., 1989], 151-2, 157, 161, 165-8, 174, 180; RS, 7:365, 366n; Easton to TJ, 17 Jan. 1805, 21 Feb. 1806; TJ to Joseph Anderson, 28 Dec. 1805; William Keteltas to TJ, 19 Jan. 1806; TJ to Easton, 22 Feb. 1806).

[1]FC: "maintained."

From Albert Gallatin

Treasury Department

SIR, December 27th: 1803.

It appears by a letter of the 16th: instant, that the Light house at Smith's Point is completed: the Contractor has left a young man on the spot to take care of the buildings; and as he will probably make a charge for his attendence, the propriety of appointing a Keeper is respectfully submitted. As a supply of Oil was ordered from Nantucket in November, it has probably already arrived at Norfolk, from whence the Collector may ship it to Smith's point as soon as a keeper shall be there to receive it.

I have the honor to be Very respectfully Sir, Yr. Obedt: Servt:

ALBERT GALLATIN

RC (DLC); in a clerk's hand, signed by Gallatin; at foot of text: "The President of the U States"; endorsed by TJ as received from the Treasury Department on 28 Dec. and "Keeper Lt. Ho. Smith's Pt." and so recorded in SJL.

CONTRACTOR: in early February 1802, Elzy Burroughs signed an agreement to build the lighthouse on Smith Point on Chesapeake Bay (Vol. 36:506).

Gallatin requested that when the OIL for the new lighthouse arrived from Nantucket, William Davies, the collector at Norfolk, should forward it "with all pos- sible dispatch" (Gallatin to Davies, 31 Dec., FC in Lb in DNA: RG 26, LL).

To George Jefferson

Dear Sir   Washington Dec. 27. 03.

The uncertainty when my note to Peyton for 558.14 D may be deposited with you, obliging me to be in a state of preparation for it, I find it better to provide & forward you the money at once, that no delay may be asked. you will accordingly recieve herein inclosed five hundred & sixty dollars to enable you to discharge the note on sight. accept my affectionate saluations.   TH: JEFFERSON

PrC (MHi); at foot of text: "Mr. George Jefferson"; endorsed by TJ in ink on verso. Recorded in SJL with notation "560 D."

For the payment to Craven PEYTON, which George Jefferson covered on 16 Dec., see TJ to Jefferson, 20 Dec., and Jefferson to TJ, 26 Dec. TJ recorded the transaction in his financial memoranda

"to pay my note to Craven Peyton 558.14 ante Aug. 11" (MB, 2:1115).

On 30 Dec., George Jefferson responded "merely to acknowledge the receipt of your favor of the 27th. inclosing 560$. which is entered to your credit" (RC in MHi; at foot of text: "Thos. Jefferson esqr."; endorsed by TJ as received 4 Jan. 1804 and so recorded in SJL).

From George Jefferson

Dear Sir   Richmond 27th. Decr. 1803

I shall forward by Mr. Richard S. Hackley, who goes on in tomorrows stage, our revised code of laws as requested in your favor of the 20th.

I am Dear Sir Your Very humble servt.   GEO. JEFFERSON

RC (MHi); at foot of text: "Thos. Jefferson esqr."; endorsed by TJ; entered in SJL as received 31 Dec.

For Richard S. HACKLEY, see Vol. 38:418-19.

From Jones & Howell

Respected Friend   Phila. 27th December 1803

Your favor of 22nd. is reced. as also one some days since, which would have been reply'd to sooner but waited for Young Stewart to pick out the Iron and files, which is at length done, as p Invoice Annex'd, and have also sent you the three sheets of Iron, agreeable to the paper reced. and we Can at any time if you give us A little previous information, supply you with such as You describe, and which you say will want next Season. we have also sent 10 Bundles more nail-rods to make up the deficit in our last Invoice, though we think the Capt. must have made the mistake.

9. Bars Iron Including Mill Spindles and Gudgeons		
at 3. 2.11. at 45/		21.64
hammermans fees on spindle mold		0.50
4 Bundles large spike rods at 2. 0. 0. at 46/6		12.40
3 sheets Iron at 62 lbs at 1/. p lb		8.27
Sundry files of various sizes		8.56
porterage		.50
		$51.87

we are Respectfully Your Friends   JONES & HOWELL

RC (MHi); at head of text: "Thomas Jefferson Esqr."; endorsed by TJ as received 30 Dec. and so recorded in SJL.

From Charles d'Ayroy Lellieret

MONSIEUR   Boston Ce 27 decembre 1803:
    Quoiqu'ayant habité depuis longtems l'amérique, J'ignore le mode a employer envers le Gouvernement que Vous représenté pour Obtenir une Concession de terre dans la partie de la *Louisiane.* Si la demande doit Vous être adréssé, ou à Monsieur le Secrétaire d'état; Si enfin il faudroit qu'elle feroit mention de la quotité qu'on désireroit avoir, ou si Vous la déterminé Vous même?
    Comme toute démarche prématurée ne rempliroit nullement le but que je me suis proposé, je forme Cette première, envers Votre excellence qui Voudra bien m'honorer d'une réponse pour que je puisse m'y conformer.
    J'ai l'honneur d'etre avec Respect de Votre excellence Votre trs Hble & trés Obt Serviteur   CHARLES D'AYROY LELLIERET

EDITORS' TRANSLATION

SIR,   Boston, 27 Dec. 1803—
    Although I have lived in America for a long time, I do not know the procedure for obtaining a land concession in Louisiana—whether the application should be addressed to you or to the secretary of state; whether it should include the quantity of land requested; or whether you determine that yourself.
    Since a premature request would not accomplish my goal, I am sending this preliminary inquiry to your excellency in hopes that you will honor me with an answer so I can take the correct measures.

I have the honor of being your very respectful, humble, and obedient servant.   CHARLES D'AYROY LELLIERET

RC (DLC); at head of text: "à Son excellence Monsieur Thomas Jefferson président des états unis Septentrionale"; endorsed by TJ as received 7 Jan. 1804 and so recorded in SJL.

From J. P. G. Muhlenberg

SIR   Philadelphia Decr. 27th. 1803—

Enclos'd I have the Honor to transmit a Letter I have just recievd from Mr. Jarvis of Lisbon—The two Pipes of Wine mentiond in the Letter, are on Board the Ship Edward, now in this Port, and will be landed, & Stor'd imediately, but as no Oppertunity offers at present, to Ship the Wine to Richmond, I have to request The President will be pleas'd to direct, whether the Wine may be Shippd to Alexandria or Georgetown, or whether it must be forwarded to Richmond, agreeably to the directions of Mr. Jarvis—Mr. Hulings at New Orleans, has forwarded, & directed to my care, one Barrell Missisippi Water, for the President, which I shall forward by the first Opportunity to Alexandria or Georgetown.

I have the Honor to be with Perfect Respect Sir Your Obedt servt
                                        P MUHLENBERG

RC (MHi); at foot of text: "The President of The United States"; endorsed by TJ as received 30 Dec. and so recorded in SJL. Enclosure not found, but see William Jarvis to TJ, 26 Oct.

In a letter of 3 Nov. to Muhlenberg, enclosed here or in a subsequent communication, William E. HULINGS reported that Hore Browse Trist had shipped to him two barrels of water from the Mississippi River intended for the president. One of the barrels had drained completely, but Hulings was able to ship the other, "said to be in bottles," to Muhlenberg (RC in MHi; see also Hore Browse Trist to TJ, 28 Sep.).

From J. P. G. Muhlenberg

SIR   Philadelphia Decr. 27th. 1803

Since forwarding my Letter of this Morning, which I had the Honor of addressing To The President—The Ship Eliza, from Cadiz arrivd in this Port—She has on Board one Butt of Sherry Wine, Shipp'd by Mr. Joseph Yesnardi—& consignd to, either the Collector of Philada. or Norfolk—I have recd. no Letter of advice, but the Captn. states, that the Wine is for The President of the U States.

I shall take the Butt in charge, until I am favor'd with The Presidents directions, in what manner it is to be dispos'd of—

I have the Honor to be with Perfect Respect Sir Your Most Obedt servt   P MUHLENBERG

RC (MHi); at foot of text: "The President of The U. States"; endorsed by TJ as received 30 Dec. and so recorded in SJL.

From Caspar Wistar

DR SIR   Philada. Decr. 27. 1803

I sincerely regret the trouble I am obliged to give you, but the inclosed were directed by the Society to be forwarded to you with a request that they might be transmitted to Mr Levingston—

With the warmest wishes for your health & happiness I am most respectfully your friend & servt   C. WISTAR JUNR.

RC (DLC); at foot of text: "His Excellency The President of the United States"; endorsed by TJ as received 7 Jan. and so recorded in SJL. Enclosures not found.

From Anonymous

SIR,   Baltimore [before 28] December 1803—

As Congress appear to want useful employment I beg leave to recommend the following subject to their consideration.

America lost an immense Sum in the course of the last War by Spoliations, and if the System which I am about to recommend had been adopted, the principal part of these losses would have been saved & the Country benefited beyond calculation—The only thing which will make our Neutrality respected, is a Law of Congress to prevent our Citizens covering property, under penaltys which will be considered superior to any investigation in an Admiralty Court. I would make the Owner & Master of American Vessells Swear to the property on entering and clearing, and that no false papers shall be exhibited or produced during the Voyage—I would also imprison the Master and confiscate Vessell & Cargo in case of fraud—

By adopting this plan, no Nation would presume to meddle with our Vessells in times of War, and our Citizens would gain immensely by trading on their own account instead of being Carriers & Coverers for the paltry consideration of Freight & Commission—

If our people had not been permitted to cover property in the course of last War, the Spoliations would not have taken place at least to any extent, and the heavy expences we were subjected to on that account would have been saved—But there are still stronger grounds in favour of my System, which is that it will save endless frauds and disputes with European Nations & enable our Citizens to purchase their produce in times of War on advantageous terms, when they find it cannot be exported on their own account under cover of our Flag & Names.—If this plan had been adopted last War, we would have purchased the produce of St. Domingo & Cuba on very low terms, instead of suffering heavily by the trade of the latter, owing chiefly to our people covering property for the Spaniards—I flatter myself you will readily see the advantages of this System, & recommend it to Congress—

I fear the Law respecting our Sailors will occasion some misunderstanding with England—I find every British Sailor that comes to the port can get a protection as an American Citizen—A few worthless fellows who can be hired for a trifle, go with the Sailors to a Notary and make Oath to their Citizenship—

RC (DLC); partially dated; endorsed by TJ as an anonymous letter received 28 Dec. and "abuse of our flag" and so recorded in SJL. Enclosed in TJ to Jacob Crowninshield, 29 Dec.

From Robert Bowie

SIR,   Council Chamber [28] December 1803

In pursuance of a Resolution of the Senate of this State, I have the honor of transmitting to you inclosed, an authenticated Copy of a law lately passed by the Legislature of Maryland, ratifying an amendment to the Constitution of the United States in the manner of choosing a President and Vice President and am with high consideration

ROBERT BOWIE

FC (MdAA: Letterbooks of Governor and Council); partially dated; at foot of text: "His Excellency Thomas Jefferson President of the United States." Recorded in SJL as a letter of 28 Dec. received from Annapolis 30 Dec. with notation "ratifn Maryld." Enclosure: "An Act to ratify an amendment to the constitution of the United States of America, proposed by congress to the legislatures of the several states" (*At a Session of the General Assembly of Maryland, begun and held at the City of Annapolis, on Monday, the 7th of November, in the year of our Lord 1803,* and ended the 7th of January, 1804, the following Laws were enacted [Annapolis, 1804; Shaw-Shoemaker, No. 6723]).

An ardent Republican and former state legislator, Robert Bowie (1750-1818) was elected governor of Maryland in 1803 and served until 1806 (ANB).

A RESOLUTION by the Maryland Senate, passed 26 Dec., requested that the governor transmit to the president the state legislature's act ratifying the Twelfth Amendment to the Constitution of the United States. The state senate passed the ratification act unanimously, while the House of Delegates approved it by a vote of 40 to 26 (*Votes and Proceedings of the Senate of the State of Maryland. November Session, One Thousand Eight Hundred and Three. Being the Third Session of* the Sixth Senate [Annapolis, 1804], 22, 26; *Votes and Proceedings of the House of Delegates of the State of Maryland. November Session, One Thousand Eight Hundred and Three. Being the First Session of This Assembly* [Annapolis, 1803], 66).

To Jonathan Dayton

Dec. 28. 03.

Th: Jefferson with his respectful salutations & the compliments of the season to Genl. Dayton, returns him the inclosed with thanks, which had been recieved by the Secy. of State. by a letter from Genl. Wilkinson at Ft. Adams Dec. 9. the troops would leave that only the next morning at Reveille, and he calculated that using all their oars, & travelling night and day, they would arrive at N. Orleans on the 16th. this seems a wonderful time for the descent!

RC (GyLeU). Not recorded in SJL. Enclosure: see Dayton to TJ, 27 Dec.

The LETTER from James Wilkinson of 9 Dec. has not been found, but Henry

Dearborn acknowledged its receipt in a letter to Wilkinson of 6 Jan. 1804 (FC in DNA: RG 107, LSMA).

From John Dickinson

MY DEAR FRIEND,   Wilmington 28th of the 12th Month 1803

Having lately found among my Papers the original Documents relating to the Convention that met at Annapolis in the Year 1786, I think it my Duty to transmit them to the Executive of the Union, and therefore I now send them.

I am entirely thy Friend   JOHN DICKINSON

RC (PHi); at foot of text: "Thomas Jefferson President"; written on verso of sheet addressed to Dickinson by George Logan. Recorded in SJL as received 31 Dec. Enclosures: (1) Resolution of Virginia, 21 Jan. 1786, appointing eight individuals to meet with commissioners from other states to take into consideration the trade of the United States, signed by Governor Patrick Henry, 6 July 1786 (MS in DNA: RG 360, PCC). (2) William Greene to Edmund Randolph, 21 Mch. 1786, acknowledging receipt of the Virginia resolution of 21 Jan. 1786 and reporting the Rhode Island legislature had passed an act "fully empowering Congress to regulate the trade of the United States" (RC in same). (3) John Langdon to Patrick Henry, 27 Mch. 1786, explaining that the New Hampshire legislature had chosen its commissioners but had not yet learned of their acceptance; the legislature is pleased that Virginia has taken the lead in the business about "a general system of commerce" (RC in same). (4) James Bowdoin to Edmund Randolph, 30 Mch. 1786, sending Massachusetts's approval for calling the convention and enclosing a resolve on the subject of 23 Mch. 1786, acknowledging receipt of the Virginia resolution and naming four commissioners from Massachusetts (RC in same). (5) Minutes of meeting of commissioners of five states, 11-14 Sep. 1786, with Dickinson unanimously elected as chairman; including their report, signed by the commissioners on 14 Sep., stating that they could not proceed without representation of other states, but they call upon the states to send commissioners to convene at Philadelphia on the second Monday of May 1787 to consider changes to the federal system; with cover sheet in Dickinson's hand: "Proceedings of the Commissioners from Virginia, Delaware, Pennsylvania, New Jersey & New York, at Annapolis in Maryland, from September 11th to Septr. 14th—1786—inclusive" and canceled: "The only enclosure is the resolve of Virginia appointing Commissioners"; notation by TJ: "sent by John Dickinson to be deposited in the public office by Th: Jefferson" (MS in same). (6) Report of the commissioners to the legislatures of Virginia, Delaware, Pennsylvania, New Jersey, and New York, 14 Sep. 1786, signed by Dickinson, calling for the states to appoint delegates to meet in Philadelphia next May "to render the constitution of the Federal Government adequate to the exigencies of the Union" (MS in same). (7) Dickinson to the president of Congress, 14 Sep. 1786, transmitting a copy of the commissioners' report to the legislatures by which they were appointed (RC in same).

To Albert Gallatin

TH:J. TO MR GALLATIN   Dec. 28. 03.

Will you be so good as to order 2 copies of the Contingent account to be made out for communicn to Congress?   Mr. Madison concurs with us in thinking it better Genl. Dearborne's case should go to Congress direct for decision.

RC (NHi: Gallatin Papers); addressed: "The Secretary of the Treasury." Not recorded in SJL.

CONTINGENT ACCOUNT: the next day, Gallatin sent TJ a brief covering note: "I enclose the account of the contingent fund" (RC in DLC; addressed in a clerk's hand: "The President of the United States"; endorsed by TJ as received from the Treasury Department on 29 Dec. and "Contingt acct." and so recorded in SJL). The official account, signed by Joseph Nourse as register, is dated 2 Jan. 1804 (see enclosure listed at TJ to the Senate and the House of Representatives, 31 Dec.).

From Kentucky Members of the House of Representatives

To THE PRESIDENT OF   City of Washington
THE UNITED STATES.   28th december 1803

Finding on a perusal of the intelligencer[1] of this day that Louisiana is Officially delivered to the French Republic, and judging that no Obstacle will prevent the peaceable possession to the United States, and contemplating the necessity that there be for an appointment of a Collector and Naval officer for the Port of New Orleans.—We the undersigned beg leave to recommend a person fitly qualified to fill either of those offices. Mr James Brown of Lexington Kentucky, This Gentleman's talents at the Bar of the Superior Courts of our State is ranked among the first practioners, as a Man of Integrity, sobriety and independent Republican principles. He is in our estimation inferior to none. We are not unaware of the inconvenience that our infant State will experience by the migration of such characters from it: but as Mr Brown has Signified his intention of moveing to the lower Country and his inclination to fill one of those offices (that of the Collector he would prefer) we cannot with hold from him this Portion of Justice which his merit entitles him to.

THOMAS SANDFORD
JOHN BOYLE
JOHN FOWLER
MATTHEW WALTON
M LYON
GEO M BEDINGER

RC (DNA: RG 59, LAR); in Fowler's hand, signed by all; endorsed by TJ: "Brown James to be Collectr. or Nav. Off. N.O." and "Kentucky delegates."

A native of Virginia, Thomas Sandford (1762-1808) resided near Covington and served in the House from 1803 to 1807. Also a Virginia native, John Boyle (1774-1835) of Garrard County served in Congress from 1803 to 1809, then as chief justice of the Kentucky Court of Appeals from 1810 to 1826. John Fowler (1755-1840), an officer in the American Revolution, moved from Virginia to Lexington, Kentucky, in 1783. He served in Congress from 1797 to 1807 and as postmaster of Lexington from 1814 to 1822. Matthew Walton (d. 1819) was a member of the Kentucky constitutional convention and state legislature before serving in Congress from 1803 to 1807. Born in Pennsylvania, George M. Bedinger (1756-1843)

settled at Boonesborough in 1779 and saw military service during the American Revolution and in the Northwest Territory. A former member of both houses of the Kentucky legislature, Bedinger served in Congress from 1803 to 1807 (*Biog. Dir. Cong.*; John E. Kleber, ed., *The Kentucky Encyclopedia* [Lexington, Ky., 1992], 66, 109-10, 350; Vol. 41:358, 359n).

Sandford sent Gallatin a separate recommendation of JAMES BROWN on 15 Feb. 1804, citing the Kentucky representatives' earlier recommendation to the president and adding that Brown's knowledge of French and Spanish "must qualify him in a superior manner" for an appointment as collector or naval officer at New Orleans (RC in DNA: RG 59, LAR; endorsed by TJ: "Brown James. to be Collectr. or Navl. off. N.O.").

[1] MS: "inlligencer."

From Meriwether Lewis

DEAR SIR,   Cahokia December 28th. 1803.

On my arrival at St. Louis, the first object to which, I called my attention, was that of collecting such information as might be in some measure serviceable to you in forming your opinions, or shaping your arrangements to effect a certain point of policy, which you expressed to me while with you at Washington last Summer; I mean that of a wish you then entertained, if possible to induce the inhabitants of Louisiana to relinquish their landed possessions in that country, and removing with their families, accept of an equivalent portion of lands on the East side of the Mississippi, with a view more readily to induce the Indians on the East, to remove to the West side of the Mississippi, and dispose of their lands on the East side of that river to the U'States. The advantages of such a policy has ever struck me as being of primary importance to the future prosperity of the Union, and therefore, I gave it my earlyest and best attention. With a view to the main object I confined my enquiries to the following subjects—The population of Louisiana, The number of emigrants from the U'States within the last year, and the proportion which that disciption of people bear to the other free white population of Louisiana. The number of Slaves and other people of colour. The quantity of lands which have been granted to, or claimed by individuals; The species of rights or claims by which the present incumbents hold these lands; The wealth of the inhabitants, and the species of property which forms that wealth; The position and extent of the several settlements, the proportion of each that are thickly inhabited (admitting as the standard, one *family* to a *square mile*); the proportion which the remaining population of each settlement, bears to the remaining quantity of square miles embraced by it. The state of agriculture, and the species and extent of the improvements made on the lands now inhabited.—

Whatever I may say on these subjects, must be understood as applicable to Uper Louisiana; the distance we are removed from the capital and settlements of the lower portion of the Province, as well as the little intercourse,[1] which takes place between the inhabitants of it's extreems at this season of the year, makes it as difficult to learn any thing in relation to Lower Louisiana, as tho' I were in Washington.—

With a view to obtain some information on these[2] subjects, I found means to obtain an introduction to Monsr. Soulard, the Surveyor Genl., and was recieved by him in a very friendly manner; he gave me many unqualifyed assurances of his willingness to serve me, and his readyness to give me any information of which, he was possessed, in

[187]

relation to the province—Monsr. S. is a Frenchman, a man of good information, an active officer, and the particular friend and confident of Colo. Lassuse; but before I proceed, in order to shew you Sir, the *good faith* with which Monsr. S. complyed with his previous declirations, as also to shew the difficulty, which in the present state of things is attendant on the procureing any accurate information relative to the state of the Province, it will not perhaps be amiss to relate, some measure in detale, the occurrences which took place at this interview between Monsr. Soulard and myself.—

In order to give[3] as great latitude as possible to my inquiries, and at the same time to avoid being thought too importunate, I prefaced my enquiries by thanking Mr. S— for his friendly dispositions, and observed that it was to be expected, that in all newly settled countrys there were but few men of general information, and that a very small proportion even of that few, were in possession of such documents as would enable them to form an accurate opinion on many interesting subjects; and concluded by observing, that the policy of the government of the U'States did not in any manner prohibit her officers or citizens from giving strangers every information relative to the government itself or the country, if therefore, my habits as a citizen of such a government, should lead me in the course of my inquiries to ask questions, which the policy of his government forbid his giving, I should feel no mortification at his withholding it, and I hoped he would feel no compunction in doing so, if he concieved his duty as an officer, or the policy of his government required it.—I then asked him if the census of Uper Louisiana had been recently taken? and if so, what was the state of the population? he told me, that an order had been lately issued for that purpose, but the returns had not yet been recieved from but few of the districts, but that he had a copy of the census taken in 1800, which he would shew me with pleasure; a few minutes after he handed me this statement, I asked his permission to take an extract of it, which was granted, he furnished me with pen, ink & paper, I set down, and had scarsely began the operation, when, (as I was afterwards informed by Mr. Hay the gentleman who acted as our mutual friend and interpreter) Monsr. Soulard exclaimed, "perhaps some person may come in," and taking hold of my hand with much apparent agitation, beged that I would desist, adding that when he had granted me permission to take an extract from that paper, the impropriety of such permission did not occur to him, he hoped I would pardon his not permiting me to do so, alledging that the jealousy of his government was such, that if it were known that he had given me permission to copy an official paper, that it would injure him with his government, I instantly desisted of course; and assured him that it was by no means my wish, that he should in order to gratify me, in the slightest manner compromit himself in the good opinion of his government; that I considered him the sole judge of the propriety, or impropriety of satisfying the inquiries I was making, and that while I should be thankfull for such information as he could consistenly with his duty give me, I should not on the other hand feel any mortification in being refused such as he might consider improper to give—this appeared perfectly to satisfy him—he then told me he thought I might state the present population of Uper Louisiana in round numbers at 10,000 souls, 2,000 of whom were slaves & people of colour, and of the remaining 8,000, two thirds of them at least were emigrants from the U'States; that the remaining third, were either French or Canadian descendants, the Spaniards and their descendants being so few in number, that they deserved no particular notice as a class of people.—

In consequence of the readiness with which Monsr. Soulard granted me permission to take a transcript of the statement of the census which he shewed me, I did not at first view, charge my memory with it's contents as I should have done, had he not so readily granted me that permission; tho' I think from the best of my recollection, that the total exceeded 7,600, for the population in 1800.—

When I extended my inquiries to the geography of the country, and asked for such information as he felt himself at liberty to give me on that subject, particularly of the interior of the country lying between the Missouri and New Mexico; he shewed me a manuscript map, imbracing a portion of the Mississippi, the Missouri from it's junction with this river to the mouth of the Osages, and the last named river in it's whole extent; I asked permission to take a copy of it, he told me he had no objection on his part, but that he must first obtain the permission of the Merchant whose property it was, and also the permission of the Commandant; desirous of knowing how Colo. Lassuse would act in such a case, I told Mons. S—, I would take upon myself to make the necessary application to the Commandant, if he would do me the favour to obtain the Merchant's permission for my copying it.—this done, I asked Colo. Lassuse on the same evening, if he would be so good as to permit the Merchants of St. Louis to give me such information as they might be disposed to give relative to the geography of the country, the request was immediately granted, and the next day I called on Monsr. S— who had been as good as his word with the merchant, whose permission he had obtained; notwithstanding the assureances which I gave Monsr. S—, that the Commandant's consent had been obtained, still he could not give me the map untill he had exacted a promise upon honour, that I would not let Colo. Lassuse know that I had such a map in my possession or from what quarter I had obtained it.—

Thus it appears to me Sir, that these people are so much accustomed to elude the eye of dispotic power, that they can do no act but this principle seems in some measure to have interwoven itself with the actuating motive; it may however be affected in some degree, in order to inhanse the obligation conferred, by inducing the person obliged, to believe, that in order to serve him they have themselves risked the displeasure of their government or the penalty of punishment; in short, whatever may be the prime spring of action among them, they move more as tho' the *fear of the Commandant*, than *that of god*, was before their eyes: Whenever information is asked from the most independant of them on any subject, the promiss to give it, is always qualified by, *so far as propryety will permit*; the measure of which *proprety* it must be understood *is the will of the Commandant.* candure obliges me to acknowledge however, that they have some reason to fear Colo. Lassuse, he has been pretty tiranical with them,— with regard to the more wealthy part of the community, the Colo. seems to have differed from his predecessors in office in respect to the policy he has observed towards them; formerly this class of people escaped punishment for almost every crime, but he has for very slight offences put some of the most wealthy among them into the Carraboose; this has produced a general dread of him among all classes of the people.—

I have no doubt, as soon as the American government takes effect in Louisiana, that many of the best informed of it's inhabitants in order to make themselves known to it, will unsolicited come forward with much interesting information, till then, every thing must be obtained by stealth. I have been thus particular to shew you in the present state of things how difficult it is to acquire information on certain[4] subjects, and the inacuracy which must necessarily attend even the little which may be obtained.—

The census as given me by Monsr. Soulard, I think is more to be relyed on than any other[5] information I have recieved on that subject. The census as known to the Spanish government itself cannot for several reasons be very accurate, and in my opinion fall considerably short of the real population.—The inaccuracy and inattention of many of their pette commandants, some of whom can neither read nor write; in many instances emigrants from the U'States pass the Mississippi, and without asking lands of the government, set themselves down and remain many months, perhaps a year, without the knowledge even of the Commandant in whose district they may be; the scattered population of a great portion of Uper Louisiana, as well as the frequent removals of the wandering emigrants from the UStates, who now form a majority of the population; all form considerations which must in some degree contribute to the inaccuracy of the census.—

I cannot learn that any of the commandants of districts keep an account of the number of persons who emigrate annually from the U'States to Louisiana, of course, what can be said on this head must of necessity be in a great measure conjectural; common opinion seems to fix the emigration of the last year at 100. families, but I believe it considerably more. I have learnt the population of the district of Cape Girardeau, for the present & some previous years with more precision than that of any other. this settlement was formed in 1795 by two families only, 45 miles above the mouth of the Ohio; taking the progressive increase of the population of this district for our data, we shal find, that by the census of 1801, they amounted to 705. souls, and in 1803 to 1,111. (this last number may be depended on for it's accuracy, I had it from the young gentleman who made out the report of the census of that district for Comdt. Lorimier who can neither read nor write); from this it appears, that the population has increased within the 2 last years 406 souls; allowing 5 souls to a family, there will be 81 families for the emigration of the two last years, the half of which is $40\frac{1}{2}$ for the emigration in the year 1803.—It may be urged however, that in order to obtain the true annual increase of population by emigration only, there should be deducted from this sum, the probable excess of births over the deaths which have taken place in that period, but I think that a sufficient allowance for this, will be found in the annual progressive increase of emigration, added to the removals which take place from the older settlements, to those more recently formed, at the same time disposing of their rights to the soil, and their improvements to later adventurers, who more wealthy than themselves purchase from and succeed them. I therefore think the increase of the district aluded to, may safely be stated at 40 families averaging 5 persons each, for the last 12 Months, ending the 31st. of October; admitting this to be the case, when we take into consideration many other districts, equally with Cape Girardeau, rapidly increasing in population by emmigration from the U'States, as New Madrid, St. Genevieve, New Bourbon, St. Louis and the country on the Maremek river, St. Ferdinand, St. Charles and particularly St. Andrew and the country lying S. of the Missouri, and between it and the uper portions of the rivers Maremek and St. Francis.—we would in such case have strong grounds to conjecture, that the emigration the last year from the UStates to Uper Louisiana was nearer 200 than 100, families; the emigration to Louisiana from any other quarter is so inconsiderable that it scarcely deserves notice.—The emigration of the ensuing year may be expected to exceed that of the last at least a third, unless some measures are taken by the government to prevent it. many persons from different parts of the U'States, particularly N. Carolina, have visited Louisiana since the cession of that country to the U'States has been made known; these persons were in serch of some eligible positions to form settlements as soon as the American government was in operation in that quarter; they appear generally pleased with the country, and will no doubt make a favourable report on their return.—

I am fully persuaded, that your wishes to withdraw the inhabitants of Louisiana, may in every necessary degree be effected in the course of a few years, provided the gouvernment of the U. States is justly liberal in it's donations. The American emigrants will be much more readily prevailed on to come into this measure than the French, the French may be said almost exclusively to be the slave holder, they own at least five sixths of that property. I fear that the slaves will form a source of some unwillingness in the French to yeald to the wishes of the government; they appear to feel very sensibly a report which has been circulated among them on this subject, that *the Americans would emancipate their slaves immediately on taking possession of the country*, this however false, is sufficient to shew the opinions and disposition of the people on that subject; there appears to be a general objection not only among the French, but even among the Americans not slave holders, to relinquish the right which they claim relative to slavery in it's present unqualifyed shape.—

The Canadian French reside almost entirely in villages situated on the banks of the Mississippi and Missouri rivers; a few individuals among them only can be said to possess wealth, and such as do, obtained it by the Indian trade; the whole of them either directly, or indirectly look to this trade as the principal source of their maintenance; the proximity of their present situations to the trade in which they are engaged, will of course produce a disposition to continue where they are; many of them are slave holders; slavery being prohibited in the Indianna Territory, (at least the further admission of any Slaves), these proprietors of slaves will be compelled to deside, whether they will reside in an adjacent part of the Indianna Territory, enjoy the benefits of their indian trade, and sacrefice in some measure their slave property, or remove with these slaves to some part of the

U'States where slavery is permitted, and sacrefice all prospects of their indian trade; thus the slaves appear to me in every view of this subject to be connected with the principal difficulties with which the government will have to contend in effecting this part of it's policy.

I know not what are the regulations, which have been, or are intended to be made by the government of the U'States in relation to the more permanent government of Uper Louisiana, but I trust I shall be pardoned for giving it as my opinion, (that of office-hunters to the contrary notwithstanding) that Uper Louisiana can be governed more for the happiness of, and justice to the people, with less expence to the mother government, and with better prospects of inforcing her future policy, by dividing it into about three counties, and incorporating it with the Indianna Territory, than by establishing it into a seperate territory, or continuing it as a part of the government of Lower Louisiana in any shape.—

In pursuing my enquiries in relation to Louisiana, any information which I may recieve and which appears to me worthy of your attention shall be forwarded to you.—

I have proposed many quiries under sundry heads to the best informed persons I have met with at St. Louis and within the vicinity of that place; these gentlemen have promised me answers in due time, but as every thing undergoes the examination of the Commandant, you may readily concieve the restraint which exists on many points.—

Some of the traders of this country from their continual intercourse with the Indians, possess with more accuracy many interesting particulars in relation to that people, than persons in a higher sphere of life among them, yet they want both leasure and abilities to give this information in any satisfactory manner in detail; in order therefore to avail myself as far as possible of their information under these circumstances, I drew out a form on paper containing 13 or 14 columns, which I headed with such subjects as appeared to me most important to be known relative to the Indians; I have some of these in circulation; and expect to recieve one or more of them in a few days.—

I have obtained three maps; one of the Osages river, before mentioned, a general map of Uper Louisiana, and a map of the Missouri river, from it's mouth to the Mandane nation; these I shall retain for some time yet, in order to asscertain by further enquiries their accuracy or otherwise; I have also obtained Ivins's and Mac Kay's journal up the Missouri, it is in French & is at present in the hands of Mr. Hay, who has promised to translate it for me; I am also promised by Mr. Hay a copy of his journal from Michilimackinack to the Assinaboin river in the north, by way (on his outward bound journey), of the S. side of Lake Superior, the River St. Louis, the River of the sand lake branch of the Mississippi, a part of the last river downwards to the mouth of the crow-wing river or river L'aile dé curbeau, and with it to the Leaf river, thence up the Leaf river to the portage of the Otter-tale Lake, thence down the Red river to it's junction with the Assinaboin river (called improperly in Arrosmith's Map *Stone Indian river*), and up this river 80 leagues to his winter establishment; on his inward bound journey; by the Assinaboin river to Red river, thence down it 18 leagues to Lake Winnipeck, and through a part of it, the river Winnipeck, Lake of the Woods, the river of the rainy Lake, the rainy Lake, and the grand portage to Michilimackinack— these I shall forward to you as soon as they are recieved.—

My best respects to your daughters, as also Messrs. T. Randolph, Eppes & Harvey, and believe me with much sincere regard—

Your Most Obt. Servt.   MERIWETHER LEWIS. Capt. 1st. U.S. Regt. Infty.

RC (PHi); at foot of text: "The President of the U'States"; endorsed by TJ as received 27 Feb. 1804 and so recorded in SJL.

Antoine SOULARD, the surveyor general of upper Louisiana in the Spanish administration of the province, continued in the same role under the United States (*Terr. Papers*, 13:71-2; Moulton, *Journals of the Lewis & Clark Expedition*, 1:5).

Maps that Lewis and William Clark compiled and sent to TJ in May 1804 may have included information from the MANUSCRIPT MAP owned by a St. Louis MERCHANT (Jackson, *Lewis and Clark*, 1:155n; Clark and Lewis to TJ, 18 May 1804).

Louis LORIMIER, a trader originally from Canada, served as militia commander at Cape Girardeau (Vol. 35:599-600).

GENERAL MAP OF UPER LOUISIANA: "A Topographic Sketch of the Missouri

and Upper Mississippi," a map by Soulard. The MAP OF THE MISSOURI RIVER probably incorporated data collected by James Mackay and John Thomas Evans (Moulton, *Journals of the Lewis & Clark Expedition*, 1:5-6, maps 4-5; Jackson, *Lewis and Clark*, 1:136n, 156n).

IVINS'S AND MAC KAY'S JOURNAL: from Mackay, Lewis and Clark probably obtained notes from travels by Mackay and Evans, who died in 1798. Lewis and Clark also got information from John Hay, although perhaps not in the form of a journal (same, 156-7n; William Henry Harrison to TJ, 26 Nov. 1803).

[1] MS: "interourse."
[2] Word overwritten in place of "the before mentioned."
[3] Lewis here canceled "myself."
[4] Word interlined in place of "many."
[5] MS: "othe."

From Philip Mazzei

28 xbre

Il bastimento che doveva partire verso il fine d'8bre, è ancora qui; onde in questo intervallo ò potuto allestire le piante, le barbatelle, e i magliuoli, che posso mandarle quest'anno. Ò messo tutto in una cassa, il contenuto della quale, come di una scatola piena di noccioli di susine, albicocche e pesche, lo vedrà nell'annessa nota.

Il motivo che à ritardato e ritarda tuttavia il do. bastimento [. . .] è di una natura che irrita sommamente la mia fibra. In altre mie precedenti ò parlato dei ladronecci di generali, commissari, comandanti di piazze e loro satelliti e indicati i complicati mezzi d'estorsione inventati a tale oggetto. Si può francamente asserire, che le armate francesi, scendendo dal Capitano al più semplice soldato ànno costantemente dimostrata tanta discretezza e morigeratezza, quanta se ne potrebbe sperare da una numerosa adunanza d'uomini dei più sensati e virtuosi, e che nei ranghi superiori l'estorsioni e ladronecci, l'avarie d'ogni genere arrivano ad un'eccesso, del quale non si à idea. Il solo pretesto dei comandanti francesi per sottomettere ad ogni sorta di avarie i bastimenti americani è la possibilità d'avere a bordo delle mercanzie inglesi. Non ci è alcuno che possa o ardisca di mostrar loro la faccia, poiché il carattere di Console non basta per farsi rispettare da certa gente né per aver adito presso i Governi, e oltre di ciò Mr. Appleton non pare atto a far rispettare neppure quello di Console. Me ne dispiace, perché gli ho creduto, e gli credo tuttavia un buono zelo. Ma lo zelo non basta; ci vogliono altre qualità, le quali par che gli manchino intieramente. Io sono il solo, a mia notizia, che procuri di dis[caglia]rlo: non si è fatto qua neppure un'amico, vive quasi affatto isolato e non è punto amato né stimato dai suoi compatrioti. Io non conosco le sue finanze, ma non le credo molto floride; e quando si è in acque basse, si richiedono talenti non comuni, una forza di carattere non ordinaria per agire in maniera da sostenere decorosamente la propria reputazione. In varie mie precedenti mi spiegai bastantemente sull'articolo dei Consolati. In quella dei 17 Aprile da Venezia dissi, che, se fosse vero[1] che la commissione per approvisionar le flottiglie nel Mediterraneo fosse data in Livorno ad altri piuttosto che al Console, bisognerebbe attribuirlo a qualche *intrigo mentre non procedesse da ignoranza o inavvertenza nel Ministro della Marina, e che non saprei cosa pensar del Console se non chiedesse immediatamente la sua dimissione.* Ora ne son certo; la commissione appartiene a 2 giovani americani, i quali essendo adesso in America, è eseguita dai 4 loro associati, 3 dei quali sono Inglesi e uno Svizzero. Così vengono tolti al Console gli emolumenti che potrebbero fornirgli i mezzi di sostenere il posto con decoro; il Console viene avvilito nell'opinion pubblica dalla detta evidente dimostrazione che il Governo non à confidenza in lui (cosa che fa tanto più specie, perchè affatto nuova) ed egli non ha il coraggio di dimettersi. Dunque ora posso dire, che non so cosa pensare; non solo del console, come pure del togliere al Consolato le commissioni, che anche in buona politica devrebbero affidargli. [. . .]

Se io dovessi dire il mio parere sul quid agendum in tale stato di cose, direi, che il console attuale dovrebbe levarsi di qui perchè ormai non può essere amato né considerato, quando ancora le sue maniere non dispiacessero [. . .] tanto ai suoi compatriotti che alla gente del paese, che non essendoci contro di lui mancanze solide, ed essendo evidente che la maggior ragione della disistima ch'ei soffre [. . .] non procede da lui, mi parrebbe giusto l'indennizzarlo con qualche altro impiego; che se uno dei d.i giovani americani, commissionati per l'approvvisionamento delle Flottiglie avesse le qualità requisite per occupare il Consolato, potrebbe darsi a quello; e che volendo darlo ad un'altro bisogna dargli anche la commissione degli approvvisionamenti.

(1.) Il Bastimento, che porterà la presente colle già dette robe si chiama *Hannah* e il capitano *Yeardsley*. Tutto dev'esser consegnato in Filadelfia al Sigr: Samuel Emery, dal quale Le verrà inviata questa lettera a Washington City, affinchè Ella possa darne le sue disposizioni.

(2.) In tempi, nei quali pare che la letteratura Toscana, o dorma, o sia sepolta, mi è venuto fra mano l'Elogio d'Amerigo Vespucci scritto 15 anni sono, il quale mi pare una delle più belle produzioni di tal genere, venuta alla luce nei nostri tempi. Mi prendo la libertà di mandarglielo, persuaso che Le piacerà.[2]

(3.) Lascio al Maggior Barnes la cura di ragguagliarla della perdita della Fregata *La Filadelfia*, comandata dal Capn. *Bainbridge*, il quale pare che abbia avuto un cattivo Piloto. Io non ne ò il coraggio. Bisognerebbe ch'io potessi non ci pensare. Quel che più di tutto mi affligge, è il timore che il Commador Preble non possa intraprendere nulla contro Tripoli, prima di ricevere un soccorso, il quale dovrebbe esser poderoso, a motivo dei preparativi fatti in questi ultimi tempi dai Tripolini.

EDITORS' TRANSLATION

28 December

The ship that was supposed to leave around the end of October is still here; therefore, in the meanwhile, I have had a chance to prepare the plants, roots, and vine stocks that I can send you this year. I have placed everything in a crate, the contents of which you will find in the attached note, along with the contents of a box of plum, apricot, and peach stones.

The reason that has delayed and keeps delaying the ship's departure is of a kind that greatly irritates my core. In previous letters I have spoken of the robberies perpetrated by generals, commissioners, commanders, and their satellites, and I have spelled out the complex strategies for vexation adopted to implement them. It would be appropriate to say that the French armies, in their lower ranks, from the captains to the mere privates have always shown such discretion and moderation as could be hoped for from a great number of the most sensible and virtuous individuals. In the higher ranks, however, extortions, robberies, and injuries of any kind reach an unimaginable excess. The sole pretext the French commanders have for subjecting American ships to all sorts of maltreatment is the possibility that they may have English goods on board. There is nobody who can or dares stand up to them, since the charge of consul is not enough to earn respect from such people, nor to have access to the governments. Furthermore, Mr. Appleton does not seem to be able to earn respect, not even for the charge of consul. It pains me, especially because I did and still do believe he is acting on good zeal. But zeal is not enough. Other qualities are needed, qualities which he seems to lack completely. I am, as far as I know, the only one who tries to get him unstuck: he has made no friends here, lives in practical isolation, and is neither loved nor valued by his compatriots. I know nothing about his finances, but I do not think he is really wealthy. And when one sails in shallow waters, one needs uncommon abilities and an extraordinary moral strength to act so as to maintain one's reputation with decorum.

In several earlier letters I think I have explained sufficiently my position on the question of consulship. In the letter of 17 April from Venice I said that, if it were true that the commission to supply the fleets in the Mediterranean Sea at Leghorn were to be given to anyone else but the consul, that should be thought as the result of some machination—unless, of course, it came from ignorance or inattention on the part of the secretary of the navy. I would not know what to think of the consul, should he not immediately ask to be relieved. Now I am certain about the matter: the commission belongs to two young Americans. Since they are now in America, it is carried out by four associates of theirs, three of whom are English and one Swiss. In this manner, the consul is deprived of the income which may provide him with the means to hold his post with decorum. Such a blatant demonstration that the government has no confidence in him (a circumstance all the more remarkable since essentially new) undermines the consul's worth in public opinion, and he does not have the courage to quit his post. What I can say now is that I know not what to think, not only about the consul, but also about subtracting the commissions to the consulship, which should be given to him, even if just for good politics.

If I were to say something about what should be done in these matters, I would say that the current consul should pack up and leave, since now he can no longer be loved nor held in esteem, not even if his manners were not so displeasing to both his compatriots and the locals. Since nothing concrete may be held against him, and since it is evident that the greater part of the lack of esteem from which he suffers is not caused by him, it would seem right that he be compensated with some other position. Finally, should one of the aforementioned young Americans, commissioned for the supply of the navy, possess the necessary qualities to hold the consulship, it should be given to him. Should one want to give that post to anyone else, this person should be given the commission of supply as well.

(1.) The ship which will carry this letter with the goods mentioned above is called *Hannah* and its captain Yeardsley. Everything should be delivered in Philadelphia to Mr. Samuel Emery, who will forward this letter to you in Washington so that you may issue your dispositions about it.

(2.) In this, age in which Tuscan literature seems either asleep or dead, I have stumbled upon the eulogy of Amerigo Vespucci, written about 15 years ago. I think it is one of the most beautiful works in its kind to come to light in our times. I take the liberty of sending it to you, as I am convinced that you will enjoy it.

(3.) I leave it to Major Barnes the task of informing you about the loss of the frigate *Philadelphia*, commanded by Captain Bainbridge, who most likely had a bad pilot. I cannot bring myself to do so. I actually wish I could take my mind off it. What torments me the most is the fear that Commodore Preble will not be in a position to begin action against Tripoli before he receives support—a support that should be powerful, on account of the preparations undertaken lately by the people in Tripoli.

Dft (Archivio Filippo Mazzei, Pisa, Italy); partially illegible; Mazzei added numbers to change the sequence of the final three paragraphs (see note 2 below); part of a conjoined series of Mazzei's drafts of letters to TJ (see Margherita Marchione and Barbara B. Oberg, eds., *Philip Mazzei: The Comprehensive Microform Edition of his Papers*, 9 reels [Millwood, N.Y., 1981], 5:437-9). Recorded in SJL as received 13 Apr. 1804. For enclosures, see below.

CONTENUTO: Mazzei compiled a list of the plant materials he sent to TJ. Along with two cases of seeds, vines, and stem cuttings of 26 varieties of grapes, plums, peaches, and apricots, he also shipped a long container of earth with several strawberry species. Mazzei enumerated the contents of the first case of fruit specimens, consisting of stems of Angelica and German apricots; Alberges, Maddelena, and breast of Venus peaches; and Malmsey, Smyrna, Galletta, Regina, Luglienga, and Tokay grapes. The second box contained pits of apricots of the Angelica, German, and early red varieties; plums of the Regina, Green Gage, Mirabelle, White Imperial, and Boccon del Re varieties; and peaches of the Alberges, Vaga loggia, breast of Venus, San Jacopo, apple, and Maddelena varieties (MS in DLC: Mazzei Papers, in Italian, undated, but labeled as a list of items sent to TJ early in 1804; translated and printed in WMQ, 3d ser., 1 [1944], 394; see also Peter J. Hatch, *The Fruits and Fruit Trees of Monticello* [Charlottesville, 1998], 50, 113, 116, 120, 121, 157, 184-8).

QUELLA DEI 17 APRILE DA VENEZIA: for Mazzei's letter of 17 Apr. 1802 regarding the navy agency at Leghorn, see Vol. 37:252-3. American consul Thomas Appleton had previously sought the appointment for himself. The current navy agent at Leghorn was the firm of Degen, Purviance & Co. (NDBW, 2:260; Madison, *Papers, Sec. of State Ser.*, 2:400; 3:274, 334-5; 4:182).

Philadelphia merchant SAMUEL EMERY was the brother-in-law of Thomas Appleton (Madison, *Papers, Sec. of State Ser.*, 5:61; 6:369).

Italian scholar and monk Stanislao Canovai wrote a eulogy of AMERIGO VESPUCCI, asserting that he, and not Christopher Columbus, deserved credit for the discovery of America. The *Elogio d'Amerigo Vespucci* was published in Florence in 1788. TJ obtained multiple copies of the book during his lifetime and took special interest in the engraved portrait of Vespucci (Sowerby, No. 4163; Vol. 12:245; Vol. 15:xxxv-xxxvi).

PERDITA DELLA FREGATA LA FILADELFIA: on 31 Oct., while pursuing a Tripolitan vessel along the coast of North Africa, the frigate *Philadelphia* ran aground on uncharted rocks near Tripoli. After efforts to refloat the ship failed, and threatened by approaching gunboats, William Bainbridge gave orders to scuttle his frigate, then surrendered to the Tripolitans. Unfortunately for Bainbridge, the Tripolitans succeeded in refloating the *Philadelphia* and took it into Tripoli harbor. Bainbridge, his officers, and his crew, totaling 307 men, became prisoners. TJ would not learn of the disaster until March 1804 (NDBW, 3:171-6; Christopher McKee, *Edward Preble: A Naval Biography 1761-1807* [Annapolis, 1972], 179-81; TJ to the Senate and the House of Representatives, 20 Mch. 1804).

Probably as an enclosure to this letter, Mazzei sent TJ a long extract of a letter that Mazzei wrote to Madison, also dated 28 Dec. (Tr in DLC: TJ Papers, 146: 25407; in Italian with some English). Mazzei sent the letter to Madison on the *Hannah* along with the items addressed to TJ (Madison, *Papers, Sec. of State*

Ser., 6:240-4; Mazzei to TJ, 27 Jan. 1804).

[1] Mazzei wrote the remainder of this paragraph as an insertion keyed to this place in the manuscript.

[2] In MS, this paragraph precedes the one labeled "(1.)." Mazzei apparently added the numbers to change the order of the final paragraphs of the letter.

Proclamation Extending Building Regulations in the City of Washington

By the PRESIDENT of the United States.

A PROCLAMATION.

WHEREAS by the first articles of the terms and conditions declared by the President of the United States on the seventeenth day of October, 1791, for regulating the Materials and manner of buildings and improvements on the lots in the city of Washington, it is provided that "the outer and party walls of all houses in the said city shall be built of brick or stone," and by the third article of the same terms and conditions it is declared, "that the wall of no house shall be higher than 40 feet to the roof, in any part of the city, nor shall any be lower than 35 feet on any of the Avenues:

AND WHEREAS the above recited articles were found to impede the settlement in the city of mechanics and others whose circumstances did not admit of erecting houses authorised by the said regulations, for which cause the operation of the said articles, has been suspended by several acts of the President of the United States from the fifth day of June 1796, to the first day of January 1804, and the beneficial effects arising from such suspensions having been experienced—it is deemed proper to revive the same, with the exception hereafter mentioned.

Wherefore, I THOMAS JEFFERSON, President of the United States, do declare that the first and third articles above recited shall be, and the same are hereby suspended until the first day of January in the year one thousand eight hundred and five, and that all Houses which shall be erected in the said city of Washington previous to the said first day of January, in the year one thousand eight hundred and five, conformable in other respects to the regulations aforesaid shall be considered as lawfully erected, except that no wooden house covering more than 320 square feet, or higher than twelve feet from the Sill to the Eve shall be erected—nor shall such house be placed within 24 feet of any brick or stone house.

GIVEN under my hand, 28th December, 1803.

TH: JEFFERSON

Printed in *National Intelligencer*, 4 Jan. 1804. MS (DLC: District of Columbia Papers); partial text only; in a clerk's hand, signed by TJ.

For the TERMS AND CONDITIONS for buildings in Washington, established by George Washington and TJ in consultation with the District of Columbia's commissioners, see Washington, *Papers, Pres.*

Ser., 9:98, and Vol. 22:89-91. In a proclamation of 25 June 1796, Washington revised the regulations to allow for the construction of wooden houses up to December 1800 and TJ renewed the suspension with some changes on an annual basis (*Centinel of Liberty and George-town Advertiser*, 15 July 1796; Vol. 33:154-55; Vol. 36:415-16; Vol. 39:335-6).

From Robert Smith

Navy dept.

SIR,

Decr. 28. 1803.

I have the honor to present for your consideration the following Gentlemen to be Midshipmen in the Navy.

Jacquelin Harvie	Virga.	Recomdd.	by Mr. Harvie
John Lyon	Md.		Colo. Stricker.
Richard Wilson	Md.		Rt. Brent Esqre.
Charles Blake[1]	Md.		Mr. Nicholson
Henry Thomas	Md.		J. Gibson Esqre.
B. F. Rittenhouse	Ca.		Genl. Smith. of Va.
Alexr. S. Dexter	R. Id.		Mr. Dexter.
Edd. Winslow	Mtts.		Doctor Eustis
Thos. Shields	Del.		Mr. Rodney.
Andw. McDowell	Vt.		Mr. Elliott.

Should you approve of these appointments the enclosed Warrants will require your signature.—

I have the honor to be, with much respect, Sir, yr ob: servt.

RT SMITH

RC (DLC); in a clerk's hand, signed by Smith; at foot of text: "The President"; endorsed by TJ as received from the Navy Department on 28 Dec. and "midshipmen" and so recorded in SJL. FC (DNA: RG 45, LSP); in a clerk's hand. Enclosures not found.

Smith wrote letters to all of the candidates for midshipman listed above, except for Charles Blake, on 2 Jan. 1804, forwarding their warrants, copies of various navy regulations, and blank oaths of allegiance to be returned to the Navy Department along with their letters of acceptance (FC in Lb in DNA: RG 45, LSO).

[1] In FC, a note records that Blake was "not warranted."

From Archibald Stuart

DEAR SIR   Staunton 28th. Decr. 1803

This will be handed to you by Doctr Cornelius Baldwin a young Gent from the State of New Jersey who has resided several years in this place and practised Physic with considerable reputation—He is desirous of becomeing an adventurer in our newly acquired Terretory on the Mississippi and should any appointment in his line be in the Gift of the executive would gladly embrace such an opportunity of introducing him selfe to public Notice in that quarter—Should he meet with such an appointment I have no doubt but he will acquit himselfe to the entire satisfaction of All concerned: & I have as little doubt of his using his utmost exertions to perpetuate the present prosperous & happy State of our public affairs

adieu I am yrs most affectionately   ARCHD: STUART

RC (DNA: RG 59, LAR); at foot of text: "The President of the U States"; endorsed by TJ as received 29 Jan. 1804 and so recorded in SJL with notation "Dr. Baldwin for Louisiana"; also endorsed by TJ: "Baldwin Dr. for emploimt N.O."

Stuart and Jacob Kinney of Staunton also sent letters of introduction for CORNELIUS BALDWIN to Senator John Breckinridge of Kentucky. Stuart's letter, dated 29 Dec., informed Breckinridge that Baldwin was planning to move to New Orleans in order to secure "a more profitable Station." Baldwin hoped to receive a federal appointment that would maintain him "untill he could acquire some Knowledge of the people & be enabled to stand upon his own legs" (same; endorsed by TJ: "Stuart Arch to mr Breckinridge"). Kinney's letter, dated 28 Dec., informed Breckinridge that Baldwin had settled in Staunton several years earlier and practiced medicine with success, but had made an unfortunate investment in an iron works. Kinney considered Baldwin "an honest industrious man" (same; endorsed by TJ: "Kinney Jacob. to J. Breckinridge").

From Louis Valentin

SIR   Nancy, December 28th. 1803.

I have the honour to send you, herewith, a copy of my treatise on the *yellow fever*. this Work is the first that had been published *ex professo* in our language, and agreeably to the desires of our first School of Physick, as you Will See it in the advertisement. Seven months ago, I had already trusted to an agent of the french government, another Work of mine the title of Which is: *Résultats de l'inoculation de la Vaccine &c.* With Some experiments on sundry domestic animals.

I Shall be Very happy if you have the goodness to accept of them. Such a favor Will add exceedingly to their Weak Worth. for the materials I gathered and the practice I acquired in the treatment of the yellow fever, I am, in a great measure, indebted to my residence for five years in your Country. it is the Sincerest Wish of my heart, that Scourge might relinquish it entirely

I remain, Sir, With the highest consideration and most profound respect

of your excellency the most humble and obedient Servant

LOUIS VALENTIN
M.D. at Nancy

RC (DLC); at head of text: "his excellency Mr. Thomas Jefferson, President of the united States of america"; endorsed by TJ as received 11 Oct. 1805 and so recorded in SJL. Enclosures: (1) Louis Valentin, *Traité de la fièvre jaune d'Amérique* (Paris, 1803; Sowerby, No. 920). (2) Louis Valentin, *Résultats de l'inoculation de la vaccine dans les départemens de la Meurthe, de la Meuse, des Vosges et du Haut-Rhin* (Nancy, 1802; Sowerby, No. 952).

Louis Valentin (1758-1829) went to Saint-Domingue in 1790 as the chief physician of the French army there. Forced from the island by the revolution in 1793, he lived in Virginia, became a member of the American Philosophical Society, and directed hospitals for French mariners until he returned to France in 1799. He studied contagious and epidemic diseases, wrote treatises on inoculation and other medical subjects, and, using his housemaids as human subjects, experimented with the transmission of the smallpox virus between humans and a variety of domestic animals for the purposes of propagating vaccine. He wrote the first biographical work on Edward Jenner (*Biographie universelle, ancienne et moderne*, new ed., 45 vols. [Paris, 1843–65], 42:453-4; Elinor Meynell, "French Reactions to Jenner's Discovery of Smallpox Vaccination: The Primary Sources," *Social History of Medicine*, 8 [1995], 287, 295, 297, 299; Louis Valentin, *Notice Biographique sur le Docteur Jenner* [Montpellier, France, 1805; Sowerby, No. 421]; Vol. 35:490-1).

To Jacob Crowninshield

SIR   Washington Dec. 29. 1803.

The inclosed has been sent to me by some person who does not chuse to give his name. the usurpation of our flag, and the practice of our merchants to lend their cover to belligerent property has been a long & crying evil. we lose the profits of doing the same business for ourselves, subject our own vessels to suspicion & vexatious searches, and are in constant danger of being embroiled with the belligerent powers on account of property which we are only made to believe to be ours, by our own citizens, sacrificing every principle of truth & patriotism to personal favour. the only means I have of giving any effect to the suggestions of the writer, is to put it into the hands of some gentleman of the legislature acquainted with the subject. on that ground I take the liberty of committing it to you, to do in it whatever your own judgment shall direct. Accept my salutations & assurances of respect   TH: JEFFERSON

PrC (DLC); at foot of text: "Mr. Crownenshield." Enclosure: Anonymous to TJ, [before 28] Dec. 1803.

To Albert Gallatin

Candidates for the office of Keeper of the Light house
at Smith's point

William Mountague. owns the land adjacent, an Antirepublican therefore inadmissible.

Lancelot L. Edwards. lives near Smith's Point. recommendd by mr Taliaferro. is he republican? is he sober? and careful & stationary at his residence?

Thomas Robinson. lives near the place. recommendd by mr Taliaferro & Genl. Mason. an old sea-captain. this is a good recommendation, but same questions as respecting Edwards

Joseph Jones Monroe, brother of Colo. Monroe. his child inherits the very land on which the light house is built, & he will live in the house belonging to it. he was known to me about half a dozen years ago. he is republican. I did not think him then a careful man, & the nature of his business (a lawyer) made him not stationary.

Wm. Nelms. lives $\frac{3}{4}$ of a mile off. recommended by Doctr. Jones as republican, honest and diligent. is he also sober?

TH:J. TO MR GALLATIN.   Dec. 29. 03.

The above is a list of the candidates for Smith's point. if the 3d. stands otherwise on an equal footing with the last, his being a sea-captain is in his favor. he seems very illiterate, which perhaps is not material. Dr. Jones probably knows them all. will you have a conversation with him on a view of the whole, and settle between you the one most preferable?

PrC (DLC). Recorded in SJL with no-   HE WAS KNOWN TO ME: see Vol.
tation "Light H. Smith's Pt."   28:45; Vol. 29:27.

From Albert Gallatin

DEAR SIR   Decer. 29th 1803

Doctr. Jones says that Joseph Monroe is perfectly worthless—Edwards extremely indolent—and Robinson having removed to Fauquier & owning no land in the vicinity never could find it convenient to return for the sake of the trifling salary. He is decidedly in favour of Nelms.

Respectfully Your obedt. Servt.   ALBERT GALLATIN

RC (DLC); at foot of text: "The President of the United States"; endorsed by TJ as received from the Treasury Department on 29 Dec. and "Nelms. Keepr. Lt. H. Smith's Pt." and so recorded in SJL.

On 31 Dec., TJ informed Gallatin, "The appointment of William Nelms to be Keeper of the Lighthouse at Smith's Point is approved." Gallatin noted that the salary was $250 and transmitted the information to the commissioner of the revenue (facsimile of RC in Patrick Evans-Hylton, *Images of America: Lighthouses and Lifesaving Stations of Virginia* [Charleston, S.C., 2005], 16; in TJ's hand and signed by him; with notation signed by Gallatin; addressed: "The Secretary of the Treasury"; endorsed: "see letter to Mr. Daviss & Mr. Nelm's same date"; not recorded in SJL). On 31 Dec., Gallatin signed letters to Nelms and Norfolk collector William Davies, informing them of the appointment (FCs in Lb in DNA: RG 26, LL).

From Thomas Leiper

DEAR SIR   Philada. Decr. 29th. 1803

Their is a report here and from the quarter I received it I believe to be true that Major Jackson is to be removed & that you would put Doctr. Bache in his place if it would give general satisfaction to the Republicans—Before I heard your opinion I was asked for mine and whilst I was a think the Gentleman mentioned several names which I most confess I did not perfectly like—He then mentioned Doctr. Bache that is the Man that will silence every republican and as for the Federalist and Tories I hope the President has been long convinced he cannot please them unless he takes from their own number—I have no doubt in my mind that the Republicans in General would be better pleased with the Executive if their were more removals and if you have any such thing in Veiw for your own sake make them all in One day for you may rely on it they will make as much noise at the removal of one as of Fifty—No doubt but the character of the Major will appear at full length drawn by himself and the question asked who is Doctr. Bache—the answer is at hand He is the Grandson of Old Franklin he is the brother of Benjamin the Aurora man he is the son of Richard who was post master all the War when it was not worth retaining and turned out by a new England faction to make room for a Mr. Hazard who is so little thought of at this present period (altho' immensely rich) as to be Voted out of the Corporation of the second Presbyterian Church. But what has Doctr. Bache done to my knowledge he was One of some 8 or Ten that first Met to Form the 4th Troop of Cavalry and from that Troop you may date the beginning of the Legion who in some Two month in respect to numbers were upon a Footing with Adams Volunteers for this action I have had more Credit for than any of my life and certainly if their is any merit in it the Doctr. most come in for his share—After this history no republican can object to the appointment—The Old Whigs were very much pleased with the favor you confered on Blair McClananghan because they knew he was in want and they do expect you will be so good as to think of him again—Have you nothing for Robert Morris a man second to none in Our Revolution—He is in want at this day—O! think of this Thing—with much esteem and perfect respect I am

Dear sir Your most Obedient Servant   THOMAS LEIPER

RC (DNA: RG 59, LAR); addressed: "Thomas Jefferson President of the U. States Washington"; franked; postmarked 30 Dec.; endorsed by TJ as received 2 Jan. 1804 and "Bache Wm. to be Survr. Phila v. Jackson" and so recorded in SJL.

4TH TROOP OF CAVALRY: Leiper was elected captain of the newly organized troop in 1798. He was major of the Horse of the LEGION organized to oppose the "Black Cockade" forces that supported the Adams administration (PMHB, 48 [1924], 281-2).

For the appointment of Blair McClenachan (MCCLANANGHAN) as bankruptcy commissioner, see Henry Dearborn to TJ, 21 July 1803.

To the Mississippi Territory Legislative Council

TO THE LEGISLATIVE COUNCIL OF
THE MISSISIPI TERRITORY.   Washington Dec. 29. 03.

I participate, fellow-citizens, in the satisfaction you express, in your address of the 19th. of November, on the result of the proceedings instituted for the relief of the states whose commerce lies through the channel of the Missisipi: and am happy in percieving the effects produced on your minds by the earnest attention of the General government to the interests of it's Western portion.

By obtaining the exclusive navigation of the Missisipi we prevent the National dissensions which rival interests there would have been ever producing, & destroy the germ of future and inevitable wars. the country too which it waters opens an invaluable field for the surplus of our population in future times.

That nations should, in friendship & harmony, take liberal & dispassionate views of their interfering interests, and settle them by timely arrangements, of advantage to both undiminished by injuries to either, is certainly wiser than to yield to short-sighted passions, which, estimating neither chances nor consequences, prompt to measures of mutual destruction, rather than of mutual benefit.

I accept your congratulations with pleasure, & pray you to be assured of my great respect & consideration.   Th: Jefferson

RC (NHi). PrC (DLC).

From J. P. G. Muhlenberg

Sir   Philadelphia Decr. 29th. 1803
I am Honor'd with Your favor of the 24th. Inst. and now beg leave to inform You, That I have this day Shipp'd for Washington, by the Sloop Unity, Captn. Allbright, the Barrell of Missisippi Water, forwarded to me by Mr. Hulings from New Orleans—The two Pipes of Lisbon, & the Butt of Sherry Wine, will be forwarded to Richmond, to the address of Messrs. Gibson & Jefferson of that place, by the Schooner Caroline, Captn. Lewis who expects to Sail on Saturday next.

I have the Honor to be with Perfect Respect Sir Your Obedt Servt
P Muhlenberg

RC (MHi); at foot of text: "The President of The U. States"; endorsed by TJ as received 1 Jan. 1804 and so recorded in SJL.

From Benjamin Smith Barton

Dear Sir,   Philadelphia, December 30th, 1803.
In answer to your letter, which I received this morning, I shall, with great pleasure and strict sincerity, communicate what I know respecting the Sulphur in Jenisseia.

I visited this bed of sulphur, or, as it is called in the country, the "Sulphur-Springs," in August, 1797. I observed a quantity of sulphur in and about the springs. The whole quantity might, perhaps, have amounted to a cart-load; I think not more. It is, unquestionably, in a state of considerable purity; for some of it, which was examined by

Dr. Priestley, was found to contain 96 *per cent*. of good and unmixed sulphur.

The whole of the sulphur that I saw, and the whole of what I could obtain any information at the time, from Captain Williamson, Mr. Thomas Morris, and other gentlemen, was, undoubtedly, derived from the water of the Springs. This water is very transparent; as much so as the clearest limestone-water. It, however, both tastes and smells, very sensibly, of sulphur. To me, it had, likewise, a very evident taste of lime. Indeed, there can be no doubt, that the sulphur is held in solution by means of the lime. The temperature of the Springs is 54 degrees of Fahrenheit's thermometer.

The sulphur is deposited by the water, in its passage out of the bason; in which it first makes its appearance. It is deposited upon the adjacent stones, leaves, mosses, &c., especially upon the mosses. The stones assume a variety of curious shapes, some of them evidently occasioned by the action of the sulphuric acid (here constantly forming, by the union of pure air with the sulphur) upon them.

I must not omit to observe, that the ground about the springs, at least on one side of them, for some distance, gives a hollow sound under the hoof of the horse. Possibly, at the place from which this sound proceeds, there is a considerable excavation, occasioned by the gradual removal of the sulphur, which is deposited by the spring. This suspicion is rendered more probable from our knowing, that the Jenisseia-country does remarkably abound in sulphur.

The above is the substance of some notes which I made on the spot. Permit me to add, that, judging by what I saw at the time, I cannot believe, that the possession of the "Sulphur-Springs" will be of any importance to the United-States. It is not easy for me to say, what quantity of the sulphur I have mentioned is deposited by the water, in the course of a month, or a year. From the small size of the Springs, however; from the transparency of the water; and from the quantity, say a cart-load, which I saw (and what I saw may be supposed to have been collecting for a very considerable length of time, as the inhabitants, in 1797, were few in number, and did not carry it away), I greatly doubt, if one quarter of a ton be deposited annually. What the bowels of the earth, in the neighbourhood of the Springs, may contain, we know not: but, with respect to the similar Springs, in Europe, we have many facts to prove, that the matters impregnating the waters, are often derived from a distant source.

Printed in *Philadelphia Medical and Physical Journal*, 1, pt. 2 (1805), 166-8; at head of text: "XXVII. Notice of the Sulphur-Springs, in the County of Ontario, and State of New-York. In a letter to the President of the United-States, from the Editor." Recorded in SJL as received 4 Jan. 1804.

YOUR LETTER: TJ to Barton, 27 Dec.

From Jacob Crowninshield

SIR   Washington 30th. Decr. 1803.

I have the honor to inclose you some ill-digested remarks on the anonymous communication which you sent me yesterday.—

I acknowledge the practice alluded to is supposed to exist among our merchants, but I assure you it is more a subject of clamour with some interested people than any thing else. If it were really carried on to the extent, and in the manner described by the writer, and had involved us in the difficulties he has refered to, it would indeed demand the prompt interference of the National Legislature. It appears to be rather the false suggestion of the belligerent nations, which has reached our ears, than the honest language of truth, and could they prescribe laws and regulations for American Commerce, at their pleasure, we might at once bow the knee, & give up all our neutral & just rights on the Seas. Notwithstanding my own opinion may seem to be, perhaps, in a trifling degree, at variance with yours as to the matter of fact, tho' I have no idea but your own convictions are similar to mine in this respect, I will with great pleasure adopt any line of conduct which you may have the goodness to point out to me on this occasion. The protection of our seamen ought to be a primary object, & I hardly know of any sacrifice I would not make, (could I act myself,) in order to prevent the flagrant violation of their rights, which we see practiced almost every day.—

With assurances of my highest respect I am Sir your devoted & humble servt   JACOB CROWNINSHIELD

RC (DLC); at foot of text: "Honble T. Jefferson. Prest US."; endorsed by TJ as received 30 Dec. and so recorded in SJL.

ENCLOSURE

Remarks on American Commerce

Remarks on the American flag & seamen.
The writer of the anonymous communication enclosed to the President, has stated "that America lost immense sums in the course of the late war by spoliations," and there can be no question about it, but he certainly attributes these losses to a wrong cause. I would ask if the 400 American vessels cap-

tured by Great Brittain previous to the ratification of Mr. Jay's Treaty, were not strictly American, how has it happened that upwards of 4 millions of Dollars have been restored to us on that account. How comes it too, that 3 or 400 sail of American vessels were adjudicated in the Vice Admiralty Courts of New Providence Burmuda, Halifax, Jamaica & Tortola, between the years '95 & 1801, & that $\frac{3}{4}$ths of these captures now remain unsatisfied, altho' the claim for restitution is equally just with the others. As the Treaty made no provission for captures subsequent to its ratification, these have not been allowed in the late settlement. The appeals are necessarily going on thro' the Superior Courts in England, but various excuses are found to delay a restoration of the property, & it is probable many vessels & cargos never will be restored, notwithstanding the fairest proofs have been given of its being American. The French captures embraced nearly 500 American vessels, & the Spaniards detained and captured 40 or 50 more, yet those who have examined this subject never doubted that the condemnations of these vessels & cargos were illegal & unjust. We have given up all expectation of recovering any thing from the French except in those cases, which are recognised by the late Convention, but the Merchts are not without hopes that something will be recovered from the Spanish Govt.—The belligerent cruisers always alledge that neutrals cover the property of their enemies, & they condemn as enemies what belongs to innocent & unoffending neutrals. If a neutral ship is loaded with a valuable cargo, it is easy enough to raise pretexts for its condemnation, it may be stated that she is bound to blockaded ports, and this will probably soon be urged respecting St Domingo, when there are few ships on that station, and when if it could be fairly examined it would be found that no real blockade had or could take place. By recent transactions of British ships of War off Martinique & Gaurdaloupe & even St Domingo, we may suppose the old system of blockade is to be enforced, & if so I fear we shall experience heavy losses. If ships are passing near these Islands, bound to other ports, it will be said that they intended to violate what they pretend[1] to call the laws of blockade, and many will be detained for adjudication, but it may well be questioned whether a belligerent squadron has a right to form a blockade at its pleasure, & if this is admitted, it surely may be doubted whether due notice ought not to be given to the neutral ship previous to her sailing. If a few ships can blockade a port or a whole Island, are neutrals safe in their Commerce. If it is to depend upon a declaration of the Commander of an inferior squadron will it not give him the power to enrich himself at the expence of the neutral & where will it end. Upon this system all France may be declared in a state of blockade, & France may retaliate upon Great Brittain, by issuing similar orders, & between them both our commerce would be annihilated.—With respect to the violation of our flag by our own Citizens covering enemies property. I can not believe the practice exists at all, or at least I doubt if it exists in any considerable degree. Our trading capital amounts to upwards of One hundred millions of Dollars upon the lowest calculation. This is fully sufficient to carry on our own commerce, as well as to purchase up a large part of the produce of the WI Islands belonging to those powers, who can not in time of War, export their own articles in their own bottoms, & it must be sold to the highest bidder, we shall then never be reduced to the necessity of taking freights for others, when we can purchase on our own account.

[209]

If necessary, Merchts can & will anticipate their capitals, & the spirit of the people is such, for commercial speculations, that they can not & perhaps ought not to be restrained.—The writer of the piece alluded to, appears to be highly in favour of the English interest, perhaps he is an Englishman, for he seems to want to find an excuse for the unjust condemnations of Amn property which took place during the late War. He says the Merchts must be made "to swear to the property on entering & clearing," & if this was done he thinks it would prevent the adjudications. Now in fact *this is always done whenever a war breaks out in Europe*, indeed all prudent Merchts take care to provide their ships with every necessary document in time of Peace as well as War. It is known as a fact that all the Merchts of Massachusetts are very particular in this respect. In addition to the usual Custom house papers the owners apply to the Notary Public or other Magistrate in the towns where they reside *& make oath to the property*. The Certificates accompany the Invoice & bill of lading, & it states every particular relative to the Cargo, who are it's owners, where it is destined, & in short nothing is omitted to prove it's neutrality. These documents then go to the Consuls of the belligerent nations and are countersigned by them. The Register is signed by the President of the US and the Custom house papers are all signed by the Collector & Naval Officer.—What more can be desired or expected, yet during the whole of last war were not vessels thus circumstanced condemned, & were there not a thousand instances of the gross violations of our flag by the belligerent ships, notwithstanding all these precautions.—My own opinion is, that our Merchts are not in the habit of covering the property of the belligerent nations. It is not for their interest to do it, whatever may be alledged to the contrary. They prefer making the profit on the shipment on their own accot. to receiving only the freight & commissions. If the cargo is their own the gain is considerable. If it is a covered freight what is the profit, a mere trifle, not worth accepting, when the other can be realised. In war time our Merchts are not satisfied with receiving a bear freight of a few hundred pounds, when it is well known, the same cargo, loaded on their own account, would produce a much larger sum. They possess sufficient funds to make the purchase, & is it at all probable they will relinquish the advantage which is known will arise to them from the sales at the port of destination. If the belligerent offers a freight it is almost universally rejected, & the produce by this means falls to us, at a cheaper price. We visit their ports with a view of supplying them with articles necessary for their consumption, & the payments are made in produce as a return cargo.

We carry Dollars Iron &c to the East Indies & China, & we take in exchange Cotton & silk goods, sugars Coffee & Teas &c. The purchases are bona fide on Amn account & risk. Can it then be said that we carry on a trade "for the paltry consideration of freight & commission." In reality I know of no trade carried on at this moment by the Amn merchts where the property is under false or disguised papers, & I doubt if it is at all practised except perhaps in some degree by the agents of English houses in the US. who possess in themselves a sort of shield in their Certificates of naturalization, & have thereby the means of covering the property of their principals in England, & so long as these men can be naturalised here, & are suffered to hold their rights of British subjects in England at the same time, I fear the evil is without a remedy.—If we *oblige* the merchts to swear to their property we shd do no more than they themselves now do voluntarily, & wd it not shew the world that we *suspected* our merchts were in the habit of covering enemies property, and had found it necessary to bind them down to positive laws, in order to prevent it, & was it adopted the consequence wd be, two vessels wd be condemned in future, where only one is at present.—

The British arbitrarily set up rules to govern the commerce of neutrals. They legislate for us without our consent. They advance the absurd doctrine that a neutral can not carry on a trade from the Colonies to the Country to which they belong. They say we must go in a particular route which they dare point out to us. They pretend to fix what is contraband of War without asking other nations whether the regulation is injurious to their particular interests or not. They declare blockaded such ports as they please without having a sufficient number of ships stationed before the port to form a close blockade. And They allow other nations to trade with them only upon a limitted and circumscribed plan. In short they are endeavouring to engross the commerce of the whole world, & to bear down the free trade of all other nations, and if we submit to mould our laws to suit their convenience, there will be no end to it, we might go on changing them from year to year, and still it would be necessary to comply with some new impositions. Commerce should be free & unshackled, it can not prosper in chains. We shall be a great commercial nation almost against our inclination, & our trade must encrease to a boundless extent if Treaties & Laws are not made to bring us back to the former dependent state, when Great Britain dictated to us as Colonies.—We ought to reserve to ourselves the right of retaliating on any of the European nations, who may be induced to violate our just rights on the ocean or to impose any extraordinary commercial restrictions on our trade, & we shd not hesitate from withholding supplies, nor refuse laying similar restrictions on their commerce with the U States. If they capture our ships the excuse will be that they were engaged in unlawful voyages, that they were bound to blockaded ports or that they were loaded with enemies property, (the best excuse of all), however fair the documents or however clear it may be that the property is American. I hope & trust this system will not be pursued by the belligerent nations in future, but if it is I am clearly of the opinion that they can be arrested by other & cheaper means than those which were adopted during the last European War.—The writer of the anonymous communication classes "*Carriers* & *Coverers*" together. They are clearly distinct. We may carry the Merchandise of other countries on our own account, & even on freight, & yet not cover it, & it is every days practice—He insinuates too that the produce of St Domingo & Cuba was charged to us at a higher price last war because we covered their property. This was not so. The produce[2] of St Domingo & Cuba was bo't at reasonable rates by our merchts and particularly in the Havana, sugar was so low as to afford great profits. It is true our merchts suffered greatly at the opening of the St Domingo trade, but their losses were chiefly owing to their sending a too abundant supply of goods at one time, & to the consequent rise of the Isld produce. Upon the whole I do not agree with the writer in any one of his positions, and so far as respects the "*Protections*," (as they are improperly called) which are given to our seamen we are equally at variance. How is "*the law* respecting our sailors to occasion a misunderstanding with England." Who are "the worthless fellows that can be hired for a trifle to go with the sailors to a Notary & make oath to the Citizenship of every British seaman who comes to our ports." In Massachusts & I believe in all the NE and middle States this can not be done to any extent. The Magistrates are very particular, & the *Collector* of the Ports wd refuse granting Protections under such circumstances. No doubt some British seamen may pass examination, but the number must be very few indeed, but a British Capt regards not your Protections, he laughs at them, & takes your seamen almost when he pleases, & I have known Amn vessels even during the prest war, very much distressed from the impressment of their seamen, & in some cases it has been difficult to get the vessels into port for the want of hands. I never yet could reconcile how we came to give protections at all, & I believe now, it would be better to refuse giving them except G Britain wd agree to respect them more than she has done for some time past. Surely our public Ships have the same right to examine the English mercht vessels, & take their seamen if found without protections, as they have to impress ours, & they can not fairly object to this *priviledge*, if they persist in their present bad habits, but this plan would not save our seamen & ought not to be followed except in the most urgent necessity. I know of no better way than to negociate with the British Govt upon the subject & get them to abandon the practice in future & restore those they have heretofore detained. It is a very unpleasant & delicate subject for Congress to legislate upon, & if any delays have taken place in that body I presume it is from this cause. Many members consider the subject as involving some important considerations, & they have no means of restraining the practice except perhaps by adopting coercive measures, which ought only to be pursued in the last resort.—

Washington 29th Decr. 1803

MS (DLC); entirely in Crowninshield's hand.

[1] MS: "prentend."
[2] MS: "poduce."

From William Lee

SIR/ Bordeaux Dec 30. 1803

I take the liberty to send you three boxes containing fruits in Brandy prunes and almonds—They go in the good Intent Capt Wallington for Philadelphia addressed to the Collecter of that port and I hope will arrive safe.—I had the honor of forwarding you ℞ the ship Genl. Washington which sailed yesterday for Boston a small bundle containing a few books directed to my care by Mr Volney—

with great respect I have the pleasure to remain your obedient servant WILLIAM LEE

RC (MHi); endorsed by TJ as received 21 Mch. 1804 and "3 boxes fruits in brandy prunes Almonds books from Volney" and so recorded in SJL.

FEW BOOKS: Volney was trying to send TJ his two-volume work *Tableau du climat et du sol des États-Unis d'Amérique*, which was published in Paris in November (Vol. 40:353n; Volney to TJ, 26 Nov.).

From Richard Stanford

DEAR SIR,   House of Rep. Dec. 30—1803

By request of Mr. J. Gales of Raleigh, N.C. I do myself the pleasure herewith to cover you a letter from Docr. Sibley, which, he thinks, may possibly throw some additional light on the subject of Louisiana.

I have the honor to be, Sir, with highest respect yr. hble. Sert.

R STANFORD

RC (MHi); endorsed by TJ as received 30 Dec. and so recorded in SJL. Enclosure: probably John Sibley to Joseph Gales, dated Louisiana, 15 Aug. 1803, providing a lengthy and highly detailed account of the population, geography, flora, fauna, and natural resources of Louisiana, which Gales received 11 Dec. from Sibley's son in Fayetteville; Sibley also states that he has been the conduit through which much of the French population learned of the sale of Louisiana to the United States and that he has worked to convince them of the "mildness of the American government" (*Raleigh Regis-*ter, 2, 9 Jan. 1804; *National Intelligencer*, 13, 16 Jan. 1804; New York *American Citizen*, 19, 21, 23 Jan. 1804).

A Republican, Richard Stanford (1767-1816) of North Carolina served in the U.S. House of Representatives from 1797 to 1816 (*Biog. Dir. Cong.*).

Joseph GALES was editor and publisher of the *Raleigh Register* (Vol. 32:60n; Vol. 37:312n). For earlier information received from John Sibley ON THE SUBJECT OF LOUISIANA, see William C. C. Claiborne to TJ, 28 Oct.

To David Leonard Barnes

SIR   Washington Dec. 31. 03.

I take the liberty of inclosing to you a petition I have recieved from Nathaniel Ingraham of your state, now suffering imprisonment at Bristol in Rhodeisland under judgment of the circuit court there. I also inclose the copy of a letter I wrote to mr Ellery on a former application in the same case. as I understand that the judges who sat in the cause are either dead or distant from the state, I shall be perfectly satisfied with the opinion of yourself alone, who acted as attorney in the prosecution. if there has been no higher degree of atrocity in the case than that which constitutes it's essence & is inseparable from it, I should be disposed to consider the intentions of the legislature as to the measure of his punishment, as fulfilled. I pray you to accept assurances of my great respect & consideration.   TH: JEFFERSON

PrC (DLC); at foot of text: "The honble Judge Barnes." Enclosures: (1) Petition of Nathaniel Ingraham, 15 Dec. (2) TJ to Christopher Ellery, 9 May 1803.

To George Clinton

DEAR SIR   Washington Dec. 31. 03.

I recieved last night your favor of the 22d. written on the occasion of the libellous pamphlet lately published with you. I began to read it, but the dulness of the first pages made me give up the reading for a dip into here & there a passage, till I came to what respected myself. the falshood of that gave me a test for the rest of the work, & considering it always useless to read lies, I threw it by. as to yourself be assured no contradiction was necessary. the uniform tenor of a man's life furnishes better evidence of what he has said or done on any particular occasion than the word of an enemy, and of an enemy too who shews that he prefers the use of falsehoods which suit him to truths which do not. little hints & squibs in certain papers had long ago apprised me of a design to sow tares between particular republican characters. but to divide those by lying tales whom truths cannot divide, is the hackneyed policy of the gossips of every society. our business is to march straight forward,[1] to the object which has occupied us for eight & twenty years, without, either, turning to the right or left. my opinion is that two or three years more will bring back to the fold of republicanism all our wandering brethren whom the cry of 'Wolf' scattered in 1798. till that is done, let every man stand to his post, and hazard nothing by change. and when that is done, you and I may retire to the tranquility which our years begin to call for, and reprise with satisfaction the efforts of the age we happened to be born in, crowned with compleat success. in the hour of death we shall have the consolation to see established in the land of our fathers the most wonderful work of wisdom & disinterested patriotism that has ever yet appeared on the globe.

In confidence that you will not be 'weary in well-doing,' I tender my wishes that your future days may be as happy as your past ones have been useful, & pray you to accept my friendly salutations & assurances of high consideration & respect.   TH: JEFFERSON

RC (CLjC); addressed: "George Clinton Governor of New York Albany"; franked and postmarked; endorsed by Clinton: "Letter from the President *private*." PrC (DLC).

Samuel L. Mitchill observed that William P. Van Ness's PAMPHLET "makes no small Conversation at Washington." The New York congressman noted that those "libelled in the most violent and acrimonious terms" were all Republicans, and he found it remarkable that he had not been "implicated at all in the squabble." The vice president, in the meantime, was giving "very pretty dinners" in Washington. Mitchill attended one on 18 Dec., and Senator John Armstrong, who was "villainously abused in the pamphlet," attended another (Mitchill to Catharine Mitchill, 21 Dec. 1803, in NNMus: Mitchill Papers).

WEARY IN WELL-DOING: "And let us not be weary in well doing: for in due season we shall reap, if we faint not" (Galatians 6:9).

[1] TJ here canceled "& side by side."

To J. P. G. Muhlenberg

DEAR SIR   Washington Dec. 31. 03.

I recieved last night your two favors of the 27th. informing me of the arrival at Philadelphia of two pipes of Lisbon wine from mr Jarvis, and a butt of Sherry from mr Yznardi of Cadiz. I will ask the favor of you to have them reshipped to Richmond to the Address of messrs. Gibson & Jefferson, who will pay freight &c from Philadelphia. that from Lisbon & Cadiz to Philadelphia shall be remitted you instantly with the duties &c the moment you will be so good as to make them known to me. I return you mr Jarvis's letter with many apologies for the trouble these private consignments of mine give you. Accept my salutations & assurances of great esteem & respect.

TH: JEFFERSON

RC (CSmH); at foot of text: "Genl. Muhlenberg." PrC (MHi); endorsed by TJ in ink on verso. Enclosure not found.

Notes on a Conversation with Matthew Lyon

Dec. 31.   After dinner to-day the pamphlet on the conduct of Colo. Burr being the subject of conversn Matthew Lyon[1] noticed the insinuations agt. the republicans at Washington pending the Presidential election, & expressed his wish that every thing was spoke out which was known: that it would then appear on which side there was a bidding for votes, & he declared that John Brown of Rhode island, urging him to vote for Colo. Burr used these words. 'what is it you want, Colo. Lyon, is it office, is it money? only say what you want & you shall have it.'

MS (DLC: TJ Papers, 113:19521); entirely in TJ's hand; follows, on same sheet, Notes on a Conversation with Charles Coffin, 13 Dec. 1803.

PAMPHLET: see George Clinton to TJ, 22 Dec.

[1] TJ here canceled "said."

To the Senate and
the House of Representatives

To the Senate and House of Representatives
of the US. of America

I now lay before Congress the annual account of the fund established for defraying the Contingent charges of government. No occasion having arisen for making use of any part of it in the present year, the balance of eighteen thousand five hundred and sixty dollars, unexpended at the end of the last year, remains now in the Treasury.

Th: Jefferson
Dec. 31. 1803.

RC (DNA: RG 233, PM, 8th Cong., 1st sess.); endorsed by a House clerk. RC (DNA: RG 46, LPPM, 8th Cong., 1st sess.); endorsed by a Senate clerk. PrC (DLC). Recorded in SJL with notation "Contingent fund." Enclosure: "Account of the Fund established for defraying the Contingent Charges of Government for the Year 1803," Register's Office, 2 Jan. 1804, noting that from the grant of $20,000 on 1 May 1802, $18,560 remains unexpended and "subject to the Orders of the President," the same balance as of 31 Dec. 1802 (MS in DNA: RG 233, PM, in a clerk's hand, signed by Joseph Nourse,

endorsed by a House clerk; MS in DNA: RG 46, LPPM, in same clerk's hand, signed by Nourse, endorsed by a Senate clerk).

Lewis Harvie delivered this message to Congress on 3 Jan. 1804. The House read and tabled the message and enclosed account. The Senate read them and ordered "That they lie on file" (JHR, 4:511; JS, 3:332).

UNEXPENDED AT THE END OF THE LAST YEAR: for the 1802 report to Congress, see Vol. 39:357-8.

From David Campbell

Campbella, State of Tennessee
Jany 1st. 1804

Dear Sir,

In reading a favourite author the other Day, the following observations made deep impressions on my mind. Man, says he, is the subject of every history; and to know him well, we must see him and consider him, as history alone can present him to us, in every age, in every Country, in every State, in life and in death. History, therefore of all kinds, of civilized and uncivilized, of ancient and modern nations, in short all history that descends to a sufficient detail of human actions and characters, is useful to bring us acquainted with our species. To teach the general rules of good policy which result from such details of actions, comes for the most part, and always should come, expressly and directly into the design of those who give such details. Having such a lesson of philosophy before me, I will not vary from the principle it inculcates. If however, I neglect any part of my duty, you will be able to supply my neglect from other sources of information, and those sources I find you have in great correctness, from reading some official Reports of the general Government. If, however, I can put into your hand a clue, which may in any measure be servicable in guiding you in the search of that truth, which may be benificial to mankind of whatever nation or language my object will be fully answered. It is true indeed I take secret pleasure in corresponding with you, because I allways receive information from your communications, and as I advance in Years my Soul thirsts more and more for knowledge: But the object of this letter is, principally to state to you, that the Cherokee Nation of Indians will not, in my opinion, exchange the Country they now occupy for any other, directly, but time, and perhaps not very remote will accomplish every object necessary for the good of the Citizens of the U. States[1] and of the Cherokee Nation. I will yet call them a Nation, though they are not alltogether independant in reality, but so in form. They will willingly relinquish all the lands North of the Tennessee for an equivalent on the Waters of the Mississipi for hunting grounds. This relinquishment will make the State of Tennessee compact, and a respectable territory; added to this it will secure the immediate occupancy of all the lands granted to individuals by the State of No. Carolina, before she ceded this part of the Country to the General Government. This will silence discontented Citizens from saying they are unjustly deprived from the enjoyment of property they payed a *bona fide* price for.

The Country in the immediate occupation of the Cherokee Indians is bounded on the South by a high ridge of mountains, On the East by the Tennessee before it forms a junction with the Holston, by far the largest River, On the North by the Te[nnessee] after it forms the junction with the before named River, which by its size and impetuosity changes the course of the Tennessee, but nevertheless looses its name. The extent of the Country from the Tennessee to the Mountains southerly, on an average, I think is not more than fifty miles, perhaps less, though it widens as you proceed Westerly, the River bearing North, the Mountains south. The Indians are fast progressing towards civilization. They have invited many Mechanics to reside among them. They also begin to teach their Children to read. I am with Sentiments of high Respect.

Your Obt. Servt.   DAVID CAMPBELL

RC (DLC); torn; addressed: "His Excellency Thomas Jefferson President of the United States City of Washington"; endorsed by TJ as received 15 Feb. and so recorded in SJL.

FAVOURITE AUTHOR: Campbell recited from Viscount Bolingbroke, *Letters on the*

Study and Use of History (London, 1752), 137-8.

THE TENNESSEE BEFORE IT FORMS A JUNCTION: that is, the French Broad River.

[1] MS: "Sates."

From DeWitt Clinton

SIR   New York 1 January 1804—

I take the liberty of introducing to you, Mr. Cutting Esqr. of this City Counsellor at Law. He is a gentleman of good character respectable standing and correct politics—and I am persuaded that you will find him worthy of your notice.

I have the honor to be With the most perfect respect Your most Obedt. Servt.   DEWITT CLINTON

RC (MHi); at foot of text: "The President of the U–S.–"; endorsed by TJ as received 9 Jan. and so recorded in SJL.

In early 1804, William CUTTING resigned as chief justice of what was called the Ten Pound Court to accept appointment to New York's chancery court. An article in the New York *Evening Post* named Cutting, who was connected to the Livingston family by marriage, among

Livingston and Clinton family members who monopolized offices in the state (New York *Daily Advertiser*, 8 Feb.; New York *Chronicle Express*, 9 Feb.; New York *Evening Post*, 25 Feb. 1804). For TJ's consideration of Cutting as a bankruptcy commissioner in 1802 and Clinton's observation that Cutting already held a lucrative state office and "ought not to be permitted to engross too much," see Vol. 37:324, 326n, 402-3, 704.

From Sir John Sinclair

Charlotte Square Edinburgh.—
DEAR SIR/   1st January.—1804.

On various accounts, I received with much pleasure, your obliging letter of the 30th of June last, which only reached me, at this place, on the 19th of November.—I certainly feel highly indebted to Mr Binns, both for the information contained in the pamphlet he has drawn up; and also, for his having been the means of inducing you to recommence our correspondence together, for the purpose of transmitting a paper, which does credit to the practical farmers of america.—

As to the Plaster of Paris, which Mr Binns so strongly recommends, it is singular, that whilst it proves such a source of fertility with you, it is of little avail, in any part of the British Islands, Kent alone excepted. I am thence inclined to conjecture, that its great advantage must arise, from its attracting moisture from the atmosphere, of which we have in general abundance in these Kingdoms, without the intervention of that agent; and the benefit which has been found from the use of this article in Kent, (one of the dryest Counties in England) tends to countenance this hypothesis.—

I hear with peculiar pleasure, that a central Society, or Board of agriculture, has been established in america, which I hope will prove of singular utility to that thriving Empire.—Regarding that important institution, and the subject of European politics in general, I beg herewith to transmit some additional observations.

Ever since I have been engaged in public life, which commenced in the year 1780, it has been my constant wish, to encourage as much as possible, an intimate connexion between the two countries, and to cultivate a friendly intercourse with the many respectable characters which america produces. In that particular I have been extremely successful; and I consider as a circumstance *of peculiar good fortune*, that it has been in my power to establish, a friendly correspondence, with the distinguished statesman, who now fills the Presidency of the United states.—

Accept of my best wishes for the happiness of the new Empire in general; and more especially of those, who are so laudably and successfully employed, in directing its councils, and promoting its prosperity.   JOHN SINCLAIR

RC (DLC); addressed: "His Highness.—Thomas Jefferson"; endorsed by TJ as received 15 May and so recorded in SJL. Enclosed in George W. Erving to TJ, 8 Mch. 1804. Dupl (DLC); in a clerk's hand, signed by Sinclair; at head of text: "Duplicate"; endorsed by TJ as

received 8 Sep. and so recorded in SJL. Enclosed in Erving to TJ, 25 June 1804.

TJ sent Sinclair a publication by John A. BINNS, a Virginia farmer, entitled *A Treatise on Practical Farming* (see Vol. 40:542n, 637, 638n).

ENCLOSURE

Observations on the American Board of Agriculture

Hints regarding the Board of Agriculture, or Central Society established in America—

The friends to agriculture and internal improvement, have heard with infinite satisfaction, that a *Board of Agriculture*, or central society, has been established in that rising Empire, and they augur from it some very important discoveries, in that most useful of all arts. From the experience however regarding such institutions, which Europe furnishes, they are convinced, that there are *two* points, which require to be particularly attended to, in the formation of that important establishment, which they beg leave to submit to the Consideration of those real patriots, who have been the means of forming it.

The first observation that occurs is this, that such an institution has hardly ever prospered, for any length of time, *without public encouragement*. The zeal of individuals flags, when the whole burden of the establishment rests upon them alone. Besides, without competent funds, great exertions cannot be made, and consequently much benefit cannot be expected. Perhaps the best of all institutions, are those, where the expence is partly defrayed by the Government of a country, and partly by private subscriptions. Individuals are thus induced to come forward, and to make exertions which otherwise they would never have thought of. It is to be hoped therefore, that this plan will be adopted in America, as one which has been already completely sanctioned by the experience of the mother Country.

In the second place, if any assistance is given by the public, it necessarily puts an end to the idea of its being merely a private Society, and it becomes "*A Public Board*," the very name of which, must give it additional respectability and weight, both at home, *and above all abroad*. There is an additional argument, in favour, both of a public grant, and of a name being given to it, importing its connection with Government; for a correspondence with agricultural Boards and Societies in *foreign countries*, would be of the Utmost service to America, in various ways, which must strike at once the mind of every intelligent individual.

One additional observation may be made, namely, that the great object of such an institution necessarily will be, *the ascertainment of facts*, and the carrying on of important inquiries, into the political, Agricultural, or Statistical circumstances of every part of the Empire. The plan therefore, of having two members from such of the different states, *formed into one body*, seems to be an excellent idea, for thus the whole nation is thus interested in the success of the Undertaking. The communications from such respectable sources also, must be extremely Valuable, and will render the transactions of the new Board of Agriculture, or central Society, an object of great interest, in Europe, as well as America.—

JOHN SINCLAIR
Charlotte Square Edino. 1st January 1804

MS (DLC); in a clerk's hand, emended, signed, and endorsed by Sinclair. Dupl (DLC); in same clerk's hand, signed and endorsed by Sinclair.

WITHOUT PUBLIC ENCOURAGEMENT: in his 30 June 1803 letter to Sinclair, TJ described the newly established Board of Agriculture as "voluntary, & unconnected with the public" (Vol. 40:637-8).

From Archibald Stuart

DEAR SIR   Staunton 1st Jany. 1804

You will receive by Doctr Baldwin a Letter from me on the subject of his intended application for some office, which may afford him a favorable introduction at New Orleans—I consider it my duty to inform you in addition to the facts stated in that Letter that the Doctr has declined his practice during the last eighteen months & engaged in the business of makeing Iron in which he has been unsuccessful & is certainly a bankrupt—

Mr Coalter and myselfe have signed a certificate in favor of Jos. Fosset jr which will probably be presented to you shortly—He is a young man of good understanding and real worth; He is robust active and enterprising, and very capable of Business   If a Commissary or Indian Trader was wanted I do not know a character that would better fill such an Office—

On the subject of Poletics we have a perfect calm in this quarter— The leaders of Our Enemies have gone too far in their opposition to make open recantations: They preserve a gloomy silence & their followers are withdrawing from them daily & at present I believe we have a decided Majority in this County—I am not without hope that the Influence of our clergy which they have exerted in deceiving the People will be greatly lessened in future: we lose no opportunity of explaining and exposing their Views—The Opposition to the Louisiana Purchase will compleat the Overthrow of the Feds   In Congress they appear to have dwindled into a Captious quibling faction

I am Dr Sir yours most affectionately   ARCHD: STUART

RC (DNA: RG 59, LAR); at foot of text: "The Honble. Thos. Jefferson Esqr. P.U.S."; endorsed by TJ as received 8 Jan. and so recorded in SJL with notation "Fosset & Baldwin for Louisiana"; also endorsed by TJ: "Baldwin Dr. Fosset Joseph junr. emploimt. Louisiana."

LETTER FROM ME: Stuart to TJ, 28 Dec. 1803.

An undated CERTIFICATE signed by Stuart and John Coalter stated that they had known Joseph FOSSET, Jr., "from an early period of his life." Formerly a clerk and merchant, Fosset was a deputy sheriff in Rockingham County and always conducted himself "with the utmost propriety & integrity." Stuart and Coalter deemed him particularly suited for a position in the Indian trade or "any quartermasters department" (MS in DNA: RG 59, LAR; endorsed by TJ: "Fosset Joseph. emploimt Louisa. commerce with Indians").

From Isaac Briggs

New Orleans, 2nd. of the
MY DEAR FRIEND,   1st. Month 1804.

Some time ago—very long after its date—the mail brought me thy favor of the 11th. of August. I had, as soon as it was possible for me, after my arrival in the Missisippi Territory, to give information which might be of any service to Gideon Fitz, taken the necessary care, by addressing a letter to him at Monticello. I have lately received a letter from him, dated at Louisville in Kentucky, which I immediately answered.

Having so arranged my business in the Missisippi Territory, that I could leave it, in progress, for a short time without injury—having, from the beginning, been a warm admirer of thy measures respecting Louisiana—and sincerely rejoicing in their glorious result—I have yielded to my inclination to see the newly acquired Country, and to see my friend William C. C. Claiborne, in his new sphere of action.

His difficulties appear to be great, and the peculiar duties of his present station extremely irksome. For many years, the Government of this country has been so administered that those channels through which the weak should have received protection in their persons and property, have been very corrupt. The administration has been made a lucrative trade through all its ramifications of Office.—Fraud towards their Prince and oppression on his subjects have been equally and systematically practised. Despotism and Licentiousness have been equally conspicuous:—An extensive aristocratic Class, wallowing in wealth and luxury, were licentious and oppressive in the extreme; for their wealth gave them influence, and the means of corruption; from interest, the latter was cherished, and the former, even the iron hand of Despotism dared not attempt to crush.

In this situation, Claiborne, as Governor ad interim, finds affairs. The people, as is usual in all cases of great and sudden change, are unreasonable in their expectations. The reputation of the American Government is so high, that they expect from it, impossibilities—they expect unbounded licence in many of their vicious, luxurious, and oppressive habits, and at the same time, the full fruition of all those blessings of Republican liberty, which never did, nor never can, long exist, except bottomed on Economy and Virtuous Manners.

So far as Claiborne's instructions enjoin him to *continue* the Spanish System of Government, although perhaps unavoidable, his duties must be unpleasant—Many parts of that system, an *honest, republican* mind, as I think his is, considering their immediate operation or their more remote consequences, must abhor. The situation of the Governor of this Country, although gradually meliorating, cannot, for years to come, if he feel for Man—for rational Liberty—for Posterity, be a happy one. Considerable time is necessary to change, radically, long established habits—The qualifications requisite in a governor, to produce such a change here, are, I believe, extremely uncommon—Inflexible integrity, mild yet firm, a virtue superior to temptation—Intelligence to discern what is right, and resolution to do it, however unpopular for the moment—Perseverance not to be fatigued by difficulties into inaction—and Patience unconquerable by perverseness in others.

My friend Claiborne's measures, thus far, appear to be popular here—But the people do not yet feel the full effects of their change of Government—all is expectancy, which will be unreasonable of course;—disappointed characters are as yet few, nor have they had time to form a party, nor to put, in motion, the engines of calumny and misrepresentation.

Claiborne has frequently expressed to me his undeviating wishes to retire to private life: having received so gratifying a proof of the President's esteem as his last appointment, he says his political ambition is now satisfied. His only remaining political wish is, that, when the President appoints his successor, as Permanent Governor of Louisiana, he may do it in such a way that the Public may unequivocally know that it is not meant as a censure upon his conduct.

My friend Trist's situation is also in many respects disagreeable— he must bear many vexations—the merchants contend for the *immediate* enjoyment of all the privileges of the commercial system of the United States—it seems in vain that they are told they must wait the pleasure of Congress.

Yet it were a pity that men of such integrity as Claiborne and Trist should withdraw, or be withdrawn, from a scene where such qualifications are so necessary—so indispensable in the production of a gradual reform.

The Divine Author of Nature has indeed made this Country a *Paradise*—but Man has converted it into a *Pandemonium*. From the mild and equitable spirit of the American Government, my hopes are sanguine. From the very commencement of our career in the new order of things here, when vice and injustice hold out, for our acceptance, their many varying snares, concealed beneath the fascinating baits of interest and pleasure, may we not, for one moment, forget the wise, monitory injunction—

"Principiis obsta, serò medicina paratur."

The number of slaves in this country is already great, and the infatuated inhabitants are in the habit of increasing it by large importations—one vessel, the Collector informs me, with slaves from Africa, is now in the river, and several more expected soon to arrive. Oh! my friend,—may I not call thee the friend of Man!—is there no way of putting a stop to this crying, dangerous, national sin? As I have ridden through some parts of this western world; and observed the numerous defiles and almost impenetrable recesses, I have reflected that these oppressed people are acquainted, far better than their oppressors, with almost every private path and every retreat—that they are already discontented and disposed to throw off their yoke, on the least prospect of success; they are capable of secresy, and many of them of considerable system. Their Masters are alarmed and think to find their safety in a rigorous discipline—in my opinion, this will but hasten the crisis, and make the catastrophe more dreadful. My mind has pursued the subject, when retired for repose; and anticipation has transferred to this country the sanguinary scenes of St. Domingo—I have, from the very bottom of my heart, adopted thy own emphatic and beautiful expressions—"I tremble for my Country when I reflect that God is just—that his Justice cannot sleep forever—and that there is no attribute of the Deity which can take part with us in such a contest."

When we make, to the world, high professions of Republicanism—hold ourselves up as the boasted Guardians of the Rights of Man—and are reproached for inconsistency—what can we answer, but

> "—Pudet hæc opprobria nobis;
> "Et dici potuisse, et non potuisse refelli."

Of all countries which I have seen, I think this would be my choice as a residence, were it not for the sanction given to slavery—"Where liberty is, there is my Country."

Nothing, I think, but a strong sense of duty has made me endure so long, nor can make me endure much longer, a separation so painful as mine, from my beloved family. My ambition, I am convinced, is not a political one—my *first* object is, the approbation of my own conscience—my *second* is the approbation of worthy men. I pray thee, to accept of my grateful acknowledgements to thyself as a Father and a Friend, of whose good opinion I am highly solicitous; and to be assured that I am not disposed to retire from my post, while the President thinks me worthy of it, nor until he finds, or I can recommend, a successor who may equally answer the President's scientific views in this country. I may, however, next summer, solicit permission to visit my family, on condition of making such arrangements in my public business that it may suffer neither injury nor delay in my absence—bearing in every respect the full responsibility of my office.

Assuring thee of the warmth and sincerity of my gratitude and esteem, I am, respectfully, thy friend,   ISAAC BRIGGS

RC (DLC); at foot of text: "Thomas Jefferson Pr: U.S."; endorsed by TJ as received 24 Jan. and so recorded in SJL. FC (NHi: Gilder Lehrman Collection at the Gilder Lehrman Institute of American History).

CLAIBORNE'S INSTRUCTIONS: see Vol. 41:632-5, 639-41.

For Hore Browse TRIST's responsibilities in New Orleans, see Vol. 41:684-5, 707. CONGRESS harmonized customs policy in the newly ceded territories with that of the rest of the country in an act of 24 Feb. 1804 (U.S. Statutes at Large, 2:251-4).

PARADISE ... PANDEMONIUM: in John Milton's epic poem *Paradise Lost*, Pandemonium was "the high Capital Of Satan and his Peers" (1.756-7).

PRINCIPIIS OBSTA, SERÒ MEDICINA PARATUR: "stand firm against the onset of the malady" (Ovid, *Remedia Amoris*, line 91).

I TREMBLE FOR MY COUNTRY: Briggs quoted from TJ's *Notes on the State of Virginia* (*Notes*, ed. Peden, 163).

PUDET HÆC OPPROBRIA NOBIS: "it shames us that these charges can be made, it shames us that they cannot be rebutted" (Ovid, *Metamorphoses*, 1.758-9).

WHERE LIBERTY IS, THERE IS MY COUNTRY: a quotation of uncertain origin, frequently misattributed to Benjamin Franklin (Ralph Keyes, *The Quote Verifier: Who Said What, Where, and When* [New York, 2006], 120).

From Israel Israel

WORTHY AND MUCH ESTEEMD SIR,   Philada. January 2d: 1804

Being informed that Removals are about to take place in the Officers of the Revenue department in this City, I am led to Request you in favor of your friend & much esteemd Citizen Cap. James Gamble, now a Senator of this State, his Modesty will prevent him from coming forward in the Accustom'd Manner, His Virtues need not be delienated by me they are known and Acknowledged by all that know him, He has Recently been Offerd an honorable place by the Governor, but I know that his Talents and Qualifications are better fitted for the Naval or Surveyors Office, he being long since and still is in the Mercantile Business,

Dr Sir if you find it necessary to make a Change, Conscious I am you will do Honor to Yourself and Oblige a numerous body of Citizens by making the above Appointment and none more so than your devoted friend   ISRAEL ISRAEL

RC (DNA: RG 59, LAR); endorsed by TJ as received 14 Jan. and "Gamble James for Survr. Phila." and so recorded in SJL.

JAMES GAMBLE had been elected to the Pennsylvania Senate in 1802 (Vol. 41:605-7).

From Brockholst Livingston

SIR,   New York 2. Jany. 1804—

Permit me to have the honor of introducing to your notice Mr. William Cutting who is on a visit to Washington—This gentleman belongs to our bar—he is an amiable & deserving young man—highly esteemed among us, & a sincere & valuable friend of the present administration—

With great respect I have the honor to be Sir, your very obedt Servt

BROCKHOLST LIVINGSTON

RC (MHi); at foot of text: "Thomas Jefferson President of the United States"; endorsed by TJ as received 9 Jan. and so recorded in SJL.

Son of Susannah French and William Livingston, the first governor of the state of New Jersey, Henry Brockholst Livingston (1757-1823) attended the College of New Jersey at Princeton, graduating in 1774. An advocate of the patriot cause, he served as an officer in the Continental Army. In 1779, he accompanied John Jay, his brother-in-law, on a mission to Spain. His long-lasting hostility toward Jay dated from this time. In the gubernatorial race of 1792, Livingston actively supported George Clinton, the successful candidate, against Jay. Livingston, who served several terms in the New York Assembly, was a member of the Democratic Society of New York, and in 1795 organized opposition to the Jay Treaty. Along with Aaron Burr, Livingston is one of those credited with organizing the Republican victory in New York in the spring of 1800, which gave the state's electoral votes to the Jeffersonians. He was admitted to the bar in New York City in 1783. In 1802, Governor Clinton appointed him to the New York Supreme Court. In 1805, he declined the nomination as U.S. judge for the district of New York. The next year, TJ named him to the U.S. Supreme Court in place of William Paterson. As a cultural leader in New York, Livingston served as a trustee and treasurer of Columbia College, as one of the founders and a vice president of the New-York Historical Society, and as a promoter of public education. In December 1800, TJ noted a characterization of Livingston as "very able, but ill-tempered, selfish, unpopular" (ANB; Richard A. Harrison, *Princetonians, 1769-1775: A Biographical Dictionary* [Princeton, 1980], 312, 397-406; Carl E. Prince and others, eds., *The Papers of William Livingston*, 5 vols. [Trenton and New Brunswick, N.J., 1979–88], 1:3, 396; New York *American Citizen and General Advertiser*, 26 Apr., 5 May 1800; Hudson, N.Y., *Bee*, 4 June 1805; New York *Evening Post*, 11 June 1805; William Keteltas to TJ, 16 Feb. 1805; Vol. 28:430-1; Vol. 31:494-5; Vol. 32:348).

In 1798, WILLIAM CUTTING married Gertrude Livingston, Brockholst Livingston's second cousin (Madison, *Papers, Pres. Ser.*, 2:116).

Notes on a Conversation with Benjamin Hichborn

1804. Jan. 2. Colo. Hitchborne of Mass. reminding me of a letter he had written me from Philadelphia pending the Presidential election, sais he did not therein give the details. that he was in company at Philada with Colo. Burr & Genl. Sam. Smith (when the latter took his trip there to meet Burr, & obtained the famous letter from him) that in the course of the conversn on the election, Colo. Burr said 'we must have a President, & a constnal one in some way.' 'how is it to be done, says Hitchborne, mr Jefferson's friends will not quit him, & his enemies are not strong enough to carry another' 'why, sais Burr, our friends must join the federalists, and give the president.' the next morning at Breakfast Colo. Burr repeated nearly the same, saying 'we cannot be without a president, our friends must join the federal vote.' 'but, says Hitchborne, we shall then be without a Vicepresident; who is to be our Vicepresident?' Colo. Burr answered 'mr Jefferson.'

MS (DLC: TJ Papers, 113:19521); entirely in TJ's hand; follows, on same sheet, Notes on a Conversation with Matthew Lyon, 31 Dec. 1803.

For the 5 Jan. 1801 letter Hichborn wrote TJ FROM PHILADELPHIA, see Vol. 32:399-400.

On 16 Dec. 1800, Aaron BURR wrote Samuel SMITH from New York: "It is highly improbable that I shall have an equal number of Votes with Mr. Jefferson, but if such should be the result every Man who knows me ought to know that I should utterly disclaim all competition." By 29 Dec., however, Burr had changed his position. Writing Smith from Trenton, Burr declared that a friend had asked "whether if I were chosen president, I would engage to resign." Although he made no reply to the gentleman, to Smith he noted, "I should not." Smith met Burr in Philadelphia the first weekend in January, before he received the 29 Dec. letter. He was surprised to learn directly from Burr that he would accept the presidency if chosen by the House (Kline, *Burr*, 1:471, 478-9, 483-4).

From Mountjoy Bayly

SIR   George Town 3d. Jany. 1804

The President will please to excuse the freedom I have taken in communicating to him the following circumstances relative to a Sulphur Spring in the Genesee—Which I made an offer off to the United States through the Secretary at War—

When I informed the Secretary of my intention to dispose of this property—he requested of me to give him a written discription of the same, which I complied with the next day, and which he informed me he would lay before the President immediately, and let me know his Opinion—I waited several days without receiving an Answer from the Secretary—I then waited on him, who informed me that he had delivered my discription of that property to the President without saying what the Opinion was—he then remarked to me that Mr. Oliver Phelps a Member of Congress from the Genesee (to whome I had referred him for a confirmation of my discription), had informed him that he had seen Colo Troop who is the Agent for that Country on his way to the City of Washington, and that Colo Troop offered Mr. Phelps the Sulphur Spring with 160 Acres of Land around the Spring for $10 Per Acre—I replied that I did not think Mr. Phelps information was correct—and to do away the prejudice which appeared to have taken possession of the Secretary's mind under an impression I supposed that Mr. Phelp's information was correct—I immediately wrote to Colo Troop on the Subject, who answered my letter decidedly contradicting the information given by Mr. Phelps to the Secretary— which I shewed the Secretary and who replied that either Colo Troop or Mr Phelps was mistaken—I then understood from the Secretary that the only Objection to purchasing the property was the want of information respecting the Quallity of the Sulphur—supposing that to be the only obstacle in the way—I referred the Secretary to Mr Williamson, who had arrived in the City, and who had been the former Agent for that Country, for the information which appeared to be the only thing wanting to determine the Secretary to make the purchase—and at the same time I informed him, that the information which he could obtain by applying to Mr. Williamson was of so respectable a nature, that it could not possibly leave a doubt on his mind as to the Quallity of the Sulphur—that Mr. Williamson had got Doctor Priestly to annallyse the same who informed him that he made a fair experiment and that it contained 96 Grains of pure Sulphur out of 100—That after informing the Secretary of the above circumstances, he without conversing with Mr. Williamson on the Subject informed me by letter of the 24th ult. that he had nothing more to say on the subject, than what he had already said—and that I was at liberty to dispose of the property.

Sir after the trouble and expence I have incurred in bringing this business before the public and that from the very best of motives— having a large, young, helpless, and friendless family, lately removed to the extreme end of the United States, with little or no means to make them Comfortable, and scarcely in a situation to return to them, to enjoy the only Consolation left me, that of participating in their distress is a situation truly painfull—when the president comes to reflect on the motive which has been the cause of my being placed in this unpleasant situation, and the great convenience that a purchase of this inexhaustible source of sulphur would[1] place in the power of the United States, I cannot but hope, that he will bestow a few moments of reflection on this important Subject, and direct such a Course to be adopted as is consistant with the public good, and at the same time do justice to the exertions of a Citizen who has devoted his time for to secure an object which he solemnly beleived to be the interest of the United States—

I have the Honor to be with high respect & Esteem the president's Humble Servt to Command   MOUNTJOY BAYLY

RC (DLC); addressed: "To the President of the United States"; endorsed by TJ as received 3 Jan. and so recorded in SJL.

SULPHUR SPRING IN THE GENESEE: see Bayly to TJ, 14 Dec. 1803.

Robert Troup (TROOP), an attorney and former federal judge, succeeded Charles Williamson as the agent of British land speculator Sir William Pulteney (ANB).

LETTER OF THE 24TH ULT.: Henry Dearborn's brief letter to Bayly of 24 Dec. 1803 is in DNA: RG 107, MLS.

[1] Bayly here canceled "give to."

From Thomas Embree

Washington county
State of Tennessee
FRIEND, & SUPERIOR;   the 3d of 1st mo. 1804

The horror & confusion occasioned in the state of Tennessee, by the method pursued to raise men to go to Louisiana, has been wonderful. The fear of being reduced to the alternative of either undertaking a grievous journey of 12 or 18 hundred miles, & much of the way through a howling wilderness, with the probability of never returning; or submiting to a fine, which to many of the citizens of a country like this, would be very distressing, hath caused many young men, & some heads of families, to leave their necessary employments, & seek refuge among strangers; whereby the burden fell on others who could not be as well spared, & many of them are fined.

Undertaking to force out the militia in this case appears to be an impolitic step; as the unreasonable appearance of it even if it had been lawful, & constitutional,[1] tends to produce seeds of disloyalty, by reducing people to an apparant necessity of disobeying. It apears to be a general opinion, as far as I am acquainted, that if force had not been attempted, men would have been easier raised.

But whether the President intended such measures to be taken or not, has been a matter of warm controversy: and I am among those (tho perhaps the minority) who contend, that, as the authority was only a request, force was not intended; seeing a request is not a command, nor order: But if the opinion should ultimately prevail, that the authority from the President was peremptory; & intended to bind the officers to use compulsory measures as the last resort, I fear it will injure his popularity. But I hope the common acceptation of the word conveyed the President's intention; for I wish for Tho's Jefferson's popularity to continue, & for him to reign as president, untill I have reason to change my opinion in regard to his merits.

If my opinion be right I shall expect the president will, for the good of the community, take speedy measures to counteract the sufferings of those who are fined, or liable to be fined, & their property, by reason of the scarcity of money, liable to be sold at so low a rate as to be very distressing to many families: But unless this be done, or some satisfactory information communicated, the contrary will probably be taken for granted, by the neighbours of

the President's real friend & respectful subject

THOMAS EMBREE

RC (DLC); at foot of text: "To Thomas Jefferson, Prisedent of U.S."; endorsed by TJ as received 15 Jan. and so recorded in SJL.

Thomas Embree (1755-1833), a Quaker born in North Carolina, settled in eastern Tennessee in 1790 and subsequently engaged in iron manufacturing. In 1797, he made a public call for the inhabitants of his state to join together and promote the gradual abolition of slavery. His call went unheeded, and Embree later relocated to Ohio with part of his family. His son Elihu remained in Tennessee, however, where he became an ardent antislavery advocate (Elihu Embree, *The Emancipator*, intro. by Ella Pearce Buchanan and John F. Nash [Jonesborough, Tenn., 1995], x-xiii; ANB, s.v. "Embree, Elihu").

METHOD PURSUED TO RAISE MEN TO GO TO LOUISIANA: see Isaac Hammer to TJ, 5 Dec. 1803.

[1] Preceding seven words, ampersand, and commas interlined.

From Albert Gallatin

DEAR SIR   Jany. 4th 1804

Will you have the goodness to examine the enclosed letter & to return it with your observations.

Respectfully your obedt. Servt.   ALBERT GALLATIN

RC (DLC); addressed (clipped): "President United States"; endorsed by TJ as received from the Treasury Department on 4 Jan. and "report on sale of lands" and so recorded in SJL. Enclosure not found, but see below.

TJ's endorsement indicates that Gallatin probably ENCLOSED a draft of the letter he sent the next day to Joseph H. Nicholson, chairman of the committee appointed on 22 Nov. to study the sale of public lands and offer amendments to the land laws. The Treasury secretary had received a 16 Dec. letter from Thomas Rodney, Robert Williams, and Edward Turner, the land commissioners at Washington, in Mississippi Territory. They pointed out problems they were encountering and suggested solutions. To detect false and fraudulent claims, they needed the power to enforce the attendance of witnesses. They advocated the appointment of a person to obtain evidence pertaining to the claims, who would "advocate the rights of the United States," for as commissioners they could not serve as both "judge and advocate." Since many of the relevant documents were in Spanish, the commissioners requested a "person capable of making a true and faithful translation on oath." Lastly, they needed an assistant clerk to record the evidence and decisions. On 5 Jan., Gallatin wrote Nicholson and enclosed the letter from the commissioners. On the subject of fraudulent and antedated Spanish grants, Gallatin noted that he had received information that the same frauds were being "attempted on a much larger scale in Louisiana." He recommended "that principles should be adopted in relation to those grants in the Mississippi territory," which would then be applied to similar cases in the newly acquired territories. Gallatin advised that the commissioners be "vested with sufficient powers to compel the attendance of witnesses" and that counsel be employed for the United States. He believed that a grant alone should not be "considered as conclusive evidence, and that in all cases where the land claimed was not occupied by or for the benefit of the grantee, at the time of, or within a limited period after the date of the grant, the burthen of the proof of its validity" should fall on the claimant. The assistance of a Spanish translator was "indispensible" to the commissioners' work, and an assistant clerk "would certainly contribute to the dispatch of the business." On 27 Jan., the committee brought in resolutions authorizing a translator and assistant clerk for both sets of commissioners in Mississippi Territory and granting the "same powers to compel the attendance of witnesses, as are now exercised by the courts of law of the United States." The Treasury secretary was designated to employ an agent to defend the rights of the United States (JHR, 4:453; *Farther Report in Part, of the Committee Appointed on the 22d of November Last, Who Were Directed by a Resolution of the House of the 24th of the Same Month, "To Enquire into the Expediency of Amending the Several Acts Providing for the Sale of the Public Lands of the United States"* [Washington, D.C., 1804], 3-11).

Petition of Joseph Goodier, with Jefferson's Order

To Thomas Jefferson President
of the United States

The petition of Joseph Goodier humbly and respectfully sheweth— That on the 3rd. instant he was convicted in the Circuit Court of the District of Columbia for Washington County of stealing a Steer the property of Daniel Carroll of Dudington and has been sentenced by the said Court to pay[1] a fine of one dollar, with the costs of prosecution and to be publickly whipped with five lashes. The circumstances under which he was convicted were so favourable that the Jury were induced to recommend him to the mercy of the Court—but the law positively requiring it the Court was under a necessity of making whipping a part of his punishment Being a young man dependant for his living on his industry and reputation in society the latter of which must inevitably suffer almost irretrievably by a public and ignominious punishment He humbly prays that the President will be pleased to pardon his Offence or at least to remit that part of his sentence which inflicts Whipping and he will ever pray &c

JOSEPH GOODIER
City of Washington
4 January 1803 [i.e. 1804]

The Jury recommended the petitioner to the Mercy of the Court, on which they ordered as slight a punishment as they could, not having the power to dispense with that part of the Law which inflicts corporal punishment; but they are willing and do respectfully recommend to the President to remit the said corporal punishment

W KILTY

W. CRANCH

N. FITZHUGH

[*Order by TJ*:]
A pardon to be issued as to the corporal punishment.

TH: JEFFERSON

Jan. 7. 1804.

MS (DNA: RG 59, GPR); misdated; recommendation of the court in a clerk's hand and signed by Kilty, Cranch, and Fitzhugh. Enclosed in Daniel Carroll Brent to TJ, 6 Jan. 1804, forwarding "papers respecting a certain Goodier now in Jail, which I am directed by the court to transmit to you" (RC in DLC; misdated 1803; endorsed by TJ as a letter of 6 Jan. 1804

received that day and "Joseph Goodier's case" and so recorded in SJL).

TJ issued a pardon of Goodier's corporal punishment on 7 Jan. (FC in Lb in DNA: RG 59, GPR).

[1] Word interlined in place of "be punished by."

From J. P. G. Muhlenberg

SIR   Philadelphia Jany. 4th. 1804.

Enclos'd I have the Honor to transmit the amount of Duties, & other charges, paid on One Butt of Sherry, & two Pipes of Lisbon Wine, which I have this day shipp'd for Richmond, by the Sloop Caroline, Captn. Lewis.

I have the Honor to be with perfect Respect Sir Your most Obedt Servt.   P MUHLENBERG

RC (MHi); at foot of text: "The President of The U States"; endorsed by TJ as received 7 Jan. and so recorded in SJL.

ENCLOSURE

Invoice for Freight and Duties

Paid freight to Washington for 1 Barrell Mississippi Water	$	.67
Porterage		.66
freight to the Owners of the Ship Eliza for 1 Butt of Sherry Wine		11.00
Do. " " Edward for 2 pipes Lisbon Do		10.50

Duties on 1 Butt Sherry Wine		55.44
Do " 2 pipes Lisbon Do		82.50
Cooperage for uncasing & Casing 1 Butt & 2 pipes in Order to have them Guaged		.75
Porterage		1.00
		$162.52

[*In TJ's hand:*]

	1. butt Sherry	2. pipes Lisbon
freight	11.	10.50
duties	55.44	82.50
	66.44	93.

46.50 per pipe

55.44 D duty @ .40 cents gives the contents of the butt to be 138½ galls. by gage

82.50 duty @ .30 cents gives 275. galls. for the 2. pipes or 137½ galls. each by gage.

MS (MHi); in a clerk's hand, calculations by TJ at foot of text; undated.

From John Page

S IR,   Richmond January 4th. 1804

I have this moment received the inclosed ratification of the amendment to the Constitution of the United States, and with pleasure hasten to transmit it to you.

I am Sir, with high respect and esteem, your obedt. servant

J OHN P AGE

FC (ViW: Virginia Governor's Papers); in a clerk's hand, signed by Page; at foot of text: "The President of the United States." FC (Vi: Executive Letterbook). Enclosure not found, but see below.

The Virginia House of Delegates overwhelmingly approved the resolution ratifying the Twelth Amendment to the United States Constitution by a vote of 128 to 8. In the senate, the resolution passed by a proportionately large margin, 17 to 1 (*Journal of the House of Delegates of the Commonwealth of Virginia, Begun and Held at the Capitol, in the City of Richmond, on Monday the Fifth Day of December, One Thousand Eight Hundred and Three* [Richmond, Va., 1804], 49; Richmond *Virginia Argus*, 4 Jan. 1804).

To Mountjoy Bayly

S IR   Washington Jan. 5. 03. [i.e. 1804]

The information first recieved as to the bed of Sulphur at Genesee was certainly such as to interest the government and make it our duty to enquire into it. this has been done. the result is that there is at the spring not more than a ton of sulphur formed, and that this is probably the deposit of ages, so that the quantity deposited annually would be no object at all. this information being from actual examination, we do not think it an object for the government to intermeddle with: at the same time we give you just credit for the readiness you have shewn to accomodate the public with the purchase, had it been expedient for them to buy. Accept my salutations & good wishes.

TH: JEFFERSON

PrC (DLC); at foot of text: "Mr. Mountjoy Bailey"; endorsed by TJ in ink on verso as a letter of 5 Jan. 1804 and so recorded in SJL.

From Benjamin Galloway

SIR.   Hagers Town Jan 5th 1804.

The foregoing is a Copy of the Impeachment which I presented to the General Assembly of Maryland in conformity to my promise made last Summer to Luther Martin. If He was not a *graceless* Chap he would feel *most sensibly*: but He is—. I am Sir with perfect Esteem & Regard

Yr obt Servt   BEN GALLOWAY

RC (DLC); written at foot of enclosure; endorsed by TJ as received 7 Jan. and so recorded in SJL.

PROMISE MADE LAST SUMMER: in July 1803, Galloway publicly called for Luther Martin's removal from office (Vol. 41:507n).

ENCLOSURE

Benjamin Galloway to Maryland General Assembly

Benjamin Galloway of Elizabeth Town Washington County and State of Maryland respectfully presents the Underwritten to the Senate and House of Delegates of the State aforesaid in General Assembly convened—

That the State of Maryland now is, and of Right has been a free and independant State ever since the fourth day of July one thousand seven hundred and seventy six. That Luther Martin now is, and has been in possession of the important office of Attorney General of the State aforesaid for upwards of twenty five Years. That said Luther Martin for a considerable Time last past has been in the almost daily practice of appearing in the Courts of Justice of said State intoxicated with spirituous Liquor, and that the Dignity of the State of Maryland is severely wounded by reason of the Appearance of its Attorney General in its Courts of Justice in said Condition—Wherefore the said Benjamin Galloway in behalf of the Citizens of said State; and with a View of removing said Luther Martin from the Office of Attorney General of said State, prays the General Assembly to take the Premises into serious Consideration, and to administer such Releif to their Country and Fellow Citizens as the united Wisdom of the Legislature, and the Dignity of the State call for with a Trumpet-like Voice.

If the General assembly should entertain a doubt as to the above mentioned Fact, so notoriously known, and so generally complained of, videlicet, the repeated Appearance of Luther Martin in Court *drunk*, the following Characters are offered, as Witnesses to prove the same.

Alexander Contee Hanson	Chancellor
Jeremiah Townly Chase	Chief Justice General Court
Richard Sprigg	Junior Judge G.C.
Henry Ridgeley	Chief Justice 1. Maryd District
Arthur Shaaff	
John Mason	
Robert G Harper	
Thomas Buchanan	
Zebulon Hollinsworth	Attornies General Court do
John Johnson	
Henry Warfeild	
Philip Barton Key	
John Gwinn	Clk General Court WS.
Thomas Harris	Assistant Clk do
Samuel H Howard	Register in Chancery
Burton Whetcroft	Clk Court Appeals
William Gibson	Clk Baltimore County—

Tr (same); in Galloway's hand.

On 14 Dec., the Maryland SENATE read Galloway's call for Martin's removal and referred it to the HOUSE OF DELEGATES, which read the statement on 2 Jan. The house ordered "That the said letter be thrown under the table" (*Votes and Proceedings of the Senate of the State of Mary-* *land. November Session, One Thousand Eight Hundred and Three* [Annapolis, 1804], 19-20; *Votes and Proceedings of the House of Delegates of the State of Maryland. November Session, One Thousand Eight Hundred and Three* [Annapolis, 1804], 85).

ws.: Western Shore.

To Louis André Pichon

Jan. 5. 04.

Th: Jefferson presents his salutations to M. Pichon, who will recieve herewith a note asking the favor of Made. Pichon & himself to dine with him on Monday next. Th:J. has written an invitation to the same effect to M. & Made. Bonaparte, & *their friends who are with them*, he has used this phrase, as while it includes the Baron de Maupertuis & M. Sotin, it might also include mr Patterson & miss Spear who he understands are with Made. Bonaparte, or any other persons of whom he is uninformed and whose company would be agreeable to

M. Bonaparte. he takes the liberty of mentioning this to M. Pichon in hopes he will have the goodness to give the explanation if necessary.

RC (facsimile in Charles Hamilton Galleries, Inc., Auction No. 98, 29 July 1976, item 152). Not recorded in SJL.

The newlyweds Jerome BONAPARTE and Elizabeth Patterson Bonaparte arrived in the national capital from Baltimore on 4 Jan. and quickly garnered attention in Washington social circles (Charlene M. Boyer Lewis, *Elizabeth Patterson Bonaparte: An American Aristocrat in the Early Republic* [Philadelphia, 2012], 17-18, 32-3; Margaret Bayard Smith, *The First Forty Years of Washington Society*, ed. Gaillard Hunt [New York, 1906], 46-7; New York *Morning Chronicle*, 5 and 11 Jan. 1804; Vol. 41:666-7, 668-9n).

BARON DE MAUPERTUIS was an acquaintance of Jerome Bonaparte from the West Indies and, according to Pichon, a relative of Bonaparte's mother. He had been nominated French consul at Rotterdam but was awaiting his instructions when Jerome met him in New York and invited him to Baltimore as a guest (W. T. R. Saffell, *The Bonaparte-Patterson Marriage in 1803, and the Secret Correspondence on the Subject Never Before Made Public* [Philadelphia, 1873], 117, 125; Carrie Rebora Barratt and Ellen G. Miles, *Gilbert Stuart* [New Haven, 2004], 254).

Pierre Jean Marie SOTIN de la Coindière, the former minister of police in France in 1797, became French commissary for Georgia in 1802. The following autumn he transferred from Savannah to Baltimore, where he witnessed the Bonapartes' Catholic marriage ceremony (*Biographie universelle*, 39:652-3; Syrett, *Hamilton*, 21:524-6; Madison, *Papers, Sec. of State Ser.*, 2:468n; Charles Edwards Lester, Edwin Williams, and Frederick Greenwood, *The Napoleon Dynasty* [London, 1853], 419; New York *Morning Chronicle*, 16 Sep. 1803).

MR PATTERSON: Elizabeth Bonaparte's father, William Patterson, did not accompany the couple to Washington. She had several brothers, including one, John Patterson, who was a frequent visitor to Wilson Cary Nicholas's household. Elizabeth's maternal aunt was Anne (Nancy) SPEAR (Helen Jean Burn, *Betsy Bonaparte* [Baltimore, 2010], 46, 58, 60, 119; Lewis, *Elizabeth Patterson Bonaparte*, 112, 188).

ANY OTHER PERSONS: according to Pichon's report to Talleyrand about the dinner, TJ also invited the brothers Robert and Samuel Smith and their wives. Samuel Smith's wife, Margaret Spear Smith, was the sister of Elizabeth Patterson Bonaparte's mother (Pichon to Talleyrand, 5 Feb. 1804, quoted in Henry Adams, *History of the United States During the First Administration of Thomas Jefferson*, 2 vols. [New York, 1889], 2:374; Vol. 41:669n).

Petition of John Duffey, with Jefferson's Order

TO HIS EXELENCY THE
PRESIDENT OF THE UNITED STATES.   [on or before 6 Jan. 1804]

Humbly sheweth unto your Exelency, Your petitioner John Duffey, That at the last Circuit Court held for the county of Alexandria, in the District of Columbia, he was tried upon an indictment found against him for keeping a disorderly house, and the Jury, without adverting to your petitioners ability to pay, found a verdict against him in favour of the United States for Two hundred dollars—in consequence of this verdict your petitioner was committed to prison, where he now is, utterly unable to pay the aforesaid fine—for all the property he has on earth, if sold, would not exceed one half of that sum; your petitioner also States to your Exelency, that he is an aged man, and to enable himself to support his family has for some years back kept a boarding house for Sailors, who unfortunately for your petitioner in some instances did not conduct themselves in as orderly a manner as they ought to have done.—in consequence whereof information was given to the grand Jury, who found the aforesaid indictment, upon which the aforesaid verdict was rendered, and by which your petitioner is consigned to perpetual imprisonment, unless your Exelency will be pleased to remit the aforesaid fine. Your petitioner has thought his duty to state also that he has been an old Soldier in the service of his country, from the year 1777, untill the conclusion of the war.—Your petitioner humbly relying upon the clemency of your Exelency, hopes the harsh sentence of this verdict will be temporised with the universally acknowledged humanity which your Exelency possesses—Your petitioner, therefore is lying at the mercy of your Exelency who he hopes will not consign him to continual imprisonment, but will remit the aforesaid fine, as your petitioner is unable to pay the same, and your petitioner as in duty bound will ever pray.

On the trial of the within mentioned Indictment, the Jury amerced the Petitioner in the Sum of Two Hundred Dollars—an application was then made to the Court for a new trial on the ground of excessive damages & Evidence was exhibited which proved that he was not worth property enough to pay the Amount of the Fine—in consequence of which the new trial was granted on Condition that he should pay the Costs & go to trial during that Term before another Jury; but the petitioner neither paying the Costs nor giving Security for this purpose, he was on application to the Court committed on the Judgment according to the usual course—The inability of Duffy to discharge the fine & Costs, appears to be the strongest Circumstance in his favor—there is, as far as our Recollection goes, an Indictment against him, not yet determined, for receiving stolen goods which may have the Effect of again causing his commitment unless he should be now released & should leave the District which is much to be desired—

The above Statement of facts is respectfully made to the president of the United States in consequence of his Note on the Subject, to John T. Mason Esquire Attorney for the District

W KILTY
N; FITZHUGH

I have only to add to the above Statement that the proof was very Strong of Duffys being a man of very bad character and of his keeping a house that was truly a nuisance to the neighbouring people

J. T. MASON

[*Order by TJ:*]
A pardon to be granted as to the rights of the US. on the judgment here spoken of, and so as not to affect the 2d indictment said to be depending.

TH: JEFFERSON
Mar. 24. 1804.

RC (DNA: RG 59, GPR); in an unidentified hand, undated, unsigned; judge's statement in a clerk's hand, signed by Kilty and Fitzhugh; Mason's statement in his hand; endorsed by TJ as received 6 Jan. 1804 and "petition" and so recorded in SJL.

EVIDENCE WAS EXHIBITED: an affidavit signed by Thomas Triplett and ten others acquainted with John Duffey stated that his property would not "fetch any thing near two hundred dollars" if sold (MS in same; undated; in the same hand as Duffey's petition, signed by all).

TJ's NOTE ON THE SUBJECT of Duffey's pardon has not been found. For his eventual pardon of Duffey, see John Thomson Mason to TJ, 21 Mch. 1804.

From Albert Gallatin

SIR/   Treasury Department January 6th. 1804.

I have the honour to enclose a copy of a Letter from the Collector of Bristol Rhode Island, and

I have the honour to be With the highest respect Sir, Your mo. Obedt: Servt.

ALBERT GALLATIN

RC (DLC); in a clerk's hand, signed by Gallatin; at foot of text: "The President of the United States"; endorsed by TJ as received from the Treasury Department on 6 Jan. and "Jonathan Russell's case" and so recorded in SJL. Enclosure not found.

The enclosed LETTER FROM Rhode Island Republican Jonathan Russell, of Providence, probably pertained to his resignation as collector at Bristol. On 24 Feb., TJ nominated Charles Collins, Jr., as his successor. The next month, TJ nominated Russell as U.S. consul at Tunis, but he declined the appointment (Vol. 34:145, 146-7n, 266, 341; Vol. 36:321, 332; TJ to the Senate, 24 Feb., 22 Mch. 1804; Levi Lincoln to TJ, 17 Apr. 1804).

From Thomas T. Hewson

SIR,   Philada Jany 6th. 1804.

I have the honour to inform you, that the American Philosophical Society, at their late meeting for the election of Officers, unanimously re-chose you President. It may not be ungrateful to you to receive this mark of the respect and esteem of Men, associated for the noble and benevolent purposes of promoting useful knowledge; and who, while engaged in furnishing intellectual stores for the mind, and in adding to the comforts and conveniencies of life, are desirous of thus giving force and stability to their labours.

I have the honour to be, Sir, with great respect, Your most obedient, humble servant,   THOS T HEWSON, Secy.

RC (MHi); at foot of text: "His Excellency Thomas Jefferson"; endorsed by TJ as received 10 Jan. and so recorded in SJL with notation "Secy. A.P.S."

Thomas T. Hewson (1773-1848) was born in London. After his family moved to Philadelphia in 1786, Hewson attended the forerunner of the University of Pennsylvania, from which he graduated in 1789, and then trained as a doctor in Philadelphia, London, and Edinburgh. He returned to Philadelphia in 1800, where he enjoyed a prestigious and public-spirited career, serving at different times as a physician or officer at such institutions as the Philadelphia Dispensary, the almshouse, the Humane Society, a prison, the Pennsylvania Hospital, and the Philadelphia College of Physicians, of which he was president from 1835 until his death. He also took a lead role in bringing *The Phar-*

macopœia of the United States of America, the first American work of its kind, to its initial publication in 1820 and in subsequently revising the work. Elected to membership in the American Philosophical Society in 1801, he served as secretary from 1803 to 1817 and 1821 to 1823, and as curator from 1817 to 1821 (Franklin Bache, *An Obituary Notice of Thomas T. Hewson, M.D., Late President of the Philadelphia College of Physicians* [Philadelphia, 1850]; Philadelphia *Gazette of the United States,* 2 Jan. 1804; Philadelphia *United States Gazette,* 12 Mch. 1807; RS, 1:609n).

On this afternoon, the APS held the LATE MEETING at which the body retained TJ as president. Robert Patterson, Caspar Wistar, and Benjamin Smith Barton remained vice presidents (APS, *Proceedings,* 22, pt. 3 [1884], 345-6).

From John Langdon

DEAR SR.   Portsmouth. Jany 6th. 1804

I was honor'd with your favor of the 22d Ult by the last mail, with Mr. Shannon's Commission inclosed, who expressed his warmest thanks for the same. This fresh mark of your goodness and attention to me at a moment when your whole time must be so much occupied by the great and important concern's of state; demands my greatful acknowledgements. The view of our Public affairs which you are pleased to give, places the United States, for prosperity and happiness, far beyond that, of any Nation on earth. The peaceable possession of that immense Teritory of Louisiana and the many and great advantages that must result to our Nation, are incalculable. the probability of peace with all the Barbary Powers, the friendship and good understanding that exists between us and the European Nations, the great unanimity, that is fast taking place in the sentiments of the Citizens of the United States must afford to every real American great reason to rejoice—It is to be lamented that two or three of the New England States with small majorities, still, present themselves moniments of Federal folly, but thanks to good Providence, they must and will soon, bow to eternal truth. Indeed Sr. when I look around, and view the whole ground, of our present happy situation and the Public proceedings in all dis[tricts I] can't help exclaiming that we are, [at this] *moment*, as happy as any Nation ever was, or, can be, considering the lot of humanity. I judge by my own feelings, and must acknowledge, that I am happy and proud of my Government—I pray you Sr. to accept of my highest consideration and respect, and sincere prayers for your Health and happiness—   JOHN LANGDON

RC (DLC); torn; at foot of text: "President of the United States"; endorsed by TJ as received 18 Jan. and so recorded in SJL.

From Ephraim Jordan and Others

TO THE PRESIDENT OF THE
UNITED STATES   [before 7 Jan. 1804]
The undersigned Inhabitants of the County of Knox Indiana Territory—beg leave humbly to recommend to the notice and patronage of your Excellency a Citizen who has long continued to deserve well of his Country.—

From the time General John Gibson, Secretary to the Territory began to reside among them in his official capacity, they have had every opportunity which familiarity of intercourse could give to be acquainted with the general and even minute outlines of his character—They have no hesitation to affirm that General Gibson forms one among comparatively few who improve upon a closer acquaintance, his benevolence and Philanthropic virtues enable him to contribute largely to the happiness of the private circle, and render him at the same time in principle and in action the firmest friend to the liberty and the prosperity of his country—It is unnecessary to call your Excellency's attention to his revolutionary services, in times of public commotion when national existence is endangered on a conspicuous theatre of action the patriot may perform important services before the public eye, and be rewarded by public approbation—but when moving in a sphere less exposed to observation in times of national peace and domestic prosperity, General Gibson has ever been among the first to exert his endeavours to promote as far as in his power the particular interests of that part of the community of which he was a member—his endeavours have not always been exerted in vain, and have met with a merited though inadequate reward, the esteem and respect of his grateful fellow Citizens—did we not flatter ourselves that General Gibson is not entirely unknown to your Excellency notwithstanding our firm conviction of his merit, we would not presume to advance among the crowd of expectants, and offer him as a fit subject for executive promotions, but influenced solely by respect for his private virtues and a knowledge of his public services, we would humbly offer as our opinion, from an acquaintance with his circumstances that his present appointment is by no means adequate either to his individual merit or his necessary domestic establishment. far be from us the presumption of dictating to the wisdom of the President the most proper reward for General Gibson's services; but we would suggest a circumstance which when known may direct your Excellency's Judgement as to one particular department in which General Gibson is well calculated to be of service to the public; he early acquired a knowledge and still retains an extensive acquaintance with the several dialects of the Indian tribes who inhabit either within or immediately surrounding the present Territory of the United States. And perhaps there is no individual in the Union better qualified for the important office of Agent for the Indian Tribes on the West side of the River Mississippi should Louisiana become the property of the United States

EPHM. JORDAN

RC (DNA: RG 59, LAR); undated, but see below; in an unidentified hand, signed by Ephraim Jordan and 59 others; addressed: "The President of the United States." Not recorded in SJL.

Ephraim Jordan (d. 1820) served with George Rogers Clark during the American Revolution. He was a justice of the peace and an officer in the Knox County militia (Logan Esarey, ed., *Messages and Letters of William Henry Harrison*, 2 vols.

[Indianapolis, 1922, repr., New York, 1975], 1:386n; *Indiana Centinel*, 15 Jan. 1820). Other signers of the recommendation included territorial judges Thomas T. Davis and Henry Vander Burgh.

This memorial was probably the "Remonstrance" to the president referred to by JOHN GIBSON in a 7 Jan. letter to Gallatin, which he states had been signed "by the judges and most of the principal Inhabitants" (*Terr. Papers*, 7:165; see Gallatin to TJ, [on or before 11 Feb. 1804]).

From Walter Saltonstall

Sᴿ   Philadelphia Jan 7th 1804
   May Your Excellency pardon the intrusion of a foreigner, and
deign to peruse the following, is the petition of respectful Sir
   Your very obedient servant   Wᴀʟᴛᴇʀ Sᴀʟᴛᴏɴsᴛᴀʟʟ

   During Mr Burges Allisons privation I taught in his academy and
since through good wishes he has accommodated me with some volumes in folio such as a Spanish dictionary and Universal penman for
my use as a Teacher; and I with pleasure seeing by your wisdom Sir
an additional territory ceded to those States inhabited by people of
other tongues I take the liberty to offer my self as an english teacher
to be sent among whom, in what part, or on what commission at any
period your excellency may think convenient.   At this time I
educate some youths the Sons of merchants and physicians (here in
latin, french, bookeeping and arithmetic and drawing of globes &c)
from whom I can have testimonials of unwearied attention to my stu-
dents and consequently of universal success, & in communicating the
art of writing all hands in use I have been happy to accomplish in a
little time.   I have been here from England since 6 years and am
between 40 and 50 & in health and activity and when the contending
nations are again in peace have thoughts at some future period to
return via France, and with the politics of those states to this time as
a stranger I have been a neuter.   The mathematical sciences I
dont profess with spaniard here since 3 years I have read and studied
so as to write their language intelligibly to them, and to construe
their writings in turn.
Coll Kirkbride a few weeks past closed his eyes reluctantly without
seeing my countryman and neighbour Fd Payne who this summer I
oft saw at his house.
From the house of John Taylor Esqr No 60 South 5th Street where
an address to me W Saltonstall will find me

Pendant votre Administration
    De cette Nation,
    Pour sa felicité;
De la Sagesse soyez vous inspiré.
De la patience, et de la philosóphie.

RC (MoSHi: Jefferson Papers); addressed: "To his Excellency Thomas
Jefferson Esqr President of the United
States City of Washington"; franked and
postmarked; endorsed by TJ as received
13 Jan. and so recorded in SJL.

Walter Saltonstall appears to have recently moved from Bordentown, New Jersey, where Burgess (sometimes spelled Burgiss) Allison operated an ACADEMY at different times during the 1790s and 1800s. The town was also the home of Joseph KIRKBRIDE, who before his death in November 1803 had been a close friend of Thomas Paine. In a Philadelphia directory for 1804, the profession of JOHN TAYLOR of 60 S. Fifth Street was listed as "gentleman" (*Philadelphia Gazette & Universal Daily Advertiser*, 16 May 1795; Trenton *True American*, 24 Nov. 1801; John Keane, *Tom Paine: A Political Life* [London, 1995], 162-4, 493; James Robinson, *The Philadelphia Directory for 1804* [Philadelphia, 1804], 233).

PENDANT VOTRE ADMINISTRATION: that is, "For the well-being of this nation you are leading, may you be inspired by wisdom, patience and philosophy."

From Thomas McKean

DEAR SIR,   Lancaster. Janry. 8th. 1804.

Yesterday I signed the Act, to ratify, on behalf of the State of Pennsylvania, an Amendment to the Constitution of the United States, relative to the choosing of a President and Vice-President of the United States. There were but nine Nays in the House of Representatives and one in our Senate, on this occasion.

The speech of Mr; Tracy in the Senate of the U.S. was sent to me, with a Letter, from that Gentleman, and also by Mr; Pickering; both letters dated the 19th. of Decemr. last: It is presumable others, of the like import, have been received by some of the Members of our Legislature. The first named Gentleman is a stranger to me, and I have not had any visit, or communication by letter or words from the latter, since I have been Governor of this State. From these circumstances it may be fairly conjectured, that no pains will be omitted in obstructing the adoption of this Amendment in other States; for these Gentlemen seem to think it an all important and dangerous measure.

I confess, I can perceive nothing dangerous or improper in the proposed Amendment, unless the precedent may encourage a too frequent attempt of the like kind, when no real necessity demands it. In this instance, a casus omissus in the Constitution is supplied, an interregnum prevented, a species of intrigue defeated and civil commotions kept at a distance. I wish the Amendment had been expressed in a more grammatical manner tho' I think the true construction of it cannot be misunderstood: In strictness, the relative refers to the next antecedent, and the words, "not exceeding three," might be strained to relate to the word, "numbers," so that the House of Representatives will be confined to the choice of a President, who had not more than three votes from the Electors. This observation may be endured in a strict Gramarian, but would be deemed a quibble in a lawyer, and hooted at by all men of plain common sense; and yet this is said by Mr; Pickering to have been demonstrated as unintelligible in the Senate, by the diversity of constructions put upon it.

We shall, if this amendment shall be adopted by thirteen States, (which I believe it will, tho' probably no more, unless the effects of party shall in the mean time cease) have our next President and Vice-President genuine Republicans, otherwise I doubt it. Several Gentlemen of the Republican party have wished to use my name as a Candidate for Vice-President, but I have absolutely declined it on public & personal considerations, and my reasons seem to have given satisfaction: As to the highest honor, it has never been hinted to me by any man, nor shall be without a positive denial: the Republicans will not think of it, and the Federalists will not so insult me as to propose it.   Accept, dear Sir, my best wishes for your health & public and private happiness.   THOS M:KEAN

RC (DLC); at head of text: "Private"; at foot of text: "His Excellency Thomas Jefferson Esq;"; endorsed by TJ as received 13 Jan. and so recorded in SJL. Dft (PHi: Thomas McKean Papers).

On 2 Dec. 1803, the Senate remained in session until late in the evening debating the proposed Twelfth Amendment. The SPEECH delivered by Uriah TRACY that afternoon was printed in pamphlet form and widely circulated as the most convincing statement of the Federalist position. He included the argument that there was no need for the amendment and that it would lead "to the selection of a less important, and more unfit person" as vice president (*Mr. Tracy's Speech in the Senate of the United States, Friday, December 2, 1803* [n.p., 1803; Shaw-Shoemaker, No. 5387]; Kuroda, *Origins of the Twelfth Amendment*, 140-1; *Annals*, 13:159-80).

CASUS OMISSUS: "case omitted" (Bryan A. Garner, *Black's Law Dictionary*, 8th ed. [St. Paul, Minn., 2004], 232).

MORE GRAMMATICAL MANNER: McKean referred to the passage that reads:

"and if no person have such majority, then from the persons having the highest numbers not exceeding three on the list of those voted for as President, the House of Representatives shall choose immediately, by ballot, the President" (MS in DNA: RG 11, RA). In the House debate on 7 Dec., Simeon Baldwin, who would soon become a Connecticut Supreme Court justice, argued that it was unclear whether the words "not exceeding three" referred to persons or numbers. The phrase precluded a number greater than three, but did it not imply "that the House might, if they chose, confine the election to two"? Roger Griswold favored striking the words out altogether. Caesar A. Rodney, John Randolph, and Thomas Sandford were among the Republicans who offered their thoughts on the construction: they saw no problem with it as rendered. Listening to the debate in the gallery of the House, Senator Timothy Pickering found the phrase UNINTELLIGIBLE and reported it as such to his correspondents (Kuroda, *Origins of the Twelfth Amendment*, 148, 214n; *Annals*, 13:678-81).

To James Monroe

A confidential opportunity offering by mr Baring, I can venture to write to you with less reserve than common conveyances admit. the 150 livres you paid to mr Chas for me shall be replaced in the hands of mr Lewis your manager here, with thanks to you for honoring what you had no reason to doubt was a just claim on me. I do not know him personally or any otherwise than by his history of our revolution, & of Bonaparte, a single copy of which he sent me. I never heard of any other being sent, nor should I have undertaken, or he expected me, to be the vender of his books here, to keep accounts and make remittances for him: if he has sent any copies for sale to my care, I have never heard of them. — Isaac Coles, son of Colo. Coles our neighbor is gone to London, Paris, &c. he asked from me a letter to you. I told him I had been obliged to make it a rule to give no letters of introduction while in my present office; but that in my first letter to you I would mention to you the reason why I gave him none. he is a most worthy young man, & one whom I had intended to have asked to be my Secretary, had mr Harvie declined the offer. you know the worth of his family.   I inclose you two letters for mr Williams, asking you from your knolege of persons and things to use your discretion for me, and deliver whichever you think best, suppressing the other.   with respect to my correspondence with literary characters in Europe, to the great mass of those who send me copies of their works, being otherwise unknown to me, or perhaps not advantageously known, I return them simple notes of thanks, sometimes saying I have no doubt I *shall* have great satisfaction in perusing their work as soon as my occupations will permit; and, where I have found the work to possess merit, saying so in a complimentary way. with Volney, Dupont, Cabanis Cepede, I had intimate & very friendly intercourse in France, & with the two first here. with Sr. John Sinclair I had the same in France & England, and with mr Strickland here. to these persons I write freely on subjects of literature, and to a certain degree on politics, respecting however their personal opinions, and their situation so as not to compromit them were a letter intercepted. indeed what I write to them in this way are for the most part such truths & sentiments as would do us good if known to their governments, and, as probably as not, are communicated to them. to the Earl of Buchan I have written one letter in answer to the compliment of a volume of his which he sent me. he is an honorable patriotic & virtuous character, was in correspondence with Dr. Franklin & General

Washington, & had every title to a respectful answer from me. I expressed myself to him in terms which were true, & therefore the more satisfactory to him. I have recieved a volume of geology, of great merit, from Faujas de St. fond. I did not know him personally, nor do I know the[1] standing he holds in society or his government; but an intimate acquaintance of his here gives me a good account of him as an amiable and virtuous man. my answer to him will be more[2] than a mere compliment of thanks, but confined to the branch of science which is the subject of his work. an opening has been given me of making a communication which will be acceptable to the emperor Alexander, either directly or indirectly, and as from one private individual to another. I have not decided whether to do it or not. this is the whole extent of the literary correspondence which I now keep up in Europe, and I set the more value on it inasmuch as I can make private friendships instrumental to the public good by inspiring a confidence which is denied to public, and official communications.

I expect this evening's post will bring us the account that Louisiana was formally delivered to us about the 16th. of December. this acquisition is seen by our constituents in all it's importance, & they do justice to all those who have been instrumental towards it. fortunately the federal leaders have had the imprudence to oppose it pertinaciously, which has given an occasion to a great proportion of their quondam honest adherents to abandon them and join the republican standard. they feel themselves now irretrievably lost, and are ceasing to make further opposition in the states, or any where but in Congress. I except however N. Hampshire, Mass. Connect. & Delaware. the 1st. will be with us in the course of this year; Connecticut is advancing with a slow but steady step, never losing the ground she gains; Massachusets has a republicanism of so flaccid a texture, and Delaware so much affected by every little topical inflammation, that we must wait for them with patience & good humour. Congress is now engaged in a bill for the government of Louisiana. it is impossible to foresee in what shape it will come out. they talk of giving 5000. D. to the Governor, but the bill also proposes to commence at the close of this session. I have in private conversations demonstrated to individuals that that is impossible; that the necessary officers cannot be mustered there under 6. months. if they give that time for it's commencement, it may admit our appointing you to that office, as I presume you could be in place within a term not much beyond that, & in the interval the Secretary of the state would govern. but the idea of the public as to the importance of that office would not bear a long absence of the principal. you are not to calculate that 5000. D. would place you by any means as much at your ease there, as 9000. D. where you are. in that station you cannot avoid expensive hospitality. where you are, altho' it is not pleasant to fall short in returning civilities, yet necessity has rendered this so familiar in Europe as not to lessen respect for the person whose circumstances do not permit a return of hospitalities. I see by your letters the pain which this situation gives you, and I can estimate it's acuteness from the generosity of your nature. but, my dear friend, calculate with mathematical rigour the pain annexed to each branch of the dilemma, & pursue that which brings the least. to give up entertainment, & to live with the most rigorous economy till you have cleared yourself of every demand is a pain for a definite time only: but to return here with accumulated incumbrances on you, will fill your life with torture. we wish to do every thing for you which law & rule will permit. but more than this would injure you as much as us. believing that the mission to Spain will enable you to suspend expence greatly in London, & to apply your salary during your absence to the clearing off your debts, you will be instructed to proceed there as soon as you shall have regulated certain points of neutral right for us with England, or as soon as you find nothing in that way can be done. this you should hurry as much as possible, that you may proceed to Spain, for settling with that court the boundaries of Louisiana. on this subject mr Madison will send you the copy of a Memoir of mine, written last summer while I was among my books at Monticello. we scarcely expect any liberal or just settlement with Spain, and are perfectly determined to obtain or to take our just limits. how far you will suffer yourself to be detained there by the procrastinations of artifice or indolence must depend on the prospects which arise, and on your own determination to accept the government of Louisiana, which will admit but of a limited delay. it is probable that the inhabitants of Louisiana on the left bank of the Missisipi and inland Eastwardly to a considerable extent, will very soon claim to be recieved under our jurisdiction, and that this end of W. Florida will thus be peaceably got possession of. for Mobile and the Eastern end we shall await favorable conjunctures. if they refuse to let our vessels have free ingress & egress in the Mobile to & from the Tombigby settlements, and if Spain is at war, the crisis there will be speedy. Fulwar Skipwith wishes office in Louisiana. but he should be made sensible of the impossibility of an office remaining vacant till we can import an incumbent from Europe. that of Govr. is the only one for which the law has made that sort of provision. besides he has been so long absent from America, that he cannot have habits and feelings, and the tact necessary to be in unison with his country men here. he is much fitter for any matters of business (below that of diplomacy) which we may have to do in Europe. there is here a great sense of the inadequacy of C. Pinckney to the office he is in. his continuance is made a subject of standing reproach to myself personally, by whom the appointment was made & on a principle of distribution solely[3] before I had collected the administration. he declared at the time that nothing would induce him to continue so as not to be here at the ensuing Presidential election. I am persuaded he expected to be proposed at it as V.P. after he got to Europe his letters asked only a continuance of two years. but he now does not drop the least hint of a voluntary return. pray, my dear Sir, avail yourself of his vanity, his expectations, his fears, and whatever will weigh with him to induce him to ask leave to return, and obtain from him to be the bearer of the letter yourself. you will render us in this the most acceptable service possible. his enemies here are perpetually dragging his character in the dirt, and charging it on the administration. he does, or ought to know this, and to feel the necessity of coming home to vindicate himself, if he looks to any thing further in the career of honor.

You ask for small news. Mr. Randolph & mr Eppes are both of Congress, and now with me. their wives lying in at home. Trist was appointed Collector of Natchez, and on the removal of that office down to New Orleans will go with it.[4] his family still remain in Albemarle, but will join him in the spring. Dr. Bache has been to N. Orleans as Physician to the hospital there. he is returned to Philadelphia where his wife is, & where they will probably remain. Peachy Gilmer has married miss House, and will go with the family to N. Orleans. mr Short has been to Kentucky & will return to Europe in the spring. the deaths of Samuel Adams & Judge Pendleton you will have heard of. Colo N. Lewis, Divers, & the Carrs are all well & their families. Sam Carr is now living in Albemarle. J. F. Mercer's quarrel with his council has carried him over openly to the Federalists. he is now in the Maryland legislature entirely thrown off by the republicans. he has never seen or written on these things to mr Madison or myself. — when mentioning your going to N. Orleans, & that the salary there would not increase the ease of your situation, I meant to have added that the only considerations which might make it eligible to you were the facility of getting there the richest land in the world, the extraordinary profitableness of their culture, and that the removal of your slaves there might immediately put you under way. you alone however can weigh these things for yourself. and after all, it may depend on the time the legislature may give for commencing the new government. but, let us hear from you as soon as you can determine, that we may not incur the blame of waiting for nothing.   Mr. Merry is with us, and we believe him to be personally as desirable a character as could have been sent us. but he is unluckily associated with one of an opposite character in every point. she has already disturbed our harmony extremely. he began by claiming the first visit from the National ministers. he corrected himself in this. but a pretension to take precedence at dinners &c. over all others is persevered in. we have told him that the principle of society, as well as of government, with us, is the equality of the individuals composing it. that no man here would come to a dinner, where he was to be marked with inferiority to any other. that we might as well attempt to force our principle of equality at St. James's, as he his principle of precedence here. I had been in the habit, when I invited female company (having no lady in my family) to ask one of the ladies of the 4. Secretaries to come & take care of my company; and as she was to do the honors of the table I handed her to dinner myself. that mr Merry might not construe this as giving them a precedence over mrs Merry, I have discontinued it; and here as well as in private houses, the pele-mele practice, is adhered to. they have got Yrujo to take a zealous part in the claim of precedence: it has excited generally emotions of great contempt and indignation (in which the members of the legislature participate sensibly);[5] that the agents of foreign nations should assume to dictate to us what shall be the laws of our society. the consequence will be that mr & mrs Merry will put themselves into Coventry, and that he will lose the best half of his usefulness to his nation, that derived from a perfectly familiar & private intercourse with the secretaries & myself. the latter, be assured, is a virago, and in the short course of a few weeks has established a degree of dislike among all classes which one would have thought impossible in so[6] short a time. Thornton has entered into their ideas. at this we wonder, because he is a plain man, a sensible one, and too candid to be suspected of wishing to bring on their recall & his own substitution. to counterwork their misrepresentations, it would be well their government should understand as much of these things as can be communicated with decency, that they may know the spirit in which their letters are written. we learn that Thornton thinks we are not as friendly now to Great Britain as before our acquisition of Louisiana. this is totally without foundation. our friendship to that nation is cordial and sincere: so is that with France. we are anxious to see England maintain her standing, only wishing she would use her power on the ocean with justice. if she had done this heretofore, other nations would not have stood by & looked with unconcern on a conflict which endangers her existence. we are not indifferent to it's issue, nor should we be so on a conflict on which the existence of France should be in danger. we consider each as a necessary instrument to hold in check the disposition of the other to tyrannize over other nations. with respect to Merry, he appears so reasonable & good a man, that I should be sorry to lose him as long as there remains a possibility of reclaiming him to the exercise of his own dispositions. if his wife perseveres, she must eat her soup at home, and we shall endeavor to draw him into society as if she did not exist. it is unfortunate that the good understanding of nations should hang on the caprice of an individual who ostensibly has nothing to do with them.   present my friendly & respectful salutations to mrs Monroe & miss Eliza: and be assured yourself of my constant affections.

Jan. 16. Louisiana was delivered to our Commissioners on the 20th. Dec.

RC (DLC: Monroe Papers); at foot of first page: "James Monroe"; endorsed by Monroe. PrC (DLC); endorsed by TJ in ink on verso. Enclosures: TJ's letters to David Williams, 14 Nov. 1803 (Vol. 41:725-8).

In a letter of 18 May 1803, Monroe reported that he had covered a payment to Jean CHAS for 30 copies of Chas's work on the American Revolution. TJ had previously received one copy of that work, as well as three different books by Chas related to Napoleon Bonaparte (Vol. 33:515-17; Vol. 36:95-6; Vol. 40:327, 393).

TJ wrote to the EARL OF BUCHAN on 10 July 1803 and thanked him for his *Essays on the Lives and Writings of Fletcher of Saltoun and the Poet Thomson* (Vol. 40:708-10).

For Barthélemy FAUJAS de Saint-Fond's *Essai de géologie*, see his letters of 12 Aug. and 20 Sep. 1803.

For the reported overture from ALEXANDER, see Vol. 38:556. In a letter of 11 Feb. 1804, Joel Barlow also indicated that the Russian emperor would welcome hearing from TJ.

BILL FOR THE GOVERNMENT OF LOUISIANA: see Bill for the Organization of Orleans Territory, [23 Nov. 1803].

I SEE BY YOUR LETTERS THE PAIN WHICH THIS SITUATION GIVES YOU: since arriving in London in late July 1803, Monroe's dispatches to James Madison repeatedly lamented the inadequacy of his salary for meeting the "incredible expences" of the city (Madison, *Papers, Sec. of State Ser.*, 5:227, 297, 337, 384, 434, 564; 6:96-7, 336-7).

CERTAIN POINTS OF NEUTRAL RIGHT FOR US WITH ENGLAND: on 5 Jan., Madison prepared a lengthy set of instructions for Monroe to guide his negotiations with Great Britain on the subject of neutral rights. Madison had already conducted informal discussions with Anthony Merry on various aspects of the subject, about which Madison felt optimistic. Despite the "many important objects" that might be included in the negotiations, Madison directed Monroe to focus his efforts on those subjects "which cannot be much longer delayed without danger to the good understanding of the two nations." To guide Monroe, Madison included "a plan of a Convention contemplated by the President," which limited itself to several key topics: the impressment of American seamen, the declaration of "fictitious blockades" by Britain, visiting and searching American vessels by the British, the right of Americans to trade with colonies at war with Britain, and "a few other cases affecting our maritime rights." As an inducement to Britain, the plan included provisions regarding the surrender of British deserters and the prevention of trade in contraband with Britain's enemies, although Monroe was to seek a reduction of the number of items considered contraband (Madison, *Papers, Sec. of State Ser.*, 6:292-308, 349-50).

For TJ's MEMOIR, see Editorial Note and group of documents on the boundaries of Louisiana (Vol. 41:321-40) and Continuation of an Examination of the Boundaries of Louisiana, 15 Jan.

INADEQUACY OF C. PINCKNEY: not only was Charles Pinckney a disappointment to TJ and Madison as minister to Spain, but the Federalist press frequently abused his personal character, especially his alleged fondness for women of low repute. The *Trenton Federalist* went so far as to describe him as "one of the greatest libertines of the age" (*Washington Federalist*, 23 Feb. 1803; Baltimore *Republican; or, Anti-Democrat*, 11 Mch. 1803; Baltimore *Federal Gazette*, 8 Apr. 1803; *Trenton Federalist*, 11 Apr. 1803; Madison to TJ, 9 Apr. 1804).

YOU ASK FOR SMALL NEWS: Monroe to TJ, 20 Sep. 1803. SAMUEL ADAMS died on 2 Oct. 1803 and Edmund PENDLETON on the 26th of the same month (Boston *Independent Chronicle*, 3 Oct. 1803; Richmond *Virginia Argus*, 29 Oct. 1803).

The feud between Governor John F. Mercer and the MARYLAND Council played out in the state's press beginning in January 1803. Mercer eventually an-

nounced that he would not run again for governor and instead contested for a seat in the House of Delegates. Reports circulated that Mercer had joined the Federalists, but one anonymous letter writer claimed that he meant "to attach himself to no sect, but to act independently" (*Publications Relative to the Difference of Opinion between the Governor and Council on Their Respective Powers* [Annapolis, 1803]; Baltimore *Republican; or, Anti-Democrat*, 28 Jan.; Easton *Republican Star, or Eastern Shore Advertiser*, 26 Apr.; *Alexandria Advertiser*, 14 July).

LOUISIANA WAS DELIVERED: word of the formal transfer of Louisiana by Spain to the United States on 20 Dec. arrived in Washington on the evening of 15 Jan. (Madison, *Papers, Sec. of State Ser.*, 6:349).

[1] TJ here canceled "footing."
[2] Word interlined in place of "fuller."
[3] Preceding six words and ampersand interlined. Change lacking in PrC.
[4] Preceding three words interlined in place of "be continued there." Change lacking in PrC.
[5] Preceding phrase in parentheses interlined.
[6] TJ here canceled "small."

To Timothy Pickering

Jan. 8. 04.

Th: Jefferson presents his compliments to mr Pickering, and has searched without success in Hutchins's Topographical Description of the Western country for the passage relative to the Northern boundary of which mr Pickering spoke to him yesterday. he imagines therefore he mistook the pamphlet to which he referred, and therefore asks the favor of the loan of it.

RC (MH); addressed: "The honble Mr. Pickering"; endorsed by Pickering. Not recorded in SJL.

TJ likely perused WITHOUT SUCCESS a pamphlet in his collection by Thomas Hutchins, *A Topographical Description of*

Virginia, Pennsylvania, Maryland, and North Carolina, Comprehending the Rivers Ohio, Kenhawa, Sioto, Cherokee, Wabash, Illinois, Missisippi, &c. (London, 1778; Sowerby, No. 525). At some point during the next several days, Pickering loaned TJ a copy of Hutchins's *An Historical*

Narrative and Topographical Description of Louisiana, and West-Florida, Comprehending the River Mississippi with Its Principal Branches and Settlements, and the Rivers Pearl, Pascagoula, Mobille, Perdido, Escambia, Chacta-Hatcha, &c. (Philadelphia, 1784). See TJ to Pickering, 13 Jan.

From John Jay AcModery

Newtown Tioga County
State of New York

Sir,   January 9th: 1804

an unfurtuanate Man addresses You with these Lines though Scarsly worthy of Your Notice on account of its Iregular stile & Compossure— But would most Humbly begg pardon for the Intrussion & wish You to exuse me for attempting to trouble You with so lenghty a Scrawlling & so poorly Connected & spelled

Sir I embarked in the Earliest Day of the American Revolution went with the faithful Genl. Montgomery the whole of his Campaign & in the Reductions of all the British post to Quebeck and at his unhapy fall in that Diresom Situation was made a Prisoner. But being a Youth not of age a Volunteer & a Son of an Eminent Tory familly in New York I soon got Liberty to Return to that City I had not ben hom more than 3 weeks when I went again into Canada as farr as three Rivers & there was defeated & then like to ben Starved & was wounded with a piece of Bomb Shell I Remained in the Servis through the whole Retread to Ticonderoga til the next Sumer in the Month of August my money being pretry much expended I then Joined the artillery with the promis of the Commanding officer of giting a Commission ere long I Continued in the War till the whole army was Regullarly Discharged I was one who allways was active in every Dangerous Expedition I had the side of Seeing Burgoine & his whole Army Surender & the Honour to Command the first field piece to Recieve them which Glories Day & the unexpressable Emotions of joy my Soul underwent on that occation is out of my power to describe— Genl. John Patterson one of the Members in Congress & first Judge of this County Can give you the Details of my Conduct in the army pretry General as wee whire most allways Staitioned togather & now are Naighbours I was takin Prisoner five times & three times wounded ones as before mentioned ones by a Musquet ball & ones by a Bayonet which had like to prove fatal to Me—I Servd. as Spy on many difficult occassions but forever discharged My trust with punctuallity and w Zeal to my country it is with Regret & Reflections only that I Could depicture those Awfull Sceens I underwent on those occations

no one could more clearrer demanstrate those feets then the Dececad Chieffs who had the Instruction of the different Missions Genl. Henry Knox & that detestable creature A. Hammilton where known to many of my Secreet Expeditions But God forbid that I should ask either of them for any favour & the Rached T. Pickering is known to a great part of it I never thought it my duty to ask my Country fo a penssion when I was Able to get my own living though great Numbers who where but Lightly wounded got a penssion during life &ce. I am Yet Able thaks be to God—But believe me hardships which I underwent through the course of the War is beginning to bear hard down on me—I was allways Sience the Revolution in Confussion til of late & am Some Yet I never could think like my father nor many of my aquaintences & am Something Chollaric in my temper on Some occations I was an Antifederalist I was a Clintonean & greatly oposd. to John Adams whereever an oppertunity would present itself I allways held that party in View as the Enemies of myself posterity & Country which often brought me into Diffuculties which terminated greatly in the loss of My property My Enemies being Numerous a few Years ago & Seeking every advantage of me So that they often put me to my shifts in Drinking a toast one day in a Harvest field directly after the fedral Juntos, had Stript me of allmost every thing by there Intreagues they thus contrivd to give me my fatal Strocke in point of property they got me entangled in the Law & there they commanded the Barr the Bench & Jurors—which makes me groan for my familly which are a wife & 3 Boyes the oldest 9 Years the 7th: Septr. last the Youngest 4 this 11th. Jany. whoes Name I Called George Washington—
Sir, the great Director of the Universe has favoured You with more then an ordinary Share of Wisdom & good furtune to Relieve & serve Your Country & espeically those that You find worthy & deserving I would Intreat Your Clemencie that Youl. be Pleasd. to Inform Yourself of Genl. Patterson & John P: Van Ness who is an old Naighbour of myn or of Governor Clinton in Respect to my Moral & Political Character & if You Should find me worthy to favour me with a Small Calling in Some of the New Aquired Teritory of Louisiana or on the late Indian purchase &ce. if only to a Reasonable tract of good fiesable Land in Some Convenient Place at or near Some of the Navagable waters in either purchase for a Reasonable Consideration I am not able to pay any great Sum after Mooving my familly that great Distance from this place—under my present circumstances I Shall with dew Submission wait the Presidents favourable Ansewr &ce

I Remain Sir Your Most Obidt. And Respectful Servant

JOHN JAY AC. MODERY

RC (DLC); at head of text: "Whorthy Friend & fellow Citizen Thomas Jefferson President of the united States of America"; addressed: "Thomas Jefferson President United States Washington City"; franked; postmarked 8 Feb.; endorsed by TJ as received 16 Feb. but recorded in SJL as received 17 Feb.

Although in the 1780s a customer apparently identified himself at a store in a neighboring county as John Jay Ac Modery, the surname of the author of the above letter may have been recognized by others as AcMoody, the name that appeared in a list of Tioga County subscribers to a 1792 version of the laws of New York and in the 1800 census for Newtown (later Elmira), New York (United States Census Schedules, DNA: RG 29; *Laws of the State of New York, Comprising the Constitution, and the Acts of the Legislature, Since the Revolution, from the First to the Fifteenth Session, Inclusive*, 2 vols. [New York, 1792], list of subscribers, v. 2; Louise Welles Murray, *A History of Old Tioga Point and Early Athens Pennsylvania* [Athens, Pa., 1908], 248).

LATE INDIAN PURCHASE: likely a reference to the recent treaty conducted with the Kaskaskias, who ceded much of the Illinois country (Vol. 41:642-3).

To James Oldham

SIR   Washington Jan. 9. 1804.

I recieved last night your letter of the day before, and now inclose you the 20. Dollars desired. I ordered from Philadelphia the three sheets of sheet iron which you supposed might be wanting. they are now on their way. if not wanting to finish the terras, they may be employed on the gutturs which are to be laid with sheet iron. they should be painted on both sides before they are laid down. Accept my best wishes.   TH: JEFFERSON

RC (CtHC); addressed: "Mr. James Oldham Monticello near Milton."

A LETTER of 7 Jan. from Oldham, recorded in SJL as received 8 Jan., has not been found.

I ORDERED: TJ to Jones & Howell, 22 Dec. 1803.

To Anne Cary Randolph

MY DEAR ANNE   Washington Jan. 9. 1804.

I recieved last night your letter of the 7th. with your Mama's postscript. as your's was the principal the answer is due to you. I am glad to find you are pursuing so good a course of reading. French, History, Morals, and some poetry and writings of eloquence to improve the stile form a good course for you. how does Jefferson get on with his French? will he let Ellen catch him? the American muse has been so dull for some time past as to have furnished nothing for our volume. I have here a pair of beautiful fowls of enormous size of the East India breed: and can get in the city a pair of Bantams. I should prefer sending you the latter, if an opportunity occurs, provided you will undertake to raise them, and furnish me a pair for Monticello. tell your Mama I shall be extremely glad to have my chair brought by Davy Bowles, as it would be impossible for me to go home in my Phaeton in the spring, and I should have to perform the journey on horseback. I shall hope therefore to recieve the chair by Davy. I am glad to hear your Aunt Jane is so near you. it will add exercise, and chearfulness to your enjoiments. give my tenderest love to your Mama & Aunt Maria, and kiss all the little ones for me. I deliver kisses for yourself to this letter.   TH: JEFFERSON

PrC (ViU: Edgehill-Randolph Papers); at foot of text: "Miss Anne C. Randolph"; endorsed by TJ in ink on verso.

AUNT JANE: Thomas Mann Randolph's sister, Jane Cary Randolph, who had moved to Glenmore, near Edgehill (see Vol. 40:453n).

The LETTER OF THE 7TH, recorded in SJL as received from Edgehill on the 8th, has not been found.

From Tompson J. Skinner

DEAR SIR   Washington Jany. 9th 1804

The Bearer Mr Easton A Citisen of New York, is Solicitous that you should become Acquainted with his Character, I am Situated at A Considerable Distance from him, But have Connections And Acquaintance in the County where he resides—

By whom I have been informed that Mr Easton was a very respectable Gentleman, of Fair Character And promising Talents, And A firm Undeviating Republican—The enclosed you will perceive is from A Gentleman whose practice is in the Same Courts, Who I consider to be Cautious, Delicate And Correct in all his Recommendations, And therefore Do not hesitate in Giving my opinion, that his Communication is Entitled to Respect

have the honor to be with Sentiments of Affection & esteem Your Humble. Servt—   TOMPSON J SKINNER

RC (DNA: RG 59, LAR); at head of text: "To President Jefferson"; endorsed by TJ as received 6 Feb. and "Easton Rufus to be Atty N.O." and so recorded in SJL with a brace connecting it to letters received the same day from Philip Van Cortlandt of 1 Feb. and Oliver Phelps of 4 Feb. Enclosure: Nathan Williams to Skinner, Washington, 2 Jan. 1804, stat-ing that he has recently met with Rufus Easton, his Oneida County neighbor and acquaintance, and is willing to render him assistance in securing him a federal appointment; Williams and Easton have practiced at the same bar, and Williams considers him "a person of good moral character, a firm republican," and "a Counsellor of respectable standing & talents, of the Supreme Court of Judicature of the State of N. York"; Williams asks that Skinner forward this information to the president, "with an intimation of the credit due to my recomendation" (same).

An influential Republican from western Massachusetts, Tompson J. Skinner (1752-1809) was a militia general and former state legislator who served in Congress from 1797 to 1799. Reelected in 1803, he resigned his House seat the following year after TJ appointed him commissioner of loans. His term of office lasted only a few months, however, terminating when TJ appointed him U.S. marshal for Massachusetts in November 1804 (*Biog. Dir. Cong.*; Paul Goodman, *The Democratic-Republicans of Massachusetts: Politics in a Young Republic* [Cambridge, Mass., 1964], 79-82; JEP, 1:471, 476; TJ to Skinner, 15 June 1804).

From David Leonard Barnes

SIR—   Providence Jany 10th 1804

I have the honour to acknowledge the receipt of your favour of the 31st ult. inclosed with the petition of Nathl Ingraham, and a copy of your letter to Mr. Ellery—It is not in my power to make a correct statement of the case decided against Capt Ingraham, without having recourse to the records, which are kept at Newport—I shall go there the beginning of February to attend the District Court, when I will obtain the necessary information, and endeavour to make the statement required—

With Sentiments of the Highest Respect I am your most Obedt Servt   DAVID LEONARD BARNES

RC (DLC); at foot of text: "Thomas Jefferson President of the United States"; endorsed by TJ as received 19 Jan. and so recorded in SJL.

From Lydia Leslie

SIR   Philadelphia January 10th 1804

The friendship you have always had the goodness to express for my late husband Robert Leslie, who about two weeks since closed a life long embittered by sickness and misfortune, has induced me to take the liberty of entreating your assistance in the present distressing situation of my affairs.

At the suit of a creditor in England for debts incurred by the partnership of Leslie and Price, an execution has been laid upon every thing we possess, and I expect the whole will shortly be advertised for sale by the Sheriff. It is needless to describe the misery of being left without any means of supporting a large family. I would gladly attempt keeping a boarding-house, but that will be out of my power if I am deprived of my furniture.

If Sir you can accomodate me with a little money for that purpose, the precise sum I leave entirely to yourself, the gratitude of the widow and children of a man whom you once honoured with your friendship, and who always regarded you with the respect and admiration your virtues so truly deserve, will be as lasting as it is unbounded. Be assured Sir that nothing but the greatest necessity could prevail on me to take the liberty of applying to you.

I will no longer Sir encroach upon your time, at present, but if your more important avocations will permit, a speedy reply will be esteemed a particular favour by

Sir Yours with respect.   LYDIA LESLIE.

P.S. You will please to direct to the north-west corner of Fifth and Arch Streets No 177.

RC (MHi); endorsed by TJ as received 13 Jan. and so recorded in SJL.

Lydia Baker Leslie (ca. 1767-1824), a native of Cecil County, Maryland, was the widow of Philadelphia clock and watchmaker Robert Leslie, with whom she had five children, including the portrait painter Charles Robert Leslie and the author Eliza Leslie. In 1793, the Leslie family moved to England, where her husband intended to improve business prospects and acquire further skills and equipment. The family returned from London to Philadelphia in 1800 and faced financial difficulties upon the dissolution of Robert Leslie's partnership with Isaac Price. As a widow, Lydia Leslie ran a boarding house in Philadelphia with her daughter Eliza, who also gave drawing lessons to support the family (ANB, s.v. "Leslie, Charles Robert"; DNB, same; Tom Taylor, *Autobiographical Recollections. By the Late Charles Robert Leslie* [Boston, 1860], 1-2, 15; *Claypoole's American Daily Advertiser*, 10 Apr. 1799; *Philadelphia Gazette*, 2 Apr. 1800, 3 Mch. 1802; *Poulson's American Daily Advertiser*, 27 Dec. 1803; *Independent Chronicle and Boston Patriot*, 7 Aug. 1824).

A MAN WHOM YOU ONCE HONOURED WITH YOUR FRIENDSHIP: Robert Leslie had visited TJ at Monticello in September 1803 (Vol. 41:565-6).

From David Meade Randolph

SIR,   Richmond 10th. January 1804

The right of appeal to your Excellency might well be questioned, were it not for a lively recollection of your singular affability towards me at a time when you supported a less elevated station, and when too, I was in the exercise of an inferior office, the honor of which it is my present object to rescue from injust opprobrium.

When it was deemed consistent with the wellfare of my country that the powers and duties of the Marshal of this district shou'd be transfered to another, I felt no emotions other than an ardent desire of evincing to the world and to my friends, that I had, in no instance betraied the confidence of your predecessors, or abused the trusts which belonged to that highly responsible office. And in pursuit of that valued object, I considered it of primary importance promptly to liquidate my Accounts Current with the United States, and to acquit myself of such monies as had, for the public benefit, been suffered to remain in my hands. Conformably with this idea, I forthwith addressed certain communications to the proper *departments* viz: of 17th & 27th May 1801—& subsequently *two* of 6th. July—19th August and 29th September of the same year—as also 8th. May, 21 August & 29th December 1802, to all which, with due humility, I beg your attention, assuring myself, that in your own high sense of honor, and sacred regard for character, I shall find that relief which facts may warrant, and which a faithful conduct shall have merited.

I have the honor to be with respectful consideration, your obedient Servant

D M RANDOLPH
Late marshal of the
district of Virginia

RC (DLC); addressed: "His Excellency Thomas Jefferson President of the United States"; endorsed by TJ as received 14 Jan. and so recorded in SJL. Enclosures: Randolph to Madison, Richmond, 6 July 1801, noting that the Treasury Department has not approved payment for his work on the census of 1800; as compensation, he requests that he be allowed to deduct $386.84 from the federal funds he still holds (Madison, *Papers, Sec. of State Ser.*, 1:385). Other enclosures not found, but see below. Enclosed in TJ to Gallatin, ca. 14 Jan. (not recorded in SJL and not found, but see TJ to Randolph, 23 Jan. 1804).

AFFABILITY TOWARDS ME: while secretary of state, TJ recommended Randolph for the collectorship at Bermuda Hundred if William Heth resigned. The vacancy did not occur. In 1791, TJ supported Randolph's appointment as U.S. marshal for Virginia (Washington, *Papers, Pres. Ser.*, 2:121n; Vol. 16:278, 279n, 352, 509; Vol. 22:189, 219).

Shortly after TJ took office, he removed Randolph as MARSHAL for packing juries and withholding money due the Treasury. Randolph's COMMUNICATIONS with the State and Treasury Departments in May and July 1801 primarily concerned payment for his work on the census of 1800 and the remission of James T. Callender's $200 fine. On 30 May, John Steele, comptroller of the Treasury, informed Randolph that he owed the U.S. $2,428.03, not including the $200 he had received from Callender (Madison, *Papers, Sec. of State Ser.*, 1:143, 236-7, 385; Vol. 33:117n, 158n, 574n, 673, 675; Vol. 34:190).

From Benjamin Vaughan

DEAR SIR,   Hallowell, Jany: 10, 1804.

Forgive the liberty which I take in introducing my cousin Mr. Robert Hallowell Gardiner to your notice, which he will claim after a time, more upon his own account, than mine. He is a young man who has not only acquitted himself honorably in his collegiate studies at

Cambridge in this state; but has travelled in several parts of Europe. Since his return, he has with great good sense, good temper, & excessive assiduity, reconciled 70 or 80 intruders upon his property to such terms, as he thought proper to prescribe to them; and he is still left possessor of nearly $\frac{3}{4}$ of the most valuable parts of a valuable township, which is the very next to that in which I reside. General Dearborn having lived in the same township with him, can say much to you of his affairs; but less than might be expected of his present character; of which the improvements have far exceeded all that the partiality of his friends could have supposed probable.

Mr. Gardiner (with his father Mr. Hallowell,) in the winter, lives in Boston; where our family was established before it had possessions in these parts, in which they have concerns which date only half a century back. In Boston & Massachusetts our ancestors rank among the oldest settlers, & were well acquainted with those of Dr. Franklin.— You see, sir, that even out of place, I feel eager to vindicate my American origin, and my ties to our antient philosophical friend.

I say nothing of the politics of Mr. Gardiner. It will to some appear a praise to neither of us, when I aver that I scarcely know them. *He* has never arrived at his opportunity for shewing them, & *I* have in certain respects passed mine. I have found him honorable, liberal, tolerant, & a firm American; & I do not know that I have a right to inquire after more.—I am confident that he will respect you as a scholar, a gentleman, and one that pursues his presumed duties; and, under such circumstances, I feel more than acquitted in making him known to you.

His companion, Mr. Gorham, was his fellow-student at College. I beg leave to name him in this letter, not only for this reason; but because I know him to be a young gentleman of good connections, amiable manners, & a literary turn.

Mr. Gardiner & Mr. Goreham will confirm to you the accounts, which our friend General Dearborn has probably given you of our retired mode of living.

With the joint respects of Mrs. Vaughan & myself, believe me, my dear sir, Your sincere & attached humble servt.

BENJN: VAUGHAN

RC (DLC); addressed: "Thomas Jefferson, President of the United States, Washington" with notation "℘ favor of R. Hallowell Gardiner Esquire"; endorsed by TJ as received 5 Mch. and so recorded in SJL.

ROBERT HALLOWELL GARDINER inherited from his maternal grandfather, Sylvester Gardiner, much of the land in the town of Gardiner in Kennebec County, Maine, on the condition that he take his grandfather's last name as his own.

Sylvester Gardiner had lost his claim to the land because of his loyalist sympathies, but it was eventually restored to him (Henry D. Kingsbury and Simeon L. Deyo, eds., *Illustrated History of Kenne-* *bec County Maine*, 2 vols. [New York, 1892], 2:601-3; Asa Dalton, "Robert Hallowell Gardiner," *Collections and Proceedings of the Maine Historical Society*, 2d ser., 1 [1890], 295-6).

From Albert Gallatin

DEAR SIR   Wednesday 11 Jany. 1804

Mr Baring has concluded, notwithstanding Mr Pichon's entreaties, not to take the stock till we shall have heard from New Orleans. He urges that it is not just that the risk, however improbable the event, of our not obtaining possession should fall on him; which he says would be the case if he gave a receipt for the stock before we know that we have possession. I offered to give him the certificates leaving the date of interest in blank, we agreeing merely that it should be filled with the day of taking possession whenever known; and I told him that next week, being the last of the three months I would insist on his taking the stock, & on his refusal would deliver it to Mr Pichon. He says that in that case he will take it, as our forcing it upon him will be a pledge of our obligation to pay even if we should not obtain possession. As Mr Pichon is much disappointed, I beg that the moment you may hear from New Orleans, you will have the goodness to drop me a line stating the day when possession was obtained.

Respectfully Your most obedt. Servt.   ALBERT GALLATIN

It was conceded by Mr Pichon in the course of the conversation, that our delivery of the stock would be a nullity in case of our not obtaining possession, as the United States were not bound by the treaty to pay if France did not comply with the Treaty.

RC (DLC); at foot of text: "The President of the United States"; endorsed by TJ as received from the Treasury Department on 11 Jan. and "Louisiana stock."

The United States was to deliver the Louisiana stock within THREE MONTHS after the exchange of ratifications of the treaty. On 21 Oct., TJ informed Congress that the exchange had taken place (Vol. 40:472-3n; Vol. 41:296-301, 552n, 583-4).

From Robert R. Livingston

I have before me your favors of the 4th & 9th of November, I do not know whether to be glad or sorry that the *marriage has not taken* effect, it might possibly have given offence, it might also have been made productive of some advantage. speaking confidentialy with one of the ministers on the subject he inquired particularly about *the probable fortune of the lady I told*[1] *him that notwthstdg the father was one of our richest*[2] *men yet her fortune of would probably be no great object to a man of his rank* (which you would believe if you saw the manner in which the family live here) but that this would be of no moment, that I would charge myself with *her marriage portion in certain arrangement*[3] *that might be made between us and thing* He understood me smiled & said that he would charge himself with the care of breaking the bussiness to *bonaparte and preparing him for it* I sincerely rejoice at the increase of republicanism with us. but how can it be otherwise when your measures & the success that attends them must force conviction upon the most prejudiced. You would be flattered if you were here to see the ground on which we stand in Europe & you would be still more flattered if you could contrast it with that we held on my arrival, since it would show that we are indebted for it to your administration. The picture you draw of national prosperity at home & the success of our negotiations abroad present us in the most respectable point of view. The following triffling incident may serve to prove it. My son in Law has gone upon a vissit to London Not only the people here but the whole corps diplomatique suppose he is gone to offer your mediation for peace, & because I stand well here & have made some fortunate guesses they believe I am in the secret of one if not of both courts & are perpetually making inquiries of when I hear from him, when he is to return &c. they even inform themselves who he vissits most in London. The Stocks have risen from this triffling incident & I have no doubt that in a proper state of things if I were empowered to make it your mediation would be accepted. But peace is yet remote the objects of controversy too uncertain to render any advances towards it possible till some misfortune happens to one or the other party.

I will not trouble you with our bussiness which however so far as the commissioners are concerned goes as ill as possible & will if some remedy is not soon applied excite the most serious discontents in a numerous class of citizens in America as it already has among those here but they deny my right to controul or even to advise with them

& if I may judge by Mr. Madisons letter they have given a very improper view both of the claims, & of the doubts that they pretend to have arisen under the treaty. I confess Sir I feel some sense of indignity, in the governments receiving advice & acting upon it without first consulting their minister, at present Mr. Skipwith is as much minister as I am in the view of our government & yet there are strong reasons for the commercial agent here, being as much under the direction of the minister as his secretary & without this he will not only be a useless, but a dangerous officer—You will find details of my bussiness in the letters to the secretary of State, together with my reasons for wishing to have my place supplied as soon as possible. No cause now exists for my making any farther sacrafices by prolonging my stay here. My affairs call me imperiously home. I must therefore Sir entreat you to comply as early as possible with my request. I had thought of Mr. Skipwith as chargé des affairs till my place could be supplied, but I find there are insurmountable objections to the appointment, both as it relates to our own citizens & to this government. recollect too Sir in your nomination that your minister has the custody of many millions. I trust Sir that if no minister is appointed in time a power will be sent me to name, or What I should prefer that you would name a charge des affairs so that I may leave this in April— Mr. McClures appointment has turned out a very unfortunate one He has obtained such a decided influence over the board of commissioners as to lead them into measures hurtful in my idea to our interests & so disgusting to every american here that it will be impossible for them to give satisfaction hereafter. They hold themselves at a distance from me I know not what is done all I know is that nothing is doing & that unwearied pains are taken to disgust the americans with the treaty but happily without effect. That I may Sir change this disagreeable subject

Let me communicate to you some very interesting discoveries of Ct Rumford who is now here & who has mentioned them to me (they are not yet published) by these it would seem that the whole bussiness of heat considered as a body is refuted, or that cold is also a body and not a negative quality. Two polished brass balls the one covered the other not, were filled with boiling water. The one that was covered with a linnen shirt grew cold in much less time than the other. both were reduced by ice to a low temperature & were carried into a room heated to 64 degrees the one that was cloathed obtained the temperature of the room first. One ball was laquered with two coats of varnish the other was left unvarnished, hot water was put in both the varnished ball lost its heat in much less time than the other An extreamly sensible thermometer of a peculiar form which Ct Rumford calls a thermescope was placed between two cylinders of brass & at equal distance from each The one was heated ten degrees above a given point & the others cooled as much below it The thermescope being equaly acted upon by both remained unchanged The heated ball was blackned & the thermometer rose because more heat was transmitted. it was covered with a thin animal substance (gold beaters skin) & the effect was the same The same experiment was reversed by puting the covering on the cold ball when the thermometer fell because more cold was transmitted if a sheet of paper was interposed between one or the other ball the thermometer rose or fell according as the interposition was to one or the other of the balls. These with a variety of other similar experiments prove that cold acts positively as well as heat, that it acts in right lines that both are repelled by polished surfaces & transmitted by animal ones, particularly when they are blackened. It is for this reason, as Rumfort alledges, that the people of hot climates are black & the bears of Siberia white. The heat of the negro passes off rapidly in the shade while his polished skin together with the evaporation of his perspiration makes him less sensible of the rays of the sun. The white bear retains his internal heat & repels the rays of cold in winter by the colour & polish of his hair & as he has no wood to cover him no cavern to retreat to in summer the same polish resists the rays of the sun which wd otherwise be insufferable in shining upon him for months together. From the facts I have mentioned he deduces many useful practical inferences. The system he builds upon it is that all bodies are in perpetual motion & act upon each other by an intervening fluid. That when a body that has more motion acts upon one that has less it renders it warmer while it looses its own heat or rather motion by being reacted upon by the body that has less motion. The ball with the shirt grows cold first because the polish of the naked one repells the rays of cold from external bodies while the shirt admits them & for the same reason the last grows warm first in a heated atmosphere. The sun which if heat was a body would be perpetualy loosing a part of its mass & by this means disorder the whole planetary system in fact sends of no rays but by its internal motion—acting thro the intervention of a fluid on other bodies renders them warm while it remains unchanged itself. The rays on the contrary sent us from the fix stars having lost a part of their motion by their distance are cold & thus diminish the heat thus the heat that the sun occasions & which would by its continual action set us on fire were it not thus counteracted The coldest nights are those on which the stars shine brightest & no clouds ward off their cold rays.

I do not know what you may think of the system, but the facts are curious & interesting. The essay will probably be soon printed in England as it has been sent by Ct Rumford to the royal society. preparations continue as ardently as ever for the descent & the army talk as familliarly of what they are to see & do in London as if they were already there. Yet I confess that I do not think *the mean adequate to the end & therefore doubt whether the expedition will be undertaken. the contrary is however the prevailing sentiment*[4] *here* Your commissions shall be attended to but Mme. Corneys tea having been some time in Quarantine has not yet reached me. I presented her your letter which she recd with great pleasure. she is at present confined & has been so this ten months by a fall by which she broke her thigh. Your friend La fayette left town yesterday after dining with me. He came down to partake of a grand fete given me by the Americans in Paris to the number of 71. all that are in Paris except McClure Mercer & Skipwith who did not chuse to honor me by their presence without my being able to assign any reason for their absence.

Mr. Tallerand & most of the ministers were present & highly pleased with their entertainment

I pray you to accept the assurances of the high esteem & sincere attachment with which I have the honor to be dear Sir

Your Most Ob hum: Servt   Robt R Livingston

RC (DLC); at foot of text: "Thomas Jefferson Esqr prest. United States"; written partly in code (see Vol. 36:208n and Ralph E. Weber, *United States Diplomatic Codes and Ciphers, 1775-1938* [Chicago, 1979], 467-77), and words in italics are TJ's interlined decipherment; endorsed by TJ as received 7 May and so recorded in SJL.

THE MARRIAGE: in his letters of 4 and 9 Nov., TJ informed Livingston of the pending—then postponed—wedding of Jerome Bonaparte and Elizabeth Patterson.

MY SON IN LAW: Robert L. Livingston, who was also acting as Livingston's secretary (Madison, *Papers, Sec. of State Ser.*, 6:340; Vol. 37:415n).

The board of COMMISSIONERS appointed under the Louisiana conventions to settle American claims against France—John Mercer, Isaac Cox Barnet, and William Maclure—had assembled in Paris in September 1803, but had accomplished little. They believed that definitive action could not be taken until the Louisiana treaty and conventions had been duly ratified by the United States, news of which did not reach Paris until 23 Dec. The incomplete state of the claims documentation further slowed their work, and they also questioned whether the 20 million francs specified to settle the claims would be sufficient. When Livingston demanded an explanation for their inaction, the commissioners replied in a 29 Oct. letter that they considered Livingston to be "unconnected with the board" and that they were responsible only to the "Administration of the United States." MR. MADISONS LETTER: Livingston's consternation over the delays in settling claims was exacerbated by a 9 Nov. letter from Madison, which informed him that the president wished Livingston to seek French consent to a suspension of claims awards until it could be determined whether the amount specified by the convention would suffice. This delay would also, Madison added, "give time for such mutual explanations and arrangements as may tend to effectuate the true spirit and object of the Convention" ([William Maclure], *To the People of the United States* [Philadelphia, 1807], 14-16, 26; George Dangerfield, *Chancellor Robert R. Livingston of New York, 1746-1813* [New York, 1960], 380-4; Madison, *Papers, Sec. of State Ser.,* 6:24-6, 222-8; Vol. 41:158-60).

The INTERESTING DISCOVERIES by Benjamin Thompson, Count RUMFORD, regarding heat transfer were read before the Royal Society of London on 2 Feb. and subsequently published as "An Enquiry concerning the Nature of Heat, and the Mode of Its Communication" (*Philosophical Transactions of the Royal Society of London,* 94 [1804], 77-182).

PREPARATIONS CONTINUE AS ARDENTLY AS EVER: that is, the expected French invasion of England (Thomas Paine to TJ, 23 Sep. 1803; William Strickland to TJ, 13 Jan. 1804).

PRESENTED HER YOUR LETTER: TJ to Madame de Corny, 1 Nov. 1803.

GRAND FETE: on 4 Jan., a committee of American citizens in Paris held a dinner in Livingston's honor at the Hôtel de Fleury to celebrate the exchange of the ratified Louisiana treaty and conventions (Dangerfield, *Livingston,* 384).

[1] In accordance with the code in MS, TJ wrote "tol din" (codes 851 and 159). The correct coding of "told" would be 851 and 139.

[2] In accordance with the code in MS, TJ first wrote "og est" (codes 1225 and 1541), then corrected it to "richest" (codes 1255 and 1541).

[3] Thus coded in MS, although TJ wrote "arrangemen."

[4] As coded in MS, the word would be "sent hi ent" (codes 379, 1434, and 1526) instead of "sent im ent" (379, 1454, 1526). TJ wrote "sent ni ent."

From Charles P. Sumner

SIR,   Boston 11 January 1804.

The approbation, with which the inclosed have been received by a number of my friends, has emboldened me to request the favor of *your* accepting them.

I offer them with great diffidence; and value them chiefly for the opportunity they afford me of making a profession of those sentiments of admiration for your character, with which—in all the sincerity of my heart—I have ever felt myself your respectful & obedient servant.   CHARLES P. SUMNER.

RC (MHi); at foot of text: "The President of The United States"; endorsed by TJ as received 20 Jan. and so recorded in SJL. Enclosure: probably Charles P. Sumner, *Eulogy on the Illustrious George Washington, Pronounced at Milton, Twenty-Second February, 1800* (Dedham, Mass., 1800), inscribed by the author to TJ; see Sowerby, No. 3276. Other enclosures not identified (see TJ to Sumner, 26 Jan.).

An attorney and Harvard graduate, Charles P. Sumner (1776-1839) was the father of future U.S. Senator Charles Sumner of Massachusetts. An early and passionate believer in the abolition of slavery and other liberal ideals, he campaigned actively for TJ's reelection in 1804. He subsequently served several years as clerk of the Massachusetts House of Representatives and as sheriff of Suffolk County from 1825 until shortly before his death (Edward L. Pierce, *Memoir and Letters*

of Charles Sumner, 4 vols. [Boston, 1877-93], 1:11-30; Anne-Marie Taylor, *Young Charles Sumner and the Legacy of the American Enlightenment, 1811-1851* [Amherst, Mass., 2001], 12-26, 29, 122).

To Albert Gallatin

THE SECRETARY OF THE TREASURY   [12 Jan. 1804]

The inclosed are furnished by the Director of the mint to be laid before Congress. the law requires they should be accompanied with the settlements which have been made relative thereto, duly certified by the Comptroller of the Treasury. duplicates of such a paper are desired with the return of these to be sent to each house by

TH:J.

RC (DLC); undated; written on address sheet of an unidentified letter, with canceled "The President of the United States" in Dearborn's hand; endorsed by TJ: "Departmt Treasury. recd Jan. 12. 04. Mint report." Not recorded in SJL. Enclosures: see TJ to the Senate and the House of Representatives, 13 Jan.

On 6 Jan., Elias Boudinot, DIRECTOR OF THE MINT, sent his annual report to the State Department (see Madison, *Papers, Sec. of State Ser.*, 6:311). Jacob Wagner forwarded it to TJ with an unsigned note: "Two copies of the annual report of the Director of the Mint. This document is required by law (2 Vol. p. 39 s. 7.) to be laid before Congress, together with the Comptroller's settlements with the officers of the Mint" (MS in DLC: TJ Papers, 146:25345; undated; entirely in Wagner's hand).

From Albert Gallatin

[12 Jan. 1804]

The Treasury report mentioned in the law is sent annually by the Comptroller, commonly in Feby.   The President may or may not transmit the enclosed as it is not the report contemplated by the law. It was sent, exactly in the shape in which the enclosed is made out, last year by the President & without any accompanying papers.

The Treasury report is altogether different in form & substance.

A.G.

RC (DLC: TJ Papers, 146:25353); undated, but in response to TJ to Gallatin, [12 Jan.]. Enclosure: see TJ to the Senate and the House of Representatives, 13 Jan.

REPORT MENTIONED IN THE LAW: Section 7 of the 2 Apr. 1792 "Act establishing a Mint, and regulating the Coins of the United States" called for the Treasury Department to adjust and settle the accounts of the U.S. Mint and once a year submit a report of the transactions to Congress, "accompanied by an abstract of the settlements," certified by the comptroller of the Treasury. Gallatin submitted the 1802 settlement from the comptroller's office to the House of Representatives on 3 Mch. 1803 (U.S. Statutes at Large, 1:246-7; ASP, *Finance*, 2:31-6; JHR, 4:392).

LAST YEAR BY THE PRESIDENT: TJ sent the 1 Jan. 1803 report by Elias Boudinot, director of the Mint, to Congress on 11 Jan. It did not include ACCOMPANYING PAPERS from the comptroller's office (see ASP, *Finance*, 2:18-21; Vol. 39:318-20).

From John Sevier

SIR   Knoxville 12 January 1804

I have the honor to Acknowledge the receipt of your letter of the 13th of December ultimo, with the inclosed copy of an Article of Amendment proposed by Congress to be added to the constitution of the United States respecting the election of President and Vice president, to be laid before the legislature of Tennessee; which will with much pleasure be complied with at their next meeting in session, and I entertain no doubt they will readily approve the measure. And I tender you assurances of my Very high respect and Consideration

JOHN SEVIER

RC (NcU: Samuel Gordon Heiskell Papers); at foot of text: "Thomas Jefferson esquire President of the U States." Recorded in SJL as received 24 Jan.

On 7 June, Sevier issued a proclamation convening the NEXT MEETING of the Tennessee legislature on 23 July. Both houses ratified the proposed Twelfth Amendment by unanimous consent on 27 July, making Tennessee the thirteenth and deciding state to do so (*Tennessee Gazette and Mero-District Advertiser*, 13 June 1804; Madison, *Papers, Sec. of State Ser.*, 7:527, 555-6; Kuroda, *Origins of the Twelfth Amendment*, 161).

To William Short

DEAR SIR   Washington Jan. 12. 04.

Mr. Lilly having lately sent me the materials for the account of your rents for the[1] year 1802. recieved by him in 1803. I am now enabled to send you an exact account of them from 1796. to 1802. inclusive; those subsequent to 1802. will be recieved by mr Price. the inequalities in those rents are to be explained. when the lands were purchased the tenants were on a fixed annual rent, & could run their fields down with corn at pleasure. Price was for life. Cornelius was till 1798. inclusive. with all those who were from year to year I had the different fields valued, and permitted them to be in corn but once in 5 years. according therefore to the fields which were in culture their rent was more or less. upon the whole this made little alteration in the amount, but it kept $\frac{2}{5}$ of the land always at rest without diminishing the rents. but what occasions a greater variation, & especially in the year 1799. was the requiring $\frac{1}{4}$ of the tobacco raised, to be paid in rent for the tobacco lands after the first year of clearing them which was rent free for the trouble of clearing. the tenants always sold the whole of their tobacco & accounted for $\frac{1}{4}$ of the price.—I also send you the articles of our account which have arisen since the date of that rendered Nov. 21. 1799. knowing that there were considerable inequalities in my monthly expenditures here, I had, in my letter of Oct. 8. 1802. stated that paiments either of 500. D. monthly or 1500. D. quarterly should commence in March 1803. and continue till the debt should be wholly paid. these were continued to October. after that there have come on me so many heavy demands for wines & other things from Europe, and this long & expensive session of Congress, that the monthly paiments were of necessity suspended. I still hoped they could have been made up at the end of the quarter; but on a rigorous view of my necessary expences through this session of Congress and for a twelvemonth foward, I find that these paiments cannot begin again till the first week of April, and that it will not be till September that I can begin to fetch up the ground lost during the suspension. on the 2d. page of the paper inclosed you will find a comparative statement of what would have been effected according to the plan of Oct. 8. 02. and what will be done by that stated in the 2d. column. in the course of the 12. months from Apr. 1804. to Mar. 1805. the lost way will be recovered, and the subsequent process hastened. I have no doubt, on as exact a view as can be taken before hand, that this arrangement can be fully complied with: I believe more can be done in autumn than here proposed: but I have thought it best to state less rather than more than can be done. however if, contrary to all expectations, some diminution should take place unavoidably, it cannot protract the final paiment but a little beyond the midsummer of the ensuing year. it is with sincere chagrin that I have found myself thus interrupted in the course of a paiment which it is the first wish of my heart to compleat. but it is useless to dwell on what I cannot alter. among the last things you do before you leave the continent, I would wish you to settle the balance exactly which shall be then due & communicate it to me in time to return you a bond for the balance before your departure, so that the subject may not rest on a simple account, but be settled by a solemn instrument. I had informed you that by my will I had charged my whole estate real & personal with this debt. the bond will of it's own nature be a charge on the whole, & will be in your own hands. besides this I will send you such a specific lien on lands as shall place you in the most perfect security[,] all this merely to guard against the event of my death. in that of my life it's discharge will be continual & not lengthy in point of time.—[o]n your return to France I must get you to inform me of the price of the Cayusac sec, and to what port it can be got most conveniently for shipping. I shall then make a remittance to our Consul at that port, & desire him to order the wine, under your auspices, that they may give me the best. Accept my affectionate salutations & assurances of great & constant esteem.

TH: JEFFERSON

RC (DLC: Short Papers); torn; at foot of first page: "W. Short esq."; endorsed by Short. Enclosures not found, but see below.

A letter of 29 Dec. 1803 from Gabriel LILLY, recorded in SJL as received 3 Jan., has not been found. TJ also recorded sending letters to Lilly on 27 Nov. and 12 and 19 Dec., all of which are missing.

In May 1802, TJ sent Short a statement regarding the RENTS he collected on Short's behalf and the agricultural plan to which he subjected the TENANTS (Vol. 37:472-4).

For TJ's account with Short RENDERED NOV. 21. 1799, see Vol. 31:513-16. As he indicated in the above letter, TJ paid the equivalent of seven monthly installments totaling $3,500 during 1803 (George Taylor, Jr., to Short, 19 Nov.

1803, in DLC: Short Papers; Vol. 40: 219, 326).

After realizing the size of his debt to Short, TJ executed mortgages on about 80 slaves and 1,000 acres of land and then made Short the principal of a corresponding LIEN, thereby securing the property from any other potential creditors (Vol. 31:503).

Cahuzac (CAYUSAC) was a relatively inexpensive red wine produced in the southwest of France that TJ had enjoyed during his time in Paris. By adding SEC, he was indicating his preference for a dryer variety (James M. Gabler, *Passions: The Wines and Travels of Thomas Jefferson* [Baltimore, 1995], 115, 206; Vol. 11:67; TJ to William Lee, 28 Apr. 1806).

[1] TJ here canceled "last."

To George Jefferson

DEAR SIR   Washington Jan. 13. 04.

There were sent from Philadelphia by Jones & Howell some time since 10. bundles of nailrod to make up the former deficiency, and three sheets of rolled iron, to your address; also by Genl. Muhlenberg of Philadelphia three pipes of wine, & from here lately 12. boxes marked TJ. and numbered 1. to 12. all to be forwarded to Monticello by water.

I have directed my manager in Bedford, mr Griffin, to get my tobacco down as early as possible, under your address. I shall be obliged to make an early sale of it, and will therefore thank you whenever you drop me a line on other subjects, to mention the price & prospect at your market. you will be so good as to attend at the proper time to engaging the hundred hams from Colo. Macon as desired in a letter of last October. Accept assurances of my affectionate esteem.

Th: Jefferson

PrC (MHi); at foot of text: "Mr. George Jefferson"; endorsed by TJ in ink on verso.

For the DEFICIENCY, see TJ to Jones & Howell, 22 Dec. 1803, and the firm's response five days later. TJ ordered HAMS in a letter of 15 Oct. 1803.

To Meriwether Lewis

DEAR SIR   Washington Jan. 13. 1804.

I wrote you last on the 16th. of Nov. since which I have recieved no letter from you. the newspapers inform us you left Kaskaskia about the 8th. of December. I hope you will have recieved my letter by that day or very soon after; written in a belief it[1] would be better that you should not enter the Missouri till the spring; yet not absolutely controuling your own judgment formed on the spot. we have not heard of the delivery of Louisiana to us as yet, tho' we have no doubt it took place about the 20th. of December, and that orders were at the same time expedited to evacuate the upper posts, troops of ours being in readiness & under orders to take possession. this change will probably have taken place before you recieve this letter, and facilitate your proceeding. I now inclose you a map of the Missouri as far as the Mandans, 12, or 1500. miles I presume above it's mouth. it is said to be very accurate having been done by a mr Evans by order of the Spanish government. but whether he corrected by astronomical observation or not we are not informed. I hope this will reach you before your final departure.—the acquisition of the country through which you are to pass has inspired the public generally with a great deal of interest in your enterprize. the enquiries are perpetual as to your progress. the Feds alone still treat it as philosophism, and would rejoice in it's failure.[2] their bitterness increases with the diminution of their numbers and despair of a resurrection. I hope you will take care of yourself, and be the living witness of their malice and folly. present my salutations to mr Clarke. assure all your party that we have our eyes turned on them with anxiety for their safety & the success of their enterprize. accept yourself assurances of sincere esteem & attachment.

Th: Jefferson

PrC (DLC); at foot of text: "Capt Meriwether Lewis." Enclosure not found, but see William Henry Harrison to TJ, 26 Nov. 1803.

[1] TJ first wrote "believing it" before altering the text to read as above.

[2] Preceding five words interlined in place of an illegibly canceled passage.

To Timothy Pickering

[on or before 13 Jan. 1804]

Th: Jefferson presents his compliments to mr Pickering and returns him Hutchins's book with thanks for the use of it. that on Louisiana he had never before seen or heard of, and it has furnished him the first *particular* information of the line agreed on by the Commrs. under the treaty of Utrecht, he has ever been able to obtain. he had, the last summer, while among his books at Monticello, prepared a Memoir tracing the rightful lines of Louisiana, on authentic documents, so far as Spain was concerned. the present information has enabled him to make the addition as to Gr. Britain which is now inclosed for mr Pickering's perusal, as he thinks it will place in a true light what ought to be done with the Vth. article of the British convention. mr Pickering will observe that if the alteration proposed is made, and the ratifications exchanged *here* the ensuing winter the running of the North Eastern boundary will not be at all delayed, as no course which can be taken could effect that demarcation till the Summer of 1785.

RC (MHi: Pickering Papers); undated; endorsed by Pickering as received 13 Jan. Not recorded in SJL. Enclosure: Thomas Hutchins, *An Historical Narrative and Topographical Description of Louisiana, and West-Florida* (Philadelphia, 1784). For other enclosure, see below.

NEVER BEFORE SEEN: it is uncertain if TJ had ever examined portions of the pamphlet by Thomas Hutchins that he requested from Pickering, but he was familiar with it. In 1792, he requested copies for William Short and William Carmichael and a third copy for his own use, a request that does not appear to have been fulfilled. The Editors in Vol. 17:123n erred in claiming that TJ corresponded with Hutchins about the pamphlet in 1784, as opposed to a different publication by Hutchins (Vol. 24:285-6; Vol. 27:737).

Under the terms of the TREATY OF UTRECHT, France restored to Great Britain territory that had been controlled by the Hudson's Bay Company. Although the treaty provided for commissioners who were to determine an exact boundary, French and British claims in Canada remained under dispute until the resolution of the Seven Years War. Hutchins, however, defined the boundary precisely by an "imaginary line" running from a point on the sea at 58 degrees 30 minutes latitude southwest to Lake Mistasim, or Mistassini, and "from thence farther South-west directly to the latitude of 49 degrees," this division forming "the true limits of Louisiana and Canada" (Hutchins, *Historical Narrative and Topographical Description of Louisiana*, 7; Parry, *Consolidated Treaty Series*, 27:484-7; Frances Gardiner Davenport, ed., *European Treaties bearing on the History of the United States and its*

Dependencies, 4 vols. [Washington, D.C., 1917-37], 3:193-206; W. J. Eccles, *France in America*, rev. ed. [Markham, Ont., 1990], 112-15, 122).

TJ may have enclosed the addendum to the draft version of his MEMOIR on the boundaries of Louisiana (see Vol. 41:322), a press copy of the draft addendum, or a different version that has not been found. Although Pickering returned the document on 16 Jan., TJ dated his draft version at 15 Jan.

To the Senate and the House of Representatives

TO THE SENATE AND
HOUSE OF REPRESENTATIVES OF THE US

The Director of the Mint having made to me his report of the transactions of the Mint for the year 1803. I now lay the same before you for your information.
TH: JEFFERSON
Jan. 13. 1804.

RC (DNA: RG 46, LPPM, 8th Cong., 1st sess.); endorsed by a Senate clerk. RC (DNA: RG 233, PM, 8th Cong., 1st sess.). PrC (DLC). Recorded in SJL with notation "Mint."

ENCLOSURE

Report of Director of the Mint

The Director of the Mint of the United States, on the commencement of the New Year, respectfully makes the following Report of the Issues of the Mint from the first January 1803 to the 31st. December of the same year.

Notwithstanding the dull prospect at the beginning of the year, Coinage of every kind, amounts in the whole to the Sum of Three Hundred and Seventy Thousand six hundred and ninety eight Dollars and fifty three Cents, as will appear in detail by the Schedule No. 1. hereunto annexed.

The current expences of the Mint have been reduced to the sum of Seventeen thousand seven hundred and five Dollars and ninety five Cents as will appear from Schedule No. 2. and the profit on the copper-coinage has amounted to Five thousand and ninety five Dollars and forty eight Cents, as appears by Schedule No. 3.

It appears to be the duty of the Director respectfully to remind the President, that in case the Loan Office in this City should be abolished by Law, that provision must be made for a Commissioner to attend the Inspection & Assaying the reserved pieces during the past year on the second Monday in February next, in the room of the Commissioner of Loans if he should be removed.

All which is respectfully submitted to the President by his Very Obt. and very Humble Servant
ELIAS BOUDINOT D.M.

Mint of the United States
Philadelphia 6th. January 1804

MS (DNA: RG 46, LPPM, 8th Cong., 1st sess.); in a clerk's hand; at head of text: "To the President of the United States"; endorsed by a Senate clerk. PrC (DNA: RG 233, PM, 8th Cong., 1st sess.). FC (DNA: RG 104, DL). Enclosures: (1) "An Abstract of Coins struck at the Mint of the United States from the 1st. January to 31st. December 1803," recording $258,377.50 in gold coins, including 8,979 eagles, 33,506 half eagles, and 423 quarter eagles; $87,118.00 in silver coins, including 66,064 dollars, 31,715 half dollars, 33,040 dimes, and 37,850 half dimes; and $25,203.03 in copper coins, including 2,471,353 cents and 97,900 half cents; making an aggregate total of $370,698.53. (2) "An Abstract of the expenditures of the Mint of the United States, from the 1st. January to 31st. December 1803," recording a total of $10,600.00 expended on salaries, $5,193.33 on wages, and $1,912.62 on incidental charges, making an aggregate total of $17,705.95. (3) "Statement of the Gain on Copper coined at the Mint of the United States from 1st Jany. to 31st. Decr. 1803," recording a net profit, after allowances for spoiled planchets and differences of weight, of $5,095.48 on the $25,203.03 in copper coins issued by the Mint for the year (MSS in DNA: RG 46, LPPM, 8th Cong., 1st sess., in a clerk's hand, including attestations by Benjamin Rush, treasurer of the Mint, 31 Dec. 1803; PrCs in DNA: RG 233, PM, 8th Cong., 1st sess.; FCs in DNA: RG 104, DL; printed in ASP, *Finance*, 2:75-7).

Lewis Harvie presented TJ's message and its accompanying papers to Congress on 13 Jan. and each house ordered them to lie on the table (JHR, 4:531; JS, 3:337).

For the recent attempt in the House of Representatives to discontinue the office of COMMISSIONER OF LOANS in the states, see Gallatin's second letter to TJ at 30 Nov. 1803 and John Randolph's letter of that date. On 24 Jan., John Wayles Eppes attempted to resurrect the measure by introducing a resolution calling for the creation of a committee to prepare a bill abolishing the office. After considerable debate, the House rejected the measure on 30 Jan. by a vote of 52 to 58 (*Annals*, 13:944, 952-9; JHR, 4:551-2, 557-8).

From William Strickland

DEAR SIR/   York. Janry: 13th: 1804.

Your letter of the 30th: of June, I received on the 22d. of October, since which time I have been waiting for a safe conveyance for my answer. I am highly flatter'd by your recollection, particularly at a period when you must be occupied by so many momentous engagements; an unwillingness to interrupt which has been the cause of my long silence. I have many times wished for an opportunity of expressing my respect for you, & congratulating you & your country on the elevated rank you now hold, equally to your own honor, & the benefit of your Country.—

I have read with attention & satisfaction the unassuming narrative of your practical farmer, & have no hesitation in confiding in what he relates. My countrymen who know nothing of the use of Gypsum will hardly give credit to the account, but I who have paid all the attention to it in my power, in the country where it is used & have witnessed the surprizing effects produced by it; can without hesitation give credit to a little more than I have seen. Confined as I am at present to a town life, in order more advantageously to educate a very numerous family, I have never been able to make the various experiments on Gypsum, which my knowledge of the application of it in America, has enabled me to plan, & which I certainly shall execute as soon as I am able; for though I could, by communicating them to others, have them sooner brought to the proof, yet should they fail under such a persons management, the practice might at once be brought into discredit, & farther trials be totally put a stop to; whereas under my own direction they might succeed, which would more than compensate for the loss of time. Certain it is that many trials on the utility of Gypsum have been made in this country, but either from injudicious management, or some peculiarity of our climate, no success has attended them, nor any benefit that can be relyed on. No country, could reap greater advantage from the use of Gypsum, than England, & this part of it in particular, since no country produces it in greater variety or purity, & within ten miles or little more of this city, it is found to the East, the South, & the West in inexhaustible quantity. While on the subject of Gypsum it may not be useless to mention, that after having witnessed the effect of it in America & wishing to ascertain the quality of what is produced here, I had a considerable quantity got in this neighbourhood, imported into N: York from Hull, & was informed by the manufacturer there, that he had never before ground any of so fine a quality, & I have heard that it answerd equally well in the use; upon gaining this information I endeavour'd to make it known to the Masters of American Vessels that it might be procured at Hull, & that were it only substituted for ordinary ballast, each vessel might take 20, or 30 tuns, by which a considerable saving might be made, that persons at Hull had usually a supply by them & that, an increased demand would insure it, but, I believe little consequence has attended my attempt, so difficult is it to make an alteration in the usual course of practice. I believe the price at Hull is generally about 20/ sterl: a tun, & it might be deliverd cheaper, & would be if the demand was increased, as it does not cost at the pitts more than 4/ or 5/.—

In return for the pamphlet you were so obliging as to send, I transmit to you, (not knowing of any thing at present more valuable to communicate) the corrected Agricultural survey of part of this County drawn up under the direction of the Board of Agriculture. It will serve as a specimen of the manner in which these surveys are drawn up, not more than a third part of which are yet published & this is thought to be one of the best. The author is a practical, Quaker, farmer residing near this City, with whom I am well acquainted & being the survey of my own country, I can vouch for the accuracy of it. It may not prove so full & complete a discription, as You or any person unacquainted with the general practice of Agriculture in this Kingdom might wish, because some practises of universal notoriety are omitted, as are also some less generally known, but which had been fully treated of in other surveys previously published; but it is as complete as was necessary for this country.—

We are involved in a war in which our existance is said to be staked against that of the Userper of France. He or we must fall; an alternative which cannot be viewed without great anxiety in consequence of the misfortunes which must befall individuals in case of a conflict, or an actual invasion, but which in a national light we survey without dismay confident in our strength & our unanimity.—Men, capable of forming a more accurate judgement, than I am, hold an invasion to be impracticable by any means now possessed by France in any numbers that can be attended with serious consequences, & even should such a body of men escape our fleet which lines the whole of their coast & our own, & which has been able to preserve its station through the worst part of the most boistrous winter we have known for some Years, they cannot foresee in the present temper of the country what impression they can make. We may litterally be called an armed Nation. Arms are offerd to every one that will take them, & they are in the hands of more than can be employed. Exclusive of that part of our regular army now at home consisting of probably not less than 80000 Infantry, & 40000 of the best cavalry in Europe, & of 80000 regular Militia, in most respects equal, in many superior in consequence of the principles of their formation, to the regular army, more than 700000 volunteers serving without pay, till called from home, are embodied & regemented. Of these more than half are completely armed & accoutred & in a high state of discipline & the rest capable of being & will be perfected in a very short time. With such a fleet & army what have we dread from an invading foe? If so circumstanced we are capable of being conquerd, we must deserve our fate & be unworthy of our independence, & you would have little to boast of, in having our blood flow in your veins.

Many think this barbarous despot, whose knowledge extends not beyond the point of his Sabre, & who would have been better qualified for King of the Franks a thousand years ago, than the Ruler of Frenchmen of the present day, will never make the attempt at invasion, but seek to injure us by other means, but it appears to me, that throwing himself upon his Fortune as he professes to have done so often before, he must risk it & that soon, for every day is adding to our strength & will be for some time to come, without as far as we can judge, in an adequate degree augmenting his. Two parties in France will urge him to the attempt; they who wish for plunder & are mad enough to think they can obtain it, & that numerous body of reflecting men, his secret enemies who detest the Tyrant, whose conduct they foresee must barbarise their country, & who expect his downfall in his failure.—Notwithstanding I speak thus confidently on our safety, I deeply lament the situation into which we are driven, not as has happend in other wars, by the ambition of Rulers, the avarice of trade, or the lust of domination, but for our self defence & to protect the civilized world from a deluge that is overwhelming it. Our cause is that of every country, that wishes to live under a moderate, an enlightend & civilized government.—As a Lover of Peace, & rational improvement I must regret seeing so many of the young & active taken from their peaceful & useful occupations, The comforts of society deranged, & habits introduced, whose tendencies are by no means desirable, & which it may not be easy hereafter to divest the country of, should their continuance prove of long duration; I can foresee worse evils as likely to arise from our present situation than it is possible for France directly to inflict us with; but for the present we must be blind to them, for self defence is the first Law of Nature.—

Lett me assure you of my sincere esteem & respect; of the happiness I shall experience in hearing of your prosperity & happiness & of those attached to you, of the pleasure I shall experience in your future recollection, & in being of any service to you, which you can point out. I recollect with unabated satisfaction the attentions I have received from you & your Countrymen; & I shall ever remain

My Dear Sir Your faithful & much obliged

Wm: Strickland

RC (DLC); addressed: "Thomas Jefferson Esqr: President of the United States of America &c &c &c"; endorsed by TJ as received 6 Apr. and so recorded in SJL.

MY LONG SILENCE: Strickland's last letter to TJ was of 16 July 1798 (Vol. 30:455-8).

YOUR PRACTICAL FARMER: John A. Binns (Vol. 40:541-2, 639-40).

I TRANSMIT TO YOU: John Tuke's *General View of the Agriculture of the North Riding of Yorkshire. Drawn Up for the Consideration of the Board of Agriculture and Internal Improvement*, published in London in 1800. The first edition of the AGRICULTURAL SURVEY was published in 1794 (see Sowerby, No. 766). In 1796, Strickland sent TJ two or three other county surveys conducted under the auspices of the BOARD OF AGRICULTURE (Vol. 29:105-6).

Syd.Edwards del. Pub.by T.Curtis. St Geo Crescent Oct.1.1804. F Sansom sculp.

Dionaea Muscipula

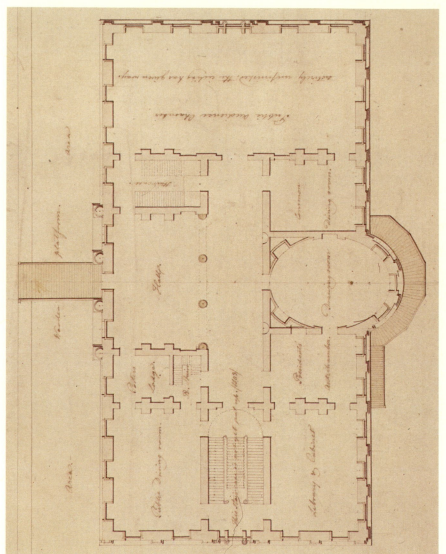

President's House Floor Plan

Elizabeth Merry

Thomas Jefferson by Amos B. Doolittle

Mr. Barnes

Dec. 12. 03.

Pay to mr Lemaire or order eighty dollars eighty

seven cents for value received on account of

your very humble servt

Th: Jefferson

80.87   Septr 199

Recu le payement E. Lemaire

Mr. John Barnes.

Order on John Barnes

A Philadelphia Baptism

A perspective View of the loss of the U.S. Frigate Philadelphia in which is represented her relative position to the Tripolitan Gun-boats when during thirty seven attacks upon her she was unable to get a single gun to bear upon them.

The Loss of the Frigate *Philadelphia*

Ironfounder.

An Iron Founder

To J. P. G. Muhlenberg

DEAR SIR   Washington Jan. 14. 04.

Your favors of Nov. 17. Dec. 29. & Jan. 4. have been duly recieved. I have desired mr Barnes to remit you 162.52 D according to the statement in your last, which he has either done, or will do immediately, and I pray you to accept my thanks for the trouble which has befallen you with these shipments. no law has yet passed for establishing a regular government in Louisiana. the Custom house of Natchez will be removed to N. Orleans with it's officers. it is as yet uncertain what government will be established & what officers necessary. probably a Govr., Secretary of the state, 3 judges, an Attorney & Marshal, and no other. of these 7. four must be lawyers, two others the first characters of our union; so that there will remain but the single office of Marshal for men of common qualifications, and I have some hundreds of applications. under these circumstances the application for mr Mackey [was] very hopeless: and as he has by letter desired me to return the papers of recommendation you forwarded to me, I take the liberty of doing it through you, as I know not his address. Accept my friendly salutations & assurances of great esteem & respect.   TH: JEFFERSON

PrC (MHi); blurred; at foot of text: "Genl. Muhlenberg"; endorsed by TJ in ink on verso. Enclosures not found.

A letter from Muhlenberg of 17 Nov. 1803, recorded in SJL as received 20 Nov. with the notation "Mackey John. employmt N.O.," has not been found. A letter of 3 Jan. from John MACKEY, recorded in SJL as received 6 Jan., has also not been found.

From Timothy Pickering

                                                                    Jany. 14. 1804.

Mr. Pickering presents his respects to the President, and requests the loan of Crozat's grant of Louisiana from Lewis XIV.

Mr. P. acknowledges the receipt of the President's observations on the northern boundaries of the U. States & Louisiana; and if any further examination of the subject should present a different view of it, to Mr. Pickering, he will take the liberty to offer the same to the President's consideration.

RC (DLC); endorsed by TJ.   For TJ's extracts of Antoine CROZAT's GRANT, see Vol. 41:332-3.

From Martha Jefferson Randolph

MY DEAREST FATHER   Edgehill Jan. 14, 1804

It was so late the other day before I could write that I had only time to add a postscript to Ann's letter to inform you of Davy Bowle's intention of going to Washington, and the offer he made of carrying your chair if you wished it; he is still here and will be on theusday, so that your intentions with regard to it may be complied with if known, on that day. he leaves this sometime next week altho I do not know when. Lilly has been here to advise with me about Kit—he is now in Charlottesville jail where he passed himself for a negro of Mr Randolph's, Lilly is afraid to take him out for fear of his going off again he thinks you wished him sold and the money laid out on another, but he says his head was so confused during, and for some time after his illness that he cannot recollect whether you gave him any orders to that effect or not; the result of the conversation however was that if he could get 120 or 25 £ before he could hear from you he should sell him rather than miss the sail but that he would be much obliged to you to let him know by the next post what you wish done with him in case of his not having been able to dispose of him. Higginbotham begged me to tell you that Stewarts goods having been attached during the time of his supposed flight the sale was to take place in a few days that with regard to himself a word from you would satisfy *him*, and no doubt the other creditors would be as well pleased to have the debt in your hands, of these however he said nothing nor do I exactly understand the use of saying what he did for Mrs Stuart being dead, and Mrs Lewis having taken charge of the girls, it appears to me of very little importance to prevent the sale of the furniture. humanity cannot be interested in the fate of a man so well able to provide for himself. and his sons are old enough to be put to any trade he chuses, nor do I believe the desire of supporting themselves to be wanting on their side, but how far they can do any thing without his concurrence or whether they can obtain that I am unable to say. I have fulfilled my commission in delivering Higginbothams message You are the best judge of what remains to be done. so much for business suffer me now to touch upon subjects more interesting and certainly more important than any business to be transacted by or, through me. we are *all* of us "as well as can be expected" Maria's spirits are bad, partly occasioned by her situation which precludes everything like comfort or chearfullness, and partly from the prospect of congress not rising till April which Mr Randolph writes us is the general opinion. I hope we shall do as well as if Mr Eppes was here but certainly her mind would be more at ease could he be with her. little Francis is doing well but it is in the best health allways that he has been attacked with those dreadfull fits; I can not help fearing them to be epileptic. the noise in the throat the foaming at the mouth and drawing back of the head certainly bear a much greater resemblance to that than convulsions which My aunt's children have been subject to. My sister Jane who held him during the last one he had two days only before Mary's birth mentioned it to me. but the distress it might occasion his parents for such an idea to get abroad determined us to confine our suspicion within our own breast's he may and I hope will out grow them time only can shew what the event will be. my own children are remarkably healthy and freer from colds than common. Ann informed you of the acquisition we have made in Jane as a neighbour we have walked to and fro repeatedly she spends much of her time with us and her husband has been as attentive as an own brother could have been he is a man of the purest heart and most amiable temper in the world adieu My Dear'est Father I must beg you to recollect that I write amidst the noise and confusion of six children interrupted every moment by their questions, and so much disturbed by [their] pratling around me that I catch myself repeatedly writing [. . .] instead of my own thoughts. that will account for, and I hope [apologize?] for any inconsistensies or repetitions in my letter, perhaps it will be deemed some excuse for not writing oftener certain as I am that it is impossible for you to doubt for one moment of the warmth of my affection I remain

with unchangeable and tender love Yours   M RANDOLPH

your letter to Anne has this moment come to hand having gone thro a mistake to Charlottesville I wish it may not have come too late for upon enquiery they tell me Davy Bowles contrary to his promise to me is gone to Richmond intending from thence to Washington. I shall hear more certainly presently and act accordingly. if St Memin comes to Washington will you remember your promise to Maria & Myself

RC (ViU); torn; addressed: "Thomas Jefferson President of the U.S. Washington"; endorsed by TJ as received 15 Jan. and so recorded in SJL.

ANN'S LETTER: a letter of 7 Jan. from TJ's granddaughter Anne Cary Randolph, recorded in SJL as received 8 Jan., has not been found, but see TJ's response of 9 Jan.

In April, TJ recorded Gabriel Lilly's sale of KIT (b. 1786), a son of TJ's slaves King and Judy Hix, for £125 to John Perry (Stanton, *Free Some Day*, 81; MB, 2:1125).

STEWARTS GOODS: in his financial memoranda, TJ recorded at 30 Jan. his agreement "to pay David Higginbotham £21. next fall for William Stewart" and serving as "security to him for do. for

20.D. more in his store" (MB, 1:1119). MRS STUART BEING DEAD: Randolph appears to be indicating the death of Mary Stewart, wife of William Stewart, although a gravestone at Monticello apparently dates her death at 5 Nov. 1805. TJ had corresponded with her in November, when trying to get her husband to return to Monticello. The Stewarts' daughters may have ended up with Mary Walker Lewis, a close friend of the Jefferson family (George Green Shackelford, *Collected*

Papers to Commemorate Fifty Years of the Monticello Association of the Descendants of Thomas Jefferson [Princeton, 1965], 260; Bear, *Family Letters*, 253n; Woods, *Albemarle*, 252; TJ to Jones & Howell, 22 Nov.).

MY SISTER JANE: that is, Jane Cary Randolph, the sister of Thomas Mann Randolph. She and her husband, Thomas Eston Randolph, had recently taken up residence in the neighborhood (Vol. 40:453n).

To Aaron Burr

Jan. 15. 04.

Th: Jefferson presents his respects to the Vicepresident and is sorry that an error of his Secretary mentioning Thursday the 17th. instead of Tuesday the 17th. in his note of invitation should have occasioned a miscomprehension of the day. mr Harvie wrote a note correcting his error, to the V. President; but lest it should not have been delivered Th:J. asks leave to expect the pleasure of his company to dinner on Tuesday the 17th. inst.

RC (NNPM); addressed: "The Vice President of the US."; endorsed by Burr. Not recorded in SJL.

Continuation of an Examination of the Boundaries of Louisiana

P.S. the Northern boundary of Louisiana, Coterminous with the possessions of England.[1]

The limits of Louisiana have been spoken of, in the preceding statement,[2] as if those established to the West & North, by the charter of Louis XIV. remained still unaltered. in the West they are so, as already explained. but, in the North, a material change has taken place. with this however it was unnecessary to complicate our subject, while considering the interests of Spain alone: because the possessions of Great Britain, & not of Spain, are coterminous with Louisiana on it's Northern boundary. we will now therefore proceed to examine the state of that boundary, as between Gr. Britain & the US.

Disputes having arisen between Gr. Britain & France as to the limits between Canada & Louisiana on the one side, & the countries of the Hudson's bay, & North Western companies on the other, it was agreed by the treaty of Utrecht (1713) Art. X. that 'Commissaries should be forthwith named by each party to determine the limits between the bay of Hudson and the places appertaining to the French, & to describe & settle the boundaries between the other British & French colonies in those parts' these Commissaries accordingly fixed the Northern boundaries of Canada & Louisiana, by a line beginning on the Atlantic, at a Cape or Promontory in 58°-30′ N. Lat. thence South Westwardly to the lake Misgosink, or Mistasin, thence farther S.W. to the lat. of 49.° North from the Equator, and along that line indefinitely. [Hutchins's topographical description of Louisiana. pa. 7.] thus the Northern boundary of Canada and Louisiana became fixed, & the latter particularly became changed to the parallel of 49.° from the Equator, instead of the highlands inclosing the Northern[3] waters running directly or indirectly into the Misipi, as settled by Louis XIV. Canada being, by the peace of 1763. transferred to England, it's Southern boundary was settled by the treaty of 1783. with the US. along the St. Croix & highlands bounding the Southern waters of the St: Laurence, the 45th. degree of latitude to the water communication between the lakes, and along that communication to the lake of the woods; whence the line of the US. was to run due West, till it should strike the Missisipi. now, according to the maps of that time, and particularly Mitchell's on* which the boundary of 1783. was predicated, the line of 49.° passes through the Southern part of the lake of the Woods:[4] and the NorthWestern point of the lake of the Woods, as observed by Thompson, Astronomer to the North West company, is in Lat. 49°-37.′ [Mc.Kenzie's 2. voyage chapt. 13.] at that lake therefore the English negotiators ceased to pursue the water communication, because, South of the latitude of that lake, they owned nothing: and to have followed the water line further Northwardly, would have broken in upon the continuity of their Southern boundary. Canada was thus closed to the West, by it's Northern & Southern limits meeting in a point in the lake of the Woods. it was at that time believed that the Missisipi, heading North of 49.° would have been intersected by that line of latitude, and our possessions consequently closed. but subsequent information rendered it probable that that river did not extend so far North; (it is now said only to 47.° 38′)[5] and consequently that there was an unclosed space between it's source & the lake of the woods. without undertaking to decide what were the

---

* the identical map used by the negociators, with their MS. marks on it, is deposited in the office of state.

limits dividing Great Britain & Spain in that quarter, we concluded it would be safest to settle, as occasions should offer, our boundary there with both nations, on the principle of 'valeat quantum valere potest' with each. having to form a convention with England for ascertaining our limits in the North Eastern quarter, we took that occasion for closing, as far as depended on her right, the vacancy in our North Western angle; & therefore proposed it to her. while negociations were going on at London for this purpose, an opportunity occurred of our acquiring Louisiana: and the stipulations being promptly concluded, a treaty for that acquisition was actually signed at Paris twelve days before that of London was concluded. but this treaty was not known to the negociators of either party at London; nor could the rights acquired by it, be affected by arrangements instituted & compleated there merely for the purpose of explaining and supplying the provisions in the treaty of 1783. in result, this acquisition rendered these explanations unnecessary, and the Vth. article respecting them merely nugatory. for England holding nothing in that quarter Southward of 49.° the line proposed in the Vth. article, from the North-Western point of[6] the lake of the Woods Southwardly to the nearest source of the Misipi, is through a country, not belonging to her, but now to the US. consequently the consent of no other nation can now be necessary to authorise it. it may be run, or not, and in any direction which suits ourselves. it has become a merely municipal object respecting the line of division which we may chuse to establish between two of our territories.[7]   It follows then that the Vth. Article of the Convention of London of May 12. 1803. should be expunged, as nugatory; and that instead of it, should be substituted one declaring that the dividing line between Louisiana & the British possessions adjacent to it, shall be from the North Western point of the Lake of the Woods, along the water edge Westwardly[8] to it's intersection with the parallel of 49.° North from the Equator, then along that parallel (as established by the treaty of Utrecht between Gr. Britain & France) until it shall meet the limits of the Spanish province next adjacent. and it would be desirable to agree further[9] that, if that parallel shall, in any part, intersect any waters of the Missouri, then the dividing line shall pass round all those waters to the North until it shall again fall into the same parallel, or meet the limits of the Spanish province next adjacent.[10] or, unapprised that Spain has any right as far North as that, & Westward of Louisiana, it may be as well to leave the extent of the boundary of 49.° indefinite, as was done on the former occasion.

Jan. 15. 1804.

MS (PPAmP); entirely in TJ's hand, including brackets; begins on final page of "An examination into the boundaries of Louisiana," 7 Sep. (see Vol. 41:329-38); endorsed as received by the American Philosophical Society on 18 Jan. 1818 and "to be published." PoC (ViU). Dft (DLC: TJ Papers, 135:23271); entirely in TJ's hand; lacks authorial note. PrC (same, 137:23692-3); undated. Tr (DLC: Monroe Papers); in Lewis Harvie's hand; undated. Tr (DNA: RG 59, TP, Orleans); in a clerk's hand; undated.

PRECEDING STATEMENT: Document II in the Boundaries of Louisiana, at 7 Sep. 1803.

The LINE of demarcation between British and French possessions that TJ discovered in Thomas HUTCHINS's *Historical Narrative and Topographical Description of Louisiana* was never agreed to by the French. The boundary discussed in Hutchins would have divided the territory of the Hudson's Bay Company (along with New Britain, or what is now Labrador and Nunivak) from the parts of Canada corresponding with Quebec on the left, or north, side of the St. Lawrence River, then extended indefinitely westward along the 49th parallel (J. P. D. Dunbabin, "Red Lines on Maps: The Impact of Cartographical Errors on the Border between the United States and British North America, 1782-1842," *Imago Mundi*, 50 [1998], 111; William E. Lass, "How the Forty-Ninth Parallel Became the International Boundary," *Minnesota History*, 44 [1975], 215-16).

American and British peace negotiators believed that the LAKE OF THE WOODS was, like the Great Lakes, part of the St. Lawrence River watershed. In this, they were following John MITCHELL's *Map of the British and French Dominions in North America* (Dunbabin, "Red Lines on Maps," 109-10).

VALEAT QUANTUM VALERE POTEST: the legal maxim meaning, let it have effect as far as it can (Bryan A. Garner, *Black's Law Dictionary*, 8th ed. [St. Paul, Minn., 2004], 1763).

VTH. ARTICLE: for the convention with Great Britain, which would have defined the boundary between the U.S. and British North America by the shortest line connecting the northwest corner of the Lake of the Woods with the nearest source of the Mississippi River, see Vol. 41:600-2. It is uncertain if TJ shared this statement declaring the fifth article NUGATORY with any of his allies in the Senate, but that body voted accordingly on 9 Feb., with Pickering and most other New England senators in the minority. The British then rejected the entire convention. The Jefferson administration subsequently worked to have the 49th parallel acknowledged as the boundary between the western portions of the United States and Canada, appealing to the Treaty of Utrecht and the commercial charter granted by Louis XIV to Antoine Crozat as the authorities for this claim. Madison asked Monroe to research the proceedings of the boundary commissioners appointed under the Treaty of Utrecht and instructed Robert R. Livingston to obtain an authenticated copy of the Crozat grant. Settling this westernmost boundary was not, however, a priority. Given, Madison wrote Monroe, "the remoteness of the time at which such a line will become actually necessary," a delay might be preferable to both parties (Lass, "How the Forty-Ninth Parallel Became the International Boundary," 215-17; JEP, 1:463-4; Madison, *Papers, Sec. of State Ser.*, 6:408, 476).

[1] Dft, PrC, and Trs lack this heading.

[2] Preceding four words lacking in Trs. In Dft TJ first wrote "hitherto spoken of" before altering the text to read as above. He made that change sometime after he created the PrC.

[3] Word interlined in Dft, lacking in PrC.

[4] In Dft TJ interlined the remainder of the sentence (including citation) in place of "& according to some later maps of Arrowsmith, it passes through the Northern part of it"; interlineation lacking in PrC.

[5] Parenthetical material interlined in Dft, with "perhaps" instead of "it is now said"; interlineation lacking in PrC.

[6] Preceding four words interlined in Dft.

[7] Sentence lacking in Dft, PrC, and Trs.

[8] In Dft TJ first wrote "along it's margin to the mouth of the River Winnipeg, and along the middle of that river" before altering the passage to read as above.

[9] Preceding eight words interlined in Dft in place of "but," with "obtain" instead of "agree"; alteration lacking in PrC and Trs.

[10] Dft and Trs end here.

From Benjamin H. Latrobe

SIR   Washington Jany: 15th. 1804.—

The following passage is contained in a letter just received from Mr Wm Stewart, by far the most wealthy & respectable Stonecutter at Baltimore. Mr Robert Stewart,—his father is proprietor of an acre, containing the best Stone on the Island. I have not yet received his proposals for supplying stone.

"I have understood ⅌ Mr Conway who was in Baltimore some time ago, that Mr D. C. Brent expects you will have to pay an advanced price for stone next Season. Mr Brent says if the Quarriers or Sellers of Stone would let him make the price he would engage to get them 10 dollars for every ton of Billstone, and 6 Dollars for every ton of Shopstone (that is inferior stone) they could raise on Acquia Creek. So that I expect he means to make you *pay* for all you get, expecting no doubt that you cannot be supplied through any other channel than his own."

I have thought it my duty to give you this information in corroboration of what I say this morning. Mr Conway is proprietor of one of the Quarries from I am in hopes to obtain a large quantity of stone at the price hitherto paid.—

I am with true respect Your faithful hble Servt

B H LATROBE

RC (DLC); closing quotation marks supplied; endorsed by TJ as received 16 Jan. and so recorded in SJL.

ROBERT STEWART, or Steuart, owned a small amount of land at Aquia Creek from which he quarried stone. Latrobe later wrote of opening a public quarry at Aquia as a means of interfering with the proposed price hike of Daniel Carroll BRENT, who operated the largest quarry there (Latrobe, *Correspondence*, 1:426-7n; see enclosure to Latrobe to TJ, 18 Feb.).

THIS MORNING: a proposed meeting between Latrobe and the president may have been the subject of an apparently misdated letter of 12 Jan. from Latrobe, recorded in SJL as received from Aquia on 13 Jan. with the notation "Jan. 19. for 12," but not found.

To Timothy Pickering

Sunday Jan. 15. 04.

Th: Jefferson presents his compliments to mr Pickering and will send him tomorrow Louis XIVth.'s charter to Crozat, the book having been sent to the Secy. of state's office to have copies of the charter made out, and the office being closed till tomorrow. he will thank mr Pickering for the return of the paper sent him, when perused, as it was a rough draught & no copy retained, and these papers are now in a course of copying to be sent by mr Bearing.

RC (MHi: Pickering Papers); addressed (clipped, obscured by binding): "The honble Mr. P[ickering]"; endorsed by Pickering. Not recorded in SJL.

The administration was copying the charter to Antoine CROZAT from an English translation of French explorer Henri Joutel's memoir, *A Journal of the Last Voyage Perform'd by Monsr. de la Sale* (Sowerby, No. 4074; Madison, *Papers, Sec. of State Ser.*, 6:408; Vol. 41:328n, 332-3).

MR BEARING: Alexander Baring.

From Alexander Baring

Monday evening. [16 Jan. 1804]

Mr Baring presents his respectfull compliments to The President and takes the liberty of assuring him that the letter he did him the honor to entrust to him and which he has received shall be conveyed to its address with the utmost care.

RC (MHi); partially dated; endorsed by TJ as received 17 Jan.

Son of London merchant and banker Sir Francis Baring, Alexander Baring (1773-1848) was sent to Amsterdam in 1794 to work at Hope & Company. French occupation forced Baring's return to London in 1795. Later that year his father and Hope & Company dispatched him to the United States to invest in land owned by William Bingham. In 1796, Baring purchased 1,225,000 acres of Bingham's land in Maine. Baring married Bingham's older daughter, Ann Louisa, in 1798 and returned to London with his family in 1801. In April 1803, he went to Paris on behalf of the Baring and Hope firms to finance the U.S. purchase of Louisiana. Baring left for the United States in August to complete the agreement. Sir Francis Baring retired late in 1804, and, in 1807, the firm became Baring Brothers & Company. By 1809, Alexander Baring was the senior partner. He served as Gallatin's intermediary during peace negotiations with the British in 1813 and 1814. In 1835, Baring became Baron Ashburton. He was called out of retirement in 1841 to serve as a British ambassador to settle the boundary dispute between the United States and Canada, which resulted in the Webster-Ashburton Treaty of 1842 (DNB; Raymond Walters, Jr., *Albert Gallatin: Jeffersonian Financier and Diplomat* [New York, 1957], 154, 266, 268, 271-3, 286, 292, 300; Robert C. Alberts, *The Golden Voyage: The Life and Times of William Bingham, 1752–1804* [Boston, 1969], 113, 310, 313, 323, 346, 433-5; RS, 7:440n).

For the LETTER entrusted to Baring, see TJ to Monroe, 8 Jan. Baring also carried a letter from Madison to Monroe of 18 Jan. (Madison, *Papers, Sec. of State Ser.*, 6:355-7).

[285]

From William C. C. Claiborne

A few days previous to my departure from Fort Adams, I had the honor to address to you a private letter, which I hope has reached you in safety.

Since my arrival in this City, my official communications to the Department of State have informed you of all events of importance, and thro' that channel I shall endeavour to keep you fully advised of such political occurrences as are worthy of notice.

I now embrace a leisure moment to write you inofficially from this City; and to observe, that the high expectations I had formed of the value of our new acquisition to the United States, are fully confirmed by my personal observations. The country on the Mississippi is fertile, happily adapted to cultivation, its productions various and abundant, the people wealthy, and in the enjoyment of all the necessaries, and many of the luxuries of life. New-Orleans is a great, and growing City. The commerce of the Western Country concentrates at this place, and there appears to me a moral certainty, that in ten years, it will rival Philadelphia or New-York. I believe the citizens of Louisiana are, generally speaking, honest; and that a decided majority of them are attached to the American Government. But they are uninformed, indolent, luxurious—in a word, illy fitted to be useful citizens of a Republic. Under the Spanish Government education was discouraged, and little respectability attached to science. Wealth alone gave respect and influence; and hence it has happened that ignorance and wealth so generally pervade this part of Louisiana. I have seen Sir, in this City, many youths to whom nature has been apparently liberal, but from the injustice and inattention of their parents, have no other accomplishments to recommend them but dancing with elegance and ease. The same observation will apply to the young females, with this additional remark, that they are among the most handsome women in America.

The promotion of education and general information in this Province, ought to be one of the first objects of the Government. I fear that if education be left entirely to the patronage of the inhabitants, it will continue to be neglected; for they are not sufficiently informed to appreciate it's value. There are some respectable characters in and near New-Orleans, who were educated in France, that have pretensions to science, but they are unacquainted with our language and Government, and I fear they will not become useful citizens for some time.

I feel solicitous to learn what form of government will be prescribed for Louisiana. I beleive myself, that a government somewhat similar to a territorial government in its *first grade*, is best suited to this Province. Some politicians who are here suppose that a military government can alone, for the present, ensure good order and harmony in this community; but I cannot assent to this opinion. The people will indeed have gained nothing by their annexation to the United States if a military system be still maintained. I believe firmly, that Louisiana may be governed without force. The inhabitants have nothing vicious in their dispositions, and have been educated in submission to the laws, and in obedience to the constituted authorities. The great body of Society being unacquainted with the American language, and strangers to our laws and customs, it is probable that partial *discontents* may arise; but I cannot suppose that *they* will be of such a nature as to render force necessary to suppress them. From the great intercourse between this Province and the United States, and the press of emigration, I entertain strong hopes that a radical change will, in a reasonable time be effected; I look forward to this change with great anxiety, for I am so great a friend to self-government that did the political safety of the Country admit of it, I could wish Louisiana to become a State tomorrow; but for the reasons already suggested, the experiment at this time would, in my opinion, be impolitic.

I believe the climate of lower Louisiana is unhealthy, but it is by no means so unfriendly to human life as has been represented. I find here a great many old people and a number of children, and in general, the people appear to possess as strong athletic constitutions as are seen in similar climates. The American troops have already experienced much sickness, and it is probable that the ensuing spring and summer will be deemed unhealthy; for the old inhabitants agree that the climate proves unfavourable to strangers.

Mrs. Claiborne ventured on a journey through the wilderness in November last, and is now with her friends in Tennessee. If the public service will admit of it, I should wish to visit that State myself in the course of the ensuing summer. When therefore, the permanent Governor of Louisiana shall have relieved me from this Post, I must entreat of you leave of absence for a few months.

Friend Briggs finding that his business in the Mississippi Territory, would admit of his absence for a few weeks, is now on a visit to this City. He is greatly delighted with the soil and situation of Louisiana, but I believe the dissipation and extravagance of the inhabitants, together with the existence of slavery, has filled his mind with much serious concern: His sentiments and conduct impress me with an opinion that he sincerely loves his country.

Col. Kirby and Mr. Nicholas left Orleans for Mobile on this morning, and will, I presume, in a few weeks transact the business of their mission; for the claims to land in Washington district are few in number. I fear Col. Rodney and Mr. Williams will have an arduous duty to perform; The claims submitted to their decision will be numerous and complicated: But being men accustomed to business and possessing much legal information, it is probable they will decide on all the claims which may be brought before them in about twelve months.

The establishment of the temporary court in the City of New-Orleans, of which I advised you in my last dispatch to the Secretary of State, has relieved me from much business, but a sufficiency still devolves upon me to occupy most of my time. It is my intention to use no more authority than the actual state of things shall require. I know that in the exercise of my present discretionary powers, the danger I have to guard against, is *the doing too much*.

I have lately obtained a sketch of the river Mississippi, from the mouth of the Yazoo river and also of the sea coast from the mouth of the Mississippi to Pensacola, and part of the coast to the West. Supposing that this Chart might be acceptable to you, I have taken the liberty to forward it under a seperate cover by this mail.

For a continuation of your private and political happiness, I pray you to accept the best wishes of,

Your faithful friend   WILLIAM C. C. CLAIBORNE

RC (DLC); in a clerk's hand, signed by Claiborne; at foot of text: "The President of the United States"; endorsed by TJ as received 15 Feb. and so recorded in SJL.

A PRIVATE LETTER: Claiborne to TJ, 8 Dec. 1803.

TEMPORARY COURT: on 30 Dec. 1803, Claiborne issued an ordinance "For Establishing A Court of Justice" in the city of New Orleans, consisting of no fewer than seven justices appointed by the governor and serving at his pleasure. Its jurisdiction extended to the recovery of debts not exceeding $3,000, with a right of appeal to the governor in cases exceeding $500. Individual justices also served as "Conservators of the Peace," with authority to decide civil cases regarding debts not exceeding $20 and to arrest and commit to trial offenders of the peace. Explaining his actions to the secretary of state, Claiborne stated that the "actual necessities of the society" led him to the measure and that he hoped it would "meet with the Presidents approbation." He sent a printed copy of the ordinance to Madison on 10 Jan. (MS in DNA: RG 59, TP, Orleans; Madison, *Papers, Sec. of State Ser.*, 6:275-6, 329, 331n).

From Albert Gallatin,
with Jefferson's Reply

DEAR SIR   Monday [16 Jan. 1804]

Mr Nourse waits for official information of the day on which possession of New Orleans was obtained for the purpose of filling the
blanks left in the certificates of the date from which they are to bear
interest. Will you have the goodness to send him a memorandum
to that effect by the bearer, as I have no evidence of the fact but a
Natchez news paper—

Respectfully Your obedt. Servt.   ALBERT GALLATIN

[*Reply by TJ*:]
the province was delivered on the 20th. of December   TH:J.

RC (DNA: RG 56, PFLP); partially   NOURSE WAITS: see note to Warrant
dated; addressed: "The President of the   for Delivery of Louisiana Stock, 16 Jan.
United States"; after adding the reply, TJ
altered the address to "Mr. Nourse."

From Joseph Lord

                                            Canaan State New York
SR.   Jany. 16th 1804

Considering the Importence of the Militia & the Confidence your
Excelency reposes in them—I think it the Duty of Every Citizen to make
all the Exertion in their power that will prove to their Advantage—
which I think will be A Sufficient Excuse for the trouble I shall give
you in communicating my Idears on that Subject—As it comes within
the limmits of your Office as Commander in Chief of the Militia to
Introduce rules of Discipline—Permit me Sr. To communicate the
within Maneskrip for your Consideration. If on Examination you find
the system worthy of your Approbation—Please to give it your Signe-
ture that I may have the benefit of the Copy which will Innable me in
my Circumstances to Draw the Proseedings of A Field Day—I have
shewn the Maneskrip to A numbor of Military carectors which have
all approved of it & wish that it might be Circulated for the Benefit of
the Militia—I shall not make any remarks on the Maneskrip it must
Speak for itself Otherwise then the Plate makes the Formation of A
Company very plain—As Children are in General Asspering after the
carector of A Soldier I think A Military Catechism would Excite that
Ambition in their young minds that it would not only learn them to

[289]

read but it would Likewise give them that knowledge into the Dutyes of A Soldier that they would be able to turn out whenever their strength would admit in Defence of the Glorious Libertyes purchased by their Fathers for them at the risk of their Lives—

Sr. If on Examenation you find the System not worthy of Practice please to make it manifest & you will much Oblige your friend & Humbl. Servt.   JOSEPH LORD AJT.

RC (ViW: Tucker-Coleman Collection); at foot of text: "To his Excelency Thomas Jefferson Esqr. President of the United States of America"; endorsed by TJ as a letter of 18 Jan. received 29 Jan. and so recorded in SJL. Enclosure not found.

Joseph Lord (1762-1844), an avid student of military tactics, wrote two works on the subject of militia instruction, *A Military Catechism* (1805) and *The Militiaman's Pocket Companion* (1821). Both publications went through multiple editions and circulated widely among militia units in New York. He served for many years as a brigade major and inspector of the Columbia County militia (Mary E. Perkins, *Old Houses of the Antient Town of Norwich, 1660-1800* [Norwich, Conn., 1895], 177; *Laws of the State of New-York, Passed at the Thirty-First Session of the Legislature: Begun and Held at the City of Albany, the Twenty-Sixth Day of January, 1808* [Albany, 1808], 346; Poughkeepsie, N.Y., *Dutchess Observer*, 15 Aug. 1821; New York *Spectator*, 14 May 1822; *Albany Evening Journal*, 27 Jan., 6 Feb., 29 May 1844).

From John Monroe

SIR.   Staunton Jany. 16. 1804.

I had the honor of writing to you in Sepr. last, by our mutual friend Judge Jones, on a Subject of great moment & high importance as it related to my self. I will here add, that an Office in either of the departments, of the law, the customs or the post Office at New Orleans will aid my view.

But Sir, on my confidence in your wish to promote the public weal in the best & most impartial manner, I rest the object of that letter. And whatever may be the decision, I shall remain satisfied; and rejoice in proportion as others are found to deserve better of their country than I do.

I now address you, Sir, merely to apprize you, That, be the result of letter of Sepr. last what it may, I am firmly resolved to remove either to the territory of Orleans, or to that of the Mississipi.

I expect to depart hence in May next.

Since writing you last fall, I have experienced a combination of opposition & oppression too powerfull for an individual to combat with success. My affairs are now brought to a crisis; And I have no resources left, but such as arise out of the energies of my mind & body.

I have long combated the bellows of adverse fortune with unabated courage, & manly exertion. I have appeared before this to have been, I now appear to be overwhelmed by the Storm of misery & distress. Yet I trust there is a renovating principle still left in the regions[1] of my mind and the exertion of my body which will support me in my calamity, and raise again above the malice of my enemies.

Before my exile from my much loved Virginia; and my absence from those choice few, who have honored me with their virtuous friendship & benevolent patronage, I hope, I trust I shall receive from you, some letters of introduction to Gentlemen in both the countries I mean to visit. Under such patronage, and with my experience, I have no doubt I shall find in the climate I am going to, and among the unknown inhabitance, that independance, which has been denied to my honest labours in my native country.—

I have not mentioned the Subject of my letter of Sepr. last to either of the heads of Departments. Perhaps I have treated those Gentlemen indelicately. Such an Idea is abhorrant to my mind. And I am ignorant of the ettiquete that may be proper on such occasions. I am not known to any of the Gentlemen, but Mr. Madison; my high esteem for, & almost unbounded confidence in him, will forever prevent me from commiting an intentional act of disrespect towards him. And I am ready and willing to make any atonement for such my ignorance. But relying on the magnanimity of his mind and the goodness his heart, I have a hope, he will believe my conduct did not originate in disrespect.

Accept my sincere wishes for your health, happiness, and a continuance of the confidence of the virtuous & honest of our Country.

I am Sir with sincere & friendly respect Yours

JNO. MONROE

RC (DNA: RG 59, LAR); endorsed by TJ as received 15 Jan. and "emploimt. Louisiana" and so recorded in SJL.

WRITING TO YOU IN SEPR. LAST: Monroe to TJ, 11 Sep. 1803.

[1] MS: "reigons."

To Craven Peyton

DEAR SIR   Washington Jan.16.04

I recieved last night from mr Higginbotham a draught of yours on me for forty seven pounds payable in April. I shall delay writing to him till the next post by which I may hear from you. I considered our settlement of Aug. 11 and the balance of 558.14 D paiable Dec. 15.

and actually paid as soon as the note was presented, as in full of the principal money due on all the purchases, and that the sum of 213.33 D for interest as settled by yourself and a note given Sep. 20[1] & since paid, as closing the whole transactions relative to the lands of the Hendersons unless John's lots should have been since purchased. knowing of no other transaction which has placed me under any further call, and being peculiarly distressed to meet others which are quite equal to all my resources, I ask the favor of an explanation from you by the ensuing post, as by the return of that I must write to mr Higginbotham. Accept my friendly salutations and best wishes.

TH: JEFFERSON

PrC (ViU); at foot of text: "Mr. Craven Peyton"; endorsed by TJ in ink on verso.

A letter from David HIGGINBOTHAM to TJ, recorded in SJL as written on 4 Jan. at Milton and received on 15 Jan., has not been found. TJ's response, re- corded in SJL under 28 Jan., also has not been found.

For SETTLEMENT of the BALANCE of $558.14, see MB, 2:1106, and TJ to George Jefferson, 27 Dec. 1803.

For the INTEREST of $213.33 on payments to the Hendersons, see Vol. 41:401.

[1] Date interlined.

To Timothy Pickering

Jan. 16. 04.

Th: Jefferson presents his compliments to mr Pickering and sends him an office copy of Crozat's grant, prepared to be sent by mr Bearing, of which he will therefore ask the return.

RC (MHi: Pickering Papers). Not recorded in SJL. Enclosure: copy of 1714 charter to Antoine Crozat (see TJ to Pickering, 15 Jan.).

From Timothy Pickering

Jany. 16. 1804.

Mr. Pickering has the honour to return to the President his memoir on the northern boundary of Louisiana. A close examination of the subject since, has convinced Mr. Pickering that the idea he took the liberty to suggest to the President, which is the basis of the memoir, and which arose in Mr. Pickering's mind on the perusal of Mr. Hutchins's observations on the treaty of Utrecht, is incorrect. He has digested his reflections on the subject; and will submit them to the

President's consideration, as soon as he can transcribe his notes—this evening or to-morrow morning.—Mr. Pickering will now only mention, that the fifth article of the British convention, all things considered, is, in his opinion, precisely what the United States should desire.

RC (DLC). FC (MHi: Pickering Papers). Enclosure: see TJ to Pickering, 13 Jan.

From Timothy Pickering

City of Washington,
January 16. 1804.

Mr. Pickering presents his respects to the President of the United States, and submits to his consideration the inclosed inquiry concerning the Northern boundaries of Canada & Louisiana. If Mr. Pickering does not extremely mistake the facts, and their necessary consequences, all dispute with Great-Britain concerning boundaries, will be forever closed, by a ratification and execution of the British convention now before the Senate: and no further negociation respecting them, for the purpose of ascertaining and confirming our existing rights, can be necessary or expedient.

RC (DLC); endorsed by TJ as received 17 Jan. and so recorded in SJL. FC (MHi: Pickering Papers); endorsed by Pickering: "Note to Mr. Jefferson Jany. 16. 1804. sent 17th."

ENCLOSURE

Pickering's Analysis of the Boundary between Louisiana and Canada, with Jefferson's Notes

An inquiry concerning the Northern Boundaries of Canada & Louisiana
By the tenth article of the treaty of Utrecht, (in 1713) Great Britain and France agreed as follows
France shall restore to Great Britain "the bay and streights of Hudson, together with all lands, seas, sea coasts, rivers and places situate in the said bay and streights, and which belong thereunto, no tracts of land or of sea being excepted, which are at present possessed by the subjects of France."
"But it is agreed on both sides to determine within a year, by commissaries, to be forthwith named by each party, the limits which are to be fixed between the said bay of Hudson, & the places appertaining to the French."

Hutchins's incorrectness is so notorious that it would be a waste of time to argue on his *very words* they would probably be found to be very loose expressions of his own very loose ideas. we have an example of it in his account of the grant to Crozat.[1]

*by an imaginary line he means a line defined in writing but not by actual demarcation[2]

"The same commissaries shall also have orders to describe and settle in like manner the boundaries between the other British and French colonies in those parts."

The only information we have of the proceedings under this article, in respect to boundaries, is that of Mr. Hutchins late Geographer, to the United States, in his "Historical narrative & Topographical description of Louisiana and West Florida, printed at Philadelphia in 1784. Mentioning the grant of Louisiana by Louis 14 to Crozat, he says (page 7) "In this grant, the bounds are fixed by the Illinois river, and the lake of that name on the North, by Carolina on the East, the gulph of Mexico, on the South, and New Mexico on the West. As to Canada or New France, The French court would scarcely admit it had any other Northern boundary than the Pole. The avidity of Great Britain was equal, but France having been unfortunate in the war of 1710, the Northern boundary of *Canada* was fixed by the treaty of Utrecht in 1713. It assigns New Britain and Hudsons bay on the North of Canada, to Great Britain: and commissioners afterwards on both sides ascertained the limits by an *imaginary line, running from a cape or promontory in New Britain, on the Atlantic Ocean in 58 degrees 30. minutes North latitude, thence South West to the lake Misgosink or Mistasim; from thence farther South West directly to the latitude of 49 degrees. All the lands to the North of the imaginary line being assigned to Great Britain and all southward of that line, *as far as the River St Lawrence*, to the French. These were at that time the true limits of Louisiana and Canada, Crozats grant not subsisting long after the death of Louis 14."

On reading the paragraph from Hutchins, the idea which first presented was, that the imaginary line from the Atlantic coast running south West to the Lake Mistasim, & thence in the same course to the 49° of latitude was to be continued on this parallel, West untill it should strike the dominions of Spain; and thus constitute the Northern boundary of Louisiana: But a further examination has manifested that idea to be erroneous.

The four first lines of the paragraph, declaring how the boundaries of *Louisiana* were fixed, refer exclusively to the grant by Louis 14 to Crozat; and have no relation to the adjustment of boundaries by the commissaries pursuant to the tenth article of the treaty of Utrecht. The words of Hutchins are "the Northern boundary of Canada was fixed by the treaty of Utrecht." Then tracing the imaginary line before mentioned, he says

"All the lands to the north of the imaginary line *were* assigned to Great Britain; and all Southward of that line, as far as the river St Laurence, to the French."—These last words evidently exclude *Louisiana*; the river St Laurence being absolutely confined to *Canada*; & lying wholly to the Eastward of Louisiana. When therefore at the close of the paragraph Hutchins says, "There were at that time (1713) the true limits of Louisiana and Canada" he plainly means, that such were the bounds of Louisiana by the grant to Crozat, and *such* the Northern boundary of Canada, as settled by the British and French commissaries, pursuant to the tenth article of the treaty of Utrecht. Indeed it was impossible that the imaginary line aforementioned, if extended Westward along the 49° of latitude, should be the Northern boundary of Louisiana; for the province of Canada intervenes between that line and all the portion of Louisiana, which according to Crozats grant, (and until 1763) lay on the Eastside of the Missisipi.

But if it were to be insisted on, contrary to the plain statement of Hutchins, (and the claim rests wholly on his statement) that pursuant to the treaty of Utrecht The parallel of the 49° of latitude, North, extended westward to New Mexico, must be deemed the North boundary of Louisiana, it is perfectly clear that both parties abandoned it by the subsequent treaty of 1763; when they fixed the source of the Missisipi as the North point of the boundary line, which following the middle of the Mississippi downwards, should thence forward separate the British territories on the East, from those of France on the West.

We have then yet to seek for the Northern boundary of Louisiana; at some period subsequent to the treaty of Utrecht. And the 4th. & 7th. articles of the treaty of 1763 appear to have decided this point.

By the Fourth Article, France cedes to Great Britain: "in full right Canada, with all its dependencies.' And by the seventh article it is declared that "to remove forever all subject of dispute with regard to the limits of the British and French territories on the continent of America; it is agreed, that for the future, the confines between the dominions of his Britannic majesty and those of his most Christian Majesty, in that part of the world, shall be fixed irrevocably by a line drawn along the middle of the river Mississipi from its source to the river Iberville, & from thence

this imaginary line after running S.W. thro' lake Mistasin till it intersected the 49th. degree was then to pursue that parallel of lat. or was not. if it was to pursue it then it does so indefinitely & becomes the Northern boundary of Louisiana. if it does not pursue it but forms at that intersection a corner of Canada, the head of the St Laurence forming the other (according to Hutchins's words) to wit at the mouth of the Utawas where it loses it's name, then these lines omit the whole of Upper Canada, and half of the Lower. see this line through L. Mistasin in a small projection in the N.W. corner of Mitchell's map[3] at the treaty of 1763. Gr. Britain & France unquestionably supposed the Missisipi to head far North of 49°. as laid down[4] by Mitchell: & their bringing their boundary thro' L. Mistasim down[5] to 49°. shews they did not mean it should stop at the parallel of the head of the Misipi but[6] that the parallel of 49°. was the boundary contemplated by them,[7] & that this dividing line between them from 49°.[8] Southwardly shd. be so much of the Misipi (between it's source & mouth) as laid below 49°.

It is admitted that the line from 58°–30′ on the Atlantic thro' L. Mistasin to it's intersection of 49°. was the Northern boundary of Canada. if Canada did [not] end at [that in]tersection, [but went] on Westward[ly to] the Misipi as here supposed, I ask what was it's Northern boundary between the intersection & the Misipi, if the 49th. degree was not? no answer can be given to this but the admission of the 49th parallel to be that Northern boundary.[9] then the Frenchman & Englishman being placed as here supposed at the[10] source of the Misipi in 47°–38′ & finding themselves 100. miles South from their acknoleged boundary of 49°. & that they could not move to E. or W. of the spot on which they stood[11] without trespassing on each others grounds, they would join hand in hand & walk due North, saying this must be our dividing line.[12]

by a line drawn along the middle this river, & the lake Maurepas and Pontchartrain to the sea.

Now it is presumed to be incontrovertible, that at this time, Great Britain & France supposed the source of the Mississipi to be far North of the 49° of latitude. Mitchells map so extends it; and the American Ministers and those of Great Britain, in fixing the boundaries of the US in the treaty of 1783, it is well known went on that ground.

Now from the above declaration of limits in the treaty of 1763, the inference appears to be irresistible that Louisiana (the only territory then remaining to France on the continent of North America) extended as far north *as that parallel of latitude which should strike the source of the Mississipi*; and the presumption is violent *that it extends no farther North*, and consequently that that parallel is its true northern boundary.

It is plain that the French, being at that source, could not step one foot eastward without treading on British ground; Canada coming up precisely to that point, and there closing with the British Hudsons bay territory. But what could forbid the British being at the *same source* of the Mississipi from advancing due West? The *source* of the Mississippi, being (as before mentioned) mutually fixed on as the Northern point from which the common boundary of the territories of the two nations should run southward, in the course of that river; and Great Britain being uncontestibly the proprietor of the Hudsons bay territory, lying Westward of the meridian of the source of the Mississipi, and Northward of Louisiana may not the parallel of latitude which strikes that source be fairly assumed as the proper boundary line of the Hudsons bay territory on one side, and of Louisiana on the Other? If France had any right to extend Louisiana farther north, would not the two powers, *when forming a treaty for the express purpose of removing forever all subject of dispute with regard to the limits of their territories*, have explicitly declared and described that extent? The answer is inevitable, *they would*.

Taking then for granted, what now appears to be clearly proved that the true North boundary of Louisiana is the parallel of latitude which strikes the source of the Mississipi, it remains to consider the important result.

The United States, under the treaty of Paris, of the 30th of April 1803, claim Louisiana as it was held by France under her treaty with Great Britain in 1763; and can set up no higher pretensions.

Now as on one hand if the source of the Mississipi, were far *above* the 49° of Latitude, The US as proprietors of Louisiana, would be gainers in territory; so the alternative is inevitable, that if the source be at any point, *below* that degree, the US must acquiesce, whatever loss of territory may ensue.

The next object then is to find the source of the Mississipi. The discoveries in that region since the treaties of 1763 & 1783, appear to have satisfied every one that the source of the Mississipi falls far short of its formerly supposed Northern Extent. Mackenzie (general history of the Fur trade) states ["]the Northernmost branch of the source of the Mississipi to be in latitude 47° 38′ North and longitude 95. 6. West, ascertained by Mr Thompson astronomer to the North West company, who was sent expressly for that purpose in the spring of 1798. He in the same year determined the Northern bend of the Missouri, to be in latitude 47° 32′ North and longitude 101° 25 West." And "the North West part of the lake of the Woods, to be in latitude 49° 37′ North, and longitude 94° 31′ West.["]

The waters of the Lake of the Woods run northerly into Hudson's Bay. Between those waters, therefore and the streams which run into Lake Superiour, there must be some high grounds, dividing the one from the other. Accordingly by inspecting Mackenzie's map, there will be seen marked a mountainous ridge, running from the North East between those two lakes; but after passing a little further west than the lake of the Woods, the ridge bends much more southward, & so continues down to the parallel of 46° and perhaps lower. Now in the same map, the most *Northern source* of the Mississipi appears to be in that mountainous ridge, to the Eastward of its great Southern bend, and is doubtless the one whose latitude was ascertained by Mr Thompson.—It also appears to be the *nearest source* to the "most Northwestern point" of the lake of the Woods; and consequently a straight line from this *point* to that *source*, will be the shortest which can be run; and thus exactly comport with the Fifth article of the convention with Great Britain, for settling boundaries with the US.

With regard to the navigation of the Mississipi, to which by the treaties of 1763 & 1783, Great Britain is intitled, it is to be observed that this stipulation, in relation to the Northern part of the River, was made on the supposition that it ran far North of the Lake of the Woods; so that the British might, on their own territory, enter upon its navigable waters. But the source of the river being south of the North Western corner of the US, the British are of course excluded from touching it, on the North except at that source: unless the stipulation in the treaties giving them expressly a right to the free navigation of the river, gives them also necessarily a right to travel over the territories of the US, or of Louisiana, to get to its navigable waters.

However this may be, it will manifestly be for the interest of the US to give them a passage to the Mississipi, if that will induce them to bring thither their furs and peltries; and they have nothing else to bring. For that object, the US instead of *excluding*, should *open a road for them.* All the furs and peltries brought by that rout would be sold to the American merchants in upper Louisiana or Indiana or in New Orleans; and furnish an important article in our commerce; which without that accomodation, would be sent to the British merchants in Canada: whence indeed they may find their way to the US, by another route.—It will be remembered that the most Northern furs are the most valuable, and these are procured from the British territories North of Louisiana. From thence come the fine beaver & otter skins so productive in the market of China; and other furs and skins so necessary in our own manufactures. The US will have them. And the only question here will be, whether the Western states, by opening a passage, will receive them by the Mississipi, or let the Northern states recieve them all by the route of the Lakes. If the European goods, necessary for the British Indian trade, can pass by the Mississipi, or the river Hudson, more conveniently than by the St Laurence, an additional benefit will accrue to the US, by the revenue to be paid on them at New Orleans or N York.

If the Fifth Article of the Convention should be expunged, or if the ratification should be clogged with any condition whatever, Great Britain may refuse to ratify any part of it; and thus a material injury result to Massachusetts and eventually to the US, by leaving unsettled their North Eastern boundaries, where on both sides grants and settlements are extending & will unavoidably interfere. If Great Britain should not now be disposed to make any dif-

if it will be our interest to give the English access to the navigable waters of the Misipi, we shall do it, without stipuln. but let us keep it in our option, till we see it is our interest.[13]

ficulty about the North Western boundary yet her situation may probably prevent her attending to a new negociation on the subject, for some time to come: And from the facts and reasons above stated, the result would probably be less favourable to the US than the terms of the present convention.

If the Convention be not ratified, then the US will be held by the 4th. article of the treaty of Amity and commerce to survey, in conjunction with Great Britain, the river Mississipi, from one degree of latitude below the falls of St Anthony, to its principal source or sources; and also the parts adjacent; and if they do not, (as they will not) find that it would be intersected by a line due West from the Lake of the Woods, why then, after all the labour, delay and expence "the two parties are to proceed by amicable negociation, to regulate the boundary line in that quarter." Great Britain may, if the question be not terminated by the ratification of the present convention, prefer the course stipulated in this 4th article of the treaty of amity and commerce; in the hope of finding the principal stream of the Mississipi stretching Westerly and terminating in a source two or three degrees of latitude farther south than the one above described as the nearest to the Lake of the Woods.

She will hazard nothing by such a survey. *The US* may lose one, two or three degrees of latitude in breadth, & in longitude from the Mississipi to New Mexico, or to the Pacific Ocean; and at the same time, give her access to the navigable waters of the Mississipi; The fear of losing which under the Fifth article of the Convention, seems to have been the only objection with the British government to concluding it in its present form. For doubtless they considered an adoption of the *nearest source* of the Mississipi, (which as before mentioned, is probably the *Northernmost*) as in the 6th article, made it in fact, the *substitute* for the *real*, that is, *the most remote* but *a more southern source* of that river.

One fact stated by Hutchins, I have omitted to notice, in its proper place. He says (page 8) that "before the treaty of peace of 1762, Louisiana on the West side of the Mississippi, extended, in the French maps, only to near 45° of latitude; a limit within which the French would not have confined their claims, had any treaty or adjustment of boundaries, furnished them with even a pretence for carrying them farther North, to the 49th. degree.

[we] have an express [right] to go to the L. of the [Woods], & Westwardly along [the] parallel of 49°. 37′. [Gr. Br.] thinks an inference [may be] drawn that she was [to come] to the navigable [part] of the Misipi. and it [is here] argued that a [right] of mere inference [is so] much stronger than [one] stipulated in express [terms], that we are in [no danger] of losing 1. 2. [or 3°] of latitude by it.[14]

another proof of the gross ignorance or inaccuracy of Hutchins. we may safely challenge any person to produce a single map, French or English, bounding Louisiana North by 45°. Mitchell's map, which was before [1762], is cut off in it's N.W. [angle] at 47°. where it leaves Louisiana still open.[15]

MS (DNA: RG 59, TP, Orleans); un-dated; in Lewis Harvie's hand, with notes in margin in TJ's hand; torn and blurred, with words in brackets supplied from Tr; quotation marks in brackets supplied from FC; endorsed by Harvie: "Notes of the President on the Boundary of Louisiana and Mr. Pickering's enquiry respecting the Northern Boundary." Tr (DLC: Monroe Papers); entirely in a clerk's hand; endorsed by Monroe: "Respecting British convention abt. boundaries; British & Louisiana—Mr Kings—ratification with exception of 5th art." PrC (DNA: RG 59, TP, Orleans). PrC (NHi: Robert R. Livingston Papers). Dft (DLC: TJ Papers, 137:23711); entirely in TJ's hand; notes only; TJ numbered the paragraphs in pencil, probably to key them in sequence to Pickering's text. FC (MHi: Pickering Papers, 38:65-71); in Pickering's hand; lacks TJ's notes. FC (same, 51:57-69); in Pickering's hand; lacks notes.

As his marginal notes and his own examinaton of the northern boundary question (printed at 15 Jan.) indicate, TJ dismissed Pickering's view that the United States ought to continue to agree to the fifth article of the convention with the British concerning the boundaries between the two nations' territories. Yet, he treated Pickering's analysis as a serious document, which members of his administration should use to contextualize TJ's opposing arguments. After receiving the document (likely the first FC identified above—see TJ to Pickering, 19 Jan., regarding the return of the manuscript), TJ drafted a set of responses on a separate sheet (the Dft). He then handed Pickering's manuscript to his secretary Lewis Harvie for copying and, after the transcript was finished, entered his responses from the Dft as marginal comments to Pickering's text (the MS). At some point, prompted perhaps by Pickering's subsequent communication of the 18th, TJ expanded and revised one of the Dft's responses, composing the revision on the verso of the same sheet of paper (see note 12). At least two transcripts of the copy in Harvie's and TJ's hands were made. Madison enclosed one to Monroe as part of a set of documents concerning the rati-

fication of the convention with the British. The press copy of a second transcript ended up with Robert R. Livingston (Madison, *Papers, Sec. of State Ser.*, 6:476-7n).

Despite the sharp critiques he made of Thomas HUTCHINS'S INCORRECTNESS, TJ was basing his insistence on the 49th parallel as the northern boundary of Louisiana in large part on Hutchins's interpretation of the results of the Treaty of Utrecht. Although erroneous, the belief that the French and British had officially settled on that boundary circulated among a number of British and Anglo-American cartographers and historians during the eighteenth century (William E. Lass, "How the Forty-Ninth Parallel Became the International Boundary," *Minnesota History*, 44 [1975], 215; Continuation of an Examination of the Boundaries of Louisiana, 15 Jan.).

LAKE OF THAT NAME: that is, Lake Michigan, which some French explorers knew as the Lac des Illinois (Louis Hennepin, *Nouvelle decouverte d'un tres grand pays situé dans l'Amerique, entre le Nouveau Mexique, et la Mer Glaciale* [Utrecht, 1697], 140).

[1] Dft: "Hutchins's incorrectness appears by his <*account*> erroneous statemt of Louis XIV's grant to Crozat. his ideas & language are so loose that it would be idle to found arguments on his *very words*."

[2] Dft: "'imaginary line.' i.e. a line not actually traced & marked."

[3] Dft: "Lake Mistasim. a S.W. line from that would strike 49th degree in Long. 75. if only the country from the intersection of that line to the St. Laurence was Canada, it would throw out the whole of upper Canada, and the Western half of Lower Canada."

[4] Dft: "as stated."

[5] Dft: "but their bringing their E. & W. boundary down," altered to "and their bringing the Northern boundary of Canada down."

[6] Word interlined in place of "which they supposed for North of 49° and consequently."

[7] Dft: "<*contempld.*> fixed in their minds."

[8] Dft: "the boundary from that," altered from "their N. & S. boundary."

[9] Dft: "the boundary."

[10] Here in Dft, TJ canceled "parallel."

[11] Preceding five words interlined in Dft in place of "source."

[12] In Dft TJ first wrote this comment as "if, placing the Brit. & Fr. agents at the course of the Misipi 47°–38′ the Brit. cd not go to the West witht. getting on Fr. ground, nor the Fr. to the E. witht being on Brit. ground, they would say to each other, here we are, 100 miles S. of our establd boundary of 49°. we can neither move to right or left, we must then march hand in hand due North to close our lines" before redrafting the comment on the reverse side of the sheet.

[13] Dft: "we shall do it as a favor, but it is better to keep the right in our power & not to treat it away."

[14] Dft: "we have <*certainly*> an express right to a line running due W from the L. of the woods. Gr. Br. has only by inference a <*line*> right to come to the source of the Misipi. we are in no danger therefore of losing 1. 2. or 3°. of Lat."

[15] Dft: "Hutchins very ignorant in sayg. that before 1762 Louisiana in the French maps went only to 45°. I have a map of 1720. copied from theirs & going to 60°. Mitchells map carries it beyond 47°. where the limit of the map leaves it open."

To the Senate and the House of Representatives

To the Senate and House of Representatives of the United States.

In execution of the act of the present session of Congress, for taking possession of Louisiana, as ceded to us by France, & for the temporary government thereof, Governor Claiborne of the Missisipi territory, & Genl. Wilkinson were appointed Commissioners to recieve possession. they proceeded with such regular troops as had been assembled at Fort Adams, from the nearest posts, and with some militia of the Missisipi Territory, to New Orleans. to be prepared for any thing unexpected which might arise out of the transaction, a respectable body of militia was ordered to be in readiness in the states of Ohio, Kentucky & Tenissee, & a part of those of Tennissee was moved on to the Natchez. no occasion however arose for their services. our Commissioners, on their arrival at New Orleans, found the province already delivered by the Commissaries of Spain to that of France, who delivered it over to them on the 20th. day of December, as appears by their Declaratory act accompanying this. Governor Claiborne being duly invested with the powers heretofore exercised by the Governor & Intendant of Louisiana, assumed the government on the same day, and, for the maintenance of law & order, immediately issued the proclamation & address now communicated.

On this important acquisition, so favorable to the immediate interests of our Western citizens, so auspicious to the peace & security of the nation in general, which adds to our country territories so extensive

& fertile, & to our citizens new brethren to partake of the blessings of freedom & self-government, I offer to Congress, and our country, my sincere congratulations.

TH: JEFFERSON
Jan. 16. 1804.

RC (DNA: RG 233, PM, 8th Cong., 1st sess.); endorsed by a House clerk. PrC (DLC). RC (DNA: RG 46, EPFR, 8th Cong., 1st sess.); endorsed by a Senate clerk. Recorded in SJL with notation "possn of Louisiana." Enclosures: (1) William C. C. Claiborne and James Wilkinson to Madison, New Orleans, 20 Dec. 1803, announcing that Louisiana "was this day surrendered to the United States by the Commissioner of France" and that the American flag was raised in New Orleans "amidst the acclamations of the inhabitants"; they enclose a copy of the "instrument of writing" that was signed and exchanged by the commissioners of both governments (RC in DNA: RG 233, PM; see Madison, *Papers, Sec. of State Ser.*, 6:192). (2) Procès-verbal, 20 Dec., in French and English, signed by Claiborne and Wilkinson as commissioners of the United States and Pierre Clément Laussat as colonial prefect and commissioner of France, certifying that on this date, "accompanied on both sides by the chiefs and officers of the army and navy, by the municipality and divers respectable citizens of their respective republics," Laussat has formally placed Louisiana in possession of Claiborne and Wilkinson in conformity to the terms and object of the treaty and conventions of 30 Apr. 1803; Laussat has delivered the keys to the city of New Orleans to the U.S. commissioners and discharges those citizens and inhabitants of Louisiana "who shall choose to remain under the dominion of the United States" from their oaths of fidelity to France (Tr in DNA: RG 233, PM). (3) Proclamation by Claiborne in English, French, and Spanish, New Orleans, 20 Dec., announcing that French and Spanish authority over Louisiana has ceased and that of the United States is established (Printed copy in same; Vol. 41:639-41). (4) Address by Claiborne to the citizens of Louisiana, 20 Dec., congratulating them on the final cession of Louisiana to the United States, an action that has secured them "a Connection beyond the reach of change, and to your posterity the sure inheritance of freedom"; the American people will welcome Louisiana's inhabitants "as brothers" and extend to them "a participation in those inestimable rights, which have formed the basis of their own unexampled prosperity"; as governor, Claiborne will work to "foster your internal happiness, & forward your general welfare, for it is only by such means, that I can secure to myself, the approbation of those great & Just men who preside in the Councils of our Nation" (Tr in DNA: RG 233, PM). Message and enclosures printed in ASP, *Foreign Relations*, 2:581-3.

The Senate and House of Representatives each received and read TJ's message and its accompanying papers on 16 Jan., with both chambers thereafter ordering them to lie for consideration. The House took no further action, but the Senate ordered 300 copies printed for its use (JHR, 4:536; JS, 3:339). They were subsequently published as *Message from the President of the United States, Accompanying Sundry Documents Relative to a delivery and possession . . . of the Territory of Louisiana. 16th January, 1804* (Washington, D.C., 1804).

To the Speaker of
the House of Representatives

Jan. 16. 04.

Th: Jefferson presents his respects to the *Speaker of the H of R*[1] and asks the favor of him, when the papers accompanying his message of this day shall have been read in his house, to be so good as to deliver them to mr Harvie, who will be waiting to carry them, with a similar message, to the other house. but one copy of them was recieved, and it was thought best not to retard the communication till another could have been made out. besides that one of the papers is original.

RC (DNA: RG 233, PM; 8th Cong., 1st sess.); at head of text: "private"; with a blank filled by Lewis Harvie (see note below); addressed by Harvie: "The Speaker of the H of R"; endorsed by a House clerk; note on address sheet in

Nathaniel Macon's hand: "(private) Mr. Beckley read this, it is private."

SPEAKER: Nathaniel Macon.

[1] Text in italics in Harvie's hand.

Warrant for Delivery of Louisiana Stock

To ALBERT GALLATIN, SECRETARY OF THE TREASURY OF THE UNITED STATES.

Whereas by an Act, passed the tenth day of November, in the year one thousand eight hundred and three, entitled "An Act authorizing the creation of a stock to the amount of eleven millions two hundred and fifty thousand dollars for the purpose of carrying into effect the Convention of the 30th. of April one thousand eight hundred and three, between the United States of America, and the French Republic; and making provision for the payment of the same"; it is, among other things, enacted "That for the purpose of carrying into effect the Convention of the thirtieth day of April 1803 between the United States of America and the French Republic, the Secretary of the Treasury be, and he is hereby, authorized to cause to be constituted Certificates of stock signed by the Register of the Treasury in favor of the French Republic or of it's Assignees, for the sum of Eleven Millions two hundred and fifty thousand dollars, bearing an interest of six per centum per annum, from the time when possession of Louisiana shall have been obtained in conformity with the Treaty of the thirtieth day of April 1803, between the United States of America and the French Republic, and in other respects comformable with the tenor of the Convention aforesaid; And the President of the United

States is authorized to cause the said Certificates of Stock to be delivered to the Government of France, or to such Person or Persons as shall be authorized to receive them, in three months at most after the exchange of ratifications of the Treaty aforesaid and after Louisiana shall be taken possession of in the name of the Government of the United States"—Now therefore Be it Known, that, I, Thomas Jefferson, President of the United States of America, by virtue of the power in me vested by the Act before recited, Do hereby authorize and require you, Albert Gallatin, Secretary of the Treasury, to cause to be delivered to the Government of France, or to such person or persons as have been authorized to receive the same, the Certificates of Stock which have been constituted in conformity with the Convention of the thirtieth day of April 1803, between the United States of America and the French Republic—: And for so doing this shall be your sufficient Warrant.

In Testimony whereof, I have hereunto subscribed my hand at the City of Washington the sixteenth day of January one thousand eight hundred and four   TH: JEFFERSON

RC (DNA: RG 56, PFLP); in a clerk's hand, signed by TJ; endorsed by a clerk as "Warrant from the President of the US to The Secretary of the Treasy." FC (DNA: RG 53, RES). Not recorded in SJL.

ACT AUTHORIZING THE CREATION OF A STOCK: see U.S. Statutes at Large, 2:245-7. Gallatin drafted this order in consultation with the president in December (see Gallatin to TJ, 19 Dec. 1803, second letter). On 22 Dec., TJ approved a document whereby Alexander Baring, acting under powers of attorney from Hope & Company of Amsterdam and Francis Baring & Company of London, and Gallatin agreed that the Louisiana stock would "be discharged by the United States, in annual Instalments of not less than one fourth part" of the whole amount of $11,250,000, with the first installment due 15 years after 21 Oct. 1803 (MS in DNA: RG 56, PFLP; dated 22 Dec. 1803; in a clerk's hand, signed by Gallatin and Baring; initialed by TJ: "Approved"). Article 2 of the 30 Apr. convention made provision for the payment of the principal "in annual payments of not less than three millions of Dollars each," with the first payment to commence in 15 years (Miller, *Treaties*, 2:513-14). The Treasury Department actually began redeeming the stock in 1812, completing payment in October 1823 (J. E. Winston and R. W. Colomb, "How the Louisiana Purchase was Financed," *Louisiana Historical Quarterly*, 12 [1929], 198-9).

On 16 Jan., upon receipt of the document printed above, Gallatin sent Joseph Nourse, register of the Treasury, an order to deliver one-third of the stock certificates, worth $3,750,000, to Baring and to transmit the remaining two-thirds to the U.S. minister to France (RC in DNA: RG 56, PFLP; FC in DNA: RG 53, RES). Baring signed a receipt for the stock the same day (DNA: RG 56, PFLP).

From Timothy Bloodworth

DEAR SIR   Wilmington January 17th 1804.

Will you be pleasd to indulge me with the freedom of a friendly Address. the Circumstance that gives rise to this request, I hope will in som Measure Apolegise for the liberty I have taken, to divert Youre attention from the great National concearns that occupy Youre Minde, in the period of the Sessions. it has been my constant, & Unremitted endeavours, to reconcile Youre inviterate Enemies to Youre Administration. firmly Believing that all Youre Measures, were pointed to the Happiness of Youre Country, divested of Sinister Views, & such has been the wisdom, & success, of Youre Measures, that Many of Youre opposers appear wiling to becom Advocates for Youre Continuance in office. among the Number of these candid proselites, I am happy to acquaint You of General Benjamin Smith, a Gentleman of effluence, Respectability, & considerable influence, who setts out tomorrow for Washington City, in order to settle the Business of the fortification begun in this place. if it should be Your pleasure to favor him with Marks of attention, I am persuaded it will confirm his attachment to Youre Person, & Administration, & if so, it will be a Means of dividing the opposition (which has been formidable in this place) & render the conquest of Republicanism More Compleat, as his Example will have a powerfull Influence on all his Adherants. I submit the subject to Youre superior information, & beg pardon for calling Youre attention to a subject so far beneath Youre Notis. An earnest desire to promote the happiness of my Country, which will in a great Measure be effected by Youre Continuance in office, has given Birth to the Measure. Not that I suppose a thousand Enemies could shake Youre Popularity, Yet the more Numerous the friends on this Occation, the less Arduous the conflict, & the Conquest will be more Compleat. I have observed with pleasure, that several persons who was against Youre Election, by passing through that City, & hearing Youre Charecter, & observing youre Conduct, have returnd Advocates for Youre Administration, & I fondly hope, it will be the case with Mr: Smith, & should this be the case, I am wel persuaded that no small Number will be Added to the Republican Interest in this District, that has heretofore laboured against the weight of Charecter, & the Influence of the Long robe, boath from the Barr, & the Pulpet.

Permit me to acquaint You that the fortification is in danger of being much Injured by the high tides, washing away the sand near the foundation of the works. much Labor has been bestow'd on the fortification, but whether or not, it would be Advisable to finish the fort, is not for me to determine.

That you may live in the enjoyment of perfect Health, & Continue to be, as You have been, a Blessing to Youre Country, is the Ardent Desire, of Dear Sir, Youre obedient Humble Servant, under Lasting obligations.   TIMOTHY BLOODWORTH

RC (DLC); endorsed by TJ as received 29 Jan. and so recorded in SJL.

BUSINESS OF THE FORTIFICATION: Benjamin Smith was traveling to Washington to negotiate a contract with the War Department for constructing improvements to Fort Johnston, located on the lower Cape Fear River near Wilmington, North Carolina. Some years earlier, Smith had acted as a security for the disgraced former collector at Wilmington, James Read, whose default left Smith deeply in debt to the federal government. Smith apparently put forward this contract proposal as a means to discharge his liability. Arriving at Washington, he presented his plans to Henry Dearborn on 3 Feb., who forwarded them to TJ. Writing Smith the following day, Dearborn informed him that the president had authorized the War Department to accede to Smith's proposal and that he "expects a faithful and punctual performance of the said agreement by the parties contract-

ing" (*Memoirs of Gen. Joseph Gardner Swift, LL.D., U.S.A., First Graduate of the United States Military Academy, West Point, Chief Engineer U.S.A. from 1812 to 1818. 1800-1865* [Worcester, Mass., 1890], 47, 51-2; Dearborn to Smith, 4 Feb. 1804, in DNA: RG 107, MLS; David Stone to TJ, 7 Dec. 1803; Bloodworth to TJ, 12 Dec.).

Also on 17 Jan., Bloodworth prepared a letter of introduction for Smith: "Permit me to Introduce to Youre Acquaintance Mr Benjamin Smith, Brigadeer General of the district of Wilmington, who is a Gentleman of Affluence, & Respectability, & has for several Years serv'd in the Charecter of Speaker in the Senate of this State. this Gentleman proposes to wait on the Secretary at War on Business of importance. With the Respect Justly due to Youre Charecter, & Station, I have the Honor to be Dear Sir, Youre Most obedient Humble Servant" (RC in MHi; endorsed by TJ as received 30 Jan. and so recorded in SJL).

From Arthur Campbell

SIR   Washington Jan. 17th. 1804

Since the acquisition of the Country West of the Missisippi I have often indulged myself in contemplations of the future greatness of the United States, different from any conceptions I had of the subject in former years. The thing is new in the annals of the World. The great matter now is, to make the wonderful event, a blessing to the human race.

With this impression on my mind, I most respectfully make an offer of my services, in governing upper Louisiana. They present survivors of[1] the American Revolution, cannot expect to see much done in their day; but some of them may begin the Work, they may give a tone to the moral and political principles of the succeeding generation, they may leave their names and example for their successors to copy from; and they may impress a grateful remembrance, who were the benefactors of mankind.

Two objects of primary importance seem—at present—to present themselves. To conciliate they present white Inhabitants, and to maintain peace with the Aborigines. Both of these, seems well understood by the Author of the Bill, lately brought forward in the Senate. It would be my pride, to second your beneficent views, in the part you will have to act, under the law.

Early in life, I acquired some knowledge, of the customs and manners of the French in Canada; and a still more intimate acquaintance with those of the Indians. for the Americans I will need no address, to gain their confidence: I am known to several of the principal Inhabitants. I can now count the same number of years, on this stage of existence, that you can, and altho I now enjoy good health and my mental powers unimpaired, yet I look for, but a few years more, and therefore conclude, that my best preparation for another life, is to be efficiently employed, in *doing good* to others.

Accept Sir The homage of my sincere Respect

Arthur Campbell

RC (DNA: RG 59, LAR); endorsed by TJ as received 22 Feb. and "for emploimt. in Louisiana" and so recorded in SJL.

A prominent landholder and leader in southwest Virginia, Campbell had been imprisoned by the FRENCH during the French and Indian War and later was appointed as an Indian agent by George Washington (DVB, 2:554-6).

[1] MS: "of of."

To Thomas McKean

Dear Sir   Washington Jan. 17. 1804.

I have duly recieved your favor of the 8th. but the act of ratification which it announces, is not yet come to hand. no doubt it is on it's way. that great opposition is and will be made by federalists to this amendment is certain. they know that if it prevails, neither a Presidt. or Vice President can ever[1] be made but by the fair vote of the majority of the nation, of which they are not. that either their opposition to the principle of discrimination now, or their advocation of it formerly was on party, not moral motives, they cannot deny. consequently they fix for themselves the place in the scale of moral rectitude to which they are entitled. I am a friend to the discriminating principle; and for a reason more than others have, inasmuch as the discriminated vote of my constituents will express unequivocally the verdict they wish to pass on my conduct. the abominable slanders of my political enemies have obliged me to call for that verdict from my country in the only way it can be obtained, and if[2] obtained it will be my sufficient voucher to the rest of the world & to posterity and leave me free to seek, at a definite time, the repose I sincerely wished to have retired to now. I suffer myself to make no enquiries as to the persons who are to be placed on the rolls of competition for the public favor. respect for myself as well as for the public requires that I should be the silent & passive subject of their consideration.—we are now at work on a territorial division & government for Louisiana. it will probably be a small improvement of our former territorial governments, or first grade of government. the act proposes to give them an assembly of Notables, selected by the Governor from the principal characters of the territory. this will, I think, be a better legislature than the former territorial one, & will not be a greater departure from sound principle.   Accept my friendly salutations & assurances of high respect & consideration.   TH: JEFFERSON

RC (PHi: Thomas McKean Papers); addressed: "His Excellency Governor Mc.Kean Lancaster"; franked; postmarked 18 Jan.; endorsed by McKean. PrC (DLC).

ADVOCATION OF IT FORMERLY: after the election of TJ as vice president in 1796, Federalists favored an amendment to the Constitution to designate votes for president and vice president as a way to keep their party in control of both offices (Kuroda, *Origins of the Twelfth Amendment*, 72, 159).

[1] Word interlined.
[2] Word interlined in place of "when."

From Henry Moore

SIR   Alexandria January 17th. 1804

I have not been much in the habit of asking favors in the course of my Life. I have now one to crave of you—

My Brother Thomas Moore has lately been unfortunate in Business owing to the Villainy of some *Great Men* in whom he reposed Confidence, and who deceived him; he has a Wife and small child looking up to him for support—he is very active and Industrious—and served a Regular Apprenticeship to Mercantile Business with Thomas Mason Brother of Genl. John Mason—He is well known to John T. Mason, Danl. C Brent & Richard Brent Esquires—If there should be any Clerkship in the City Vacant, or any appointment to be made in the Western Country, will you be so good as to make Interest for him You are already acquainted with the Character of his father Cleon Moore You have understood he fought the Battles of his Country, and took a very active part under the immediate eye of Genl. Washington, in the acquirement of our just rights, by which our Necks were freed from the Yoke of the British Tyrant, and our Country now justly claims the preeminence over all the World—

I have several times addressed myself to you in a free and unreserved manner; my reason is I know you with all other natives of America who are truly friends to their Country and to Mankind in general; to be an Enemy to unnecessary formality & show—

I pray you excuse my freedom, and accept my best wishes for your happiness and prosperity as well here as hereafter, during your Political Career, and after you retire to the Beautiful Shades of Monticello to pass your declining years in the Reflections that arise from the approbation of our own Conduct, and when conscious we have done all in our power for the Benefit and happiness of our fellow Mortals—I am this moment called off, or would have transcribed this Letter—therefore you will excuse the bad Writing—

I tender you the homage of my highest consideration & respect & Believe me to be very respectfully Your Obt. Servt.

HENRY MOORE

Son of Cleon Moore of Alexandria—

Judges Kilty & Cranch & Fitzhugh can satisfy you as to my Brothers capacity for Business &c—

RC (DNA: RG 59, LAR); addressed: "Thomas Jefferson Esquire President of the U.S. Washington City"; franked and postmarked; endorsed by TJ as received 19 Jan. and "Moore Thos. emploimt." and so recorded in SJL.

Henry Moore established a broker's office in Alexandria in 1797 and subsequently became a lawyer. In 1800, he succeeded his father as notary public in Alexandria. Two years later, he announced that he was relocating to Kentucky, but his tenure there was apparently short-lived and he returned to Alexandria (Miller, *Alexandria Artisans*, 1:342; *Alexandria Advertiser*, 1 Nov. 1797 and 2 May 1808; Alexandria *Times; and District of Columbia Daily Advertiser*, 31 July 1800; *Washington Federalist*, 19 May 1802; CVSP, 9:115).

SEVERAL TIMES ADDRESSED: Moore wrote two letters to TJ in June 1801, one of which has not been found (Vol. 34:319n).

From William Short

Jan. 17.— [1804]

Jefferson.—Ansr. his of 12—change of time &c—has not changed my determination that this shd be no inconvenience to him—of course at liberty to act as he pleases on it—the only inconvenience to me not to be able to direct myself the vestment—state of France—of sea & of my affairs with G.J. may perhaps make me stay another year— pleasure of my residence in my own country shall often regret it—the most abundant source tho being considered by all as an Ame. Cit. to all intents & purpose—one only exception, regret the more as it is where I shd. the least have expected it—the report as to Strobel contradicted—as to the bank directors & Mason—Wish he cd. be inured to their sentiments that wd. surprize—they shew the adherence of men of property—well the heads of Govt could see into the hearts of all—they would not find their most dangerous enemies & best friends where they expect—will write to the owner of Cahusac by first letter— this will avoid the delay

FC (DLC: Short Papers); partially dated; entirely in Short's hand, consisting of an entry in his epistolary record. Recorded in SJL as received from Philadelphia on 20 Jan.

After his return to the United States in 1802, Short carried a message from Monroe to TJ that may have conveyed a request for a consular post for Short's acquaintance Daniel STROBEL. TJ subsequently recommended Strobel for an appointment as U.S. consul in Antwerp (Madison, *Papers, Sec. of State Ser.*, 4:573-4; Vol. 40:719n; Daniel Strobel, Jr., to TJ, 20 July 1805).

For a sense of what Short may have written concerning MEN OF PROPERTY, see TJ's response of 23 Jan.

From Caspar Wistar

DR SIR   Philad Jany. 17. 1804

I beg leave to present to you Mr Thos. Benger a native of Newfoundland who has resided many years near this city & is greatly respected here—He will be interesting to you on account of his efforts to improve the mode of preparing our black oak bark for exportation as a dye stuff & he goes to Washington to apply for a patent for his improvement. As Mr Benger can give you more information than I can do, relative to this new subject of Commerce, I will not tresspass upon your valuable time with any observations upon it.

With the warmest sensations of gratitude & esteem I beg leave to subscribe myself your obliged friend & servt

C. WISTAR JUNR

RC (DLC); at foot of text: "His Excellency The President of the United States"; endorsed by TJ. Recorded in SJL as received 24 Jan.

Later in the month, Thomas BENGER received a patent for "improvement in preparing quercitron or black oak bark for exportation or home consumption, for dying or other uses" (*List of Patents*, 39; Madison, *Papers, Sec. of State Ser.*, 6:355).

From Thomas Worthington

SIR   Washington Jany 17th 1804.

I am requested by the Governor of Ohio to enclose to you a resolution passed by the Legislature of that state

You have no doubt been informed of the agreement of that Legislature to the amendment proposed to the constitution of the United States   The law giveing their assent to the amendment has been officially transmitted by the Governor to the Speaker of the H of Representatives of the U. States & by that house deposited in the office of the secy of State—

I take this oppertunity of offering you my sincere congratulations on the possession of Louisiana—With sincere Respect & esteem I have the honour to be Sir your Obt St—   T WORTHINGTON

RC (DLC); at foot of text: "The president of the U States"; endorsed by TJ as received 17 Jan. and so recorded in SJL. Enclosure: resolution of the Senate and House of Representatives of Ohio requesting that Governor Edward Tiffin forward a certified copy of the legislature's act of 30 Dec. 1803 declaring assent to the proposed Twelfth Amentment to the Speaker of the U.S. House of Representatives (see *Acts of the State of Ohio: Second Session of* the General Assembly . . . *One Thousand Eight Hundred and Three* [Chillicothe, 1804], 56-9; *Journal of the Senate of the State of Ohio: Second Session of the Legislature held under the Constitution of the State, A.D. 1803* [Chillicothe, 1803], 65; *Journal of the House of Representatives of the State of Ohio. Second Session of the Legislature held under the Constitution of the State, A.D. 1803* [Chillicothe, 1803], 66-9).

From Albert Gallatin

DEAR SIR   Jany. 18th 1804

Mr Harvie called on me this evening to inform me of his being selected to carry the stock to France and wishing that this might be ready to morrow. The Stock is ready; but there are two circumstances to be attended to.

In the course of the transaction, I have always reminded Mr Pichon that we were neither bound to transmit the stock nor liable for any accidents which might attach to the transmission; but that desirous of assisting in every thing which was convenient for the French Government, we would transmit the stock in such manner & by such means as he would himself select: and I have obtained from him an official letter stating that the Warrant of the Secretary to the Register of the Treasury to deliver one third of the stock, and to transmit the other two thirds, was to be considered & held as a complete fulfilment of the engagement entered into by the United States to transfer the stock within three months after the exchange of[1] ratifications; and in the same letter which is also signed by Baring & Addressed to the Register, this officer is directed by them to transmit the stock by the first public vessel or safe opportunity. It was at the same time verbally agreed that Mr Pichon should pay the extra expence of the provision vessel touching at a French port, and also that the stock should be placed under the care of an officer of our navy. The selection of your private Secretary must appear so eligible to him that he certainly will not object; but I think that in order to guard against any possible accident it is proper to obtain his assent in writing to Mr Harvie being the bearer.

The other consideration is that of expence. Doubting, as we were not bound to transmit the stock, of the authority of incurring expence for that object, I put down a few days ago in a small additional estimate of appropriations sent to the Committee of ways & means, an item, for the printing & transmission of the certificates, of 1500 dollars. In the mean while it seems proper that the expence should not be larger than necessary. By the arrangement with Mr Smith, as an officer was to be the bearer, no other would have been incurred than the price of his passage to & from Europe; and it was intended that he should leave the stock to our Consul at the first French port and should proceed in the provision ship to Gibraltar where he might join the squadron if wanted, or return in the vessel. If Mr Harvie shall go is it intended that the same course should be followed? or is he to go to Paris? In either case is he to receive a compensation [. . .] paying his passage? and if so from what fund [shall it] be paid if the proposed appropriation should not pass? I will call to morrow morning on you, but send this letter in order that you may be ready to decide as Mr Harvie told me that he wished to go immediately as far as Richmond. Should he, when arrived there, find it inconvenient for family reasons not to proceed, provision must also be made for the mode of transmitting the stock from thence to Norfolk.

I enclose the sketch of a letter intended for Mr Pichon.

With sincere respect & attachment Your obedt. Servt.

ALBERT GALLATIN

RC (DLC); torn; addressed: "The President of the United States"; endorsed by TJ as received from the Treasury Department on 19 Jan. and "mr Harvie's mission" and so recorded in SJL. Enclosure not found.

The letter of 16 Jan. that Louis André Pichon and Alexander Baring ADDRESSED TO THE REGISTER, Joseph Nourse, called for the stock to be transmitted to Robert R. Livingston "by the first vessel belonging to or chartered by the United States which may be bound to France or any other safe opportunity." In the meantime, Nourse was to keep the certificates in his custody, "it being understood and agreed that your delivery of one third of the said certificates, and the warrant of the secretary of the Treasury authorizing you to transmit the remaining two thirds are a fulfillment of the engagement taken on the part of the United States" (FC in DNA: RG 53, RES; J. E. Winston and R. W. Colomb, "How the Louisiana Purchase was Financed," *Louisiana Historical Quarterly*, 12 [1929], 233).

ASSENT IN WRITING TO MR HARVIE: on 20 Jan., Pichon informed Gallatin that enlisting the president's private secretary to deliver the Lousiana stock "cannot but be extremely acceptable to Me." He requested that Gallatin "lay before the President my best and most respectfull acknowledgements for a determination which while it ensures the transmission of the Stock, cannot fail to be highly gratifying to the Chief Consul of France" (Tr in DLC; endorsed by TJ as received from the Treasury Department on 20 Jan. and "mr Harvie's mission"; FC in DNA: RG 53, RES). The act of 14 Mch. 1804 included a $1,500 appropriation to cover the expense of PRINTING and TRANSMISSION of the certificates (U.S. Statutes at Large, 2:264-5). The administration expected a provision ship sailing from NORFOLK to serve as the conveyance for the stock (NDBW, 3:321-2).

[1] Preceding two words interlined.

From Timothy Pickering

City of Washington
January 18. 1804.

Mr. Pickering presents his respects to the President, and returns the copy of Crozat's grant from Louis XIV. with his thanks. The grant is not what Mr. P. supposed, of the *province* of Louisiana, but a *monopoly* of its *commerce*, for 15 years; with some specific property therein, the value of which, and its tenure, were to depend on his labour and expence in cultivation and improvement. But in relation to boundaries, the description of the province is not sufficiently definite; appearing, on the western side of the Mississipi, to be applicable no farther northward than to the lands watered by the Missouri, and on the eastern side no farther than the Illinois; the country north of the Illinois being a part of Canada, or New-France: But its utmost extent northward can be only to embrace the country watered by the Mississipi above the Missouri. And Mr. P. conceives that nothing can be gained by assuming for the northern boundary of Louisiana, the highlands which divide the waters of the Mississipi from those which run into Hudson's Bay. There seems little room to doubt, but that a parallel of latitude striking the northern source of the Mississipi which is nearest to the Lake of the Woods, would leave all its other sources to its south, and comprehend a considerable range of country to the north of them.

Considering all the Hudson's Bay territory North of *Canada* as indisputably assigned to Great Britain under the treaty of Utrecht; and all the country, to which France had any pretensions, *east of the Mississipi* (except the island of New-Orleans)—by the treaty of Paris of 1763;—the only question remaining (if indeed any remained) between G. Britain & France, would respect the boundary between Louisiana & that part of the Hudson's Bay territory which adjoins it on the North. And notwithstanding the long detail yesterday submitted to the President, Mr. Pickering wishes, by way of illustration, to present the subject in one more point of view.

Let France be still considered as the proprietor of Louisiana, and consequently, pursuant to the treaty of 1763, that the Mississipi, from its source downward, is the common boundary of that province on the west, and of the British territory on its east side; and the limits of the Hudson's Bay territory, where it joins the north side of Louisiana, undefined:—Let each of those two Powers stand at the source of the Mississipi, and contend about their common boundary line from thence westward. Let France attempt to incline it to the North of West; and Great Britain make an equal effort to incline it South of West; their rights, and consequently their moral powers, being equal:— What would be the result?—They must necessarily concur in moving precisely on a middle line; and that is the parallel of latitude which touches the source of the Mississipi. Like two equal powers in mechanics, applied to move one body, each drawing it towards itself, but each exactly counteracted by the other,—the body moves on precisely in a middle line between them.

RC (DLC); endorsed by TJ. FC (MHi: Pickering Papers, 38:72-73). FC (same, 51:71-74). Recorded in SJL as received 18 Jan. Enclosure: copy of charter to Antoine Crozat (see TJ to Pickering, 15 and 16 Jan.).

BY WAY OF ILLUSTRATION: although there is no evidence that Pickering here enclosed it, he drew a map demonstrating the 47° 37′ boundary line that he believed appropriate. The line extended indefinitely from the northernmost source of the Mississippi River, six minutes above what the map displayed as a northern tributary of the Missouri. The boundary constituted something of a midway point between the northwest corner of the Lake of the Woods and a tributary of the Mississippi, well to the south of the northernmost source. Although he did not label the tributary, Pickering appears to have had the St. Peter's, or Minnesota, River in mind. In the longer analysis he enclosed two days earlier, Pickering worried that if negotiations over the northwest boundary were reopened, the British might be emboldened to pursue a more remote and more southern source of the Mississippi as an appropriate boundary marker (MS in MHi: Pickering Papers, 51:77-8; endorsed by Pickering: "Sketch, to represent N. West Boundaries").

To Joel Barlow

DEAR SIR   Washington Jan. 19. 04.

Permit me to introduce to your friendly attentions the bearer mr Harvie. he is a young gentleman of the first order of talents, education, standing, and prospect in our country. he is the son of my particular friend, and with a view to prepare him for the public scene on which he will shortly enter, I invited him to become a member of my family for about a twelvemonth, in order that he might gain a general view of our affairs. he has lived with me as a secretary, and avails himself of a special occasion of making a short visit to France & England, & to return in autumn. he is a discreet & highly honourable young man. he can give you perfect information as to the state of politics & parties here. in particular he can satisfy you that federalism is in it's last agonies, & that we want nothing now but for you to come & write it's history. a more instructive lesson can never be offered to our country. and this is the spot where alone it can be written. Marshal is engaged in writing a libel on republicanism under the mask of a history of Genl. Washington. the antidote is reserved for you. you will find this a pleasant residence, good society, living in a plain unexpensive way: and the climate really excellent. in hopes it will not be long before you see us, I tender you my friendly salutations and assurances of great esteem & respect.   TH: JEFFERSON

RC (MH); addressed: "Joel Barlow esq. Paris"; with notation "by mr Harvie," which TJ canceled with notation "mr Harvie has declined going"; endorsed by Barlow. PrC (DLC). Recorded in SJL and connected by a bracket with entries for Robert R. Livingston, Pierre Samuel Du Pont de Nemours, and Fulwar Skipwith at 19 Jan. and George W. Erving at 20 Jan.; TJ later canceled the Livingston, Skipwith, and Erving entries.

As indicated by TJ's note on the address sheet, Lewis HARVIE, in the end, declined going to Paris. His decision was known by 4 Feb., when Gallatin queried TJ on how the stock should be sent. On 7 Feb., Gallatin informed Joseph Nourse that it "not being practicable for Harvie to go to France," John B. Nicholson, a Navy midshipman, would give a receipt for the stock certificates and deliver them to Lieutenant James T. Leonard in New York. Robert Smith gave Nicholson his assignment on the same day, noting that if Leonard could not carry the dispatches, "you are to proceed with them to France yourself, under such instructions as you may receive from the Secretary of the Treasury." On 7 Feb., Gallatin also informed Madison of Harvie's decision and noted that he needed passports for Nicholson and Leonard as soon as possible, as Nicholson was directed to depart for New York the next day. On 13 Feb., Leonard gave Nicholson a receipt for the stock certificates. Leonard delivered the stock to Robert R. Livingston on 25 Apr. He also delivered the correspondence and dispatches he carried to Paris for TJ and Madison, including this letter to Barlow (Gallatin to Nourse, 7 Feb. 1804, in DNA: RG 56, PFLP; receipts signed by Leonard and Livingston in same; NDBW,

3:396; Madison, *Papers, Sec. of State Ser.*, 8:575-6; Barlow to TJ, 26 June; Leonard to TJ, 8 Aug. 1804).

MY PARTICULAR FRIEND: John Harvie of Belvidere (Vol. 39:363n).

For TJ's 1802 attempt to convince Barlow to write a HISTORY to counter John Marshall's *Life of George Washington*, see Vol. 37:400-1 and Vol. 38:406-7.

To Pierre Samuel Du Pont de Nemours

DEAR SIR   Washington Jan. 19. 1804.

Mr Harvie, a young gentleman who has lived with me since the departure of Captn. Lewis on his expedition up the Missouri, making a short visit to Paris, I have thought I ought not to deny him the advantage of your acquaintance. he has fine talents, great information, is moral & honourable. he is destined by his genius, acquirements and standing in society to run the career of political honour in our country, and perhaps no young man has entered on it with better prospects. your attentions & counsels[1] will be useful to him & gratifying to me. he carries the stock created for the purchase of Louisiana, and by the delivery of that closes the transaction, the country having been delivered to us on the 20th. of December. this acquisition, by removing from us all prospect of necessary war, has given great joy to our country; in which I am sure of your sincere participation. mr Harvie will be able to give you our political details, and to inform you that federalism is here in it's last agonies. as you know all the wickedness of it's principles, you will feel an interest for us in this information. we are preparing a form of government for the Territory of Orleans. by this name we call the lower division of Louisiana, which will be divided from the upper by an East & West line 10. miles North of Nachitoches on the Red river, about the Lat. of 32°. we shall make it as mild & free, as they are as yet able to bear, all persons residing there concurring in the information that they are neither qualified, nor willing, to exercise the rights of an elective government. the immense swarm flocking thither of Americans used to that exercise, will soon prepare them to recieve the necessary change. present me respectfully, to Made. Dupont, and accept my affectionate salutations, and assurances of constant esteem.

TH: JEFFERSON

PrC (DLC); at foot of text: "M. Dupont"; endorsed by TJ in ink on verso.

[1] Word and ampersand interlined.

To Timothy Pickering

Jan. 19. 04.

Th: Jefferson presents his compliments to the honble mr Pickering
and returns him the paper on the subject of boundary with thanks for
the communication. he acknoleges the ingenuity of the views it presents, but thinks they can be combated on very solid ground, and that
it is our duty to meet them. he thinks it impossible that an express
stipulation that we shall go to the N. Western point of the lake of the
Woods in 49°–37′ and thence due West, can ever be made to give
way to a mere inference that Gr. Br. was to come to the navigable
waters of the Missisipi, which inference she has already given up in
the convention before us, and is shewn to be not a necessary one, as
her right of navigation to the source would have been admitted &
satisfied by her obtaining from Spain a right to enter the river at it's
mouth. should Gr. Br. delay the rectification of the Vth. article, she
will certainly not refuse to leave it for a separate convention & ratify
at once so much of this as relates to the North Eastern angle, which
we shall urge her to do, so as to run that line in 1805. which is as early
as it could be done, were we now to ratify this convention.

RC (MHi: Pickering Papers). PrC (DLC). Enclosure: see enclosure to Pickering to
TJ, 16 Jan. (second letter).

From Thomas Appleton

SIR   Leghorn 20th January 1804.

The two letters you did me the honor to write under date of the 5th
and 13th of July last, have lately reached my hands.—In the course of
a month an opportunity will present for Baltimore, by which conveyance I shall reply particularly to both, and likewise ship the Wine you
are desirous to obtain, as that quality can only be procured at florence.

By the same vessel you will receive, Sir, a small case containing
a few bottles as samples of the best wines which are the growth of
Tuscany.—I am in hourly expectation of an answer from a friend at
Rome whom I have charged, in the manner you have directed me,
with the business relative to Madme. Cerachy.

I have requested my brother-in-law Saml. Emery of Philadelphia, to receive from on board the Ship Hannah Capt. Yardsly bound to that port, and forward to you, two small cases, and an earthen Vase of strawberry plants, I have shipped by the desire of Mr. Mazzei. —

Accept Sir the assurances of the high respect and esteem with which I am Your devoted Servant TH: APPLETON

RC (MHi); at foot of text: "The President of the United States Washington"; endorsed by TJ as received 13 Apr. and so recorded in SJL. FC (Lb in DNA: RG 84, CR, Leghorn); with postscript: "N.B. The above was sent by the Ship Hannah and sailed 6th. february."

TJ's letter of 13 JULY to Appleton is recorded in SJL but has not been found.

To William Brent

SIR   Washington, Jan. 20. [04.]

The departure of mr Harvie for Europe within a day or two, will leave the office of my private secretary again vacant. a continuance of the same sentiments with respect to yourself, induces a repetition of the offer, under the possibility that the reasons on your part for declining it may not continue. I shall willingly admit every accomodation which may reconcile the few duties it will superadd to the prosecution of your present pursuits. an answer in the course of a day or two will oblige me. Accept my salutations & best wishes.

TH: JEFFERSON

PrC (DLC); torn; at foot of text: "Capt. William Brent"; endorsed by TJ in ink on verso.

When it became clear that Meriwether Lewis would step down as secretary to assume command of the western expedition, TJ made an OFFER of the post to Brent, who had inquired about the position at the beginning of TJ's presidency. Brent turned it down in February 1803, citing the need to establish himself in business (Vol. 33:241-2; Vol. 39:598n).

From George Clinton

DEAR SIR   Albany January 20th. 1804.

I am highly gratified by the generous and very friendly Sentiments expressed in your Letter of the 31st: of last Month—It was far from my Intention however to have given you the trouble of replying to the one I addressed to you.

I most sincery[1] wish the pleasing hope you cherish of the increase of republicanism may be realized in its full extent; but candor oblidges me to confess that my expectations are less sanguine. this difference may be owing to the despondency incident to old Age and ill health and I shall rejoice to find myself misstaken—I calculate little upon the Return of deserters at this late Hour, shou'd they come back it will be from interested Motives, and tho they may increase our Numbers they will add nothing to our strength and by deceiving us into a false calculation of our Force our exertions will be relaxed—If this shoud be the Case their return will be an Injury—The prevailing Itch for Office threatens much Danger from the discord which competions[2] always occasion; besides everyone of this numerous & sordid Tribe of Office Hunters has, in his own Opinion, a strong Claim to the favours of Government either for what he has done, said or Thought—They cannot (& ought not) all be gratified and disapointment will put an end to their patriotism—In this State we are however at present able to effect any good Thing we please to undertake and as it is uncertain how long this may be the Case it will be wise in us to embrace this favourable Juncture & fill the important Office I now hold with some suitable Character not so far advanced in Years and enjoying a better share of health—Under this impression it is my Intention to decline a reelection—prudential Considerations however forbid publishing this determination at present—The partiality of my Friends who overrate my Services & personal influence will I am apprehensive be opposed to this Measure, but as they must be sensible that my health (delicate at best) is impaired, by the incessant Care & confinement which the Duties of this Office impose on me—I flatter myself this will induce them to acquiese.

I intreat you to be assured that when releived from Command, invalid as I am, I shall return to the Ranks and with unabated Zeal assist in defending the ground we have gained

With high Respect & Esteem I am yours Sincerely

GEO: CLINTON

RC (DLC); endorsed by TJ as received 29 Jan. and so recorded in SJL.

[1] Thus in MS.
[2] Thus in MS.

ONE I ADDRESSED TO YOU: Clinton to TJ, 22 Dec. 1803.

To Nicolas Gouin Dufief

SIR   Washington Jan. 20. 1804.

I am desirous to obtain two copies of the New testament in Greek or Greek & Latin, both of the same edition exactly; and two others in English, both also of the same edition; and all four of the same format, that they may admit being bound up together. the format to be either 8vo. or 12mo. but the latter of preference. will you be so good as to endeavor to procure these for me? Accept my salutations and best wishes.   TH: JEFFERSON

PrC (DLC); at foot of text: "Mr. Dufief."; endorsed by TJ in ink on verso.

The COPIES OF THE NEW TESTAMENT were intended for "The Philosophy of Jesus," TJ's assemblage of English-language biblical verses (EG, 45-9; TJ to Joseph Priestley, 29 Jan.).

To Thomas T. Hewson

SIR   Washington Jan. 20. 1804.

The renewed evidence of regard which I recieve through you from the American Philosophical society, calls for my grateful acknolegements. the suffrage of a body of men, of the first order of science, associated for the purposes of enlightening the mind of man, of multiplying his physical comforts improving his moral faculties, and enlarging the boundaries of his knowledge in general, is a testimonial which I cherish among those most dear to me.

After making my just acknolegements to the society for their favors, I add congratulations on the enlarged field of unexplored country lately opened to free research. should the unknown regions of Louisiana attract the attentions of the friends of science, such facilities and patronage as are within the limits of it's authority will be cordially afforded by a government founding it's security & best hopes in the knolege of it's citizens, not in their ignorance.

I pray you to present my high respect to the society, and to accept yourself assurances of my great consideration.

TH: JEFFERSON

RC (PPAmP); addressed: "Mr. Thomas T. Hewson Secretary of the A. Philosophl. Society Philadelphia"; franked and postmarked; endorsed for the APS. PrC (DLC).

PRESENT MY HIGH RESPECT: TJ's message was read before the assembled members at the American Philosophical Society's meeting of 3 Feb. (APS, *Proceedings*, 22, pt. 3 [1884], 347).

From Thomas McKean

SIR   Lan: Jany. 20th. 1804

I have the honor to transmit to you, an exemplified copy of an Act of the General Assembly of the Commonwealth of Pennsylvania entitled "An Act to ratify on behalf of the State of Pennsylvania, an amendment to the Constitution of the United States relative to the choosing of a President and Vice President of the United States" and am, with great consideration, and respect,

Sir, your most obedt. Servant   THOMAS M:KEAN

FC (Lb in PHarH); at foot of text: "Thomas Jefferson President of the United States." Recorded in SJL as received from Lancaster on 25 Jan. with notation "ratifn. S." Enclosure: see below.

EXEMPLIFIED COPY: on 20 Jan., Timothy Matlack, master of the rolls for

Pennsylvania, certified a copy of the Pennsylvania act to ratify the Twelfth Amendment as approved by McKean on 7 Jan. (DNA: RG 11, RA). As noted in SJL, TJ sent the document to the State Department.

To the Portsmouth, Virginia, Baptist Society

GENTLEMEN   Washington Jan. 20. 04.

It is some time since I recieved a letter from you of which it has not been in my power sooner to make the acknolegements justly due for it.

The satisfaction which you express, on behalf of the Baptist society of the town of Portsmouth, with the course of the present administration in general, and particularly with the substitution of economy for taxation, & the progress and prospect exhibited of the discharge of our public debt within a convenient period, is a proof of that soundness of political principle which your society has manifested generally through our Union: and the preference you give to the late acquisition of territory by just & peaceable means, rather than by rapine & bloodshed, is in the genuine spirit of that primitive Christianity, which so peculiarly inculcated the doctrines of peace, justice, and good will to all mankind.

The important services for which our country is indebted to the talents and integrity of my fellow-labourers, merit, as they have recieved, your just praise: and the expression of it adds much to the satisfaction I derive from the approbation of measures to which they so [universally] contribute. if it be ambition zealously to pursue the advancement of the public liberty & prosperity, we feel that ambition and deem it lawful and laudable; and we covet no honour beyond that which will follow a faithful discharge of the duties of our nation.

I pray you to accept, for yourselves, & the society of which you are members, assurances of my great respect.　　TH: JEFFERSON

PrC (DLC); blurred; at foot of text: "Messrs. Davis Biggs & John Foster." I RECIEVED A LETTER FROM YOU: the society addressed TJ on 12 Nov. 1803 (Vol. 41:710-11).

From Thomas Bedwell

SIR,　　　　　　　　　　　　　Philada Jany 21st 1804.

altho I am conscious that I am guilty of great impropriety in thus taking this liberty of addressing you, yet I have presumed notwithstanding, depending as an apology only on the supposed importance of a discovery which I thought too interesting if successful not to communicate—Having had repeated opportunities in a particular manufactory to observe the effects of a solution of Iron upon the parts of Oaken Vessels, in giving them solidity and the means of resistance to the action of the Atmosphere; I was led step by step to an investigation of the same, and which was rather accelerated by an additional proof which I conceived I had obtained—Vessels whose plank and Timbers have been destroyed by the length of time they have been in employ, together with the action of the Worm, have uniformly when broke up exhibited the following curious facts, that altho the Timber with which the Vessel had been formd was evidently in a high state of decay, Yet wherever an Iron Bolt, spike or large piece of that Metal was introduc'd, the wood to the distance of a few inches around was undecay'd and untouch'd by the Worm it had also assumed an indurated appearance bordering upon a petrifactive nature, and in all cases strongly attach'd to the Metal, this circumstance added to the afore-recited observations stimulated me to make som regular experiments to bring forward proofs of its utility and application—In the course of these experiments I have successively try'd the effects of the Solution of Iron in the Acids of Vitriol Salt and Nitre, from the Whole of these I always found, that the Wood after long immersion was much hardened, and had assumed a Black or dark Blue appearance, this change of colour I had expected from the well known action of the Gallic Acid on solutions of Iron, with this I found that the effect of the Metal had produced a still greater and more essential alteration, it had introduced and lodged in the pores of the Wood an irreducible precipitate evidently calcareous and Metalic, which added both to its weight as well as solidity—Satisfied with the variety and results of my experiments, I presumed it might be of real service in preserving such Timber as might be employed for the Building Sea Vessels, Bridges &'c but felt at the same time assured that the Modes I had made use of were too expensive, and difficult, for common Use I now varied my process in such a manner as to reduce it to a system of Economy—I placed my Wood in a suitable vessel and kept it below the water by loading it with small pieces of Iron Ore, of the hard or Mountain kind, I continued it in this state for Three Months, at the expiration of which I took it out and let it dry thoroughly. I now found it was of a Black colour to within a few lines of the center and so excessively hard as hardly to admit the action of a good knife—The Colour had penetrated by different shades to near the middle, which was in its first state from which to the outside edge the various effects of meliorations were extreemly evident—succeeding so far in the economy of the process and without sensibly altering the nature of it, I have presumed that works of considerable magnitude might be set on foot at a very small expence—Pits might be sunk in a soil capable of retaining water at the bottom of which might be introduced a layer of Iron Ore, upon that layers of Timber and Ore &&& might be placed till the same were filled allowing room for Water to form the upper surface at least one foot over the whole, it might now be left in this situation for Nine—Twelve or Eighteen Months, as the Bulk of Timber might require—The advantage I expect to result from this mode of treatment would be, not only an additional solidity to the wood but a property of resistance capable of securing it from the attack of the Worm to which may be added, that the Gallic Acid would be exhausted or rendered inert; consequently Iron Bolts spikes &c might be again introduced with perfect safety—

This Sir is the purport of my address to you and in which I have been as brief as possible so as to convey my Idea. should you conceive it of sufficient merit to engage your Notice I shall esteem myself particularly and highly honoured—for the above Sir give me leave to add, that I expect no kind of reward or pecuniary gratification, notwithstanding which I should esteem it a happy circumstance should my abilities as Assayer and Mineralist be thought of sufficient weight to attract your notice, and as in this instance of offering them to your consideration I might not be thought too presuming, permit me to add I can produce every testimony of Character from Men of the highest Respectabillity—with the Greatest Respect

I have the Honr. to remain Your Excellency's most Humble & Obdt Servt   THO BEDWELL

[323]

RC (DLC); endorsed by TJ as received 25 Jan. and so recorded in SJL.

Thomas Bedwell (ca. 1748-1831) held several patents, both in his own name and in partnership with others, for improvements in tanning, dyeing, and evaporation. In his varied career, he manufactured sulfur for Continental forces during the American Revolution; participated in business partnerships in linen printing, engraving, printing, tanning, and dye manufacturing; and promoted ventures in coal and lead mining before finally settling as a druggist in Philadelphia (*List of Patents*, 4, 10, 24, 34; Paul H. Smith and others, eds., *Letters of Delegates to Congress, 1774–1789*, 26 vols. [Washington, D.C., 1976–2000], 4:518; *Pennsylvania Evening Post*, 30 May 1775, 16 July 1776; *Pennsylvania Packet*, 14 Aug., 25 Sep., 30 Dec. 1779; Philadelphia *Independent Gazetteer*, 5 July 1783; *Dunlap's American Daily Advertiser*, 17 Aug. 1793; *Albany Gazette*, 25 July 1796; *Philadelphia Inquirer*, 15 Nov. 1831; Vol. 27:804).

From Anne Cary Randolph

Edgehill Jan. 21 1804

I recieved my Dear Grand Papa's letter but it was too late to answer it' Jefferson will not let Ellen catch him for he is now translating the history of Cyrus by Xenophon I will very gladly untertake to raise a pair of Bamtams for Monticello if you will send them to me I am very sorry to inform you that the plank house is burnt down John Hemming's was here last night and he told us that the floor of the hall and the Music gallery was burnt up and that it was as full of plank as it could of which not one inch was saved your ice house will be full by ten oclock today I suppose you have heard of Aunt Bolling's death Aunt Virginia is engaged to Cousin Wilson Cary and Aunt Hariet to a Mr Hackley of New York adieu My Dear Grand Papa your affectionate Grand daughter ACR

RC (MHi); endorsed by TJ as received 24 Jan. and so recorded in SJL.

PLANK HOUSE IS BURNT: John Wayles Eppes also received word from TJ's daughter Mary, who noted "the misfortune that has happen'd at Monticello" with "the burning of the plank house just after it had been completely fill'd with the flooring plank & timber for the cornices" (Mary Jefferson Eppes to John Wayles Eppes, 21 Jan., in ViU: Eppes Family Papers).

Thomas Mann Randolph's sister VIRGINIA married Wilson Jefferson Cary in August 1805 and moved to Carysbrook in Fluvanna County. Harriet Randolph, another sister, married Richard S. HACKLEY, a New York merchant who became a U.S. consul (DVB, 3:115-16; Vol. 35:266n; Vol. 38:418-19).

To Meriwether Lewis

My letters since your departure have been of July 11. & 15. Nov. 16. and Jan. 13. yours recievcd are of July 8. 15. 22. 25. Sep. 25. 30. & Oct. 3. since the date of the last we have no certain information of your movements. with mine of Nov. 16. I sent you some extracts made by myself from the journal of an agent of the trading company of St. Louis up the Missouri. I now inclose a translation of that journal in full for your information. in that of the 13th inst. I inclosed you the map of a mr Evans, a Welshman, employed by the Spanish government for that purpose, but whose original object I believe had been to go in search of the Welsh Indians, said to be up the Missouri. on this subject a mr Rees of the same nation, established in the Western parts of Pensylvania, will write to you. N. Orleans was delivered to us on the 20th. of Dec. and our garrisons & government established there. the order for the delivery of the Upper posts were to leave N. Orleans on the 28th. and we presume all those posts will be occupied by our troops by the last day of the present month. when your instructions were penned, this new position was not so authentically known as to affect the complection of your instructions. being now become sovereigns of the country, without however any diminution of the Indian rights of occupancy, we are authorised to propose to them in direct terms the institution of commerce with them. it will now be proper you should inform those through whose country you will pass, or whom you may meet, that their late fathers the Spaniards have agreed to withdraw all their troops from all the waters & country of the Missisipi & Missouri, that they have surrendered to us all their subjects Spanish & French settled there, and all their posts & lands: that henceforward we become their fathers and friends, and that we shall endeavor that they shall have no cause to lament the change: that we have sent you to enquire into the nature of the country & the nations inhabiting it, to know at what places and times we must establish stores of goods among them, to exchange for their peltries; that as soon as you return with the necessary information, we shall prepare supplies of goods and persons to carry them and make the proper establishments; that in the mean time, the same traders who reside among or visit them, and who now are a part of us, will continue to supply them as usual: that we shall endeavor to become acquainted with them as soon as possible; and that they will find in us faithful friends, & protectors. although you will pass through no settlements of the Sioux (except seceders) yet you will probably meet with parties of them. on that nation we wish most particularly to make a friendly impression, because of their immense power, and because we learn that they are very desirous of being on the most friendly terms with us.

I inclose you a letter which I believe is from some one on the part of the Philosophical society. they have made you a member, and your diploma is lodged with me; but I suppose it safest to keep it here, & not to send it after you. mr Harvie departs tomorrow for France, as the bearer of the Louisiana stock to Paris. Capt. William Brent takes his place with me. Congress will probably continue in session through the month of March. your friends here & in Albemarle as far as I recollect are well. Trist will be the Collector of N. Orleans, & his family will go to him in the spring. Dr. Bache is now in Philadelphia & probably will not return to N. Orleans. Accept my friendly salutations & assurances of affectionate esteem & respect.

Th: Jefferson

PrC (DLC); at foot of first page: "Capt Meriwether Lewis." Enclosures not found, but see TJ to Lewis, 16 Nov. 1803, and John Vaughan to TJ, 21 Nov.

YOURS RECIEVED: TJ gave incorrect dates for several of the letters received from Lewis. That of 26 July 1803 he called 25 July, and he identified Lewis's of 8 and 13 Sep. by their dates of receipt, 25 and 30 Sep., respectively.

According to popular legend, the WELSH INDIANS were the descendants of Prince Madoc of Wales, who allegedly discovered and colonized America in the twelfth century. Enthusiasm for the myth of Madoc's North American descendants reached its peak in the late eighteenth and early nineteenth centuries, and it was popularly believed that Welsh-speaking Indians resided along the upper reaches of the Missouri River. The legend inspired mapmaker John Thomas Evans to leave Wales to seek out his imaginary kinsmen in the 1790s. Among the other Welshmen taken with the story was Morgan John Rhys (REES), a radical Baptist minister who raised money in Wales to spread the gospel among the Welsh Indians before emigrating to America himself in the late 1790s, where he became acquainted with Evans and his mission. Rhys traveled widely in the United States before abandoning his ministry and settling in Somerset County, Pennsylvania, where he died in December 1804 (DNB, s.v. "Madog ab Owain Gwynedd" and "Rhys, Morgan John"; W. Raymond Wood, *Prologue to Lewis and Clark: The Mackay and Evans Expedition* [Norman, Okla., 2003], 40, 42-6, 193-5).

From Joseph Clay, Jacob Richards, and Frederick Conrad

SIR   Washington 23d. Jany. 1804.

Our friend and colleague Michael Leib has signified to us his intention of retiring from public duties. As we are most immediately connected with him, we feel it due to him, to ourselves, and to our common cause, to offer to you our sentiments, and our recommendation of him to your attention. Carrying with him into retirement nothing but the bruises of warfare and the consciousness of having faithfully performed his duty, permit us to ask of you another reward for him, your approbation of his conduct in an appointment in case of vacancy, to one of the ministerial offices in Pennsylvania, dependant upon you. We conceive that he is entitled to such a situation on the score of his services, of his fitness, and of public confidence. Persecuted and reviled for years by the utmost rage and malice of our political opponents, he has notwithstanding met with the constant support of the genuine friends of our principles and of the constitution, and to their reiterated approbation of him evinced in his repeated elections, we beg leave to refer in corroboration of our own sentiments and of our own testimonial in his favor.

It can hardly have escaped your notice that a party whose object it is, in conjunction with the federalists, to overthrow the existing state of things, is coming fast into existence and strength in our State. We consider this party as equally hostile with those with whom they are combined, to the true interests of our country; if some decisive countenance be not given to those who have heretofore braved the tempest, we much fear that listlessness may succeed to activity, apathy to vigor, and the usual energies being withdrawn, the triumph of faction may be the result. This we sincerely deprecate, and with deference we suggest, that the notice of our friend will, in our quarter, have a salutary influence against such an evil.

We are not ignorant that our friend has enmity and opposition to encounter even from some who profess attachment to our cause; for this we might be, in some measure, able to account. We might trace it to fear lest his talents and the confidence reposed in him by the public, should enable him to frustrate the designs of those who are desirous of possessing unlimited controul over the affairs of Pennsylvania; a fear which, in some instances, has produced hostility which not even the gratitude due for personal obligations has been able to eradicate.

Sincerely attached to your administraton and personally to you, we have, under the influence of this attachment declared our sentiments with a freedom, which, we trust will not be displeasing; if however we have erred in this opinion, we flatter ourselves that you will pardon the honest error of our zeal, and believe us when we assure you of our high respect and regard.

JOSEPH CLAY
JACOB RICHARDS
FREDK CONRAD

RC (NHi: Gallatin Papers); in Clay's hand, signed by all; addressed: "The President of the United States"; endorsed by TJ as received 23 Jan. and "Leib Michael to be in Customs Phila" and so recorded in SJL.

Joseph Clay from Philadelphia, Jacob Richards (1773-1816) from Delaware County, and Frederick Conrad (1759-1827) from Montgomery County were all first-term congressmen from Pennsylvania. Richards and Conrad served two terms. Clay, elected to a third term, resigned in 1808 to become a bank cashier. Richards, a University of Pennsylvania graduate, returned to the practice of law and received a commission as colonel of the Delaware County militia. Conrad, who earlier had served in the legislature, was appointed prothonotary and clerk of courts for Montgomerty County in 1821 (*Biog. Dir. Cong.*; *Kline's Carlisle Weekly Gazette*, 10 Nov. 1802; *Aurora*, 7, 26 Sep. 1804, 6 Sep. 1806; Reading, Pa., *Berks and Schuylkill Journal*, 17 Feb. 1821; Vol. 38:523, 524n).

IN CONJUNCTION WITH THE FEDERALISTS: in the fall of 1802, William Duane and others began accusing the more conservative Republicans of joining with the Federalists, especially in opposition to Michael Leib and in support of Thomas McKean (Higginbotham, *Pennsylvania Politics*, 61-5; Vol. 38:407-8, 421-2).

From Albert Gallatin

DEAR SIR   Jany. 23 1804.

It seems, upon the whole, more eligible that Mr Harvie should take his passage in a private vessel than in that which will be chartered from Norfolk. Mr Pichon thinks so, and I agree with him. Will you have the goodness to give the information to Mr Harvie, in order that he may make his arrangements. I will, if agreeable, write to the Collectors of New York and Baltimore in order to know what vessels will sail shortly for France or Holland, and on their information, the most proper for Mr H. to embark may be selected and his passage engaged. He may in the mean while, if he thinks proper go to Richmond in order to make his money arrangements; and it will be sufficient if he shall be here on the 1st Feby.

Respectfully Your obedt. Servt.   ALBERT GALLATIN

RC (DLC); at foot of text: "The President of the United States"; endorsed by TJ as received from the Treasury Department on 23 Jan. and "mr Harvie" and so recorded in SJL.

From Craven Peyton

DEAR SIR   Stump Island 23d Jany. 1804

I am sorry I did not get yours of the 16. instant time enough to of answered it by the return post. the draught given in favour of Mr. Higingbathom was on accompt. of corn furnished, all othar accompts being fully settled between us. at the time my giveing the draft I named to Mr. Higingbathom your convenience was to be consulted that I had rathar be pushed for money then for you to be. I will still meet the amt. at the time if it shoud not be convenient for you to do so. you will please let me no by post.

with great respt. yr. mst. Obt   C PEYTON

RC (ViU); endorsed by TJ as received 30 Jan. and so recorded in SJL.

MR. HIGINGBATHOM: that is, David Higginbotham.

To David Meade Randolph

SIR   Washington Jan. 23. 1804.

An appeal to the Executive, when justice is understood to be refused by any department, is always proper. on the receipt of your letter of the 10th inst. I inclosed it to the Secretary of the Treasury for explanations. the business lying within the Comptroller's line of duty, he has returned the answers which I now inclose you, and from which it would seem that the final liquidation of your account awaits certain explanations from yourself which have not yet been recieved. the settlement being thus placed within your own power, will I presume be finally closed with the promptitude which you desire. Accept my respectful salutations.   TH: JEFFERSON

PrC (MHi); at foot of text: "David M Randolph esq."; endorsed by TJ in ink on verso. Enclosure not found.

To Martha Jefferson Randolph

MY DEAR MARTHA   Washington Jan. 23. 04.

Our Milton post not having come in last night, we are without news from you. I suppose he has been delayed by the weather, a severe snow storm having begun yesterday morning & still continuing. the snow is supposed to be now a foot deep, and is still falling with unabated fury. as it is the first, so I hope it will be the last of our severe winter weather. it is so tempestuous that I presume Congress will hardly meet to-day; & the rather as they have nothing pressing. the little before them will permit them to proceed at leisure, and finish when they please, which I conjecture will be about the 2d. week of March. I expect that mr Eppes will leave it before it rises in order to be with Maria at the knock of the elbow in February. I hope

she will keep up her spirits. should she be later than she has calculated, perhaps we may all be with her. altho' the recurrence of those
violent attacks to which Francis is liable, cannot but give uneasiness
as to their character, yet be that what it will, there is little doubt but
he will out-grow them; as I have scarcely ever known an instance to
the contrary, at his age.—On Friday Congress give a dinner on the
acquisition of Louisiana. they determine to invite no foreign ministers, to avoid questions of etiquette, in which we are enveloped by
Merry's & Yrujo's families. as much as I wished to have had yourself
& sister with me, I rejoice you were not here. the brunt of the battle
now falls on the Secretary's ladies, who are dragged in the dirt of
every federal paper. you would have been the victims had you been
here, and butchered the more bloodily as they would hope it would
be more felt by myself. it is likely to end in those two families putting
themselves into Coventry until they recieve orders from their courts
to acquiesce in our principles of the equality of all persons meeting
together in society, & not to expect to force us into their principles of
allotment into ranks & orders. pour into the bosom of my dear Maria
all the comfort & courage which the affections of my heart can give
her, and tell her to rise superior to all fear, for all our sakes. kiss all
the little ones for me, with whom I should be so much happier than
here; and be assured yourself of my tender & constant love.

Th: Jefferson

RC (NNPM); at foot of text: "Mrs. M.
Randolph." PrC (ViU: Edgehill-Randolph
Papers); endorsed by TJ in ink on verso.

KNOCK OF THE ELBOW: TJ to Mary
Jefferson Eppes, 26 Dec. 1803.

On Friday, the 27th, a large body of congressmen, presided over by Samuel Smith,
gave a DINNER in honor of the peaceful
acquisition of Louisiana. The president,
vice president, department heads, and
other officers of government were invited.
TJ was escorted by several members of
both houses and leaders of the Washington militia to Stelle's Hotel, the place of
the banquet. A discharge of artillery announced his arrival, and a band played

"Jefferson's March" to welcome him.
"An assemblage so numerous," one paper
wrote, "to celebrate an event, at once so
glorious and so happy, may not occur
again for centuries to come" (Washington *Universal Gazette*, 2 Feb.).

BRUNT OF THE BATTLE: TJ was undoubtedly referring to a letter printed
initially in Philadelphia's *Gazette of the
United States* in which Dolley Madison,
Margaret Smith, Hannah Gallatin, and
especially Dorcas Osgood Dearborn faced
ridicule for offending Elizabeth Merry
(*Gazette of the United States*, 13 Jan.; Canons of Official Etiquette, [after 22 Dec.
1803]; TJ to William Short, 23 Jan.).

To William Short

Your favor of the 17th. is duly recieved; and consoles me under the chagrin of the necessity which had come upon me, contrary to my calculation but it will not lessen the devotion of my efforts to the main object. I had just before the reciept of your letter fallen on a bundle of papers which I had brought with me from Monticello to put into your hands. but they escaped my recollection & notice while you were here. they are now inclosed, and compose the whole of those I possess which concern your affairs.—you will have seen by the newspapers that there is something of etiquette between the diplomatic gentry & us. that there exists such a subject of disagreement is true. but every particular[1] fact respecting it which I have yet seen in any newspaper is false. mr & mrs Merry, M. & Mde. Yrujo claim at private dinners (for of public ones we have none) to be first conducted to dinner & placed at the head of the table above all other persons citizens or foreigners, in or out of office. we say to them, no; the principle of society with us, as well as of our political constitution, is the equal rights of all: and if there be an occasion where this equality ought to prevail preeminently, it is in social circles collected for conviviality. nobody shall be above you, nor you above anybody. pèle-mele is our law. as there is no lady in my family, I had made it a point when I invited female company to get the favor of one of the Secretary's ladies to come & take care of them; and as she was considered in some measure as assisting in the honors of the table, I led her to table myself, and naturally placed her by me. all others followed pele-mele. this had gone on for three years without exciting any jealousy that it was intended to give a rank to those ladies over their fellow citizens. it was generally understood, as a personal compliment to the lady who was so kind as to take the charge of my company of the other sex. you were present at the first & only dinner to which mr & mrs Merry have been invited by me. the next place they dined at was mr Madison's, where as in all private societies here, the pele-mele is the law; and[2] mrs Merry, happening, from the position where she was seated, not to be the foremost, Merry siesed her by the hand, led her to the head of the table, where mrs Gallatin happening to be standing, she politely offered her place to mrs Merry who took it without prudery or apology. since this she has declined dining, except at one or two private citizens', where it is said there were previous stipulations; she did not come here on the Newyear's day, where every person[3] of note, foreign or domestic, meets to interchange the compliments of the season, all mixed in the same room without the possibility of ceremony; and it is said the two families (Merry's & Yrujo's) mean to put themselves into Coventry until further orders from their court. mrs Merry's jealousy was the first admonition to me that my usage, at my social dinners, could be misconstrued into an attribution of precedence to the ladies of the Secretaries, and I have from that moment changed it, taking now by the hand whomever position places in my way; and those ladies themselves were the first to approve the change, as they had never pretended to precedence over their fellow citizens or others.[4] I thought it more honorable if an act of mine could be construed into a departure from the true principle of equality, to correct it at once & get into the right road, rather than by perseverance in what was incorrect, to entangle myself in inconsistencies. I presume the courts of these agents will have too much good sense to attempt to force on us their allotment of society into ranks or orders, as we have never pretended to force on them our equality. our ministers with them submit to the laws of their society; theirs with us must submit to ours. they plead the practices of my predecessors. these practices were not uniform: besides I have deemed it my duty to change some of their practices, and especially those which savoured of anti-republicanism. I have ever considered diplomacy as the pest of the peace of the world, as the workshop in which nearly[5] all the wars of Europe are manufactured. on coming into the administration I dismissed one half of our missions, & was nearly ripe to do so by the other half. the public opinion called for it, & would now be gratified by it: and as we wish not to mix in the politics of Europe, but in her commerce only, Consuls would do all the business we ought to have there, quite as well as ministers. certainly we have not suffered by the change at Lisbon, or Berlin, as to any legitimate concerns we had at either place. I do not however expect that the policy of London or Madrid will be to drive us into a completion of the a-diplomatic system. in all this business, Pichon has had the good sense to keep himself entirely aloof from it, and to go on as he had done for three years before. I did not mean when I entered on this subject to have detained you so long with it. but I am not sorry I have possessed you of the whole of it because you are much in society, and we really wish that it should be known to all correctly & according to truth. those especially who read the Gazette of the US. need to be set to rights, for in the long[6] statement which appeared in that paper about a week ago, there was not one single fact which was not false. I am happy to hear from you that there are some at least of our monied corps who do not maintain a spirit of opposition to the national will. every object of our wish, at home or abroad, is now satisfactorily accomplished, except the reduction of this mass of anti-civism which remains in our great trading towns. it is the only thing which ought now to occupy us, because tho' not $\frac{1}{25}$ of the nation, they command $\frac{3}{4}$ of it's public papers. that they should acquiesce in the will of the great majority is but a reasonable expectation, and no man knows the pressure which I have withstood to cover them from the besom of the public desire, I mean, as to a general sweep from office. those removed by me, otherwise than for default, are not more than one twenty fifth part of the whole I found[7] in office. yet for this twenty fifth I am the single object of their accumulated hatred. I do not care for this now. I did at first, because I had believed they would have had the justice to be satisfied that I did so little when goaded to do so much. they can never now excite a pain in my mind by any thing personal. but I wish to consolidate the nation, and to see these people disarmed either of the wish or the power to injure their country. the former is far the most desireable: but the attempt at reconciliation was honourably pursued by us for a year or two, & spurned by them, and never given up till it was seen to be desperate.

what you say induces me to hope this is not as universal as I had supposed. however that the body of them are in active opposition, we may conclude from the aspect of their newspapers which must be in unison with the minds of those who maintain them. above all the Gazette of the US. is evidence of this fact; because it is palpable that not only printers, but a body of writers, must be employed at the expence of individuals in publishing that paper, the most abandoned as to truth or decency of any one that ever was published in the US. this is palpable because it is a fact well known that no paper is maintained in this country by it's annual subscriptions. the advertisements constitute the whole profits of these papers. now the Gazette of the US. has scarcely ever a single advertisement. 4. pages of solid matter in small type, a great proportion of it original, & the whole so false and malignant, as shews it is prepared for the purpose of exportation, and to poison the minds of foreign countries against their own, which is too well informed to drink of the dose. still as long as a hope remains that either their own interests, or a despair of changing the nature of our government, will produce acquiescence voluntarily, this is devoutly to be attended as the most desireable way of doing, what must be done in some way, consolidating the nation.

If you pass another twelvemonth here, we shall hope to see you again in the South, and I think you cannot pass the months of August

& September in a more healthy place than Monticello where we shall all be happy to see you. Congress is likely to continue a couple of months longer. Accept my friendly salutations and assurances of constant affection.

TH: JEFFERSON

RC (MdBJ-G); at foot of first page: "Mr. Short"; endorsed by Short. Enclosures not found.

LONG STATEMENT WHICH APPEARED IN THAT PAPER: an "Extract of a letter from a gentleman at Washington, dated 2d January 1804," was published in the *Gazette of the United States* on 13 Jan. and was reprinted in the *Washington Federalist* on 30 Jan. The editors of the *Gazette* prefaced the account of repeated diplomatic slights to the Merrys by Washington society, claiming that Americans had "an unalienable right to be informed of the etiquette of our court" and reminded readers that during the last session of Congress, TJ had invited British chargé Edward Thornton to dine with him in the company of Thomas Paine. They queried, "What can be Mr. Jefferson's motives for these outrageous insults?"

[1] Word interlined.
[2] TJ here canceled "it happened that."
[3] Word written over "citizen."
[4] Preceding two words interlined.
[5] Word inserted in margin.
[6] Word interlined.
[7] Preceding two words interlined.

From David Austin

RESPECTED SIR.   Norwich, Cont: Jan'y 24th: 1804

The experience I have had of your candor, induces me to address you once more, on the State of the Nations, & on the state of our own Nation, in particular.

The peace of European Nations is not yet attained: nor can it be attained unless the means appointed to produce it, be carried to them or they come to us. —

I have a mind to clothe the pacific operations of your administration, with a glade of prophetic light, such as I perceive the Nation is entitled to receive, from the medium of providencial atmosphere in which it moves.

Could a station be given me at Washington, of easy employment, such as might afford but a decent support, I could, by illustrations of the prophetic aspects, soon cause our own nation, & other nations to see that the principles of the Pacific Economy, now sought by Divines & Philosophers were hidden, like a vein of silver, in the crevices of our National Rock.

Yesterday I prepared an Oration, introduced, as though delivered at the Capitol, on occasion of the accession of Louisiania &c to its relation to the U: States. — I think it would gratify you not a little, to hear it pronounced. — Should you haply find for me a place, at Washington, & leave me now & then an occasional opportunity for a display of the import of certain events as they pass in the light of pro-phetic inscription, I believe the present administration would find no occasion to repent the opportunity given for the illustration. The fact is your own mind seems in a perfect train, for the attainment of all the good which the powers of civil policy & philosophy can give: but in reference to a state, for which the Clergy of all denominations are looking, & which none of them can reach, suffer me to say, simply political administration scarcly is capable to reach it.—

I think the mind of the Moral & spiritual part of our Nation might as well be drawn towards the City of Washington, as the political: & as it were, the whole Nation launch into an higher state of elevation: such as should shew to nations abroad, that such things are done for us, as a Nation, as to the same extent were never done before.—

Your candid & modest remark, on casting your eye upon certain illustrations of the State of the Nations, which I had the honor to lay before you; invited my mind to a more candid adoption of a principle, more favorable to your interest, than before I had done. You said "it ought to succeed, beyond the present state of things was in the womb of providence, undoubtedly, Providence would raise up instruments to bring it about," or in words to that effect.—

The only question, now is whether opportunity shall be given for this development, under the patronage of the National wing: or whether it shall be left to generate its own existance in the New-England States.—

If through the Medium of national administration, pacific principles on the higher grade of moral expectation should be conveyed, it is evident that the Unity of National mind might more rapidly be pro-duced, than though truth, ever so evident, was left to the weight of its own innate powers.

I submit these thoughts, with all diffidence, for your consideration, & can assure you that nothing will be found in my views, discordant to the interests of the present administration; my hope being, that an accumulation of Moral good might be the effect of those labors to the Nation, of which your disposition & administration present so good a political copy.—

My residence is at Norwich; at which place, I should think myself honored by receiving the smallest testimony of yr. good Will:

& am with all esteem; & prayers for your prosperity.—

DAVID AUSTIN

RC (DLC); addressed: "Th: Jefferson Esqr. P:U:S. City of Washington"; franked; postmarked "Chelsea Landing in Norwich," 26 Jan.; endorsed by TJ as received 3 Feb. and so recorded in SJL.

The source of TJ's alleged REMARK to Austin is unknown. While residing in Washington from 1801 to 1802, Austin sent TJ several unsolicited writings and frequently offered to discuss them with the president in person (Vol. 34:279, 349-52, 463; Vol. 35:138-41, 176-8; Vol. 36:271-2, 395-6).

From Albert Gallatin

[on or before 24 Jan. 1804]

Is it proper to submit this letter to the Attorney general in order to examine whether prosecutions may be instituted under the Statute for actual opposition to the Marshal in the exercise of his legal functions? Or is it better not to notice the acts & to let the prosecutions for the riot take their course in the State courts?

Respectfully submitted   ALBERT GALLATIN

RC (DLC: TJ Papers, 146:25373); undated, but see below; at foot of text: "The President."

TJ's response to Gallatin of 24 Jan. and Levi Lincoln's opinion of [25 Jan.], which TJ recorded in SJL with the notation "Plymouth riot," indicate that the LETTER was one from Henry Warren, customs collector at Plymouth, Massachusetts, to the secretary of the Treasury, now missing. On 23 Dec., the *Columbian Courier, or Weekly Miscellany* at New Bedford provided information on the "*Riot at Plymouth*," noting that it took place at a public auction conducted by the deputy marshal on 16 Dec., where forfeited rum and molasses were being sold. A "mob" of 150 to 200 participants was determined "to abuse any person who should over bid the original owners." At least two individuals made bids and both were, reportedly, "shamefully abused." One had to be rescued "from the hands of the ruffians" by his friends, being "in so mangled and exhausted a situation that his life was at first despaired of." The observer hoped "that the instigators of so daring an outrage on the laws" would be punished.

To Albert Gallatin

TH:J. TO MR GALLATIN.   Jan. 24. 1804.

Mr. Harvie concludes not to go to Richmond. I think it would be best for you to write to Baltimore & N. York for information of every vessel in port, and to sail soon, & on what day, for any port on the Western coast of the Continent of Europe. this being known we can take our choice, and, without any previous engagement of passage, mr Harvie can arrive at Baltimore or N. York 24. hours before the departure of the vessel chosen, & engage his passage. N. York seems the port at which he would be soonest disengaged from British enterprize here; and the ports of Europe South of the channel those where he would be least likely to fall in with them on the European coast; the channel being probably full of their cruisers. of this however we have time enough to consider.—I have sent mr Warren's letter to the Atty Genl for his opinion.

other Questions to be considered, in the event of a British cruiser falling in with the vessel in which mr Harvie will be.

1. shall he throw the papers overboard on his vessel being brought to? or trust to an examination in hopes of liberation.

2. if detained, shall he deliver the stock to liberate his vessel? shall he accompany the stock to England? or abandon it & carry to Paris the information of what has happened?

RC (NHi: Gallatin Papers); addressed: "Mr. Gallatin." PrC (DLC).

WRITE TO BALTIMORE & N. YORK: on this day, Gallatin wrote to Robert Purviance, collector at Baltimore, requesting immediate information on any American vessels at the port "bound to France or Holland on which a passage may be obtained for a gentleman who goes with public dispatches." A vessel whose char-

acter and cargo were "clearly neutral" was "preferable." Gallatin required the precise time when the vessel expected to sail, "but the object for which the information is wanted need not be mentioned further than may be necessary to ascertain whether a passage can be obtained" (Gallatin, *Papers*, 9:181).

For WARREN'S LETTER, see the preceding document.

From Gideon Granger

Jan: 24. 1804—

G Granger presents his Compliments to the President—he returns Mr. Eppes letter—Joseph Jones Esq is P.M. at Petersburg.—

He is fearfull that the line of Intelligence from Fort Adams to New Orleans will stop on the first of next month and as he has no Authority to act on the Subject he has suggested it that the President (if he sees proper) may direct Govr Claiborne to continue the line untill provision shall be made by[1] law for a regular Mail.—

He incloses a Letter fm W Judd Esq & takes the liberty to remind the President that Perpoint Edwards considers himself a Candidate for the Office of Commissioner under the Spanish Convention lately ratified or rather by the Senate advised, to be, ratified.—

he wishes this representation to be considered as strictly limited to the *fact* as he feels the impropriety of even an intimation of an opinion in favor of his friend.—

RC (DNA: RG 59, LAR); endorsed by TJ as received 23 Jan. and "Edwards Pierpoint. to be Commr. to Spain." Enclosure: William Judd to Granger, 5 Jan., requesting an appointment as a district

or supreme court judge in the new territory, if Indiana is divided by Congress; he continues, "I know my Own Tallents and Verily believe should appear to Advantage as first Majistrate in such a State, but conclude there are others of more prominent Character that the President will nominate"; note by Granger at foot of text: "Mr. Judd is a Gentleman of about 60 years of Age has for many years been a respectable but not a great Lawyer—he lost his Inheritance & the labors of his life by purchasing Georgia Lands—he is a Stedfast Republican of fair Character—G Granger" (same; endorsed by TJ: "Judd Wm. to be judge of Detroit. his letter to mr Granger"). Other enclosure not found, but see below.

The John Wayles EPPES LETTER probably pertained to the post office at Petersburg. On this day, Granger wrote John Grammer, postmaster there since 1783, that he believed the public interest would be "promoted, by the appointment of a new postmaster" and that he had, consequently, appointed JOSEPH JONES in his place (FC in Lb in DNA: RG 28, LPG; *Washington Federalist*, 27 Feb., 1804; Stets, *Postmasters*, 267).

OFFICE OF COMMISSIONER: John M. Pintard, the former U.S. consul at Madeira, wrote to Madison on 4 Feb. from Georgetown, South Carolina, to remind the secretary of his earlier application for an appointment as one of the commissioners to Spain (RC in DNA: RG 59, LAR, endorsed by TJ: "Pintard John M. to mr Madison. Commr. to Spain"; Vol. 39:438n).

[1] MS: "my."

Notes on Lewis Harvie's Mission

[24 Jan. 1804]

Harvie Lewis.

to be allowed 38.05 D per month for months, his passage there & back, also his passage[1] from the seaport to Paris with the stock, as would have been paid to a special person by our Consul who should have employed one to carry it on.

if taken & carried to England, such extra expence to be allowed him as would have been allowed to the Lieutt. destined for that service in the same case.

MS (DLC: TJ Papers, 130:22422); entirely in TJ's hand; undated; on verso of undated memorandum by Robert Smith (see below).

TO BE ALLOWED: TJ drew his calculation for the payment his secretary would receive from an undated note by Robert Smith. Before Harvie took the job, the administration had planned for a naval officer to deliver to France two-thirds of the stock certificates allocated for the purchase of Louisiana and apparently determined that half pay and rations would serve as salary for the job. According to Smith's figures, half pay and rations for a lieutenant would total $38.05 (same).

IF TAKEN & CARRIED TO ENGLAND: see TJ to Gallatin, 24 Jan.

[1] TJ here canceled "by land."

To the President of the Senate

TH: JEFFERSON TO THE
PRESIDENT OF THE SENATE Jan. 24. 1804.

Governor Claiborne's letter accompanying this is communicated merely for information. some of the matter, proper for the hearing of the house, would yet be improper for the press. over two passages, which are personal, blank papers are fixed, because they are not important enough for closed doors, nor proper even to be read with open ones. will you be so good as to return the letter, when read, to mr Harvie who will be waiting to communicate it to the other house?

PrC (DLC); at head of text: "Private." Not recorded in SJL.

On 23 Jan., the Senate had elected John Brown of Kentucky as PRESIDENT pro tempore due to Aaron Burr's absence on account of illness (JS, 3:343).

CLAIBORNE'S LETTER: see the next document.

To the Senate and the House of Representatives

GENTLEMEN OF THE SENATE AND OF THE HOUSE OF REPRESENTATIVES

I communicate, for your information,[1] a letter just recieved from Governor Claiborne, which may throw light on the subject of the government of Louisiana, under contemplation of the legislature. the paper being original, it's return is asked.   TH: JEFFERSON
Jan. 24. 1804.

RC (DNA: RG 233, PM, 8th Cong., 1st sess.); endorsed by a House clerk. PrC (DLC). RC (DNA: RG 46, LPPM, 8th Cong., 1st sess.); endorsed by a Senate clerk. Recorded in SJL with notation "Claiborne's lre." Enclosure not found, but see below.

LETTER JUST RECIEVED: in his diary entry for 24 Jan., John Quincy Adams recorded that the Senate received and read a "letter from Governor Claiborne to the Secretary of State." This was Claiborne's letter to Madison of 2 Jan. 1804, which reported in detail on the difficulties he faced in establishing a temporary government in Louisiana. Chief among the

impediments were the overwhelming inefficiency and corruption of the late Spanish government, which Claiborne believed to be too far gone to continue or reform. "The original principles of that system have been long lost sight of," he wrote in his 2 Jan. letter. "It had scarcely a nerve not wounded by corruption." The ignorance of the general population and the decadence of the territory's planters and merchants added to the problems, leaving Claiborne to declare that "the principles of a popular government are illy suited to the present state of Society in this province." In his brief tenure, Claiborne had undertaken a few tangible reforms, such as sanctioning Pierre Clément Laussat's replacement of the Spanish cabildo with a new municipal government and establishing a temporary court system, but he nevertheless emphasized the need for "the early establishment of some permanent government for this Province." Claiborne's quandary, as well as the general difficulty the Republicans experienced in creating a government for Louisiana, amused Federalist representative Manasseh Cutler of Massachusetts. "By letters from the new Governor, Claiborne, it seems that a republican government will not do there," he wrote to his son-in-law on 26 Jan. "It seems a little odd for red-hot democrats to become advocates of one that is perfectly despotic" (Adams, diary 27 [1 Jan. 1803 to 4 Aug. 1809], 65, in MHi: Adams Family Papers; Madison,

Papers, Sec. of State Ser., 6:274-8; William P. Cutler and Julia P. Cutler, *Life, Journals, and Correspondence of Rev. Manasseh Cutler, LL.D.*, 2 vols. [Cincinnati, 1888; repr. Athens, Ohio, 1987], 2:160-1).

Lewis Harvie delivered TJ's message to each chamber on 24 Jan. The Senate and the House of Representatives each read TJ's message and its enclosed letter on that day. The Senate ordered the message to lie for consideration, while the House directed that Claiborne's letter be returned to the president (JS, 3:344; JHR, 4:550).

[1] Preceding three words interlined in RC in RG 46, where TJ first wrote "I communicate herewith."

From Samuel Smith

SIR/   Senate Chamber, 24 Jany. 1804

I recieved a Letter last Night from Mr. Patterson requesting me to remind you of your polite Intention of giving him a Letter to Mr. Livingston on the Subject of his Daughter's Marriage with Mr. Bonaparte—I believe an Oppertunity will offer in a few Days that he wishes to embrace. I am Sir

with Respect Your friend & servt.   S. SMITH

RC (DLC); endorsed by TJ as a letter of 24 Jan. received on the 23d and so recorded in SJL.

LETTER TO MR. LIVINGSTON: for TJ's earlier comments to Robert R. Livingston on the marriage of Jerome Bonaparte and Elizabeth Patterson, see Vol. 41:666-9, 690.

From James Taylor, Jr.

SIR   Norfolk Jany 24 1804

I have just receivd a few Cases of champaign. I do not profess myself a judge of its quality; but those who do, say it's excellent. Shall I reserve a few Cases for yourself & freinds? the price 72$ ℔ doz.

I have receivd from Mr Barnes of G. Town an order on this Branch for $94.88. the balance of your account—

a pipe of Wine ordered for you by Mr. Newton is arrived, it is thought to be of a Superior quality. If you want another pipe, I have

some imported from the same House, such as Mr. Madison now drinks,
I think not inferior—I am with great respect

Yr: ob: servt   JA TAYLOR JR

RC (MHi); endorsed by TJ as received 31 Jan. and so recorded in SJL.

From Nicholas Febvrier

Washington Goal

MAY IT PLEASE YOUR EXCELLENCY   Jany. 25. 1804

I am cover'd with confusion when I think it should be my Fate to
engage Your Attention from the grand Interests of the Nation even
for a Moment; but when I know & your People know that one of
Your great & noble Traits are Humanity & Philantrophy, it gives Me
confidence.

The humane Howard an English-Man visited the Cells of the miserable; I have every sentiment to believe, He participected of more
ectatick Bliss in his Tour from Acts of beneficence to the unfortunate,
than at the Levèes of proud & gilded Palaces; It is in this confidence
I have presumed

An unfortunate adopted Citizen, a Native of Martinico presents
his Picture; the War & its calamities have reduced from a State of
Affluence to Indigence this Caracter: His Creditors have pressed &
placed Him not only in a dishonorable but a distressing Situation,
Altho' He believes they are sensible He has sufficient to pay all his
just claims: His aged Cheeks are flushed with Crimson when He
thinks He has been under the Necessity of petitioning for the benefit
of that humane & generous Law which protects the Debtor in this
Territory: He has given up for the benefit of his Creditor *his All*;
every Property whatever, wherein He is in the least interested: He
notwithstanding complains not at Fate, but endeavours to bear up as
Man ought to do, with Dignity: Retrospection will however at times
impil an involuntary Sigh—A Tear—it is Sympathy that vibrates like
the Chords of the tuned Instrument, 'tis the Fate of his native Countryman that strikes upon his Heart Strings; Who have been hurled
into that Vortex of destruction by the same Great & Wonderful[1]
Power. What? a Native Frenchman not to oppose a Torrent of Calamity, an Host of Foes? Mon Dieu, Lewis the XVI with all his accumulated guilt sufferd the Guillotine with Patience, resignation &
dignity; Ought He, can He complain.

My Son will intrude upon Your public Duties, I have Three, my
good Sir; Two of them now resident at Martinico, Who received

[341]

their Education at George Town College, at which place I am known to the most respectable Citizens.

I flatter myself Francis will have confidence to stand in Your Excellency presence if peritted & communicate to You our Situation, *An Extreamity of Necessity at the Moment.*

Simular Applications I am sensible are too numerous; 'tis impossible You can indulge Your feelings in every Instance.

With Ten Thousand Apologies and a grand Prayer for the great national Interests of my adopted Country, as well as for Honor Prosperity & Happiness to the Man, under who's arraignments & influance We Free People stand so highly exalted and respected amongst the Nations, I conclude. I repeat a prayer for Your Excellency & Household, & Subscribe Myself

The unfortunate Citizen   NICH'. FEBVRIER.

RC (DLC); addressed: "To His Excellency Thomas Jefferson Esqr President of the *United States*"; endorsed by TJ as received 30 Jan. and so recorded in SJL.

In 1793, Nicholas Febvrier owned a plantation near Annapolis, and at some point he acquired a property near Georgetown, which was exposed to public sale in 1803. He took an oath as an insolvent debtor on 6 Feb. 1804., after which he returned to Martinique, likely dying there by 1806 (*Maryland Gazette*, 10 Jan. 1793;

Georgetown *Olio*, 14 July 1803; *Washington Federalist*, 27 Jan. 1804; Susannah Febvrier to TJ, 8 Jan. 1805 and 16 Apr. 1806).

The English reformer John HOWARD visited prisons throughout Great Britain and on the Continent while advancing the cause of improving conditions for prisoners (DNB).

[1] Febvrier wrote "Wonder-" at the end of a line but then failed to complete the word on the next line.

From Levi Lincoln

SIR   Washington Jany   1804 [25 Jan.]

I have examined the questions referred to my consideration by your note of yesterday—By the Constitution of the US. offences against it and the laws made in pursuance thereof are cognizable by the federal Courts—All crimes or misdemeanors, which are not such by this constitution, or to which the jurisdiction of the federal Courts, is not by law, expressly extended, are, it is conceived triable by a State judiciary only—

Under the clause giving the authority to make all laws necessary & proper for carrying the powers vested in the national Govt. into execution, is the 22. Sec of the act for the punishment of[1] certain crimes agt. the US.—This Sec. provides that if any person or persons shall knowingly and wilfully *obstruct, resist,* or *oppose* any officer of the U.S.

in serving or attempting to serve or *execute* any mesne process, or warrant, or any rule or *Order* of any of the courts of the U.S. or any *other legal* write *or process whatsoever*, or shall assault or beat or wound any officer or other person duly authorized in serving or executing any rule *or order process* or warrant aforesd., every person so knowingly and wilfully offending in the premises, shall on conviction thereof, be emprisoned not exceeding twelve months & fined not exceeding three hundred dollars —

In the 71st. Sec of the act of the 2d of March 1799 for regulating the collection of duties on imposts & tonnage (V. 4. p 391) It is provided that if any person shall forcibly resist, prevent, or impede any officer of the customs, or their deputies, or any person assisting them, in the execution of his duty such person so offending shall for every such offence be fined in a sum not exceeding four hundred dollars

By the 90th Sec. of the same law (p. 430) It is provided that all ships or vessels goods wares or merchandise, which shall *be condemned* by virtue of this act &c shall be *sold by the Marshal*[2] *or other* proper officer of the Court, in which the condemnation shall be had, to the *highest bider*, at *public auction*, by order of such court &c—

The foregoing recited parts of the laws of the U.S. are those alone, it is beleived, which can, on any principles, be construed to embrace; or to extend to the outrage committed at Plymouth. Of the applicability of the provisions of the aforesd. 71. Sec. of the law, I have very serious doubts — I have mentioned it, because, at first blush, it seemed to apply, and may have from others a less confined construction. It is true, the stealing of goods after the condemnation & before the sale, which the collector had seised & stored, may be considered, in its bearings & effects, as really a resistance and impediment to an officer of the customs, or his assistance, in the execution of their duty, yet I conceive it is not that direct personal resistance and impedement which the law contemplated. But should it be considered as applicable, it would reach every part of the Plymouth transaction—

The Marshal, who by the 90th Sec. of the cited law, who is to sell *by the order of a Court* condemned goods, wares and Merchandise, to the highest bider, at public auction, is both an officer of the federal Court, and of the US. within the intent of the sd 22 Sec. of the first mentioned act; and the *order* of the Court, in which the condemnation of the goods has been had to the Marshal for their sale, is also an *order or legal* process within the letter, as well as within the reason & meaning of this sec. of that law—

It is therefore to me perfectly clear that the persons who deterred the people from biding on the goods, who threatening[3] insulting and intimidating those who did bid, assaulted & beat Crocker, abused the officer, and endeavoured to intimidate & embarrass him in the *execution of his order for to make* the sales have been guilty of a very aggravated *obstruction, resistance & opposition* to an officer of the U.S. and are liable on an indictment by a federal Court to be convicted fined & imprisoned—

In addition to this offence agt the US. of an obstruction to its officer, in the Execution of his duty—there appears to have been three other distinct offences committed agt. the State in which these transactions took place as mentioned in the Collectors letter—and as such triable only under the authority of that State

The taking of the two hodgsheads of rum from the Store on the 14th. was undoubly feleneous (even if by the former owner,[4] as is supposed, or by the consent of the store keeper,) and an highly aggravated theft—The threatenings insults assaults beatings and other outrages at the sale was a violent high handed riot, involving all who were present for the unlawful purpose of preventing a fair sale, or were actually concerned aiding or countenancing the acts of violence which took place.—The losing of the horses, in the evening, was a malicious mischeif constituting a legal misdemeanor, and furnishing a third ground for a state indictment in the County which has been disgraced by the wantonness of a few—

Under these circumstances would it not be desirable to divide the criminal processes which it may be thought proper to commence? Should prosecutions both State & national be instituted and be conducted with firmness, ability, moderation & prudence (as I have no doubt they would be from my knowledge of the gent. who would manage them) they would lead to some useful disquisitions disclosures, and avowals in open Court—

A few of the leaders, or principals being tried before the federal Court at Boston, a few others well selected on account of their habitual opposition to the execution of the revenue laws and to Govt. before the State courts at the place where the offences were perpetrated would probably be a more useful exhibition both of the firmness and fairness of Govt. as well of its magnanimity & mildness (as it would be more convenient to the offenders themselves) than to carry all who ought to be[5] tried to a distance from home with the Witnesses—It is possible from prejudice & connections, there would be a difficulty in the jurys agreeing to convict, taken from Plymouth & its neighbourhood on evidence sufficiently strong. But it is certain in such a case there would not be twelve persons in one panel who would agree to acquit—The consequence would be a continuance & trials from Court to Court, which would hold the offenders under bonds, under expence and under a kind of suffering, which might be as useful to the individual & the public as would be a conviction at the first term—

It is possible the persons who stole the rum & those who injured the horses may not be discovered, and altho the opposers of the Marshal, May by the same act of opposition have been also guilty of a riot against the laws of their own state, yet as it may be thought severe to punish them both ways, or rather for both offences; and as the district Attorney may think it his duty to prosecute all who may be deemed worthy of punishment in the federal Court, & the Attorney Genl of the State may from delicacy, not think it proper to anticipate, or interfere with, prosecutions which may be grounded on the transactions of the 16th, would it not be advisable by letter to the collector or the district Atty to suggest to them the expediency of a consultation with the Atty Genl. of the State on the proprietors of prosecuting some of the offenders of the 16th as *Oppugnators*[6] to an officer of the US, in the federal Court; and others as *federal* rioters in the Courts of the State

I am sensible that some of the above remarks are not answers to the stated questions but as they associated with them, and are applicable to the subject matter I have taken the liberty of submitting them.

I have the honor to be Sir most respectfully Your Obt Servt

LEVI LINCOLN

Please to excuse the accident to the enclosed

RC (DLC); partially dated, but see below; postscript in margin of first page; addressed: "The President of the United States"; endorsed by TJ as received 26 Jan. and "Plymouth. riot at. Atty Genl.'s opn" and so recorded in SJL.

NOTE OF YESTERDAY: on 24 Jan., TJ informed Gallatin that he had sent Henry Warren's letter to Lincoln, but TJ's query to the attorney general is not recorded in SJL and has not been found.

For Section 22 of the 30 Apr. 1790 ACT FOR THE PUNISHMENT OF CERTAIN CRIMES, quoted here by Lincoln, see U.S. Statutes at Large, 1:117. Sections 71 and 90 of the 2 Mch. 1799 act FOR REGULATING THE COLLECTION OF DUTIES are in same, 1:627, 678, 696-7. For the pagination as cited by Lincoln, see *Acts Passed at the Third Session of the Fifth Congress of the United States* (Philadelphia, 1799).

TJ appointed George Blake the U.S. DISTRICT ATTORNEY for Massachusetts in July 1801 (Vol. 35:300-1n). ATTORNEY GENL OF THE STATE: James Sullivan (ANB).

[1] MS: "of of."
[2] MS: "Marsal."
[3] MS: "theatening."
[4] MS: "owne."
[5] Word lacking in MS.
[6] Lincoln underlined this word, and "federal" later in the sentence, with two strokes.

From Henry Dearborn

War Department

SIR,   26th: January 1804.

I have the honor of proposing for your approbation, Erastus Granger of Suffield (Connecticut) as Agent for the Six Nations of Indians—vice Capt: Callender Irvine resigned—

I am with Sentiments of respect &ca.

FC (Lb in DNA: RG 107, LSP); in a clerk's hand.

Dearborn wrote ERASTUS GRANGER on 30 Jan., informing him of his appoint-

ment as agent to the Six Nations and enclosing copies of his commission and instructions (FC in Lb in DNA: RG 75, LSIA).

Notes on a Conversation with Aaron Burr

Jan. 26.   Colo Burr the V.P. calls on me in the evening, having previously asked an opportunity of conversing with me. he began by recapitulating summarily that he had come to N.Y. a stranger some years ago, that he found the country in possn of two rich families, (the Livingstons & Clintons) that his pursuits were not political & he meddled not. when the crisis however of 1800. came on, they found their influence worn out, & sollicited his aid with the people. he lent it without any views of promotion. that his being named as a candidate for V.P. was unexpected by him. he acceded to it with a view to promote my fame & advancement and from a desire to be with me, whose company & conversation had always been fascinating to him. that since that those great families had become hostile to him, and had excited the calumnies which I had seen published. that in this Hamilton had joined and had even written some of the pieces against him. that his attachment to me had been sincere and was still unchanged, altho many little stories had been carried to him, & he supposed to me also, which he despised, but that attachments must be reciprocal or cease to exist, and therefore he asked if any change had taken place in mine towards him: that he had chosen to have this conversn with myself directly & not through any intermediate agent. he reminded me of a letter written to him about the time of counting the votes (say Feb. 1801) mentioning that I[1] his election had left a chasm in my arrangements, that I had lost him from my list in the admn, &c. he observed he believed it would be for the interest of the republican cause for him to retire; that a disadvantageous schism would otherwise take place; but that were he to retire, it would be said he shrunk from the public sentence, which he never would do; that his enemies were using my name to destroy him, and something was necessary from me to prevent and deprive them of that weapon, some mark of favor from me, which would declare to the world that he retired with[2] my confidence. I answered by recapitulating to him what had been my conduct previous to the election of 1800. that I never had interfered directly or indirectly with my friends or any others, to influence the election either for him or myself; that I considered it as my duty to be merely passive, except that, in Virginia, I had taken some measures to procure for him the unanimous vote of that state, because I thought any failure there might be imputed to me. that in the election now coming on, I was observing the same conduct, held no councils with any body respecting it, nor suffered any one to speak to me on the subject, believing it my duty to leave myself to the free discussion of the public: that I do not at this moment know, nor have ever heard who were to be proposed as candidates for the public choice, except so far as could be gathered from the newspapers. that as to the attack excited against him in the newspapers, I had noticed it but as the passing wind; that I had seen complaints that Cheetham, employed in publishing the laws, should be permitted to eat the publick bread & abuse it's second officer: that as to this, the publishers of the laws were appd by the Secy. of state, witht. any reference to me; that to make the notice general, it was often given to one republican & one federal printer of the same place, that these federal printers did not in the least intermit their abuse of me, tho' recieving emoluments from the govmt, and that I had never thot it proper to interfere for myself, & consequently not in the case of the Vicepresident. that as to the letter he referred to, I remembered it, and[3] believed he had only mistaken the date at which it was written; that I thought it must have been on the first notice of the event of the election of S. Carolina; and that I had taken that occasion to mention to him that I had intended to have proposed to him one of the great offices, if he had not been elected, but that his election in giving him a higher station had deprived me of his aid in the administration. the letter alluded to was in fact mine to him of Dec. 15. 1800. I now went on to explain to him verbally what I meant by saying I had lost him from my list. that in Genl Washington's time it had been signified to him that mr Adams, then V. President, would be glad of a foreign embassy; that

Genl. Washington mentd it to me, expressed his doubts whether mr Adams was a fit character for such an office, & his still greater doubts, indeed his conviction that it would not be justifiable to send away the person who, in case of his death, was provided by the constn, to take his place; that it would moreover appear indecent for him to be[4] disposing of the public trusts in apparently buying off a competitor for the public favor. I concurred with him in the opinion, and, if I recollect rightly, Hamilton, Knox & Randolph were consulted & gave the same opinions. that when mr Adams came to the admn, in his first interview with me he mentioned the necessity of a mission to France, and how desireable it would have been to him if he could have got me to undertake it; but that he concieved it would be wrong in him to send me away, and assigned the same reasons Genl Washington had done; and therefore he should appoint mr Madison &c. that I had myself contemplated his (Colo. Burr's) appointment to one of the great offices; in case he were not elected V.P. but that as soon as that election was known, I saw it could not be done for the good reasons which had led Genl. W. & mr A. to the same conclusion, and therefore in my first letter to Colo. Burr after the issue was known, I had mentioned to him that a chasm in my arrangements had been produced by this event. I was thus particular in rectifying the date of this letter, because it gave me an opportunity of explaining the grounds on which it was written which were indirectly an answer to his present hints. he left the matter with me for consideration & the conversation was turned to indifferent subjects. I should here notice that Colo. Burr must have thot I could swallow strong things in my own favor, when he founded his acquiescence in the nominn as V.P. to his desire of[5] promoting my honor, the being with me whose company & conversn had always been fascinating to him &c. I had never seen Colo. B. till he came as a member of Senate. his conduct very soon inspired me with distrust. I habitually cautioned mr Madison against trusting him too much. I saw afterwards that[6] under Genl. W's and mr A's admns, whenever a great military appmt or a diplomatic one was to be made, he came post to Philada to shew himself, & in fact that he was always at market, if they had wanted him. he was indeed told by Dayton in 1800. he might be Secy. at war: but this bid was too late. his election as V.P. was then foreseen. with these impressions of Colo. Burr there never had been an intimacy between us, and but little association. when I destined him for a high appmt, it was out of respect for the favor he had obtained with the republican party by his extraordinary exertions and success in the N.Y. election in 1800.

MS (DLC: TJ Papers, 113:19521); entirely in TJ's hand; follows, on same sheet, Notes on a Conversation with Benjamin Hichborn, 2 Jan. 1804.

LETTER WRITTEN TO HIM: see Vol. 32:306-7. The letter of 15 Dec. 1800 is also printed in Kline, *Burr*, 1:469-70.

INTEREST OF THE REPUBLICAN CAUSE FOR HIM TO RETIRE: in December 1803 and January 1804, Burr's supporters were actively campaigning to retain him as vice president on the 1804 Republican ticket (Kline, *Burr*, 2:822-3n; TJ to Abraham Bishop, 15 Dec.). For the maneuvers of the Clinton and Livingston families to have Burr's name removed from the ticket, see Kline, *Burr*, 2:822-3n.

In the 2 Mch. 1797 conversation between TJ and Adams, the president-elect reportedly noted that it was "the first wish of his heart" to send TJ on the MISSION TO FRANCE; Adams then noted the reasons he "supposed it was out of the question" (Vol. 29:551-3).

FAVOR HE HAD OBTAINED WITH THE REPUBLICAN PARTY: for the party's choice of Burr as the vice presidential candidate in 1800, see Vol. 31:556-7n.

[1] TJ here canceled "had destined."
[2] TJ here canceled "the."
[3] Word interlined in place of "but."
[4] TJ here canceled "use" or "usi."
[5] TJ here canceled "supp."
[6] TJ here canceled: "he was always go."

To Charles P. Sumner

Washington Jan. 26. 04.

Th: Jefferson presents his compliments to mr Sumner, and his thanks for the pamphlets he inclosed which he will read at his first moment of leisure, &, he does not doubt, with satisfaction. he begs leave to add his acknolegements for the obliging expressions in mr Sumner's letter.

RC (MH). PrC (MHi); endorsed by TJ in ink on verso.

MR SUMNER'S LETTER: Sumner to TJ, 11 Jan.

To Littleton W. Tazewell

DEAR SIR   Washington Jan. 26. 1804.

The pressure of my business has put it out of my power sooner to acknolege the reciept of your favr of Dec. 9. I had for some time ceased to make partial paiments towards the debt due to mr Walsh, under the purpose, when I should touch it again, to make a compleat discharge of it. the state of things in England had made me suppose he would not be desirous of removing money from this to that country till the threatened crisis had passed, and had induced me, in my calculations, to place the discharge of that debt about the end of the present year. your information that he has no particular anxiety as to it's very speedy collection, and your polite accomodation of the time to my arrangements, will induce me still to keep the same period in view, unless any necessities of mr Walsh should call for an earlier attention to it, in which case I shall certainly exert myself to fulfill his wishes. my own anxieties will not permit me to interpose any unnecessary delay.

You are now placed in the midst of mercantile men. may we at length hope that that body of men, percieving that we aim at preserving the public faith & paying it's debt honestly, at protecting commerce & enlarging it's field, at an intercourse with France & England, peaceable, friendly and rigorously impartial and equal, at such economical arrangements as, while they support effectual government, will prevent the laying new burthens on commerce & agriculture, will become satisfied with the order of things which the nation has chosen to establish? I know no *principle* in which these gentlemen differ from us; because I am not willing to ascribe to them the desire to change the form of government entertained by some prominent characters. Accept my friendly salutations & assurances of respect.

Th: Jefferson

RC (DLC); addressed: "Littleton W. Tazewell esq. Norfolk"; franked and postmarked; endorsed by Tazewell. PrC (MHi); endorsed by TJ in ink on verso.

mr walsh: that is, Wakelin Welch, Jr. (Tazewell to TJ, 9 Dec. 1803).

now placed: Tazewell moved from Williamsburg to Norfolk in 1802 (Vol. 31:230n).

To Joseph Yznardi, Sr.

Dear Sir   Washington Jan. 26. 04.

I wrote you last on the 10th. of May, and since that have recieved your several favors of Apr. 4. July 9. & 19. and Oct. 22. and very lately another letter written in Octob. subsequent to that of the 22d. but without particular date. with the two last came the butt of Pale Sherry to Philadelphia, from which place it is now on it's way to Richmond in Virginia to be forwarded to Monticello. if the quality is equal to that of the Xeres sin color which you furnished me before, as I doubt not it is, I shall not begrudge the price which you consider as high. but as the stock of wines I have now on hand, will permit my keeping those I get hereafter until they ripen, I will adopt your advice of taking hereafter those of the same quality but of less age, and keeping them to their proper age. I propose therefore, when I remit you the price of the pipe just recieved, to add to it the amount of another which you would be so good as to send me in the course of the current year, of the same quality but less age & consequently cheaper and to do the same annually hereafter which will be a sufficient supply for me[1] of that kind of wine.

The other matters contained in your last letter of October have been communicated to the Secretary of State, within whose department they lie and will be under consideration in due time. Accept my friendly salutations and assurances of great esteem and respect.

TH: JEFFERSON

PrC (DLC); at foot of text: "Joseph Yznardi esq."; endorsed by TJ in ink on verso.

LETTER WRITTEN IN OCTOB.: actually Yznardi to TJ, 3 Nov. 1803.

[1] Preceding two words interlined.

From Albert Gallatin

[27 Jan. 1804]

The general direction of the prosecutions which it may be thought proper to institute seems to fall within the province of the Attorney general; and I presume that it will be necessary for him to delegate to the district attorney the discretionary power of deciding to what extent they should be instituted.

In doing this, it seems important that the district attorney should in the first place obtain in writing the statement of the Marshal or deputy marshal, and also a knowledge of the other evidence which may with certainty be obtained—that no prosecution should be instituted in the federal courts except in cases where the evidence of an offence agt. the United States is positive, and where no doubt is entertained that a conviction will take place—and that, according to Mr Lincoln's suggestion, the dist. attorney should be instructed to confer with the atty. general of the State—

A.G.

RC (DLC: TJ Papers, 146:25372); undated. Recorded in SJL as received from the Treasury Department on 27 Jan. with notation "Plymouth riot."

LINCOLN'S SUGGESTION: see Lincoln to TJ, [25] Jan.

To Hammuda Pasha, Bey of Tunis

GREAT AND GOOD FRIEND,

I received in due time your letter of the 7th of September repeating the request of a frigate of 36 Guns with which on a former occasion, I had informed you that circumstances did not permit us to comply. I am under the necessity of stating that these circumstances continue, and that our naval force being only proportioned to our exigencies we cannot with prudence lessen it[1] by parting with any portion of it. I should regret much a misconception of our motives on this occasion. We set a just value on your friendship, as we do on that of all other nations with which we have intercourse: and as we presume those nations do on ours. These mutual friendships, and the interest arising out of them, are equivalents the one for the other, and authorize equal expectations, equal claims, and rights on both sides. Of our dispositions towards yourself in particular, we have not been wanting in proofs, in addition to the faithful fulfilment of our Treaty, nor shall we on proper occasions, fail to continue reasonable manifestations of them,[2] according to the rules we observe in our intercourse with Nations.

Such being our regard for you, it is with peculiar concern I learn from your letter of Sept 14 that Mr Cathcart, whom I had chosen to succeed to the place of Mr Eaton near you, and chosen from a confidence in his Integrity, experience, and good dispositions, has so conducted himself as to incur your displeasure. In doing this, be assured, he has gone against the letter and spirit of his instructions, which were, that his deportment should be such as to mark my esteem and respect for your character, both personal and public, and to cultivate your friendship by all the attentions and services he could render. So soon as he went out of this line, he was out of the line of his duty, and his acts are disclaimed as in opposition to his orders. On his return to the United States he will be made sensible how far in this he departed from the intentions of his employers. The consideration that the bands of peace between Nations[3] ought not to be burst asunder by the hasty and unauthorized acts of a public Agent was worthy of your wisdom and justice and the acquiescence in the transaction of our affairs by Mr Davis until an Agent could be sent with formal authorities, manifested a desire of maintaining a good understanding, which being reciprocal,[4] is auspicious to our peace. In selecting another character to take the place of Mr Cathcart, I shall take care to fix on one who I hope will better fulfil the duties of respect and esteem for you, and who in so doing only, will be the faithful representative and organ of my earnest desire that the peace and friendship so happily subsisting between our Countries may be firm and permanent: And I pray God, Great and Good friend that he may have you under his holy keeping.

Done at Washington in the United States of America, this 27th day of January 1804.

FC (Lb in DNA: RG 59, Credences); in a clerk's hand; at head of text: "Thomas Jefferson, President of the United States of America, To the Most Illustrious and Most Magnificent Prince, the Bey of Tunis, the abode of happiness"; below signature: "By the President, James Madison Secretary of State." PrC (DLC); a Dft, partially dated, day of month left blank; at foot of text: "Hamuda Basaw, Bey of Tunis." Tr (CSmH); in Richard O'Brien's hand. Tr (Christie's, New York City, 2002); in an unidentified hand. Recorded in SJL at 24 Jan.

ON A FORMER OCCASION: in his letter to Hammuda of 14 Apr. 1803, TJ declined the bey's request for a frigate from the United States. Hammuda's letters to TJ of 7 and 14 Sep. 1803, received by TJ on 16 Nov. and 11 Dec., respectively, have not been found (Vol. 40:196-7; Vol. 41:738).

TJ appointed James Leander CATH-CART as consul at Tunis in April 1803. Upon his arrival there on 2 Sep., and fol-

lowing brief negotiations on the subjects of the frigate and annuities, Hammuda abruptly refused to accept Cathcart as consul, blaming him for the war with Tripoli and wishing the president to appoint instead "a man that is not known in the other parts of Barbary." The bey agreed, however, to allow George DAVIS, a U.S. navy surgeon, to continue to act as temporary consul until he received answers to his letters to TJ. Cathcart left Tunis on 8 Sep. (Madison, *Papers, Sec. of State Ser.*, 5:391-8, 408-18; NDBW, 3:43, 47-8; Vol. 40:153n, 196-7, 257-8, 647).

[1] Preceding 15 words interlined in PrC in place of "the present aspect of affairs does not render it prudent for us to lessen our naval force."

[2] Remainder of sentence interlined in PrC.

[3] Preceding two words interlined in PrC.

[4] Word interlined in PrC in place of an illegible cancellation.

From Philip Mazzei

27 Genn. 1804.

Mandai a bordo del bastimento Hannah la cassa delle piante, vid., barbatelle, e magliuoli; la scatola coi noccioli; un vaso colle fragole d'ogni mese; e in un sol plico la mia del 23 8bre con un'aggiunta del 28 xbre; un altra mia a Mr. Madison, e l'Elogio d'Amerigo Vespucci. Ma poichè il Capno. Yeardsley non à potuto ancor partire, Le dirigo un'altro plico, contenente un'Opuscolo, che il Conte Gio: Potocki mi à dato per Lei, e una lettera per il Bellini, che ne include una delle sue sorelle con altri fogli: concernenti affari di famiglia. L'autor dell'opuscolo, che si è trattenuto 2 mesi in Firenze per farlo stampare, è quel mio debitore, di cui Le parlai in 2 precedenti, la prima sul punto di partir ⅌ Pietroburgo, e l'altra dopo il mio ritorno. Ella può averlo veduto dalla Pr. Mar. Lub; dall'Ab. Morellet, e dalla Duchessa d'Enville, ove veniva spessissimo. La vecchia Duchessa l'amava molto e lo stimava ancor più, poichè l'Ab. Barthelemy diceva, che era il più erudito giovane che avesse conosciuto. Egli à grand' ingegno ma la sua testa sbalestra. Non à mai potuto, star fisso un'ora intiera nella medesima cosa. La sua impazienza fa sì, che i suoi scritti abbondano in errori ortografici, come vedrà. Quantunque io non sappia la quarta parte di quel ch'ei sa della lingua francese, glie ne corressi moltissimi nell'Operetta che stampava mentre io ero a Pietroburgo sull'istoria primitiva dei popoli della Russia, che qua viene stimata dal mio amico Fabbroni o da altri versati in cose di tal natura. Dopo la mia partenza ne offerse la dedica all'Imperatore, il quale gli rispose con tal gentilezza, che io mi determino a includerlene la copia, persuaso che Le piacerà di vedere un saggio di quanto Le ò detto di quel degno Principe. Certo è, che il minimo Principe dell'Impero crederebbe di abbassarsi troppo, scrivendo in quello stile ad un privato.

In questo momento ricevo da Livorno una lettera del Maggior Barnes, nella quale mi dice: "I have received certain advise that Commodore Preble has taken & carried into Syracuse a Tripoline Bombard with 70 men. I hope he may soon take as many as to equal our prisoners in number at Tripoli."

Credo che s'inganni sulla supposizione che gli cambierebbero; e quando ancora gli cambiassero, non ci darebbero il solo Capitano per mille della lor canaglia. Desidero ardentemente di veder arrivare, *il più presto possibile*, un buon rinforzo d'America.

Il Capno. Yeardsley à detto a Mr. Appleton, che partirà tra 3, o 4 giorni; che avrà gran cura del vaso colle fragole, che l'à fatto metter nella sua camera, che la farà innaffiare quando bisogna, mettere allo scoperto quando pioverà. Io l'ò fatto avvertire, che non richiedono troppa umidità. Siccome abbiamo qui un'inverno più dolce del solito varie delle dette piante nel vaso ànno già fiori, e una ve n'è col frutto.

È uso quasi universale d'innestare gli Albicocchi su piante di Susini. L'avverto, che riescono molto meglio, più vegeti, e di maggior durata, quando sono innestati su piante dell'istessa natura. Son portato a credere che sarebbe l'istesso in ogni genere di piante.

Mi confermo al solito. Tutto suo,   Filippo Mazzei

EDITORS' TRANSLATION

27 Jan. 1804.

I have sent on board of the Hannah the trunk with the plants—that is, the roots and the vine stocks, the box with the fruit stones, and a pot with strawberries of every month. In the same parcel I have added my letter of 23 Oct., with an addendum of 28 Dec., together with another letter for Mr. Madison and the *Elogio d'Amerigo Vespucci*. Since, however, Captain Yeardsley has not yet been able to leave, I am addressing you another parcel, which contains a booklet that Count Potocki has given me to be passed on to you and a letter for Mr. Bellini, which contains another one by his sisters along with other papers concerning family business affairs. The author of the booklet, who has remained two months in Florence to have it printed, is the person indebted to me of which I spoke to you in two previous letters, the first as I was about to leave for Petersburg, and the other after my return. You may have had a chance to see him at the Princess Lubomirska's; at the Abbé Morellet's, and at the Duchess of Enville's, where he was very often in attendance. The old duchess loved him dearly and esteemed him even more, since Abbé Barthélemy was used to saying that he was the most learned young man he had ever met. He has great intelligence, but his mind is off balance. He has never been able to keep his focus one hour on the same thing. His impatience is such that his writings are rife with spelling mistakes, as you will see. I don't know a fourth of what he does about the French language, and yet I have corrected a great deal of those mistakes in the booklet he was printing while I was in Petersburg on the early history of the Russian peoples, which my friend Fabbroni and others well versed in such matters here hold in esteem. After I had left, he offered to dedicate it to the emperor, who answered him with such grace that I have decided to include a copy of that message. I am certain that you will appreciate seeing a proof of what I have written you about that worthy prince. Certainly the smallest prince of the empire would think to be lowering himself too much, if writing in that style to a private citizen.

I have just now received from Leghorn a letter by Major Barnes, in which he writes: "I have received certain advise that Commodore Preble has taken and carried into Syracuse a Tripoline bombard with 70 men. I hope he may soon take as many as to equal our prisoners in number at Tripoli."

I think he is mistaken on the supposition that they would exchange prisoners. What is more, should they agree to the exchange, they would not release even the captain alone for a thousand of their rabble. I am so eager to see coming *as soon as possible* a good reinforcement from America.

Captain Yeardsley told Mr. Appleton that he will set sail in three or four days and that he will take great care of the strawberry pot. He has had it stored in his room, will have it watered when needed and brought outside when it will rain. I have let him know that this kind of plant does not require too much moisture. Since we have a milder than usual winter here, many of the aforementioned plants already bear flowers and there is one that already has fruits.

The custom of grafting apricots on plum trees is almost universally accepted here. I advise you that they actually have better outcome, resulting in stronger and longer lasting plants, when they are grafted on trees of the same nature. I am inclined to think that the same would apply to any kind of plants.

I confirm I am as always, all yours   FILIPPO MAZZEI

Dft (Archivio Filippo Mazzei, Pisa, Italy); partially illegible; part of a conjoined series of Mazzei's drafts of letters to TJ (see Margherita Marchione and Barbara B. Oberg, eds., *Philip Mazzei: The Comprehensive Microform Edition of his Papers*, 9 reels [Millwood, N.Y., 1981], 6:919-20). Recorded in SJL as received 13 Apr. 1804. Enclosure not found, but see below.

UN VASO COLLE FRAGOLE D'OGNI MESE: Mazzei sent the everbearing but small-fruiting Alpine strawberry, known to produce fruit several months of the year. In 1810, TJ remarked that he was disappointed in its yield, guessing it would "take acres to yield a dish" (Peter J. Hatch, *The Fruits and Fruit Trees of Monticello* [Charlottesville, 1998], 167; RS, 2:481-2; Vol. 34:306-7n; TJ to Mazzei, 18 July 1804).

UN ALTRA MIA A MR. MADISON: for Mazzei's letter to Madison, see Mazzei to TJ, 28 Dec. 1803.

UN'OPUSCOLO: Mazzei sent TJ one of the 100 copies of Jan Potocki's *Dynasties du second livre de Manethon* published in Florence in 1803. TJ paid John March to have the work leather bound in August 1805 (Sowerby, No. 2; statement of account with March, 30 Sep. 1805).

PR. MAR. LUB: Elizabeth Lubomirska, known as the Princesse Maréchale, was Potocki's mother-in-law from his first marriage (Margherita Marchione and others, eds., *Philip Mazzei: Selected Writings and Correspondence*, 3 vols. [Prato, Italy, 1983], 3:314, 617; François Rosset and Dominique Triaire, *Jean Potocki* [Paris, 2004], 108, 111; Vol. 12:387; Vol. 13:104; Vol. 14:446).

SULL'ISTORIA PRIMITIVA DEI POPOLI DELLA RUSSIA: Potocki's *Histoire primitive des peuples de la Russie* was published in St. Petersburg in 1802 and included his letter of dedication to Alexander I, for which the emperor named him his private counselor (Jean Potocki, *Écrits politiques* [Geneva, 1987], 156-7).

TRIPOLINE BOMBARD: on 23 Dec. 1803, the American warships *Constitution* and *Enterprize*, under the command of Commodore Edward Preble, took possession of the ketch *Mastico* off the coast of Tripoli. Although sailing under Turkish colors with a Turkish captain, the vessel also carried two Tripolitan officers, several Tripolitan soldiers, and some 42 African slaves belonging to the bey of Tripoli and other Tripolitan merchants. After further investigation, Preble discovered that the ketch was Tripolitan, and that the vessel and its crew had played an active role in the capture of the *Philadelphia* and the plundering of its crew. Many of the African slaves were apparently intended as gifts from the bey to the Ottoman sultan. Taking his prize to Syracuse, Preble renamed it the *Intrepid* and added the ketch to the Mediterranean squadron. It would subsequently play a vital role in the burning of the *Philadelphia* in March 1804 (NDBW, 3:289, 294, 300, 310-11, 371, 374, 378; Christopher McKee, *Edward Preble: A Naval Biography, 1761-1807* [Annapolis, 1972], 184-5, 189-91; Joseph Barnes to TJ, 4 Feb., 16 Mch. 1804).

From Thomas T. Davis

DR SIR   Danville Jany. 28th 1804

By Major Barbee I send you a lump of Salt broken from the Salt mountain on the Arkansas River[1] by Mr. Choto a French Gentleman at St. Louisa; it was of at least 4. lb weight when given me but many peices have broken off. The other p[. . .] sent you is what I suppose to be Plaister of Paris & is in immense quantities on the Missouri. Major Barbee is a man of Great respectability.

I am respectfully Your Obt Sevt.   THO. T DAVIS

RC (DLC); torn at seal; addressed: "The Honble Tho: Jefferson City of Washington" with notation: "Hond. by Major J. Barbee"; endorsed by TJ as received 6 Mch. and so recorded in SJL.

MAJOR BARBEE: probably Joshua Barbee of Danville, a major and brigade inspector in the Kentucky militia (*Register*

of the Kentucky State Historical Society, 28 [1930], 4; Thomas Speed, *The Political Club, Danville, Kentucky, 1786-1790* [Louisville, Ky., 1894], 83-4).

MR CHOTO: either Auguste or Pierre Chouteau (see Davis to TJ, 5 Oct. 1803).

[1] Preceding four words interlined.

To James Dinsmore

DEAR SIR   Washington Jan. 28. 04.

I return you the drawings for the architrave of the front of the gallery, with a preference of that marked b. with the rounded listel. I do not approve of cutting the wall, not even the cellar wall, to make a space for the descent of the clock weights; but would have them advanced into the room so as to descend clear even of the cellar wall. should the box in this case encroach too much on the window, we may avoid the eye sore by leaving them unboxed, to descend naked till they get to the floor whence they may enter a square hole & go on to the cellar floor.

The loss of so much plank by fire & otherwise is one of the most afflicting circumstances I have had to meet in the whole course of my building: & the only term to it seems to be the conclusion of the work. to cover the kiln-house with slabs will be only to require double time & fuel to season with and probably to consign another kiln full to the

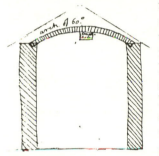 flames. we must therefore purchase bricks somewhere, cost what they will, to cover the house with an arch as here represented. it will take about 1500. whole bricks, clinkers. the gable ends may be closed with stone, leaving in the Southern one a smoke hole as is shown in this drawing, so that stopping that and the firehole at the bottom of the other end, a fire may be extinguished in a moment for want of air, even if it has already made some progress. so the external[1] covering of wood may burn down without affecting the plank. speak to mr Lilly to get the bricks, and to mr Hope to do the work as soon as the weather will admit, and in the mean time endeavor to[2] make a new provision of plank. John Perry proposes to get the scantling for the N.W. offices this winter, which I should prefer if it can be secured from waste. I am afraid the flooring plank he was to lay upstairs is among that lost, and that we shall not have those rooms ready for the plaisterer. Accept my best wishes.   TH: JEFFERSON

RC (H. W. Lende, Jr., San Antonio, Texas, 1988); at foot of text: "Mr. Dinsmore." Enclosures not found.

Dinsmore likely enclosed DRAWINGS FOR THE ARCHITRAVE intended for Monticello's entrance hall in a letter of 21 Jan.,

recorded in SJL as received 24 Jan. but not found. That letter also must have offered suggestions for the installation of the Great Clock in that room. Powered by two cannonball-like WEIGHTS, which were strung on ropes and descended into the basement below and which also set off the hourly striking of a Chinese-inspired gong, the clock was completed according to TJ's specifications in 1793 and installed in the renovated Monticello in 1804 or 1805. TJ purchased weights for it in July 1804 (Susan R. Stein, *The Worlds of Thomas Jefferson at Monticello* [New York, 1983], 376-7; MB, 2:1131).

Dinsmore had likely provided details on the burning of the plank house at Monticello, about which Anne Cary Ran-dolph also reported in her letter of 21 Jan. CLINKERS are bricks whose surface has become vitrified through exposure to intense heat (OED).

A letter of 19 Jan. from JOHN PERRY, recorded in SJL as received 24 Jan., has not been found.

[1] Word interlined.
[2] TJ here canceled "provide."

From Nicolas Gouin Dufief

MONSIEUR,   à Philadelphie ce 28 de Janvier. 1804

Mr Bocquet, artiste de mérite & auteur d'un plan interessant de la Capitale du pays de nos nouveaux frères, s'est chargé de vous remettre lui même la présente, & un paquet qui contient les livres que vous m'avez demandés—

J'aurais bien désiré pouvoir vous adresser une édition du nouveau testament en Anglais, aussi Jolie que l'édition Grèque & latine de Londres, mais telle qu'elle est, elle vaut beaucoup mieux que l'édition Américaine de Boston—

Je finis en faisant les vœux les plus ardens pour que l'année qui Commence soit pour vous une Suite non Interrompue d'événemens heureux, & en vous priant d'agréer avec votre bonté ordinaire mes Sentimens inébranlables d'estime, de respect, & de réconnaissance

N. G. DUFIEF

Le prix des livres est Comme Suit

2 exempl. du Testamt.	G. & L.	5.	D
2 D	Angl.	1 25	
		6.25	

EDITORS' TRANSLATION

SIR,   Philadelphia, 28 Jan. 1804

Mr Bocquet, a talented artist and author of an interesting map of the capital of our new brothers' country, volunteered to give you this letter, along with a package containing the books you requested.

I would have liked to be able to send you an English edition of the New Testament as attractive as the Greek and Latin edition from London, but this one, such as it is, is still much better than the American edition from Boston.

I conclude by extending my most fervent wishes that your new year be a continual series of happy events, and asking you to accept, with your char-

acteristic kindness, my unwavering sentiments of admiration, respect and
gratitude.   N. G. DUFIEF

The books are priced as follows:
2 copies of the New Testament in Greek and Latin   5.00 dollars
2 copies in English   1.25
                                                      6.25

RC (DLC); at foot of text: "Le Président des Etats-Unis"; endorsed by TJ as received 4 Feb. and so recorded in SJL.

MR BOCQUET: undoubtedly the artist and designer whose work "A View of New Orleans Taken from the Plantation of Marigny" was hung in the dining room at Monticello. At this time, he was identified most often as John L. Boqueta (or Boquet) de Woiseri, the name that appeared in advertisements for engraved versions of the above-named painting and of his PLAN INTERESSANT of New Orleans. While in Washington, Boqueta received TJ's permission to dedicate the engrav-

ings to the president and also convinced the Senate to subscribe for an engraving of the plan, which was to be hung in the Senate Chamber (Philadelphia *Aurora*, 23 Feb. 1804; *New-York Commercial Advertiser*, 17 Apr. 1804; New York *Daily Advertiser*, 7 Mch. 1805; JS, 3:355; Vol. 41:illustration).

The editions of the NOUVEAU TESTAMENT EN ANGLAIS were King James Version texts printed in Dublin in 1791 and 1799. Evidence indicates that TJ cut passages from both editions in compiling "The Philosophy of Jesus," the original of which has been lost (EG, 45-6).

From William Dunbar

DEAR SIR   Natchez 28th. Jan: 1804

I have the pleasure of transmitting you a few imperfect notes relating to the Missisippi and the Alluvial Country thro which it passes. I am sensible they contain remarks of trivial importance, but believing almost every thing relating to this Country to be *now* very interesting to the United States, I have considerably enlarged my notes since the cession of Louisiana, & do now suffer them to escape from my hand, flattering myself that their imperfections will be veiled by your indulgence. Should you think them not unworthy of being read before the Philosophical Society, you will be pleased to transmit them, at your leisure, to that respectable body.—I have added the results of three years meteorological observations, but have forborn to subjoin any notes concerning the influence of Seasons, as they would be little more than a repetition of what the Society is already in possession of. I have only noticed two Phenomena, one produced by the Sun, the other by the Moon.—My Amanuensis being a frenchman little acquainted with english, you will be pleased to excuse errors hastily corrected.

I am concerned to observe that a resolution has been submitted to Congress by a Committee, of which our own Delegate is a Member, which resolution goes to deprive Jefferson College of 30 acres of land granted by the late Congress and to give the same to the City of Natchez: The Town of Natchez is not in distress, the Corporation has been empowered by this legislature to levy taxes, more than sufficient for their expences, upon all property within the liberties of the town. —The College is in absolute poverty: The Trustees, reckoning upon the thirty acres (near the town) as an object immediately productive, have passed a resolution, to prepare plans & contract for the erection of the most necessary buildings; if the 30 acres are taken away, the progress of the College must be arrested. Our public treasury has been so poor (& so unreasonable an aversion from paying taxes prevails) that the College has received no aid from the territory: private Contribution has not gone beyond the narrow Circle of a few public spirited individuals; the section reserved by Congress will not very speedily be productive; hence if our newly created town Corporation obtains a victory over the College, the poor Seminary will be absolutely nipped in the bud.

With the highest Consideration I have the honor to be Your most Obedt. Servant   WILLIAM DUNBAR

RC (DLC); endorsed by TJ as received 29 Feb. and so recorded in SJL. Dft (Lb in Ms-Ar: William Dunbar Papers). Enclosures not found, but see below.

TJ forwarded Dunbar's enclosed NOTES on the Mississippi River and his METEOROLOGICAL OBSERVATIONS to the American Philosophical Society, which read them at its meetings of 6 and 13 Apr. 1804. The society subsequently published both papers in the sixth volume of its *Transactions* as "Description of the river Mississippi and its Delta, with that of the adjacent parts of Louisiana" and "Monthly and annual Results of Meteorological Observations made by William Dunbar, Esq. at the Forest, 4 Miles East of the River Mississippi, in Latitude 31°. 28s. North, and Longitude 91°. 30s. West of Greenwich" (APS, *Transactions*, 6 [1809], 165-89; APS, *Proceedings*, 22, pt. 3 [1884], 350; TJ to Dunbar, 13 Mch. 1804; TJ to Caspar Wistar, 24 Mch. 1804).

RESOLUTION HAS BEEN SUBMITTED: on 9 Nov. 1803, the House of Representatives received a petition from the mayor and aldermen of the city of Natchez, asking that title to certain vacant property in and adjacent to the city be confirmed to

them. The land in question, however, had already been set aside for the support of Jefferson College, as authorized under section 12 of the 3 Mch. 1803 act "regulating the grants of land, and providing for the disposal of the lands of the United States, south of the state of Tennessee." A House committee reported in favor of the Natchez petition on 15 Dec. and presented a resolution to repeal the portion of the 1803 act regarding lands set aside for Jefferson College. Dunbar, however, challenged the city's authority to determine land titles in Natchez and subsequently presented his own petition, which the House received on 26 Jan. 1804 and which claimed that a lot in Natchez had been granted to him by the Spanish government in 1797. The House referred assorted papers to a new committee, which on 10 Mch. recommended that the portion of the 1803 act that set aside lands for the benefit of Jefferson College "be suspended until further order be taken thereon by Congress" (JHR, 4:440, 489, 553, 565, 632; ASP, *Public Lands*, 1:162-3, 185-7, 194-6; U.S. Statutes at Large, 2:234, 305; *Terr. Papers*, 5:426-7).

OUR OWN DELEGATE: William Lattimore.

NEWLY CREATED TOWN CORPORATION: the Mississippi Territory legislature incorporated the city of Natchez on 10 Mch. 1803 (Harry Toulmin, *The Statutes of the Mississippi Territory, Revised and Digested by the Authority of the General Assembly* [Natchez, 1807], 128-35).

From Lemuel Sessums

University of N, Carolina

PATRON OF MANKIND,   January 28th. 1804

I ardently beg that you peruse this letter and reflect on the situation of a family which I shall attempt to describe. My Father is a man, aged fifty six, of independent circumstances, My Mother is a woman, aged forty five, of laudable affections. They live in the town of Tarborough in this state; I am now a student here and having perhaps more acqured knowlege than my Father have been pitched upon to write this letter; We have in family five whites as we know of, one of my Brothers left Tarborough in the year 95, we have occasionally heard from him, the last time was March 1803; in which month I had a loving Brother that departed this life, which was the occasion of much distress in the family, particularly between my loving Father and affectionate Mother. A Captain by the name of William Rickard was through this state in the year 95 gathering troops to go to the westard to guard against the attacks of the Indians or Spaniards, he was in Tarborough and my Brother, unfortunate for him and distressfull to the family, happened to be intoxicated. Rickard being a recruiting officer, and of a pretty flattering tongue persuaded him to enlist, he pleased with the idea of being usefull to his country accepted of the offer when in that situation. He enlisted for five years, his time was up in the year 1800 in the month of august. The september of the same month, My Father and myself started after him, we went as far as Nashville, we there heard that he had enlisted a second time and for five years more. At the news of this, Oh most excellent Sir, judge the sensations of a venerable Father! his lips quivered like a leaf, his countenance displayed the mingled emotions of sorrow, anger and affliction, in fact he was deprived of his natural reason a considerable time. My Brother was then at the Natches five hundred miles from Nashville, my Father was so disappointed at his conduct, so far from home and having a numerous family of whites and blacks to attend to, thought proper to return; so we were deprived of the pleasure of seeing him. He has since written to my Father giving the cause of his conduct which was as follows. That he was at the distance of twelve hundred miles from home, that he was in indigent circumstances, without money, without friends and the most disagreeable of all reflections was, that he thought he was forsaken by his once loving Father. Oh heavens, placing myself in his situation, I behold all its horrors, all its miseries. I at one moment imaginarily behold him gasping under the agonies of death produced by melancholy reflection, at another acting like a furious madman, engaging in all the follies and precipitancies of youth. But need I attempt to describe these things which you very well know? On account of the death of one of my Brothers, on account of the age of my parents and the anxiety they have to see *him* once more before death who is now at fort Adams. I most humbly petition by their request and with my own desire, that you release him from the service of the united states, that you direct a letter to me with such powers that my Father or myself may go and bring him home. On this occasion you have an opportunity to shew your compassion, let me entreat you to extend to him that pity which a human being deserves, reflect my Most Worshipfull Sir on the numerous inconveniences, the miseries and oppressions attendant on the life a soldier. under the direct command of a tyranical captain, obliged to obey his orders Just or unjust, more enslaved than the blacks of this country and lastly deprived of all the comforts of this life. His situation is not as bad as that of my loving Parents, their feelings on this occasion I cannot describe. the afflictions of Parents so situated are unknown to me, because I never experienced them; But let me tell you my dear Sir, I have frequently been in their company and heard them converse about him until the tears trickeled down their cheeks, absobed in grief, they were deprived of utterance. Oh, mentally and bodily afflicted, What would be their Joy, should you grant a release? What pleasure would they derive from seeing once more the child of their bosom? What inexpressible satisfaction would there be upon a meeting. But alas now what melancholy thoughts, what number of sorrows attend their disturbed souls? insted of their affliction decreasing old age appears to strengthen it, neither the light of the day nor the darkness of the night can obliterate his remembrance. He is absent and he never will return unless by your interposition. Grant Oh for heavens sake grant our most humble request. I shall write no more, words I am persuaded will not have any effect upon your mind.

suffer me then to subscribe my name with sentiments of the highest respect, greatest esteem and sincere love.

LEMUEL SESSUMS

N.B. My Brother who is the soldier is named Roderick Sessums and my Father Solomon Sessums.

RC (MoSHi); addressed: "To his Excellency Thomas Jefferson President of the united states City of Washington"; postmarked Chapel Hill, 29 Jan.; endorsed by TJ as received 8 Feb. and so recorded in SJL.

A member of the senior class at the University of North Carolina, Lemuel Sessums (ca. 1784-1804) died on 5 Mch., at the age of 20 (Raleigh *Minerva; or, Anti-Jacobin,* 19 Mch.; *Wilmington Gazette,* 27 Mch.).

To James Walker

Sir   Washington Jan. 28. 1804

Your letter of Oct. 1. was recieved in the course of that month, altho' the delay of compleating my mill will not only lose me the intermediate rent, but endanger rival establishments getting the start, yet my absence from home rendering it impossible for me to make other satisfactory arrangements, I must acquiesce in the delay of another twelvemonth as you propose, and expect you to begin for me in autumn next. by that time mr Hope will have done the walls, and mr Perry the covering & carpenter's work generally. I must therefore get you to lay off the exact spot for the mill house for mr Hope, furnish him with a plan, and give mr Lilly a bill of scantling, which he will have sawed at the saw mill if compleated, or by hand if not compleated. I presume the sooner the ground is laid off the better, that mr Lilly may commence digging the foundation. possibly he may find blowing to do in it. you can also be so good, when you are there as to advise him about the canal, which has not yet been properly compleated, & the wing dam. from defects in both I understand the water does not get to the mill in proper quantity. Accept my best wishes

Th: Jefferson

PrC (MHi); at foot of text: "Mr James Walker"; endorsed by TJ in ink on verso.

TJ received Walker's LETTER of 1 Oct. on 16 Oct. 1803 (Vol. 41:460).

To Timothy Bloodworth

Dear Sir   Washington Jan. 29. 1804.

I thank you for the seed of the fly trap. it is the first I have ever been able to obtain, and shall take great care of it. I am well-pleased to hear of the progress of republicanism with you.[1] to do without a land tax, excise, stamp tax & the other internal taxes, to supply their place by economies, so as still to support the government properly & to apply 7,300,000 D. a year steadily to the paiment of the public debt; to discontinue a great portion of the expences on armies & navies, yet protect our country & it's commerce with what remains; to purchase a country as large & more fertile than the one we possessed before, yet ask neither a new tax, nor another souldier to be added, but to provide that the country shall by it's own income pay for itself before the purchase money is due; to preserve peace with all nations, and particularly an equal friendship to the two great rival[2] powers France & England, and to maintain the credit & character of the nation in as high a degree as it has ever enjoyed, are measures which I think must reconcile the great body of those who thought themselves our enemies; but were in truth only the enemies of certain jacobinical, atheistical, anarchical, imaginary caracatures, which existed only in the land of the raw head & bloody bone beings created to frighten the credulous. by this time they see enough of us to judge our characters by what we do, and not by what we never did, nor thought of doing, but in the lying chronicles of the newspapers. I know indeed there are some characters who have been too prominent to retract, too proud & impassioned to relent, too greedy after office & profit to relinquish their longings, and who have covered their devotion to monarchism under the mantle of federalism, who never can be cured of their enmities. these are incurable maniacs, for whom the hospitable doors of Bedlam are ready to open, but they are permitted to walk abroad while they refrain from personal assault.

The applications for Louisiana are so numerous that it would be immoral to give a hope to the friends you mention. the rage for going to that country seems universal. Accept my affectionate salutations & assurances of great esteem & respect.   TH: JEFFERSON

PrC (DLC); at foot of text: "Timothy Bloodworth esq."

[1] Preceding two words interlined.
[2] Word interlined.

I THANK YOU: TJ is replying to Bloodworth's letters of 12 Dec. 1803 and 17 Jan. 1804.

From Timothy Bloodworth

DEAR SIR   Wilmington January 29th 1804

I am Solicited by the Freinds of Mr George Gibbs of New York, formerly of this Town, to mention to the President the Charecter of that Gentleman, who I am inform'd has Made Application for the appointment of Navy Agent.

In compliance with their request, I beg leav to observe, that Mr Gibbs has during the Course of his Life supported the Charecter of an Honest Man, Much Esteem'd in this place, for his Steady habits,

& rectitude of Conduct. he was Brought up from his early youth to the Merchantile Business, & was considered a proficient in his calling. but has been unfortunate by seling his Stock in Trade, to a Mr Barkley, who became Bankrupt, & drew Mr Gibbs into the Vortex. on this occation he Conducted with much propriety, & obtain'd a Certificate of Bankruptcy. having no More to Add on this subject, shall conclude by expressing an Ardent wish for youre Health, & Happiness. With Sintiments of Gratitude, & perfect Esteem, I remain Dear Sir.

Youre Obedient Humble Servant.

TIMOTHY BLOODWORTH

RC (DNA: RG 59, LAR); endorsed by TJ as received 12 Feb. and "Gibbs John. to be Navy Agent N.Y." and so recorded in SJL.

Before declaring bankruptcy and moving to New York, GEORGE GIBBS had been in business with John Barclay in Wilmington (*Wilmington Gazette*, 3 Sep. 1801, 10 Mch., 20 May 1803).

Daniel Ludlow, the NAVY AGENT at New York, resigned in November 1803. John Beekman was appointed his successor the following month (NDBW, 3:241, 303).

To Mary Jefferson Eppes

MY DEAREST MARIA   Washington Jan. 29. 04.

This evening ought to have brought in the Western mail, but it is not arrived. consequently we hear nothing from our neighborhood. I rejoice that this is the last time our Milton mail will be embarrassed with that from New Orleans; the rapidity of which occasioned our letters often to be left in the post-offices. it now returns to it's former establishment of twice a week, so that we may hear oftener from you: and in communicating to us frequently the state of things I hope you will not be sparing, if it be only by saying 'all is well.' I think Congress will rise the 2d. week in March, when we shall all join you. perhaps mr Eppes may sooner. on this I presume he writes you. it would have been the most desireable of all things could we have got away by this time. however I hope you will let us all see that you have within yourself the resource of a courage, not requiring the presence of any body.—since proposing to Anne the undertaking to raise Bantams I have recieved from Algiers two pair of beautiful fowls, something larger than our common fowls with fine aigrettes. they are not so large nor valuable as the East-India fowl, but both kinds, as well as the Bantams are well worthy of being raised. we must therefore distribute them among us; and raise them clear of mixture of any kind.

all this we will settle together in March, and soon after I hope we shall begin the levelling, and establishment of your hen-house at Pant-ops. give my tenderest love to your sister; to all the young ones kisses, to yourself every thing affectionate.   TH: JEFFERSON

RC (Mrs. Harold W. Wilson, Miami, Florida, 1964); addressed: "Mrs: Eppes Edgehill near Milton"; franked; postmarked 30 Jan.

I HAVE RECIEVED FROM ALGIERS: see Richard O'Brien to TJ, 8 Oct. 1803.

From Bishop James Madison

DEAR SIR   Williamsburg Jany. 29h. 1804

Our College having just lost it's Professor of Mathematics, I am extremely anxious to procure, if possible, a Person for that office, who shall be, in every Respect, perfectly qualified. It has occurred to me, that Mr Mansfeild, the Author of the ingenious Dissertations, with which you favoured me, might be induced to accept the office. As you are acquainted with him, & probably, have some Knowledge of his Circumstances, I thought I should not trespass too much upon your Goodness, to beg the Favour of you to inform me, whether you supposed such a Place would be agreable to him. I recollect that you mentioned, he had been appointed to execute a Business, which would necessarily take some Time; but should he return by the Fall, & reasonable Expectations be entertained, that he wd. then become one of our Body, I have no doubt, the Place might be Kept open for him; especially, if his private Character be worthy of his distinguished Talents.—The Emoluments may be rated at 1.000$ pr an:—too little—indeed, to attract Men of real Talents; but we do not abandon the Hope of a more adequate Remuneration.—

Perhaps there may be within your Knowledge some other Person, whom you could recommend; if so, the Information would be considered as an additional Proof of your Desire to befriend Science.

In the Report, which I have presented to the Executive of this State, I flatter myself, that I have already demonstrated the Invalidity of the Claim of Maryland.

Permit me to congratulate you upon the happy Termination of all our Anxieties relative to Louisiana; & I will not refrain from adding, that I beleive, in the Estimation of Reason & of common Sense, the Beginning, the Progress, & the End of that great Acquisition, reflect the highest Honour upon the present Administration—I am, Dr Sir, with sincerst Respect & Esteem

Yr. Friend & Sert   J MADISON

RC (DLC); endorsed by TJ as received 4 Feb. and so recorded in SJL.

The COLLEGE of William and Mary's professor of moral philosophy, Robert Andrews, had long doubled as MATHEMATICS instructor at the cash-strapped institution. The INGENIOUS DISSERTATIONS appeared in Jared Mansfield's *Essays, Mathematical and Physical* (J. E. Morpurgo, *Their Majesties' Royall Colledge: William and Mary in the Seventeenth and Eighteenth Centuries* [Williams-burg, Va., 1976], 183, 216; Vol. 31:280n; Vol 40:412n).

REPORT: Madison sent letters of 4 Nov. and 13 Dec. 1803 to Governor John Page concerning the commission appointed to investigate Maryland's claims on territory controlled by Virginia. Page enclosed them in a communication of 10 Dec. 1805 to the House of Delegates (Vi: Executive Communications to the Speaker of the House of Delegates; Vol. 38:325-6, 338n; Vol. 40:533-4).

From Samuel Morse

DEAR SIR,   Savannah, January 29, 1804.

As I have engaged to notice the defects as well as the good qualities of any candidate recommended to office, it is proper that you should know the following fact.

Capt. Choate purchased in Liverpool a quantity of glass and crockery ware for his own use, On the way home, his mate, Guthrie, persuaded him that he ought not to pay duties "when such a fellow as Putnam had command of the cutter, and suffered goods every day to be run." Choate hearkened to him, *gave* him, the goods, and they were smuggled ashore. Guthrie has, since, been united with Putnam, & threatened a prosecution, but it was supposed the proof was not sufficient.

I am persuaded Choate heartily repents of the transaction and will never again be guilty of a similar. As it came to my knowledge since I wrote in his favour, I believe it would be a neglect of duty to suffer it to pass.

Every body is looking for the removal of Putnam; though I receive some censure for the part I have acted against him: not on his account, but from a supposed coalition with Mr. Gibbons. I know I am doing my duty and am fully supported by my conscience.

There are two individuals who, I think, would not make improper candidates for the place. Alexander Wyly, son of the late Col. Wyly, a revolutionary character; and Benjamin Webley, who was himself a revolutionary character. Their particular claims have not been investigated, nor have they been spoken with on the subject.

Accept the assurance of my highest respect.   S. MORSE

RC (ViW: Tucker-Coleman Collection); at foot of text: "Mr Jefferson"; endorsed by TJ as received 15 Feb. and so recorded in SJL.

I WROTE IN HIS FAVOUR: Morse's recommendation of Captain Thomas Choate has not been found.

TJ appointed Henry PUTNAM master of the Georgia revenue cutter in March 1802 upon the recommendation of Senators James Jackson and Abraham Baldwin and Congressman John Milledge. Accusations that Putnam was a convicted thief appeared in Federalist newspapers soon after the appointment. TJ recommended that Putnam bring suit against the *Washington Federalist* in order to clear his name. On 8 Apr. 1803, the newspaper reported that Putnam had brought suit against its proprietors "for a *libel* against his *fame good name and reputation*" (*Washington Federalist*, 8 Apr. 1803; *Newburyport Herald*, 22 Apr. 1803; George R.

Lamplugh, *Politics on the Periphery: Factions and Parties in Georgia, 1783-1806* [Newark, Del., 1986], 171-2; Vol. 37: 388-9).

I HAVE ACTED AGAINST HIM: Morse supplied TJ with new charges against Putnam; see Notes on Henry Putnam's Case, printed at 13 Feb. The Republican newspaper editor was criticized for his SUPPOSED COALITION with Thomas GIBBONS, a Federalist described by Jackson as "one of the most violent British Partizans in Georgia." Putnam publicly horsewhipped Gibbons in Savannah after finding that he was the source of the 1802 allegations (Lamplugh, *Politics on the Periphery*, 171-2; Madison, *Papers, Sec. of State Ser.*, 1:175-7; Gallatin to TJ, 16 Feb.).

To Joseph Priestley

DEAR SIR   Washington Jan. 29. 04.

Your favor of Dec. 12. came duly to hand, as did the 2d. letter to Dr. Linn and the treatise on Phlogiston, for which I pray you to accept my thanks. the copy for mr Livingston has been delivered[1] together with your letter to him, to mr Harvie, my secretary, who departs in a day or two for Paris, & will deliver them himself to mr Livingston, whose attention to your matter cannot be doubted. I have also to add my thanks to mr Priestly, your son, for the copy of your Harmony, which I have gone through with great satisfaction. it is the first I have been able to meet with which is clear of those long repetitions of the same transaction as if it were a different one, because related with some different circumstances.

I rejoice that you have undertaken the task of comparing the moral doctrines of Jesus with those of the ancient Philosophers. you are so much in possession of the whole subject that you will do it easier & better than any other person living. I think you cannot avoid giving, as preliminary to the comparison, a digest of his moral doctrines, extracted in his own words from the evangelists, and leaving out everything relative to his personal history and character.[2] it would be short and precious. with a view to do this for my own satisfaction, I had sent to Philadelphia to get two testaments Greek of the same edition, & two English with a design to cut out the morsels of morality, and paste them on the leaves of a book, in the manner you describe as having been pursued in forming your Harmony. but I shall now get the thing done by better hands.

I very early saw that Louisiana was indeed a speck in our horizon, which was to burst in a tornado, and the public are unapprized how near this catastrophe was. nothing but a frank & friendly development of causes & effects on our part, and good sense enough in Buonaparte to see that the train was unavoidable, and would change the face of the world, saved us from that storm. I did not expect he would yield till a war took place between France and England, and my hope was to palliate and endure, if messrs. Ross, Morris &c. did not force a premature rupture, until that event. I believed the event not very distant, but acknolege it came on sooner than I had expected. whether however the good sense of Buonaparte might not have seen the course predicted to be necessary & unavoidable, even before a war should be imminent, was a chance which we thought it our duty to try; but the immediate prospect of rupture brought the case to immediate decision. the denoument has been happy: and I confess I look to this duplication of area for the extending a government so free and economical as ours, as a great achievement to the mass of happiness which is to ensue. whether we remain in one confederacy, or form into Atlantic and Missisipi confederacies, I believe not very important to the happiness of either part. those of the Western confederacy will be as much our children & descendants as those of the Eastern, and I feel myself as much identified with that country, in future time, as with this: and did I now foresee a separation at some future day, yet I should feel the duty & the desire to promote the Western interests as zealously as the Eastern, doing all the good for both portions of our future family which should fall within my power.

Have you seen the new work of Malthus on population? it is one of the ablest I have ever seen. altho' his main object is to delineate the effects of redundancy of population, and to test the poor laws of England, & other palliations for that evil, several important questions in political economy, allied to his subject incidentally, are treated with a masterly hand. it is a single 4to. volume, and I have been only able to read a borrowed copy, the only one I have yet heard of. probably our friends in England will think of you, & give you an opportunity of reading it. Accept my affectionate salutations, and assurances of great esteem & respect.   TH: JEFFERSON

PrC (DLC); in ink at foot of first page: "Dr. Priestly."

UNDERTAKEN THE TASK: Priestley's final work, *The Doctrines of Heathen Phi-* *losophy, Compared with Those of Revelation* (Sowerby, No. 1528; Joseph Priestley, Jr., to TJ, 20 Dec. 1804).

SENT TO PHILADELPHIA: TJ to Nicolas Gouin Dufief, 20 Jan.

The NEW WORK of Thomas Robert Malthus was the second edition of *Essay on the Principle of Population*, published in 1803. TJ had read reviews of the first edition, which was published anonymously (Vol. 35:533n; TJ to Thomas Cooper, 24 Feb. 1804).

[1] Word interlined in place of "forwarded."

[2] TJ first wrote "his history" before altering the passage to read as above.

To James Taylor, Jr.

SIR   Washington Jan. 29. 1804.

Immediately on the reciept of your favor of Dec. 29. I desired mr Barnes to remit you 94.68 D the balance due to you which I presume he has done.   I used formerly to be supplied from Norfolk with moulded candles of Myrtle wax, sometimes indeed so adulterated as to be unfit for use, but sometimes pure & good. when such, I prefer them for my own use to any candle on account of their cleanness & fragrance. if you could furnish me with 100. ℔. of sufficiently pure, & of the larger size I should be glad of them.   I have been so troublesome to my friend Colo. Newton with my cyder commissions & others, that I have avoided trespassing on him this year: but were you to meet with Hughs's crab cyder, genuine & good, 3. or 4 barrels would be very acceptable. but they must come double-cased, or they will come half-water, as has happened on the way from Norfolk with all I have had hitherto from thence. Accept my salutations & respects.

TH: JEFFERSON

PrC (MHi); at foot of text: "Mr. Taylor"; endorsed by TJ in ink on verso.

Taylor's FAVOR, recorded in SJL as received 7 Jan., has not been found. A pre-

vious letter from Taylor of 22 Nov. 1803, recorded in SJL as received 2 Dec., and TJ's response of 3 Dec. have also not been found.

To Joseph Lord

Washington Jan. 30. 04.

Th: Jefferson presents his compliments to mr Lord, and returns him his Manuscript. neither his time nor qualifications permit him to undertake to pass a judgment on compositions, & still less on those of the character of the within, which have been less his study than [. . .] others. he thanks him for the communication.

PrC (DLC); torn; month interlined in dateline in place of "Dec."; initially endorsed by TJ in ink on verso as a letter of 29 Jan., then altered to 30 Jan. Recorded in SJL under 29 Jan.

HIS MANUSCRIPT: see Lord to TJ, 16 Jan.

From Henry Moore

Alexandria Columbia
Jany 30th. 1804

SIR,

I had this pleasure a few days since; and have now to inform you that the person, in whose behalf I solicited your assistance, has this day moved to this place, and will have it in his power to maintain his Family by keeping a small Grocery Store, and taking five or six Boarders

I pray you excuse my Freedom in thus addressing you; and accept assurances of the high consideration and respect with which I have the Honor, to subscribe myself—

Very Respectfully Sir Your Obedt. Servt.

HENRY MOORE
of Cleon

RC (DNA: RG 59, LAR); endorsed by TJ as received 1 Feb. and so recorded in SJL.

FEW DAYS SINCE: Moore to TJ, 17 Jan.

From Sally Palmer

HONERED SIR

Hudson 30th january 1804

I pray you will pardon the boldness And pitty the Distressis of a poor disconsolate Widdow left a lone with three small Children And have nothing to support my self and them But my own labour the inhuman phizition That attendid my husdband in his sickness Has siesed my furniture and will expose it for sail Unless I Can procure money anugh to defray His Chargis hear I am a lone woman not A relative to apploy to in my distress and what Method to take to save what littel property I have Got I know not I ther fore take the boldness to seek for mercy at your hands hoping your Honner will pitty my afflictions and send me A small sum of money to relieve my present Distress and I hope the supream giver of all things will reward you for the kindness you will Do me and my fervent prayrs shall be raisd to heavin Continuly for your long life and Prosperity

Your Honners Humble servt

SALLY PALMER

RC (MHi); addressed: "Mr. Thomas Jefferson President of the united states Washington"; franked; postmarked Hudson, N.Y.; endorsed by TJ as received 6 Feb. and so recorded in SJL.

To Craven Peyton

DEAR SIR   Washington Jan. 30. 04.

Soon after my letter of the 16th. had gone off, your contract for corn occurred to me, which I had not recollected before. I saw at once that your draught must have been founded on that; and before the reciept of your letter of the 23d. which is only this moment come to hand, I returned the draught with an acceptance to mr Higginbotham & with explanations of the cause of delay, and assurances of taking it up at maturity. Accept my friendly salutations & assurances of esteem.   TH: JEFFERSON

RC (Goodspeed's Book Shop, Boston, 1946); at foot of text: "Mr. Craven Payton." PrC (ViU); endorsed by TJ in ink on verso.

From William Thomson

Manchester 30th Jany 1804.

I take the Liberty, Sir, of presenting you with a copy of the letters of Curtius, written by John Thomson of Petersburg. Perhaps the affection of a brother, may render him blind to the imperfections of this little work, yet he flatters himself, you will esteem it worthy the small space it shall occupy in your Library—The present edition contains a concise account of the life of the Author, written by his friend Mr. Hay. It contains but few incidents which can interest, for he had scarcely placed his foot on the threshold, when the door was closed forever on him. In soliciting your acceptance of this copy, I feel myself justified, under the belief that the works of genius are always acceptable to you, but more especially, those which are the productions of our own country. I am, Sir, with great respect, yours,

WILLIAM THOMSON

RC (MoSHi); endorsed by TJ as received 3 Feb. and so recorded in SJL. Enclosure: *Letters of Curtius, Written by the Late John Thomson of Petersburg* (Richmond, 1804; Sowerby, No. 3526).

At this time, William Thomson, a lawyer, was selling his property in Manchester, Virginia, and settling the estates of his father and brother in preparation for a move out of the state. Instead, he ended up in Abingdon, where he lived for about three years. Following in his brother's footsteps, he published a series of highly critical letters addressed to John Marshall, substituting the pseudonym "Lucius" for his brother's "Curtius." Sometime after sending TJ his work *A Compendious View of the Trial of Aaron Burr* in 1807, Thomson moved to the Mississippi Territory, where he curried favor among Republican leaders in the area. William C. C. Claiborne reported naming him attorney general for Orleans Territory in August 1808, but although he remained on a list of Claiborne's appointments as of 21 Apr. 1809, it is unclear if Thomson, apparently offended by a perceived snub from Claiborne, ever assumed the duties of the office (Richmond *Virginia Argus*, 12 Feb. 1803, 4 Jan. 1804, 10 June 1807; *Aurora*, 21 Nov. and 1 Dec. 1807; *Terr. Papers*, 5:629; 9:798, 837; Rowland, *Claiborne Letter Books*, 4:239-41; Thomson to TJ, 7 Oct. 1807).

TJ was well familiar with the LETTERS OF CURTIUS, having requested a copy of the first edition in 1799 (Vol. 31:14-15n).

To Barthélemy Faujas de Saint-Fond

SIR   Washington Jan. 31. 1804.

You have given me great pleasure by sending me your excellent volume on geology. it might otherwise have been long unknown to me; as we are late here even in hearing of the new publications of Europe. altho' my engagements leave me time to read scarcely any thing, yet I could not resist the subjects of this volume. I had paid considerable attention some five & twenty years ago to the fossile bones on the Ohio. at that time that country was little explored, much less was known of the bones than at present, & they had been less the subject of discussion with the literati of Europe. M. de Buffon had given a first opinion that they were not the bones of an Elephant, in which Hunter had concurred. but M. de Buffon afterwards changed his opinion, and with this latter opinion Daubenton concurred. We had, for the ground of our judgment here, only the grinders, a few bones, & the climate they were found in. the grinders were marked by strong differences from those of the elephant: the bones were of vastly greater volume: the climate too rigorous for the elephant we knew. these differences were thought sufficient to deem this animal of a different genus. yet as genera & species are mere matters of definition, depending on the characteristics which each author of a system assumes as his rule of distribution, there can be no real objection to assigning to the American animal a chamber in the apartment of elephants, and to the Mammoth another and a distinct one, it being understood that ulterior comparisons shew them to be distinct species. your distribution of these animals therefore into 4. species, the Asiatic, the African, the Mammoth, and the American, is well calculated to reconcile opinions, & has just claims to adoption. the objections derived from climate may be solved, either, 1. by supposing that some great convulsion of our globe, some displacement of the ocean perhaps, has transported these remains from the places of original deposit to those where they are now found: altho' it would perhaps be remarked as singular that the same convulsion had brought none of the bones of the Asiatic or African elephant here, nor left any of those of the Mammoth, or American, there. or 2. by supposing that nature may have distinguished the different species of elephants by differences of temperament, as we see done in the case of the brown bear, & the white sea-bear: and in that of the round-horned elk, of America, & the palmated elk (called Moose in America) the former of which does not exist here North of 42.° nor the latter South of that line. between these two solutions every one will be able to satisfy himself with the classification you have so judiciously proposed.

The remains of the Megalonyx were discovered here in 1796. we had then never heard of the animal of Paraguay, whose skeleton is mounted at Madrid. we had only the foreleg compleat, & the claws, of ours, to guide us. we naturally therefore brought him into comparison with the clawed animals already known; and, of these, with the lion as the largest. it was not till 1797. that we obtained some knolege of the description by messrs. Cuvier & Roumé of the animal of Paraguay, & that through the imperfect channel & coarse engraving of an English magazine. these gentlemen having the whole skeleton before them, and particularly the teeth, as well as the claws, had found that, according to those methods of arrangement which assort quadrupeds by their teeth & claws, this one would take his station with the Sloth. nature deals only in individuals. classification is the mere work of man, to help his research and recollection, and different zoologists have assumed different characteristics for classification. hence it has happened that all of these methods sometimes associate species the most unlike in their general characters. the present instance is remarkable, as it brings together what nature has placed in her extremes, that is, the Bradypus, the slowest & most helpless of all animals, with the Megalonyx, in all probability the most powerful which has existed. in an arrangement which, like M. de Buffon's, presents animals in groupes, according to their general and most obvious analogies, I presume the Megalonyx would take his stand, where we had reviewed him, at the head of the Unguiculated column. still I think with you he had better be kept in reserve, as an animal sui generis, until further information may enable us to place him among companions with whom he will appear not dissorted.

A journey of discovery undertaken here will probably produce some further information as to the Megalonyx & other animals, lost as well as living. it's immediate object is to explore the Missouri river to it's source, proceed thence to the nearest river leading Westward, & descend that to the Pacific ocean; so as to give us with accuracy the geography of this interesting channel of communication across our continent. the labour & perils of this journey, the athletic constitution it required, hardy habits, knolege of Indian manners, and address in managing them, excluded from the enterprise men merely scientific, whose habits render them generally unequal to such an undertaking. Capt. Lewis, to whom I confided it, is perfectly equal to the Astronomical duties: and tho' neither a regular botanist, zoologist, or mineralogist, has been so accurate an observer of all the subjects of these departments existing here, that he will not lose his time in noting things already known. he will select such only as are new to this part of the world. he will particularly give a good account of new animals. this party, consisting of about 12. persons, will probably return at the close of 1805.

I am in hopes of being able, the ensuing summer, to send other parties up the principal branches of the Missisipi and Missouri; the Red river, Arcansa, the Padoucas, Panis, & the Missisipi itself. the objects will be the same with those confided to Capt. Lewis. these also will require two years to accomplish their mission, some of these rivers extending 1000. or 1200. miles from their mouths, and into a country as yet unexplored by whites. it will give me great pleasure if these enterprises should produce materials for extending the bounds of knolege, and enable us to yield to our elder brethren in science some return for the accumulated stores of twenty centuries which we have recieved from them.

I pray you to accept my salutations and assurances of great respect and consideration.   TH: JEFFERSON

RC (Sotheby's, 2002); at foot of first page: "M. Faujas de St. Fond."

For the VOLUME ON GEOLOGY, see Vol. 41:187-9.

UNGUICULATED COLUMN: that is, animals with nails or claws (OED).

JOURNEY OF DISCOVERY: Faujas de Saint-Fond published a French translation of the closing paragraphs concerning the western expedition of Lewis and Clark in the 1804 edition of the journal of the Muséum d'Histoire Naturelle. The following year, an English translation of this extract appeared in the *Philosophical Magazine* of London. Several American newspapers subsequently reprinted the secondhand translation, which included some differences in phrasing from the original (*Annales du muséum national d'histoire naturelle*, 5 [1804], 316; *The Philosophical Magazine: Comprehending the Various Branches of Science, the Liberal and Fine Arts, Agriculture, Manufactures, and Commerce*, 21 [1805], 280-1; New York *American Citizen*, 10 Dec. 1805; New York *Republican Watch-Tower*, 11 Dec. 1805; Boston *Democrat*, 18 Dec. 1805).

To Lafayette

MY DEAR FRIEND   Washington Jan. [31. 1804]

The rarity of my letters to you will satisfy you how difficult it is for me to write a letter; as you must be conscious of the impossibility of my wanting the inclination. since I wrote you last I have recieved mr Tracy's book on Ideologie and as you were so good as to be the channel of communication *from* him, so I must ask you to do the same *to* him, by rendering him my thanks for this mark of his attention; & for the pleasure I shall have in reading it at my first leisure moment. you must be so good as to deliver my friendly respects to Mde. de Chastellux also, on whose behalf you as well as herself wrote to me. the compensation to the Baltimore family was from the British government, not from that of Maryland, who confiscated poorly & simply. if the British government has mistaken the true representation of Lord Baltimore, they alone can correct it. I know I ought to write a letter to Mde. de Chastellux myself; but my dear friend I have now a thousand letters before me to each of which I ought to write an answer, & to any one of which it would be easy: but to all it is impossible, and I am obliged thus to make one letter answer many, & be burthensome to some friends & apparently unjust to others. I must now hasten to your own affairs. some of us are very anxious to get leave to shift the location of your lands to the neighborhood of N. Orleans, or even to the Kaskaskia purchase. we are afraid to propose it by itself. but if any bill should be before the legislature which would properly admit the introduction of such a provision, we shall not fail to try it. but the opportunity is uncertain. a location as near to N. Orleans as any vacant lands could be found, would be truly precious, as that country will settle rapidly & solidly. there it would be a noble settlement for any member of your family, should you never think of coming yourself. this will be delivered you by mr Harvie, my secretary, a young gentleman of family, fortune, personal virtue & distinguished talents, who is happy in an opportunity of presenting you his respects. deliver mine, avec empressement, to Mdes. de la Fayette & de Tessé, and be assured of my constant & affectionate attachmt & respect.   TH: JEFFERSON

PrC (DLC); torn; at foot of text: "M. de la Fayette."

Madame DE CHASTELLUX hoped to recover an indemnification that she believed was owed to her son, a descendant of the Lords Baltimore (Vol. 40:486n).

AVEC EMPRESSEMENT: eagerly.

To La Valette

Washington Jan. 31. 04.

I recieved with very great pleasure, my dear Sir, your favor of September 11. forwarded by mr Wheaton. it was the first authentic information I had recieved of you since I left Paris in 1789. and since that epoch what a croud of events have we seen! what a necrology! what could assure me you were not involved in it? but you are alive, in good health, & happy, and it is from yourself I learn it. I sincerely rejoice at it, always recollecting with pleasure the many proofs I recieved of your friendship at Baltimore now twenty years ago, as well as our friendly intercourse at Paris. I shall continue to nourish for you those friendly sentiments of those days, and tho' my vocations here may not permit me to repeat it in letters, nor to give length to the present expression of it, yet they will not be the less fervent & constant. this will be delivered you by mr Harvie, my Secretary & friend, of great merit and talents, and will therefore safely convey to you my affectionate salutations & assurances of great respect.

TH: JEFFERSON

PrC (ViW: Tucker-Coleman Collection); at foot of text: "Genl. La Vallette"; endorsed by TJ in ink on verso.

To Louis Pio

DEAR SIR   Washington Jan. 31. 1804.

Since my departure from Paris in 1789. I have at different epochs recieved letters from you, informing me of your health, and residence at that place. the busy scenes of life in which I have been constantly engaged here, have not permitted me to do justice to my feelings for my old friends beyond the Atlantic, by assuring them by letters of the continuance of my affections for them. in truth I have been under the necessity of abandoning the attempt to keep up my European correspondencies, in order to fulfill my more urgent duties here. nevertheless my affections & good wishes for them are ever the same, as if I could oftener express them. I am sorry to learn that the course of the revolution has left you in a less easy situation than it found you. what shipwrecks of life, fortune & happiness have marked it's devastating course? the issue of it has certainly not been what was originally proposed: but at this distance we are not competent to estimate it's final effect on the happiness of the nation. the happiness of our own experiment manifests itself from day to day. the present conveyance by mr

Harvie my secretary, offering me a certain conveyance, I could not deny myself the pleasure of recalling my self to your recollection, and of assuring you of the continuance of my friendship for you, and of my affectionate consideration.　　　　　TH: JEFFERSON

P.S. lest you should have sent me the only copy you had of the inclosed paper, I return it after having perused it with satisfaction

PrC (DLC); at foot of text: "M. Pio." Enclosure not found, but see Pio to TJ, March 1803 (Vol. 40:122-4).

To Andrew Ellicott

DEAR SIR　　　　　　　　　　　　　　Washington Feb. 1. 1804.

The Western boundary of Louisiana, after getting a certain distance from the sea, being the high lands inclosing all the waters running into the Missisipi or Missouri, I think it probable Congress will enable me to send two or more parties the next summer to ascertain some of the most important points in that contour. one will probably ascend the Red river from it's mouth to it's source, pass on to the Arcansa at it's head & descend that to it's mouth, ascertaining with astronomical precision the longitude & latitude of each source, and laying down the rivers themselves in the same way you did the Missisipi. another party should in the same way delineate two of the most important of the Southern branches of the Missouri. according to Arrowsmith these should be the Padoucas & Panis rivers. but it is difficult with our present information to say which they should be. Capt Lewis will give us the Missouri: and when we settle the source of the Missisipi with the British, I think to have that river surveied down to the mouth of Ohio. for the two first mentioned enterprises I shall want two proper characters. astronomy enough to take the latitude & longitude, the latter by lunar observations, is indispensible, this being the main object of the enterprize. bravery, prudence, habits of hardy living, some knolege of Indian character, a degree of knolege of the subjects of botany, Nat. history & mineralogy, would be useful qualifications, & the more of them the person possessed the better. do you know any persons qualified to take charge of such enterprises? what would be the fitness of mr Gillespie who was with you formerly, for such a matter? I pray you to designate to me as many of the persons within your acquaintance as have the essential talent, and to particularise which of the subordinate qualifications they also possess. what do you think of the methods I suggested in my letter to you of

Feb. 26. of last year, for taking lunar observations without a time piece? I have not been able to convince myself of their inadequacy. Accept my salutations & respects. Tʜ: Jᴇꜰꜰᴇʀꜱᴏɴ

RC (DLC: Ellicott Papers); addressed: "Andrew Ellicot esq. Lancaster. Pensva"; franked. PrC (DLC).

ᴘᴀᴅᴏᴜᴄᴀꜱ & ᴘᴀɴɪꜱ ʀɪᴠᴇʀꜱ: that is, the Kansas and Platte Rivers (see TJ to Meriwether Lewis, 16 Nov. 1803).

Surveyor David ɢɪʟʟᴇꜱᴘɪᴇ served with Ellicott on the commission to survey the southern boundary of the United States in the late 1790s. He was the son of Congressman James Gillespie of North Carolina (Andro Linklater, *The Fabric of America: How Our Borders and Boundaries Shaped the Country and Forged Our National Identity* [New York, 2007], 122, 151-2, 156-7, 164; Powell, *Dictionary of North Carolina Biography*, 2:299).

TJ's ʟᴇᴛᴛᴇʀ to Ellicott of 26 Feb. 1803 has not been found (Vol. 39:640).

From George Hay

Sɪʀ, Richmond. February 1. 1804

Mr. Carr informs me, that you were acquainted with the Character, and respected the talents of the late Mr. Thomson. I therefore take the liberty, of begging your acceptance of a Copy of the new Edition of the letters of Curtius: to which is prefixed a short sketch of his life, hastily written by myself.

The way in which the parties in *the dialogue* are mentioned, is intentionally, vague. The inquisitorial power of public opinion is not so immediately felt, but is almost as formidable, as that which has been established by law in other Countries. I did not therefore think it prudent to Communicate to the World that *these parties* were Mahomet and Jesus Christ.

The history, to which Mr. T. intended to have devoted his time and talents, has been since undertaken, and I understand, accomplished by the present chief justice. It is not wonderful that *Curtius* and *General Marshall*, should have been both, ambitious of literary fame; but it is somewhat singular, that the views of both, should have been almost at the same time, directed to the same object.

Viewing you, at this moment, only as the friend of literature and genius, I will offer no apology for giving you the trouble of reading this lengthy letter.

I am, with great respect, Your mo. ob. Serv. Gᴇᴏ. Hᴀʏ

RC (MHi); endorsed by TJ as received 4 Feb. and so recorded in SJL. Enclosure: John Thomson, *The Letters of Curtius, Written by the Late John Thomson of Petersburg* (Richmond, 1804; Sowerby, No. 3526).

In his preface, Hay referred to the ᴅɪᴀʟᴏɢᴜᴇ "between the two most memorable personages that have ever appeared among men" and noted that Thomson, while never allowing the sheets out of his hands, read it out loud to Hay, who was "astonished and delighted" by it. The preface also mentioned Thomson's collection of information for a HISTORY, presumably about the American Revolution and early republic. John MARSHALL, the target of Thomson's Curtius letters, published the first three volumes of his *Life of George Washington* in 1804 (Thomson, *Letters of Curtius*, v-vi, viii).

To Jean Baptiste Say

SIR   Washington Feb. 1. 1804.

I have to acknolege the reciept of your obliging letter, and, with it, of two very interesting volumes on Political economy. these found me engaged in giving the [leisure moments I rarely find] to the perusal of Malthus's work on population, a work of [sound] logic, in which some of the opinions of Adam Smith, as well as of the [economists], are ably examined. I was pleased, on turning to some chapters where you treat the same questions, to find his opinions corroborated by yours. I shall [proceed] to the reading of your work with great pleasure. in the mean time the present conveyance, by a gentleman of my family going to Paris, is too safe to permit a delay in making my acknolegements for this mark of attention, and for having anticipated to me a satisfaction which the ordinary [course] of literary [communications would not] have given me for a considerable time.

The differences of circumstance between this and the [countries] of Europe furnish differences of fact whereon to [reason,] in questions of political economy, and will consequently produce [sometimes a difference of result]. [there,] for instance, the quantity of food is fixed, or increasing in a [slow] & only [Arithmetical ratio], and the [population is limited by the same] ratio. [supernumerary births] consequently add only to your [mortality]. here the immense extent of uncultivated and fertile lands enables every [man,] who will labour, to marry young, & to raise a family of any size. our food then may increase geometrically, with our labourers, and our births, however multiplied, [become effective].—Again, there the best distribution of labour is supposed to be that which places the manufacturing hands alongside of the agricultural; so that the one part shall feed both, & the other part furnish both with clothes & other comforts. would that be best here? [egoism], and first appearances say yes. Or, would it be better that all our labourers should be employed in Agriculture? in this case a double or treble portion of fertile lands would be brought into culture; a double or treble [creation] of food be produced, & it's surplus go to [nourish the now perishing] births of Europe, who in return would manufacture and send us in exchange our clothes & other comforts. morality listens to this, & so invariably do the laws of nature [. . .] our duties & interests, that when they seem to be at variance, we ought to suspect some fallacy in our reasonings. in solving this question too we should allow it's just weight to the moral & physical preference of the agricultural, over the manufacturing, man. my occupations permit me only to ask questions. they deny me the time, if I had the information, to answer them. perhaps, as worthy the attention of the author of the Traité d'economie politique, I shall find them answered in that work. if they are not, the reason will have been that you wrote for Europe; while I shall have asked them because I think for America.   Accept, Sir, my respectful salutations & assurances of great consideration.   Th: Jefferson

PrC (DLC); blurred and faint; at foot of first page: "Mr. Say."

TJ received Say's undated LETTER on 3 Nov. 1803. Say enclosed his two-volume

Traité d'économie politique (Sowerby, No. 3547).

GENTLEMAN OF MY FAMILY: Lewis Harvie (TJ to Joel Barlow, 19 Jan.).

To James Taylor, Jr.

DEAR SIR   Washington Feb. 1. 1804.
    I recieved last night your favor of Jan. 24. and thank you for your attention to me as to the Champagne you have recieved. my desire to take of it must depend entirely on it's quality. if fine I should be willing to take 30. dozen: but if not fine, it would be useless here. will you be so good as to send me a single case of it by the first possible conveyance by water, so that I may try it, and will instantly give you an answer. but I would wish you in the mean time not to miss the sale of the whole should you have an offer; because I should not otherwise feel myself at the perfect liberty I wish to be at, to purchase or not according to it's quality. as the ice in the Patomak may for some time prevent the arrival even of the sample, I think if 4. bottles were well packed in a light box, they would come safely by the stage, as quickly as a letter by the post, and I could decide on recieving them.   The pipe of Madeira you will be so good as to forward at your convenience. the single one will suffice for me this year as the increased taste for French wines lessens the consumption of Madeira. Accept my salutations & assurances of respect.   Th: Jefferson

PrC (MHi); at foot of text: "Mr. James Taylor"; endorsed by TJ in ink on verso.

From Philip Van Cortlandt

SIR, Washington Feby. 1. 1804

Rufus Easton Esqr. who will present this has informed me that he is an Applicant for an Office under the Territory of Louisiana and has expressed a desire that I should communicate the knowledge I have respecting him—

I remember meeting Mr. Easton one morning at Oneida and was favorably impressed which produced enquiry and was informed that he resided at Rome and was a Councellor at law of respectable reputation, and I have lately received a letter from Mr. D. Clinton giving me Similar information with a request that I shold introduce him to the members of the State and to afford him every proper Attention and patronage in conjunction with them—this is therefore intended as an Assurance of my Esteem for Mr. Easton and my concurrance with my Colliegues in Sentiment.

Please to Accept the tribute of my high Respect & Esteem
PH. V. CORTLANDT

RC (DNA: RG 59, LAR); endorsed by TJ as received 6 Feb. and "Easton Rufus to be Atty N.O." and so recorded in SJL with a brace connecting it to letters received the same day from Tompson J. Skinner of 9 Jan. and Oliver Phelps of 4 Feb.

From Madame de Corny

le 2 fevrier 1804.

je naurois pas le meilleur thé du monde, la quantite, la jolye boette qui le renferme ne Seroient pas tout ce quil y a de mieux que je crirois encor mille fois *Merci* pour le Souvenir seulement; Ce n'est point une vaine parole, je pense a Vous chaque matin, et Cette habitude m'est vraiment douce Si les malaises du soir, la nécessité de Consoler ma vie me font repetter 2 fois cette boisson tant aimée, encor je paye hommage a Celuy qui me l'a procuré. au milieux de tant daffaires et si importante, avoir songé a moi est dun prix infini—donnez moi donc souvent a lire des discours si sage si eloquent, lheureux president qui peut rapeller tout le bien quil a fait et tout celuy quil prépare, mon Compliment pouroit arriver trop tard après la réelection, je trouve donc prudent de vous lenvoyer davance, il est impossible que la reconnoissance public mette de linexactitude dans son choix pauvre montechillo vous voilà abandonné pour toujours, je vous prie, monsieur, d'indulger une nouvelle fantaisie, C'est de menvoyer un dessein du point de vue le plus favorable de Ce lieu qui a fait vos delices je nay jamais regardé avec indifference le dessein de mont vernon jugez que dinteret réuni pour celuy qui moffrira le tableau fidelle dune maison que vous avez bati, dun parc que vous avez planté. un de vos enfans loccupe til? que jamais il ne soit neglige je vous en prie.

je recois bien surement des lettres fort aimable de ma cher angelique est ce que je quitterai Cette valée sans la revoir? Sa fille Kruger aime lamerique Son mariage la voila avec un enfant C'est un lien bien fort je nespere plus quelle mamene sa mere Cette mere vous laimiez bien, aimez la toujours elle le meritte, Que vous importe tout Ce qui Se passe autour delle vous ete au dessus de Cela et C'est justice que je vous demande pr elle.

Vos filles sont surement bien mariee leurs maris sont ils près de vous loeil vigilant dun pere peut il les diriger

je nabuserois jamais de vos bontees et je ne me permetterai de vous recommander que dhonnetes gens. mais ce bon Mr de corny mavoit accoutumee au plaisir dobliger la solitude extrème dans laquelle je vis, le nouveau monde qui mentoure, laccident qui en Cassant mes os a rompu le peu de societe que j'avois, me prive de tout moyen detre util C'est un besoin pr mon coeur et jay pris la liberte de vous recommander 1° Mr le det pour lequel vous me faitte bien regretter quil ne Soit pas en amerique et 2° Mr Foncin qui a servi chez vous avec distinction

je suis encore bien empêché dans ma marche et lhyver tout entier est perdu pour les progres il faut les ajourner aux chaleurs. et, influeront telles sur mes vieux muscles. . . cela n'est pas demontré

adieu mon cher monsieur je voudrois vous avoir bien persuade de ma gratitude et des sentiments damitie que je vous ai donné pr toujours   DE CORNY

EDITORS' TRANSLATION

2 Feb. 1804

Even if this were not the best tea in the world, and in such quantity, and enveloped in the prettiest possible box, I would still shout thank you a thousand times, simply for the thought. It is not an exaggeration to say that I think of you every morning and this habit is very pleasant. When evening discomforts and the need for consolation make me pour two more cups of this drink I love so much, I once again praise the one who procured it for me. The fact that you thought of me, amidst so many important responsibilities, is infinitely precious to me.

Please give me such wise and eloquent speeches to read as often as possible. It is a fortunate president who can evoke all the good he has done and all that he is planning. Since my congratulations might arrive too late after the reelection, I think it prudent to send them in advance. Public gratitude cannot err in its choice.

Poor Monticello, abandoned forever. I beg you, Sir, to indulge a new fantasy. Could you send me a drawing of the place that has been your delight, done from the most favorable perspective? I never look at the drawing of Mount Vernon without being moved. Imagine how much more deeply I would feel for an accurate drawing of the house you built, in a garden you planted. Does one of your children take care of the garden? I beg you not to let it be neglected.

Of course, I receive very affectionate letters from my dear Angelica. Shall I leave this vale without seeing her again? Her daughter Cruger likes America. She is married with a child. That is a strong link. I no longer dare hope that she will bring her mother back to me. You used to like her mother. Keep cherishing her as she deserves. Do not be concerned about what goes on around her. You are above that; all I ask for is justice.

Your daughters surely have good marriages. Are their husbands nearby? Can a father's watchful eye guide them?

I would never take advantage of your kindness, and would only allow myself to recommend honest people to you. But the good Mr. de Corny showed me the pleasure of helping others. The extreme solitude in which I live, the new world that surrounds me, the accident of breaking my bones that also interrupted the little company I had, deprive me of any way of being useful. Since my heart needs to be useful, I take the liberty of recommending first Mr. Ledet, for whom you make me regret that he is not in America; and second Mr. Foncin, who served your country with distinction.

I still cannot walk and there is no way to progress during the winter. I must wait until warm weather, but will the warmth help my old muscles? It is not certain.

Farewell, my dear sir. I hope I have convinced you of my gratitude and of the friendship I have always had for you.   DE CORNY

RC (DLC); ellipses in original; endorsed by TJ as received 6 June and so recorded in SJL.

LE MEILLEUR THÉ: see TJ to Madame de Corny, 1 Nov. 1803.

DES DISCOURS SI SAGE: TJ probably sent a copy of his annual message to Congress delivered on 17 Oct. 1803 (Vol. 41:534-40).

MA CHER ANGELIQUE: Angelica Schuyler Church. Her daughter, Catherine Church Cruger, had a son, Eugene, in 1803 (New York *Evening Post*, 5 Feb. 1831). In a letter to Madame de Corny in January 1803, TJ noted that Angelica Church was Alexander Hamilton's sister-in-law (Vol. 39:418).

From William Eaton

Washington City
SIR,   Feb. 2d. 1804.

At an early period of our rupture with Tripoli Mr. Cathcart suggested to me the plan of using Hamet Bashaw, the legitimate sovereign of that regency, then an exile at Tunis, as an instrument in favor of the United States to chastise the perfidy of our enemy, his brother, who had usurped the Government—

I did not then enter decidedly into the measure, doubting whether any construction of my original instructions from Government would authorize the discretion—But Mr. Madison's instructions of May 20th. 1801 (exhibit A.) having removed this obstacle I entered into engagements with the Bashaw to that effect; conditioned that on being restored to his dominion he should place the usurper and family into our hands as hostages of a perpetual peace: and I sketched the project to the Department of State in my report of Sep. 5th.—Those instructions were delivered to me by Commodore Dale at Portofarine, forty miles from Tunis, on the 18th Augt. while I was yet under a suspense of the Bey's order to quit his kingdom for refusing to state his demand to the Government for 10,000 stands of arms—The moment of our squadron's appearance on the coast was peculiarly favorable, both as it respected Tunis and Tripoli: it checked for a moment the arrogance of the former, and it gave a paralytic shock to the latter. The enemy was securely calculating on the booty he expected from American captures. He had no apprehension of a force so near him; and was consequently unprepared to counteract its operations. His best corsaires, comprising his chief naval force and the chosen strength of his turkish soldiery, were either blockaded at Gibraltar; or were at sea not in a capacity to return immediately to his assistance. He had but a few guns, badly mounted, on his castle batteries; not soldiers to man them; and scarcely a sentinel on their ramparts. His interior was agitated by dissentions; and his capital distressed by famine. Of this last circumstance, however, I was not informed until after the departure of the Commodore for his station: it had been carefully concealed from me until the alarmed commerce of Tunis betrayed it in a demand of the Bey for my passports of safe conduct to his merchantmen bound to that port with provisions. At once to sieze the advantages which the occasion offered and to silence the Bey's demand for passports, which, if granted, would, according to Barbary exclusive privileges, have covered the property at all events, I announced Tripoli in a state of blockade; & dispatched an express vessel to the Commodore with the information. He confirmed the declaration of the blockade, and pledged himself for its support; but, nine days afterward, Sep. 6th. appeared in the road of Tunis on his way to Gibraltar, having left the enemy's coast by reason of sickness in his ship. He left with me, however, a letter of instructions to keep up the idea of a blockade until his return with the squadron; which would be immediately on receiving fresh orders from Government: for he doubted whether the orders he then held would authorize him to coerce the enemy. I did so; but never saw him after. The friendly Bashaw grew despondent.

On the 3d Nov. I gave him some encouragement, as reported to the department of State Dec. 13th.

Being myself in a very imperfect state of health from the convalescence of a fever, which had reduced me very low the preceeding summer, my physician advised me to take a sea voyage. Accordingly I embarked in the United States transport George Washington and proceeded to Leghorn, where was put into my hands the President's letter to the Bey of Tunis in answer to his demanding forty 24 pound battery guns; which conveyed, in a language sufficiently intelligible, a resolution *no longer to owe to dishonarable concessions our right to navigate the seas freely*. This Mr. Cathcart and myself received as assurance of the approbation of Government of our measures, and as an encouragement to perseverance.—Hearing from Tunis that overtures of reconciliation had been made by the ruling Bashaw of Tripoli to his exiled brother it was resolved that I should return immediately to Tunis in order to defeat his designs. Accordingly, 28th. Feb. I embarked in my own arm-ship, The Gloria, and arrived the 12th. March following; found Hamet Bashaw actually on the point of embarking for Tripoli, under the escort of forty armed Tripolitans; having been refused further supplies of provisions by the Bey of Tunis. This Bey demanded for Hamet and retinue my passports—and renewed his demand for passports for his merchantmen to Tripoli. I could neither grant the one nor the other—He, as usual, menaced me with war and personal vexations. I desired to communicate this state of things to the commanding officer on the coast. There was no American vessel of war near; and it would be improper to confide the information to accidental conveyance. There were then with me at the American house Doctor William Turner and Mr. Charles Wadsworth of the navy, and Captains George G. Coffin and Joseph Bounds, American masters of vessels, whom I consulted; and with their advice (exhibit C.) dispatched the Gloria to the commanding officer with a detail of facts, and suggested to him the exertions I thought necessary to prevent the friendly Bashaw falling into the hands of the enemy; and at the same requested that he would give the Gloria a warrant to act under my orders *until the arrival of the Commodore*. The ship fell in with Captain McNiell, the only officer on the coast, three days after leaving port; who approved of my measures; sent the ship back with his warrant and orders to act offensively against Tripolitans; and went himself in search of the Bashaw. In the mean time I had wrought upon the Sapatapa, Bey's minister, to countenance and aid my project in consideration of my promise to give him $10,000. *on condition of his fidelity and of its success*. He confessed to me it was the intention of the enemy Bashaw, by this illusive overture, to get possession of his brother in order to destroy him; and he permitted my Dragoman, under an injunction of secrecy, to communicate the plot to Hamet. This determined him to go to Malta under a pretext of evading the Swedish and American cruisers. He arrived safely; dismissed his escort; and reported himself to me. Having now gained what I considered the most important point in our plan, the security of the friendly Bashaw, I immediately dispatched the Gloria to convey the intelligence to our commodore and Government, as detailed in my letter of 4th. Apl. 1802 & inclosures. But what was my astonishment to learn that, on her arrival at Gibraltar, instead of meeting there a squadron prepared to sieze this advantageous position, to find a solitary commander of a frigate, without having surveyed the ground, ready to stamp defeat and pass censure on the measure! Captain Murray dismissed my ship in a manner most injurious and disgraceful to me; and proceeded to Tunis, where he arrived early in June, and tarried six days with me without signifying anything of his proceedure at Gibraltar; though he expressed his dissent to the plan concerted with Hamet Bashaw. The Gloria arrived a day or two after the Constellation's departure. But a general discontentment prevailed among the crew. Two of them had been taken off by Cap. Murray at Gibr.—two or three others deserted at Tunis—and all were unwilling to go to sea, it being known that sundry enemy cruisers were out—

During these transactions, it seems, the Sapatapa had betrayed to the ruling Bashaw of Tripoli the plot of his brother with the Americans and Swedes (for the Swedish Admiral embraced the project) to dethrone him. This certainly had the influence to induce him to propositions of peace, first through the mediation of the Bey of Tunis and then of the Dey of Algiers; and to call to the defence of his city as many of his moors and arabs as were submissive to his orders.

Captain McNiell had had an interview with Hamet Bashaw at Malta, and promised him his succour—Captain Murray also, sometime in August, after being better informed, saw and engaged to him his co-operations; and I held my position at Tunis in daily expectation of the Commodore's arrival until the deserters, abovementioned, promulgated the transactions which took place at Gibraltar in a manner that they became known to the Sapatapa—It was a matter of exultation at the court of Tunis that the *American Consul* was abandoned by his countrymen; and the occasion was siezed to *humble his pride*! My project with Hamet Bashaw was considered as blown out—And the Sapatapa now required an immediate settlement. I had, the preceeding year, been compelled in order to prevent a rupture, to take on myself the charge of a cargo of oil laden by the Sapatapa on board the Ann Maria; and had made very considerable cash payments on that and other accounts; besides bringing forward, at the particular desire of the minister, a small American ship calculated for a cruiser with a part cargo of coffee and sugar, which arrived late in Dec. or early in January, but which he would not receive because I refused my passports to his Tripolitan coasters.—On presenting my accounts he struck out the sum before stated as conditionally engaged for his *secret service*. Against this I remonstrated, alledging that he had forfieted right to the claim on account of having shifted his ground; offered himself as the mediator of peace for the enemy; and, as I believed, betrayed to him the whole affair. He affected not to understand any thing about this subject—But insisted on the deduction as an *error*. We had frequently before compared accounts, and agreed. The case went before the Bey. I demanded that the Sapatapa should produce his books in evidence—He said he kept none; *he was not a trader*: but swore *by the head of his master* that his statement was honest. His master, of course, gave judgement against me. There is no appeal from that decision Nor could I obtain forbearance. The minister, when retired from the hall of justice, said, with a sarcastic cant *"We know how to keep Consuls to their promises!"* The ship and merchandize which had been rejected by the Sapatapa, now sunk in value by the event of peace, could not be converted into cash. The expense of the Gloria had continued from the 1t. of March without produce; and I saw no immediate relief from this expense; for I could obtain no information from the Commodore. It was in this dilemma that I applied to the commercial agent of the Bey for a loan of $34,000. on a credit of six months, $2,000 of which were discounted by him for use—Thus stood affairs with me until the 8th. September 1802, when the Bey, as if sedulously calculating to harrass my feelings, concived the project of ordering my ship to America with a letter to the President demanding a thirty-six gun frigate. The letter was accompanied to me with his passport to the ship as a protection against Tripolitans, and with his peremptory order to dispatch her without delay—I availed myself of this protection, at the risque of the Bey's resentment, to send the ship to Leghorn; and ordered the crew discharged—

Though our ships of war had now all left the coast I still kept up a correspondence with Hamet Bashaw, till at length he arrived at Derne and was affectionately received by his subjects, who renewed their allegiance to him—He now sent agents to me with this intelligence; and was soon after joined by a nephew, who had been banished to Cairo, at the head of a multitude of mountain Arabs: so that the

Bashaw found himself with a force sufficient to act against the usurper, and only waited the arrival of our squadron to blockade him by sea; when he would move and invest him by land. His agents had been with me sixty days, incog. when Commodore Morris appeared, for the first time, Feb. 22d. 1803, in the road of the Goulette for the purpose of contesting the reclamation of the Bey of Tunis of property belonging to his subjects taken upon the imperial polacca, the Paulina—The Commodore went on shore under the pledge of the Bey's honor that he should be treated with the same distinctions as officers of the same rank of other friendly powers—After some discussion he satisfied the Bey's claims, as was supposed; and he entered into some engagements with those Agents, as ℔ enclosure D.—In the mean time I had exhibited to him a view of my affairs; mentioned to him what I supposed would be the balance due on my note to the Bey's agent, and the cause in which it originated—He expressed his entire satisfaction with my proceedings, and his opinion that Government would indemnify me; for he had freequently heard the Bey's agent confess that the minister had defrauded me. He was requested, on going to pay his visit of Congee to the Bey, to say something to the minister, to whom in fact the money was going, to engage his forbearance until I could receive relief from America. This, he said, he would do—And every thing seemed to have resumed a tranquil appearance at Tunis. But the next morning the Bey's agent came forward with additional claims on the prize; some trifling articles of no great value. A contest of words, contradictions and reproaches, ensued on the subject. The parties became incensed. The Commodore left the American house; and, instead of going to take leave of the Bey as is always customary and for which purpose carriages were waiting, passed his course for the marine to embark. It was at this moment of irritation and distrust that the Agent followed after, refused him a passage in his sandals to the Golette, and demanded payment of the balance on my note: His reasons for so doing are stated in certificate E. The next day, at the palace, I remonstrated with the Bey against this violation of faith and outrage against the dignity of my nation, mingling on the occasion something of those feelings which a sense of the personal indignities I had suffered at his court could not but excite in my own breast, with such plainness as to produce my expulsion from his kingdom: at the same time this Bey bore testimony, in the presence of all the Americans present, to the zeal and integrity of my conduct as an agent; but alledged that *my head was too obstinate*, and that he *must have a Consul with a disposition more congenial to Barbary interests.* (His minister had often said he believed me the sole cause of their not getting a vessel of war from the United States; and, as I am informed by Mr. OBrien, had said He would *work my ruin*) Though I felt no regret in leaving the country, The manner in which I was hurried away left many of my individual concerns unsettled, vastly to my injury. The prohibitions to which I had been previously subjected by the Government in consequence of my adherence to positions relative to the commerce of this regency with the enemy, which duty compelled me to hold, had operated also greatly to my disadvantage; For I had let go every thing but what I thought would effect the honor and the interest of my Country—

Having gone through this statement of events which produced the items in my account now before your Excellency, I have only to beg it may be considered, that I have been but the chief acting agent of a measure which was recommended and urged, not only by Mr. Cathcart an Agent of the Government best acquainted with the probabilities of its success, but by every other Agent and citizen of the United States whom I consulted on the subject: a measure adopted by every commanding officer who has appeared on the station; and approved by the Executive (as ℈ exhibit B.)—and that I have taken no steps in the business but what resulted from the station on which I was placed and the nature of my duty, and what have met the concurrence of my Colleague, Mr. Cathcart, and other officers of Government with whom I could consult. That so far as my Agency had any influence on the measure it succeeded; and that if we have not experienced all the advantages calculated to result from its success it ought to be attributed to the *lâcheté* of a commander over whose conduct I had no controle. That it was not apprehended any expense would ultimately accrue to the United States from this measure; that such expenses as should be incident to its prosecution would be defrayed out of its success; and that it would be a public saving both of life and property: as would eventually have been the case had it been pursued with suitable energy—

I ask leave further to remark, that my ship was to be employed on this emergency only till the *arrival of the Commodore*. But it was impossible to immagine that his arrival would be delayed eleven months after the plan was mature for execution; or that, on his arrival and finding it in that stage, he should make no effort to give it effect. He was entreated to send only one of his ships with the agents to the friendly Bashaw in order to encourage his perseverance until he could bring the whole squadron to co-operate with him. This was refused on a pretext that the ships were on short rations and must all accompany him to Gibraltar to provision. This may have been the case; but it is nevertheless true that the whole squadron lay nine days after arriving at that port without taking in even a biscuit or a bucket of water—It is true that the first appearance of this commodore before Tripoli was not till the 22d of May 1803—And it is equally true that during the seventeen months he commanded the whole force of the United States in the Mediterranean he was only nineteen days before the enemy's port. I certainly feel no inclination to act the part of an informer; nor would I state these facts were it not that those delinquencies have most deeply affected me; rifled me of my honor; and, for ought I can percieve, reduced me to extreme poverty. Whereas, had I been supported with that integrity which was due to the confidence of the Government in the Commander I should have saved both my honor and my property; my country would have experienced lasting benefits from my exertions; and he would have enjoyed the satisfaction of self approbation—I should at least have saved myself the mortification of this appeal to the equity and the commiseration of your Excellency.

It is believed the project with Hamet Bashaw is still feasible. The very circumstance of his *existence* is evidence of his holding a position formidable to the usurper, for it is well known that a turkish despot never suffers a rival to exist whom he can destroy—And I must be permitted still to adhere to the opinion which has influenced my conduct in this affair, that it is the most eligible way of securing a permanent peace with that regency; for there is *no faith in treaties with the ruling Bashaw*!

I have the honor to be with profound respect, Sir, your Excellency's most Obedient & very humble Servant   WILLIAM EATON

RC (DNA: RG 59, CD, Tunis); at head of text: "His Excellency The President"; endorsed by TJ as received 3 Feb. and so recorded in SJL. Enclosures: (1) Madison to Eaton, 20 May 1801, informing Eaton that the president has determined to send a navy squadron to the Mediterranean in response to the hostile designs of the bey of Tripoli; since Eaton has long urged the exhibition of a naval force along the Barbary coast, Madison adds that the president has "every reason to expect the utmost exertions of your prudence and address, in giving the measure an impression most advantageous to the character and interests of the United States"; the means for effecting this object, however, must be left "in a great degree" to Eaton's knowledge of local circumstances (Madi-son, *Papers, Sec. of State Ser.*, 1:199-201). (2) Statement by George G. Coffin and Charles Wadsworth, dated 22 Aug. 1802 on board the frigate *Boston* off Alicante, stating that following discussions with Eaton in March 1802 at the consular house in Tunis, they approved of Eaton's plan to prevent Ahmad Qaramanli's reconciliation with his brother Yusuf, the reigning bey of Tripoli, and his suggestion to send the *Gloria* to sea with dispatches for Captain Daniel McNeill of the *Boston* to effect the purpose; Coffin and Wadsworth also advised Eaton to retain the *Gloria* in service thereafter for sending dispatches or to facilitate his escape from Tunis in case his actions should anger Hammuda; Doctor William Turner of the frigate *Philadelphia* and Captain Joseph

Bounds of the *Gloria* were also present at these conferences and were in agreement with Coffin and Wadsworth (ASP, *Claims*, 1:330). Other enclosures not identified.

Born in Connecticut, William Eaton (1764-1811) served as a non-commissioned officer during the American Revolution and earned a bachelor's degree from Dartmouth College after the war. Rejoining the army in 1792, he served as a captain in the Northwest Territory, where he impressed his commanding officer, Anthony Wayne, with his military skill and his aptitude for Indian languages. Returning east in 1795, Eaton made useful political contacts with Timothy Pickering and others, which helped him weather a court-martial in 1796. His connections and self-taught introduction to Arabic language and culture led to his appointment as the American consul at Tunis in 1797. Soon after his arrival in the Mediterranean, Eaton began to promote his plan to oust the reigning bey of Tripoli, Yusuf Qaramanli, and replace him with his elder brother, Ahmad. Resigning his office in 1803, Eaton returned to the United States to press his scheme in Washington and also to seek settlement of his convoluted public accounts. Returning to the Mediterranean in 1804 in the vaguely defined role of navy agent for the Barbary regencies, Eaton joined Ahmad in Egypt in early 1805 and proceeded to assemble a polyglot army to march on Tripoli and topple Yusuf. Under Eaton's leadership, and with the assistance of the American navy and marines, the mercenary army marched 500 miles across the North African desert and captured the port city of Derna in April 1805. Within weeks, however, Eaton was informed that a peace had been negotiated between the United States and Yusuf, and that he was to evacuate Derna. He returned to America in November 1805 and was widely feted, but remained bitter over the Tripolitan treaty and his belief that it had betrayed Ahmad and the honor of the United States. In 1807, Eaton was a witness for the prosecution in the conspiracy trial of Aaron Burr, but his testimony failed to impress the court. He returned to his home in Massachusetts, resentful and embittered,

where his intemperate outbursts and increasingly dissolute lifestyle soon alienated former supporters and eroded his once heroic reputation (ANB; JEP, 1:249; NDBW, 4:120; Louis B. Wright and Julia H. Macleod, *The First Americans in North Africa: William Eaton's Struggle for a Vigorous Policy Against the Barbary Pirates, 1799-1805* [Princeton, 1945], 151-98; Vol. 40:647-53).

PLAN OF USING HAMET BASHAW: for Eaton's long-digested plan of using Ahmad Qaramanli to overthrow his brother, see Vol. 38:347n; Vol. 39:494-5n; Vol. 40:92, 93n, 647, 650. For earlier consideration by TJ, Madison, and the Treasury Department of Eaton's accounts while consul at Tunis, see Notes on William Eaton's Accounts, Vol. 40:647-53.

PRESIDENT'S LETTER TO THE BEY OF TUNIS: TJ to Hammuda Pasha, 9 Sep. 1801 (Vol. 35:240-1).

For Eaton's purchase, and subsequent sale, of the armed ship GLORIA on his own account, see Vol. 38:367-8n and Vol. 40:649.

WILLIAM TURNER, surgeon on the frigate *Philadelphia*, had been left in charge of American affairs at Tunis in early 1802 during Eaton's absence. CHARLES WADSWORTH was purser of the frigate *Boston*. GEORGE G. COFFIN and JOSEPH BOUNDS were captains of the merchant ships *Anna Maria* and *Gloria*, respectively (NDBW, 1:614, 648; 2:16, 21, 78, 95, 168, 240; ASP, *Claims*, 1:330; Vol. 38:368n).

SAPATAPA: Yusuf Sahib-at-Taba, the principal minister of the bey of Tunis (Vol. 38:347n; Vol. 40:95n, 647).

SWEDISH ADMIRAL: Olaf Rudolf Cederström (Vol. 36:667n).

For Hammuda's 8 Sep. 1802 LETTER TO THE PRESIDENT, see Vol. 38:365-8.

IMPERIAL POLACCA, THE PAULINA: in January 1803, the U.S. schooner *Enterprize* had seized the polacre *Paolina* near Malta, claiming that its cargo was bound for Tripoli. Hammuda protested the capture to Eaton, however, asserting that part of the cargo belonged to one of his subjects at Djerba and demanding restitution for the loss (NDBW, 2:344-6, 350-5, 364-5, 383; 3:341-6; Madison, *Papers, Sec. of State Ser.*, 6:632; 7:341n, 520n; Vol. 40:576).

LÂCHETÉ: cowardice.

From Albert Gallatin

DEAR SIR   Feb. 3. 1804

Hartshorne has recovered 750 dollars damages against the United States for the trespass committed in lighting the beacon near Sandy hook; and he will renew his actions continually on the same ground. The damages are absurd, as the injury done by hanging a lanthern on the beach of his barren tract could not be estimated at one cent; and our expectation had all along been that every jury, especially in New York, would give nominal damages. At present, however, as the New Jersey legislature has done nothing, there are but two ways, either to order the light in the beacon to be discontinued or to accede to his terms which are about ten times higher than the highest price Govt. ever gave for land for light houses. Either way is bad enough, and in order to place the whole subject before you I enclose the whole correspondence with Hartshorne, Gelston & Bloomfield.

Respectfully Your obedt. Servt.   ALBERT GALLATIN

RC (DLC); at foot of text: "The President of the United States"; endorsed by TJ as received from the Treasury Department on 3 Feb. and "Hartshorne's case" and so recorded in SJL. Enclosures not found, but see below.

The Sandy Hook lighthouse, in New Jersey at the entrance to New York harbor, stood on four acres of land ceded to the United States, but authorities found it necessary to erect two beacons on land still owned by proprietors, the principal being Richard HARTSHORNE. Gallatin asserted that Hartshorne refused "to sell on reasonable terms." In 1801, the owners thought $2,000 an appropriate sum. In August 1802, after the first beacon was erected, they brought suit and obtained $100 in damages for trespass. RENEW HIS ACTIONS: on 16 Feb., David Gelston, the collector in charge of Sandy Hook, informed Gallatin that Hartshorne had commenced two new suits against him for trespass (*New-York Evening Post*, 6 Apr. 1804; Gallatin, *Papers*, 47:1056-7; Vol. 35:738; Gallatin to TJ, 15 Nov. 1805).

DAMAGES ARE ABSURD: Gallatin held Brockholst Livingston, a New York Supreme Court justice, responsible for the $750 award against the United States (Gallatin to TJ, 9 May 1805).

On 18 Feb., Gelston informed Hartshorne that the lights were TO BE DISCONTINUED and, if he required it, the two beacons would be immediately removed. Hartshorne replied that the proprietors thought the enhanced safety provided by the beacons would encourage the government to negotiate. He wanted it understood "that if any injury should result to individuals, or the public from the removal of those lights, it may not be attributed to the proprietors, who have always been, and are still willing to sell the property to the public for a reasonable price." Newspapers noted that William P. Schenck, the lighthouse keeper at Sandy Hook, had received orders "not to light the two beacons on the point of that place." The report continued: "We do not know the cause of this extraordinary measure. Those lights are of as much consequence as that in the Light-House" (*New-York Commercial Advertiser*, 3 Mch.; *New-York Herald*, 7 Mch.; *New-York Evening Post*, 6 Apr. 1804; Vol. 38:446-7n). On 11 Apr., Gelston wrote the Treasury secretary that large meetings were being held and he was "pressed hard to permit the beacons to be lighted." He continued, "I feel an anxiety to hear from you, as I can say nothing to the repeated applications." The beacons were soon operating again. Gallatin convinced insurance companies to make a private agreement with Hartshorne to continue the lights until the dispute was resolved. The NEW JERSEY LEGISLATURE subsequently passed an act to enable the government's purchase of the land (Gallatin, *Papers*, 9:489; Gallatin to TJ, 15 Nov. 1805).

From George Logan

DEAR SIR   Feby. 3d: 1804

I received last evening the enclosed Letters from two of your sincere friends. should it not be convenient to you to write to Dr. Priestley, I will with pleasure communicate to him any information on the subject of his Letter you may wish to have conveyed to him. His favorable opinion respecting your administration is flattering; and I am happy to say it is a sentiment gaining ground amongst our best Citizens.

I am with sentiments of great respect Your Friend.

GEO: LOGAN

RC (DLC); endorsed by TJ as received 3 Feb. and so recorded in SJL. Enclosures not found, but see below.

As Logan indicated here and as TJ mentioned in a letter of 24 Feb. to Thomas Cooper, Logan enclosed a letter from Joseph PRIESTLEY.

From Joseph Barnes

Livorno Feb. 4th. 1804

On my return from Naples a few days since, Mr Jefferson, I found my friend Mr Mazzei had some favorite Vines &c and Letters to send to the President of the U.S. and requested me to find a Vessel which would convey them with care; On my arrival in Leghorn I fortunately found the Hannah nearly ready to sail, and arranged with the Master, Yardsley, to take them on board, who I have no doubt will pay every attention to them—I saw them delivered safe to Mr Appleton, who will address them to his Brother in Law at Philadelphia—Cap. Yardsley will charge no freight.

During my stay at Naples I had several interviews &c. with General Acton, Prime Minister of the Kingdom of the two Sicilies, whose disposition relative to forming a Treaty of Commercial relations with the United States I found equally favorable, but rather disappointed by the delay!

My friend Mr Mazzei having forwarded one copy, & myself another, of the Letter of General Acton to me, and having written so fully on the subject in my former Letters it would be presumption in me to trouble Mr Jefferson further relative thereto at present: Therefore I shall only suggest, that *had* I power, I am persuaded of the essential services I could render my Country—I could only assure General Acton, that those Matters required deliberation, and that no question the requisite powers would soon arrive—In two of my former Letters I took the Liberty of suggesting to Mr Jefferson, that in order to render essential services with the Government of the two Sicilies, 'tis indispensably necessary I should *reside* at *Naples*, being the *Seat* of Government, as all important objects are effected by *favor* & *personal* exertion with such Governments as those. And, I need not repeat the Assurance, to the President, that my chief Motive & primary wish has ever been to *promote* the good of my *Country*, & the *interest* & *happiness* of my fellow Citizens, and *not* influenced by *any* pecuniary consideration.—My worthy friend Mazzei, who certainly is one of the *most* zealous friends & admirers of Mr Jefferson, & defenders of the Government of the U.S., is extremely solicitous that I should be near him, our sentiments being generally coincident, & suggested his intention of writing to Mr Jefferson on the subject—*were* I influenced by pecuniary motives, I should certainly prefer the Consulate of Leghorn to any in the Mediterranean; but *no* consideration would *induce* me to make an overture of this Nature *contrary* to the Interest of[1] Mr Appleton, with whom since my residence in this Country I have been in the habits of friendship & intimacy—Nevertheless, should *any* circumstance *induce* the President to *change* the residence of Mr Appleton to France, for instance, which unquestionable is the Country for which he is *best* calculated & qualified, I flatter myself Mr Jefferson will not consider it presumption in me to suggest, that from the consideration of being near my friend Mazzei, for whose Talents, Political knowledge, & knowledge of Mankind, I have the highest respect, I should be extremely happy, & *wave many* other considerations; thro whose influence & my exertion the presumption is, we should succeed especially in these Countries—In fine the *summit* of my wishes being the *good* of my Country, & *happiness* of my Country-men, My desire is to be more useful or to be on a more extensive & important[2] Theatre of Action than my present situation in Sicily; the distance, place or Country I should not Mind, even were it to Tunis or Constantinople, provided this object could be obtained & Mr Jefferson should consider I could be more useful.—

Mr Mazzei, in conjunction with me, has already written to the Court of Russia relative to the *Black Sea*, the opening of which to the American Flag would be[3] an immence object to our commerce. Such a commission as I took the Liberty of suggesting in my former Letters for Italy or to Constantinople, the Black Sea &c would be productive of much good to the United States, consequently of happiness and Glory to Mr Jefferson—Being persuaded many good Commercial arrangements may be *made* in places at present scarcely known—and the more especially as the Grand Signeur will not Acknowledge a Consul from any Country which has not some Commercial Arrangement with the Port, consequently our Consul is not Acknowledged at Smyrna.—Nor can any Flag pass into the Black Sea whose Government has not an understanding with the Grand Signeur.—

Knowing the *ardent zeal* of Mr Jefferson for the Glory, true interest & happiness of our common Country, I *anticipate* the Mortification he will have experienced on the unfortunate intelligence of the *Loss* of the U.S. Frigate Philadelphia, especially as it will flatter the Vanity & *highten* the pretentions of the Tripolines, and *increase* the *obstacles* to the desired object *Peace*—'tis unnecessary for me to detail the particulars, as Mr Jefferson will have recd. them, but only to State that in *my* Opinion disgrace ought to be attached to all who should surrender under any circumstances to those Barbarians—Much more important would it have been to the United States, had the Crew of the said Frigate *Sunk* Gloriously to the *bottom*, or *ascended Gloriously* in *the Air*, *rather* than have Yielded. This would have made a *forcible* impression on the Minds of these barbarians, of our *determined Spirit*, to succeed or perish in the attempt.[4]—

I am happy to have it in my power, and anticipate with Much pleasure the Satisfaction Mr Jefferson will receive from the advice, which I have recd. from my Agent at Palermo dated the 8th Ulto., of Commodore Preble having taken & carried into Syracuse a Tripoline Vessel with 70 men carrying Presents for the Grand Signeur at Constantinople, and, that thro' the exertions of my Agent he got 20 days off the Quarantine, as the people put on Board the prize were indispensible to Commodore Preble.—

I have also the pleasure of informing Mr Jefferson, that this Morning a dispatch arrived to Mr Appleton, from our Minister, Mr Livingston, at Paris, containing instructions from the First Consul of France to the French Commissary General at Tripoli to interfere in behalf of *our* fellow Citizens *in chains* there; which no question will have a happy effect. I have in consequence been arranging all the Morning the most expeditious & safe means of forwarding it to my Agent in Messina, with directions to consign it personally to Commodore Preble, or his Agent at Syracuse—which is 90 miles distant from Messina—Mr Livingston observes in his Letter, that Bounaparte took up the Matter so warmly that he wrote the dispatch himself; the consequences being to us *important*, every Caution relative to the quick dispatch & safe delivery of the said dispatch is the more essential— The President will excuse me for suggesting the necessity consequent on this Misfortune, *not* of making any Overtures, but of *increasing* our force, *redoubling* our vigilance, *assuming* a more hostile appearance, & *Menacing* those Pirates with eternal[5] unless they will meet us in rational considerations of Peace & Amity—which may be affected the means of the arrangements which I heretofor took the Liberty of suggesting in my former Letters practicable with the Neapolitan Government; & that too with little if any additional Expence to the United States—Such measures would tend to *Lessen* the hope & necessarily *increase* the desire of Peace in those Barbarians.—

Permit me to say, I should do *injustice* to my feelings were I to close this Letter without expressing the *high* gratification I have recd. in learning from the Address of the President presented to Congress on the 17th Octr. 1803—the prosperous & increasing State of the Union—and the still more pleasing prospect, not only of the *dissolution* of the *funding system* in a few years, (which I had anticipated in my Letter dated Decr. 22d 1800 would be amongst the happy effects of the Election of Mr Jefferson to the Presidency) but from the Grand System of political Economy introduced by Mr Jefferson, & pursued by the Representatives of the People from a general co-incident of sentiments, that a fund may be Established, the interest of which would be equal to the exigences of the Government, consequently taxes rendered[6] This is highly practicable from the National Lands alone by Means of a system of Leasing them at stipulated prices, or of holding them 'till they should command certain prices; and appropriate the sum of the proceeds, say in Loan offices in the respective States, to Lend Money on real estates, or otherwise, which would produce the Annual Sum requisite, or the *desideratum*, which would be unexampled in the History of Nations, & cause the United States to be the Envy & admiration of the World—wishing this & every good contemplated may be the result, and that Mr Jefferson may preside to the complition—I have the honor to be

with the highest considerations of respect Mr Jefferson's Obedt. Servt. J: BARNES

P.S. In course of this Month I expect to depart again for Naples, on my route for Sicily, where I hope to meet some dispatches from the department of State—

RC (DLC); at head of text: "H.E. Thos. Jefferson. President of the U.S."; endorsed by TJ as received 13 Apr. and so recorded in SJL.

GRAND SIGNEUR: Selim III, the Ottoman sultan (Vol. 33:563n).

OUR CONSUL: TJ appointed William Stewart consul at Smyrna in 1802 (Vol. 37:205n, 348).

INSTRUCTIONS FROM THE FIRST CONSUL: on 16 Jan., Talleyrand instructed the French commissary general at Tripoli, Bonaventure Beaussier, to "put all in train" to alleviate the crew of the *Philadelphia* and obtain their release. Beaussier was also to make known to Yusuf Qaramanli that the conflict between Tripoli and the United States had "more than once excited the solicitude of the First Consul," and that Bonaparte "desires that a solid and advantageous peace to both parties, may speedily put an end to the War that at present divides them." Robert R. Livingston sent a copy of Talleyrand's instructions to Thomas Appleton with directions to forward them as soon as possible to Commodore Edward Preble, who was to carry them to Beaussier at Tripoli (NDBW, 3:332; Madison, *Papers, Sec. of State Ser.*, 6:357-8, 359n).

[1] Barnes here canceled "my friend."
[2] Word and ampersand interlined.
[3] Word interlined in place of "offer."
[4] Preceding four words interlined in place of an illegible cancellation.
[5] Thus in MS.
[6] Thus in MS; Barnes probably omitted a word as he started a new page.

From William Bradley

MAY IT PLEASE YOUR EXCELLENCY

Washington Goal
4h. feby. 1804

This represents an unfortunate Mechanic confined in Washington Goal—the Tale is plain & simple—& Testimony of the Truth may be fully substantionated at the Moment He is now under durance relative to a Building He has erected in the Vicinity of the West-Market—the Subject in some degree may be familiar to Your Ear—He has only to say the Confinement adjudged to Him He suffers with Patience, He is fearful He has acted with Impropriety & upon a full explination of the Business He has been made sensible of having opposed Your Proclomation—May it please Your Excellency, our little all has been collected together, the Labor of a Number of Years has been thrown into this Building if Permission is not suffered by You good Sir to proceed; We shall not only be miserably reduced but the House Which We at presint occupy; by the Corporation of George Town is order'd within these few days to be removed, it rests in the Market House Square at George Town—We shall in consequence suffer more I fear than our ability[1] can maintain.

I have a Wife with Children; Who's Caracter for Industry & every action to make themselves respectable in society stands unimpeached—I cannot have the Honor of Approaching Your Excellency to petition for Relief upon the premises but Mrs. Bradley Who has been a fond and affectionate Wife & Who has brought two Daughters into Society Whom I am proud to claim, will if permitted into Your presence be able more fully to explain our very unfortunate Situation—Consider Sir 'tis our all & if we shall not be able to proceed We must again commence the World—With every Wish for Your Comfort, prosperity & Happiness

I remain Your most Obd Servt   WM. BRADLEY

RC (DLC); addressed: "To His Excellency Thos. Jefferson Esqr President of the United States"; endorsed by TJ as received 4 Feb. and so recorded in SJL; also endorsed by TJ: "confined for contempt of court, therefore left to the judges who *can* remit."

In December 1803, the U.S. Circuit Court for the District of Columbia upheld an attachment of contempt against William Bradley for violating an injunction issued by Thomas Munroe, the superintendent of the city of Washington. The court ordered Bradley into "close custody" for a term of six days and to stand further committed until the costs upon the attachment had been paid (William

Cranch, *Reports of Cases Civil and Criminal in the United States Circuit Court of the District of Columbia, from 1801 to 1841*, 6 vols. [Boston, 1852-53], 1:157-8). Bradley may be the person of the same name who wrote TJ a letter dated 11 Jan. 1803, recorded in SJL as received 12 Jan. from Washington, that has not been found (Vol. 39:639).

YOUR PROCLAMATION: see Proclamation Extending Building Regulations in the City of Washington, 28 Dec. 1803, which restricted the size, height, and location of wooden houses in the city.

[1] Bradley first wrote "than that ability of our Family" before altering the text to read as above.

From the Earl of Buchan

SIR,   Edinburgh, February fourth 1804.

Your letter of the tenth of July last is just what I expected from the figurative as well as official reppresentative of the virtuous Washington.

I perused it, and re-perused it with sensibility as containing fully, & emphatically the uniform opinion I have entertained concerning the subjects of it.—retired as I am, & have long deliberately been from the busy world of politics I enter not the less into the interesting contemplation of what may be eventually productive of good or of evil to mankind and by means not perceptible to common eyes I have constantly endeavoured to do good to my country and to society. May I beg your acceptance of the enclosed token of my esteem. It is the ribbon and badge of our family order of the cross crosslet of Marr & being revived on the anniversary of Washington last year when it was celebrated here in my house on the 22d. of February in the presence of the Americans then resident at Edinburgh is bestowed on those who venerate the memory and emulate the conduct of that distinguished Citizen and Statesman.

accept illustrious President of the assurances of my high consideration & respect. BUCHAN.

RC (DLC); endorsed by TJ (torn). Recorded in SJL as received 15 May 1804. Enclosed in George W. Erving to TJ, 8 Mch. 1804.

Buchan, a distant relative of the Fairfax family, liked to claim kinship ties to George WASHINGTON. In 1791 the earl sent his "cousin" a snuff box presumably carved from the wood of an oak tree in which William Wallace had taken shelter during the battle of Falkirk. Until at least 1817, Buchan continued his custom of giving annual Washington birthday addresses to

Americans in Edinburgh (Washington, *Papers, Pres. Ser.*, 11:255n; *Harvard Library Bulletin*, 5 [1951], 367-8; Vol. 16:xxxii-iii).

The heraldic crest of the CROSS CROSSLET OF MARR, or a combination of a cross and a sword, symbolized unshakeable faith (John Burke, *Encyclopædia of Heraldry, or General Armory of England, Scotland, and Ireland*, 3d ed. with suppl. [London, 1844], n.p.).

MY HOUSE: Dryburgh Abbey (Vol. 40:709n).

From Peter Carr

DEAR SIR. Richmond. Feb. 4th. 1804.

Mr. John Comegys, a merchant of Baltimore, will deliver this—during my stay, and illness there last spring, I was indebted to him, for his very friendly attentions. He will remain in Washington a few days, and has requested this introductory letter. I am just on the wing for Albemarle; Accept assurances, my dear Sir, of affectionate attachment. P. CARR

RC (DLC); endorsed by TJ as received 15 Feb. and so recorded in SJL.

JOHN COMEGYS was a merchant and importer of dry goods and British wares. He later presided over a subscription campaign to raise funds for a Baltimore monument dedicated to the memory of

George Washington (Baltimore *Federal Gazette*, 22 Apr. 1802, 6 May 1803; James Robinson, *Baltimore Directory for 1804* [Baltimore, 1804], 11; Baltimore *American and Commercial Daily Advertiser*, 4 Apr. 1805, 15 July 1814, 4 July 1815).

From Albert Gallatin

DEAR SIR 4th Feby. 1804

I enclose a letter from Mr Simons respecting the new slave importation law. Is it proper that he should collect the duty of $12\frac{1}{2}$ p% on merchandize? or ought he to be instructed not to do it?

As Mr H. declines going with the Stock, the question recurs, in what manner shall it be sent? There are two ways. Either a navy officer may be sent with it instead of Mr H.; or the Stock may be sent to New York by one of the clerks to be delivd. to the collector, and to be sent, as dispatches, by two different vessels bound to France, one third in each vessel.

The bundle to be directed to the American Consul's care at the port of delivery with instructions to forward it by first safe opportunity to the Minister of the U. States at Paris. I would have waited on you; but the sinking fund report has absorbed so much of my time as to have rendered my presence necessary at the office the whole morning. It is important, however, that no further delay should take place in the transmission of the stock, and immediate measures will be taken to effect it in whichever mode you will think most eligible

Respectfully Your most obt. Servt.   ALBERT GALLATIN

RC (DLC); at foot of text: "The President of the United States"; endorsed by TJ as received from the Treasury Department on 4 Feb. and so recorded in SJL with notation "negroes imported"; also endorsed by TJ: "Symonds' qu. if negroes are merchandize." Enclosure not found.

The NEW SLAVE IMPORTATION LAW passed by the South Carolina General Assembly on 17 Dec. 1803 lifted the ban on the importation of slaves from Africa. From the reopening of the slave trade in 1804 until its prohibition by Congress in 1808, Charleston imported more than 75,000 African slaves. By 1807, up to $390 was paid for an imported slave. TJ probably asked the attorney general for an opinion on the question posed by Gallatin, for according to SJL, Levi Lincoln wrote to the president on 6 Feb. on the subject "whether negroes merchandize." TJ referred Lincoln's letter, which has not been found, to the Treasury Department. The South Carolina act spurred a debate in Congress, where on 14 Feb., Representative David Bard of Pennsylvania introduced a resolution calling for a $10 tax to be "imposed on every slave imported into any part of the United States." This was the sum allowed under the ninth section of the first article of the Constitution. Thomas Lowndes of South Carolina led the opposition to the resolution. After two days of debate and an unsuccessful attempt to postpone action, the House ordered the Committee of Ways and Means to bring in a bill. On 16 Feb., John Randolph presented a bill "laying a

duty on slaves imported into the United States." After another day of debate, the House defeated Lowndes's motion to postpone consideration until the next session of Congress. They, however, agreed, by a 56 to 50 vote, to William Findley's motion to postpone action until the second Monday in March. The House did not consider the bill again during the session (*Acts and Resolutions of the General Assembly of the State of South-Carolina. Passed in December, 1803* [Columbia, S.C., 1804], 48-53; James A. McMillin, *The Final Victims: Foreign Slave Trade to North America, 1783-1819* [Columbia, S.C., 2004], 86-7, 94-5, 105-6; *Annals*, 13:991-1010, 1012-20, 1024-36; JHR, 4:582).

MR H.: Lewis Harvie.

DIRECTED TO THE AMERICAN CONSUL'S CARE: on 8 Feb., after it was determined that an American officer would most likely carry the stock and dispatches to Bordeaux, Gallatin wrote instructions to William Lee, the U.S. consul there. He requested that Lee assist the carrier in the safe delivery of the stock and noted that the "usual mode of travelling must be preferred." If the local French prefect wanted to alter or "accelerate the transmission, any extra-expense of that kind must be defrayed by the French Government." If the carrier arrived at any other French or Dutch port, Gallatin ordered that the local U.S. consul "lend him the assistance required" (Gallatin, *Papers*, 9:419).

SINKING FUND REPORT: on Saturday, 4 Feb., the commissioners—John Brown of Kentucky, president pro tempore of the Senate, Madison, Lincoln, and Gallatin—signed the letter transmitting the detailed report prepared by the Treasury Department to Congress. The Senate and House received it on Monday, the 6th. The doc-uments were read in the Senate and ordered to lie for consideration. In the House the report was read and referred to the Committee of Ways and Means (ASP, *Finance*, 2:84-101; JS, 3:343, 350-1; JHR, 4:567).

From Gideon Granger

Feb: 4. 1804

G Granger presents his Complimts to the President & returns the Letter from Mr. Ellery to Mr. Madison. he has permitted the Senators from R.I. to read the same. They[1] appear to think the old Gentleman has coloured well.

G Granger incloses a Letter he recd. from New York last mail from a very respectable Merchant in that City.

Isaac Kibbe Esq. who is spoken of in the Letter was some 12 or 14 years Since a Citizen in the County of Hartford in Connecticut from which place he removed to New York where by intensive commercial pursuits, he has, as I have ever understood, acquired a fortune & pretty much retired from business 2 or three Years since. He is a middle aged Man, of a very ready and active Mind of fair character and I believe exceeded by but few if any in Knowledge of Accts. & of commercial Affairs, particularly with the Spaniards—

RC (DNA: RG 59, LAR); endorsed by TJ as received 4 Feb. and "Kibbe Isaac to be Commr. to Spain" and so recorded in SJL. Enclosures: (1) William Ellery to Madison, Collector's Office, Newport, 19 Jan. 1804, expressing concern that efforts are afoot to remove him from office; he contends, "my official conduct has been faithful in every respect, and for the truth of this I dare appeal with confidence to the Treasury Department"; his political principles are the same as those he "avowed at a time which tried mens souls" and when he signed the Declaration of Independence; he never was "a partizan" and his old age disposes him "to rest and peace"; during his first years as collector of customs, his net income "was not equal to the salary of a boatman, and that to subsist my family I was obliged to sell that part of my real estate which the British had not destroyed during the revolutionary war"; at 76 years of age, he has not the resources to start a new business; with great economy, his office now affords a bare maintenance for his family; Ellery appeals to Madison to lay his letter before the president, acknowledging that "I cannot think so lightly of his humanity as to conceive it possible that he should remove me from office" (RC in DLC: Madison Papers, endorsed by TJ: "Ellery Wm. to mr Madison"; Madison, *Papers, Sec. of State Ser.*, 6:367-8). (2) William Kibbe to Granger, New York, 30 Jan. 1804; presuming "some respectable Republican Mercantile Gentlemen will be appointed" to the commission to implement the Convention with Spain, he recommends his brother Isaac Kibbe; his brother was "at the first origins of modern Federalism, a Republican" and continues "uniformly the same"; he is "as able a Negotiator & well informed Merchant" as any in New York City and "is as well informed in the Commerce between this Country & Spain and

Europe in general as perhaps any Man in the Country"; Kibbe also notes that it will be "important to the Harmony, Stability and Security of Goverment" to appoint commissioners from New England and that no Republican "Mercantile Character can be found, whose appointment will have so favourable an impression" and "so much Influence" with the Connecticut River settlements (RC in DNA: RG 59, LAR).

William ELLERY, customs collector at Newport, Rhode Island, remained in office until his death in 1820 (Madison, *Papers, Sec. of State Ser.*, 6:368n). SENATORS

FROM R.I.: Christopher Ellery and Samuel J. Potter (*Biog. Dir. Cong.*).

In 1790, ISAAC KIBBE represented Enfield, Connecticut, in the state's general assembly. By 1794, he had relocated to New York City (Hartford *Connecticut Courant*, 17 May 1790, 24 Mch. 1794). Samuel Osgood, naval officer of the port of New York, also recommended Kibbe (Osgood to TJ, 22 Feb., recorded in SJL as received from New York on 1 Mch. with notation "Kibbe Isaac. Commr. to Spain," but not found; Vol. 40:257n).

[1] MS: "The."

From James Houston

SIR   Philadelphia 4 Feby. 1804

Altho I am unaquinted with you in person and being but a farmer and you in the first charector of Statesmen yet I hope you will not be offended at my freedom in presenting the inclosed for your consideration and my instruction whether to proceed or not I am a stranger in this Citty and when I had wrote my jornal knew not whether to let it lay by or not having little or none aqaintance in Congress to communicate my thoughts in writeing unto for the Member from the District I belong unto which is Maj. Lewis I never have seen to my knoledge but once I liev in Rockbridge Cty Near to the line of Augusta Cot. by reading the within you will know what has brought and detains me here (afflicted with Cancer) Meditating what to do I thought of the time as mentioned in my Jornal when I took Mercury and had my Cancer eate out with arsenac as you may see by the inclosed turn seven leaves read page first and 2d when confined at that time passed away time when pain admited in reading Docter Franklins life and your Notes on Virginia diverted my pains as I thought at times and was much pleased to think that men would spend so much labour for the good of others instruction and improvment but wished to see something wrote on Cancers could procure none but Buckan and he leaves it in doubt whether cureable or not I thought if it was in the power of Medcean to try experiments and have sufferd much and think my relation of things perhaps would be of service to some poor afflicted persons in like complaints I know writers only plough the soil for envy you have felt that by one paragraph in your Notes which I always esteemed one of the most beatifull parts of your book but we should always try to be doing good when it is in our power for weeds will always mix less or more amongst wheat If you think this worthy of Notice please to write me an answer by post directed to me Phl. No 42 Market Street for I expect to be in this place untill last of March then to return to Rockbridge if any thing was don I could go in Stage if required and let Congress behold my face and I could obtain I suppose Doctor Rushes description of My Cancer when I came to this place as he viewed me but have not conversed with him of late what I have wrote (except this letter to yourself) have read over to Docter Tate for his approbation this therefore is unto you a Virginian the place where I was born and raised to manhood and fought as Malitiman to defend my native land therefore I hope you will not be digusted at me for writing to you so freely Col. Andrew Moore of Rockbridge and many in that and Augusta Cty Mr. Colter & others[1] knows me very well and was acquainted something with my situation while under this complaint. My circumstances are but midling having been now two full years a heavy expece to my family having no slaves they are working hard for money to supply me And I could not well go to the Federal Citty for it is expensive but if thought best would try if my expences was paid but would except of no other reward for what I could do would be contributed to this institution in hopes it would relieeve some in like distress as I have had

What I have wrote is wholy my own invetion And all founded on truth the words that others spoke are mostly put down in my jornal when any other person is included my familys letters would show that in my relation of things I built on truth and a foundation for every line there put down I often veiwed my case almost like one cast upon an Iland and having no hope unless by chance some Vessal would light my way and now I am in hopes the Vessel is come and have an Anxiety that thousands of my fellow creatures scattered over this American Island may have a passage as well as myself My poetry some may think has too many lines on religion Mixed through it but they ware the natural reflections that flowed on my mind for I composed most poetry when under the most pain which was for six or seven months and often was dredfull to bear as pr Jornal Docter Tates pills are easy taken outward application but seldom not much to suffer and in the corse of some months the Cancer rots and generally falls out then runs for some time and in Sex eight ten and twelve months the constitution is clear of the complaint D Tate says it is a constitutional disorder works like the Veneral disease that will kill if not cured at some time or other and he has found the means to purge it away if they are not too farr gon in the compl mine was in my head to the bone round the corner of eye $\frac{3}{4}$ of Inch betwixt eye and nose part of both upper and under eye lids ware eate away when I came to Tate could for some months after my Cancer fell out blow aire out of the wound at corner of eye and in one place the Docter said there wase hole through scull bone but whether or not I cannot assert positively but I know the hole was deep and some persons almost fainted to look at me all is healed now but a small hole between nose and corner of eye Otherwise I am healthy active and lively as almost any of my age could expect   from a Countryman of yours confined in this citty and humbly submit this for your consideration and if no more is to be don please to return my papers by post if you pay any postage write to me and I will [. . .] it. With confidence yours &c.

JAMES HOUSTON

RC (MHi); torn; addressed: "Thos Jefferson President US Washington"; franked and postmarked; endorsed by TJ as received 9 Feb. and so recorded in SJL. Enclosure: see below.

In a narrative written to accompany the poetic journal that described his medical history, James Houston identified his age as 52 when he began composing the journal. He had suffered from symptoms of cancer since 1789. He may have been the individual of that name who paid taxes in Rockbridge County on a slave, six horses, and 12 head of cattle in 1782 (James Houston, *A Plan for the Ladies Fund, in the United States of America, for the Relief of Those Afflicted with Cancers* [Philadelphia, 1804], 12-13; Oren F. Morton, *A History of Rockbridge County Virginia* [Staunton, Va., 1920], 373).

PRESENTING THE INCLOSED: Houston evidently was sharing a version of the journal cited above. Written in verse, it chronicled Houston's ordeal with CANCER. Houston had it published about a month later, along with a plan for raising funds to purchase and make public the methods that he believed had cured him (Houston, *Plan for the Ladies Fund*, 17-19).

BUCKAN: a reference to the oft-published and widely read work of the English physician William Buchan, *Domestic Medicine*, which included a chapter on the treatment of cancers (*Domestic Medicine: or, a Treatise on the Prevention and Cure of Diseases by Regimen and Simple Medicines* [Philadelphia, 1784], 356; Sowerby, No. 891).

Houston received an apparently successful course of treatment in Philadelphia from Dr. James TATE, who administered pills and also "some tincture" applied to the lint wrapping for the affected area. After a five-week period during which the wound appeared to worsen and discharged fluid, the cancer began to recede. Crediting the pills, Houston asked Tate to reveal his pharmaceutical formula for the benefit of other sufferers, but Tate insisted that doing so would destroy his livelihood. Houston hoped that the sale and distribution of his pamphlet would help raise the $50,000 that Tate claimed as the price for making his methods public. In 1794, Tate had cured George Washington of a cancerous spot, drawing similar praise for his talents as a physician (Houston, *Plan for the Ladies Fund*, 17-19; Washington, *Papers, Pres. Ser.*, 17:580-1n).

[1] Preceding 11 words interlined.

From James Jackson

Sir, Washington, Feby 4h, 1804.

I wished much yesterday to have an opportunity to mention a desire of Captain Eatons, to return again to the Barbary coast; and to acquaint you with his character as far as I have known him—He was in Georgia in 1795, & 1796, with the rank of Captain in the Army, and commandant of the Station at Coleraine—and was at length persecuted from that state, by the Federal and Yazoo Party's, with Gaither, his Colonel, and Seagrove, Superintendant of Indian affairs, at their head—and I believe his attentions to Republicans in general, and to myself and the Georgia Commissioners at the treaty of Coleraine in particular, principally led to place him in the back ground, with those people, and his open and decided opposition to Col Gaither, and other Officers taking shares in that most infamous & corrupt speculation, confirmed their determination to destroy him—In repeated conversations I have heard him speak of you Sir, & other characters, supposed in the opposition, with the highest respect, & that before Officers of different sentiment who have indirectly threat'ned him for it—as far as he dared to go—he did go—and candidly declared to me, his predilection for the republican cause.

Mr Eaton tells me that he has laid a memorial before you, on the situation he finds himself in—respecting a settlement of his accounts, which he says, if not allowed, must beggar him and his Family—a Wife and several Children—The Ship Gloria—he deemed absolutely necessary, and that she was warranted to act by the authority of a Naval Commander of the United States—of this however I shall not pretend to offer an opinion, I barely wish to place the Character of Captain Eaton in the light, I viewed him, whilst in Georgia, in the Years mentioned and to recommend him to you, should a vacancy of Consul for the barbary States, present itself—You are however the best Judge of his conduct at Tunis; and the firmness with which he sustained the American reputation, and resisted the repeated demands, and importunities of the Tunisian Bashaw.

I am Sir with the highest respect, Your obedt Servt

JAS JACKSON

RC (DNA: RG 59, LAR); at foot of text: "The President of the U States"; endorsed by TJ as received 4 Feb. and "Eaton to be Consul in Barbary" and so recorded in SJL; also endorsed by Daniel Brent.

While on army duty in GEORGIA in 1796, William Eaton was charged with several misdeeds by his commanding officer, Henry GAITHER, including speculation, disobedience, misuse of supplies, and defrauding the troops under his command.

Eaton vehemently denied the accusations, claiming they were the result of Gaither's personal animosity and jealousy. Although a court-martial found Eaton guilty of only a minor charge, Gaither had him confined for a month, then ordered him to Philadelphia, where Secretary of War Timothy Pickering refused to confirm the sentence and left Eaton's status in the army unchanged (Charles Prentiss, ed., *The Life of the Late Gen. William Eaton* [Brookfield, Mass., 1813], 20-53).

LAID A MEMORIAL BEFORE YOU: Eaton to TJ, 2 Feb. 1804.

NAVAL COMMANDER: Daniel McNeill.

From Frank Nash

DEAR FRIEND   [on or before 4 Feb. 1804]

what delight did you see daylight at midnght yong at my sight but however others has thought that it might be daylight before night as well as at midnight but dear Sir it must be that what is wright is wright whether it be midnig or at daylight but if you please you will keep your pleasures allike untto the day as well as the night or shall I be with a flight

Dear friend if it is to se the land and sea I would sea them free as I might du I would sea them free by daylight tu but if I should sail on the sea I would sail on the sea as I might tu but if I should travel on on the lanand I would travel on the land as I might du du mind daylylight and let midnight be out of sight   FRANK NASH

Tomorrow Tomorrow put eth Its tender leaves and seth what shall I be why if it was for time why if it ws pleasures why if it was for treasures why if it was for wisdom why if it was for want why if it was for wit why if if heavene be of want and likewise wit yet your wayays cannot be allways wise you prove friendly but it is to be what I might be but like a fool I am as I might be and so from day light till till night as

Bears and lions Delight to growl and fight for it is thier too but children you should not [learey] each other echothers to

Silver and gold its cullous [hoth] If win gold [tu my Reply] Say this or I say america

amen

RC (MHi); with ink smudges, words poorly formed; undated, but see below. Perhaps enclosed in Nash's letter of 12 Sep. or 29 Nov. 1803.

Nash perished at sea on a ship that set sail from London on 4 Feb. (*New-York Commercial Advertiser*, 20 Mch. 1804; Vol. 41:377n).

From Oliver Phelps

Sir,   Washington Feby 4th. 1804

I take the liberty to notice to your Excellency Rufus Easton Esquire a Citizen of the State of New York a young gentleman of talents and respectability, who has been meritorious in the Republican cause.—

He wishes for the appointment of District Attorney for N. Orleans— Living some distance from Mr. Easton I am not so well acquainted with his legal knowledge but from information received from Gentlemen of the first respectability of the State of New York I have no doubt of his being very reputable in the line of his proffession, and well qualified to discharge the duties of that office—

I have the honor to be Sir with high esteem and respect your Obedt. Servant   OLIVER PHELPS

RC (DNA: RG 59, LAR); at foot of text: "His Excy the President of the U States"; endorsed by TJ as received 6 Feb. and "Easton Rufus to be Atty N.O." and so recorded in SJL with a brace connecting it to letters received the same day from Tompson J. Skinner of 9 Jan. and Philip Van Cortlandt of 1 Feb.

Connecticut native Oliver Phelps (1749-1809) was a successful merchant before entering land speculation on a grand scale. With his partner, Nathaniel Gorham, he gained title to millions of acres in western New York from the state of Massachu- setts in 1788. But the speculation proved unsustainable and the two men eventually lost most of the land. Phelps nevertheless moved to New York, settling in Ontario County and serving a single term in Congress from 1803 to 1805 as a Republican. As a Connecticut native and Burrite, however, Phelps did not possess TJ's esteem. He was the Burrites' candidate for lieutenant governor of New York in 1804, but was soundly defeated (DAB; Kline, *Burr*, 2:835-8, 850-4; Vol. 36:82n; Vol. 37:460-1, 517; Vol. 39:222; Vol. 40:592; Phelps to TJ, 10 Apr. 1804).

From Ephraim Kirby

SIR   Fort Stoddert. Feby 5th. 1804

After an uncommonly fatigueing and hazardous[1] journey, of four months, I reached this place in company with my associate, Mr. Nicholas, on the 26th. day of last month. At every step, impediments unforeseen were presented, and our passage protracted to a length beyond[2] every calculation. I commenced my journey in September. It was then supposed that I had taken ample time to accomplish it by the middle of November. It does not, however, appear that the public service will suffer by the delay. The people have been preparing their business to lay before the Board,[3] and it will probably be now dis- patched within the same compass of time, which it would have re- quired, had the board convened at the time appointed.

I had the honor to address to you a letter from Natchez, in which I said, that the Commission of Register of the Land Office for the County of Washington, committed to my charge,[4] was filled with the name of Joseph Chambers, an inhabitant of the County.—I discovered at Natchez, that he was the only person in this part of the Mississippi Territory[5] on whom the appointment could with propriety be confered. Since my arrival here, I have seen nothing which leads me to doubt the correctness of my first information.[6] Mr. Chambers has commenced his official duty and the business of the Board is progressing in a favourable and agreable manner.

In the letter which you did me the honor to write on the 15th. of July, Fort Stoddert was named as the place for the Board of Commissioners to hold their session, from which it has been presumed to be the place designated for the Registers Office. Capt. Schuyler, the present commandant of the Garrison has done himself great honor, by his prompt exertions to accomodate the Board[7] with every convenience for the discharge of its duties. He caused to be fitted up in the Barracks, suitable[8] rooms for the office of the Register, and other purposes. A removal from this place, at the present time would derange and retard the public business. It is said that Fort St. Stephens is more in the centre of population, and will be a more convenient place for the permanent establishment of the office after the Board of Commissioners have closed the business of their appointment.—Of this you will doubtless receive more particular and correct[9] information from the Register.

The queries subjoined to your letter of the 15th. of July have received attention. A short time will enable me to answer them with some degree of accuracy.—

I have the honor to be with great respect Your most Obedt. Servt.

EPHM KIRBY

Dupl (DLC); at head of text: "duplicate"; at foot of text: "The President of the United States"; endorsed by TJ as received 22 Mch. and so recorded in SJL. RC (same); endorsed by TJ as received 9 Apr. and so recorded in SJL.

LETTER FROM NATCHEZ: Kirby to TJ, 16 Dec. 1803.

[1] RC: "hazardous and laborious."
[2] RC: "exceeding."
[3] RC: "Board of Commissioners."
[4] RC: "which you had been pleased to entrust to my care."
[5] RC: "in the county of Washington."
[6] RC: "I am confirmed in the correctness of that impression."
[7] Remainder of sentence lacking in RC.
[8] RC: "convenient."
[9] RC: "accurate."

From Daniel Smith

Sir,   Sumner county Feb. 5th. 1804.

Tho' late in my congratulations with you on the acquisition of Louisiana they are not the less ardent on that account. How greatly is our chance encreased to remain at peace with foreign nations! to what a degree are they excluded from tampering with our indians! how bright the prospect of encreasing population and commerce.

A bill, I understand, is on its passage in Congress for the government of the Territory of Orleans, and the appointment of a suitable person as governor will claim your attention. Permit me on this occasion to call up to your recollection your friend Mr. Andrew Jackson with whom you are acquainted—He is a well wisher in a high degree to the welfare of the United States, possesses very acute parts, and firm decision, and I trust would answer your expectation.—Not knowing what other characters may be recommended to you for that purpose, I have taken the liberty to mention his name as an act due to merit. you will have at any rate more characters to choose from.

I am Sir with great respect and esteem Your obedt. Servt.

DANL SMITH

RC (DNA: RG 59, LAR); at foot of text: "Thos. Jefferson Esq. President of the U.S."; endorsed by TJ as received 22 Feb. and "Jackson Andrew to be Govr. Louisiana" and so recorded in SJL.

To Abraham Bradley, Jr.

Feb. 6. 04.

Th: Jefferson will thank mr Bradley to inform him of the days & hours of departure & arrival of the mail between Washington and Milton, according to the establishment reverted to since Jan. 31.

RC (Kenneth W. Rendell, Inc., Catalogue No. 48, 1970, Item 131); addressed: "Mr. Bradley Post office." Not recorded in SJL.

DEPARTURE & ARRIVAL OF THE MAIL: Bradley was the assistant postmaster general (Vol. 41:267-8n).

From Thomas Cooper

DEAR SIR   Northumberland Feby. 6. 1804

It is with much regret I inform you of the decease of Dr. Joseph Priestley this morning at 11 oClock. He retained his faculties, his cheerfulness, his kindness to the last moment; he died without pain; it was a gradual falling asleep. He wd. have been 71 in March.

Knowing how much he respected you, and believing, that in common with those who know how to appreciate uncommon attainments uncommon Industry and a life of uncommon utility, that you also bore high respect for your departed friend, I hasten to communicate to you the intelligence. May your life long continue to be useful as it has been, and your end be as cheerful as his. Believe me very sincerely and respectfully your friend   THOMAS COOPER

RC (DLC); endorsed by TJ as received 16 Feb. but recorded in SJL as received 17 Feb.

YOUR END BE AS CHEERFUL AS HIS: an account of Priestley's final days, probably written by Cooper, explained that after his health had worsened to the extent that "he was unable to speak," Priestley rebounded enough to meet with friends and family members to whom he expressed happiness at the prospect of his impending death. On the morning of the 6th, he dictated revisions to some pamphlets, concluding "That is right, I have now done." Thirty minutes later he asked to be moved to a cot, where he soon "breathed his last so easily, that those sitting close to him, did not immediately perceive it" (*Aurora*, 18 Feb. 1804; Robert E. Schofield, *The Enlightened Joseph Priestley: A Study of His Life and Work from 1773 to 1804* [University Park, Pa., 2004], 400-1).

From Charles Philip, Baron de Hanstein, with Jefferson's Note

                                    Unterstein in Eichsfeld, which now
                                    appertains to the King of Prussia,
MY LORD!   near Gottingue, the 6th. Febr. 1804.

Your Excellence pardon, if I humbliest implore Your Known generosity and complaisance.

My father in law, Stephan Wilkinson, had all his fortune lost, consisting of 8000 pounds in the American war by the ardent love and great adherence to the King of England, and there-above was taken away him a part of 3000 pounds by Captain Wolf, but the most considerable part he has lost by the troops of the united provinces of Nord-America, and he left for fear all, what had could erect and support his suffering heirs. It is true, General Howe did assure him in

King's name, to compensate all the loss from England, but the Death of my father in law, travalling for Great-Britain, did darken each prospect to his suffering childern. I, Major Charles Philipp Baron de Hanstein, officer of the Hessian armies in America, married the daughter of Mr. Stephan Wilkinson, Christiana, wrote to England and pray'd a gracious repair of the lost fortune, and I obtained the answer, I must produce an attest of the President of the American provinces, which certifies the loss of my father in law. Often I wrote, but my repeated letters were in vain, I believe, because they are not arrived, and the more that, because we have eight years since recieved no letters from the brother in law of my wife, the merchant Mr. John Anderson to New-York. Therefore I intreat Your Excellence, to have the grace of drawing a reverse, that my father in law, Mr. Stephan Wilkinson has left behind the worth of 8000 pounds, at the same time I beseech also Your Excellence humbliest to inform us of the fate of the merchant Mr. Anderson. For that extraordinary condescendence and grace of Your Excellence I will be thankfull all my lifetime and solicit instantly from heaven the well-fare of Your Excellence, and You will make happy a suffering family. In deepest submission I remain till death
   Your Excellence obedient Servant

          CHARL PHILIP BARON DE HANSTEIN
          Major

[*Note by TJ*:]

these offices of humanity are proper for a[1] governmt to lend a hand to, where the individual has no other resource. recommended therefore to the attention of the office of State   TH:J

RC (DNA: RG 59, MLR); in same hand as Christiana de Hanstein's unsigned letter to TJ of 22 June 1804, signed by Baron de Hanstein; with TJ's note below endorsement; endorsed by TJ as received 15 May and so recorded in SJL with notation "S." Also endorsed by Jacob Wagner.

Hanstein's wife, CHRISTIANA, had written George Washington in 1794 regarding her family's Loyalist claim on the British government. Washington referred the matter to Secretary of State Edmund Randolph, who forwarded the letter to members of her family in the United States (Washington, *Papers, Pres. Ser.*, 15:279-80, 288). She would later seek TJ's assistance in the matter (Christiana de Hanstein to TJ, 22 June 1804).

Madison wrote Hanstein on 21 June, informing him that his letter to the president had been referred to the State Department, which made enquiries regarding the family of JOHN ANDERSON. Madison enclosed a letter received as a result of those enquiries, but added that it is "neither usual nor convenient" for the executive departments "to ascertain the facts & procure the certificates" necessary to establish the claim. Madison forwarded a copy of Hanstein's letter to Anderson, "leaving it to his care to exicute your wishes in this particular" (Madison, *Papers, Sec. of State Ser.*, 7:346).

[1] Word interlined in place of "the."

From Joel Yancey

DEAR SIR   Albemarle February. 6. 1804
I have it in contemplation to remove to the Louisiana country, and provided I thought myself qualified for the execution of any public business in that country that wou'd be adequate to the support of a genteel family, I believe I shou'd so far rely on my acquantaince with you as to request the favour of you to mention me that department in whose gift offices of that nature are, provided none shou'd offer that you may prefer, and you shou'd conceive me adequate to the functions of an office of the above description, I wou'd very gratefully acknowledge your assistance[1] so far as wou'd exclude Sacrifice of Sentiment. I am very respectfully your
   Most Obdt. Servt   JOEL YANCEY

RC (DNA: RG 59, LAR); endorsed by TJ as received 10 Feb. and "for emploiment in Louisiana" and so recorded in SJL.

Joel Yancey (1773-1838), a native of Albemarle County, served as one of the sheriffs who collected taxes on lands in the county. In that capacity he received payments from TJ for taxes on property in Fredericksville Parish, including Shadwell. TJ also drew on Yancey as a source of cash, to be repaid through Gibson & Jefferson in Richmond, where the sheriffs deposited their collections. Yancey represented Albemarle County in the Virginia General Assembly in 1805-6. He moved to Kentucky, served in that state's legislature, and won election to the U.S. House of Representatives in the Twentieth and Twenty-first Congresses (*Biog. Dir. Cong.*; Leonard, *General Assembly*, 239; Woods, *Albemarle*, 357-8, 384; MB, 2:1024, 1025, 1026, 1027, 1038-9, 1079, 1105, 1106, 1107; Vol. 32:127-8; Vol. 35:349-50; Vol. 38:449; Vol. 41:405; Craven Peyton to TJ, 8 Dec. 1803). Another Joel Yancey supervised TJ's Poplar Forest and Bedford County lands (RS, 4:318n).

[1] MS: "assitance."

From Allan B. Magruder

SIR,   Lexington, Kentucky—[before 7 Feb. 1804]
It is with great diffidence that I have taken the liberty to send you a Series of Reflections on the late Cession of Louisiana, to the United States. They were digested and Commited to paper, last Summer, during the pendancy of that Negociation of Which, you are the parent; & Which, in its Ultimate issue, has added the most important advantages to our Country.—
   Be so obliging, therefore, as to accept the pamphlet, Which I have the honor to send you. It is a Small testimony of the Sincere devotion I feel for an administration, Which, in every respect, Comports with the true genius & felicity of the American Nation.—

I am, Sir, with great respect, your mo: Ob Sevt

ALLAN B. MAGRUDER

RC (ViW: Tucker-Coleman Collection); undated; endorsed by TJ as received 7 Feb. and so recorded in SJL. Enclosure: Allan B. Magruder, *Political, Commercial and Moral Reflections, on the Late Cession of Louisiana, to the United States* (Lexington, Ky., 1803; Sowerby, No. 3472), dedicated "To Thomas Jefferson, Esquire, as a testimony of high approbation, for his patriotic efforts to elude the calamities of war, upon the late question, relative to the free navigation of the Mississippi."

Allan B. Magruder (1775-1822), a lawyer from Lexington, Kentucky, had requested TJ's aid in 1791 in obtaining a clerkship in the Treasury or War Department. He was the author of a lengthy laudatory essay on the "Character of Thomas Jefferson," which first appeared as an unsigned piece in the *Kentucky Gazette* in 1800. After TJ's election, it was widely reprinted from the London *Morning Post* and reappeared in 1803 in American newspapers and in two issues of the *Medley; or, Monthly Miscellany*, a short-lived Lexington periodical. Magruder briefly considered writing a history of the Indian wars in the west as well as a biography of George Rogers Clark, but set aside the projects when he became involved in pol-

itics. He relocated to Orleans Territory, where he became a federal agent investigating land claims in the western district from July 1805 until his removal the following year, possibly because of intemperance. An elected delegate to the Louisiana constitutional convention in 1811, he chaired the committee to compose the document and was chosen as one of the two agents to convey the new Louisiana constitution to President Madison. Magruder won election as the first U.S. senator for his state (Lexington *Kentucky Gazette*, 29 May 1800, 11 Oct. 1803; New York *Chronicle Express*, 23 June 1800; Boston *Independent Chronicle*, 28 Oct. 1802; New York *Evening Post*, 1 June 1822; *Biog. Dir. Cong.*; AHR, 35 [1930], 297; Warren Billings and Edward F. Haas, eds., *In Search of Fundamental Law: Louisiana's Constitutions, 1812-1974* [Lafayette, La., 1993], 10, 13, 14, 19, 157; Jared William Bradley, *Interim Appointment: W. C. C. Claiborne Letter Book, 1804–1805* [Baton Rouge, La., 2002], 369; *The Medley; or, Monthly Miscellany* [June and July 1803], 111-15, 124-9; Gallatin, *Papers*, 12:647, 649; 24:246, 291; RS, 1:642n; Vol. 27:794n; Magruder to TJ, 10 Sep. 1804; Albert Gallatin to TJ, 19 Mch. 1806).

From Mathieu Dumas

Au Quartier Général à Ostende le 17.
Pluviose an 12 de la République française
[i.e. 7 Feb. 1804]

MONSIEUR,

En m'appuyant auprès de votre Excellence de la recommandation de nos anciens amis et Compagnons d'armes de la mémorable guerre de l'Indépendance, comme aussi du souvenir de votre bienveillant accueil, Lorsque J'eus l'honneur de vous voir en France chez le Général Lafayette, Je pris la Liberté de vous recommander il y a quelque tems une affaire à laquelle toute ma famille, mes neveux, les enfans de ma belle Soeur Eugénie Delarue, née Beaumarchais, et mes propres enfans Sont également intéressés. C'est la juste répétition de la créance de feu Beaumarchais Sur le congrès des Etats-unis pour fournitures dans les premiers tems de la guerre, conformément au compte arrêté Sur le rapport du Ministre des finances, Hamilton.

Les conclusions du dernier rapport de Monsieur Galatin Loin d'infirmer ce premier arrêté de compte, n'y opposent qu'une présomption du payement d'un Million fondée Sur des témoignages équivoques, Sur de véritables calculs de probabilité dont nous pouvons enfin démontrer l'erreur; l'hypothèse dont Mr. Galatin S'était Servi, dumoins pour Suspendre un prononcé définitif, avait pour baze des informations recueillies bien avant l'époque de Son Ministère d'une manière incomplète, sinon fraudulense, dans les Bureaux des affaires étrangères de notre Gouvernement, alors qu'il n'y avait réellement point de Gouvernement en France, à l'époque de nos plus grands troubles et d'un désordre honteux dans l'Administration Supérieure.

Mais Sous un Gouvernement réparateur, J'ai obtenu des recherches plus exactes, un témoignage authentique invoqué par Mr. Galatin lui-même, enfin l'autorisation à la Légation française de Soumettre à votre Excellence ces Documents, ces titres certains à votre Justice, à votre généreuse intervention.

C'est au Général Bernadotte que j'avais remis l'année dernière la demande de mon beau frère, le Gen. Delarue, et la mienne; il avait reçu particulièrement des Instructions de notre Ministre des Relations Extérieures qui a bien voulu les transmettre au Général Thureau, notre Ambassadeur près de votre Excellence; et celui ci, après avoir pris une connaissance approfondie de notre réclamation, veut bien se charger de vous offrir, en la fesant valoir officiellement, l'hommage particulier de ma respectueuse Reconnaissance.

Salut & Respect.   MATHIEU DUMAS

EDITORS' TRANSLATION

                             At the headquarters in Ostend,
                             17 Pluviose Year 12 of the Republic
SIR,   [i.e. 7 Feb. 1804]

Our friends and comrades in arms from the memorable War of Independence recommended me to your excellency. Remembering your kind welcome when I had the honor of seeing you in France at General Lafayette's, I took the liberty, some time ago, of entrusting you with a matter that concerns my whole family: my children and my nephews, who are the sons of my sister-in-law, Eugénie Delarue, née Beaumarchais. It concerns the justified claim from the late Beaumarchais's trust to the United States Congress for payment of equipment during the early days of the war, as outlined in the report by Secretary of the Treasury Hamilton.

Mr. Gallatin's final report did not invalidate the first claim. It merely opposed payment of one million, which was based on ambiguous evidence and calculations that we can now demonstrate to have been erroneous. The hypothesis Mr. Gallatin used to postpone a decision was based on information gathered long before his term as secretary in an incomplete, if not fraudulent, fashion by the foreign ministry of our government, during the period of our greatest troubles, when France had no real government and there was a shameful disorder in the higher administration.

Under a restored government, I have obtained more precise information, testimony from Mr. Gallatin himself, and authorization from the French legation to submit these documents, these accurate claims, to your excellency for your justice and generous intervention.

Last year, I gave General Bernadotte my request and that of my brother-in-law, General Delarue. He received authorization from our foreign affairs ministry to transmit it to General Turreau, our ambassador. After studying our request, he agreed to present it to you, in his official capacity, along with my respectful gratitude.

Greetings and respect. MATHIEU DUMAS

RC (DLC); on Dumas's printed letter-head stationery as councillor of state and chief of staff, with blanks filled for place and date; in a clerk's hand, closing and signature by Dumas; English date supplied; at head of text: "A Son Excellence, Monsieur Jefferson, Président des Etats-unis de l'Amérique Septentrionale"; endorsed by TJ as received 19 Nov. and so recorded in SJL.

Mathieu Dumas (1753-1837), a close friend of Lafayette, joined the French army in 1773 and was an aide-de-camp to General Rochambeau during the American Revolution. He held a variety of military and government positions during and after the French Revolution. By 1803, he was a councillor of state and serving as chief of staff under General Louis Nicolas

Davout. He later served as minister of war to Joseph Bonaparte and as intendant-général of the army during the ill-fated French invasion of Russia in 1812 (Tulard, *Dictionnaire Napoléon*, 574, 628; Vol. 32:252; Vol. 40:415-16).

For Dumas's involvement in pressing the claim of the heirs of Pierre Augustin Caron de BEAUMARCHAIS, see Vol. 32:252; Vol. 40:415-16; Vol. 41:384-5, 526.

DERNIER RAPPORT DE MONSIEUR GALATIN: see Gallatin to TJ, 17 Oct. 1803 (Vol. 41:543).

GÉNÉRAL THUREAU: Louis Marie Turreau de Garambouville was named the new French minister plenipotentiary to the United States in December 1803. He would not arrive in Washington until November 1804 (Madison, *Papers, Sec. of State Ser.*, 6:156, 157n; 7:531n; 8:275).

From Louis Gex-Oboussier

Switzerland in Indiana Territory
le 7e. fevrier 1804.

J'ai l'honneur de transmettre sous ce plis à Votre Excellence une lettre de recommandation à votre adresse dont la famille Reymond a été favorisée par M. Louis Porta; cette famille originaire comme moi du Pays de Vaud et acheminée pour le Kentucky a eut le malheur de perdre Son Chef à Lancaster de Pensylvanie en Août 1802. privée de toutes ressources la Veuve Reymond a dû bounder deux de Ses enfans chés un Sellier de dite Ville, dès lors Son fils ainé a aidé par Son travail à l'entretien du reste de la famille.

La ruine presque totale du Commerce de la Suisse m'ayant decidé à quitter Vevey que J'habitois, à renoncer à mon état de Négotiant et à passer dans ce Pays pour me rapprocher de mes Compatriotes Dufour; en passant à Lancaster en Juillet dernier la Veuve Reymond Se decidat à m'accompagner et elle se trouve maintenant aupres de moi avec trois de Ses enfans; mes moyens pécuniaires étant tres minimes, je me suis joint à mes amis Dufour et à un autre Vaudois nommé aussi Reymond pour acquérir conjointément 1111. acres de terre in Section No. 15. et fractions No. 22 et 27. situé sur Indian Creek et la riviere de l'ohio à 8. mille en sus de l'embouchure du Kentucky-river, ma famille composée de mon Epouse et de 6. enfans doit m'y Suivre dans le courant de cette année et jusques allors la Veuve Reymond et ses trois enfans resteront aupres de moi et m'aideront au défrichement que j'ai commencé.

Je prens la liberté de me recommander ainsi que cette famille à la haute protection de Votre Excellence; nous nous proposons de cultiver ici la Vigne comme nos Compatriotes Dufour, S'il étoit possible que nous pussions jouir de la meme faveur qui leur a été accordée par le Congrés. Votre Excellence peut compter Sur les efforts que nous ne cesserons de faire pour la mériter.

Je prie Votre Excellence d'excuser ma démarche et d'agréer l'hommage de la respectueuse Consideration de Son très humble & très obeissant Serviteur.   L. GEX-OBOUSSIER

EDITORS' TRANSLATION

Switzerland, in Indiana Territory
7 Feb. 1804

I have the honor of transmitting to your excellency a letter of recommendation that Mr. Louis Portas graciously wrote on behalf of the Reymonds. This family, originally from Vaud like me, and heading toward Kentucky, had the misfortune of Mr. Reymond's death in Lancaster, Pennsylvania, in 1802. Left with no resources, his widow was obliged to apprentice two of her children to a saddlemaker. Since then her eldest son has been working to help support the rest of the family.

After the almost complete collapse of Swiss commerce I left Vevey, where I lived, gave up my business as a trader, and came to this country to join my compatriots, the Dufours. When I traveled through Lancaster last July, Mrs. Reymond decided to accompany me here. She is now with me, as are three of her children. Given my limited financial resources, I went into partnership with my friends the Dufours and another person from Vaud, who is also named Reymond. Collectively we purchased 1,111 acres of land in section 15 and parts of sections 22 and 27, on Indian Creek and the Ohio River, eight miles below the mouth of the Kentucky River. My wife and six children are arriving later this year. Until then, Mrs. Reymond and her three children are staying with me and helping clear the land.

I take the liberty of asking your excellency's protection for me and for the Reymond family. We plan to grow vines here as our Swiss compatriots, the Dufours, do. If we could benefit from the same privileges Congress granted them, your excellency could be assured that we would work diligently to deserve your favor.

I beg your excellency to forgive me for approaching you and to accept this sign of respectful esteem from his very humble and obedient servant.

L. GEX-OBOUSSIER

RC (DLC); addressed: "A Son Excellence Monsieur Jefferson Président des Etats unis à Washington federal City"; franked; endorsed by TJ as received 23 Feb. and so recorded in SJL. Enclosure: Louis Portas to TJ, 6 Apr. 1802 (Vol. 37:185-6).

Louis Gex-Oboussier was among the Swiss immigrants to settle in the New Switzerland colony of Swiss vinedresser John James Dufour. The settlement had recently moved from Kentucky to southern Indiana after Dufour's vineyards in the first location failed. Gex-Oboussier es-

tablished his own vineyard and produced wine in small quantities for several years, but without great success. In 1826, he left the settlement and moved to the utopian colony of New Harmony (James L. Butler and John J. Butler, *Indiana Wine: A History* [Bloomington and Indianapolis, 2001], 72-5, 83, 96, 118; Vol. 32:529-33; Vol. 36:373-6; Vol. 37:185-6).

ACCORDÉE PAR LE CONGRÈS: in 1802, Congress granted Dufour and his associates the right to purchase up to four sections of land in southern Indiana at two dollars per acre, without interest, and payable by 1 Jan. 1814 (Vol. 36:376n).

To George Jefferson

DEAR SIR   Washington Feb. 7. 1804

Doctr. Wardlaw has requested me to remit you a sum of 72. D 87½ c to be subject to his orders. I therefore now inclose you seventy five dollars to cover his draught. not having heard anything of my tobo. yet from mr Griffin, my manager at Poplar forest, I write to him again this day to hasten it down, tho' I am not without hope it is with you or on it's way. I shall have occasion for it's proceeds by the last of next month or beginning of the following. Accept my affectionate salutations.   TH: JEFFERSON

by another lre of same date
desired 400. b. coal

PrC (MHi); at foot of text: "Mr. George Jefferson"; with notation of other letter added in ink; endorsed by TJ in ink on verso.

A letter of 3 Dec. 1803 from William WARDLAW, recorded in SJL as received 4 Dec., has not been found. A letter from TJ to Wardlaw, recorded in SJL at this day, is also missing. On the same day in his financial memoranda, TJ recorded sending George Jefferson the $75 for Wardlaw (MB, 2:1119).

A letter of this day to Burgess GRIFFIN was recorded in SJL but has not been found.

ANOTHER LRE OF SAME DATE: TJ recorded only one letter to George Jefferson, with the notation "coal."

From Lacépède

le 17. pluviôse, an 12.
[i.e. 7 Feb. 1804]

MONSIEUR LE PRÉSIDENT

La lettre que j'ai l'honneur d'écrire à votre excellence; vous sera présentée par le général thureau membre de la légion d'honneur, et notre ambassadeur auprès de vous. Il offrira de ma part à votre excellence, un exemplaire de l'histoire naturelle des cétacées que je viens de publier. J'ai l'honneur de vous prier, Monsieur le président, de réunir cet hommage à celui que M. livingston a eu la bonté de vous faire parvenir en mon nom, à l'exemplaire de l'histoire des poissons, qu'il vous a adressé. Je desire vivement que ces ouvrages vous rappellent quelquefois qu'en europe personne n'éprouve pour vous une plus haute estime et ne s'honore plus de votre amitié. Notre ambassadeur m'a promis de saisir toutes les occasions de vous parler de mon admiration et de mon dévouement. C'est un brave et habile militaire dont on estime beaucoup les lumières, les talents et le caractére. Il travaille à un grand ouvrage qui ne contribuera pas peu à la gloire de la France, et particulièrement à celle de notre armée. Il est digne d'élever le monument qu'il a conçu et qui est déjà avancé. J'envie comme tous les vrais amis de l'humanité, l'avantage qu'il va avoir de contribuer à resserrer les nœuds qui unissent les deux premières nations des deux mondes. Je m'associe par mes vœux, à ce beau ministère.

Il me tarde bien d'apprendre le succès de l'important voyage que vous m'avez annoncé l'année dernière. Combien ses résultats seront utiles aux sciences naturelles et aux sciences politiques qui ne valent qu'autant qu'elles dérivent des premières! Quelle grande et belle tâche va remplir votre nation, en portant successivement, sur toute la surface de l'amérique septentrionale, tous les bienfaits de la raison perfectionnée, avec la moindre somme possible des inconvéniens attachés aux progrès de la civilisation! Puisse votre nation être toujours dirigée dans les grands mouvemens aux quels la nature des choses la destine, par des hommes tels que vous!

Agréez, Monsieur le président, ma vénération et mon respect.

B. G. ET. L. LA CEPÈDE

EDITORS' TRANSLATION

17 Pluviose Year 12
[i.e. 7 Feb. 1804]

MISTER PRESIDENT,

The letter I have the honor of writing to your excellency will be delivered by General Turreau, our ambassador to you and a member of the Legion of Honor. He will bring your excellency a copy of the natural history of cetaceans that I have just published. I have the honor of asking you, Mister President, to add this tribute to the history of fish which Mr. Livingston kindly sent you on my behalf. I ardently hope these books will remind you that no one in Europe holds you in higher esteem or is more honored by your friendship than I. Our ambassador promised to seize every occasion to tell you of my admiration and devotion. He is a skilled, courageous soldier whose mind, talent and character are much admired. He is pursuing an important work that will contribute considerably to the glory of France and especially our army. He is qualified to complete the monument he has conceived, which is already quite far along. Like all true friends of humanity, I envy his opportunity to help strengthen the ties that unite the two premier nations of the two worlds. He has my best wishes to this admirable mission.

I am impatient to hear about the success of the important journey you told me about last year. The results will be so useful to natural science as well as to political science, which itself is only valuable to the extent that it derives from natural science. What a great and noble task your country will fulfill by gradually carrying across the whole surface of North America all the benefits of perfected reason accompanied by the fewest possible downsides of the progress of civilization. May your nation always be led by men like you in the great undertakings to which it is destined!

Accept, Mister President, my devotion and respect.

B. G. ET. L. LA CEPÈDE

RC (DLC); English date supplied; endorsed by TJ as received 19 Nov. and so recorded in SJL.

Louis Marie Turreau (THUREAU) de Garambouville evidently delivered Lacépède's recently published *Histoire naturelle des cétacées* when he assumed his duties as French minister to the United States in November 1804. Lacépède sent TJ the fifth volume of the natural history on fish (POISSONS) the previous July (Madison, *Papers, Sec. of State Ser.*, 8:275; Vol. 41:115-16).

QUE VOUS M'AVEZ ANNONCÉ: TJ to Lacépède, 24 Feb. 1803 (Vol. 39:576-9).

To Wilson Cary Nicholas

TH:J. TO MR NICHOLAS.   Feb. 7. 04.

Reflecting on the proposition as to upper Louisiana which you mentioned as likely to unite all, and as it has been further explained by a map in the hands of mr Smith, I think it may be made to do. it is the better as it will sink the name of Louisiana, which might entertain hankerings on both sides the Atlantic. but something more energetic on that side the river must be provided than the ordinary provisions on this side, adapted to their exposed situation and to the object of preventing settlements. I send you a sketch, which under familiar names, may give the necessary authority. I confess that in giving the brevet to the County Lieutt. I have a hope of sliding into the regular corps some select characters, worthy of trust, say Captains, Majors, & perhaps one Colonel. if this is wrong, strike out the brevet.—do not let the paper be seen in my handwriting, as the Feds would make a text of it.[1]—would it not be well to take this occasion of raising the salaries of those two Governors? they are really inadequate to any stile of living which is not shabby & afflicting to the incumbent. Missisipi should be at least 3000. D. Indiana 2500. D. and Detroit 2000.

RC (NCooHi). PrC (DLC).

MR SMITH: probably Senator John Smith of Ohio, who had previously supplied TJ with information on Louisiana

and New Orleans (Vol. 40:186-7; Vol. 41:173-4, 291-2).

[1] TJ originally ended the letter here, before repositioning the dateline and continuing the text.

ENCLOSURE

Draft Section of Bill for Organization of Upper Louisiana

Each of the portions of country on the Western side of the river Missisipi hereby annexed to the Indiana & Missisipi territories shall be divided into counties by their respective Governours, under the direction of the Pres. of the US. as the convenience of the settlements shall require, & subject to such alterations hereafter as experience may prove more convenient. the free[1] inhabitants of each county between the ages of _____ and _____ shall be formed into a militia, with proper officers, according to their numbers, to be appointed by the Governour, except the Commanding officer, who shall be appointed by the Pres. of the US. and who whether a captain, Major, or Colonel Commandant, shall be the County Lieutenant, and, as such, shall under the Governor, have command of the regular officers & troops in his county, as well as of the militia, for which purpose he shall have a regular brevet commission giving him such command, and the pay and emoluments of an officer of the same grade in the regular army. he shall be specially charged with the emploiment of the military & militia of his county, in cases of sudden invasion or insurrection, and until the orders of the governor can be recieved; & at all times with the duty of ordering a military patrole, aided by militia if necessary, to arrest unauthorised settlers in any part of his county, or persons who, not having been settled therein on the _____ day of _____ shall be found without a passport from the Governor of the territory, and to remand the same to the Governor to be dealt with according to law, destroying at the same time the buildings, enclosures & property found on such unauthorised settlement: and on any repetition of the offense thereafter by the same person, the Governor shall be authorised to commit the offender to jail there to remain until he shall give security for his good behavior for 3. years, of which a repetition of the same offence, in any part of the sd territories on the Western side of the river Missisipi, shall be a breach.

PrC (DLC: TJ Papers, 138:23854); undated; entirely in TJ's hand.

HEREBY ANNEXED: this draft formed the basis for an amendment to the bill to divide Louisiana and provide for its temporary government, which Nicholas introduced in the Senate on 9 Feb. (see TJ's draft bill at 23 Nov. 1803). Nicholas's amendment, in a modified form, was subsequently incorporated into section 12 of the final version of the bill as approved by the Senate on 18 Feb. and enacted by Congress on 26 Mch. It differed, however, with TJ's "sketch" in several particulars. The residue of Louisiana not included in the Orleans Territory would be called the district of Louisiana and would come under the executive authority of the governor of Indiana alone. The area would be divided into districts instead of counties. Free inhabitants between the ages of 18 and 45 were to be formed into a militia. TJ's term "County Lieutenant" was replaced with "commanding officer." The commanding officer of each district was to have a BREVET COMMISSION giving him rank and pay equal to the regular army. Most of TJ's specifics regarding the removal and punishment of unauthorized settlers were included in Nicholas's amendment, but were removed from the final version of the act. Instead, section 12 authorized military patrols and militia to arrest unauthorized settlers found in their respective districts, "and to commit such offenders to jail to be dealt with according to law" (Nicholas's amendment, 9 Feb., printed for the Senate [Washington, D.C., 1804; Shaw-Shoemaker, No. 7575]; bill as read in the House of Representatives, 20 Feb. [Washington, D.C., 1804; Shaw-Shoemaker, No. 7406], 10-13; U.S. Statutes at Large, 2:287; JS, 3:353, 359-60).

[1] Word interlined.

From James Powell

SIR   New York Febury 7 = 1804

I Canot suffer my self to entertain a doubt but that you wil be pleased to excuse this adress, with the same chearefulness you would acknowlidge a like obligation, Information assures me, Sir—That you are an ageid resident of Virgenia, and doubtless of extensive information—I shal ever be readey to acknowlidge it as a singular favour dun me—if it is in your power to afford me aney information of my Hor. Fathers family. My father Joseph Powell (at the time he left Maryland his parential abode about 1754) was the onely son of Thomas and Peggy Powell, sum of the erely setlers on the Potomake River (Tho originally from Whales England) my father lernt the Carpenters trade of one Isack Oakson at Anapolis—he had one sister whose name was Martha. Aney information You may have to afford me on this or aney other ocation shal be gratefully Acknowlidged as a want of candure, or Initention from severil like aplications I hope wil farther pleade as an apoligie for this intrudeing on your more immediate and Important Concernes

Sir, With sentiments of esteeme I remain Yours to Serve

JAMES POWELL

RC (DLC); at foot of text: "Mr Thomas Jefferson Esqr, President of the United States"; endorsed by TJ as received 9 Feb. and so recorded in SJL.

James Powell, a son of Emma and Joseph Powell, acted on behalf of his mother and brothers Thomas and Joseph to lay claim to the original Maryland property entailed by their grandfather Thomas Powell, which had fallen under the jurisdiction of the federal district. TJ's re-

sponse to James Powell of 10 Feb. was recorded in SJL but has not been found. Powell wrote about his situation to the newly inaugurated President Madison in 1809 and noted that he had "adrest To Mr. Thomas Jefferson Late President of the U.S., who politely Refered me To Bishop Madison President of William and Marys Colidge whose answour Nither I nor my Elder Brother Mr. Thomas Powell have not been so fortunate as To Receive" (Madison, *Papers, Pres. Ser.*, 1:60-2).

From David Meade Randolph

SIR,   Richmond 7 February 1804

I am thankful for your ready attention to my last letter—I should not again intrude on your patience but to counteract an effect so unjustly produced in your mind, by a charge of Mr. Duvall's, who asserts that I had "persisted in a refusal to exhibit the necessary vouchers" by which alone my purpose cou'd be answered. Assured of your liberality, and determined to refute unmeritted censure, I beg your perusal of the enclosed correspondence as the only possible means to which from the singularity of circumstances, I can have recourse.

The object in view can never be relinquished—I shall therefore, shortly make personal application to the proper department, where you will be so good as to deposit the enclosed—and in any result, I shall be mindful of the honor bestow'd on your respectful & Obedt. Servant

D M RANDOLPH

RC (DLC); at foot of text: "Thos. Jefferson Esqr."; endorsed by TJ as received 11 Feb. and so recorded in SJL. Enclosures: (1) Randolph to William Marshall, "Clerk of the Courts of the United States in the district of Virginia," Richmond, 29 Jan. 1804, explaining that his accounts with the U.S. Treasury remain unsettled because Gabriel Duvall accuses him of refusing to provide the necessary vouchers; "I pray you to furnish me everything within your power towards an

explanation," Randolph pleads, "and as much in the form of a *voucher* as possible"; the former U.S. marshal notes that all he has is "a fair record of abstracts"; he cannot provide any other evidence than that which Marshall furnishes (Tr in same; in Randolph's hand; at head of text: "Copy"; on same sheet as next enclosure). (2) Marshall to Randolph, 5 Feb., noting that he does not have it in his power to give Randolph what the Treasury Department considers "a Voucher";

he observes that most of the unsettled items were sums paid to witnesses summoned by the United States; as clerk he always kept a record and certified those who attended; examining Randolph's abstracts, Marshall finds "that they are all certified by me and passed by the Judge"; he recalls that he never "certified any acct. without Knowing that the witnesses did attend and that you did pay for their attendance, but tis impossible for me to give at present a more particular detail of it"; Marshall notes that in February 1801, John Steele expressed satisfaction with the explanation that he gave him regarding "monies paid to witnesses on the part of the United States" and that those accounts were settled; "I know you have no other Voucher in your possession and I know the officers of the Treasury are satisfied that is the case," Marshall states,

"and that the certificate of the Judge ought to be by them conclusive evidence that the money was paid and that the witnesses were summoned," but still the Treasury obstinately persists and he cannot see that Randolph has any redress; Marshall laments that Randolph "did not have the transaction closed" when it was in his power "& when the then Comptroller seemed disposed to an equitable adjustment" (Tr in same; in Randolph's hand; at head of text: "answer"; begins on same sheet as Enclosure No. 1).

MY LAST LETTER: Randolph to TJ, 10 Jan. TJ replied on 23 Jan.

For the Treasury secretary's negative response to Randolph's request that the president DEPOSIT THE ENCLOSED at the Treasury Department, see Gallatin to TJ, 13 Feb.

From William Alexander

RESPECTED SIR   Charleston 8th. February 1804

Allow A Youth to Address you his Father was held in Carolina with esteem, his Son has met with Misfortunes to A Considerable Sum

The Youth who now addresses you must observe my deceased parents (Alexr. Alexander & *Wife*) have Left some small competency to me but having the family of Wife and Child Induces me to Supplicate you for an Appointement of Any Kind in Carolina My Adged Grand Mother was with Enjoyment (altho at the Adge of Eighty Seven) At the Moment I Mentioned that you had appointed my Uncle her Son, James Anderson as Commercial Agent at Cette in France, Permit me Sir to beg your Excuse for My Intrusion, Allow me to mention My Most Respected Father was the class mate of the Rt Revd Bishop White, was Usherd by our Respected Country Man, Coln Laurens, in Business at the Time of his first appearance in Carolina, From the Repeated Losses that I have Sustained Induces me to request some small Post of Appointiment, further Respected Sir Allow me to Observe, Our Late President Mr Adams, Appointed my Deceased Brother as Midshipman in our Early Navy, by which means he lost his early Life,

By the Loss of My Mother, for the Consolation of Three Sisters I have Appointed the Honble Judge Wm Johnson, to be the Protecter of them, myself having A family, to him for my Carracter, or General

Gadesden, you can write, or the Collector, with every hopes that you may give me some Appointment, I subscribe Humbly Sir

WILLIAM ALEXANDER

RC (DNA: RG 59, LAR); endorsed by TJ "for office" and so recorded in SJL at 18 Mch.

Charleston lumber merchant and factor William Alexander was the son of schoolmaster Alexander Alexander and his wife, Rachel. His parents died in 1800 and 1803, respectively (Charleston *City Gazette and Daily Advertiser*, 3 Feb., 31 July, 31 Dec. 1800, 27 May 1801, 14 June 1803; Philip M. Hamer and others, eds., *The Papers of Henry Laurens*, 16 vols.

[Columbia, S.C., 1968-2003], 6:115n, 592n).

BISHOP WHITE: Episcopal bishop William White of Philadelphia (ANB). COLN LAURENS: Henry Laurens.

MY DECEASED BROTHER: Alexander Alexander, Jr., was appointed a midshipman in 1799 and resigned the following year. He died in November 1803 (NDQW, Dec. 1800-Dec. 1801, 315; Charleston *City Gazette and Daily Advertiser*, 17 Nov. 1803).

From David Leonard Barnes

SIR—   Providence Feby 8th 1804

In compliance with my promise in my letter of the 10th ultimo, I will now endeavour to state the principal matters in Capt. Ingraham's case

John West Leonard commenced two actions in the District Court of Rhode Island, one against James D'Wolf as owner, the other against Nathaniel Ingraham as Master of a vessel employed in the slave trade—The action against Ingraham was for receiving on board Seventy slaves—The action against D'Wolf came on first—The Atty produced the Depositions of Thomas Cook and and Samuel Arnold, copies of which are hereto annexed—The Deft then produced Capt Ingraham, who swore that he had no written orders from the Deft— and that his verbal orders from him were, if he took gold dust, ivory, camwood &c, to go to Havanna to market—but if he took slaves, to go to Savannah—that having taken slaves, he was absolutely on his way to Savannah, when he was captured by a British Privateer, off the hole in the rock, & carried into New Providence, and condemmed— Several Masters of vessels swore, that it was not uncommon to make the hole in the rock, in a passage from Africa to Savannah—On this evidence the Deft was acquitted—The cause against Ingraham was continued on the motion of the Atty to obtain from New Providence, a copy of what Ingraham had sworn to in his protest there, and in his answers to the standing interrogatories, as well as a copy of his log-book if it could be obtained—Having received a Commission as

District Judge before the next Term, I certified the cause to the Circuit Court, in which it was tried at the November Term, 1801, at Newport—The Commission sent to New Providence was returned executed, at a very considerable expence to the Atty—I have extracted from the papers annexed to the Commission, such parts as serve to show the real destination of the vessel, & send them hereto annexed— I send also annexed copies of the Depositions produced on the part of the Atty—These Depositions, and the papers from New Providence, contain nearly if not quite all the evidence used in the cause—The Jury returned a verdict for 14,000 dollars, on the only count in the declaration, which was for receiving seventy slaves on board, with which the Court, & all disinterested men seemed to be content— Judgment was rendered and execution issued, and at the return Term the next Spring, Ingraham was committed to the prison at Bristol, where he resided—In conformity to the law on that subject, he obtained the liberty of the prison yard, which includes the Court-House, the Church, and a very considerable tract of land in a pleasant part of the Town—but I believe he has not the liberty of going into any private home—He has but little if any property—has a wife and four or five children, the oldest a boy about 13 or 14 years old, the youngest is quite small—His Mother lives at Bristol in a house with another of her sons, who has some property, though not more than is necessary for his own family—

Having stated the proceedings & evidence in the cause, I hope my having been concerned as Attorney, will be a sufficient apology for not giving an opinion as to the propriety or impropriety of granting the prayer of the petition—

To prevent all mistakes relative to the papers before refered to, I have annexed them under my Seal—

With Sentiments of the Highest Respect I have the Honour to be, Your most Obedient Servant   DAVID LEONARD BARNES

RC (DNA: RG 59, GPR); at foot of text: "Thomas Jefferson President of the United States"; endorsed by TJ on final page of enclosures as received 19 Feb. and so recorded in SJL with notation "Ingraham's case." Enclosures: (1) Deposition of Thomas Cook, a "Mariner of Lawful age" of Shrewsbury, Monmouth County, New Jersey, given at Providence, Rhode Island, 10 Jan. 1801, in the case of Leonard v. D'Wolf; at Newport, Rhode Island, in January 1800, Cook joined the sloop *Fanny*, owned by James D'Wolf, on a voyage to the coast of Africa; D'Wolf said the vessel was going for ivory and camwood, but on the morning of the sloop's departure, Cook learned that the *Fanny* was going for slaves; D'Wolf refused to discuss the cargo and threatened to jail the crew if they did not board; the *Fanny* sailed to Africa, picking up slaves at the Galinhas and water at Sierra Leone, and then sailing for Havana; on its return, the sloop was taken by a British privateer and carried to New Providence; once in port, the *Fanny*'s captain told the crew that they would have to provide for themselves; Cook subsequently made his way to New York; in response to questioning by the plaintiff and defendant, Cook affirmed that Nathaniel Ingraham was captain of the *Fanny* during its entire voyage; the sloop reached the coast of Africa in March 1800, but Cook could not say when it sailed from there; the *Fanny* took 73 black slaves on board, of whom 66 remained at the time the sloop was taken to New Providence; Cook understood that Ingraham owned 4 of the slaves and the mate owned 2, and that 15 were "on freight marked on the Buttock with the Letters W.D.," which Cook understood meant they belonged to "William Dalton a trader on the Coast"; the remainder were "Cargo Slaves" who had been purchased with the proceeds of the outward cargo; before leaving Bristol, Cook neither saw D'Wolf on board the *Fanny*, nor heard him give directions regarding the voyage; the *Fanny* left Bristol with a cargo of rum and tobacco as well as a number of irons "for both hands & feet," which were used on "the greater part of the Men slaves" acquired in Africa; Ingraham handled the business of purchasing and receiving the slaves; at New Providence, Cook received no wages from Ingraham; at New York, Cook joined the crew of the revenue cutter *Governor Jay* under the command of Captain John West Leonard; Cook had traveled to Rhode Island on his own business with Captain Leonard, Lieutenant John Wade, and Samuel Arnold; Cook was not promised money for coming to Rhode Island and he knew nothing of Leonard's suit against D'Wolf until after he arrived there (Tr in same; in a clerk's hand, including Cook's signature by his mark and attestation by Caleb Harris, chief justice of the Court of Common Pleas, County of Providence). (2) Deposition of Samuel Arnold, a "Mariner of Lawful age" of Albany, New York, given at Providence, 10 Jan. 1801, in the case of Leonard v. D'Wolf; on 30 Jan. 1800, D'Wolf asked Arnold and others to ship in the *Fanny*, which D'Wolf stated was bound for the coast of Africa for camwood and ivory, or gold dust and ivory (Arnold does not recall which); on board the *Fanny* at Bristol, the crew discovered "a Grating for Locking down Slaves"; the sloop's mate, William Richmond, told them the grating was for one of D'Wolf's ships that was in the African slave trade; the *Fanny* sailed on 4 or 5 Feb. and arrived off the African coast after 25 or 30 days; the sloop took on slaves at the Galinhas and Cape Mount, then departed for Havana about 6 July; after 40 or 50 days, the *Fanny* was taken off Abaco by a British privateer and carried to New Providence; once in port, Ingraham advised his crew to "look out for ourselves" and Arnold subsequently shipped in a brig bound for Havana; before the *Fanny* left Bristol, Arnold saw "a number of Irons vizt Cuffs for the hands & feet" brought on board; when some of the crew refused to board if the sloop was going for slaves, D'Wolf threatened them with jail and declared that the sloop's business was not their concern; in response to questioning by the plaintiff and defendant, Arnold states that he did not know the intended voyage of the sloop as described in the portage bill he signed, because he could not read; that Ingraham was captain on the *Fanny* during the entire voyage, that he transacted the business of purchasing and receiving the slave cargo, and that 73 slaves had been taken on board; Arnold understood that 4 of the slaves were Ingraham's, 2 were Richmond's, 15 branded with "W.D." on their buttocks belonged to "William Dalton," and the remainder were cargo slaves; the *Fanny* carried a cargo of rum and tobacco from Bristol, and almost all of the male slaves were put in irons during the sloop's voyage from Africa; Arnold had no prior acquaintance with Leonard and came to Rhode Island only for his wages from the *Fanny*; Arnold is testifying at Leonard's request and knew nothing of the suit against D'Wolf before yesterday (Tr in same; in a clerk's hand, including Arnold's signature by his mark and attestation by Harris). (3) "Extract from Nathaniel Ingraham's protest at New Providence dated 23 August 1800," stating that he sailed in the *Fanny* from Sierra Leone on 6 July 1800, bound for Havana with a cargo of slaves (Tr in same; in Leonard's hand). (4) "Extracts from Nathaniel Ingraham's answers to the

Interrogatories in the Court of Vice Admiralty at New Providence," in which Ingraham states that the *Fanny* was taken by the privateer schooner *Jason* on 21 Aug. 1800 near the "hole in the rock" on the island of Abaco; that the *Fanny*'s voyage began at Bristol, Rhode Island, and was to end at Havana, where Ingraham was to deliver up the vessel and cargo and discharge the hands; the *Fanny* sailed from Bristol on 2 Feb. 1800, bound for the Galinhas with a cargo of rum, tobacco, and flour, which was there to be discharged to "a Mr Dalton, a Mr Hall, and other British subjects residing there"; the *Fanny* took on board its cargo of slaves and proceeded to Sierra Leone for wood, water, and provisions, whence it sailed 6 July for Havana; "Walter Dalton," a British subject residing at the Galinhas, was the shipper and owner of 15 of the slaves, and 4 slaves died on the passage; the remaining slaves were consigned to David Neagle of Havana "for the account risque & benefits" of James D'Wolf & Brothers as Dalton's agents; the remaining slaves, "except the adventures," were owned by the D'Wolfs and consigned to Neagle "for the real account, risque and benefit of said James D'Wolf & Brothers, and none else"; Ingraham swears that the slaves taken on board, "except the adventures," belonged to D'Wolf; among Ingraham's papers on board was a letter from Dalton to Neagle, which said the slaves, "except the adventures," would become the property of the D'Wolfs once unloaded at Havana (Tr in same; in Leonard's hand). (5) Copy of "Capt Nathaniel Ingraham's directions," ordering him to proceed to the coast of Africa and make the best trade possible on the windward part of the coast, touching first at the river Galinhas; Ingraham thereafter to proceed to Havana and deliver the vessel and cargo to Neagle and discharge and pay the crew; if trade is found to be bad on the windward coast, Ingraham is at liberty to proceed leeward (Tr in same; in Leonard's hand). (6) Copy of "Capt. Nathl Ingrahams Orders," extracted from the portage bill, or agreement, dated 13 Jan. 1800, between Ingraham and the crew of the *Fanny*, describing the sloop's intended voyage as from Bristol to the coast of Africa, then to Havana and home (Tr in same; in Leonard's hand). (7) Deposition of Cook, given at Providence, 10 Jan. 1801, in the case of Leonard v. Ingraham, repeating much of the information provided by Cook in his deposition in the suit against D'Wolf in Enclosure No. 1 (Tr in same; in a clerk's hand, including Cook's signature by his mark and attestation by Harris). (8) Deposition of Arnold, given at Providence, 10 Jan. 1801, in the case of Leonard v. Ingraham, repeating much of the information provided by Arnold in his deposition in the suit against D'Wolf in Enclosure No. 2 (Tr in same; in a clerk's hand, including Arnold's signature by his mark and attestation by Harris).

The HOLE IN THE ROCK, or Hole-in-the-Wall, was a navigation landmark on the extreme southern point of Abaco Island in the Bahamas (Edmund M. Blunt, *The American Coast Pilot*, 10th ed. [New York, 1822], 261-4).

To William Eaton

SIR   Washington Feb. 8. 04.

I find, on conversation with the Secretary of state that your papers are before the Auditor, not the Comptroller as I had believed, that the Auditor has asked the opinion of the Secretary of State on certain points, which opinion being unfavorable to you, you wish a revisal of it. altho' it be as yet interlocutory only yet as it will direct the final decision, I have proceeded to consider it.

The first point is that which respects your vessel the Gloria, employed by you first to carry intelligence, & then to be used as additional to our armed force in the Mediterranean. the situation of affairs in the Mediterranean has led us to permit the Consuls there to employ advice-boats for communicating promptly important information. but as it is an expensive mode of conveying intelligence, they resort to it on their own responsability. they are therefore to see that the vessel they employ is the least expensive which is competent to the object, and that the occasion be of sufficient importance to justify a special dispatch boat. your vessel, the Gloria, was much more expensive than[1] was necessary. and as to the 2d object, the employing her as additional to our navy, the legislature alone can add to, or diminish our naval force. the Secretary of the navy decides, & I think correctly, that we should not be justifiable in leaving to the executive agents to decide what additional force they shall[2] call into service for the operations committed to them with a given force. as to this article therefore, the Executive will carry it's indulgence to the utmost justifiable point, in allowing you for your vessel while employed as an advice-boat.

The 2d. question respects a sum of 10,000. D. which you agreed to give to the Tunisian minister, if he would favor the restoration of the Ex-Bashaw of Tripoli, & the restoration should be effected, without which he was to have nothing: & you had agreed with the Ex-Bashaw that he should repay the money if he was restored. so that in either event, it was not to fall on the US. the Ex-Bashaw & ourselves having a common enemy, might justifiably harmonize in our operations. but the subsidising an ally, rests with the legislature only, here, as it is known to do in England. but this question is unnecessary. the US. were only to pay in the first instance *after* the restoration of the Ex-Bashaw. he never was restored; therefore by the very terms of your contract the US. had nothing to pay to the Minister. but it seems that on certain mercantile transactions between yourself & the minister, he had money of yours in his hands, and retains it under pretext of this contract. but the pretext being groundless, it is as if he refused to pay you without offering any pretext. the US. never became securities that he should pay you what he might fall in your debt in your mercantile dealings. it will indeed be a proper occasion for them to lend their aid in recovering the money through your successor, as they would to any other individual in like circumstances; but this is the utmost to which they are bound.

FC (DLC); in TJ's hand; at foot of first page: "Mr. Eaton"; at head of text: "not sent." Not recorded in SJL.

Although TJ apparently never sent the above letter, its opinions coincide with those of Madison in his 11 Feb. letter to the AUDITOR of the Treasury, Richard Harrison, regarding Eaton's accounts. In it, Madison stated his belief that Eaton's contingent expenses should be allowed and that his demand regarding the ship GLORIA, which was properly rejected by the Navy Department, could be settled by the Treasury "at a reasonable rate" for the period during which Eaton employed it as a vessel "for giving and receiving intelligence." Like TJ, Madison flatly re-jected Eaton's charge for $10,000 prom-ised to the TUNISIAN MINISTER, Yusuf Sahib-at-Taba, which, Madison declared, "is under all circumstances of the case not admissible under any proper exercise of the discretion vested in the Execu-tive" (Madison, *Papers, Sec. of State Ser.,* 6:465-6; Vol. 40:649-50).

[1] TJ here canceled "should."
[2] TJ here canceled "employ."

From Christopher Ellery

Senate Chamber Feby. 8th. 1804—

C. Ellery again ventures to intrude upon the precious time of the President with a request that he may be considered as among the friends of Mr. Seymour, who, as he understands, is recommended for some office in the lately acquired territory. C. Ellery is not intimately acquainted with Mr. Seymour, but well knows that his family is one of the most respectable in Connecticut. He begs to observe also that Mr. Seymour is conversant in mercantile affairs, and has the spanish language, as well as a knowledge of spanish manners & customs, gained by a residence of two or three years in Havana

With his highest respects C. Ellery tenders to the President his warmest wishes for his health & happiness—

RC (DNA: RG 59, LAR); torn at en-dorsement; endorsed by TJ as received 9 Feb. and "[Seym]our   for N.O." and so recorded in SJL.

In 1801, Ledyard SEYMOUR, the young-est son of Hartford mayor Thomas Sey-mour, wrote TJ from Havana, where he lived for several years. An 1804 document recommending him for office has not been found, but in 1805 he applied di-rectly to TJ for a position (Dexter, *Yale,* 2:379; 5:37; Vol. 35:546-8; Ledyard Sey-mour to TJ, 14 June 1805).

From David Leonard Barnes

SIR—   Providence Feby 9th 1804—

I take the liberty to inclose an original Letter from the Secretary of the Treasury, intrusted to my care by Capt Leonard, to show the countenance he received from the Government in the prosecutions he commenced—The treatment he received at the [. . .] trial, as he came out of the Court House in the evening, I presume he has stated in his Letters to the Treasury Department in the Spring of 1801—

The inclosed letter belonging to Capt Leonard, I should like to have it returned to be delivered to him—

With Sentiments of Great Respect I have the Honour to be your most Obedt Servt   DAVID LEONARD BARNES

RC (DLC); torn; at foot of text: "Thomas Jefferson President of the United States"; endorsed by TJ as received 19 Feb. and so recorded in SJL with notation "Leonard's case." Enclosure not found.

TREATMENT HE RECEIVED: John West Leonard's suit against James D'Wolf for slave trading commenced 4 Feb. 1801 in the U.S. district court for Rhode Island at Newport, where a sympathetic jury quickly acquitted D'Wolf the following day. While leaving the courthouse after the first day of the trial, Leonard was "roughly handled" by a group of unidentified persons, but escaped serious injury (*Philadelphia Gazette*, 14 Feb. 1801; Jay Coughtry, *The Notorious Triangle: Rhode Island and the African Slave Trade, 1700-1807* [Philadelphia, 1981], 222-4, 226; Barnes to TJ, 8 Feb.).

From John Barnes

Geo: Town 9th. feby. 1804.

The President, having been pleased to intimate a desire to be informed—when JB. should wish to remove to Philada it may be proper, for JB. to state to the President, His reasons, that will Operate, against the possibility of JB. fixing upon the precise time, and thereby avoid, the many, & great inconveniency, extra exps. & probable Loss, that would unavoidably attend such, a removal—at the present Crisis—should accident, or, unforeseen disappointmt. intervene, to impede his intended Negociation, on his Arrival at Philadelphia, (of which, the President is in part already apprized Off)—

As JB.'s first Operation at Philada agreable to His premeditated plan, must *Commence*, from the stability, of his *Bank*, or *Stock Capital*—as without this Essential, it would be in Vain to Attempt it—at any time, yet in Order to form, a possible conjecture, for JB.'s removal from hence (under present existing Circumstances) His first Arrangemt. here—would be to close immediately—his daily store sales, and give notice—say, 1st March, to quit his dwelling House, Allowing 2 or 3 Mos for settling & adjusting his outstanding a/c. and disposal of remaining stock of Merchandize Househd: furniture &c.— would bring him, nearly to the 1st. July—should then, any Alarm, of a prevailing fever at Philada (as was unhappily the Case last year,) His situation would indeed become serious—if not ruinous—destitute—of the many Comforts, & conveniencies, He now partake of.

Under these impressions, JB. cannot, think it, either prudent, or advisable, to risque his shattered *Bank*.—His little All! on so adventrous a prospect, but rather—Content himself, in the Hope of a more favorable One, mean while it is His wish—to Consolidate, his scattered property, as circumstances will best permit, and by degrees—invest it, Occasionally in the most productive public funds, or Stocks: reserving, such a proportion—as $\frac{1}{4}$ or $\frac{1}{5}$. say $1000. for his immediate Cash Articles—with another—1000. on Credit, in Order to furnish, his present, Usual demands—while here, and little employmt. for himself, without any extra expence—on his Store a/c—with these Views & resources, by a frugal Observance and perseverance, He may at least meet, in part—His daily engagemts. & expenditures— flattering himself with its meeting—the President's approval—as His greatest Consolation—and with it, his best endeavours still—to preserve it.

with the highest Respect & Esteem—I am Sir your most Obedt. & very humble Servt: JOHN BARNES.

RC (ViU: Edgehill-Randolph Papers); addressed: "The President, U States"; endorsed by TJ as received 11 Feb.

REMOVE TO PHILADA: for Barnes's long-considered plan to retire from business in Georgetown and remove to Philadelphia, see Vol. 38:479, 499-500; Vol. 40:583, 636-7, 661.

To Henry Dearborn

TH:J. TO GENL. DEARBORNE.   Feb. 9. 1804.

It is represented to me on the part of a person of the name of Solomon[1] Sessum living at Tarburgh in N. Caroline, in independant circumstances, but himself & wife both old, that Roderick Sessums their son was, in the year 1795, during a fit of intoxication, enlisted by a Captn. Rickard then recruiting in that quarter. that being at Natchez in 1800, when his time was to expire, the father with his only remaining son sat out to bring him home. they got as far as Nashville, where they learned that the son finding himself at such a distance from home without money or the means of getting back, enlisted a second time. the father afflicted by this to the derangement of his mind for some time, returned home: the family is represented as being in a very unhappy state, the parents old & anxious once more to see their son, who being now in the 4th. year of his second term of five years, they pray may be discharged & restored to them.   every thing connected with a regular soldiery is so unpopular with citizens at large, that every occasion should be taken of softening it's roughnesses towards them. in time of peace, when the service admits a little relaxation, & there is time to recruit, I think it would have a good effect to indulge citizens of respectability in cases like the present. perhaps justice to the public may require a stoppage of pay to the amount of a just proportion of the bounty money according to the time he has to serve. I submit all this to your discretion not wishing that any rules should be violated which the public good may require to be inflexibly adhered to.   affectionate salutations.

RC (PHi: Daniel Parker Papers); addressed: "The Secretary at War"; endorsed by Dearborn. PrC (DLC). Recorded in SJL as a letter to the War Department with notation "Sessum's case."

REPRESENTED TO ME: Lemuel Sessums to TJ, 28 Jan.

[1] Word interlined.

To Henry Dearborn

TH:J. TO GENL. DEARBORNE   Feb. 9. 1804.

Considering that we have shortly to ask a favour ourselves from the Creeks, the Tuckabatché road, may we not turn the application of Hawkins to our advantage, by making it the occasion of broaching that subject to them? he might be directed to say to them that we furnish with pleasure the several articles which he has asked for their use: that there is nothing we have more at heart than to assist them in all their endeavors to provide for the maintenance and comfort of their families. that our dispositions to render them neighborly kindnesses are increased by the necessity we shall be under of asking indulgences from them which are rendered necessary by our late acquisition of New Orleans. that it is becoming indispensible for us to have a direct communication from the seat of our government[1] with that place, by a road which, instead of passing the mountains through Tennissee & the Chickasaw & Choctaw country, shall keep below the mountains the whole way, passing along the lower side of the Currahee, by Tuckabatchee, Fort Stoddart, & the mouth of Pearl into the island of New Orleans. that we do not mean to ask this favor for nothing, but to give them for it whatever it is worth; besides that they will have the advantages of keeping taverns for furnishing necessaries to travellers, of selling their provisions & recieving a great deal money in that way: and that on this subject we shall have to give him a particular instruction soon for making the proposition to them.

It seems to me that the favour they have asked furnishes a conciliatory opening for our proposition, which going to them abruptly might otherwise be recieved with displeasure. will you be so good as to consider this, and to do finally what you think best?

RC (PHi: Daniel Parker Papers); addressed: "The Secretary at War"; endorsed by Dearborn. PrC (DLC). Recorded in SJL as a letter to the War Department with notation "The Creeks."

APPLICATION OF HAWKINS: on the previous day, the War Department received a letter of 1 Jan. from Benjamin Hawkins, U.S. agent to the southern Indian nations. The letter has not been found, but a clerk noted that it enclosed a "schedule of articles necessary" for the Creek agency. In a letter of 11 Feb., Dearborn informed Hawkins that "Orders have been given for having the Articles innumerated in the lists transmitted by you, forwarded as early as possible" and advised him "to embrace the earliest opportunity for sounding" the Creeks on the prospect of allowing a road through their territory. The secretary of war repeated TJ's expressions of friendship for the nation and the president's ideas on the payment and the advantages that the Creeks might obtain by such an allowance (DNA: RG 107, RLRMS; Dearborn to Hawkins, 11 Feb. 1804, DNA: RG 75, LSIA).

[1] Preceding six words interlined.

From William Fleming

DEAR SIR,   Richmond, 9[th Febru]ary, 1804

Although I am not in the habit of soliciting favours, either for my self or friends, an apology may perhaps be expected for my troubling you on the present occasion, as I doubt not you are assailed with addresses of the kind, from all quarters of the union.

My only motive is to serve a respectable and worthy gentleman in the state of Kentucky—Mr. John Logan, nephew of the treasurer of that state, who wishes to better his fortune by becoming an adventurer in the Louisiana country; and aspires at the office of a surveyor, should there be one vacant in that territory.

I have reason to fear that this will be a fruitless application, but shall be much gratified if it proves successful.

For the principles, character, and connexions of mr. Logan I beg leave to refer you to mr. John Breckinridge, who is well acquainted with them all.—

With great respect and esteem, I am dear sir Your obed. servant

WM FLEMING.

RC (DNA: RG 59, LAR); torn; endorsed by TJ as received 12 Feb. and "Logan John to be Surveyor in Louisiana" and so recorded in SJL.

From Albert Gallatin

[9 Feb. 1804]

Shall I answer that no determination having taken place Mr Baldwin will be considered as an applicant—or that arrangements have already been made for the New Orleans hospital?   A.G.

RC (DLC); undated; at foot of text: "The President"; endorsed by TJ as received from the Treasury Department on 9 Feb. and "Baldwin Dr. to hospital of N.O." and so recorded in SJL.

TJ and Senator John Breckinridge received letters recommending Dr. Cornelius BALDWIN, which they evidently shared with Gallatin. Baldwin delivered Archibald Stuart's letter of introduction to the president on 29 Jan. (see Stuart to TJ, 28 Dec. 1803, and note).

From Henry W. Livingston

Thursday—Feby. 9th. 1804

Mr. Livingston has the honor to send enclosed to the President of the United States, a Remonstrance, which he received yesterday, addressed to the President and signed by several Citizens of Hudson in the State of New York

RC (DNA: RG 59, LAR); endorsed by TJ as received 9 Feb. and so recorded in SJL with notation "petn of citizens of Hudson. Malcolm to continue Collector."

Henry Walter Livingston (1768-1810), of the Upper Manor branch of the Livingston family, graduated from Yale in 1786 and practiced law in New York City. He spent the early 1790s in Paris as private secretary to Gouverneur Morris, then

the U.S. minister to France. Livingston served in the New York Assembly before being elected as a Federalist to the Eighth Congress, narrowly defeating the incumbent John P. Van Ness. He served two terms in the House of Representatives (*Biog. Dir. Cong.*; John L. Brooke, *Columbia Rising: Civil Life on the Upper Hudson from the Revolution to the Age of Jackson* [Chapel Hill, 2010], 72, 316, 403, 478; Vol. 37:460-1n, 517).

ENCLOSURE

From William Jenkins and Others

Hudson Jany 27th. 1804

The Remonstrance of the Subscribers Republicans, Owners and Masters of Vessels, and other citizens of the city of Hudson in the County of Columbia & State of New york respectfully sheweth

That they have with much regret been informed that an Attempt is about to be made to remove Henry Malcolm Esqr from the office of Collector of the Customs for the Port of Hudson and to have Moses Younglove appointed in his stead

The Subscribers beg leave to state that should this removal take place it will be in direct opposition to the opinions & wishes of a very large majority of the Citizens of this place and nearly the whole of the mercantile interest and whatever differences may exist among them on many topics yet in this we may almost say that there is but one voice which is most decidedly against the proposed removal—We are happy that this occasion affords us an opportunity to pay our tribute of respect to Doctor Malcolm's capacity promptitude Industry and impartiality for all which he is as Eminently distinguished in his public capacity as he is for his Virtues in his private one

Without wishing to derogate from the merits of Doctor Younglove we cannot but Express our opinion that there is a vast difference between his qualifications for the Office in question & those of Doctor Malcolm the present incumbent—

The official conduct of Doctor Malcolm has so far as our knowledge Extends given universal satisfaction and we have never heard his Talents Integrity or Prudence impeached. Upon this subject many of us can speak from a personal knowledge derived from a long & intimate acquaintance—As we know of no complaint against the present Collector as his manners capacity punctuality & Every other necessary qualification are unquestioned We can conceive no useful End to be obtained from a change though we have much to fear if such Event should happen—If however more need be said we can state that Doctor Malcolm at an Early period of our revolutionary war entered into the service of his Country first as Surgeon in the naval and afterwards in the Land Service and continued to act in the latter till near the close of the contest—He has a large & increasing family of young children and is very much dependent on his office for their Support—He was appointed to the office in 1795 during the Presidency of Geo. Washington Esq and has become intimately well acquainted with all the duties of it—Doctor Younglove has but recently moved into this City & though we are far from calling in question his probable qualifications We cannot omit observing that by our Laws his Residence has not been sufficiently long to Entitle him to be a Citizen of this City

He is we believe wholly unacquainted with mercantile business and having heretofore resided in the Country We are led to conclude that he is entirely deficient in the knowledge of the various important duties which will be required of him—He is in Circumstances as we have been informed not to require the office, his family consisting only of himself & his wife. Under these Circumstances we most Earnestly intreat that the removal may not take place—neither the Interest of the Government, the Promotion of the Republican Cause or Sound Policy demand it—and we hesitate not to say that the greatest violence would by such a measure be committed upon the Feelings of a large & respectable number of the most steady and influential friends of the present just & benignant administration whose toleration will continue to secure the Esteem it has Excited   Wm Jenkins

RC (DNA: RG 59, LAR); in Jenkins's hand and signed by him and 71 others; at head of text: "To Thomas Jefferson Esqr President of the United States of America"; endorsed by TJ as received 9 Feb. and "Malcolm Henry Collectr. Hudson. not to be removd."

William Jenkins (1771?-1805) and Marshal Jenkins, Jr., who also signed the remonstrance printed above, were the sons of Marshal Jenkins, one of the early settlers at Hudson, New York, who built and owned ships and was engaged in other commercial and manufacturing enterprises. William joined his father in commercial firms until the spring of 1804. Jenkins was also affiliated in commercial activities, including trade in rum and sugar, with members of the Wiswall family, two of whom also signed this remonstrance (Stephen B. Miller, *Historical Sketches of Hudson* [Hudson, N.Y., 1862], 18-19, 30, 36, 115; Hudson *Bee*, 15 Feb. 1803; 15 May, 11 Sep., 13 Nov. 1804; 18 June 1805; Vol. 27:605).

In 1802, prominent Hudson Republicans sought the removal of HENRY MALCOLM, a Federalist (Vol. 38:33-4, 501-2, 520-1; Vol. 39:155n). Correspondence recommending Moses YOUNGLOVE as col-

lector at Hudson has not been found. Younglove came from Canaan, in Columbia County, where he established and served as clerk of the Canaan Democratic Society in 1794 and 1795. He was elected to the state assembly in 1801, serving one term (John L. Brooke, *Columbia Rising: Civil Life on the Upper Hudson from the Revolution to the Age of Jackson* [Chapel Hill, 2010], 314-17, 537n; Alfred F. Young, *The Democratic Republicans of New York: The Origins, 1763-1797* [Chapel Hill, 1967], 397; Philip S. Foner, ed., *The Democratic-Republican Societies, 1790-1800* [Westport, Conn., 1976], 237-9, 243-6).

From David Leonard Barnes

SIR   Providence Feby 10th 1804

After delivering my letter of the 8th inst. at the Post Office, I found I had omitted to return Capt Ingrahams petition,—I therefore inclose it,—and have the honour to be with high Respect

Your Obedient Servt   DAVID LEONARD BARNES

RC (DLC); at foot of text: "Thomas Jefferson President of the United States"; endorsed by TJ as received 19 Feb. and so recorded in SJL with notation "Ingraham's case." Enclosure: Petition of Nathaniel Ingraham, 15 Dec. 1803.

From Jean Étienne Boré

MONSIEUR LE PRÉSIDENT

DES ETATS UNIS   Nlle. Orléans ce 10 fevr. 1804

nommé à la place de maire de cette ville par le préfet colonial et Commissaire de la république française quand il prit possession du pays, Jaurais desiré être en etat de Justifier aux yeux de mes concitoyens cet acte de confiance par autant de talens que de Zêle; mais, apres avoir eté Jusqu'a l'âge de 30 militaire, Jay depuis eté constamment occupé de faire valoir mes terres Sur mon habitation, et Jétais arrivé à l'age de 63 ans Sans m'être exercé activement dans la carriere publique. nous en étions à peu pres tous à ce meme point Sous la domination éspagnole. cependant, Mr. Le Gouverneur Claiborne a jugé à propos de me continuer dans la place de Maire.

à ce titre Je me trouve; pour le moment, tenu des devoirs envers mon pays comme envers le Gouvernement americain: Si vous ne recevez de moy quelques observations utiles au bien de la Louisiane, quelqu'autres Louisiannais vous le fera. Je Suis à la tête du corps municipal de la capitale de cette province; c'est a dire du Seul corps qui y éxiste, du Seul qui y Soit composé de proprietaire et de citoyens: J ay qualité pour vous parler de leurs interets.

Je n'hésite donc pas Monsieur le President, à acquitter ma conscience, en me permettant d'entrer aujourd'huy dans quelques dètails avec vous et en vous mettant à portée de voir notre Situation et nos dispositions par d'autres yeux que des yeux ètrangers ou nouveaux parmi nous.

La France nous a tirés des mains d'agens cupides et de celles d'un Gouvernement apathique: nos vies et nos fortunes étaient à leur merci ou à L'abandon et notre prosperité commerciale et agricole etait entravée: celle cy Se relevera d'elle même par la Simple influence de la liberté; mais celles-la exigeoient de Suite une police ordinaire vigeureuse, et des tribunaux de justice versés dans nos loix civiles et qui restassent quelques tems en permanence continuelle pour vider une infinitee d'affaires arrierées et en Souffrance

nous Sommes dans une impastience extrême des Bills qui doivent fixer notre organisation interieure. Le besoin S'enfait ressentir de plus en plus chaque Jour. Nous avons une confiance éxtrême dans la Sagesse du Congrés dans la votre, Monsieur le president, qui, apres avoir fait négocier notre union à la fédération, aurés a coeur qu'elle tourne à notre bon heur. Vous Serez jaloux de cimenter des Sentimens de fraternité entre la Louisiane et les autres ètats que vous Gouvernez, entre leurs habitans et Les Louisianais.

J'ai vu avec infiniment de peine qu'il S'en est manifesté de differens ces jours derniers. il est tres facheux de commencer ainsy. ce n'est pas au Sein des plaisirs, dans des bals, au milieu d'un Cercle nombreux de femmes qui en faisaient le charme, et l'ornement, qu'on devait S'attendre a voir èclore cet esprit de trouble et de division. Les torts, il faut que vous Sachiez la verité, ont été favorisés ou même accrus par ceux à qui il appartenait de les réprimer. des têtes chaudes des gens avides d'influence n'importe a quel prix, y ont beaucoup contribué: ils contribuent tous les jours à induire en erreur les dépositaires du pouvoirs et à leur faire faire de fausses demarches.

Joserai vous le representer Mr. Le President il est indispensable que les chefs de la Louisiane possedent la langue française comme l'anglaise: S'ils eussent eü cet avantage, nous naurions pas éprouvé les évenemens qui ont produit une Si mauvaise Sensation et le cours des affaires ne languirait pas et ne Serait point exposé à des embaras Sans nombre.

nous avons vu l'instant où le corps municipal était forcé de vous porter à cet égard Ses vives réclamations: Mr. Claiborne débuta des le principe par nous insinuer que nous devrions rédiger nos actes publics en anglais. un retour Sur luy même; d'apres le mécontentement que cette proposition excita nous fit renoncer à vous adresser Monsieur Le President le mémoire de plaintes que nous avions déja dressee à ce Sujet et prèserva nos libertés de cette atteinte. un Gouvernement despotique par Sa nature les a tres longtems respectees: que ne devons nous pas attendre d'un Gouvernement republicain ou les principes des droits naturels ont tant de Sauvegardes et auquel nous nous associons aujourd'huy Sous les garanties d'un traité qui contient des Stipulations Sacrées en notre faveur. nous nous flattons généralement que nous Serons èrigés en ètat Séparé, aussitot qu'il Sera constaté que nous avons une population Suffisante; nous ne doutons pas qu'en attendant on ne nous donne ce que vous appelés *votre Second dégré* de Gouvernement. C'est l'objet continuel de nos esperances et de nos entretiens parmi tout ce qui éxiste de Louisiannais. nos pères ont découvert, peuplé, dèfrichè ce pays: il est arrosé de notre Sang et de nos Sueurs; nous l'avons fait fleurir malgré les obstacles: dignes Jusqu'a present d'un meilleur Sort, nous l'attendons des états unis. ils appreciront l'acquisition qu'ils ont faite, et ils Séforceront de nous la rendre chêre. ils en ont le bon moyen, en nous donnant une Constitution conforme à nos besoins, à nos voeux, a nos droits.

c'est un des plus ancien habitans, un proprietaire un père de famille, un homme indépendant, un vrai patriote qui vous tient ce langage au nom de Ses concitoyens et de Son pays.

J ay l'honneur d'estre avec un profond Respect Monsieur Le President votre tres humble et tres obeissant Serviteur   BORÉ

E D I T O R S '   T R A N S L A T I O N

To the President
of the United States   New Orleans 10 Feb. 1804
The colonial prefect and commissioner of the French Republic named me mayor of this city when he took possession of the territory. I would have wished to be in a position to justify this act of confidence in the eyes of my compatriots through equal measures of talent and zeal. But unfortunately, after serving in the army until age 30, I was fully involved in cultivating my land and reached the age of 63 without having exercised public service. Under Spanish rule almost all of us were in the same position. Governor Claiborne nevertheless saw fit to renew my appointment as mayor.

In this role I find myself obligated to my country and to the American government. If I do not communicate my recommendations about Louisiana, other Louisianans will do so. As the head of the municipal government of the capital of this province, in other words of the only existing local government, the only one composed of landowners and citizens, I am in a position to speak to you about their interests.

I thus take it upon myself, Mister President, to assuage my conscience by explaining certain details so you can learn about our situation and preferences from us rather than from foreigners or newcomers. France saved us from rapacious agents and an apathetic government. Our lives and fortunes had been at their mercy or in ruins; our commercial and agricultural livelihood had been curtailed. Prosperity will come back on its own, in the context of freedom, but our lives and fortunes require a vigorous police force and tribunals that are familiar with civil law and convene for extended periods to resolve an endless number of matters that have been pending and delayed.

We are desperately impatient for laws to establish our internal organization. We feel that need more keenly every day. We have utter confidence in the wisdom of Congress and in yours, Mister President. After negotiating our entry into the union, you want us to succeed. You want to foster fraternal feelings between Louisiana and the other states you govern, between their inhabitants and the Louisianans.

I have observed, with infinite pain, that disputes have come to light in recent days. It is unfortunate to begin like this. We would not expect to see this spirit of discord and division emerging among pleasures and dances, in the midst of a large circle of women who make up their charm and beauty. You need to know the truth. The disputes have been fostered and even fomented by those whose responsibility it is to control them. The hotheadedness of people who are greedy for influence at any price contributes in large measure. These people are responsible for misleading those in power and having them undertake inappropriate measures.

I am taking the risk of telling you this, Mister President. It is essential that the leaders of Louisiana speak French as well as English. If they had had that advantage, we would not have witnessed the events that produced such a bad impression; things would not be languishing and we would not be in such difficulty.

We came to realize that the municipal government had to bring you its specific demands. Mr. Claiborne began everything by insinuating that we should compose our public acts in English. His proposal aroused such opposition that he reversed himself and spared us this infringement on our liberty. We thus refrained, Mister President, from sending you the list of grievances we had drawn up. The previous, despotic government respected our liberty of language. How much more we expected from a republican government which has so many safeguards for natural rights and to which we are now joined under the protection of a treaty that contains sacred stipulations in our favor. We take pride in believing that we will become a separate state as soon as our population is sufficient. Meanwhile we have no doubt that you will provide what you call your "second degree" of government. That is the unwavering goal of the hopes and conversations of all Louisianans. Our fathers discovered, settled, and cleared this land. It is watered with our blood and sweat. We made it flourish despite the obstacles. We deserve better conditions, and expect them from the United States. The American nation will value its acquisition and work to enhance it. It can do so by giving us a constitution that conforms to our needs, our wishes and our rights.

As one of the earliest inhabitants—a landowner, father, independent man, and true patriot—I say this on behalf of my compatriots and my country.

With profound respect, Mister President, I have the honor of being your very humble and obedient servant.   BORÉ

RC (DLC); endorsed by TJ as a letter of 20 Feb. received 9 Apr. and so recorded in SJL. Dupl (DNA: RG 59, TP, Orleans); at head of text: "Dupta"; endorsed by TJ as received 20 Apr. and "to be filed in Secy. of State's office."

Jean Étienne Boré (1741-1820) was born at Kaskaskia in the Illinois country. Educated in France, he settled permanently in Louisiana in 1776 and eventually established a plantation near New Orleans. After the collapse of the colony's indigo industry, Boré shifted to sugar cane and has been credited as the first Louisiana proprietor to oversee the successful production of granulated sugar. His introduction of sugar cane with a shorter growth cycle helped ensure the crop's subsequent viability by allowing planters to avoid the winter frosts that had previously hindered large-scale efforts. In a letter of 25 Feb. 1799 to Andrew Ellicott, which Ellicott evidently shared with TJ, Boré detailed some of his growing techniques. Named mayor of New Orleans by French prefect Pierre Clément Laussat, Boré continued in office under William C. C. Claiborne but resigned the post in protest against the congressional law organizing Orleans Territory. He remained a conspicuous leader of the French Creole planter elite, helping organize efforts for immediate statehood. After turning down an appointed position on the territory's legislative council, he was later elected to that body and also served in the territory's assembly (Boré to Andrew Ellicott, 25 Feb. 1799, RC in DLC: TJ Papers, 105:17999-18001; New York *American Citizen*, 21 Aug. 1804; *Orleans Gazette and Commercial Advertiser*, 5 Feb. 1807; Glenn R. Conrad, ed., *Dictionary of Louisiana Biography*, 2 vols. [New Orleans, 1988], 1:90; Pierre Clément Laussat, *Memoirs of My Life*, trans. Sister Agnes-Josephine Pastwa, ed. Robert D. Rush [Baton Rouge, 1978], 23-4, 51-2; Thomas N. Ingersoll, *Mammon and Manon in Early New Orleans: The First Slave Society in the Deep South, 1718-1819* [Knoxville, Tenn., 1999], 193-4).

s'EN EST MANIFESTÉ DE DIFFERENS CES JOURS DERNIERS: on 8 Jan., disagreements over whether Anglo-American or French dances would take precedence at a New Orleans public ball devolved into what Claiborne described in a letter to Madison as a "*fracas*" and Laussat in his memoirs as "bedlam." At another ball, a similar disagreement was further fueled by James Wilkinson's detainment of a French Creole shopkeeper and a French naval officer, over which some 30 "Americans and Frenchmen scuffled with each other," according to Laussat. A report by Claiborne and Wilkinson pinned blame on the aggressiveness of some French officers and "troublesome young Men from Bordeaux," pointed out that great efforts had been required to avoid bloodshed, and indicated their suspicion that Laussat was sowing discontent among the Creoles as well as hope that French control would one day be restored. Laussat, for his part, blamed the weakness and confusion of American leaders, especially Claiborne, and also thought that Daniel Clark was manipulating discord behind the scenes. At Boré's suggestion, Claiborne ordered a small detachment of militia to be stationed at the ballroom during all subsequent social events (Madison, *Papers, Sec. of State Ser.*, 6:330, 416-17, 449-53; *Terr. Papers*, 9:177-82; Laussat, *Memoirs of My Life*, 92-6; Rowland, *Claiborne Letter Books*, 1:351-2).

Under the provisions of the Northwest Ordinance, territorial government proceeded from a first stage, in which all political leaders were appointed, to a SECOND degree of government, in which citizens elected a legislative council and a house of representatives. This transition was contingent upon the adult free male population of a territory reaching 5,000 individuals (Evans, No. 20779). For TJ's own criticism of the first stage of territo- rial governance as it related to Mississippi Territory, see Vol. 31:336, 337n; Vol. 34:560-2.

From Mary Jefferson Eppes

Edgehill february 10th

Your letters My dear Papa have been long unanswered but while low in spirits & health I could not prevail on myself to do it, the hope however of soon[1] seeing you & Mr Eppes for the time is now ap- proaching makes me feel all of happiness that anticipation can give in my present situation, it is indeed only by looking forward to that much wish'd for moment that I acquire spirits to support me in the tedious interval, but to be with you both again would compensate for any suffering

in the mean time I have a favor to beg of you that I hope will not be refused, it is one which my sister as well as myself is deeply inter- ested in, we had both thought you had promised us your picture if ever St Mimin went to Washington, if you did but know what a source of pleasure it would be to us while so much separated from you to have so excellent a likeness of you you would not I think refuse us, it is what we have allways most wanted all our lives & the cer- tainty with which he takes his likenesses makes this one request I think not unreasonable, he will be in Washington the middle of this month & I cannot help hoping you will grant us this one favor.   I am very much afraid you will be disappointed in getting your faeton, Davy Bowles went to Richmond intending to return here before he went on, but it is so long since he left us that as his wife is now staying in Richmond it is most probable he has hired himself there.   Your acacias are very beautiful My dear Papa, there are eight of them very flourishing, that have changed their foliage en- tirely, they have remain'd in my room, so the warmth of which I be- lieve they are indebted for their present flourishing state as they ap- pear to be more delicate the smaller they are. I wish you could bring us a small piece of your geranium in the spring if it is large enough to admit of it. perhaps Mr Eppes could more conveniently take charge of it than yourself. Adieu dearest Papa we are all well here & all most anxious for the happy moment that will reunite us again after this long separation believe me with the tenderest love yours ever

M EPPES

RC (MHi); endorsed by TJ as received 15 Feb. and so recorded in SJL.

LOW IN SPIRITS & HEALTH: in a letter to her husband, Mary elaborated on her condition: "my health has been growing gradually worse, I have puked up a great deal of bile which I suppose is the cause of it, but am afraid to take any thing in my present situation, tho' my stomach is so weak that it scarcely retains any thing" (Mary Jefferson Eppes to John Wayles Eppes, 6 Feb. 1804, RC in ViU).

In November 1803, engraver Charles Balthazar Julien Févret de Saint-Mémin (ST MIMIN) advertised that he would leave Washington by the 20th of the month and requested that persons desiring a likeness by his physiognotrace make their application before that time. TJ did not sit for a portrait until the engraver returned to town the following November (*Washington Federalist*, 25 Nov. 1803; *National Intelligencer*, 12 Nov. 1804; Bush, *Life Portraits*, 51-3).

For TJ's ongoing interest in ACACIAS, see Vol. 39:337.

ADIEU DEAREST PAPA: this was the last letter that Mary would write to her father before her death on 17 Apr. from complications following childbirth (see TJ to Madison, 17 Apr. 1804).

[1] Word interlined.

From Albert Gallatin

[10 Feb. 1804]

Israel Ludlow the Regr. Land office is dead

The applicants are

—Kilgore who has for 18 months done the duties of the office with great correctness.

—Symmes, the judge's son, recommended by Smith & Morrow.

As the office is kept shut, & the sales & paymts. stopt, an early appointmt. is necessary   A.G.

RC (DNA: RG 59, LAR); undated, but written on verso of Enclosure No. 2. Enclosures: (1) Charles Killgore to Gallatin, Cincinnati, 23 Jan., informing the Treasury secretary of the death of Israel Ludlow; although Killgore has conducted business for Ludlow, the land office is now shut as he does not "think it proper to transact any business untill some appointment is made"; he assures Gallatin that if he receives the appointment, he can give any security the government requires (RC in same). (2) Ohio senator John Smith and Representative Jeremiah Morrow to Gallatin, Washington, 10 Feb., announcing the sudden death of Ludlow, "making it indispensable to appoint a successor" as soon as possible; both recommend Daniel Symmes as "well qualified to do the duties" of the office (RC in same, in Smith's hand, signed by Smith and Morrow; *Biog. Dir. Cong.*).

Charles Killgore (KILGORE), a Federalist, began corresponding with Gallatin and submitting land office returns on behalf of Ludlow in September 1802. The president sent Killgore's nomination to the Senate on 24 Feb. His commission is dated the 29th. When Killgore died in 1807, TJ appointed Republican Daniel SYMMES, nephew of John Cleves Symmes, to the office (commission in Lb in DNA: RG 59, MPTPC; Gallatin, *Papers*, 7:531, 582; 8:25, 584, 698; John Cleves Symmes to TJ, 5 Oct. 1807; Thomas Henderson to TJ, 6 Oct. 1807; TJ to the Senate, 2 Dec. 1807).

To James Houston

Washington Feb. 10. 04.

Th: Jefferson presents his salutations to mr Houston, and in compliance with the desire expressed in his letter of the 4th. returns him his journal. he is happy that mr Houston has got into the hands of the person who is certainly the most able he could have found in the unfortunate complaint under which he labours. with respect to any application to Congress, it would be inefficient, because the Constitution allows them to give no other reward for useful discoveries but the exclusive right for 14. years: and the care of the public health is not among those given to the general government, but remains exclusively with the legislatures of the respective states. he congratulates mr Houston on his prospect of recovery, and sincerely wishes it may be compleated.

PrC (DLC); endorsed by TJ in ink on verso. Enclosure: see Houston to TJ, 4 Feb.

EXCLUSIVE RIGHT: Houston and his publisher entered the title of his pamphlet into the clerk's office of the federal district of Pennsylvania, and in a letter of 10 Apr. to Madison, Houston requested copyright protection. Proceeds from the sale of the pamphlet, along with funds raised by lottery, would, Houston hoped, "reward those who make New discouverys in Medcen" (*Aurora*, 10 Apr. 1804; Madison, *Papers, Sec. of State Ser.*, 7:33).

From Carlos Martínez de Irujo

Friday evening [10 Feb. 1804]

The Marquìs of Casa Irujo regrèts it is not in his power to have the pleasure of accepting Mr. Jefferson's invitatiòn for Tuesday next.

RC (MHi); partially dated; endorsed by TJ as received 10 Feb. and so recorded in SJL.

NOT IN HIS POWER: Madison, in a private letter to James Monroe of 16 Feb., reported, "The Marquis d Yrujo joined with Merry in refusing an invitation from the president and has throughout made a common cause with him not however approving all the grounds taken by the latter. His case is indeed different and not a little awkward; having acquiesced for nearly three years in the practice agst. which he now revolts" (Madison, *Papers, Sec. of State Ser.*, 6:486).

From David Jackson, Jr.

Much respected Sir—   Philadelphia. Feby 10th 1804

Upon enquiry, understanding it was deemed expedient, that some changes should be made in the Custom House Department, and beleiving that in a Representative Government like ours, it is of the first consequence that Offices should be filled by men, whose characters, private, as well as public should be invulnerable; as a Citizen of this District, if such a change should be contemplated in the Custom House Department of this City, I feel emboldened from my knowledge of the Republican Character of James Gamble Esqr. to take the liberty of presenting him to your veiw—

Mr. Gamble is one of our Shipping Merchants—the public confidence has long been reposed in him, by their choice of him Successively to the elective offices of Representative to the State Legislature, and Senator for this District, which latter station he now fills to the satisfaction of his Constituents—

Referrences for a knowledge of Mr. Gambles, political standing may be made to Mr Maclay, Dr Logan, Mr Findley, Mr. Anderson & Mr. Conrad of the Pennsylvania Delegation—

Fully sensible that removal from Office, is an easy matter compared, with replacing, with Characters, generally satisfactory—under this veiw beleiving Mr. Gamble to unite many personal, as well as public qualifications, for a vacancy of the above nature, should it take place— I have no hesitation in Saying should it comport with your Excellency's veiws to appoint him, that it would give general satisfaction—

I remain your fellow citizen & Supporter   David Jackson

RC (DNA: RG 59, LAR); endorsed by TJ as received 13 Feb. and "Gamble James. customs. v. Jackson" and so recorded in SJL.

TJ's endorsement indicates that he considered James Gamble as a candidate to replace William Jackson, the Federalist surveyor at the custom house in Philadelphia. Gamble had previously applied to TJ for the office of surveyor or naval officer (Vol. 40:93n; Vol. 41:605-7).

From Elizabeth House Trist

Dear Sir   Pen Park Feby 10th 1804

I have heard from different quarters that Doct Bache wou'd certainly supercede Major Jackson in the Office of inspector of the Port of Philadelphia few things cou'd have delighted me more—for various reasons in the first place it will be a situation that wou'd enable him to provide for his family in his native City—which wou'd render Mrs Bache extremely happy as she has numerous and near relatives that are very dear to her, the children will also by an intercourse with their connections derive advantages, when by a seperation they wou'd scarsely be remembered—the Doctor by being placed in a situation that wou'd free him from pecuniary embarrasments—wou'd be a different Character, and if he perform'd his publick duty well his indiscretions (admiting that he was still prone to them) wou'd be lost in the Vortex of a populous city

I think too that it wou'd be a gratification to the republicans as well on his own account as being a Grandson of Docter Franklin and I am sure he will merit as much, and be more satisfactory to *We* the people than that imperious Scotch Tory—I really am so interested in the event that I am on tip toe for a confermation of the report—The duties of my Son precludes the possibility of his leaving that country till July his anxiety as well as our own for a reunion has detirmined us to bid Adieu to Albemarle the beginning of next month in hopes of being in readiness for an early Spring voyage Browse has arranged matters for us to embark from Philad I shou'd have prefered Baltimore tis too agonizing to take leave of ones friends without the most distant hope of ever seeing them again that consideration wou'd induce me to forego the pleasure of once more visiting my natal place We have had Snow upon the ground for two weeks most part of the time the weather moderate and clear fine for the Farmers tho bad for visiting, you hear oftner than we do from Edge Hills. we sent the day before yesterday to enquire after the health of the family all well but Mrs Eppes who had a fall attended with no bad effects but spraining both her ancles,—Notwithstanding we have had a *respectable* winter in point severity, There are many down with those fevers that prove generally so mortal which greatly surprises me it rages most among the Blacks Mr Eppes has I hear several down with it. I hope you continue to enjoy good health and sperits that those blessings may be long preserved to you is the sincere wish of your much
   Obliged friend   E. Trist

RC (NcU: Nicholas Philip Trist Papers, Southern Historical Collection); addressed: "The President City Washington"; endorsed by TJ as received 17 Feb. and so recorded in SJL.

THOSE FEVERS: in letters of 21 Jan. and 6 Feb. to John Wayles Eppes, Mary Jefferson Eppes reported that many of the enslaved workers at Pantops were suffering from "the nervous fever," possibly an indication of an outbreak of typhus (RCs in ViU; Vol. 14:359n).

From Joel Barlow

DEAR SIR   Paris 11th Feby 1804.

The enclosed letters from Mr Laharpe to Mr Stone and from Mr Stone to me are in my opinion of sufficient consequence to be communicated to you. this Laharpe is a Swiss Republican of An excellent character and an enlightened mind. he was the tutor of Alexander the present Emperor of Russia; having returned to his own country on the Accession of Paul he became one of the Directors of the Helvetic Republic. but by the last revolution in that country he was driven out and now cultivates a little estate at Plessis Piquet, near Paris,

I mention this least you might confound him with the Laharpe formerly of the French Academy and correspondent of Paul & possibly of your acquaintance while you resided here. That Laharpe afterwards turned royalist and fanatic and is since dead. The one now in question has the singular merit of having enriched with the purest principles of liberty and morals the mind of the chief of a powerful empire. Alexander maintains a confidential correspondence with Laharpe, and it appears to me from what I have seen of his letters that he has an ardent desire to ameliorate the condition of mankind that, his great study is to find out and adopt the most prudent measures, by instruction and otherwise, to restore every class of the Russian people to that state of equality which nature intended for men in Society.   He is well acquainted with the English litrature and language, with our revolution and history; with your character principles, And Administration. He has mentioned you with particular respect in several of his letters, And the paragraph here extracted from one of his letters, Laharpe assures me, is sincerely intended by the Emperor as an invitation or an overture to a correspondence direct with you, which his veneration for your character would not suffer him to begin without first ascertaining that it would be agreeable to you, if this disposition to communicate with you be cultivated on your part it may produce very happy effects.

A young man mounted on the throne of so great a nation as[1] Russia, who by their constitution is absolute, and who from his age may reign many years, will have the means, if properly directed, of propagating those principles and reducing to practice those ideas which may go far towards harmonising nations and promoting a more social and rational order of things than mankind have hitherto experienced. You are sensible that the best dispositions will produce little effect if the mind has not embraced the simple principles which govern the great work of Civilization, and if it does not perceive them to be demonstrable as those of the exact sciences, And it is hardly to be supposed that so young a man, educated in the midst of Aristocracy can be sufficiently informed to enable him to do all the good that his power might command and that the present State of things requires from his situation,   What we are is the result of education. I mean the daily and hourly education of our lives, we recieve and emit the Atmosphere of Ideas which Surround us, we are govern'd by them, and we sometimes furnish a useful one and add it to the general mass in circulation. It is therefore of immense importance that this Atmosphere should be kept as pure as possible.

You have been nourished in the purest political region of our globe, your genius has added to the general stock of knowledge your reputation, experience and the station you fill command respect, and your principles and opinions will be contemplated, weighed and digested with more attention than those of any other man perhaps now alive, more than even yours would be, were you in another situation. we are always anxious to read and consider the opinions of the chiefs of nations, believing them to be in some measure those of the people they govern, hence it is from those high stations that useful principles can be delivered to the world to the greatest advantage,   Knowing the liberality of your mind and believing that you will not doubt the purity of my zeal, I am sure you will excuse me if I point out some of the topics on which I think your communications with the young Emperor would be likely to produce the best effects. I believe him to be well disposed, ambitious of doing all the good in his power, but his situation is exceedingly[2] delicate. It would not do for him to alarm the privileged orders by attempting at present anything like a free representative legislation perhaps not even to let it be known that he desires the complete emancipation of the Serfs. But there are other principles leading directly to civilization, which being slow in their progress and already in some degree admitted in Europe, do not so much alarm the Nobles and priests; such as the liberty of the press, and the education of the people in general, which is of infinitely more consequence than institutions for the higher sciences alone.

On the Subject of interior national economy there are roads, bridges, canals for easy communication, so much encouragement, as a perfect protection will give to agriculture and manufactures, establishments of industry for the poor and aged, workhouses united with confinement for criminals, as in some of our states, and a general reform and Amelioration in criminal jurisprudence. A perfect liberty of interior commerce from one extreme of the Empire to the other, is likewise to be learned from us. *But Above all the liberty of the Seas* is a subject on which he must want information System and Support, he has this object particularly at heart; and it is one which tends more directly to the civilization of Europe and the tranquility of America than any other, The restrictions on commerce, the expence of military navies, and the almost perpetual wars which they excite Are severely felt in Europe. and the chiefs of nations who shall devise and carry into effect the means of reforming an evil so alarming will have rendered more Service to the world and acquired more glory to themselves than can well be imagined on any other subject,

Russia and the United States have no foreign possessions to protect, and their exports apply directly to the necessities of the manufacturing nations, whose industry they nourish by consuming its products. this renders them both powerful in their moral as well as their physical means of defence; And their example would have great weight with the minor nations whose interest it would be to follow it, These circumstances make it peculiarly proper as well as interesting to the world, that their two governments should come forward with a plan for the liberty of the seas which could not be resisted. The effects in favor of humanity to be produced by such a System are incalculable. they would be no less felt in the interior of every particular nation than in the great scale of public tranquility among the several nations. In which latter View it must certainly be considered as an indispensible step towards a permanent peace,

Fortunately for this system it is easy to demonstrate that it is the source of the wealth of nations, and of individuals, as well as the foundation of their peace. And the Arguments are such as to carry more undeniable conviction to ordinary minds than those of most other principles of Republicanism.   Each of the two governments in question are likewise remarkable for extending over an immense territory & their population is rapidly increasing. Russia will have a population as preponderating in one hemisphere as that of the United States in the other. this makes it still more important that all good principles Should be cultivated by them both with particular Zeal; and this not only for the benefit of the Vast numbers which will compose their own nations, but because it will give them a Vogue, and command their reception with all their neighbours even to the greatest part of the world,   There is one subject familiar to all americans, but appreciated only by a few thinking men, which I never have seen developed with that energy and detail which it merits I mean the *Federality* of our System of Government. this is not at all understood in Europe even in theory. Their best writers dont know what we mean by it, And it appears to me that even in America its advantages are seldome adverted to, ill understood, & not cherished by any of us in the manner they deserve. For my own part, I consider it so essential to political liberty that I dont see how our other most inveterate and best inculcated principles could be preserved without it. Without the Federal part I Should despair of the preservation of the representative part of our system. If this principle were better understood by the Philosophers in Europe we should not see so many of the former believers in the progressive improvement of Society now despairing of that consoling doctrine; If it were well understood in America we should hear no more of that blasphemy which we have often heard of a Seperation of States, dissolving the Union, &c. &c. we should no more find our citizens frightened at seeing our government extending itself over the Missisippi, or even to the western Ocean; provided, it be done by peaceable & honest means, by the consent of all parties concerned.

I ask your pardon for so long a letter & remain with perfect respect Dear Sir your most obedient Servant,   JOEL BARLOW

The bad state of my wife's health & some business I had in England did not permit us to return to America last season, we hope to be more fortunate this year—

You may address your letter for the Emperor with perfect confidence under cover to Mr. +Laharpe at Plessis Piquet near Paris covered again to the american agent here directing him if he should not know Mr. Laharpe to enquire of Mr Stone English Bookseller; write in english or french as you think proper—

+ Frederic Cesar Laharpe

Dupl (DLC); in clerk's hand, signed by Barlow; at head of text: "Copy"; endorsed by TJ as received 5 July and so recorded in SJL. RC (same); at foot of first page: "Mr. Jefferson"; endorsed by TJ as "dupl." received 13 July; lacks authorial footnote. Enclosures: (1) Frédéric César de La Harpe to John Hurford Stone, Plessis Piquet, France, 20 Oct. 1803, praising TJ as "one of the the most admirable members of the noble society of men who share a desire for universal enlightenment and freedom," La Harpe writes that Alexander I of Russia shares many of the same principles and has indicated his admiration for Jefferson; La Harpe believes that allowing the two leaders to reach a "mutual understanding" will benefit human welfare; the emperor has recently expressed in a letter to him "I would be very grateful if you could introduce me to Jefferson, and I would be truly honored"; La Harpe hopes Stone will fulfill this request (RC in same, in French; Dupl in same, in Barlow's hand, in French). (2) Stone to Barlow, Paris, 20 Oct. 1803, reporting the enclosure of a just-received letter from La Harpe indicating the Russian emperor's wish to develop "a more intimate acquaintance with Mr. Jefferson"; as Barlow is well connected to the president, Stone entrusts the letter to Barlow, who is to consider it "a charge in favor of mankind" and who can communicate it to TJ in the way he deems most proper (RC in same; Dupl in same, in Barlow's hand, follows on same sheet Dupl of Enclosure No. 1).

For extracts from an earlier communication from the English expatriate John Hurford STONE regarding the relationship between Frédéric César de La Harpe and his former pupil ALEXANDER I, emperor of Russia, see Vol. 38:554-6.

THE LAHARPE FORMERLY OF THE FRENCH ACADEMY: a reference to the Enlightenment man of letters Jean François de La Harpe. For about 15 years, he served as French literary correspondent to Paul I, then heir to the Russian throne. La Harpe published four volumes of his correspondence with Paul in 1801 (Christopher Todd, *Voltaire's Disciple: Jean-François de La Harpe* [London, 1972], 23, 49, 70).

[1] MS: "a." RC: "as."
[2] RC: "extremely."

From Albert Gallatin

[ca. 11 Feb. 1804]

This man is totally incompetent & ought not to have been appointed.

Yet to an application made in favour of a personal friend of mine & who is well qualified I have answered that considering the age & circumstances of Gibson it would be cruel to remove him. I was also led to form a better opinion of Gibson than ever I had before from his candour in giving his evidence in the Logan controversy, considering the time (1798) when he gave it.   A.G.

RC (DNA: RG 59, LAR); undated, but see TJ to Gallatin at this date; written on address sheet of John Gibson to Gallatin (see enclosure); endorsed by TJ: "Gibson John. to mr Gallatin. to be continued in office." Enclosure: Gibson to Gallatin, Vincennes, 7 Jan., citing the remonstrance "signed by the Judges and most of the principal Inhabitants" of the territory and sent to the president (see Ephraim Jordan and Others to TJ, [before 7 Jan.]), Gibson requests reappointment to the office he now holds "or to any other the President may think me worthy of"; Gibson notes that he is "advanced in life" and has a family depending on him, and if he should not be reappointed "it would Expose them and myself to the greatest distress" (RC in same).

THIS MAN: John Gibson, appointed secretary of Indiana Territory by John Adams in May 1800 (Vol. 39:78n).

PERSONAL FRIEND OF MINE: probably John Badollet. In March, William Findley, John Smilie, and Gallatin recommended Badollet as register of the land office at Vincennes (Gayle Thornbrough, ed., *The Correspondence of John Badollet and Albert Gallatin: 1804-1836* [Indianapolis, 1963], 13, 25-6; Findley and Smilie to TJ, 28 Mch.; Gallatin to TJ, 28 Mch.).

For Gibson's deposition IN THE LOGAN CONTROVERSY, dated 4 Apr. 1800, see Vol. 31:477-80.

To Albert Gallatin

TH:J. TO MR GALLATIN.   [11 Feb. 1804]

I have always proposed to re-appoint Genl. Gibson to his present office, wherein I hear of no complaint against him. neither his age nor understanding entitle him to any thing beyond that, & equal to his antient military rank.

I personally know those who recommend Dr. Baldwin. Kinney is a good man, but as a federalist feels no great interest in our making good appointments. judge Stuart is my intimate friend & eleve. he would not lead me into a scrape. accordingly in his letter there is not one word of Baldwin's talents, & from a conversation or two with the latter, I should suspect him to be ignorant. the best person I know for the Hospital at N. Orleans is Doctr. Barnwell of Philadelphia. he applied the last year; and I had a book of his to judge him by, and from that concluded his talents perfectly adequate & beyond what we could expect to get for that place. I wrote to Philadelphia, to Dr Wistar particularly to learn his character. his report was strongly favorable. but as it proved that Bache would accept, he was preferred. there is a Doctr. Wallace, who stands next to Barnwell among the candidates; but he is a Virginian. Baldwin had better be informed that no appointment being made, no other answer is ever given to any body.

Among the candidates for the lighthouse at Old point comfort, Capt Eli Vickery seems decidedly the best. there is a mr Bingham from Richmond well recommended. but it must be quite out of his line, whereas Vickery is an old sea captain. nothing is said of the politics of either but both are recommended by the best republicans. if you know no reason to the contrary, appoint Vickery.

I think it would be well to consult mr Huger as to Capt Tucker Howland for the lighthouse on North Island. should he know nothing against him, I suppose he must be appointed on mr Stevens's recommendation.

There are two matters, which were the subjects of conversation between us the first year of our being in the administration, & which were reserved for future consideration; which as I always forget to mention when I see you, I will now notice in writing. one was the adopting some means of ascertaining the *exports* from & the *imports consumed* in, each state respectively. this would be an element in our political arithmetic which it might be useful to possess in the various estimates & views of our affairs. I remember you thought, prima facie, it could be done without great trouble. the other was the laying before Congress at some time of every session a Calendar of 1. the interest of the public debt paid in each year. 2. the principal paid, or added. 3. the principal remaining due at the end of each year. this Calendar to be carried back as far as possible, even to the commencement of the present constitution if practicable. this would be laborious; but could not some one, of abilities & dispositions proper for it, be selected & employed on it solely until compleated? Would it not be useful also to oblige our successors, by setting the example ourselves of laying annually before Congress a similar calendar of the expenditures 1. for the civil, 2. the military, 3. the naval departments, in a single sum each? the greatest security against the introduction of corrupt practices & principles into our government, which can be relied on in practice, is to make the continuance of an administration depend on their keeping the public expences down at their minimum. the people at large are not judges of theoretic principles, but they can judge on comparative statements of the expence of different epochs. when you shall have bestowed some thought on these subjects we will have conversation on them. affectionate salutations.

RC (NHi: Gallatin Papers); undated, with date supplied from PrC; endorsed by a clerk. PrC (DLC); date added by TJ in ink at foot of text. Recorded in SJL at 11 Feb. with notation "Gibson. Dr. Baldwin. Vickery. Howland. callendar of publick debt—do. expenditures—exports & imports."

ENTITLE HIM TO ANY THING BEYOND THAT: see Ephraim Jordan and Others to TJ, [before 7 Jan. 1804], where John Gibson is recommended as an agent to the Indian tribes west of the Mississippi.

For Jacob Kinney's and Archibald Stuart's letters for Cornelius BALDWIN, see Stuart to TJ, 28 Dec. 1803 and 1 Jan. 1804.

William BARNWELL applied to TJ for the marine hospital position at New Orleans on 15 Mch. 1802. He had already sent TJ a copy of his 1802 book entitled *Physical Investigations & Deductions, From Medical and Surgical Facts* (Vol. 36:432; Vol. 37:75). I WROTE TO PHILADELPHIA: see TJ to Caspar Wistar, 22 Mch. 1802, and Wistar's reply, Vol. 37:112-13, 205-7. James W. WALLACE received recommendations from George Wythe, Richard Brent, and Philip R. Thompson (Vol. 41:304-5, 363-4, 369-70).

The recommendations for the LIGHTHOUSE AT OLD POINT COMFORT have not been found.

LIGHTHOUSE ON NORTH ISLAND: Daniel Stevens, lighthouse superintendent, revenue inspector, and supervisor of the revenue for South Carolina, informed William Miller, commissioner of the revenue, that the keeper of the Georgetown lighthouse, John Shackleford, was resigning on 31 Mch. Stevens enclosed an application from Tucker Howland and a certificate signed by Savage Smith, Samuel Smith, George Heriot, and William Heriot, commissioners of pilotage for the port of Georgetown, recommending Howland as a "fit & proper person to take charge of the Light House on North Island." Both were dated 16 Jan. Stevens requested that Miller submit the enclosures to the president for his approbation (RCs in DNA: RG 59, LAR, endorsed by TJ: "Howland Tucker. lt. house North isld. S.C."; ASP, *Miscellaneous*, 1:278, 287, 306; N. Louise Bailey and others, eds., *Biographical Directory of the South Carolina Senate, 1776-1985*, 3 vols. [Columbia, S.C., 1986], 1:717; 3:1509-12, 1634). For the results of Gallatin's consultation with South Carolina congressman Benjamin Huger, see Gallatin's note at 9 Mch.

From Albert Gallatin

Dear Sir   Saturday 11 Feby. 1804

It is necessary to know where Eli Vickery lives in order to notify him of his appointment to keep the Old Pt. Comfort light house.

The enclosed you have already seen, and I have already communicated my opinion of Davies's inability which is rather felt than susceptible of positive proof. The emplymt. of clerks of inferior abilities is known already at the Treasury. I might write to Gatewood if, it shall be your opinion that on his testifying the truth of the allegations, Davies shall be removed: it is proper to state that Gatewood was the candidate for the office when Davies was appointed and is of course inimical to him. Your idea to suffer the man to die appears to me dangerous. The last six months that a man, who is not fit for the office, remains in it are always those during which confusion of accounts and delinquency either take place or encrease beyond bounds. Witness Habersham, Holmes, Bird, Lamb, Delany, E. Livingston &a. Gerry is the only instance to my knowledge where a delinquency of several years standing had not encreased for the 4 or 5 last he was in office. Whenever a successor shall be appointed, it is desirable that he may have activity, assiduity & competent talents; for Norfolk may now be ranked amongst the large ports; and the office of collector if well executed will require the constant attention of the officer. The only man who has been mentioned to me is Tazewell, by whom I do not recollect, but, I believe, by Mr. Madison.

I have this year, with much labour, laid the foundation in the report on the sinking fund of the *public debt calender* by stating with perfect correctness the application during the year 1802 to principal and interest. I had intended to add to it the State of the debt at the commencemt and end of the year; but the Statements prepared for that purpose did not please me and I had not time to correct them before the report must necessarily be made. I have them now on hand in order that they may appear in next year's report; and I may set any clerk, with very little superintendence, to pursue the subject, on the same plan, from year to year back to any given year.

I am afraid that an account of coastway exports cannot be correctly obtained; and if obtained would not give the true amount of produce of each State. Thus Alexandria exports (to other States) Maryland tobacco & flour and Pennsylvania flour—Baltimore exports much Pennsylva. produce—Petersburg a considerable quantity of N. Carolina do. &a. I will, however take the subject under consideration &

see whether any returns may be required from the collectors which will assist in forming an Estimate—.

With respect Your obedt. Servt. ALBERT GALLATIN

RC (DLC); at foot of text: "The President of the United States"; endorsed by TJ as received from the Treasury Department on 11 Feb. and "Vickery—Davies.—calendar of public debt—exports & imports" and so recorded in SJL. Enclosure not found, but see below.

YOU HAVE ALREADY SEEN: perhaps Gallatin was returning the letter from Virginia congressman Edwin Gray of 30 Dec., which TJ received on 2 Jan. The letter has not been found, but TJ noted in SJL that it regarded "Bedinger v. Davies Collectr. Norfolk." Daniel Bedinger, a firm Republican, had served as the first surveyor and inspector at Norfolk. He resigned after local Federalists prevailed and President Adams decided not to appoint him collector at the port in 1797. Instead, Otway Byrd was chosen (JEP, 1:11, 14, 104, 111; Carl E. Prince, *The Federalists and the Origins of the U.S. Civil Service*, [New York, 1977], 12, 107-11; Vol. 29:386-7). Adams appointed William Davies collector at Norfolk in December 1800, after Byrd's death. Gallatin expressed misgivings over the collector's handling of estimates and repairs at the marine hospital. When seeking information for an appointment in 1802, Gallatin requested that TJ recommend other correspondents near Norfolk to relieve him "from the inconvenience of writing" to Davies. The Treasury secretary now considered writing Philemon GATEWOOD, the naval officer at Norfolk (JEP, 1:11, 14, 357; Vol. 38:178, 180n, 482).

John HABERSHAM, collector at Savannah, died in office in November 1799 in debt to the Treasury Department. He was succeeded by James Powell, who was removed by TJ in 1801 for having never rendered an account. Appointed collector at Charleston, South Carolina, in 1791, Isaac HOLMES was removed by John Adams in 1797 for failing to remit to the Treasury hundreds of thousands of dollars in duties collected (*Augusta Herald*, 27 Nov. 1799; JEP, 1:330; Gallatin, *Papers*, 22:257; Vol. 29:567n; Vol. 33:220, 677). For the financial difficulties Byrd (BIRD) experienced as collector at Norfolk, see Vol. 37:285, 287n, 429. Adams dismissed John LAMB, collector of customs at New York, in 1797, after the discovery of a shortfall in his accounts. His deputy reportedly embezzled the funds and fled to Europe (Vol. 40:167n). Sharp DELANY, customs collector at Philadelphia, was forced to resign in 1798, after it was found he owed the Treasury at least $86,000, which he could not repay (Prince, *Federalists*, 88). For the removal of New York district attorney Edward LIVINGSTON in the summer of 1803 for his failure to remit about $44,000 to the Treasury, see Vol. 38:122, 123n; Vol. 40:545-6; Vol. 41:63. In the summer of 1802, TJ reluctantly removed Samuel R. GERRY as collector at Marblehead after finding he was delinquent in his payments to the Treasury (Vol. 36:195-6, 205; Vol. 38:41, 180-9).

In late December 1803, Littleton W. TAZEWELL informed Madison of Davies's "fast declining health." At the same time, Tazewell requested that he be considered as an applicant for the Norfolk collectorship (Madison, *Papers, Sec. of State Ser.*, 6:220-1).

Statement D of the 1804 REPORT ON THE SINKING FUND consisted of an account for 1802 "of the fund provided for the payment of principal and interest of the public debt" (ASP, *Finance*, 2:91).

From Albert Gallatin

DEAR SIR   Feb. 11. 1804

I enclose for your consideration the letters intended in Hartshorne's & Putnam's cases. Please to return them with your opinion.

With respect your obedt. Servt.   ALBERT GALLATIN

RC (DLC); addressed: "The President of the United States"; endorsed by TJ as received from the Treasury Department on 13 Feb. and "Putnam. Hartshorne" and so recorded in SJL. Enclosures not found, but see below.

HARTSHORNE'S & PUTNAM'S CASES: see Gallatin to TJ, 3 Feb., and Notes on Henry Putnam's Case at 13 Feb.

To George Hay

Washington. Feb. 11. 04.

Th: Jefferson presents his salutations to mr Hay, and his thanks for his works of mr Thompson the irreparable loss of whom never occurs to his mind without producing the deepest regret. he prays mr Hay to accept his respects & assurances of high consideration.

PrC (MHi); endorsed by TJ in ink on verso.

THANKS: Hay to TJ, 1 Feb.

From George Jefferson

DEAR SIR   Richmond 11th. Febr. 1804

I have to acknowledge the receipt of your favor of the 7th. inclosing 75$—The coal you require shall be forwarded by the first opportunity; there are however but few vessels I believe, which go from here to Alexa. and fewer still to Washington.

only 14 hhds of your Tobacco are yet down. the price now is from 6 to 7$ according to quality, *or the opinion of it*. I hope yours may be *supposed* to be of the first.

the wine & some iron from Philadelphia arrived only a few days ago.

I am Dear Sir Yr. Very humble servt.   GEO. JEFFERSON

RC (MHi); at foot of text: "Thos. Jefferson esqr."; endorsed by TJ as received 15 Feb. and so recorded in SJL.

From John Rice Jones

SIR/   Vincennes, Indiana Territory 11th Feby. 1804

The within vocabulary, and another Copy, was put into my hands sometime since, for the purpose of inserting, in the Languages of any of the Indian Tribes I was acquainted with, the names of the several words therein comprised; which, when done, I was requested to forward to you—The other Copy has been delivered, many months since, to a gentleman of St. Louis, a considerable Trader with the osage nation, who promised me to fill it up with the words of that Tongue—As soon as it is finished, which will be soon, it shall be forwarded—

I would have done myself the honor of sending you, the inclosed one, of the miamia Language, long since, had I not been informed that you were already furnished with one; which however from the Information of Capn Lewis, who I had the pleasure of seeing at Cahokia a few days ago, appears not to be true.

Some part, perhaps the whole of the Information contained in the "emancipated American," has, I doubt not, been communicated to you by Capt Lewis, who informed me of his Intention of doing so— For fear it has not, I take the liberty of inclosing a newspaper, wherein that piece has been inserted, for your perusal, and of assuring you that, from the best Information I could obtain on the spot, it does not in the least exaggerate the Conduct of the late Spanish officers, and that the Charges alledged against them, can most, if not all of them be substantiated.

Should you wish to have vocabularies of the Languages of any of the other Tribes in these parts, I shall think myself honored in receiving your Commands and with pleasure obey them.—

With Sentiments of the most profound respect I have the honor to be Sir, your most obedient and very humble servant

JNO RICE JONES

RC (DLC); at foot of text: "Thos. Jefferson, Esqr. Prest. of the United States"; endorsed by TJ as received 6 Mch. and so recorded in SJL. Enclosures not found.

John Rice Jones (1759-1824) was born in Wales and trained as a lawyer in London before emigrating to the United States in 1784. He soon settled out west, becoming commissary for American troops at Vincennes and acquiring land there and at Kaskaskia. He became the first attorney general for the Indiana Territory and later served on Indiana's legislative council. After splitting politically from William Henry Harrison, he led efforts to make Illinois a separate territory. Dedicated to the expansion of slavery into the region, he settled eventually on the west side of the Mississippi, where he held mining interests, and was named to the legislative council of Missouri Territory. He served in Missouri's constitutional convention in 1820 and after statehood

[457]

was appointed to the Supreme Court of Missouri (Charles E. Burgess, "John Rice Jones, Citizen of Many Territories," *Journal of the Illinois State Historical Society*, 61 [1968], 67-8, 80-1; JEP, 2:9, 601-2).

GENTLEMAN OF ST. LOUIS: likely Auguste Chouteau, who was permanently settled in the city, but possibly his half-brother Pierre Chouteau, who spent much of his life among the Osage but may have then been in St. Louis (Vol. 41:473n; Meriwether Lewis to TJ, 26 Mch. 1804).

Jones was implicating Charles Dehault Delassus, the LATE SPANISH lieutenant governor for upper Louisiana, in a scheme to issue land grants dated before the Span-

ish retrocession to France. Jones reported on the "iniquitous and fraudulent Grants" in a letter of 21 Jan. to Thomas T. Davis, judge of the Indiana Territory. An anonymous communication from Kaskaskia to Gallatin, dated 18 Oct. 1803, also reported a number of large, back-dated land grants made by Spanish officers. An extract from this letter appeared in a congressional report and was reprinted in newspapers. Isaac Briggs reported on similar issues confronting American administrators in lower Louisiana (*Terr. Papers*, 7:168-9; ASP, *Public Lands*, 1:173; New York *American Citizen*, 18 Feb. 1804; Vol. 41:350).

To Allan B. Magruder

Washington Feb. 11. 1804.

Th: Jefferson presents his salutations to mr Mc.Gruder, and his thanks for his pamphlet on Louisiana. altho' he has not yet gone through it, he percieves very extensive views of the subject taken, and various considerations worthy of attention. that the opening such an extent of country for the future spread of our descendants, will add to their happiness, and enlarge the mass of men living under free & national government, can be doubted by none. those are now living who will see that country contain double or treble the present population of the United states.

PrC (ViW: Tucker-Coleman Collection); endorsed by TJ in ink on verso.

HIS PAMPHLET ON LOUISIANA: *Political, Commercial and Moral Reflections, on the Late Cession of Louisiana, to the United States*, enclosed in Magruder to TJ, [before 7 Feb.]. In this 150-page essay, Magruder described the political, agricultural, and commercial advantages

of Louisiana and its future economic development. His vision for the future of Louisiana included a moral argument for using the land to relocate and civilize Indians and to colonize emancipated blacks (Junius P. Rodriguez, ed., *The Louisiana Purchase: A Historical and Geographical Encyclopedia* [Santa Barbara, Calif., 2002], 211-12).

From Lyman Spalding

SIR,   Portsmouth Feby. 11th 1804

Shall I again presume to call one moment of your important time, to so small a subject, as the bill of Mortality for Portsmouth, for 1803, which I beg you to accept.

I am Sir your most obt humble Servt.   L. SPALDING.

RC (DLC); at foot of text: "The President of the U.S."; endorsed by TJ as received 22 Feb. and so recorded in SJL. Enclosure: Spalding, "Bill of Mortality, for Portsmouth, Newhampshire, for A.D. 1803," recording the number and causes of death as well as the ages of the victims (printed copy in same).

AGAIN PRESUME TO CALL: Spalding had sent TJ annual compilations of vital statistics for Portsmouth for the previous two years; see Vol. 36:626 and Vol. 39:566.

To Thomas Sumter, Sr.

Feb. 11. 04.

Extract of a letter from Philadelphia

'Mr. Burr is here. he and P. Butler are much together. several federal characters of note are here also; among whom is one of the Pinckneys. all visit him.'

Extract of another letter from Philadelphia.

'During mr Burr's stay here he saw much company: among others mr P. Butler in particular. I strongly suspect some arrangements have been made to defeat the proposed amendment, as the latter is about to leave, or has already left this for Carolina. the amendment is before the Jersey legislature. I understood a decision was expected this day. mr Burr has been at Trenton since yesterday.'

Th: Jefferson communicates the above to Genl. Sumter in confidence, merely that he may understand his colleague. clandestine influence on the governor, to prevent his calling the legislature, is the only thing to be apprehended; & this only because it will prevent that state from the opportunity of pronouncing it's will, whatever it may be. this communication being for Genl. Sumter's private information, Th:J. begs him to burn it, and to accept his friendly salutations.

PrC (MoSHi: Jefferson Papers); endorsed by TJ in ink on verso.

Aaron BURR left Washington on 29 Jan. and arrived at Philadelphia on 1 Feb., remaining until 7 Feb. before departing for New York (Matthew L. Davis, *Memoirs of Aaron Burr, with Miscellaneous Selections from his Correspondence*, 2 vols. [New York, 1836-37], 2:274-6).

The New Jersey LEGISLATURE ratified the Twelfth Amendment to the Constitution of the United States on 22 Feb. Governor Joseph Bloomfield forwarded an attested copy of the act to the State Department the following day (*Acts of the Twenty-Eighth General Assembly of the State of New-Jersey . . . Being the Second Sitting* [Trenton, 1804], 284-6; Madison, *Papers, Sec. of State Ser.*, 6:506).

CALLING THE LEGISLATURE: on 3 Mch., Governor James B. Richardson of South Carolina issued a proclamation convening a special session of the state legislature on 10 May to consider the proposed Twelfth Amendment (Charleston *City Gazette and Daily Advertiser*, 8 Mch. 1804; Richardson to TJ, 1 June 1804). Following his message on the opening day of the session, Richardson presented the legislature with two letters from Pierce Butler, dated 6 Dec. 1803 and 3 Apr. 1804, that detailed his opposition to the amendment (FCs in PHi: Pierce Butler Letterbooks, 1787-1822; Charleston *Carolina Gazette*, 18 May 1804).

To Solomon Sessums

SIR   Washington Feb. 12. 04.

I recieved three days ago a letter of Jan. 28. from your son Lemuel Sessums stating circumstances which rendered the discharge of your son Roderick Sessums from his military engagements a reasonable indulgence to you on the part of the government. an order has accordingly gone from here for his discharge. the last returns we possess are of about three months ago, when he was at Natchez, from whence he has consequently gone with his company to New Orleans. I wish to yourself and family an early & happy reunion with him.

TH: JEFFERSON

PrC (MoSHi: Jefferson Papers); at foot of text: "Mr. Solomon Sessums"; endorsed by TJ in ink on verso.

Solomon Sessums of Tarboro, North Carolina, died in 1817 (New York *Spectator*, 19 Dec. 1817; Lemuel Sessums to TJ, 28 Jan. 1804).

AN ORDER HAS ACCORDINGLY GONE: on or about 10 Feb., Henry Dearborn directed Thomas H. Cushing to order the discharge of Roderick Sessums, a private serving in Captain John Bowyer's company (FC in Lb in DNA: RG 107, LSMA; Heitman, *Dictionary*, 1:235).

From George W. P. Custis

SIR   Mount Washington, 13th of Feby 1804

Perceiving by the detail of Public Affairs that a Bridge is contemplated by the Government, whereby the Counties of Washington & Alexandria shall be united, & other objects of National moment effected. I have done myself the honour to address your Excellency on this subject, & beg leave to propose for your consideration whether the ground immediately below the spot intended for the University & from thence to any part of the Mt Washington Estate may not afford as desirable a situation as any other.

It may not be improper to add, that the Channell at this place is more narrow, & the water less deep, than in any other part of the Potomak, & the difference in width of the River is so evident as to need no illustration. These objects are certainly momentous on the score of expence, and whether the foundation[1] of the piers on each side of the Channell, may not tend to deepen the same, & thereby assist rather than prevent the Navigation, can be determined by those conversant in such matters—

I beg leave (for a more complete & satisfactory explanation) to refer yr Excellency to the Public Ground appropriated for the University, from whence you will be able to judge of the various situations which will present themselves to yr veiw & estimate them according to the dictates of yr wisdom & their relative circumstances—

I have the honour to Subscribe With becoming Respect Yr Very Obt Sevt   GEORGE W P CUSTIS

RC (MHi); at foot of text: "The President of the US"; endorsed by TJ as received 16 Feb. and so recorded in SJL.

George Washington Parke Custis (1781-1857) was the adopted grandson of George Washington and the future father-in-law of Robert E. Lee. His Alexandria County estate became the site of Arlington National Cemetery. Custis gained renown as a playwright (ANB; Robert M. Poole, *On Hallowed Ground: The Story of Arlington National Cemetery* [New York, 2009], 11-12).

The House of Representatives was currently considering a petition to establish a company for erecting a BRIDGE across the Potomac River between the southwest end of Maryland Avenue and "Alexander's island." A counter-petition from Georgetown opposed the measure as detrimental to the trade of that town. No decision on the matter was reached before the end of the session (JHR, 4:525, 544, 556, 569, 576, 583).

The SPOT INTENDED for a long-contemplated national UNIVERSITY in Washington was bound by 23d and 25th Streets and E Street, with its southern boundary on the Potomac River (RCHS, 19 [1916], 100; 51-52 [1951-52], 27).

[1] MS: "founation."

To Henry Dearborn

Feb. 13. 1804.

Th: Jefferson with his friendly compliments to Genl Dearborne returns him Govr. Mc.kean's letter; to whom he may say for the Govr's satisfaction that the letter had been communicated to Th:J. who said that some vague intimation of the purport mentd in the letter had been formerly[1] dropped to him, but it was so little noted that neither the person, nor manner can now be recollected: that satisfied the fallen party could never rise again but by dividing the republicans, Th:J. has been entirely on his guard against these idle tales, and considers Govr. Mc.kean's life & principles as sufficient[2] evidence of their falsehood, and that he may be perfectly assured that no such insinuations have or can make an impression on his mind to the Governor's disadvantage.

RC (CtY); endorsed by Dearborn. PrC (DLC). Not recorded in SJL. Enclosure: Thomas McKean to Dearborn, 8 Feb., refuting a long letter he understood the secretary of war had received or read "giving an account of the origin and design of a third party" composed principally of the state officers of Pennsylvania "with the Governor at their head, to oppose the re-election of Mr. Jefferson as President, and to further the election of the Governor to that office"; McKean recalls refuting the allegation with a smile the first time he heard the charge, but now learning from another quarter that the "tale" had been circulated in Washington, he felt it "not improper," but necessary, to assure Dearborn that it was "an insidious and wicked fabrication; that no Officer of this State ever hinted such a thing"; McKean notes that he "never had an overture respecting this affair from Whig or Tory, Republican or Federalist, or any person whomsoever"; he believes that all of his state appointees are "sincere friends to the present President" who will do their utmost to see that he is reelected; in April 1802 and October 1803, some Republican members of Congress and a friend had sought to put his name forward as a vice presidential candidate, but he firmly and convincingly refused the overtures for personal and public reasons; lastly, McKean pleads for the name of the letter writer, noting "Such base Incendiaries and Intriguers ought not to be concealed; what must the President think of a professed friend if such a story should reach his ears?"; only through exposure could the "malignant design" and "abominable Lie" be defeated (FC in PHi).

TO WHOM HE MAY SAY: in his 20 Feb. response to McKean, Dearborn noted that he had shown the governor's letter to the president, who wanted McKean to know that "although some vague intonation of the report alluded to had been made to him it was so little noticed that neither the person or manner can now be recollected, that being satisfied that the fallen party would never rise again but by dividing the republicans, he had been on his guard against their Idle tales." TJ considered the governor's "life & principles as sufficient evidence of their falshood," and McKean therefore "may be perfectly assured that no such insinuations have or can make any impressions on his mind" to the governor's "disadvantage." Dearborn informed McKean that he had overheard the "very lengthy" letter read, but the handwriting was unknown to him, and he was "not permitted to know the name of the writer." The author was apparently intimately acquainted with the leading state officers. Minute circumstances were detailed to show how the governor "had been induced to consent to be a candidate for the Presidency." Dearborn had conferred with William Findley and one or two other Pennsylvania congressmen. They assured him that the "whole story was unfounded, and especially that part of it which related to Your Excellency." Dearborn thought Findley knew who the writer was. He evidently resided in Lancaster and had been a recipient of the governor's patronage (RC in PHi).

[1] Word interlined.
[2] Word interlined in place of "better."

From Nicholas Febvrier

George Town

MAY IT PLEASE YOUR EXCELLENCY   Feby. 13: 1804

My Son attends to receive Your Excellency's Answer to a Lettr. some time since delivered You—I blush when I think that my Necessity should be such as to make Me call on the humane & charitable I am penyless & of course Friendless—

May God bless You

Adieu

if You cannot assist Me, You can forgive Me—I remain wishing if Possible an exaltation to Your Glory

I am the Unfortunate   NICHOLAS FEBVRIER

RC (DLC); endorsed by TJ as received 13 Feb. and so recorded in SJL. LETTR. SOME TIME SINCE DELIVERED: Febvrier to TJ, 25 Jan.

From Albert Gallatin

DEAR SIR   13. Feby. 1804

I regret that you entered into a correspondence with D. M. Randolph on the subject of his accounts. The enclosed letter of the clerk is so indecent as relates to the Comptroller that I do not like to show it to him. The account of rejected items consists on various charges, either unauthorized by law or unsupported by vouchers. The judges have in many instances authorized &[1] certified payments without any colour of law; and those payments have always been rejected. Hall late Marshal of Pennsylva. has now an application before Congress for similar advances. Perhaps also, in Mr. R.'s case, he cannot produce the receipt of the witnesses &c. for their attendance; and the clerk can only certify to their having attended & not to their having been paid. I do not perceive Mr. R.'s right to ask you to deposit this letter in the Treasy. dept. If he wants to deposit any thing there let him do it himself. To make the President his channel of communication is disrespectful to him & appears to me a bad precedent. If, however, you think it best that it should be so deposited please to return it; and I will refer it officially to the Comptroller—

Respectfully Your obedt. Servt.   ALBERT GALLATIN

RC (DLC); endorsed by TJ as received from the Treasury Department on 13 Feb. and "D. M. Randolph" and so recorded in SJL. Enclosures: David Meade Randolph to TJ, 7 Feb., and enclosures.

LETTER OF THE CLERK: William Marshall to Randolph, 5 Feb. (Enclosure No. 2 described at Randolph to TJ, 7 Feb.).

In March 1801, TJ removed John HALL as marshal of Pennsylvania. In his APPLICATION to the House of Representatives presented on 11 Jan. 1804, Hall sought "reimbursement of certain extraordinary expenses" incurred by him during the discharge of his official duty, for which he had received no allowance. The Committee of Claims reported against the petition a week later (JHR, 4:526, 540). For Hall's unsuccessful petition to Congress in 1801, see Vol. 33:206n.

[1] Preceding word and ampersand interlined.

From John Langdon

SR.   Portsmouth Feby 13th. 1804

It is more than probable that The impeachment of Judge Pickring will end in his removal, should this take place I would beg leave to recommend, John Saml. Sherburne Esq the present District Attorney, to take his place as Judge, this gentleman was Active, and lost one of his legs in our revolution, has an independant fortune, practiced the law for a long time, correct in his principles, and is, in all respects, better qualified for the place then any other man that I know of in the State. —

I have the honor to be with the highest respect and consideration. Sr. Your Oblig'd Hbl Sert   JOHN LANGDON

RC (DNA: RG 59, LAR); at foot of text: "The President of the United States"; endorsed by TJ as received 24 Feb. and "Sherburne John Saml. to be district judge v. Pickering" and so recorded in SJL.

Near the end of the previous session of Congress, on 2 Mch. 1803, the House of Representatives approved a resolution of IMPEACHMENT against U.S. district judge John Pickering of New Hampshire, whose erratic behavior, alcoholism, and deteriorating mental health had led to calls for his removal by Langdon and other Republicans. On 20 Oct., the House appointed a committee to prepare articles of impeachment against Pickering. Presenting four articles to the House on 27 Dec., the committee charged Pickering with behaving "contrary to his trust and duty" as a judge, ignoring or violating federal laws, and injuring the public revenue. In addition, the committee accused Pickering of being "a man of loose morals and intemperate habits," who appeared on the bench in "a state of total intoxication" and frequently invoked the name of God "in a most profane and indecent manner." After electing 11 managers to conduct the impeachment on its behalf, the House presented the articles to the Senate on 4 Jan. 1804 and the upper chamber organized itself into a court of impeachment on the same day. Dining at the President's House on 5 Jan., Federalist senator William Plumer of New Hampshire queried TJ on the Pickering case. Plumer readily admitted that the judge was insane, but asked the president whether insanity was a sufficient cause for impeachment and removal from office. TJ replied that if the charges against Pickering in the articles of impeachment were proven, "that will be sufficient cause of removal without further enquiry." Plumer then steered the conversation toward the preliminary inquiry by the House of Representatives into the "expediency of impeaching" Supreme Court Justice Samuel Chase. TJ admitted to knowing little about the proceedings, but opined that the

House would probably consider Chase's conduct during the treason trial of John Fries and the sedition trials of Thomas Cooper and James Thomson Callender, especially the Callender trial. Plumer, who feared the actions against Pickering and Chase were part of a broader Republican attack on Federalist judges, recorded that TJ closed their conversation by declaring, "This business of removing Judges by impeachment is a *bungling way*." On 12 Jan., the Senate ordered Pickering to appear before them on 2 Mch. to answer the charges against him. Upon receiving the summons, Pickering reportedly "expressed his determination of claiming his trial by *battle*" and asked the Senate sergeant at arms "to be the bearer of his challenge to Jefferson." He then declared his intention of going to Washington in order to "convince Jefferson if he does not again retreat beyond the Allegany that other men besides Cornwallis can fight." Despite his assertions, however, Pickering would not appear at his impeachment trial (JHR, 4:383-4, 411, 503, 507-9, 510, 513-14, 515, 516; JS, 3:494-507; Everett Somerville Brown, ed., *William Plumer's Memorandum of Proceedings in the United States Senate, 1803-1807* [London, 1923], 100-101; Peter Charles Hoffer and N. E. H. Hull, *Impeachment in America, 1635-1805* [New Haven, 1984], 206-13; Lynn Warren Turner, *The Ninth State: New Hampshire's Formative Years* [Chapel Hill, 1983], 209-18; Jeremiah Mason to William Plumer, 29 Jan. 1804, William Plumer Papers, NhHi; Vol. 37:462-3; Vol. 39:368, 422-5, 443-4; Vol. 40:372-3n).

From Nathaniel Macon,
with Jefferson's Note

SIR   Washington 13 Feby 1804

By the last mail I received inclosed; After reading I will thank you to return it, I have written to another friend for information concerning the grapes as soon as I hear from him, you shall be informed, whether more sorts can be obtained

I am with very great respect Sir Yr. most obt. Sert.

NATHL MACON

[*Note by TJ:*]

William Hawkins to mr Macon. Warren county Feb. 4. 04.

there are but 2. kinds of grapes remaining.

one, oval, purple, early ripe

the other round, white.

Dr. Brehon is supposed to have taken cuttings of all the various kinds which Colo. Hawkins had.

enquiry shall be made—

RC (DLC); endorsed by TJ as received 13 Feb.; TJ's note subjoined below text of Macon's letter.

WILLIAM HAWKINS was a nephew of Benjamin Hawkins (COLO. HAWKINS); Powell, *Dictionary of North Carolina Biography*, 3:75.

From J. P. G. Muhlenberg

SIR   Philadelphia Febry. 13th. 1804.

As president of the Vine Company; I am requested by the Managers, to sollicit The President of the U States, to Honor the Company, by becoming a Subscriber,

I should not have become troublesome on this occasion, but knowing how much, Institutions of this kind have been patronisd by you—I have taken the liberty to enclose a Subscription paper—permit me to observe, that the affairs of the Company are now in a flourishing situation, & the Institution bids fair, to become very beneficial to our Country.

I have the Honor to be with perfect Respect Sir your Obed Servt

P MUHLENBERG

RC (MHi); at foot of text: "Thomas Jefferson Presidt, U States"; endorsed by TJ as received 16 Feb. and so recorded in SJL. Enclosure not found.

The VINE COMPANY of Pennsylvania promoted the production of wine (New York *Commercial Advertiser*, 12 Aug. 1802; Philadelphia *Gazette of the United States*, 30 Apr. 1803; *Aurora*, 31 Jan. and 9 Feb. 1804).

Notes on Henry Putnam's Case

[on or after 13 Feb. 1804]

Henry Putnam.

Allworthy. a sailor on board Revenue cutter. Mar. 7. 03. the cutter took a load of corn on board at Savanna, for Putnam who was on her[1] and carried it to his plantn near Beaufort S.C. &[2] where took on board $2\frac{1}{2}$ bales of cotton, went up the river to Salter's a negro importer.[3] there took on board 6. negroes, which he landed below Savanna in the night Mar. 20. & the next night sent the Cutter's boat down for them, brought them up & delivd them to Muir Mc.Kay & co.

Walters. confirms the taking the negroes on board, but havg left the vessel off the harbour of Savanna he does not know what was done with them. Putnam sells liquor to his men. he took wood as well as cotton on board in S.C. to bring to Savanna. sells duck to them for trowsers.

(allen) another witness on board confirms as to cotton & negroes & that on Lt. Allen's remonstrating to Putnam, he said he should be well paid for it.

[466]

Stuart & Jackson mariners on board prove a gross abuse of a boat-swain [who afterwds died]

Morse. lre Nov. 13. 1803. merchants in the negro trade have insinu-ated in his hearing that they had no fear of interruption from the Cutter as the Capt. might be easily quieted.—Mitchell master of a slave ship, *is reported*, to have said in presence of 2. witnesses who can be produced[4] he was obligd to give Putnam 500. D to be at the Southward when he arrived. the cutter was to the Southward, and the cargo of negroes were landed & are now on the public wharves for sale.

do. Jan. 11. 04. it is said, & proveable, that within the last month, Putnam visited a brig at sea, without Manifest or other paper, con-taining negroes & rum, and forbid it to be entered in his log book. he has now a negro on board the cutter obtained in this way.—he siezed a schooner, & left her witht a guard, & she went off to sea in the night. connivance presumed—

do. Jan. 13. can be proved he boarded Salter's ship, containing ne-groes, and let her pass.—the schooner before mentd. brought slaves. Putnam was bribed to let her go. while she was at the mouth of the river, 2 of the men run away, came on board the Cutter & gave in-formation. Putnam being absent, Allen Lt. sent & siezed her, & brought her up to Savanna. he took her out of Allen's hands, and she went off in the night a 2d time. the Counsel for the schooner informed Morse of this.   a prosecution is instituted in the Superior court of Georgia.   —he stole a watch during the war from Saybrook. he steals lumber from the wharves now. he has made over all his property to cover it from his creditors. he has obtained perjury by subornn of which an official copy exists.

---

1. 1803. Mar. 3. this is proved.
2 selling liquor to his men. is proved
3 ill usage of boatswain is proved
4 his visiting a Brig at sea, without papers, & not enterg in Log book
5 Mitchell's case.
6 the case of the Schooner
7 the subornation of perjury

} susceptible of proof.

MS (ViW); entirely in TJ's hand, in-cluding brackets; undated, but after re-ceipt of Gallatin's note of 11 Feb. (third letter) with enclosures; endorsed by TJ: "Putnam's Case. Savanna."

Thomas Alworthy (ALLWORTHY) be-came an authorized pilot on the Savan-nah River in 1807. In the same year, the United States won a suit against him for resisting and striking an officer of the revenue cutter (*Republican; and Savannah Evening Ledger*, 16 June, 21 July, 15 Aug. 1807; 15 July 1809).

MUIR MC.KAY & CO.: that is, Mein, Mackay & Company, the Savannah mercantile firm of William Mein and Robert Mackay. Pierce Butler, one of the firm's major clients, purchased slaves imported by the company in 1803 (Walter Charlton Hartridge, ed., *The Letters of Robert Mackay to His Wife Written from Ports in America and England, 1795-1816* [Athens, Ga., 1949], 254n, 268-9n; Malcolm Bell, Jr., *Major Butler's Legacy: Five Generations of a Slaveholding Family* [Athens, Ga., 1987], 132, 535, 536).

LT. ALLEN'S REMONSTRATING: Thomas Allen was appointed mate of the Georgia revenue cutter in 1802 (Vol. 37:52, 53n).

On 1 Dec., TJ sent Gallatin the letter from Samuel MORSE of 13 Nov. 1803 (now missing). He did the same later with Morse's letters of 11 and 13 Jan. 1804, both recorded in SJL as received from Savannah on 3 Feb., but not found. Gallatin returned all three to TJ on 11 Feb.

[1] Preceding four words interlined.
[2] TJ here canceled "brought back."
[3] Preceding three words interlined.
[4] Preceding eight words and numeral interlined.

To Caesar A. Rodney

Th: Jefferson requests the favour of *Mr. Rodney* to dine with him *on Wednesday the 15th. inst.* at half after three.

Feb. 13. 04.

The favour of an answer is asked.

RC (IHi); printed form, with blanks filled by TJ reproduced in italics; addressed by TJ: "Mr. Rodney."

From Aaron Vail

L'Orient the 13th. February. 1804

I have recd. from on board the Schooner Citizen of George Town, Capt. Wm. Lawson, two boxes shipp'd by order of the President of the U.S., one address'd to Madame de Tessé & the other to Mr. R. R. Livingston Paris.

A. VAIL

RC (MoSHi: Jefferson Papers); endorsed by TJ: "Tessé Made. de."

TWO BOXES: on the conveyance of TJ's shipment, see Vol. 41:674. For the plants and seeds TJ sent to MADAME DE TESSÉ and for the tea shipped for Madame de Corny under cover to Robert R. LIVINGSTON, see Vol. 41:644-6, 668.

Vail's letter to TJ of 10 Jan. 1804, recorded in SJL as received from Paris on 2 Aug. 1804, has not been found.

From Cato West

DEAR SIR,   February 13th. 1804

I take leave Respectfully to address you upon a subject Interesting to me and as I concieve much so to the Government. — Upon the arrival of the first part of the Tennessee Regiment of Volunteers Majr. Witherspoon the Officer Commanding informed me, he had no means of procuring Forage for the Horses of his Corps and that he knew of no person in the Regiment Authorized, for that purpose and solicited my Immediate attention to that object as the Horses were much injured and reduced by forced Marches, and then suffering; at the same time handed me a letter from Genl. Wilkenson requesting me to do all in my power for the accommodation and Comfort of that Patriotic band of Soldiers. The application of the Officer supported by the Genls. request with my own inclination, determined me to provide for subsisting the Horses of that Corps — And I accordingly Employed Majr. F. L. Claiborne for that service, in hopes however it would not long be necessary for me to act on that Business, presuming that a Quarter Master or Agent duly Authorized would soon appear for the purpose.

But when Colo. Doherty arrived with the residue of the Troops he informed me there was no such Character attendant on his Regiment and solicited in a pressing manner a Continuance of supplies of Forage, and also some other articles of inconsiderable value, necessary for the use of his Regiment.

Upon this subject I wrote early to the Secy. of War, and also to Genl. Wilkenson, and Govr. Claiborne in New Orleans. From the Secy. I have recieved no answer — From the Genl. I recd. an answer with his thanks for my Interposition on that Occasion and soliciting in a pressing manner a Continuance of my attentions to that Corps and directed me to draw upon the Secretary of War for the amount of my disbursements — I also recd. a letter from the Govr. approving of what I had done on the Occasion — I have however postponded drawing Bills in hopes of being favoured with the Answer of the Secretary of War with more direct Authority to draw for the amount due for those Supplies — But some Money having been Borrowed by my Agent for the purpose of purchasing those supplies and in all cases where purchases have been made Immediate payment was promised, will oblige me to draw very soon, but shall previously or at the same time Transmit the Accounts with all necessary Vouchers for their support in the Usual mode of similar Business, trusting that no difficulty will arise to me in obtaining due payment thereupon and that my proceedings herein will meet your approbation and all others concerned. For the information of Government and to explain my conduct fully in this measure I shall transmit with the accounts a Copy of the Correspondence with Genl. Wilkenson and others relative thereto, trusting thereby to remove if not prevent any Impressions which could possibly be made to my disadvantage—The prices charged for supplies of Forage to those Troops may be thought high, but when it is Known that all the Articles of liveing are extremely dear in this Country it will Readily be accounted for, and if it were necessary Proof could be made that the prices charged are not higher than is customary. I am aware of the Impropriety of an Officer's traveling out of the line of his legal duties even when he may do good, but the Extreme exigency of this case, was such that I could not hesitate in determining what part to take. I have stated to you Sir Briefly my proceedings on this Occasion trusting that you will please to excuse the Liberty thus taken in addressing you out of the Common mode, which has arose from a fear of Difficulties which might prove Injurious to me, and this solicitude has been excited by the Omission of the Secretary of War to answer my Communication above mentioned.

I am Dear Sir with very great Respect and much Esteem your Friend &c. CATO WEST

RC (MoSHi: Jefferson Papers); addressed: "Thomas Jefferson President of the U.S. Washington"; franked; postmarked 17 Feb.; endorsed by TJ as received 13 Mch. and so recorded in SJL.

A native of Virginia, Cato West married a daughter of Thomas Green and migrated with the Green family to the Natchez district in the early 1780s. Together with his brothers-in-law Abner Green and Thomas Marston Green, West headed an influential Republican faction in the Mississippi Territory, whose members led the opposition to Federalist governor Winthrop Sargent and later became rivals of Governor William C. C. Claiborne and his supporters. TJ appointed West secretary of the Mississippi Territory in 1803, and he became acting governor of the territory later that year following Claiborne's departure for Louisiana. He actively sought a permanent appointment as governor, but was bitterly disappointed when TJ instead chose Robert Williams for the post in 1805. West subsequently resigned as secretary and largely withdrew from public life (Dunbar Rowland, *Encyclopedia of Mississippi History*, 2 vols. [Madison, Wis., 1907], 2:950; Robert V. Haynes, *The Mississippi Territory and the Southwest Frontier, 1795-1817* [Lexington, Ky., 2010], 39-40, 62-3, 76-83, 104-7; *Terr. Papers*, 5:414; Vol. 39:594, 615, 634; Vol. 40:103-4n; Vol. 41:350).

From Alexandre Baudin

Nouvelle Orlians Le 14 fevrier 1804

Alexandre Baudin habitant planteur à eu lhonneur de faire une Petition en datte du 31. Janvier et 7. du Courant Réclament de la Justice et de l'Equité de votre honnorable Personne de faire Jouir aux habitans Sucrier et Cultivateur de Cannes à Sucre des Privilèges que les loix des Indes leurs accorde et sous la Sauvégarde de la qu'elle ils ont Etablis leurs Manufactures et Plantacions, vue que le tribunalle de Justice nomé Provisoirement à la ville de la Nouvelle Orlians par Son Excélance le Gouverneur Claiborne *Inore les dites loix et Privileges*, et la dittes cours N'etant Compausé que de Negocient qui ne Conaissent Nulement les loix ni les cour de la Jurisprudence, ne prenant en outre Aucqune Conciderations de la Pausitions affligente ou ce trouve Lhabitant Cultivateur, qui dans le moment Actuel ne peut trouver à vendre Sa denrée qua terme, lachant Journellement des Exécutions contre leurs Propriétés; et va Sen Suivre une Ruine Generalle et Un Abandon de diverse Plantacions de Sucre qui ne peuvent Exister qu'en etant protégé par le Gouvernement Actuelle, de la même maniere qu'elles letoient par les loix Existantes sous le Gouvernement Expagniol, le peticionaire tant dans son nom privée qu'en celui de plusieurs habitans ces Concitoyens me Chargent de Suplier de nouveaux de votre honorable Personne de dèlivrer le plutot possible des ordres Provisoires au Gouverneurs de cette Province de ne point Enlever aux habitans les Privileges qui empaichent, et Prohibe, et Rendent Nulles toutes les saisis, et Ventes Judiciaires, de leurs terres, Negres, et Ustencilles Nécessaires aux traveaux de leurs Sucrerie, offrant à lavance et Conformement aux sages Précautions, des loix en leurs faveurs de Remettre Anuellement le Produit de leurs Récoltes à quoi le Peticionaire à voulus ce Conformer Ainsy que plusieurs habitans qui ce Sont endaité auprés des divers Capitalistes qui prestent leurs Argent à Un pour cent par mois, pour former leurs Etablissements. Concequent à quoi Mr. le Gouverneur Claiborne ne veut faire attencion, malgré les Répresentacions que lui a fait le Supliant Ainsy que plusieurs habitans, Alleguant qu'il ne peut Prandre sur lui Pareilles Chauses; et pérmet que la Cour qu'il à Elu fasse Saisir les habitans debiteurs, qui sont journellement Condamné Sur des loix Americcquaines à ce que disent les Menbres compausent la ditte cour de Justices, et sans les avoir fait promulguer avent de les mettre en vigeur, ce qui forme un dèsordre Genéral, et entrainéra Une Ruine totale de grands nombres d'habitans qui ne fondent leur Sauvégarde que Sur les Sages Précautions et les Promptes ordrés que votre honorable

Personne, voudra faire passer au Gouverneur de cette Province à quoi le peticionaire Ainsy que ces Concitoyens à lieu d'esperer pour le bien Géneralle des Cultivateurs.

Et suis avec Respect, Monsieur le President, Votre trés humble & trés hobeissant Serviteur.   A BAUDIN

EDITORS' TRANSLATION

New Orleans, 14 Feb. 1804

I, Alexandre Baudin, plantation owner, had the honor of petitioning you on January 31 and February 7 to ask your honorable person for justice and fairness in giving sugar cane planters the rights that are accorded by the Laws of the Indies and under whose protection they founded their plantations and refineries. The provisional court, established in New Orleans by his excellency Governor Claiborne, is unfamiliar with these laws and privileges. The court is composed entirely of businessmen who do not know anything about the laws or jurisprudence. They take no account of the devastating position in which the planters find themselves. Currently, the planters cannot sell their sugar and they receive daily citations against their property. This will lead to widespread bankruptcy and abandonment of the sugar plantations. The plantations can only survive with government protection, like the protection they had under the laws of the Spanish government.

In my name and that of several fellow citizens who asked me to plead on their behalf, I ask your honorable person to give provisional orders, as soon as possible, to the governors of this province not to abrogate the laws that prevent, forbid, and void all seizures and court sales of planters' land, slaves, and the tools necessary for the operation of their sugar refineries. We ask you to provide, at the same time, and in accord with prudent safeguards, laws requiring us to deliver the product of our harvest each year. We wish to conform fully to these laws. Several planters borrowed money at one per cent per month to set up their refineries. Then Governor Claiborne refused to hear their case, claiming that he could not take such causes upon himself. He is allowing the court he named to seize the debtors; they are then fined daily according to American laws that the members of the court did not promulgate but are now applying. The result is widespread disruption that will cause the ruin of a large number of planters who entrust their well-being to the wise protection and prompt orders your honorable person shall give to the governor of this province. This petitioner and his fellow citizens are hopeful that you will do so for the welfare of the planters.

Respectfully, Mister President, I am your very humble and obedient servant.   A BAUDIN

Dupl (DNA: RG 59, MLR); endorsement effaced; at head of text: "A L'honnorable Thomas Jefferson Président du Congrés des Etats Unis de l'amerique"; at foot of text: "*Duplicata*"; endorsed by TJ as received 2[3] Apr. and "Original sent to Govr. Claiborne to report upon. this duplicate to be filed in Office of state.

Th:J." RC not found but recorded in SJL as received 16 Apr.

Born in 1755 in Île de Ré, France, Alexandre Baudin was living in Louisiana by 1793, having possibly moved there from Saint-Domingue. An experienced sailor, who had during the 1780s commanded a ship transporting Acadians to Louisiana and who likely had experience importing slaves to the West Indies, Baudin was granted a permit to import slaves into the colony. He arranged for a shipment from Africa in 1795, but the ship arrived after the imposition of a total ban on slave importation, and Baudin lost an appeal to the municipal government of New Orleans to allow the shipment. Undeterred, he continued to engage in the slave trade and acquired a plantation in Metairie, north of New Orleans, which he was forced to sell because of indebtedness. He also owned land in Pointe Coupee (Michèle Rivas, "Un navigateur-naturaliste d'origine poitevine célèbre en Australie, méconnu dans sa patrie: Nicholas Baudin [1754-1803]," *Revue Historique du Centre-Ouest*, 5 [2006], 84, 87, 89-90; *Acts Passed at the First Session of the Seventh Legislature of the State of Louisiana* [New Orleans, 1825], 82; *Orleans Gazette and Commercial Advertiser*, 8 Sep. 1809; *New Orleans Argus*, 17 May 1828; Paul F. Lachance, "French Louisianians and the Slave Trade, 1706-1809," in Charles Vincent, ed., *The African American Experience in Louisiana: From Africa to the Civil War* [Lafayette, La., 1999], 125; Thomas N. Ingersoll, *Mammon and Manon in Early New Orleans: The First Slave Society in the Deep South, 1718-1819* [Knoxville, Tenn., 1999], 185-6, 416n; Gabriel Debien, "The Saint-Domingue Refugees in Louisiana, 1792-1804," in Carl A. Brasseaux and Glenn R. Conrad, eds., *The Road to Louisiana: The Saint-Domingue Refugees, 1792-1809*, trans. David Cheramie [Lafayette, La., 1992], 149).

FAIRE UNE PETITION: TJ did not record receiving a communication of 31 Jan. from Baudin, but according to SJL he received on 12 Mch. a letter of 1 Feb., which he likely enclosed in his letter of 14 Mch. to Levi Lincoln. TJ also enclosed material related to Baudin's case to William C. C. Claiborne on 18 Mch. Baudin's communication of 7 Feb. is recorded in SJL as received 26 Mch. with the notation "inclosd papers to Govr. Claiborne, referrg to March 18." TJ enclosed that document to Claiborne on 27 Mch. (see note to TJ to Claiborne, 18 Mch.). None of Baudin's papers that TJ forwarded to Lincoln or Claiborne has been found.

A statute of Spain's Laws of the Indies (LOIX DES INDES), the most complete compilation of which was published in 1680, shielded refiners of sugar from the seizure and sale of movable property such as slaves and milling equipment, except by the crown. The law also barred sugar producers from renouncing this privilege (*Recopilacion de leyes de los reynos de las Indias*, 5.14.4).

For the provisional court that Baudin criticized, see Claiborne to TJ, 16 Jan. NEGOCIENT QUI NE CONAISSENT NULEMENT LES LOIX NI LES COUR DE LA JURISPRUDENCE: Claiborne based his appointments to the court largely on his sense of the members' potential loyalty to the United States. Four were Anglo-American merchants with no legal training, and only one of the Creole members had intensive knowledge of Spanish legal procedure. Meeting for the first time on 10 Jan., the court adopted rules largely in keeping with Anglo-American procedure, particularly with regard to the use of writs and execution of judgments (Mark F. Fernandez, "The Rules of the Courts of the Territory of Orleans," *Louisiana History*, 38 [1997], 68-73; Mark F. Fernandez, "Local Justice in the Territory of Orleans: W. C. C. Claiborne's Courts, Judges, and Justices of the Peace," in Warren M. Billings and Mark F. Fernandez, eds., *A Law Unto Itself? Essays in the New Louisiana Legal History* [Baton Rouge, 2001], 87-9).

From Andrew Ellicott

DEAR SIR,   Lancaster Feby. 14th. 1804.

I ask pardon for not acknowledging the receipt of your two last letters before this:—the delay has been occasioned by the press of business in the land-office, which during the session of our Legislature is such, that we have not a moment to spare for either recreation, or paying that attention to our friends which decency appears to require. I have however directed my attention to the subject of your letters, and will give you my opinion in 8 or 10 days.—

I am sir with great esteem and respect your sincere friend

ANDW. ELLICOTT

RC (DLC); at foot of text: "T. Jefferson President U.S."; endorsed by TJ as received 16 Feb. and so recorded in SJL.

YOUR TWO LAST LETTERS: TJ to Ellicott, 23 Dec. 1803, 1 Feb. 1804.

To Albert Gallatin

TH:J. TO MR GALLATIN   [14 Feb. 1804]

Eli Vickery lives at Norfolk. if the letter be addressed to the care of Colo Thos. Newton, it will be handed him.

RC (DNA: RG 26, MLR); undated, but endorsed by a clerk as a letter of 14 Feb. from the president; addressed: "The Secretary of the Treasury." Not recorded in SJL.

This undated note is in response to Gallatin's query at 11 Feb. (second letter). Gallatin forwarded TJ's answer to John Brown, a clerk in the office of William Miller, commissioner of the revenue, who handled lighthouse correspondence (Gal-

latin, *Papers*, 10:255). Gallatin wrote Brown, on the same sheet, below the president's note: "Eli Vickery is appd. keeper of the light house at Old Point Comfort—His salary the same as for Smith's point—He & the Collector of Norfolk to be notified—A.G." The endorsement indicates that letters were written to Vickery and William Davies on the 14th. William Nelms received $250 as the lighthouse keeper at Smith's Point (Gallatin to TJ, 29 Dec. 1803).

From Albert Gallatin

DEAR SIR   14 Feby. 1804

Although I wrote you that I thought Marshal's letter indecent, I would be very sorry that you should commit yourself in giving an opinion of that kind which might bring your name in the newspapers & make you appear as a party in a mere question of accounts between the treasury and an individual. Nor is it certain that there will be no obstacle to a settlement with the treasury: I think myself that it will not be finally adjusted without a suit. Permit me, to suggest for those reasons, the suppression in your letter of the words between crotchets and the substitution of more general expressions such as "It does not appear however that any intervention of mine be necessary to transmit to that department any certificates in support of your claim, and the enclosed sheet is returned to be disposed of as you shall think proper" or any thing which may throw the transaction in its proper channel—

With respectful attachment Your obedt. Servt.

ALBERT GALLATIN

The New Orleans revenue bill passed yesterday and will probably be presented to morrow for your approbation. The following subjects will require immediate attention.

1. The appointment of officers vizt. Collector, Nav. officer & Surveyor.

2. The propriety of erecting the Mobile country into a separate district, fixing, for the present, the custom house at Fort Stoddart or near the 31° of latitude

3. The manner in which the collector of N. Orleans shall be instructed to consider that part of W. Florida claimed as part of Louisiana and especially Baton rouge & other settlements on the Mississippi & lake Pontchartrain.

From a conversation with W. Nicholas, I believe that he will be pleased in seeing Robt. Nicholas receiving an office on Mobile in preference to one at N. Orleans; provided that the emoluments be about equal. In the present situation of the country, the two offices of collector of customs at Fort Stoddart and Receiver of public monies for the land office there would be about equal to the place of Surveyor at N. Orleans—

RC (DLC); addressed: "The President of the United States"; endorsed by TJ as received from the Treasury Department on 14 Feb. and "D. M. Randolph. officers N.O.—Mobile.—Ro. C. Nicholas" and so recorded in SJL.

I WROTE YOU: Gallatin to TJ, 13 Feb.

SUPPRESSION IN YOUR LETTER: TJ evidently sent Gallatin a draft of a letter to David Meade Randolph, which has not been found. For the letter the president sent, see TJ to Randolph, 23 Feb.

TJ signed the NEW ORLEANS REVENUE BILL, or "Act for laying and collecting duties on imports and tonnage within the territories ceded to the United States, by the treaty of the thirtieth of April, one thousand eight hundred and three, between the United States and the French Republic, and for other purposes," on 24 Feb. IMMEDIATE ATTENTION: the last section called for the act to commence 30 days after passage (U.S. Statutes at Large, 2:251-4; JHR, 4:600).

COLLECTOR OF N. ORLEANS SHALL BE INSTRUCTED: see Gallatin to TJ, 25 Feb. (first letter).

From Craven Peyton

DEAR SIR,   Stump Island 14th. Feby. 1804
since the receipt of yours of 16. Jany. I made propositions to John
Henderson saying I woud. give him for all his proparty what two
good impartial men shoud. value it at, that is in & about Milton, the
proportion in dispute for two attorneys to give there opinion to the
value in writing respecting the Justness of his claim & for the proparty to be valud. accordingly. I was induced to do this thinking it was
for the best as Mr. Higingbothom informed me Millar was to give
Henderson a considerable sum for his mill seat provided he coud.
dissolve my Bill. his motion was made at last Court. the Court was
divided of course my bill was not dissolved. he means to come on at
the next court shoud. he then not succeed he will give me an answar
to my propositions, which are now submitted to you for your instructions to me respecting them, as the oald Mill is now intirely still I am
induced to make you some propositions respecting her, which are I
will again try to purchase the shears which are in the hands of the
legatees which are of age together with the Widows thirds. I will pay
half the purchase Money & be at half of every expence, give my own
services gratis, provided you woud. permit me to have one half of the
profits which I think woud. be great although the shears coud. not be
had for less than about Six times the sum you thought them worth Or
I will with equal pleasure make the purchase intirely for you, though
I think nothing of this coud. be done untill every description of claim
which J. Henderson has coud. be settled his holding several shears in
the Mill which he woud. have valued provided the above propositions are carried into affect with him, will you be so good as to enclose
a draft on Gibson and Jefferson payable the 10th apl. it being in part
for Corn for Fifty Pounds.
 with much Respt. Y. mst. Obt   C PEYTON

RC (ViU); endorsed by TJ as received For the ongoing concerns of Peyton and
22 Feb. and so recorded in SJL.   TJ over the Henderson MILL SEAT, see
               Vol. 40:283, 304-5, 504 and Vol. 41:400.

From Albert Gallatin

DEAR SIR   Feby. 15. 1804
 Wilson Nicholas called again on me this morning, and seems to
prefer an office in New Orleans for his nephew. Yet there is a difficulty,
as we must have all the custom house officers at N Orleans immedi-

ately, and the business of the Comrs. at Mobile will not be terminated till in the course of the summer & perhaps later.

The vacancy on the bench occasions already conjectures & half applications. Wade Hampton is anxious for Mr Julius Pringle. Of that gentleman whom I never saw I know only that he was considered when pleading before the Supreme Court of the United States as extremely wild, and that he has assisted the Yazoo companies with his professional advice, a circumstance which may perhaps have some weight with Mr Hampton. The importance of filling this vacancy with a republican & a man of sufficient talents to be useful is obvious; but the task is difficult. As there are now two circuits without a residing judge, (the circuit of Virga. & N. Cara. having yet two) the person may be taken from either. If taken from the 2d district Brockholst Livingston is certainly first in point of talents &, as he is a State judge, would accept. If taken from the 6th district, unless *you* know some proper person, enquiry will be necessary. Parker the dist. atty. seems qualified but he is a federalist. I am told that the practise is as loose in Georgia as in New England and that a real lawyer could not easily be found there. But S. Cara. stands high in that respect at least in reputation.

With great respect Your obedt. Servt.   ALBERT GALLATIN

RC (DLC); at foot of text: "The President of the United States"; endorsed by TJ as received from the Treasury Department on 15 Feb. and "Ro. C. Nicholas. Pringle" and so recorded in SJL.

VACANCY ON THE BENCH: writing on 26 Jan., Alfred Moore informed Madison that he was resigning as associate justice of the Supreme Court due to the "ill State of my health." Appointed to the court in December 1799, the justice from North Carolina requested that Madison "make known my resignation to his Excellency the President" (Madison, *Papers, Sec. of State Ser.*, 6:392; JEP, 1:325).

John Julius PRINGLE, South Carolina's attorney general, was admitted to the Supreme Court bar in 1796 (DHSC, 1:260; Vol. 34:6, 7n).

TWO CIRCUITS WITHOUT A RESIDING JUDGE: Gallatin prepared a table to show the Supreme Court justice assigned to each U.S. judicial circuit ("Presiding judge") and the justices' residence by circuit ("Residing judge"). In the First

Circuit (New Hampshire, Massachusetts, and Rhode Island), William Cushing presided and was also resident; in the Second Circuit (Connecticut, Vermont, and New York), William Paterson presided and none of the justices was resident; in the Third Circuit (New Jersey and Pennsylvania), Bushrod Washington presided and Paterson was resident; in the Fourth Circuit (Delaware and Maryland), Samuel Chase presided and was resident; in the Fifth Circuit (Virginia and North Carolina), John Marshall presided and he, Washington, and Moore were resident; in the Sixth Circuit (South Carolina and Georgia), Moore presided and no justice was resident. In both instances in which Moore's name appeared in the table, Gallatin wrote *"resigned"* (MS in DLC: TJ Papers, 146:25352; undated; entirely in Gallatin's hand, including endorsement "Circuits").

For TJ's 1801 description of Thomas PARKER as a South Carolina Federalist who was "able" and "unmedling," see Vol. 33:513, 514n.

Memorial from Alexander Richards

To the President
of the United States   New york Feby. 15th. 1804—

The Memorial of Alexander Richards of the City of New York Merchant, in behalf of Oliver Hecks and Henry Rous of the same City Mariners and Citizens of the United States

Respectfully sheweth

That the said Oliver Hecks and Henry Rous sometime in the Month of September in the Year One thousand eight hundred and two sailed from the Port of New York on board of the American Schooner called the Beaver fitted out by and belonging to your Memorialist on a Voyage to the Island of Jamaica, the former in the capacity of Master and the latter in the capacity of Mate of the said Schooner—That in the prosecution of that Voyage being at Sea near the Bahamian Banks they fell in with two small Boats having on board twenty four Persons who proved to be Spaniards belonging to a Spanish Ship which had been wrecked the day before on the said Banks and who were immediately taken on board the Schooner and treated with all the kindness and humanity due to their distressed and helpless condition.—

Your Memorialist further begs leave to represent that the want of a sufficient Supply of Provisions and Water would have rendered it imprudent to have prosecuted the said Voyage with such an increased Crew—Wherefore and in compliance with the earnest solicitations of the said Spaniards the Schooner put into the Port of Nevitis in the same Island where they were landed and from whence the Schooner soon afterwards and without receiving or claiming any compensation or reward for the Services they rendered departed for her Original Port of destination but the Winds proving adverse and little progress having been made in the Voyage during the space of thirteen days it was found necessary at the expiration of that period owing to the extraordinary Consumption which had taken place of Provisions and Water to put into Port for a Supply of those Articles—

With a view to obtain such supply the Schooner thereupon went into the Port of Holgen in the same Island where permission to sell six Barrels of Flour in order to supply her necessary wants being asked for was granted by the Governor and that Quantity was accordingly landed in an open and undisguised manner but immediately thereupon the Master Mate and Crew of the Schooner were seized, stripped of their Cloathing and thrown into Prison and there confined for the space of four Months and although they were then liberated both Vessel and Cargo were found to have been sold without Trial or Condemnation and the Proceeds appropriated by the Spanish Officers there to their own use or to that of the Govenment and every effort to regain them proved unavailing—

Under these Circumstances the Master, Mate and one Seaman whose name is not known to your Memorialist proceeded to the Havanna in order there to obtain restitution of the property lost and redress for the Injuries which they had thus sustained—but such restitution and redress being demanded they were again thrown into Prison by order of the Governor of the Havanna where without a Trial or the form of one they have endured a rigorous and humiliating Confinement for more that twelve Months last past and where they still remain without even the Prospect of relief—Their Situation having been represented by Letter to your Memorialist whose Aid and Intercession have been solicited in their behalf he deems it his Duty to lay their Complaint before your Excellency and to solicit in their behalf such Interference and remonstrance as may be effectual not only to restore to them their Liberty and Property but also to procure for them as the peaceful and unoffending Citizens of a friendly Nation such full and ample redress and Indemnification for the Losses, Sufferings and Indignities which they have experienced as Outrages so audacious and unprevoked entitle them to demand.—

Your Memorialist therefore humbly prays that such Measures may be taken for these Purposes as your Excellency shall in your Wisdom judge expedient

And your Memorialist shall pray   ALEXR. RICHARDS

RC (DNA: RG 76, Claims against Spain); in a clerk's hand, signed and dated by Richards; endorsed by a clerk. Enclosed in Richards to Madison, 15 Feb. (RC in same; printed in Madison, *Papers, Sec. of State Ser.*, 6:484).

Alexander Richards was a merchant in New York who outfitted ships for the Caribbean trade. He was likely the individual of that name who worked as an army contractor during the Quasi-War with France. The *Beaver* was not the only vessel of his to run into problems in Cuba. In 1801, he reported the loss to Spanish privateers of about $13,000 worth of goods from the brig *Friendship*. Richards retained Alexander Hamilton in his efforts to gain restitution from insurance underwriters for the losses of the *Friendship*, the *Beaver*, and another vessel (New York *Mercantile Advertiser*, 7 May 1800, 8 Dec.

1801; *Longworth's American Almanac, New York Register, and City Directory, for the Twenty-Seventh Year of American Independence* [New York, 1802], 299; *Longworth's American Almanac, New York Register, and City Directory, for the Twenty-Ninth Year of American Independence* [New York, 1804], 236; Syrett, *Hamilton*, 24:428; Julius Goebel, Jr., and Joseph H. Smith, eds., *The Law Practice of Alexander Hamilton*, 5 vols. [1964-81], 2:773; 5:320-1).

OLIVER HECKS was probably the New York-based ship master and captain identified as Oliver Hicks in many advertisements from 1805 until his death in 1823. HENRY ROUS was listed as a shipwright in 1802 (*New-York Gazette and Advertiser*, 28 Dec. 1805; New York *Mercantile Advertiser*, 14 Oct. 1819; New York *Spectator*, 15 July 1823; *Longworth's American Almanac* [1802], 306).

In a letter of 29 May to the Marqués de Someruelos, the GOVERNOR and captain general in Havana, Madison repeated the information in Richards's memorial and insisted that the mariners' petition "tho' supported only by their own allegations has claimed the serious attention of the President." The secretary of state requested that Someruelos look into the matter and administer a just settlement (Madison, *Papers, Sec. of State Ser.*, 7:262).

From William Short

Feb. 15. [1804]

Jeffn.—As to papers he sent me—Price is to give him directions as to Durret &c—Anthony—If he shall not receive the back rents to give Price a list—he to acot. with Mr. G. Jef.—The affair of the etiquette—the gaz. of U.S.—the no advertisements explained—inclose the paper from J V Stap—Gerry's letter to me left at N. York—My first object was to enquire after Harvie as have no ansr. from him

FC (DLC: Short Papers); partially dated; entirely in Short's hand, consisting of an entry in his epistolary record. Recorded in SJL as received from Philadelphia on 19 Feb. Enclosure not found.

TJ enclosed some of Short's financial PAPERS in his letter of 23 Jan.
Short and his Indian Camp manager Joseph PRICE were trying to convince one of Short's tenants, John DURRETT, to relinquish his lease in exchange for a dif-

ferent plot of land. Durrett had previously inquired about purchasing land from Short (Joseph Price to Short, 13 Jan. 1804, DLC: Short Papers; Vol. 40:107).
ANTHONY: possibly a reference to Anthony Giannini, another of Short's tenants, who wrote Short in December to warn him about Price's efforts to control all the best land in the neighborhood and to implore Short to allow him to remain a tenant (Anthony Giannini to Short, 23 Dec. 1803, DLC: Short Papers).

From William Wingate

DEAR SIR.   Haverhill Mass: Feb: 15. 1804.

As the Intrest and welfare of my Country is always Uppermost on my Mind, I now Sincerely Congratulate You And our Republican Brethren and Country, for the invaluable Acquisition of Louisiana to the United States, (an immense rich fertile and extensive Teritory) without the expence of a *Single drop of blood*, for which I wish *You* in behalf of myself and Country the best of Heavens blessings both here and hereafter is all I can give You in return, except rendering You and our Common Country my future best Services, provided I Should be So happy As to Merit Your Confidence and Approbation—Sir I can with propriety Affirm that I have Uniformly thus far devoted my Life to Serve the Intrest of My Country and Republican Brethren to the extent of my Abilities & influence, permit me Sir to Say, the President of the United States has nor can do no more—Sir, I Cannot Concent to Undervalue myself or wound my feelings so much As to Solicit my Republican friends here or at Washington for to Solicit an Office for me Under the General Goverment, especially on the principle of obtaining me a Comfortable living, it is true that They generally know that I am both needy and deserving, also lost my property by a Combination of my Federal enemies in Hancoks day and Since, with *no other view* but to destroy my *Republican influence*, Such Sir has Sacredly been my Misfortune—My friends have often proposed for to Solicit an Office for me, my Wish has always been and now is for to obtain one by my own merit, I expected that my friend Carr would have obtained the *Collectors* Office at Newbury port, if He had Succeeded I Should have found business with him, As he has failed, it is now my Wish and desire to obtain the Office Mr. Hodge now holds in Newbury port, the President no doubt has often been informed that Mr. Hodge is an open Enemy to Mr. Jefferson, His Administration and our present Republican form of Goverment, if this be true, the Sooner he is removed the better, I ask is it not owing to Such Clogs in the great Wheel that makes it go round So heavily in this Common Wealth—Shall here observe, that our friend Carr is a very Usefull Spoke in our State Legislature, besides Mr. Carrs Son in Law is now a Collector, for those two important reasons I do not think it So proper and Usefull for to Appoint Mr. Carr into Mr. Hodges Office as to Appoint Some other person, delicacy forbids my Saying any more on the Subject, being Sensiable that it belongs Solely to the Presidents Province to Judge of the necessity of removing and Appointing all Such Officers—

I beg leave only to add that in Case I Should be Appointed into *any* Office that it would be the height of my Ambition to do the business Correct, and to give the President, my friends and all Concerned General Sattisfaction, and always Cheerfully to Acknowledge the favor with feeling Gratitude—As I am desirous to know my prospect, if the President Should Judge it proper and can make it Convenient to return me an Answer, I now pledge my Sacred Honor with regard to Secrecy—

Sir, I duly received Your Letter Containing my papers by the hand of Mr. Varnums Son in Law, I was happy to find that my information met Your Approbation, And now return You my Sincere thanks for the friendly expressions mentioned in Your Letter—

Sir, Believe me to be Sentiments of the most Sincere Esteem and Respect Your Most Obedient Humble Servant—

WILLIAM WINGATE

NB. Newbury port (or Portland) would be my Wish to reside, if the President Should appoint any other place or Office I Shall Cheerfully Submit—

P.S.

Sir, I Concluded at the instant I was Sealing this letter, for to inclose Duplicates of two letters I refered to in my former letter, and were not inclosed, as their Contents respects the President also will shew my Political Ideas, have taken the liberty to inclose them, but in full Confidence with regard to Secrecy, and as they are of no use to me, you need not return them—I hope sir, your Candor will excuse the expressions used in them, also pardon me for taking the liberty of inclosing them—

RC (DNA: RG 59, LAR); at foot of text: "The President of the United States"; endorsed by TJ as received 25 Feb. and "for office in Mass." and so recorded in SJL. Enclosures: (1) Wingate to Joseph B. Varnum, dated Haverhill, 6 Dec. 1802, suggesting that TJ "may *Immortalize His Name* and *Fame* throughout the Civilized parts of the Globe" by completely revising the nation's import laws; Wingate believes national wealth is derived from agriculture, domestic manufacturing, and exports, and that laborers and mechanics will always emigrate to countries that offer them the best employment and the most freedom; Wingate suggests that Congress remove the duties on salt, Bohea tea, and brown sugar and add them to the duties on other teas and luxury items; he also adds a long list of manufactured goods upon which "A duty of 100 per Cent at least" should be placed in order to provide employment for American mechanics and laborers; conversely, raw materials not raised in America should be imported with very low duties or no duty at all; Wingate also recommends a bounty on the production of domestic hemp; if Varnum finds his remarks "worth notice," Wingate asks that they be communicated to the president (Tr in same; in Wingate's hand). (2) Wingate to Varnum, dated Haverhill, 19 Jan. 1803, urging that the president and heads of departments remove the "*Internal Enemies cloathed* with *power*" from federal office; the so-called Federalists have "Sworn on every occasion" to supplant liberty with monarchy and oppression, and for "*any Republican ruler* to *prefer* or *promote* an *open Enemy* in *preference* to an *open Friend*" strikes Wingate as "ingratitude of the blackest die"; John Hancock won no new friends by promoting his enemies and neglecting his supporters, and instead laid the foundation for the Essex Junto and the Federalist party in Massachusetts; Wingate claims to have been an early and consistent promoter of the Republican cause in Massachusetts and has recently urged the formation of "*County Meetings,*" which he believes will help Republicans in both Massachusetts and New Hampshire; Wingate is also "feelingly alarmed" by the present crisis in national affairs, especially respecting Louisiana, and urges Varnum and his fellow Republicans to resist the temptation to lead the nation into an unjust war; Varnum should take no action until he knows "the *minds* of the *People*" on the subject and thereby avoid a repetition of the disgraceful Jay Treaty, which was "*Secretly effected* and *falsly imposed* on the *People*"; Federalists in Congress are attempting to increase expenditures and "*lessen our only Revenue*" in order to force the president to levy internal taxes and thereby, in Wingate's opinion, prevent his reelection; Federalists cannot be thwarted nor the Republicans supported unless the president and his cabinet "*actually remove every Secret* and *open Enemy out of office*" (Tr in same; in Wingate's hand).

For previous recommendations to appoint Francis CARR surveyor at Newbury-

port in place of Michael HODGE, see Vol.
39:153n and Vol. 40:586, 588-9n.

YOUR LETTER CONTAINING MY PA-
PERS: TJ to Wingate, 25 Feb. 1803.

MY FORMER LETTER: Wingate to TJ,
7 Feb. 1803.

From Joseph Anderson

DEAR SIR   Senate Chamber Feby 16th. 1804

In a letter from Governor Claiborne (which was laid before the Senate) he express'd a wish, that some *Compliment* might be paid to the troops of the Mississipi Territory—for their promptitude, in turning out, and descending the River—I have several times since intended to adress you upon the Subject—but have felt delicate, least you might think it an improper interference—My respect for you, and a desire that no Jealosy shou'd be created in the minds of my fellow Citizens must plead my apology—permit me therefore to Suggest—(Shou'd you think proper to Comply with Governor Claibornes request) that it wou'd be adviseable, to pay *at least* a Similar *Compliment*, to the Tennessee Volunteers who march'd to Natchez— Without intending to detract from the merits of the Mississipi Volunteers—it cannot be denied—that those of Tennessee have undergone much greater fatigue—and must be equally entitled—

In order to exhibit a View of *their tour*—I take leave to inclose a letter, which I recd. by last mail—from the Colonel who Commands the Tennessee Volunteers—he is much respected in our State—and has deservedly the Character, of a Judicious, mild, and prudent man— from my knowledge of the dispositions of Military men—I have no hesitation in saying, that a Seasonable Compliment—from their *Commander in Chief*—is always grateful, and will greatly tend, to create emulation and lessen the recollection, of past fatigue—

With Sentiments of verey high Consideration—I am very respectfully   JOS: ANDERSON

RC (DLC); addressed: "The President of the United States"; endorsed by TJ as received 16 Feb. and so recorded in SJL. Enclosure not found.

LETTER FROM GOVERNOR CLAIBORNE: in his letter to Madison of 2 Jan. 1804, William C. C. Claiborne lauded the conduct of the Mississippi Territory volunteers who participated in the occupation of New Orleans. Claiborne suggested that a "complimentary communication" from the president "would be a just tribute to their merits" (Madison, *Papers, Sec. of State Ser.*, 6:278; TJ to the Senate and the House of Representatives, 24 Jan. 1804).

COLONEL WHO COMMANDS: George Doherty (see TJ to Dearborn, 29 Feb. 1804).

From Richard Claiborne

Washington M.T.
16. February 1804.

Sir

Prompted by considerations as are thought to be of importance, and encouraged by the situation of the public business, in which they are concerned—Commissioner Williams, and surveyor General Briggs, go to make some communications to Government, which it is believed will be useful.

From the more deliberate and confidential conversation of these Gentlemen, than by writing,—you will be better informed,—of the necessary amendments to the land law for this Territory,—of the present effects of this law,—of the popular schism here which is less dangerous, than a certain insidious Junto; the persons and characters of whom, you will be informed of,—of the genius and manners of the Inhabitants, here, and in Louisiana,—and many other Topics, unnecessary for me to touch upon.

One object I have in writing to you, Sir, is, concerning Mr. Williams and Mr. Briggs—nor would I touch upon men's characters but to do them honor—reposing what I have to say, in your own breast, for they entertain no idea that I write as I do, and I would avoid, in appretiating them, any unfavorable allusion to others.

Mr. Briggs is esteemed for his morals, his scientific, patriotic, and useful talents; and I know of no man more likely, in this quarter, to be useful than Mr. Briggs.

With respect to the business of the board of Commissioners, the legal abilities, and the talent for originating and arranging, which Mr. Williams has evinced, will be felt very much by his absence,—besides, his manners, his judgment, his integrity, and his great goodness of Heart—will render him popular in any community.

It only remains for me to finish my passage down the Mississippi, to complete my ideas of the most important country that ever blessed the face of the Globe! But I shall be prevented for some time by the public business I am engaged in, which I shall cheerfully discharge at the relinquishment of every other consideration.

Mr. Briggs will inform you with respect to his Brother's plan of inland navigation; and I heartily wish him success; but I hope the collapsing Paddle will be found useful after all, which will be seen when the experiments are made. There is no manner of doubt that the Mississippi and its waters afford a field for the exercise of every exertion in this way. The patronage and approbation I had the honor to meet with in the City of Washington, to my invention, will stimulate me to do every thing in it that I can, as public business will aford me intervals of leisure. Convenient and effectual *Force* is all that is wanted; for the means of *application* are yet easier than perhaps have been brought forth.

I pray you Sir, to receive a continuation of the long and undeviating respect and esteem I have entertained for you.

R CLAIBORNE

P.S. I cannot but repeat that Mr. Williams is of importance here—as the claimants will likely decline attending to their claims so much as if he was present.

RC (DLC); at foot of text: "Thomas Jefferson Esquire"; endorsed by TJ as received 11 Sep. and so recorded in SJL.

For the motivation behind the journey of Robert WILLIAMS and Isaac BRIGGS to Washington, see Briggs to TJ, 27 Feb. 1804.

A CERTAIN INSIDIOUS JUNTO: the Republican faction in Mississippi led by Cato West and members of the Green family (see West to TJ, 13 Feb. 1804).

PUBLIC BUSINESS I AM ENGAGED IN: Claiborne was clerk to the commissioners of the land office in Adams County. He had also been appointed postmaster at Washington (*Terr. Papers*, 5:300-1; Stets, *Postmasters*, 155).

For Claiborne's INVENTION of a boat propulsion system, see Vol. 38:271-2; Vol. 39:140; Vol. 40:373-4, 404.

From Thomas Cooper

SIR   Northumberland February 16. 1804

Before your Letter arrived Dr Priestley was dead: of which I informed you hastily on the same afternoon.

The work you mention of Mr Malthus, I have perused with deep interest and melancholy conviction of the general truth of his Theory, but I cannot help thinking he carries it much too far. Granting the tendency of the procreative passion to increase the human species far beyond the ratio of the increase of Subsistence; this cannot supercede the benefits that may arise from improvements in the Science of Government, and in all the Arts that contribute to the comforts of human existence, nor do I think that he allows sufficiently for a studied and improved system of gradual emigration. All the first part of his Book is evidently nothing to the purpose, for altho' in every actual State of human Society, population has a tendency to overrun subsistence, it is impossible not to see the obvious improvements of which uncivilized nations are susceptible, when we compare them with those European societies which have made any tolerable use of the progress of human knowledge. I fear his preventive check to population, altho' it may operate among thinking men, will ultimately blend itself with

the check of Vice; for in the Mass of young people the checks to marriage untill middle life, will induce in my opinion the inevitable prev-
alence of licensed Prostitution, which I think full as bad as infanti-
cide. I am in hopes that as knowledge increases, and the effects of the
natural tendency to procreate become fully understood in their relation to civil Society, means will be discovered to counteract the excess
without the recurrence to a system of impossible abstinence, to vice,
or to misery. We are yet in the infancy of Knowledge respecting political Œconomy.

Malthus's remarks on the Tables of population, his observations
on the corn Laws and the poor Laws are just; & he has unfolded the
principles of these branches of political Œconomy better than his
predecessors. But his general Ideas have been forestalled by Sr James
Steuart, Adam Smith, and Arthur Young; and most of them are
found, tho' not in sufficient detail, in the treatise of Herenschwand
"Discours fondamentel sur la Population"; a book which notwithstanding some mistakes both in fact and reasoning, has not yet been
superceded.

I remember well conversing with you at Dr Logan's at German
Town, just after I had perused the first edition in 8vo of Malthus's
(then anonymous) essay on the principle of Population, and it seemed
to you that a well regulated System of gradual Colonization might
prove an effectual remedy, without adding to the inevitable mass of
human Misery. I sincerely wish some of his opponents in England
would consider this Remedy more fully, for as the Question stands as
he has rested it, the whole System of human Affairs is too gloomy for
a benevolent mind to rest upon.

Our Legislature of Pennsylvania is at present more remarkable for
good Intentions than extensive information, and the measures they
are adopting to supercede the necessity of Law and Lawyers altogether if they can, disturb in no small degree the harmony that did
and ought to subsist between them and the Governor. I think they
make more haste than good speed, but I foresee that they are bent on
passing some acts founded on principles, which the Governor thinks,
and the Supreme Court of our State have decided to be unconstitutional. This will lead to an investigation shortly, tho' perhaps not this
Session, how far the Judges of our Courts have a right to decide on
the constitutionality of a Law passed by the Legislature. The Judges
say the Constitution is a part of the Law of the Land which they are
bound by their oaths to recognize: their opponents say, that the Constitution is merely a Beacon set up by the people, to direct the Course
of their Representatives in the making of Laws. This may lead to a

Convention here, which I should have no objection to, if we could throw more knowledge into our representation than they have evinced for these two Years past.

There are strong suspicions that our chief magistrate in consequence of these disputes, shews more inclination to federalists and federalism than the Republicans ought to approve, but I confess I do not see the evidence of his defection, tho' he is certainly much vexed at the present conduct of our Party.

Believe me Sir, with sincere respect Your friend

THOMAS COOPER

RC (DLC); endorsed by TJ as received 23 Feb. and so recorded in SJL.

On this day, Cooper wrote another letter to TJ, recorded in SJL as received 14 Mch. with the notation "Jacob Hart. Survr. Louisa." but not found.

YOUR LETTER: TJ to Joseph Priestley, 29 Jan. Cooper reported Priestley's death in his letter of 6 Feb.

IDEAS HAVE BEEN FORESTALLED: in addition to Adam Smith, Cooper referred to James Steuart, author of *An Inquiry into the Principles of Political Oeconomy*, and the English agricultural reformer and writer Arthur Young, with whom TJ was well familiar (Sowerby, Nos. 705, 3555). Building on the work of Steuart, Smith, and Young, Jean Herrenschwand (HERENSCHWAND), a Swiss-born economist who worked at different times for the French government, published in London in 1786 *De l'economie politique moderne. Discours fondamental sur la population* (Joseph J. Spengler, *French Predecessors of Malthus: A Study in Eighteenth-Century Wage and Population Theory* [Durham, N.C., 1942], 290-6).

The LEGISLATURE OF PENNSYLVANIA and Governor Thomas McKean split over the latter's vetoes of the "Hundred Dollar Act," which would have vested more power in local justices of the peace, and a bill creating an arbitration system that would have displaced judges and juries in some cases. In January, the legislature overrode McKean's veto of a different bill involving justices of the peace and passed a revised version of the Hundred Dollar Act. McKean allowed the legislation to pass without his signature (Higginbotham, *Pennsylvania Politics*, 51-3, 65-6; Vol. 39:473-4n).

From Albert Gallatin

DEAR SIR   Feby. 16 1804

Gen. Jackson called last night and stated that a true bill having been found agt. Putnam, although he believed him innocent & persecuted, yet he thought he ought to resign: and he wishes that idea to be communicated to him. Is that proper under present circumstances? I have sketched a letter to the Collector, which, if it shall meet with your approbation, I will show in the first place to Gen. Jackson & then transmit.

The General is warm against Morse for having coalesced with Gibbons. Him I have once seen, and that he is a bitter federalist and was so not twelvemonth ago I do know. Morse's object appears, however, to have been altogether laudable & his motives are certainly pure.

Gen. Jackson says that he will recommend a successor who is now harbour master of Savannah; his name I think Wymbley or Wimbleton, he will write on the subject. Choate would not do—He is also very desirous that the dist. atty. Mitchell should be judge supreme court; if taken in S. Cara., he recommends Gaillard the late Speaker.

Respectfully Your obt. Servt.   ALBERT GALLATIN

RC (DLC); at foot of text: "The President of the United States"; endorsed by TJ as received from the Treasury Department on 16 Feb. and "Putnam. Wibley. Mitchell. Gilliard" and so recorded in SJL. Enclosure not found.

It is not clear if Gallatin actually sent a letter regarding the Henry Putnam case to Thomas de Mattos Johnson, the COL-LECTOR at Savannah (Vol. 39:158n). On 5 Mch., Putnam wrote Gallatin that he had submitted his resignation on 17 Feb., effective the first day of April 1804, the end of the quarter. He assured the Treasury secretary that he had always faithfully discharged his duties, noting that he had "made more Seizures during the time" than "by any Officer in the same department on the Continent." He was being driven from office by "the Enemies of the Present Administration" and was resigning "to prevent the possibility of the

Slightest imputation, arriseing only from the Tongue of Slander Touching the *President That unequald good man.*" Putnam requested that Gallatin show his letter to James Jackson (RC in DNA: RG 59, LAR; endorsed by TJ: "To mr Gallatin" and "Putnam Henry. resigns cutter in Georgia").

HARBOUR MASTER OF SAVANNAH: Benjamin Webley. In an undated note, Gallatin wrote: "If the President intends that Wybley should be appointed Master of the revenue cutter, it will be sufficient for him to direct that a commission be prepared in his name—The appointment is, by law, in the President alone—A.G." (MS in same; entirely in Gallatin's hand). TJ entered Webley's appointment on his list at 26 Mch. (see Vol. 43: Appendix I).

Jackson influenced TJ in the appointment of David Brydie MITCHELL in 1802 (Vol. 37:52, 391, 409).

To the Senate and the House of Representatives

To the Senate and
House of Representatives of the US.

Information having been recieved some time ago, that the public lands in the neighborhood of Detroit required particular attention, the Agent appointed to transact business with the Indians in that quarter was instructed to enquire into, and report the situation of the titles and occupation of the lands private and public in the neighboring settlements. his report is now communicated, that the legislature may judge how far it's interposition is necessary to quiet legal titles, confirm the equitable, to remove the past, and prevent future, intrusions, which have neither law nor justice for their basis.

TH: JEFFERSON
Feb. 16. 04.

RC (DNA: RG 46, LPPM, 8th Cong., 1st sess.); endorsed by a Senate clerk. PrC (DLC). RC (DNA: RG 233, PM, 8th Cong., 1st sess.); endorsed by a House clerk. Recorded in SJL with notation "lands at Detroit." Enclosure: Charles Jouett to Henry Dearborn, Detroit, 25 July 1803, enclosing a report on the settlements at Detroit and its vicinity, which includes concisely "all those facts concerning which I imagined the Government would wish to be informed"; for each settlement, Jouett provides details on its location, geography, population, economic activities (or lack thereof), and land tenure; the population is overwhelmingly Canadian; claims to land titles largely originate from Indian grants as early as the 1770s, as well as a handful of French grants from the 1740s and 1750s; some residents are squatters; almost no titles were confirmed by the French or British; although legal title to most of the occupied lands is questionable, Jouett found that most of the inhabitants consider themselves and their neighbors to be freeholders (MS in DNA: RG 233, PM, endorsed by a House clerk; printed in ASP, *Public Lands*, 1:190-3); see also Notes on Charles Jouett's Report on Detroit, [ca. 17 Feb. 1804].

For the INFORMATION received previously regarding public lands in the vicinity of Detroit, see Vol. 36:24, 500, 607.

THE AGENT: in 1802, the War Department appointed Charles Jouett agent for Indian affairs in the Northwest and Indiana Territories and agent for examining and managing claims at Detroit and its environs (Dearborn to Jouett, 27 July, 7 Sep. 1802, in DNA: RG 75, LSIA; Vol. 39:258n).

TJ received Jouett's REPORT under cover of a letter from Dearborn dated 17 Feb.: "I have the honor herewith to enclose Two copies of a Report made by Charles Jouett Esqr. Indian Agent at Detroit, in relation to the Titles of land at Detroit & its vicinity, the periods at Which they were settled &Ca. &Ca." (RC in DLC, in a clerk's hand, signed by Dearborn, at foot of text: "The President of the United States," endorsed by TJ as received from the War Department on 17 Feb. and "Jouett's report on Detroit" and so recorded in SJL; FC in Lb in DNA: RG 107, LSP). Lewis Harvie delivered TJ's message and its accompanying papers to the Senate and House of Representatives on 17 Feb. The Senate ordered them to lie for consideration, while the House referred them to a committee formed in Nov. 1803 to consider amending acts for the sale of public lands (JS, 3:359; JHR, 4:453, 456-7, 584). The message and report were printed on the order of the House as *Message from the President of the United States, Transmitting a Letter and Report from the Agent Appointed to Transact Business with the Indians . . . 17th February 1804* (Washington, 1804).

From Edward Thornton

Thursday 16 February 1804.

Mr Thornton presents his Respects to the President of the United States, and is sorry that he cannot have the Honour of waiting on him on Friday next.

[489]

RC (MHi); addressed: "To The President of the United States"; endorsed by TJ.

Upon Anthony Merry's arrival in Washington and presentation of his credentials, Edward THORNTON had Lord Hawkesbury's permission to return to England, but stayed in America until July 1804 (Malcolm Lester, *Anthony Merry Redivivus: A Reappraisal of the British Minister to the United States, 1803-6* [Charlottesville, 1978], 18-19).

From George Wolcott

EXCELLENT SIR—   Saybrook Feby. 16th. 1804

I have received the Commissions your Excellency has been pleased to honor me with—appointing me Surveyor of the Customs—and Inspector of the Revenue for the Port of Saybrook—I accept them with gratitude and to the best of my ability shall faithfully discharge the Trust reposed in me

I am Excellent Sir most respectfully your Obedient Servt.

GEORGE WOLCOTT

RC (DNA: RG 59, MLR); addressed: "His Excellency Thomas Jefferson President of the United States Washington City"; franked; postmarked 20 Feb.; endorsed by TJ as received 25 Feb. and so recorded in SJL with notation "accepts" and "S."

George Wolcott (ca. 1752-1822), a Windsor, Connecticut, native, was the older brother of Alexander Wolcott, Republican leader and customs collector for the Middletown district, of which Saybrook was a port. The newly appointed surveyor was noted for having been removed as deputy sheriff in Hartford County for his political opinions during the "reign of terror." The Federalist press criticized the administration for appointing another Wolcott to office, especially since he lived in the country "fifty miles" from Saybrook. Wolcott relocated to the port, where he remained in office the rest of his life (Hartford *Connecticut Courant*, 14 Mch. 1804; Hartford *American Mercury*, 22 Mch. 1804; New London *Connecticut Gazette*, 6 Feb. 1822; Vol. 40:85, 86n).

To Henry Dearborn

TH:J. TO GENL. DEARBORNE   Feb. 17. 04.

Altho' the communication of the within to me might be considered as confidential, yet it is so important that Wilkerson's maneuvres should be understood that I send it for your perusal, in confidence also. he is turning on us the batteries of our friends in aid of his own. the business of the Commission terminated on the 16th. of Jan. when the order for the upper posts was given, as that compleated the delivery of possession. how long his military duties may keep him there you can best judge. but in my opinion he should understand that his powers as Commr. terminated with the delivery of the last[1] order, and that he should be brought away as soon as possible, or I should not wonder if some disturbance should be produced to keep him there. be so good as to return the inclosed immedly. affectte. salutations.

PrC (DLC). Recorded in SJL as a letter to the War Department. Enclosure not found.

ORDER FOR THE UPPER POSTS: on 16 Jan., in accordance with instructions from Dearborn and Madison, William C. C. Claiborne and James Wilkinson sent orders to Captain Amos Stoddard at Kaskaskia regarding the transfer and occupation of upper Louisiana. Stoddard was first to act as France's commissioner for receiving the province from Spain, then as the agent of the United States to take charge of "the several Posts, Territories & Dependencies" that had been transferred from France to the United States. Until Congress made provision for a permanent government, Stoddard was to exercise both the civil and the military functions formerly exercised by the Spanish commandants. Such functions, however, were to be kept "carefully separated & distinct." To that end, Claiborne commissioned Stoddard civil commandant at St. Louis, while instructions regarding military affairs were to come from the "Commander in chief of the American Troops." Arriving at St. Louis on 24 Feb., Stoddard formally received upper Louisiana from Spain in the name of the French Republic on 9 Mch., then assumed control for the United States the following day (*Glimpses of the Past*, 2 [1934-35], 80-2, 92, 95-7; Vol. 41:632-5).

[1] Word interlined.

From Henry Dearborn

War Department
SIR,   February 17th. 1804

I have the honor to submit the following statement, for the purpose of shewing the necessity of an Act of Congress authorising the appointment of Six Surgeons Mates, in addition to the number authorised by the Law of the 16th. of March 1802, fixing the Military Peace Establishment—

The Posts recently established, in addition to the twenty five contemplated at the late organization of the Army, & for which Surgeons Mates will be required, are Plaquemines, Atacapas, Opelousas, Natchitoches, Arkansas, New Madrid, St. Louis & Chikago.—I take the liberty, Sir, of suggesting also, the propriety of such alteration on amendment being made in the Law fixing the Military Peace Establishment, as will authorise the President of the United States to cause Malt liquor, to be issued to the Troops of the U.S. instead of Ardent Spirits, at such Posts & for such part of the year as shall be deemed useful—There can be no doubt but ardent Spirits will be found very injurious to the health of the Troops at many of the Southern Posts & especially at New Orleans & its vicinity—An equivalent in good

Malt liquor or light Wine would contribute greatly to the health of the Troops; but long & obstinate habits will probably render legal authority necessary, for effecting the proposed substitution—

With respectful consideration I am Sir, your Obedt. Servt

H. DEARBORN

RC (DLC); addressed: "The President of The United States"; endorsed by TJ as received from the War Department on 17 Feb. and "Surgeon's mates.—ration of malt liquor v. spirits" and so recorded in SJL. FC (Lb in DNA: RG 107, LSP).

On 26 Mch., Congress amended the MILITARY PEACE ESTABLISHMENT act of 1802. The revised act authorized the president to appoint up to six additional surgeon's mates and to substitute rations of rum, whiskey, or brandy with malt liquor or "low wines" (U.S. Statutes at Large, 2:290).

From Simon Didama

DEAR SIR!   Oldenbarneveld February 17th. *1804*.

how my Friends their hearts and mine did rejoice as soon we were informed of the happy event taken place into the city of New-Orleans, and Louisiana. in taking possession of that country in such a Pacificq and Amiable manner, an event dear Sir! on which every one whose heart beats for the well-being of this Country, and all the Friends of Humanity and Liberty have great reason to rejoice, and to be thankfull towards your Administration, and a Government who are always endeavouring to devote their best and properest means for the good and best Intrest of this Happy, blessed, and beloved Country.

Notwithstanding dear Sir! after this all has happened, how glad should We all have been to receive an answer from you, on Thomas Paine, Esqr. on Our plan we did take the Liberty in sending it over, inclosed on your address the Seventeenth day of October last. because my Friends and I, are left in an Uncertainty at present, not knowing what to do, or not, till we should be informed there could be a good chance in settling that country (Louisiana) with Sober, honest, and Industrious People who are willing to spend their life time under the influence and Protection of this Government; the best and happiest we have reason to suppose, for Human beings upon this Globe.

We Humbly beseech you Dearest Sir! as a true beloved Friend, and Father of your Country, once more to be so generous in sending the inclosed to Thomas Paine, Esqr. the obligations and respect we should be under will be answered by us with blessings of gratitude. and if it is in your power Dear Sir! (as we really believe it is) to assist us in our undertakings, please to be so kind to inform us what proper means we shall have to pursue, and if there may be any need for us in coming to the City of Washington, in order to know what arrangements, plans, divisions or terms on which the Lands we have in view may be made, or Sold. we Humbly pray to inform us of it, as soon it is possible. I shall be ready to come immediately on the first information we shall receive and if our undertaking may succeed, as we are sure it shall, on account of the great and extensive correspondence, Friends, and acquintances we have in Holland, and in these Republicq. it would be a great and sattisfactory improvement not only for this country but also for those who wish to deal and join with us in our object, on which with all the Ambition due on such an undertaking we immediately will begin to take at hand, and heart, all possible means we shall have in our power, in order to have the Lands cleared, and settled with such individuals, who with their industry may live very happy and contented on it.

reason Why we insist and are so desirous to get an answer from you on Thomas Paine, Esqr. is this; because if our object could be obtained, some of us should be inclined to proceed to Europe, as soon as possible; in order to get settlers from there, while on the other hand some of us should be willing to go immediately unto the spot, to have improvements made, on account we are so far ready with our Plan, that if it may succeed, our Friends can have in the course of two months Hundred hands ready to clear Lands, and building Log-houses to receive a great number of Families from our native country.

With all the Honour and respect due to your Honorable and worthy Character, besides the high Station you hold in these Republicq. and after recommanding myself into your Friendship and Esteem,

I remain Dear Sir! your most Humble and Obedient Servant

Simon Didama

My address Simon Didama, phisician at Oldenbarneveld (Town of Trenton) near Utica, County of Oneida, State of New-york.
NB I do know there are a great number of French inhabitants into Louisiana. I am acquinted with that language, so it may be there a great service to me.

RC (DLC); addressed: "Thomas Jefferson, Esqr.: president of the United States. City of Washington"; franked; postmarked Utica, New York, 21 Feb.; endorsed by TJ as received 1 Mch. and so recorded in SJL.

From Gideon Fitz

SIR   Washington M.T. Feb. 17th 1804

After my most humble acknowledgments & respects—I have to inform you that from the repeated accounts of the disagreeableness which attended travellers though the wilderness road: we at length thought it mought be most prudent to go on to the falls of the Ohio and come down by water we arrived there the 5th Novm. where we had no opportunity of leaving untill the 23d Decem. and on the 30th Jan. we landed at Natchez in a few days after proceeded on to this place where I found Mr. Briggs at his office I also have the honor of acknowledgeing his most agreeable and kind receiption—He has also extended his goodness so fare as to put his office books &c. in my care untill he returns in which time I shall have the opportunity of some considerable improvement as also he gave Mr Nelson the gentleman with whoom I board instructions not to ask or require any money of me before his return—I find the common necessaries of life in this Country extremely high our travelling expences also has been very high indeed and I also must confess I found miself considerable alarmed when we first arrived here and found the business which we came on in its present situation tho we must now content ourselves as well as possible and wait the result of a second consideration—

I now have the honor to acknowledge miself your most humle and Obed servt   GIDEON FITZ

RC (DLC); at foot of text: "Mr Tho. Jefferson P.U.S."; endorsed by TJ as received 20 Apr. and so recorded in SJL.

For the recent incidents of DISAGREEABLENESS on the road between Nashville and Natchez, see Vol. 41:33-4, 46, 295.

From Peachy R. Gilmer

           Pen Park.

P R GILMER To MR. JEFFERSON.   17th. Feby. 1804

I contemplate removing to Louisiana, in March or April next; my pecuniary affairs will render any appointment of sufficient emolument to support me, very acceptable

If my abilities and other requisite qualifications are such as to entitle me to promotion, I pledge myself to discharge the duties of any office to which I may be appointed, with my best ability and with punctual fidelity

If the appointment of attorney for the Orleans district has not been made it will be prefered to any other—provided my experience and talents are deemed adequate to the discharge of the duties, attached to that office

If however from either of these causes it should be impossible or improper to bestow it upon me, any other will be thankfully received, whether in Lower or uper Louisiana

I have the honor of an acquaintance with several gentlemen of the first respectabelity, now in Washington, from whom Mr. J. may get any information, that may be required, either as to my moral and political principles, or talents

I am sorry to add one to the numerous applications of this nature, which I know are constantly made;—

My view in this communication is merely to enrol my name on the list of Applicants, and well assured that the President will act with perfect propriety, whether in giving, or withholding an office; neither event can lessen or encrease the high esteem and regard, with which I am—   PEACHY R GILMER

RC (DNA: RG 59, LAR); endorsed by TJ as received 22 Feb. and "to be Atty Genl. N.O." and so recorded in SJL.

Son of TJ's friend and doctor George Gilmer and brother of Francis Walker Gilmer, who was one of TJ's protégés, Peachy R. Gilmer (1779-1836) attended William and Mary and then studied law under his brother-in-law William Wirt. He lived in Henry County for a number of years before establishing a law practice in the town of Liberty (later Bedford). He appeared on a slate of presidential electors for James Monroe in 1808 and may have run unsuccessfully for a seat in Virginia's Convention of 1829-30 (Richard Beale Davis, *Francis Walker Gilmer: Life and Learning in Jefferson's Virginia* [Richmond, Va., 1939], 360-6; Richmond *Virginia Gazette*, 4 Oct. 1808; *Alexandria Gazette*, 3 June 1829; *National Intelligencer*, 22 Apr. 1836).

To Rufus King

SIR   Washington Feb. 17. 04.

I now return you the M.S. history of Bacon's rebellion with many thanks for the communication. it is really a valuable morsel in the history of Virginia. that transaction is the more marked as it was the only rebellion or insurrection which had ever taken place in the colony before the American revolution. neither it's cause nor course have been well understood, the public records containing little on the subject. It is very long since I read the several histories of Virginia. but the impression remaining in my mind was not at all that which this writer gives; and it is impossible to refuse assent to the candor & simplicity of his story. I have taken the liberty of copying it, which has been the reason of the detention of it. I had an opportunity too of communicating it to a person who was just putting into the press a history of Virginia, but still in a situation to be corrected. I think it possible that among the antient MSS. I possess at Monticello I may be able to trace the author. I shall endeavor to do it the first visit I make to that place and if with success I will do myself the pleasure of communicating it to you. from the public records there is no hope, as they were destroyed by the British, I believe very compleatly, during their invasion of Virginia. Accept my salutations and assurances of high consideration & respect   Th: Jefferson

RC (NHi); at foot of text: "Rufus King esq."; endorsed by King as received 22 Feb. and "M.S. of Bacons Rebellion in Virginia." PrC (DLC).

King enclosed the manuscript HISTORY OF BACON'S REBELLION in a letter of 20 Dec. 1803.

TAKEN THE LIBERTY OF COPYING: for TJ's personal copy, see Preface to a Manuscript on Bacon's Rebellion, printed at 10 Mch. TJ may have sent a copy to John Daly Burk, who published the first volume of his HISTORY OF VIRGINIA in 1804.

The second volume, which included much material and analysis on Bacon's Rebellion, appeared the following year. Burk is credited as the first chronicler of Virginia to portray Nathaniel Bacon as a patriot whose resistance to gubernatorial authority anticipated many of the ideals of the American Revolution (John Daly Burk, *The History of Virginia, From Its First Settlement to the Present Day*, 4 vols. [Petersburg, Va., 1804-16]; Brent Tarter, "Making History in Virginia," VMHB, 115 [2007], 7-8; DVB, 2:402).

Notes on Charles Jouett's Report on Detroit

[ca. 17 Feb. 1804]

Jouett's report of 1803. respecting the settlements at Detroit.

Otter creek	24. farms & families
River Raison	121.
Sandy creek	16.
Rocky river	2.
River Huron	1.
Ecorce or Bark river	16.
river Rouge	43.
to Detroit	23.
Detroit. 4. as.	
Gros-isle	10.
to Gros Point	60.
to Milk river	24.
to river Huron	30.
river Huron	34.

to Sinclair river	2
Sinclair river	12
	20
	438

MS (DLC: TJ Papers, 137:23713); undated, but see below; entirely in TJ's hand, including endorsement: "Detroit."

JOUETT'S REPORT: although TJ dated his message to Congress on the subject of

Charles Jouett's report 16 Feb., he received the report from Dearborn on the 17th; see TJ to the Senate and the House of Representatives, 16 Feb. 1804.

Notes on Supreme Court Candidates

1804. Feb. 17.   Characters of the lawyers in S.C.   W.H. T.S.

John Julius Pringle }
Waities. }

these are the two principal of those called republicans. they are of old standing, and highest reputn. Pringle was wavering once, was even with the federalists, but got back again. but both are so moderate, that they only vote with the republicans; they never meddle otherwise. Pringle is so rich that he confines his practice to Charleston, & it is thought would not accept a commission which should call him from there. Waities is so sickly that he would not be able to ride. neither would possess the confidence of the republicans.

William Johnson.

a state judge. an excellent lawyer, prompt, eloquent, of irreprocheable character, republican connections, and of good nerves in his political principles. about 35. years old. was speaker some years.

Trisvan.

a state judge. of equal respectability, or very nearly so, & indeed in every qualification as Johnson. same age. but of such total feebleness of body as to be quite unfit.

Gilliard.

was speaker of the assembly. equal in talents to Johnson, but more Jacobinical. all his connections were revolutionary tories, & their estates confiscated. they got something back again, at least his father did. this young man was educated abroad. he returned soured agt. those then in power for what his family had suffered. he found he had nothing to hope from them, and joined those who now constitute the republican party. his conduct while in the assembly was uniformly firm, almost vindictive; yet in an instance or two, from family influence or interest he has swerved a little from sound principle. upon the whole, his standing is not quite as respectable as that of Johnson.

MS (DNA: RG 59, LAR); entirely in TJ's hand; endorsed by a clerk.

W.H. T.S.: Wade Hampton and Thomas Sumter, Sr.

Thomas Waties (WAITIES), a former law student of John Julius Pringle, had served as an associate judge on the South Carolina Court of Common Pleas since 1789 (*S.C. Biographical Directory, House of Representatives*, 3:753-5).

WILLIAM JOHNSON represented Charleston in the South Carolina General Assembly from 1794 until 1799, when he was elected to the state court of common pleas (*S.C. Biographical Directory, House of Representatives*, 4:322-5; Vol. 34:7n).

Like his colleague Johnson, Lewis Trezevant (TRISVAN) had studied law under Charles Cotesworth Pinckney and was elected to the state court of common pleas in 1799 (John Belton O'Neall, *Biographical Sketches of the Bench and Bar of South Carolina*, 2 vols. [Charleston, S.C., 1859], 1:68-71, 73).

Theodore Gaillard (GILLIARD) served in the South Carolina House of Representatives, where he was twice elected speaker. TJ had appointed him a bankruptcy commissioner in 1802 (*S.C. Biographical Directory, House of Representatives*, 4:220-1; Vol. 37:512, 513n, 699, 711).

From Henry Dearborn

SIR   [18 Feb. 1804]

orders were early[1] given for the necessary supply's of provisions for the volunteers from Tennessee. on their arrival at Natchez, it was a general opinion that they could take provisions with them sufficient for their Journey through the woods and they made no objection that I have heard of to that part of the arrangement. they certainly had sufficient time before they marched, for furnishing themselves aboundantly.—In Genl. Wilkinsons letters, you see what measures had been taken for their return; they cannot be paid until their Muster & pay rolls are received & adjusted. I long ago requested the Govr. to have the proper rolls made out immediately on their return and forwarded, on which they would be paid without delay.

H. DEARBORN

P.S.

what perticular compliment ought to be paid them and in what manner, must rest on mere opinions, they as a body are certainly not intitled to any great compliment on the score of promptitude, their sufferings have undoubtedly been considerable. when they return if their conduct shall appear to have been correct or proper generally, it may be useful & just, to address some mark of approbation to the Commanding Officer, to be published by him or by some other proper person in the newspapers of that State.   HD—

RC (DLC); undated; endorsed by TJ   [1]MS: "ealy."
as received from the War Department on
18 Feb. 1804 and "Tennissee militia" and
so recorded in SJL.

From Benjamin H. Latrobe

DEAR SIR,   Washington Feby. 18h. 1804

Since I last had the honor to wait upon you nothing has occurred upon which I felt myself authorized to take up your time, and though I have often been in your house, I have not found it necessary to trespass upon your leisure for directions.—

In the mean time, every thing has been prepared to begin the roof as soon as the Weather promises to be fair.—The lead for the Gutters has been cast & the iron Work prepared. My time has been employed in the accounts in the designs necessary for the ensuing season, and principally in the negociations for stone.

I now take the liberty to send you a sheet of sketches which explain the effect of different dispositions of the plan of the House of Representatives, lighted a la Halle de Bled.—

The best proportioned room would be the circle of 80 feet No. III. But its excessive rise above the Balustres renders it perhaps inadmissible, independently of the narrowness of the intercolumnation if 32 Columns be the number adopted.

No II in which the Intercolumnation is in the mode of Eustyle gives columns too slight in appearance for the weight of the dome, & lowers the room too much. The Elliptical room No. IV has all the faults formerly enumerated with very slender Columns.

In No I I have taken great pains to ascertain the line in Perspective of a Dome upon an Eliptical plan, segment 120 Degrees, Columns (as in Doctor Thornton's plan 3 feet Diameter), as it would appear along the Pensylvania avenue. It must be observed that the Capitol hill is only 78 feet above the tide,—though its abruptness gives it the air of much greater altitude, & that therefore any roof projecting much above the parapet is seen easily at the distance of $\frac{1}{2}$ a mile which distance reduces the angle of Elevation to a very few degrees.—

I take the liberty to lay these sketches, and a paper on the State of the Stone contracts before you this evening & will wait upon you early tomorrow morning.—

I have been very seriously ill for the last fortnight of an species of intermitting headach, which has contributed to delay my business. I am with true respect Your very hble Serv   B HENRY LATROBE

RC (DLC); addressed: "The President of the Un. States"; endorsed by TJ as a letter of 18 Feb. received 17 Feb. and so recorded in SJL. Enclosed sketches not found.

LAST HAD THE HONOR: likely the meeting Latrobe mentioned in his letter of 15 Jan.

Latrobe was trying to resolve the design deficiencies he perceived in the PLAN for the south wing of the Capitol, which suffered in his view from the EUSTYLE scheme, in which columns were spaced no more than two and a half column diameters apart from each other, a scheme he found incompatible with the ELLIPTICAL plan (OED, s.v. "eustyle"; Allen, *History of the United States Capitol*, 52, 55-6; Vol. 40:127, 129-30).

ENCLOSURE

Sources of Stone for the Capitol

[on or before 18 Feb. 1804]

State of the Prospect of procuring Stone for the Capitol for the Year 1804.—

1. From Messrs. Brent & Cook.—These Gentlemen are the only contractors who may with certainty be relied upon. They require an advance of 2000.$ on a contract made with them Feby. 17h. 1804 for 1000 Tons delivered in Washington, at 8.$ ℔ Ton for all stone of one Ton & under,—8.25 above one Ton to 1½ Ton & 8.75$, for all stone of greater weight.—The *average* of their supply will probably cost 8.$ 10cts. which is 44 Cents ℔ Ton more than last Year. But should the public Quarry yield good Stone, the bills may be so regulated as to take no stone of them exceeding 1 Ton weight.

2./ The public Quarry,—is opened & promises well. We may depend on 600 Tons good stone at 7.$ 25 Cents average.—The *next* season, I flatter myself to be entirely supplied from thence.—

3./ We have bought for Cash a quantity of stone ready quarried at Acquia, about 150 Ton, which when brought hither will cost only 5.$ ℔ Ton.—

4./ Robertson has contracted to deliver from a very good Quarry now open 400 Ton of extra-fine stone for the Cornice & Capitals at 9.$ ℔ Ton. I consider this as an advantageous Contract as that species of stone does not appear in any other Quarry. Of this stone I expect with certainty not more than 250 Ton as Robertson is not entirely to be depended upon.—

5./ Stewart at Acquia,—labors under disadvantages in working his Quarry, which render the fulfillment of his contract for 250 Tons precarious. this stone however is very good, & he will make a great exertion this season. 8$ ℔ Ton

6. Conway of Acquia has good stone, but having no great force, may not perhaps compleat his Contract for 300 Tons.—8$ ℔ Ton

7. Richardson of Fredericsburg has an excellent Quarry, & were he not engaged in building the New Jail, might furnish a very large Quantity of Stone. But I fear he will disappoint us, & as he wants a large advance, I hesitate about contracting for 500 tons at 7$ 66. cts.—the Quantity & terms which he offers.

Cook & Brent enter into their Contract, *at the risk* of its being avoided if no appropriation be made by Congress to the prosecution of the public Works.—

Recapitulation.—

		Tons
Cook & Brent,		1.000
Public Quarry		600
	Ton	
Robertson, contract	400, —say—	250
Stewart, do	250. —say—	100
Conway do	300 —say—	200
Richardson offers	500	000
Purchase by Cash at Acquia		150
Total to be depended upon		2.300

This quantity will compleat the South wing,—according to the best judgement I can form, on a subject the most complicated & difficult to be calculated, that can be conceived.

As I have said above,—I expect the public Quarry to compleat the work in future Seasons.
                                          B HENRY LATROBE
                                          survr. Public Bldgs U.S.—

MS (DLC); undated; addressed: "The President. U.S."; endorsed by Latrobe "Prospect of Freestone for the public buildgs for the *Year. 1804.*"

Daniel Carroll BRENT and John Cooke (COOK) operated one of the principal quarries at Aquia Creek. Other quarriers included William ROBERTSON, Robert Steuart (STEWART), and Thomas B. CONWAY. Latrobe had recently learned that the quarry of George RICHARDSON was not nearly as extensive as Richardson claimed (Latrobe, *Correspondence*, 1:426n-7n; Latrobe to TJ, 15 Jan.).

From John Thomson Mason

DEAR SIR   Washington 18th Feby 1804

I some time ago took the liberty to enclose to you a letter from my much esteemed friend James Brown of Kentucky expressive of his Wish to serve the United States in their newly acquired territory at the Mouth of the Mississippi. At the request of the same Gentleman I beg leave to make it known to you, that his services, if desired, may be commanded in the Revenue department, either as Collector or Naval Officer, if it is contemplated to establish such there.

I am constrained here to trouble you with a few remarks that regard myself only. My friend the Marshal of this District mentioned to me some time ago, that he had intimated to you, my willingness to serve the United States in these newly acquired regions.

It is true I have very serious thoughts of visiting that Country, but it is in the first place to explore it. Upon this visit, should I determine to remove there, which must depend entirely upon circumstances, that determination will not be the result of views personal to myself individually, influenced by those only, I should remain where I am, my object in going thither, will be the comfortable establishment of sixteen Nephews and Nieces, who are from particular Circumstances placed under my protection, and together with my own growing family seem in some degree to depend upon my own personal exertions

With these objects, should the emegration take place, reflection teaches me, that my whole time and my utmost exertions will be necessary to their attainment. Under this conviction I am determined, should I go, not to embarrass myself with any public or professional business whatever, but to confine my views wholly and exclusively to a comfortable settlement for those whose interests are as dear to me as those of my own family. At my time of my life, now in my fortieth year, it is as much as I can expect to accomplish by every exertion in my power.

I am sure you will pardon the intrusion made upon your time by this explanation from one who is with

Great respect and sincere attachment Your friend & Servt

JOHN T. MASON

RC (DNA: RG 59, LAR); endorsed by TJ as received 20 Feb. and "declines appmt in Louisiana" and so recorded in SJL.

For the letter by JAMES BROWN OF KENTUCKY, see Mason to TJ, 5 Oct. 1803.
MARSHAL OF THIS DISTRICT: Daniel Carroll Brent (Vol. 33:345n).

From Thomas Munroe

Superintendants Office
SIR,   Washington 18 February 1804

The enclosed representation having been this day delivered to me to be laid before you, it may not be improper for the following observations to accompany it.

A man by the name of Jenkins, tenant of Samuel Davidson an Original proprietor claims the right of retaining possession of the part of the City mentioned in the representation, under that part of the Deed of Trust, of which the enclosed is a Copy, and accordingly keeps the same enclosed as a Corn field—. The Cattle, horses and hogs of the Citizens get into this field, and it is said Jenkins frequently kills them—. Several Applications have been made to me for prompt redress under your Authority, and I have told the Applicants they must resort to the Judicial authority, it being the Opinion of the Attorney of the District "that so soon as Appropriations & designations were made by the President whether for streets or other public purposes, and so soon as Lots were sold to individuals, from that moment did the right of the Original proprietor to possess the land so disposed of cease" I have frequently communicated this to Davidson, Jenkins and the persons who have made complaints, as long ago as April last but Jenkins still keeps up his enclosures and justifies it under his landlords construction of the deed of Trust; altho' he admits the streets are designated by the plan of the City, and that lots have been sold in their vicinity; but he contends these lots must be required for actual improvements, that the streets must become necessary for the convenience of the improvers of the lots, or of the public in such degree as to make it manifestly necessary that the Original proprietor should relinquish his possession—.

I have always supposed that these streets were notoriously known as such, and that the plan of the City was a sufficient designation of them, but perhaps you, Sir, may deem it proper to make some declaration on the subject to be published that the Court may have the less hesitation in acting, & Offenders have better information.—

I have the Honor to be with the utmost respect, Sir Yr mo Ob Hum Servt   THOMAS MUNROE

RC (DLC); endorsed by TJ as received 18 Feb. and "inclosures" and so recorded in SJL. Enclosure not found, but see below.

On 13 Apr. 1803, Munroe wrote Thomas JENKINS regarding a written complaint he had received from a number of "respectable inhabitants of this city," that Jenkins's enclosures were obstructing several streets, including "Eleventh street west." He asked Jenkins to allow free passage on the streets so as to "render unnecessary a resort to compulsory measures." A week later, Jenkins proposed erecting gates across the streets. In a letter of the 21st, however, Munroe

explained that the complainants could not accept this solution because of the "injuries which they apprehend would, unavoidably, tho' unintentionally be done to your crops by persons, horses & cattle passing through the fields unprotected by fencing on each side the road or street." He repeated his advice to remove the obstructions to the streets voluntarily. Many years later, a Thomas Jenkins certified that a "trespassing stray" horse had gotten into his enclosures in the district and requested the owner to "prove property, pay charges, and take him away" (Munroe to Thomas Jenkins, 13 and 21 Apr. 1803, DNA: RG 42, LRDLS; *Washington Gazette*, 31 May 1821).

From Thomas Munroe

18 February 1804

T Munroe being informed that the President is engaged with the Secretaries would not ask his signature to the enclosed requisition were he not much urged by Colo. Cooke & Colo. Brents son who are waiting at the Office on their way to Virga. to get $2000 on their Contract for freestone provided the President sanctions the advance— there are $9,944 of the $50,000 in hand—Mr. Latrobe thinks, and says he will write to that effect, that after the payment of the $2000 to Messrs. Cooke & Brent, enough of the $9944 will be left to pay outstanding demands, and to meet the expenses on the Presidents House, & the other expenses which, from conversation with the President he understands it to be necessary to give a preference to out of the unexpended balance—will the President, therefore, if he approves it & deems it necessary say—"The above mentioned advance to Messrs. Cooke & Brent may be paid"

RC (DLC).

COLO. BRENTS SON: either William Brent or Thomas Ludwell Lee Brent, the eldest children of Daniel Carroll Brent

(W. B. Chilton, "The Brent Family [Continued]," VMHB, 17 [1909], 195).

For the ADVANCE to the Aquia Creek quarry owners John Cooke and Daniel Carroll Brent, see the enclosure to Benjamin H. Latrobe's letter of this day.

Notes on a Cabinet Meeting

1804. Feb. 18. Present the 4. Secs. & Atty Genl.

it is agreed we shall consider the settlements on the Misipi[1] from Iberville up to our line, as our territory, as to importations and exportations thro' the Misipi,[2] making Baton rouge a port of delivery. so also as to what shall come thro' Ponchartrain

that the militia of Colour shall be confirmed in their posts, and treated favorably, till a better settled state of things shall permit us to let them neglect themselves.

that an intimation shall be given by Claiborne to Morales that his continuance in that territory is not approved by the Government.

that the remaining Span. troops shall be desired to withdraw.

that Fort Stoddert shall be a port of entry.

that Monroe shall be instructed to negociate as to our lines with Spain, & the extention of territory Eastwd. viz. 1. to the Perdido. 2. to Apalachicola. 3. all E. Florida. that according to the greater or less extent he may give of the following equivalents. 1. relinquish our right from the Rio Bravo, Eastwardly towards the Mexican river. 2. stipulate that a band of country of given breadth shall be established between our white settlements, to be unsettled by either party for a term of years.[3]

3. 1,000,000. Dollars

as to Stevens's accounts, opinions seem not to be satisfactorily formed except by mr Gallatin that there is no fund applicable, & mr Madison that the foreign intercourse fund is applicable. with this last I concur.

MS (DLC: TJ Papers, 131:22677); entirely in TJ's hand; follows, on same sheet, Notes on a Cabinet Meeting of 4 Oct. 1803.

MILITIA OF COLOUR: in a 17 Jan. letter to Madison, William C. C. Claiborne enclosed an address he received from "the free *people of colour*," dated New Orleans, January 1804, and bearing 55 signatures. Identifying themselves as "free Citizens of Louisiana" and natives of the province, the memorialists expressed their "lively Joy" at becoming part of the United States. "We are duly sensible that our personal and political freedom is thereby assured to us for ever," and they expressed their confidence "in the Justice and Liberality of the Government towards every Class of Citizens which they have here taken under their Protection." The memorialists had been employed in military service under the previous government and respectfully offered their services to the new government "as a Corps of Volunteers agreeable to any arrangement which may be thought expedient" (Madison, *Papers, Sec. of State Ser.,* 6:351; *Terr. Papers,* 9:174-5). Writing on 20 Feb., Dearborn informed Claiborne that, after careful consideration of the delicate subject, it had been decided to allow him to continue or renew the "Corps of the Free men of color" as he saw fit. Dearborn added, however, that it would not be prudent to increase the corps, but rather to diminish it "if it can be done without giving offence." The officers should be chosen with due regard for their respectability, integrity, and popularity. The corps might also be presented with a standard or flag "as a token of the confidence placed in them by the Government" (FC in Lb in DNA: RG 107, LSMA).

In a private and confidential letter to Claiborne dated 20 Feb., Madison informed him that the removal of Juan Ventura MORALES, the former Spanish intendant at New Orleans, to some other part of the country "would be agreeable to the President." Citing "his temper and his treasures, his connections and his views," the administration deemed Morales to be a potentially "mischievous member of the society." The means for encouraging Morales's departure from Louisiana, however, were left for Claiborne to determine (Madison, *Papers, Sec. of State Ser.,* 6:496-7).

SPAN. TROOPS: in his 20 Feb. letter to Claiborne, Dearborn stated that it was presumed that Spanish troops and their officers, both civil and military, had already left New Orleans and its vicinity. If this was not the case, Claiborne was to use "prudent and reasonable measures" to effect the complete Spanish evacuation of Louisiana as soon as possible (FC in Lb in DNA: RG 107, LSMA).

E. FLORIDA: an undated, unsigned manuscript in TJ's papers, entitled "Notes sur la floride," extolled the economic, strategic, and political value of acquiring both Floridas, especially East Florida. Writing in French, the unidentified author asserted that the peninsula contained interior lands well suited to the cultivation of a variety of crops, as well as valuable forests and coastal fisheries. Its proximity to key navigation routes gave East Florida strategic importance, while possession of both Floridas would end disputes over the southern boundary of the United States and provide greater security against foreign invasion or hostile Indians. The author further suggested that existing slaveholders could establish themselves in the Floridas, and that free blacks and mulattoes could be banished there as well. The friends of slavery ("Les Amis de l'Esclavage"), the author continued, had little fondness for the present government, so concentrating them in the south would lessen their influence on the other states. The author urged the acquisition of the Floridas, given their potential importance to the United States, even if it meant exchanging them for the part of Louisiana west of the Mississippi River (MS in DLC: TJ Papers, 235:42230-1).

[1] Preceding three words interlined.
[2] Preceding three words interlined.
[3] Preceding five words interlined.

From Thomas Sumter, Sr.

Satuor'y, 18th. Feby. 1804—

T Sumter Beg leave to mention to the President of the United States—that Mr. Mullegan of Charleston So Carola. is Anxious to have an appointment under the Governt. to be instituted in the County. of Louia. to wit, Marshall—

at a suitable time other Communications will be submitted on this Subject—

RC (DNA: RG 59, LAR); addressed: "The President of the United States"; endorsed by TJ as received 18 Feb. and "Mulligan to be Marshal Louisiana" and so recorded in SJL.

TJ appointed Francis Mulligan (MULLEGAN) a bankruptcy commissioner for South Carolina in 1802 (Vol. 37:711; Vol. 39:633). For his earlier solicitations for office, see Vol. 39:586n.

To Caspar Wistar

DEAR SIR   Washington Feb. 18. 04.

Having recieved the inclosed essay on public education from it's author, the revd. mr Knox, &, as I presume with a view that it should be communicated to the Philosophical society, I take the liberty of putting it under cover to you for that purpose, and to present you my salutations & respect.   TH: JEFFERSON

RC (William Reese Company, New Haven, Connecticut, 2001); at foot of text: "Doctr. Wistar." PrC (DLC); endorsed by TJ in ink on verso. Recorded in SJL with notation "Knox's essay." Enclosure: Samuel Knox, An Essay, on the Means of Improving Public Education, Adapted to the United States (Frederick, Md., 1803).

Samuel KNOX, an Irish-born Presbyterian minister and Maryland educator, had previously sent TJ a copy of An Essay on the Best System of Liberal Education, which was published in 1799 in Baltimore. Its publication was the result of a competition held in 1797 by the American Philosophical Society in which Knox shared a prize with Samuel Harrison Smith for the best essay on education. Knox was also the pseudonymous author, signing himself as "A Friend to Real Religion," of A Vindication of the Religion of Mr. Jefferson, and a Statement of His Services in the Cause of Religious Liberty, printed separately as a pamphlet in Baltimore in 1800 as well as appended to William Pechin's edition of TJ's Notes on the

State of Virginia (ANB; DAB; APS, Transactions, 4 [1799], iv, vii; Sowerby, No. 1114; RS, 2:174n).

IT SHOULD BE COMMUNICATED: the 1803 octavo essay, which Knox dedicated to TJ as president of the United States, president of the APS, and "the Liberal Patron of Science and Humanity," appeared in a list of donations from individuals to the society printed the next year (APS, Transactions, 6, pt. 1 [1804], xiv).

From "Your Freind"

[on or before 18 Feb. 1804]

Keep the Good of your Country at heart and do well and the Lord will reward you   YOUR FREIND

RC (DLC); undated; addressed: "Optimo Viro in hac patria Esquire qui est salvator patria sua et maximus Amicus humani Generis hoc Tempore—Federal City, Washington" (that is, "the Best Man in this country, Esquire; who is the savior of the human race at this time, a friend of his own country, and a great man") and "mail"; stamped; above address in pencil in unidentified hand: "This must be intended for the present President of the US"; endorsed by TJ as received from an anonymous writer on 18 Feb. and "Latin inscription" and so recorded in SJL.

From John Armstrong

SIR/   Cincinnati February 20th. 1804

Captain Lewis on his way to the Westward called on me and requested that I would at the proper season furnish you with some cuttings, from my Nursery, which you will receive herewith,

No. 1. 2. 3. & 4 were sent me from detroit two years since. No. 5 & 6 are from bearing trees in my Orchard—

No 1 Large White apple—tied with a White string

No. 2 Large Red apple tied with a red string

No. 3 Pumgray an apple much admired and will keep the year round tied with a blue string

No. 4 Calvit apple which is without comparison the best apple that ever was Eaten—tied with a green string

No. 5 Ox Eye striped apple ripe in the fall, highly flavoured weighs from 16 to 20 Oz—tied with a yellow string

No. 6 Egg Plumb as large as a hens egg light coloured rich & Sweet with a small stone will succeed by engrafting on a Damson, Wild Plumb or Peach stock—

I generally cut my cions at this Season of the year, and place one end of the cuttings about two inches in the ground in a perpendicular position and there let them remain until the proper season for placing them into the stock—I practice Tounge Grafting, and seldom lose five trees out of one thousand, have had trees to bear the second year after ingrafting them—

It would oblige me if thro some of your friends I could obtain a few cuttings of the Virginia Cyder apple generally called Hughes Crab with a description of the fruit—

While I have the honor to be with due respect your Obd. Servt.

JOHN ARMSTRONG

RC (MHi); at foot of text: "His Excellency Thomas Jefferson"; endorsed by TJ as received 6 Mch. and so recorded in SJL.

John Armstrong was married to Tabitha Goforth, the daughter of William Goforth, on whom Meriwether LEWIS relied for information about the mammoth excavations at Big Bone Lick. News of the legendary produce of Armstrong's NURSERY in Columbia, Ohio, circulated beyond Cincinnati in 1802 (Jackson, *Lewis and Clark*, 2:684-5; Peacham, Vt., *Green Mountain Patriot*, 27 Oct. 1802; *Philadelphia Repository*, 6 Nov. 1802).

The pomme gris (PUMGRAY) was a dessert apple that came from French North America. The CALVIT apple was an anglicized form of the Calville Blanc d'Hiver variety that had been introduced into the Michigan territory by the French. The EGG PLUMB, or Yellow Egg, was a variety of the magnum bonum plum known for its golden yellow hue, large shape, and usefulness in preserving and baking. TJ tried to graft it with the popular DAMSON or Damascene cultivar (Peter J. Hatch, *The Fruits and Fruit Trees of Monticello* [Charlottesville, 1998], 49, 76-8, 112, 114). CIONS: scions.

To Albert Gallatin

DEAR SIR   Washington Feb. 20. 04.

Expecting that mr Madison & yourself would be able with a little discussion to make up an opinion on Dr. Stevens's case, I had not given it any serious consideration. I have now however done so and I send you the result, asking the favor of you to make any observations to which you may think it open in matters of fact, inference, or omission. on receipt of these I will give it a final consideration in order to bring the subject to a close. accept affectionate salutations.

TH: JEFFERSON

PrC (DLC); at foot of text: "The Secretary of the Treasury." Recorded in SJL with notation "Dr. Stevens's case."

DR. STEVENS'S CASE: on 24 Dec. 1803, Richard Harrison, at the auditor's office, notified Madison that he concurred with the opinion that although Edward Stevens went to Saint-Domingue with a com-

mission as U.S. consul general, "his powers were in fact those of a Minister and that his *Expenses* while on the mission were to be reimbursed by the United States." Stevens had submitted an expense statement totaling $27,325, including $20,350 for travel and household maintenance, but he had supplied no vouchers. Thus, the auditor noted, they could not be "admitted consistently with the Rules which generally govern in settlements at the Treasury." Harrison suggested that Stevens's original agreement be modified to allow an annual sum "judged reasonable, & sufficient" to cover his expenses. Comptroller Gabriel Duvall concurred. On 27 Dec., Harrison again wrote Madison: "I am still decidedly of Opinion that whatever allowance he is to have, whether in the shape of compensation, or as a Reimbursement of *Expenses* must be fixed by some superior Authority before it can be admitted by the Accounting Officers of the Treasury" (Madison, *Papers, Sec. of State Ser.*, 6:209-10, 236). Stevens submitted his accounts in April 1802 when John Steele was comptroller. Steele also raised questions about the expenditures (see same, 3:96-7, 134, 150-1; 8:563).

ENCLOSURE

Memorandum on the Edward Stevens Claim

Doctr. Stevens having been sent by the preceding administration in 1798. to St. Domingo, with the Commission of Consul general, and also with authorities as an agent additional to his[1] Consular powers, under a stipulation that his expences should be born; an account of these is now exhibited to the Secretary of state and the questions arise Whether the paiment can be authorised by the Executive, and out of what fund?

The constitution has made the Executive the organ for managing our intercourse with foreign nations. it authorises him to appoint & recieve Ambassadors, other public ministers, & consuls. the term *minister* being applicable[2] to other agents as well as diplomatic, the constant practice of the government, considered as a commentary, establishes this broad meaning; and the public interest approves it; because it would be extravagant to employ a diplomatic minister for a business which a mere rider could execute. the Executive being thus charged with the foreign intercourse, no law has undertaken to prescribe[3] it's specific duties. the permanent act of 1801. however, 1. when he uses the agency of a Min. plenipo. or Chargé, restricts him in the sums to be allowed for outfit, salary, return & a secretary, and 2. when any law has appropriated a sum for the *contingent* expences of foreign intercourse, leaves to his discretion to dispense with the exhibition of the vouchers of it's expenditure in the public offices.[4] under these two standing provisions, there is annually a sum appropriated 'for the expences of intercourse with foreign nations.' the *purposes* of the appropriation being expressed by the *law* in terms as general as the *duties* are by the *constitution*, the application of the money is left as much to the discretion of the Executive, as the performance of the duties: saving always the provisions of 1801.

It is true that this appropriation is usually made on an estimate, given by the Secretary of state to the Secretary of the Treasury, & by him reported to Congress. but Congress, aware that too minute a specification has it's evils as well as a too general one, does not make the estimate a part of their law, but gives a sum in gross, trusting the Executive discretion for that year, & that sum only. so, in other departments, as of War for instance the estimate of the Secretary specifies all the items of cloathing, subsistence, pay &c of the army: and Congress throw this into such masses as they think best, to wit, a sum in gross for cloathing, another for subsistence, a third for pay &c. binding up the executive discretion only by the sum, & the object generalised to a certain degree.[5] the minute details of the estimate are thus dispensed with in point of obligation, & the discretion of the officer is enlarged to the limits of the classification[6] which Congress thinks it best for the public interest to make. in the case before us then, the sum appropriated may be applied to any agency with a foreign nation, which the constitution has made a part of the duty of the President,[7] as the organ of foreign intercourse.

The sum appropriated is generally the exact amount of the estimate, but not always. in the present instance, the estimate, being for 1803. was only of 62,550. D. (including two outfits) and the appropriation was of 75,562 D. leaving a difference of 13,012 D.

If indeed there be not enough of this appropriation left to pay Dr. Stevens's just demands, they cannot be paid until Congress shall make some appropriation applicable to them. I say his *just* demands: because by the undertaking of the then administration to pay his expences, justice as well as law will understand his *reasonable* expences. these must be tried by[8] the scale which law & usage have established, whereon the Minister, Chargé, & Secretary are given as fixed terms of comparison. the undefined agency of Dr. Stevens must be placed *opposite* to that term of the scale, with which it may fairly be thought to correspond: and if he has gone beyond that, his expences should be reduced to it. I think them beyond it, and suppose that Dr. Stevens, viewing himself as a merchant, as well as a public agent, found it answer his purposes as a merchant to apply a part of his reciepts in that character in addition[9] to what he might reasonably expect from the public, not then meaning to charge[10] to his public character the extraordinary stile of expence which he believed at the time he could afford out of his mercantile profits.

TH: JEFFERSON
Feb. 19. 1804

PrC (DLC); endorsed by TJ. Dft (same). Recorded in SJL as a communication to the Treasury Department with notation "Dr. Stevens's case."

SENT BY THE PRECEDING ADMINISTRATION: for Edward Stevens's appointment in February 1799 and his mission, see Vol. 31:44, 45n, 49; Vol. 33:447; Vol. 37:234-5, 455-7.

PERMANENT ACT OF 1801: that is, the act of 10 May 1800, entitled "An Act to ascertain the compensation of public Ministers." The act gave the president the power to settle accounts under any law making an appropriation for contingent expenses of relations with foreign nations and to make "a certificate of the amount of such expenditures as he may think it advisable not to specify, and every such certificate shall be deemed a sufficient voucher for the sum or sums therein expressed to have been expended" (U.S. Statutes at Large, 2:78-9). For the SUM

APPROPRIATED in 1803 for the expense of foreign relations, see same, 2:214. The estimate of $62,550 for the "diplomatic department" is included in *Letter from the Secretary of the Treasury, Accompanying a Report and Estimates of Appropriation for the Service of the Year 1803* (Washington, D.C., 1802), 5.

[1] Preceding three words interlined in place of "not at all comprehended within the."

[2] Word interlined in Dft in place of "constantly applied."

[3] Word interlined in place of "delineate" in Dft.

[4] See TJ to Gallatin, 21 Feb., for his instructions to cancel the remainder of the paragraph and substitute text in its place. In Dft, TJ canceled the remainder of the paragraph and wrote in the margin: "To give the Executive the *means* of fulfilling the constitutional duty of maintaining the foreign intercourse, and even

to *supply* the *authority*, if the constitutional words be deemed inexplicit or defective, a sum is annually appropriated for the expences of intercourse with foreign nations. if we consider this as giving the *means* only of fulfilling the constitutional duty, then it leaves their application to his discretion as generally, as the constitution had left the duties. if, as in some other cases, the appropriation intends, by the same words, both to legalize the object, and give the means, then the latitude of the expression here used, gives the same latitude of execution, saving always the general regulations of the act of 1801."

⁵ In Dft, TJ first wrote "by the sum and the purpose," which he changed to "by

the sum and the general object" before altering the passage to read as above.

⁶ Dft: "general classification."

⁷ In Dft, TJ first wrote "which the constitution has made a part of his duty" before altering the passage to read "which either the constitution or the appropriation has made a part of the duty of the President."

⁸ Preceding two words interlined in Dft in place of "reduced to."

⁹ Preceding two words interlined.

¹⁰ In Dft, TJ first wrote "not then thinking of charging the whole" before altering the text to read as above.

From Albert Gallatin

DEAR SIR   20 Feb. 1804

I enclose a number of papers relative to the removal of   Banning Collector at Oxford Maryland. Of the propriety of his removal there never was a doubt; but the Republicans would not agree about a successor. They have now all united in favor of John Willis, and as even Mr Nicholson who was the warmest supporter of the other candidate agrees to it, there cannot, I think, be any difficulty in it. The late removal of Selby has rendered the Repub. more impatient at the continuance of Banning.

Respectfully Your obedt. Servt.   ALBERT GALLATIN

RC (DLC); at foot of text: "The President of the United States"; endorsed by TJ as received from the Treasury Department on 20 Feb. and "Banning Collector at Oxfd. Maryld. to be removd Willis to be appointed" and so recorded in SJL. Enclosures: (1) Joseph Telford and Philemon Willis to Gallatin, Easton, Maryland, 7 Mch. 1803, stating again their complaints against the collector Robert Banning, who refused to give a second bond unless the first was paid or to provide certificates to allow reshipment; Telford and William Meluy's shipment of cotton was detained at Baltimore when the officer there informed them certificates were "absolutely necessary" and nothing could be done "with the Cotton untill it was taken back to Mr. Ban-

ning" to procure the certificates; Banning showed a letter, reportedly from the Treasury secretary, indicating that Gallatin "approved of his conduct" with the bonds; a few days later Banning confronted Willis and observed that the Treasury secretary had written him "that what we stated in our first Letter to you were lies"; the writers continue: "we do assure you we did not believe him in this, more than we did the paragraph he shewed us, which stated, you approved of his conduct in compelling us to pay off our first Bonds (tho' not due) before he wou'd suffer us to Bond for the second Cargo" (RC in DNA: RG 59, LAR). (2) Samuel Dickinson, William Harrison, and Joseph Newcome to Gallatin, Easton, 9 Mch. 1803, recommending John Willis in place of the officer at Oxford; recommendations have already been sent to Robert Wright, Joseph H. Nicholson, and Gabriel Duvall, and others will be sent in a few days; Willis's appointment would "oblige a Generous Public" (RC in same; endorsed by TJ: "Willis John. v. Banning Collector of Oxford"). (3) Samuel Smith to Gallatin, 11 Mch. 1803, endorsing a petition in favor of John Willis as collector in place of Banning, whose "Removal Can do no Injury," but "the Obliging of the respectable Gentlemen who subscribe the memorial may and will do much good" (same). (4) Caleb Stanfield, Thomas Pamphilon, and Richard Barnaby to Gallatin, Oxford, 22 Mch. 1803; thinking that a new appointment will soon be made to replace the naval officer at Oxford, they recommend John Willis, an established citizen of the port, who "is a man of business real merit &c." and "the only friend that we had to mr. Jefferson's Election" (same; for TJ's note on address sheet, see below). (5) Statement by William Meluy, Easton, 19 Apr. 1803, recalling the August 1802 encounter between Telford and Philemon Willis and Banning over bonds; Meluy states that Banning later produced a letter which he said was from Gallatin approving of his conduct; Telford later informed Meluy that he did not think the letter was from the Treasury secretary, and Meluy observed that "if it was, it must have been in answer to an improper statement of his Business, and if Mr. Banning had let him read the whole of the letter, he might have soon determined what it alluded to"; Meluy then recounts a case in which cotton from Anguilla was delayed at Baltimore because Banning had not issued the necessary papers; enclosed in Wright and Nicholson to Gallatin, Easton, 19 Apr., endorsing Meluy, Telford, and Philemon Willis as persons in whom "full faith may be given to any facts stated by them"; after making full inquiry into Banning's conduct, Wright and Nicholson believe "that he ought to be removed from office" and that "his Removal will give general Satisfaction" (same). (6) Nicholson to Gallatin, Easton, 21 Apr. 1803, noting that, as promised, he has made "enquiry into the Pretensions of John Willis as successor to Banning";

as Willis's letters indicate, he is "excessively ignorant and conceited, and totally unfit for the place"; Nicholson recommends Edward Markland for the office, describing him as "a sober, steady judicious man, with an unexceptionable Character" who will "prove an excellent Officer" and "give general Satisfaction"; Nicholson reports "a universal Disgust prevailing against Banning" and believes "Willis has been recommended more with a View of getting Banning out, than from any Opinion of his own fitness"; he recommends that no time should be lost in removing Banning, as he "is really odious to our Friends and disliked generally by Federalists" (same; endorsed by TJ: "Markland Edwd. v. Banning Collectr. Oxford"). (7) Memorial by Robert Orvill, William Rose, Edward Lloyd, John Hardcastle, all members of the Maryland legislature, William Whitely, a state senator, and four others to Gallatin, 10 May 1803; believing that the present naval officer at Oxford is to be removed, they recommend John Willis as a resident of the port who is well qualified for the office and "bears the Character of an honest, Steady, sober Man" with commercial experience; he is "an excellent Scholar, writes an excellent hand, and we think he is a Man of firmness and Integrity, and know him to be a Zealous Supporter of the Present Administration" (same). (8) Thomas Coward and 14 others to Gallatin, undated; as captains and owners of vessels trading at Oxford, they recommend John Willis, a resident of the port, as fully qualified to fill the office of naval officer when the long expected removal of the present officer takes place; they note the "great disadvantage of the present officers not residing at the place where the office is kept, and the delay occasioned frequently, by his deputy not having a Sufficient Knowledge of the business"; they believe Willis to be a man of integrity and ability and a strong friend and supporter of the present administration (same; endorsed by Gallatin). (9) Lloyd, Rose, Coward, and four others to Gallatin, Talbot County, 30 Jan. 1804, apologizing for once again writing about the collector's office at Oxford, but they understand that Gallatin has received new information about transactions at the port; although John Willis and Markland are both qualified and good Republicans, they support Willis because the collector's office remains at Oxford, the place of his residence; "two-thirds of the friends in the district" think that Willis is entitled to a preference and "that he is in every respect fully quallifed to perform the several duties attached to the office" (same). (10) Nicholson to Gallatin, [ca. 20 Feb. 1804], enclosing "a Letter last night recd. in Relation to the Collector's office at the Port of Oxford" (perhaps Enclosure No. 9); Nicholson states "You had probably better give the place to Willis" (same).

In an undated note to the president written on the address sheet of Nicholson's letter to the Treasury secretary (see Enclosure No. 10) that Gallatin headed: "Oxford. John Willis agreed on as successor to Banning" and "Collector of the district of Oxford Md. and Inspector of the revenue for the port of Oxford," Gallatin wrote: "The propriety of the removal is respectfully submitted—Mr Banning has acted in one instance with great impropriety & his removal would long ago have been submitted, had it not been for the disagreement about a proper successor—Albert Gallatin" (MS in DNA: RG 59, LAR); at foot of text: "The President of the United States"). For papers calling for Banning's removal that Gallatin had shared with TJ in April 1802, see Vol. 37:387-8.

For the removal of William SELBY, collector at Snowhill, Maryland, see Vol. 41:729-30 and Nicholson to TJ, 29 Nov. On the address sheet of Enclosure No. 4, above, TJ noted: "Banning Collector of Oxford. Maryld charges against him 1. refusing credit unless a bond not due was paid. 2. denying a certificate for draw back 3. lives 12. miles off, which occasions inconvence"; see also TJ to Gallatin, 21 Feb.

From Benjamin H. Latrobe

SIR,   Washington, Feby. 20th. 1804

On the 4th. of April 1803, I had the honor to lay before you a general report, on the State of the public Buildings in this City. I now beg leave to submit to you an account of the progress that has been made in the works directed by you in consequence of that report: and in order more clearly to explain the subject, I beg to recapitulate concisely what I formerly stated.

I. *On the North Wing of the Capitol.*

On a careful survey of the North wing of the Capitol it was found, that the want of Air & light in the Cellar story, had began to produce decay in the Timbers,—that the roof was leaky, & the cielings & walls of several of the Apartments were thereby injured,—that it would be impossible to render the Senate Chamber, the extreme coldness of which was matter of serious complaint, more warm and comfortable without the construction of stoves or furnaces below the floor for which purpose it would be necessary to carry up additional flues, and to remove a very large quantity of rubbish from the Cellars:—and that the Skylights were extremely out of repair.

During the course of the last Season therefore openings have been made into all the Cellars, the decayed timbers have been replaced where immediately necessary,—the floors that required it have received additional support, the Senate Chamber has been rendered more comfortable by the introduction of warm air,—by the erection of a stove,—by the exclusion of cold air from the Cellar by plaistering,—and should the plan adopted after the experience of the present Session be approved, another Stove is ready to be put up:—All the Cellars have been cleared and the rubbish removed. In respect to the roof, the best repairs which could be made without unroofing the whole wing, have been made, and the leaks rendered of less importance:—but the early meeting of Congress, and the magnitude, & the doubtful completion as to time, of a thorough repair by taking off the whole upper part of the roof,—induced me to postpone this operation. Every preparation however is made, and the lead which covers so great a part of the roof will contribute greatly to defray the expense of this thorough repair.—

The sky lights have also been *only* repaired, but it is necessary to substitute in their room Lanthorn lights, with upright Sashes and close tops. This Work has also been deferred, and for the same reasons.

General repairs of those parts of the building which were hastily & slightly executed previously to the removal of the seat of Government were also necessary, and they have been made.—

II. On the South Wing of the Capitol.

On the 4h. of April 1804, it was necessary to report to you,—that on opening, in order to examine the Walls of the Cellar story of the South wing of the Capitol the workmanship was found to have been so unfaithfully performed, as to render it absolutely necessary to take them down to the foundation, and that even the greatest part of the Materials were too bad to be used again.—Previously therefore to the commencement of the work upon this Wing all the old external Walls were removed. The new Work was executed with the best Materials and in the most durable manner that could be devised.—Great disadvantages were encountered at the commencement of the Season. The long intermission of public Work, had scattered the Workmen, and the supply of materials was difficult and tardy. The work however which has been done, is considerable. The Walls have been raised to nearly half the heighth of the Ground story. The preparations for further progress,—should the Legislature direct the same, are also great, and materials are now collected on the Spot nearly sufficient, and already prepared to finish the external Walls of the lower story. The rapidity and greater oeconomy with which the work will in future proceed are also an advantage gained. A system for the supply of materials is now organized,—a great number of excellent Workmen are collected, and the expense of Machinery, scaffolding, & utensils defrayed.—

The Hall in which the House of Representatives are now assembled was erected as part of the permanent building. I am however under the necessity of representing to you, that the whole of the Masonry from the very foundation is of such bad workmanship and materials, that it would have been dangerous to have assembled within the building, had not the Walls been strongly supported by shores from without.—For easy examination the Wall has been opened in several places, and an actual inspection will immediately explain the state in which it is.

Besides the Work done to secure the present Building,—it has been lighted in the best manner which the construction of the roof will admit,—in order to remedy the diminution of light by carrying up the external Walls.—The encrease of the number of the Members of the House this session, rendered it necessary to take up the Platform, and to enlarge the space for seats. This has also been done, & forms part of the Expenditure of the Season.

In my former report, I took the liberty to suggest the propriety of considering whether any & what improvement of the original plan of the Work, might be necessary for the better accomodation of the House of Representatives in the South Wing of the Capitol, so as to bring the Offices attached to the house nearer to the Legislative Hall. The attention You have already been pleased to give to this subject encourages me to suggest the necessity of an ultimate decision previously to the Commencement of the Work of the ensuing Season.

III. The President's house.—

Agreeably to Your desire that the Monies appropriated by the Legislature should be devoted as much as possible to the erection of the Capitol & to the accomodation of the Legislature,—the expenditure on the President's house has been kept as low as possible.

In my former report to You on this building I state;—that the Roof & gutters were so leaky as to render it necessary to take off all the Slating; to take up all the gutters & to give them much more current, and to cover the building with Sheet iron, as uniting safety against fire with Oeconomy;—To strengthen & tie together the roof which having spread, has forced out the Walls;—to put up the Staircase, which was already prepared;—to sink a Well for the purpose of procuring good Water, of which the house was in absolute Want;—to glaze those Apartments which required it, & to complete some accomodations wanted in the Chamber story.

All these Works, except the complete repair of the roof have been done. The work on the roof is however in progress, and the funds remaining in hand are estimated to be sufficient to complete this object.—

The superintendant of the City has favored me with the necessary information to give the following Statement of Expenditures, up to this day.—

1.	The expenditure of monies out of the fund of 50.000$, on the roads, and on objects not placed by You under my direction,		4.832	63
2./	On the North wing of the Capitol,			
	a. In repairs	$1.573.22½		
	b. On the Senate Chamber	1.168.34½		
			2.681	57
3.	On the South Wing			
	a. Repairs &c of the Hall of Representatives	555.13½		
	b. Materials, Labor & Superintendance of the Work of the South Wing	31.190.23½		
		31.745.37	31.745	37
4.	On the President's House. Repairs, and Works Enumerated above		2.251	67
5.	Balance, estimated to be sufficient to discharge unsettled & outstanding accts.—to complete existing contracts of last Season,—to pay advances on new Contracts, & prepare to lay in a Stock of new materials		8.488	76
			50.000	

The above statement, collected in many instances from running, and unsettled accounts, is necessarily liable to corrections in detail,—which cannot however in any case, materially affect the results stated.—

The Season is now at hand in which preparations for the Work of the present Year should be made. I therefore respectfully submit the premises to Your consideration,—and am

Your faithful humble servt.,

B HENRY LATROBE
surveyor of the public Buildings
of the United States at Washington.

P.S. I beg leave to add, that to compleat the Work *in freestone* of the South wing,—which is the most expensive part of the building, the sum of 30.000$ will be sufficient, according to the best Estimate which can be made.

RC (DNA: RG 233, PM, 8th Cong., 1st sess.); at head of text: "To the President of the United States"; endorsed by Latrobe and a House clerk. PoC (DNA: RG 46, LPPM, 8th Cong., 1st sess.); endorsed by Latrobe and a Senate clerk. Enclosed in TJ to the Senate and the House of Representatives, 22 Feb.

Latrobe preferred LANTHORN LIGHTS, or small, open structures at the top of a roof or dome, to skylights because he be-

lieved them less subject to leaks and less vulnerable to summer heat (Carl R. Lounsbury, ed., *An Illustrated Glossary of Early Southern Architecture and Landscape* [New York, 1994], 205-6).

The temporary structure in which the HOUSE OF REPRESENTATIVES met, known derisively as the "oven," was contained within the foundation of the south wing but was never intended as a PERMANENT BUILDING (Allen, *History of the United States Capitol*, 55-6).

From Caesar A. Rodney

[. . .]

HONORED & [. . .]   Feby. 20. [1804]

[. . .] attachment which I feel [. . .] your administration, & for [. . .] state the reasons which have [. . .] me absolutely to decline being [. . .] [for] the seat I now hold, at the ensu[ing] [. . .]

When [I agre]ed to stand a poll for Rep: to Cong. it [. . .] consequence of very pressing solicitations & from a beleif, which the opinions of others had impressed on my mind, that I might possibly turn out Mr. Bayard, who had been so extremely violent, as to rouse not only political, but to excite personal feeling against him. At the time I was dependent on my profession alone for the support of a numerous family & I was well aware of the fatal effects it would have on my practice & which I have since felt. The times I thought called for the sacrifice & I was [willing?] [. . .] I was successf[ul] [. . .] & its champ[. . .] the mark of Repu[. . .] [. . .] our flag. The few [. . .] [. . .]ings of this description [. . .] a dozen, I believe to be worn [. . .]. They ought to be consider[. . .] [. . .]

Stripped [. . .] by tories & toryism of a large estate [. . .] my uncle Cæsar Rodney with whom [. . .] well acquainted, thro the friendship & [. . .] [Gov]ernor McKean from purely patriotic motives I was enabled to commence life in my professional character. By my practice I have maintained not only myself & family but my father & sister, together with the family of an Aunt for a number of years. And should before this, have acquired a competence had not an attack of the yellow fever in 98' brought me to the verge of the grave & laid the foundation of a state of extreme ill health which contin[ued] [. . .] 1800. 1801. I was [. . .] & indeed afterw[ards] [. . .] my profession with [. . .] am now in the [. . .] [be]tter state of health [. . .] & can therefore [. . .] with increased assiduity [. . .] me to this step at this period. I have [. . .] [. . .]ved that my present situation is ruinous [. . .] business. Recollect the judges are [. . .] [. . .]al & I have no favor to expect now [. . .] it from the Court: Another reason which I cannot fully explain but which you will feel the force of, in consequence of a change of disposition on the part of one who ought to aid & assist me produced too by federal intrigue, my family situation is so altered that I would not for any consideration be dependent for a single dollar. This reason with a man of independent mind is insuperable & with me it has been conclusive, ever since I was [. . .] not suffer [. . .]

[. . .] that I should not be [. . .] I was first set up, & [. . .] resolution they have [. . .] again & you will perceive [. . .] from Read Montgomery & A[. . .] [. . .] I have been pressed. They are a few of [. . .] number I have received. Mr. Read [. . .] you know. Dr Alexander has been once [. . .] for Governor & once for Rep. to Cong. T. Montgomery has been our candidate for Governor also.

I enclose you also letters from my friends J. Warner & H. Niles which contain some material information. As to Vaughan who submitted to a public cow-skinning from a *Fed.* sometime ago & Mendenhall who has lately submitted to a caning from a Republican, they are of themselves too contemptible to be named. But to me the authors of the [. . .] Clane, for the [. . .], now leagued [. . .] mischief excites in [. . .] [be]cause they have no [. . .] but on the subject of [. . .] the game which this infamous [. . .] to play at the last Boro[ugh] [. . .], when the barge-men were all ma[. . .] [. . .] [. . .]te. They consider Wilmington as the [. . .] of Republicanism & endeavor by little [. . .] difference about market houses spring water & strict regulations to create division, in hopes that in time it will extend itself to politicks. Mr. Dickenson who had been too long imposed on by the artifice & sycophaney of Vaughan gave me when I visited home a dinner at which the principal Republicans of the Borough & its vicinity were invited. J. Warner, Dr. Tilton. Dr. Alexander &c &c. This was the signal for Bayard & B[. . .] [. . .] [. . .]fest that conn[. . .] [. . .] [. . .]isted & it is [. . .] to them.

[. . .] [appear] at public meetings. [. . .] [. . .]ble to revolutionise Ke[. . .] [. . .] electors of Prest. & V. Prest. [. . .] a fair opportunity of att[. . .] [. . .] I shall not fail to improve.

Tho' I [. . .] promise myself to be of so much use & importance, as you have been partial enough to me, to suppose, yet after an acquaintance with the rules of the house & the forms of proceeding & understanding the temper of members I could be of much more service than hitherto. Thus far I have endeavoured to pursue that unassuming course which should not excite the least jealousy & to adopt that line of conduct which might enable me to heal any [. . .] [. . .]ing acquired in a [. . .] house & attained [. . .] endeavour to imitate [. . .] by associating with the [. . .] in their different lodgings & [. . .] very great subject before it [. . .] house. This is the proper [. . .] [num] erous a body. It would require [. . .] time but it would be well [. . .] heretofore been principally occupied in writing letters [. . .] I seldom write less than a dozen [. . .] hoping it will produce a good effect. [I will] thank you to return this as I have not time to copy it

Yours most Sincerely C. A. RODNEY

RC (DLC); torn, large portions of text lost; partially dated; endorsed by TJ as received 21 Feb. and so recorded in SJL, which also indicates that the letter was written at Washington. Enclosures not found.

PRESSING SOLICITATIONS, including one from TJ, convinced Rodney to run for the congressional seat held by James A. Bayard (Vol. 37:330, 386-7; Vol. 38:638). In a letter to TJ in 1800, Rodney sketched his early career, including the loss of the LARGE ESTATE he inherited from his uncle Caesar Rodney and the role of Thomas McKean as "a second father" (see Vol. 32:370-1). George READ, Thomas MONTGOMERY, and Archibald ALEXANDER pressed Rodney to run for reelection. In early 1804, Rodney informed his friends and Delaware's Democratic nominating conference that under no circumstances would he

run again. The Democratic-Republicans, however, had already met at Dover on 20 Jan. and unanimously selected him as their candidate. Read and John WARNER were among the New Castle conferees at the meeting. On 13 Feb., Rodney explained to Read: "My profession is my sole support & my only dependence." Bayard reminded his political opponent that losing the 1802 election meant he was now "employed in the homely drudgery of making money," while Rodney was "in the refined and elegant pursuit of attaining honour and reputation" (John A. Munroe, *Federalist Delaware, 1775-1815* [New Brunswick, N.J., 1954], 232-3; Bayard to Rodney, 10 Dec. 1803, in "James Asheton Bayard Letters, 1802-1814," *Bulletin of the New York Public Library,* 4 [1900], 230; Wilmington *Mirror of the Times, & General Advertiser,* 4 Feb. 1804).

From James Taylor, Jr.

SIR Norfolk Febry 20th. 1804

I have deferred answering your favors of 29 Jany & 1 feb: in hopes of being able to give you information that the myrtle wax candles coud be procured—I have made enquiry wherever there was a chance of procuring the wax, & have several people looking out for it, but fear I shall not succeed—Colonel Cook of Surry has promised to send me a few barrel of Cyder, if he can get such as is worth sending to you; your directions respecting the casing shall be attended to—the pipe of Wine & one box of champaigne shall be sent by Butler, it would be better to request some person in Alexr. to attend to reshipping the articles sent from hence—Colo: Newton has been very much indisposed since his return & is still confind—I am respectfully

Yr: ob: Sert.   JA TAYLOR JR

RC (MHi); endorsed by TJ as received 27 Feb. and so recorded in SJL.

COLONEL COOK OF SURRY: probably a member of the Cocke family, which had played a prominent role in Surry County for many years. Possibilities include Richard Cocke, whose home was actually in neighboring Isle of Wight County, and John Hartwell Cocke, who had ties to Norfolk through his wife (Norfolk *American Beacon*, 20 Feb. 1816; "The Cocke Family of Virginia [Henrico]," VMHB, 5 [1897], 71, 73, 78).

SENT BY BUTLER: likely Tristram Butler, who in November had handled a shipment for TJ from Norfolk to Alexandria (Edward Johnston to TJ, 23 Nov. 1803).

From Antoine Louis Claude Destutt de Tracy

a auteuil prés paris ce 1er. Ventose an 12.

MONSIEUR,   (21 fevrier 1804)

Le General la Fayette me mande qu'il a bien voulu vous faire hommage de ma part, d'un ouvrage qui traite de la formation de nos idées; mais qu'il ne vous est pas parvenu. je regrette que la Seconde edition que l'on prepare ne Soit pas encor faite, par ce qu'elle contiendra quelques additions importantes. en attendant j'ai l'honneur de vous envoyer de nouveau la premiere; et j'y joins une Seconde partie que j'ai publiée depuis, et qui traite de l'expression de nos idées. la troisieme a laquelle je travaille, traitera de leur deduction; et complettera le Sujet.

j'attache un grand interest a ce que cet ecrit ait l'avantage d'etre connu de vous. je n'ose esperer qu'il merite le Suffrage que j'ambitionne le plus dans le monde; mais j'aime à me flatter que l'homme d'etat et le philosophe eclairé qui fait le bonheur d'un grand peuple et contribue puissamment aux progrés de l'humanité toute entiere, verra avec indulgence et bienveillance quelques recherches qui ont pour but d'assurer la marche de l'esprit humain, et de donner enfin une base incontestable a toutes Ses connoissances.

j'ai l'honneur de vous Saluer avec respect et admiration

DESTUTT-TRACY

[520]

Auteuil, near Paris. 1st Ventose, Year 12
SIR   (21 Feb. 1804)

General Lafayette informs me that he sent you my book, as I requested, about how ideas are formed, but that it did not reach you. To my regret, the second edition, which will contain some important additions, is still in preparation and not yet complete. In the meantime, I have the honor of sending you another copy of the first volume along with a second part that I published later, concerning how ideas are expressed. The third and final part, which I am working on now, treats how they are deduced. That will complete the project.

It is very important to me that this work have the advantage of being known by you. I do not dare hope that it deserves the approval I most desire in the world, but I like to flatter myself that the statesman and enlightened thinker who is responsible for the well-being of a great people and who contributes powerfully to the progress of all humanity, will view with indulgence and good will this research which seeks to advance the human spirit and to provide, at last, an indisputable base of all knowledge.

I have the honor of greeting you with respect and admiration.

DESTUTT-TRACY

RC (DLC); endorsed by TJ as received 30 Apr. 1805 and so recorded in SJL. Enclosures: (1) Destutt de Tracy, *Projet d'éléments d'idéologie à l'usage des écoles centrales de la Republique Française* (Paris, 1801). (2) Destutt de Tracy, *Élémens d'idéologie. Seconde partie. Grammaire* (Paris, 1803).

Antoine Louis Claude Destutt de Tracy (1754-1836) served as colonel of a regiment in the French military under the ancien régime. A deputy for the nobility in the Revolutionary-era Estates General, he renounced his title and embraced the movement for liberal reform, becoming a key figure among less radical leaders such as Lafayette and Volney and at one point publishing a rebuke to Edmund Burke's critique of the Revolution. He was second-in-command of the cavalry in Lafayette's Army of the Center in 1792. While in prison during the Terror, he began the philosophical work that became the basis for *Éléments d'idéologie*, the first volume of which he published in 1801. Destutt de Tracy became a member of France's National Institute of Arts and Sciences in 1795 and in 1808 was elected to the Académie Française. Named

to the Conservative Senate of France in 1799, he retained his association with liberal reformers, whom Bonaparte termed the Idéologues, and took a particular interest in public education. During his retirement years, TJ corresponded with Destutt de Tracy often and prepared a translation of a later work, *A Treatise on Political Economy*. Using manuscripts sent to him by Destutt de Tracy, TJ in collaboration with William Duane also saw to publication an anonymous English version of *A Commentary and Review of Montesquieu's Spirit of Laws* (Emmet Kennedy, *A Philosophe in the Age of Revolution: Destutt de Tracy and the Origins of "Ideology"* [Philadelphia, 1978], xi, 14-19, 29, 35-7; *Dictionnaire de Biographie Française*, 22 vols. [Paris, 1933-   ], 11:115-16; RS, 1:262-3n; 3:3-4; Vol. 36:481n; Vol. 38:615n).

TJ reported to Lafayette that he had not received the first volume of Destutt de Tracy's examination of ideology (OUVRAGE QUI TRAITE DE LA FORMATION DE NOS IDÉES) but in a subsequent letter informed Lafayette that the book had arrived (Vol. 41:665-6; TJ to Lafayette, 31 Jan.).

To Albert Gallatin

TH:J. TO MR GALLATIN   Feb. 21. 04.

I return you mr Nicholson's letter because it is chiefly on private topics. the two charges against Banning, that he refused to let duties be bonded unless a bond not due were paid, and the neglecting to give such a certificate on cotton as might authorise a drawback, (when too a re-exportation was not, at the time, thought of) appear to be founded on single acts, not habitual practices. they seem fit subjects for demanding legal indemnification, rather than immediate removal. the circumstance of his residing 12. miles off is more serious, as it must probably produce habitual inconvenience. I wish more of the trouble which has been taken by Willis's friends to prove his fitness, had been applied to a specification of the acts of wrong or negligence of Banning.

I find on reading again the paper I wrote hastily & sent you yesterday I have not kept, as distinct as I should have done, the two separate grounds of authority on which the practice in the department of state has been deemed to be solidly founded. the following amendment will convey my meaning more correctly. 2d paragraph, 1. 13. strike out 'under these two &c. to the end of the paragraph, and insert 'To give the Executive the *means* of fulfilling the constitutional duty of maintaining the foreign intercourse, and even to supply the *authority*, if the constitutional words be deemed defective or unexplicit, a sum is annually appropriated 'for the expences of intercourse with foreign nations.' if we consider this as giving the *means* only of fulfilling the constitutional duty, then it leaves their application to his discretion as generally as the constitution had left the duties. if, as in some other cases, the appropriation intends, by the same words, both[1] to legalize the object, and give the means, then the latitude of the expression here used, gives the same latitude of execution, saving always the general regulations of the act of 1801.'

PrC (DLC). Recorded in SJL with notation "Dr. Stevens's case."

NICHOLSON'S LETTER: the only letter found from Joseph H. Nicholson to Gallatin in February 1804 is that described as Enclosure No. 10 in Gallatin to TJ, 20 Feb. PRIVATE TOPICS: after Nicholson agreed to support John Willis, he added, in a second, short paragraph: "I wish you would send me a Letter in the form of an answer to one from me relative to the Pre-emption Rights—direct to me as Chairman &c." Nicholson headed the committee appointed on 22 Nov. 1803 to consider preemption rights and other issues raised by petitioners from Ohio. On 17 Feb., the committee was directed to inquire into reducing land prices in Mississippi Territory for those settlers who held "a right of pre-emption only" (RC in DNA: RG 59, LAR, 12:0429; JHR, 4:453, 541, 583-4). For the committee's mandate, see Gallatin to TJ, 4 Jan.

SENT YOU YESTERDAY: see Memorandum on the Edward Stevens Claim,
printed as an enclosure at TJ to Gallatin,
20 Feb.

[1] Word interlined.

From Albert Gallatin

DEAR SIR   Feby. 21 1804

Doctor Stevens's case shall receive a full & candid investigation.
But it embraces several important considerations both as to constitution & law and as to facts; and I fear that I may not have time to apply
my mind to it, before the numerous congressional subjects with
which I am still engaged shall have been disposed of; So far as relates
to this department it must go through two stages vizt. settlement of
accounts, and payment. Although from the general superintendence
vested in the Secretary, there is no impropriety in his interference,
and it may even be his duty in certain cases to interfere in questions
arising in the settlement of accounts; in this instance, whatever my
opinion may be, I certainly will yield to yours, if, after a full examination, you shall differ; and will, if Mr Duvall assents,[1] give to that part
of the business any direction you may think eligible. Permit me, at
the same time, with perfect respect and great deference to your judgment, to say that, so far as relates to payment, this being a question
of appropriation of which the Secrety. of the Treasury is, in the nature of things, left sole judge, and for which he is alone responsible,
it seems to me just that, on that point, he should be permitted to act
in conformity with his own view of the subject. In saying this, I do
not, by any means, intend to prejudge the case, on either of the questions arising under it, farther than I have already done, and I certainly will reconsider them with great attention.

I enclose some letters respecting Banning which left a very unfavorable impression on my mind. I have no doubt that, after having
misconstrued the law, he misrepresented the opinion I had given. I
have seen him; he is an extremely weak young man: of his incapacity
you need not entertain any doubt; his only qualification is to write a
good hand; and he is extremely obnoxious.

I enclose a letter just received from Mr Davies the collector of Norfolk. Does it require any answer?

The letters to Mr Rodney are returned—I will write immediately
to Mr M'Creery respecting Molier. If a Frenchman is to be chosen,
D'Herbigny may I think be trusted. He is generally esteemed, writes

English with sufficient correctness and is with us—an American much more than a Frenchman.

Respectfully Your obdt. Servt.   ALBERT GALLATIN

RC (DLC); at foot of text: "The President of the United States"; endorsed by TJ as received from the Treasury Department on 21 Feb. and "Stevens. Banning. Davies. d'Herbigny" and so recorded in SJL. Enclosures not found.

HE MISREPRESENTED THE OPINION I HAD GIVEN: see Enclosures No. 1 and No. 5 described at Gallatin to TJ, 20 Feb., for the report that Banning showed his critics a letter in which Gallatin reportedly approved of the collector's conduct. The letters to Thomas RODNEY perhaps pertained to the appointment of an

assistant clerk, a translator, and an agent to defend the rights of the United States by investigating land claims, all positions requested by the Mississippi Territory commissioners (see Gallatin to TJ, 4 Jan.). I WILL WRITE IMMEDIATELY: see Gallatin to TJ, 22 Feb.

D'HERBIGNY: Pierre Derbigny, an attorney who settled in New Orleans in 1797 (Gallatin, *Papers*, 8:605-6; RS, 4:631-2).

[1] Preceding four words interlined.

From Wilson Cary Nicholas

DEAR SIR   Washington Feb. 21. 1804

I was yesterday informed by both the Senators from R. Island, that there state was very much discontented; with all the most valuable offices remaining in the hands of Federalist's; and from recent letters they did fear, *that* spirit wou'd manifest itself, by a rejection of the amendment to the constitution. the Legislature will meet in a week. I presume the rule that you have adopted of giving to the federalists a proportion of offices, must be applied to the states seperately, for if in apportioning the offices between the parties, it shou'd so happen that none but federalist's, shou'd hold offices in particular States, and those States happen to be republican as is the State of R. Island, it cou'd not fail to be a source of great uneasiness. There is no part of America where the conflict of parties has been greater than in that State. This perhaps may make it necessary to make some sacrifice to appease the republicans. I have so often experienced your indulgence that I flatter myself, you will pardon the liberty I have now taken, and ascribe it solely to the solicitude I feel that your administration shou'd give general satisfaction to our friends.

I am Dear Sir with the greatest respect your humble Servant

W. C. NICHOLAS

RC (DLC); endorsed by TJ as received 21 Feb. and so recorded in SJL.

The Rhode Island LEGISLATURE convened on 27 Feb. and ratified the proposed Twelfth Amendment on 1 Mch. (*Providence Phoenix*, 3 Mch. 1804; Ku-

roda, *Origins of the Twelfth Amendment*, 160).

Order for Pardon of Nathaniel Ingraham

Feb. 21. 1804.

The act of 1794. under which this prosecution was, inflicted pecuniary punishment only (to wit 200. D. for each slave) and no imprisonment. since that, another act (1800. c. 51) has limited the pecuniary forfeiture to 2000. D. and substituted imprisonment not exceeding two years. the prisoner having no property, his imprisonment until he shall pay 14,000. D. would be perpetual. it seems proper therefore *as far as the executive has authority*, to apply to this case the spirit of the act of 1800. and to consider the two years imprisonment which the party has already suffered, and the 7000. D. for which he will be still answerable to the Prosecutor, as having more than filled up the measure of punishment which the existing laws make the maximum. let a pardon therefore issue for whatsoever the US. may pardon, leaving the rights & the remedies of the prosecutor untouched.

TH: JEFFERSON

MS (DNA: RG 59, GPR); entirely in TJ's hand, written at foot of Petition of Nathaniel Ingraham, 15 Dec. 1803.

For the ACT OF 1794 and the ACT OF 1800 regarding the slave trade, see U.S. Statutes at Large, 1:347-9, 2:70-1; Vol. 39:400-1n.

THE PROSECUTOR: John West Leonard.

TJ issued his PARDON of Ingraham on 24 Feb., remitting and releasing to him the government's interest in the $14,000 judgment against him (FC in Lb in DNA: RG 59, GPR).

From Éleuthère Irénée du Pont de Nemours

Eleutherian Mill,
near Wilmington (Del.)
february 22th 1804.

MONSIEUR LE PRESIDENT,

Monsieur le Secretaire de la guerre a bien voulu me faire part de la reponse du Docteur Hunter relativement aux epreuves qu'il a faites du Salpêtre du gouvernement et dont le resultat est que l'impureté des divers Salpetres qui sont dans les magasins ne devait être que de $4\frac{1}{2}$ à $6\frac{1}{4}$ pour cent. Cependant les echantillons qui m'ont été remis par le général Irwin, et sur lesquels j'ai fait à plusieurs reprises des experiences très exactes, contenaient de 7 à 21 pour cent de Substances etrangeres au Salpêtre, ainsi que j'ai eu l'honneur de vous l'ecrire le 20 Juillet dernier. Ces echantillons etant encore entre mes mains il eut été facile de constater si cette Singuliere difference provenait du Salpêtre Soumi aux épreuves ou de l'inexactitude que le docteur ou moi aurions pu mettre dans nos experiences; mais le général Dearborn ajoutant que Monsieur Hunter proposait au gouvernement d'entreprendre à Ses fraix le raffinage de deux cent milliers de Salpêtre aux conditions de rendre dans les magasins quatre vingt dix livres de Salpêtre pur pour chaque cent livres de brut, et le ministre me faisant l'honneur de me proposer ce travail aux mêmes conditions, J'ai du Simplement repondre qu'il ne m'etait pas possible d'accepter et que je croyais même que le gouvernement ne pouvait faire aucune operation plus profitable que d'en charger le docteur Hunter.

Maintenant que cette affaire est ainsi terminée, Je crois Monsieur le President devoir à votre bienveillance pour mon Pere, aux encouragements que vous avez bien voulu me temoigner, et je me dois à moi même, de Soumettre à vos lumieres la preuve que la demande que j'avais faite de trente pour cent pour couvrir les dechets et fraix de Raffinage n'etait nullement extravagante, quoique si eloignée de l'offre nouvelle que le gouvernement vient de recevoir. D'après la lettre du Ministre de la guerre le Docteur Hunter estime l'impureté du Salpêtre à 5 pour cent terme moyen entre les diverses qualités, il évalue les dépenses de raffinage à cinq autres livres pour cent et S'engage en conséquence à rendre au gouvernement 90 Livres de Salpêtre pur par chaque cent livres de brut. quelques procédé que le docteur puisse employer pour le raffinage du Salpêtre, et en Supposant les epreuves qu'il a deja faites parfaitement exactes, il sera forcé d'ajouter au dechet d'impureté, qu'il croit être de 5 pour cent, un autre dechet d'environ $3\frac{1}{2}$ causé par l'humidité contenue dans le Salpêtre brut, et ensuite la perte inévitable occasionnée pendant le raffinage, par l'evaporation et par le coulage des vaisseaux, par la quantité de Salpêtre qui S'attache au muriate de Soude et aux écumes, ou qui reste combinée dans les dernieres eaux-meres, dechet que Chaptal estime dans son ouvrage être de 7 pour cent et qui souvent n'est pas moindre de dix. Il eprouvera donc un dechet de raffinage dont, d'après ses propres données, la plus faible estimation ne pourrait être moindre de $15\frac{1}{2}$ pour cent, Sans y comprendre aucun fraix, et qui rendrait très difficile le retour de 90 livres pour cent dans les magasins à moins que le docteur ne posseda pour cela un Secret particulier, Secret dont l'importance meriterait bien tout le travail et les encouragemens que le gouvernement pourrait lui donner.

L'administration des Poudres de France qui dirige toutes les raffineries de Salpêtre a fixé à 30 livres pour cent le dechet de raffinage qu'elle alloue à ses preposés, toutes les dépenses etant payées par elle. Lorsque j'ai proposé au gouvernement de raffiner le Salpêtre des magasins de Philadelphie et de Supporter tous les fraix sans autre retribution que la même deduction de 30 livres pour cent, Je n'avais pu le faire qu'en raison de la Superiorité qu'a en général le Salpêtre de l'Inde sur celui fabriqué en Europe et qui m'avait paru pouvoir compenser la difference des fraix, et que, parceque le ministre m'avait assuré que le Salpêtre de qualité inferieure etait en trés petite proportion dans les magasins. J'avais cru faire au gouvernement une proposition raisonable et trés moderée et meriter ainsi à ma manufacture la protection et les encouragemens dont elle etait digne Sous les autres rapports.

En me permettant, Monsieur le President, de vous Soumettre les observations precedentes je n'ai nullement en vue d'obtenir un travail que le gouvernement repugnerait à m'accorder, mais Seulement de me Justifier à vos yeux sur la grande difference qui existe entre mes propositions et celles du docteur Hunter et sur mon refus d'accepter la preference que le Ministre avait bien voulu m'offrir aux mêmes conditions.

J'ai l'honneur d'être avec un profond respect, Monsieur le President Votre tres humble et très obeissant Serviteur

E. I. DU PONT DE NEMOURS.

EDITORS' TRANSLATION

Eleutherian Mill, near Wilmington (Del.)
MISTER PRESIDENT,   22 Feb. 1804

The secretary of war has informed me of Dr. Hunter's response concerning his tests on the government's saltpeter. His results indicate that the impurity of different types of saltpeter in the reserves is only about $4\frac{1}{2}$ to $6\frac{1}{4}$ percent. Yet the samples General Irvine gave me, and on which I have done several very precise experiments at different times, contained from 7 to 21 percent of substances foreign to saltpeter, as I had the honor of informing you on July 20. Since these samples were still in my possession, it would have been easy to note whether this significant difference came from the saltpeter that had been submitted for testing or from inaccuracies that Dr. Hunter or I could have incorporated into our experiments. General Dearborn then added that Mr. Hunter proposed to refine the saltpeter in the warehouse to obtain 90 pounds of pure saltpeter for every 100 pounds. The secretary offered me the contract on the same conditions. I was obliged to respond that it was simply not possible to accept and that I thought the least expensive solution was to entrust the task to Dr. Hunter.

Now that the matter is concluded, I believe I owe it to myself, Mister President, given your good will toward my father and your encouragement to me, to prove that my proposal of 30 percent to cover waste material and refining costs was not at all excessive, despite the discrepancy with the offer the government has just received. According to the letter from the secretary of war, Dr. Hunter estimates the impurity of the saltpeter at about 5 percent and the cost of refining at another 5 percent. He thus commits to returning 90 pounds of saltpeter for every 100 pounds of gross weight. Whatever means the doctor uses to refine the saltpeter, and assuming his previous experiments to be totally accurate, he will be forced to increase the 5 percent impurity rate by another $3\frac{1}{2}$ percent caused by moisture in the unrefined saltpeter, by inevitable loss during refining through evaporation, leakage from the containers, and saltpeter that attaches to sodium and scum or stays in the last bath. Chaptal estimates this loss to range from 7 percent to as much as 10 percent. Based on Dr. Hunter's own estimates, he will thus have a waste factor of at least $15\frac{1}{2}$ per cent, not including his costs. This would make it very difficult to return 90 pounds for every 100 in the warehouses, unless the doctor has some special secret. If he does, the secret is so important that it warrants all the work and help the government can give him.

France's gunpowder administration, which operates all the saltpeter refineries, has established 30 percent as the authorized rate of waste, plus expenses. When I proposed to refine the saltpeter in the Philadelphia warehouses and cover all costs without any other remuneration than this same 30 percent deduction, I could do so only because saltpeter from India is generally superior to Europe's. That seemed to compensate for the cost difference, since the secretary assured me there was very little inferior quality saltpeter in the warehouses. I felt my proposal was reasonable and my company deserved the protection and encouragement it had earned in other matters.

By taking the liberty of sending you these observations, Mister President, I do not seek to obtain a contract that the government does not wish to give me. I simply seek to explain the significant difference between my proposal and Dr. Hunter's and my refusal to accept the conditions the secretary offered me.

With profound respect, Mister President, I have the honor of being your very humble and obedient servant.   E. I. du Pont de Nemours

RC (DLC); at head of text: "A Son Excellence Monsieur Jefferson President des Etats-Unis"; endorsed by TJ as received 27 Feb. and so recorded in SJL. Dft (DeGH).

la reponse du docteur hunter: in a letter dated 11 Feb., Henry Dearborn informed du Pont of the results of chemist George Hunter's tests on the purity of saltpeter stored in the public magazine at Philadelphia, as well as his terms for clarifying one hundred tons of the same (FC in Lb in DNA: RG 107, MLS).

To Albert Gallatin

DEAR SIR   Feb. 22. 1804.

The papers you last sent me place Banning's conduct in a more unfavorable point of view than those before communicated. about Davies we will converse the first time we meet. As to Doctr. Stevens's case I am sure we shall ultimately come to a result in which we can all harmonise. whether in every case there be, or be not, an appeal from the Comptroller to the Secretary of the Treasury, & from the Secretary to the President, and generally from every head of a department to the President, in order to produce an Unity of action, are questions of speculation which I am sure that in practice we never shall have occasion to decide. the construction of our government makes the head of a department and the President mutual Counsellors. if the case is difficult, usage establishes the practice of a general consultation. there never has arisen a case and I am persuaded never will, where the respect we mutually entertain for the opinions of one another will not produce an accomodation of opinion. in the present case I verily believe the ground of the difference of your opinion from ours is that you judge of the acts for foreign intercourse from impressions that have remained in your mind, which do not correspond with the law. I will pray you, before you look to any other part of the subject, to consider well that act (1801.) you will find it gives no authority to pay money. it only forbids paiment beyond certain limits in certain cases. it supposes the power to pay up to those limits as already existing. there never was a dollar paid under that act: and if a power to pay cannot be found somewhere else, we have been paying even the 9000. D. a year without authority. you will see that if that act were torn out of the book, it would not affect this question. that we are restricted by that act, but derive no authority from it at all; except indeed when we should want to settle without voucher the expenditure of monies granted by Congress for *contingent* purposes expressly and eo nomine. but of all this you will think at your leisure. affectionate salutations.

TH: JEFFERSON

PoC (DLC); with notations by TJ on verso:
"1790. July 1. I. 128.
<1792. May 8. II. 124.>
1793. Feb. 9. II. 159.
1794. Mar. 20. III. 16.
1796. May 30. III. 348.
1798. Mar. 19. IV. 69.
1800. May 10. V. 188" and, in pencil:

"See Act 1 July 1790 biennually contd. to <May 10. 1800> act Mar. 19. 1798 which was superseded by apprn. [act] of May 7. 1800 by Act May 10. 1800 which is permanent, & to be continued with the annual apprn. Mar. 3. 1801" (see Memorandum on the Edward Stevens Claim, enclosed in TJ to Gallatin, 20 Feb.). Recorded in SJL with notation "Banning. Stevens."

PAPERS YOU LAST SENT ME: see Gallatin to TJ, 21 Feb.

CONSIDER WELL THAT ACT: TJ was again referring to "An Act to ascertain the compensation of public Ministers" of 10 May 1800 (U.S. Statutes at Large, 2:78-9; TJ to Gallatin, 20 Feb.). Section

2 of the act gave the president the authority to accept certificates in lieu of vouchers. Payment of the certificates, however, required an appropriation BY CONGRESS FOR CONTINGENT PURPOSES (U.S. Statutes at Large, 2:78-9).

From Albert Gallatin

DEAR SIR   22 Feby. 1804

The enclosed is the only answer which could be obtained from Mr M'Creery.

Can the N. Orleans revenue law be transcribed in order to have it ready by Monday's mail. I presume that, if it cannot be done immediately in Mr Madison's office, I may have the loan of it to morrow for that purpose.

I enclose the first return from Mr Trieste, which you will have the goodness to return as it belongs to the files of the office. It does not appear to me, especially taking into view that Sect. of the law now before you which repeals the duties on exports, that those duties (on exports to U.S.) which shall have been collected before the law is in force can be remitted by any but legislative authority. But I doubt the legality of having collected that on exports to Spain.

Respectfully Your obedt. Servt.   ALBERT GALLATIN

RC (DLC); endorsed by TJ as received from the Treasury Department on 22 Feb. and "Molier. N. Orleans revenue bill. Trist's return" and so recorded in SJL. Enclosure: William MacCreery to Gallatin, 22 Feb. 1804; responding to the Treasury secretary's query of 21 Feb., the Maryland congressman notes that "in the capacity of Notary Public, of money Broker, of Merchant and Shopkeeper" at Baltimore, Henry Molier "was uniformly unfortunate," causing MacCreery to conclude "that his talents for business are very limited"; he thinks, however, that Molier would be "very usefull in a subordinate capacity"; MacCreery admits: "As to his morals, I know nothing—nor do I remember to have heard his honesty impeach'd" (same). Other enclosure not found.

REPEALS THE DUTIES ON EXPORTS: see Section 3 of the 24 Feb. revenue act (U.S. Statutes at Large, 2:252). In his 27 Feb. instructions to Hore Browse Trist, Gallatin noted that articles exported from New Orleans TO SPAIN before 25 Mch., the day the revenue law would commence, "ought not to have paid the export duty.— In case where that duty may have been levied on such exportation to Spain, it must therefore be refunded" (Terr. Papers, 9:192-3).

From Robert Lawson

DEAR SIR,   Bacon Branch Feby 22nd. 1804.

I do with unequivocal sincerity return my thanks for your benevolent acts of kindness to me. If it had not been for the thirty dollars plac'd by you in the hands of the then Governor Monroe, I should have had not any cloaths at all: and he well knowing that there was no prospect of my return to Kentucky in any short time, thought it could not be better applied. My eldest son from Kentucky is now in Richmond; but has not the means to carry me out—Nor do I know how this can be done, but by the contributions of the Benevolent, who will consider my afflict'd, and absolutely dependent situation on the Hand of private bounty. With a view solely to this object, I am constrain'd to send forward several Letters beging Charity.

Mrs. Caphart with whom I have boarded for nearly twelve months, well knowing my situation, undertakes on foot to deliver those Letters, if she can see the persons to whom they are address'd. She is upwards of sixty, has nothing to pay her Rent, and purchase common necessaries, but by spining. The mony allow'd her by the Cincinnati on my account for board, from my disabled state of body and her trouble—I well know does not enable her to lay up one penny at the years end. She has had a great proportion of trouble with me. I wish from her kind attention it was in my power to reward her for it. She has under gone heavy afflictions for the greater part of her life. Her late Husband was for twenty years, in an absolute and unhappy state of insanity, and she attended him all that time. Her character she will shew.

On her shewing you Letters, I am confident (Sir) that you will be so good as to instruct her in the way of finding the Gentlemen, if in place. There is one paper open: Be so kind as to read it. It describes nothing but facts, and yet they are but hints comparitively speaking to what I have long suffer'd, and do now suffer: But in my afflictions of body or mind, they have to congratulate you and your patriotic co-adjutors, for the great and beneficial effects to the Citizens of the United States, under a virtuous administration of the national Government. May God long preserve you in Health, and may you have to the latest posterity, Thanks of cordial Gratitude.

I remain with every Sentiment of Gratitude, respect, and Esteem, Dear Sir, your much oblig'd, and most obedt. Servt

RO: LAWSON

Will you be so good as to write a few lines by Mrs. Caphart.

[531]

RC (ViW: Tucker-Coleman Collection); addressed: "His Excellency Thomas Jefferson Esqr President of the United States" and "favd. by Mrs. Caphart"; endorsed by TJ as received 6 Mch. and so recorded in SJL.

For TJ's BENEVOLENT ACTS OF KINDNESS to Lawson, see Vol. 34:398, Vol. 37:520, and Vol. 38:48-9. On 20 July 1802, TJ directed that $30 be conveyed to Lawson by James MONROE; see Vol. 38:110-11.

Beginning in June 1801, the Virginia Society of the Cincinnati deemed that Lawson's infirmities made him incapable of supporting himself and appropriated an annual sum of $200 paid to William DuVal for his support. Lawson began to board with MRS. CAPHART near Richmond in March 1803. As a result of an earlier illness and exposure to extreme cold in his previous lodgings, he developed ulcers in his feet and legs and was not able to wear shoes or socks. Lawson addressed a memorial to the Society of the Cincinnati on 9 Dec. 1803, acknowledging their support to him, requesting additional aid so that he could return to Kentucky in the spring, and soliciting some additional compensation for his caretaker. In a letter of the same date, DuVal certified that Mrs. Caphart had contracted with the society for Lawson's board, clothes, and laundry for £60 a year. He attested that Lawson was "well treated and lives comfortably" although he "continues helpless and unable to Walk." Since June, Mrs. Caphart had been washing and dressing his sores, a "Trouble which was not in our Contract." DuVal concluded that, "So long as Mrs Caphart treats the General of the same Attention & humanity it appears to me that the Cincinati could not better his Condition by Removing him." Lawson died in Richmond on 28 Mch. 1805. His funeral was held at the state capitol, and he received burial with the honors of war for his "gallant and meritorious services in the revolution." The society decided upon Lawson's death to "forget the injustice he has done to himself—& cordially remember which is due to his former Military Rank & Character" (Edgar Erskine Hume, *Papers of the Society of the Cincinnati in the State of Virginia 1783-1824* [Richmond, 1938], 229-30, 292; Richmond *Virginia Gazette*, 30 Mch. 1805).

To the Senate and
the House of Representatives

To THE SENATE AND
HOUSE OF REPRESENTATIVES OF THE US.

I communicate to Congress, for their information, a report of the Surveyor of the public buildings at Washington, stating what has been done under the act of the last session concerning the city of Washington, on the Capitol and other public buildings and the highway between them.   TH: JEFFERSON
                                                              Feb. 22. 1804.

RC (DNA: RG 233, PM, 8th Cong., 1st sess.). PoC (DNA: RG 46, LPPM, 8th Cong., 1st sess.). FC (DLC). Recorded in SJL with notations "Expenditures on buildings &c. at Washington" and "copied with the double pen of Hawkins." Enclosure: Benjamin H. Latrobe to TJ, 20 Feb. 1804.

Lewis Harvie delivered this letter and REPORT to the Senate and House on 22 Feb. The Senate ordered both to lie for consideration, while the House referred the report to a committee consisting of Philip R. Thompson, John Smilie, Benjamin Huger, John Campbell, and Richard Cutts. On 13 Mch., the House approved a resolution and ordered the committee to draw up a bill allocating $50,000 for the public buildings. The bill passed the House three days later and after some interference in the Senate passed that body on 27 Mch. (JS, 3:363; JHR, 4:593, 646-7, 655; *Annals*, 13:299-300, 305-6).

As indicated by his notation in SJL, this was TJ's first recorded use of the polygraph machine invented by John Isaac Hawkins, who transferred the rights to the invention to Charles Willson Peale. While he waited for one of his own, TJ borrowed the polygraph of Benjamin H. Latrobe, much to Latrobe's and his "Wifes inconvenience, whom," Latrobe reported to Peale, "I have now restord to her former post of Copying Clerk" (Latrobe, *Correspondence*, 1:436).

To George W. P. Custis

SIR   Washington Feb. 23. 04.

On the reciept of your letter I rode to the Hamburg hill from whence you suppose a bridge may be advantageously thrown across the river. comparing this with the other positions, below and above, which have been proposed, I observe that in proportion as they lengthen the road they shorten the bridge. it will rest with the legislature to decide at which place or places they will authorize the establishment of a bridge. the inhabitants of Georgetown think their interests will be much injured by any bridge below their port. in this clashing of interests between different points of the territory to all of which I sincerely wish prosperity, I hold myself aloof from medling, no law calling on me to do otherwise. should it be made my duty to take any part in it, I shall certainly place every local interest out of view and regard the general interest only. Accept my salutations and respect.   TH: JEFFERSON

PoC (DLC); at foot of text: "George W. Custis esquire."

YOUR LETTER: Custis to TJ, 13 Feb. 1804.

From Albert Gallatin

DEAR SIR   Treasury Dept. 23 Feby. 1804

I have the honour to enclose a memorial requesting the removal of Moses Kempton Collector of Burlington, together with a certificate of E. Tucker (formerly Surveyor of Little Egg harbour whilst this last port was attached to Burlington, and afterwards Collector of sd. little Egg harbour when erected into a district, from which last office he was removed for charging more in his account than he paid to his boatmen) charging sd. Kempton with having altered three receipts, which were vouchers to his accounts, thereby charging the U. States with 63 dollars more than he had paid.

I immediately requested the Register to select amongst Kempton's accounts those receipts and to communicate them with any other information on the same subject which he might possess. His letter together with the altered receipts and Kempton's apology when the alteration was discovered is enclosed.

That he (K.) altered the receipts, and that he kept the money in his possession, until after the alteration had been discovered, and without paying it over to E. Tucker; which, if the motive he assigns for his conduct is the true one, he ought to have done; is fully proven. The only plea in his favour is that which he makes, that when he settled with E. Tucker, he forgot that he had then altered the receipts & received the overplus. How far that plea should be considered as sufficient is submitted.

It appears that the fraud or alteration was discovered at the Treasury and not by E. Tucker who does not seem to have known the fact till written to, on the 12 July 1797, by the Comptroller. That E. Tucker, who is now the complainant, feels resentment agt. Kempton, and was himself removed, not for altering receipts, but for taking receipts for greater sums than he paid, must be remembered, but does not affect the evidence on the files of the treasury agt. Kempton.

Respectfully Your obedt. Servt.   ALBERT GALLATIN

Please to return the papers enclosed in the Register's letter.

RC (DLC); at foot of text: "The President of the United States"; endorsed by TJ as received from the Treasury Department on 24 Feb. and "Kempton Moses. collectr. Burlington to be removed" and so recorded in SJL. Enclosure printed below. Other enclosures not found.

MOSES KEMPTON took office as collector at Burlington, New Jersey, in 1795

(JEP, 1:194, 195). Ebenezer TUCKER served as surveyor of Little Egg Harbor from 1789 until 1796, when he became collector of the newly erected district. After TJ's election, Tucker led a successful campaign to have William Watson, his successor as collector at Little Egg Harbor in 1799, replaced by Silas Crane, a Republican (JEP, 1:10, 18, 212, 213, 326, 327; Vol. 35:365-6; Vol. 37:345-6).

ENCLOSURE

Memorial of Burlington, New Jersey, Republican Citizens

The Memorial and Representation, of the Subscribers, republican Citizens, of the district of Burlington, in the State of New Jersey, respectfully Sheweth.—

That we have beheld with considerable regret for some time past, Moses Kempton Esquire, in Occupancy of the Office of Collector of the Customs, for this District; and pray that he may be succeeded by William H. Burr Esquire: for the following reasons.—1st The said Moses Kempton is a violent

Federalist, and a rigid persecutor of Republicans; as a proof of which we state the following facts; On the 10 February 1802 William Pearson, (in company with William Coxe both members of the Legislature, & violent friends of order) was arraigned at the Bar of the Court, of Quarter Sessions of this County, for waylaying, and inhumanly beating, a respectable republican Citizen, viz. Ebenezer Tucker Esquire, on the Question of the Court (of which Mr Kempton was a member) what sum the said Pearson should be fined for the Outrage, the said Kempton voted for the culprit to pay the insignificant sum of *10. Cents*; when William H Burr Esquire, and other Republican members, voted that Pearson should be fined from 500 to 800 Dollars, see[1] the True American of the 30 March 1802.—2nd. We very much doubt the said Kemptons Honesty and Integrity, and refer the President to the Certificate of Ebenezer Tucker Esqr. marked A.—3d. William H. Burr Esqr. the person recommended[2] to succeed Mr. Kempton, is a true Republican. A Man of property, Integrety, and Respectability.

We presume it would superfluous, in us, to remind the President, how Expedient it is to remove from power, and Influential Offices, men of Mr Kemptons Character and violence; and for men to succeed them, who are just and moderate, and who are not only attached to Republican Men, but to Republican measures.—

We therefore in behalf of ourselves, and the Republican Citizens of this District, for the reasons, and proofs aforesaid, pray that Mr Kempton may be succeeded by William H. Burr Esqr., which favor will be gratefully acknowledged by.—

AMOS HUTCHIN
District of Burlington
May 25th. 1803.

RC (DNA: RG 59, LAR); in a clerk's hand, signed by Amos Hutchin, George Painter, William Hyer, John Brognard, John Rogers, William Wood, George Githens, Caleb Burr, and David C. Bryan; at head of text: "To the President, of the U. States"; endorsed by TJ as "Burlington Memorial" received 24 Feb. 1804 and "Burr Wm. H. to be Collectr. Burlington v. Kempton" and so recorded in SJL. Enclosure not found.

WE HAVE BEHELD WITH CONSIDERABLE REGRET: TJ evidently conferred with James Sloan, first-term Republican congressman from New Jersey, about the removal of Moses Kempton. Sloan sent out a query and received several responses. On 13 Mch., Joseph Budd wrote from Mount Holly that Kempton was "a Determined federalist" who does "all that he Can for the federal Interest." Budd concluded: "he ought not to hold any appointment to office" under the federal government (RC in DNA: RG 59, LAR; endorsed by TJ: "Kempton Moses. to be removd"). Stephen C. Ustick observed that during the election of 1800, Kempton was one of the "most active in opposing the Jefferson or Democratic Ticket, and promoting the Federal Ticket by reading Addresses in the Market place, as well as using his own personal influence to the utmost of his power" (Ustick to Sloan, Burlington, N.J., 15 Mch., in same; endorsed by TJ: "Kempton Moses to be removd. Ustick's letter to mr Sloane"). Ustick served as secretary of the Burlington County meeting of the Democratic Association that met in August 1803 and nominated WILLIAM H. BURR as one of their candidates for the assembly and Budd for the council. Ustick's appointment as postmaster at Burlington later in 1804 gave "universal satisfaction to the friends of Republican Government" (Trenton *True American*, 3 Oct., 5 Nov. 1803; Stets, *Postmasters*, 167).

WILLIAM PEARSON assaulted EBENEZER TUCKER on 28 Jan. 1802 (Newark

Centinel of Freedom, 9 Feb. 1802; see also Vol. 37:210-11). INSIGNIFICANT SUM OF 10. CENTS: in the end, Pearson was fined $1 by the court. The fine recommended by the 23 justices present varied from $800 to 5 cents (Trenton *Federalist &*

New-Jersey State Gazette, 16 Feb. 1802; Trenton *True American*, 12 Jan., 23 Feb., 2, 30 Mch. 1802).

[1] MS: "se."
[2] MS: "rcommended."

To George Jefferson

DEAR SIR   Washington Feb. 23. 04.

I believe I mentioned to you a considerable time ago that 10. boxes and 2. kegs were sent from hence to your address. I find they have but just now left Alexandria, as by the inclosed bill of lading. be so good as to have them forwarded to Monticello by water. Accept affectionate salutations.   TH: JEFFERSON

PrC (MHi); at foot of text: "Mr. George Jefferson"; endorsed by TJ in ink on verso. Recorded in SJL with notation "bill lading 10. boxes 2. kegs." Enclosure not found.

MENTIONED TO YOU: perhaps TJ to George Jefferson, 13 Jan.

From George Jefferson

DEAR SIR   Richmond 23d. Febr. 1804.

I am desired by Mr. John H. Craven to request the favor of you to procure & forward him 2.$\frac{1}{2}$ bushels of clover-seed, as there is none to be had here.—I fear I shall not be able to get a vessel to take so small a quantity of coal as you require; it being but seldom that such small ones offer, as could take no more, & not often that larger ones partly engaged, are to be met with. say then if you please, if I may send a larger quantity? and the most I may send—if I can do no better. no more of your Tobacco has yet come down.

I am Dear Sir Yr. Very humble servt.   GEO. JEFFERSON

RC (MHi); at foot of text: "Thos. Jefferson esqr."; endorsed by TJ as received 27 Feb. and so recorded in SJL.

To David Meade Randolph

SIR   Washington Feb. 23. 04.

As it appeared from your letter of Jan. 10. that you thought there was a denial of justice to you in the Treasury department, it became my duty to ask the explanations which have taken place. these now shew that the way is open to a settlement with the department directly[1] without any further intervention of mine. I may add of a certainty that you will find a perfect disposition there to decide on your case with impartiality, according to the rules of evidence which have been established in the Treasury of long standing, which are necessary for the public security, and which are of universal application. Accept my salutations and respect.   TH: JEFFERSON

PoC (DLC); at foot of text: "David M. Randolph esquire."

EXPLANATIONS WHICH HAVE TAKEN PLACE: see Gallatin to TJ, 13 and 14 Feb.

[1] Word interlined.

To David Leonard Barnes

SIR   Washington Feb. 24. 04.

I thank you for the trouble you have been so good as to take in Ingraham's case. it has given more than I had meant, as I should have been perfectly satisfied with your opinion alone. I now return the letter which you desired to have again. I have ordered a pardon as to whatsoever appurtains to the US. leaving the interests of the prosecutor untouched. accept my respectful salutations and assurances of great consideration.   TH: JEFFERSON

RC (CtY); addressed: "The honble David L. Barnes Providence"; franked; postmarked 23 Feb. PoC (DLC); endorsed by TJ. Recorded in SJL with no-

tation "Ingraham's case." Enclosure not found, but see Barnes to TJ, 9 Feb.

ORDERED A PARDON: see Order for Pardon of Nathaniel Ingraham, 21 Feb.

To Thomas Cooper

DEAR SIR   Washington Feb. 24. 04

I have duly recieved your favors of the 6th. and 16th. and learnt the death of Dr. Priestly with all that regret which the termination of so good and so useful a life necessarily inspires. all late accounts of him had given me apprehensions for him. not indeed that the continuance of life could be important to him, but as every year added to it was usefully employed for the general good of mankind. we may consider him as a patriarch in science the like of whom cannot soon be lost. I sent him last summer a copy of a letter I had written to Dr. Rush, with a Syllabus of a comparative view of the morals of Jesus & of the antient philosophers, with a wish that he would undertake the execution of such a work. he did so, & his last letter to Dr. Logan informed him[1] he had compleated the work. I mention this subject to introduce a request that you will be so kind as to take measures to prevent my letter & syllabus from ever getting into other hands. you know that if I write as a text that two and two are four, it serves to make volumes of sermons of slander and abuse.   A review of Malthus's anonymous tract had given me great prejudices against his principles. but he has greatly mended their appearance in his last work. he has certainly furnished some sound corrections of former errors, and given excellent views of some questions in political economy. but I think with you he is particularly defective in developing the resource of emigration. were half the money employed under the poor laws in England, laid out in colonising their able bodied poor both the emigrants and those who remained would be the happier. from the singular circumstance of the immense extent of rich & uncultivated lands in this country, furnishing an increase of food in the same ratio with that of population, the greater part of his book is inapplicable to us, but as a matter of speculation. Accept my friendly salutations and assurances of great esteem and attachment.

PoC (DLC); at foot of text: "Thomas Cooper esq."

SENT HIM LAST SUMMER: Vol. 40:251-5. In a letter of 3 Feb. to TJ, George

LOGAN shared a letter he had received from Joseph Priestley.

[1]TJ first wrote "last letter to me informed me" before altering the text to read as above.

List of Nominations from Albert Gallatin

[24 Feb. 1804]

6 Collins *Charles* Collector of the district of Bristol R.I.
and Inspector of the revenue for the port of Bristol
7 *John* Willis Collector of the district of Oxford
and Inspector of the revenue for the port of Oxford
4. *Alexr* Bailey Collector of the district of Natchez
& Inspector of the revenue for the port of Natchez
3. Garland *Wm.* G Surveyor of the port of New Orleans

and Inspector of the revenue for the port of N. Orleans
2. <u>Morgan</u> *Benjamin* Naval officer of the port of N. Orleans
1. <u>Trist</u> Collector of the District of

MS (DNA: RG 59, MCL); undated; in Gallatin's hand, with first names and numbers added by TJ rendered in italics; endorsed by Gallatin: "Nominations" and by TJ: "Nominations Feb. 24. 04."

TJ added the numerals to the list above as he prepared to transmit the names to the Senate (TJ to the Senate, 24 Feb.).

According to SJL, on 6 Feb. Rhode Island senator Christopher Ellery wrote TJ recommending "Collins to be Collec-tor v. Russel" at the DISTRICT OF BRIS-TOL, but the letter has not been found. See Gallatin to TJ, 6 Jan. 1804.

ALEXR BAILEY COLLECTOR: that is, Alexander Baillie (Gallatin, *Papers*, 9:946).

Philadelphia merchant Chandler Price wrote Alexander J. Dallas on 14 Oct. 1803 praising his former partner Benjamin MORGAN, who had moved to New Orleans in 1800 and was suitable for an office (Gallatin, *Papers*, 8:894).

To Bishop James Madison

DEAR SIR   Washington Feb. 24. 1804.

This is the first moment it has been in my power to answer your letter of Jan. 29. I do not know whether you are apprised that Mansfield has been made Surveyor general of the US. and went last summer with his family to Indiana. his salary is 2000. D. but I do not know that he is satisfied with his situation. he knows he is to be called on to make surveys of certain waters in that quarter which he views with dismay as beyond his physical force. it is possible therefore he might prefer the tranquil situation you propose for him. should he do so, I should not object to it, because he would be doing more good in raising up many mathematicians than in performing the functions of a single one. of his strength in Mathematics his book is a proof. his character is irreproachable. his morals and conduct correct & pure. should you therefore think proper to write to him on the subject you are free to say that it is with my consent, and that I shall be perfectly satisfied whatever may be his determination, as in either position he will be rendering important services to the public. Accept my affectionate salutations and assurances of great esteem and respect.

TH: JEFFERSON

PoC (DLC); at foot of text: "Bishop Madison"; endorsed by TJ.

Jared MANSFIELD, whom Madison sought for the mathematics chair at the College of William and Mary, reported to TJ concerns over his health and a preference for a position in the Corps of Engineers (Vol. 41:676-7).

To J. P. G. Muhlenberg

DEAR SIR   Washington Feb. 24. 1804.

I am sorry to be obliged to return the inclosed without my signature. as soon as I came into the administration applications came to me from all parts of the states to become a contributor to the various buildings, establishments, institutions, & enterprizes undertaken in the different states, & I began by complying with them. but I very soon found that no resources whatever would be adequate to meet these applications; and I was under the necessity of laying it down as a law for myself, to confine my contributions of this kind to the state in which my property lies, & to the district in which the seat of government makes me a resident. within this district, where every thing is to be done, the calls are quite sufficient to absorb every thing which it's inhabitants can spare. for these considerations I withold with regret the act you desired, and I trust you will think the ground sufficient. Accept my friendly salutations and assurances of great esteem and respect   TH: JEFFERSON

PoC (DLC); at foot of text: "Genl. Muhlenberg." Enclosure not found, but see Muhlenberg to TJ, 13 Feb.

To Caesar A. Rodney

DEAR SIR   Washington Feb. 24. 04.

I recieve with sincere grief your letter of the 21st. and lament the necessity which calls for your retirement, if that necessity really exists. I had looked to you as one of those calculated to give cohesion to our rope of sand. you now see the composition of our public bodies, and how essential system and plan are for conducting our affairs wisely with so bitter a party in opposition to us, who look not at all to what is best for the public, but how they may thwart whatever we propose, tho they should thereby sink their country. talents in our public councils are at all times important; but perhaps there never was a moment when the loss of any would be more injurious than at the present. the condition of our affairs is advantageous. but it is also true that we are now under a crisis which is not without hazard from different quarters at home and abroad. but all this you understand perfectly: and if under such circumstances you withdraw [I shall] believe that the necessity which occasions it is imperious and shall lament it most sincerely. Accept my affectionate salutations

TH: JEFFERSON

RC (CtY); torn, words in brackets supplied from PoC; addressed: "The honble
Caesar Rodney." PoC (DLC).

LETTER OF THE 21ST: that is, Rodney's letter of 20 Feb. received by TJ on
the 21st.

To the Senate

TO THE SENATE OF THE UNITED STATES

I nominate Hore Browse Trist of the Missisipi territory to be collector of the district of Missipi.[1]

Benjamin Morgan of New Orleans to be Naval officer of the port of
New Orleans

William G. Garland of New Orleans to be Surveyor and Inspector of
the revenue for the port of New Orleans.

Alexander Bailey of the Missisipi territory to be Collector of the district, and Inspector of the revenue for the port, of Natchez.

Charles Kilgore of the state of Ohio to be register of the land office at
Cincinnati.

Charles Collins junior[2] of Rhodeisland to be Collector of the district,
& Inspector of the revenue for the port of Bristol in Rhode island.

John Willis of Maryland to be Collector of the district, and Inspector
of the revenue for the port of Oxford.

Meriwether Jones of Virginia to be Commissioner of loans for the
state of Virginia.

TH: JEFFERSON

Feb. 24. 1804

RC (DNA: RG 46, EPEN, 8th Cong.,
1st sess.); with an emendation by Samuel
A. Otis (see note 2 below); endorsed by a
Senate clerk. PoC (DLC); TJ placed a
check mark alongside each name. Recorded in SJL with notation "nomins.
Trist &c."

When Lewis Harvie delivered this message on Friday, 24 Feb., the Senate dispensed with the rule, immediately considered the nominations, passed a resolution
confirming the appointments of Trist,
Morgan, and Baillie (BAILEY), and or-

dered the clerk of the Senate, Samuel A.
Otis, to deliver the resolution to the president. The senators confirmed Garland and
Collins on 25 Feb., Killgore and Willis
on 29 Feb., and Jones on 9 Mch. (JEP,
1:464-6).

[1] TJ originally left a blank for the name
of the district, which he filled in the RC
but left open in the PoC.

[2] Word interlined by Otis (see TJ to
Otis, 25 Feb.) and interlined by TJ as
"junr" on PoC.

From William C. C. Claiborne

Dear Sir,   New-Orleans Feby 25th. 1804.

Mr. Isaac Briggs and Mr. Robert Williams are now in this City, and propose taking their passage (by Water) for the Seat of Government in two or three Days. I cannot omit so favorable an opportunity to write you an unofficial and private Letter.—The causes which induce these Gentlemen to leave Natchez, they will themselves explain. I do sincerely regret the excuse for their departure, but under existing circumstances their presence in the Missisippi Territory could be of no public service. I believe the Register (Mr. Turner) has not used all that diligence in registering Claims, which his Duty enjoined, and that on this account, the Commissioners found themselves unable to proceed to Business;—But on this point, Mr. Williams can inform you more particularly.—

Since my private Letter of the 5th. of Feby, every thing here, has remained in tranquility; Except it be, the Intrigues of a small but aspiring *Party*, who wish to raise to the Office of Governor of lower Louisiana a Gentleman who (in their opinion) would be disposed to confer on each and every of them, some official favours.—This *Party* supposing that I might (possibly) be in the way of their favorite candidate, have endeavoured to render me personally *unpopular*, but failing in this Object, they have recently reported (as a certainty) that the confidence of the President in me, was either lost or considerably diminished, for I would shortly be superseded as Governor of lower Louisiana.—Some of my Creole friends (Natives of the Province) who have heard this Rumor, express great regret for my misfortunes;—I find, that when a Spanish Governor of Louisiana was superseded, a more lucrative or higher office was given him, unless indeed he had lost the confidence of his Government, and it being now reported and believed, that I am order'ed to Natchez, the Impression is said to be general, that *I am in disgrace.*—

It is true, that the incessant Toil and anxiety of Mind, which I have experienced since my residence in this City, united with the heavy Expences attending House keeping, & an opinion (I entertained) that Congress would observe great œconomy in the Salaries allowed to Territorial officers, had obscured to my view, many of the charms, which others see in the office of permanent Governor of lower Louisiana, and that another Appointment had appeared to me, more elligible.—

But I must confess Sir, that the *Confidence* of the present Administration, is to me an inestimable Treasure, and therefore it is, that the

Reports, (or rather the *Impressions*) of the Day, have Occasioned me some Inquietude.—I fear, however, I was wrong in introducing this subject, and I must offer you an Apology. My feelings led me imperceptibly on—And the Topic being introduced, I could not sooner restrain my Pen.—

Mr. Briggs and Mr. Williams will be enabled to give you much Information concerning Louisiana, & the Interests & Wishes of the Inhabitants.—I find, that a complete Representative Government would be most pleasing to the French Inhabitants—they have been encouraged by Mr. Laussat to expect similar political privileges to the Citizens of the United States, and I believe very little part of an independent state, would equal the expectations which are formed; and yet I find, that the greatest advocates for a complete Representative Government in lower Louisiana, entertain serious doubts as to the capacity of the people to govern themselves.

The inhabitants of West-Florida, I understand, are becoming restless under the Spanish Government; some late Taxes which are imposed, have excited great Clamour, and the wish is general, that the U. States may speedily take possession of that District.

Accept I pray you, my best wishes for a continuance of your private and public happiness.

I am Dear Sir, With great Respect Your faithful friend

WILLIAM C. C. CLAIBORNE

RC (DLC); at head of text: "Duplicate"; at foot of text: "Thomas Jefferson President of the U. States"; endorsed by TJ as received 9 Apr. and so recorded in SJL.

LETTER OF THE 5TH. OF FEBY: a letter from Claiborne to TJ dated 5 Feb. 1804

has not been found, nor is one recorded in SJL. A letter from Claiborne dated 7 Feb. is recorded in SJL as received 13 Mch. from New Orleans with notation "to be Govr. Louisa. or Misipi," but has also not been found.

From Joseph Fenwick

SIR   Bordeaux 25 February 1804.

From what Mr. Skipwith has mentioned to me on his intention of going to Louisiana, the american Consulate at Paris may soon become vacant.—The late events that have taken place here in trade, may also occasion a vacancy at Bordeaux; if so, I beg leave to offer you my services for either of these places.

I could enter into the office with the lesson of experience, & the best connexions in this Country: the times & position of things, require a person to exercise its functions with consideration & independence: I have no personal interest in navigation and the resolution never again to meddle with it; and if I do not deceive myself I cou'd acquit the duties of the office, with credit to my Country, & advantage to its commerce.

with the greatest consideration & respect I have the honor to be Sir your most devoted Servant   JOSEPH FENWICK

RC (DNA: RG 59, LAR); at head of text: "Thomas Jefferson Esquire President of the United States Washington"; endorsed by TJ as received 28 Apr. and "to be Consul at Bordeaux or Paris" and so recorded in SJL.

Joseph Fenwick was relieved of his position as American consul at BORDEAUX in 1797 (Madison, *Papers, Sec. of State Ser.*, 1:94-6; Vol. 33:334, 596).

From Albert Gallatin

DEAR SIR   Feby. 25th 1804

Will you have the goodness to examine with strict attention the enclosed instructions to Mr Trist, and send them to me, with your observations, in time to be transcribed and forwarded by Monday's mail—.

Respectfully Your obedt. Servt.   ALBERT GALLATIN

RC (DLC); at foot of text: "The President of the United States"; endorsed by TJ as received 25 Feb. and "instrns to Collector of N.O." and so recorded in SJL. Enclosure: see below.

A partial draft of Gallatin's INSTRUCTIONS TO Hore Browse Trist is located in Gallatin's papers at the New-York Historical Society (see Gallatin, *Papers*, 9:328). Entitled "Secretary's Instructions to the collector at New-Orleans, Dated Feb. 27. 1804," it is a sketch of several of the paragraphs of his instructions. There are no markings by TJ on the sheet and it is not in a state of completion to be TRANSCRIBED. Gallatin began his sketch by noting that U.S. vessels coming from France and Spain or their colonies had to unload only at New Orleans, with French and Spanish ships "on the same footage." U.S. vessels "coming from any country on this side the Cape of Good Hope" were allowed to proceed to Natchez if bound for that port. These instructions pertained to the sixth section of the 24 Feb. revenue

law and were included in the second paragraph of Gallatin's letter to Trist. Gallatin went on to observe that until the revenue act went into effect on 25 Mch., articles exported to Spain "ought not to pay the export duty." Under the cession, Gallatin explained, the United States was claiming West Florida to the Perdido River, but "All articles of the growth of the disputed territory may be freely imported into the ports of N.O. & Bayou St. John as American produce." Gallatin outlined the rules for smaller vessels "employed solely in the river or Lake trade." They were designed to promote friendly intercourse for those residing within the contested territory. In a separate paragraph, Gallatin noted "No foreign vessel must be permitted to proceed higher up than N.O." He concluded: "Two objects to be kept in view: To prevent any gross attempt to smuggle: and to abstain from any act which might endanger the peace of the U.S." The 27 Feb. letter as sent by Gallatin to the New Orleans collector is printed in *Terr. Papers*, 9:192-7.

From Albert Gallatin

DEAR SIR   Saturday afternoon [25 Feb. 1804]

I could not obtain a copy of the revenue law for New Orleans and am informed that it was sent to you. I was obliged to close the instructions without it & may have omitted some important particulars. I will thank you to send it when you return the sketch of instructions. If both could be sent to my house some time to morrow, it would accelerate the business.

Respectfully Your obedt. Servt   ALBERT GALLATIN

RC (DLC); partially dated; addressed: "The President of the United States"; endorsed by TJ as received from the Treasury Department on 25 Feb. and "revenue law N.O." and so recorded in SJL.

COPY OF THE REVENUE LAW: see TJ to Gallatin, 26 Feb. In his 27 Feb. letter to Hore Browse Trist, Gallatin enclosed the

New Orleans revenue law of 24 Feb. entitled "An Act for laying and collecting duties on imports and tonnage within the territories ceded to the United States" and the 25 Feb. "Act relating to the recording, registering and enrolling of ships or vessels in the district of Orleans" (*Terr. Papers*, 9:192; U.S. Statutes at Large, 2:251-4, 259-60).

To Samuel A. Otis

                                                      Feb. 25. 04.

Th: Jefferson asks the favor of mr Otis to permit him, by his secretary to correct a nomination sent in yesterday by adding to the name of Charles Collins the word 'junior.'

RC (DNA: RG 46, EPEN, 8th Cong., 1st sess.); addressed: "Mr. Otis"; endorsed by Otis.

Otis entered the correction on TJ's list (see note to TJ to the Senate, 24 Feb.).

To Craven Peyton

DEAR SIR   Washington Feb. 25. 04

Your favor of the 14th. must have lost a post or two somewhere, this being the first which admits an answer. with respect to the old mill it is as impossible that she should ever go again as that water should run uphill. therefore let it belong to whom it will it can never be any thing more than an insulated spot of ground surrounded by mine. the only reason for offering to purchase the old materials is merely to consolidate the possession. I would not therefore be willing to give more than I formerly mentioned to you: & still less to embark in any scheme of working the old mill, which can no more be done than if she were on the top of the hill. consequently I would not chuse to leave J. Henderson's shares in her to valuation, because valuers might have ideas of the possibility of setting her to work & might value her accordingly. neither would I leave to valuers the estimating his interest in the new situation, because however the court of Albemarle may decide, I know that by carrying the matter before the district court the case is a sure one, if there be nothing in it of which I am unapprised. it would be substituting valuers unacquainted with the law, and liable to mistake it instead of judges who cannot mistake it in so plain a case. their opinion too would be preferable to that of two lawyers, one of whom would be named by the other party. upon the whole therefore I prefer letting the thing take the course it is in; only keeping mr Barber and mr Carr on the alert to give us the benefit of a decision by the district court if necessary. I shall be with you towards the end of the next month.

I inclose you the note you desire for £50. in part paiment for corn. Accept my friendly salutations.   Th: Jefferson

RC (facsimile in Sotheby's, Catalogue No. 6761, 13 Dec. 1995, Lot 193); at foot of text: "Mr. Craven Peyton." PoC (ViU); endorsed by TJ.

Report on Meeting of Republican Caucus

[25 Feb. 1804]

Geo. Clinton	67
Langdon	7
Breckeridge	20
Levi Lincoln	9
Gid: Granger	4
Saml. McLay	1
	108

A Committee of one from each State, N. Hampshire & Connt. excepted, to enquire what measures are proper to be adopted to prevent the election of Vice President interfering with that of President—to report next Saturday.

Some Western & some Jersey Members refused to stand pledged at first but there was a tacit Acquiescence understood to be given by the act of balloting.

No names were announced before the ballots were counted.

MS (DLC: TJ Papers, 119:20583); undated, in an unidentified hand; endorsed "Washington"; endorsed by TJ: "Caucus of republicans. Washn. Feb. 25. 04."

On the evening of 25 Feb., a caucus of congressional Republicans met in the Capitol to choose the party's nominees for the forthcoming presidential election. Chaired by Senator Stephen R. Bradley of Vermont, the meeting unanimously nominated TJ for president by a voice vote. It then proceeded to the choice of a vice president. George CLINTON was the most prominent candidate, but strong support also existed among western members for John Breckinridge. Reporting on the proceedings, John Randolph observed that "our western brethren have discovered that they want something more than the free navigation of the Mississippi." To avoid any potentially divisive debates, a vote by ballot was called without any formal nominations being made. After the first ballot, Clinton was nominated by what the *National Intelligencer* described as "a very large majority" (Randolph to Monroe, 28 Feb., DLC: Monroe Papers; *National Intelligencer*, 29 Feb.; New York *American Citizen*, 2 Mch.; Noble E. Cunningham, Jr., *The Jeffersonian Republicans in Power: Party Operations, 1801-1809* [Chapel Hill, 1963], 103-8).

The COMMITTEE appointed to promote the success of the Republican ticket consisted of Wilson Cary Nicholas of Virginia, Abraham Baldwin of Georgia, John Breckinridge of Kentucky, Thomas Sumter, Sr., of South Carolina, William Cocke of Tennessee, Samuel Smith of Maryland, John Condit of New Jersey, Andrew Gregg of Pennsylvania, Samuel L. Mitchill of New York, Nathaniel Macon of North Carolina, Caesar A. Rodney of Delaware, Joseph Stanton, Jr., of Rhode Island, and Gideon Olin of Vermont (New York *American Citizen*, 2 Mch.; *Aurora*, 6 Mch.).

To Mary Jefferson Eppes

Washington Feb. 26. 04.

A thousand joys to you, my dear Maria, on the happy accession to your family. a letter from our dear Martha by last post gave me the happy news that your crisis was happily over and all well. I had supposed that if you were a little later than your calculation, and the rising of Congress as early as we expected, that we might have been with you at the moment when it would have been so encouraging to have had your friends around you. I rejoice indeed that all is so well. Congress talk of rising the 12th. of March, but they will probably be some days later. you will doubtless see mr Eppes & mr Randolph immediately on the rising of Congress. I shall hardly be able to get away till some days after them. by that time I hope you will be able to go with us to Monticello and that we shall all be there together for a month: and the interval between that and the autumnal visit will not be long. will you desire your sister to send for mr Lilly and to advise him what orders to give Goliah for providing those vegetables which may come into use for the months of April, August & september. deliver her also my affectionate love. I will write to her the next week. kiss all the little ones, and be assured yourself of my tender and unchangeable affection.

RC (Mrs. Harold W. Wilson, Miami, Florida, 1963, on deposit ViU); signature clipped; addressed: "Mrs. Eppes at Edgehill near Milton"; franked. PoC (ViU: Edgehill-Randolph Papers); signed and endorsed by TJ.

HAPPY ACCESSION TO YOUR FAMILY: Mary gave birth to a daughter, named after her, on 15 Feb. (*Thomas Jefferson's Prayer Book*, ed. John Cook Wyllie [Charlottesville, 1952], plate 9).

A LETTER of 17 Feb. from MARTHA Jefferson Randolph, recorded in SJL as received 22 Feb. from Edgehill, has not been found.

To Albert Gallatin

TH:J. TO MR. GALLATIN   Feb. 26. 04.

You are so much the best judge of the propriety of adding 25. D. to the salary of the light housekeeper at New London that whatever you determine thereon I will approve. is a vault necessary to keep oil which is not to be eaten? usage must have settled this point. the building a wharf meerly to land their oil at would seem to be the fore horse of a very long team. how many places are there in the US. where we land something or another at, and where a wharf would make the landing more convenient. if the salt water overflows their well, they should keep it out by a high curb. I sent the N.O. revenue laws to the office of state on Thursday morning with directions to make out a copy for you which you have doubtless recieved. I now inclose a copy of the register law and return the rough draught of your instructions to the Collector. I think it would be well to charge him more particularly with the duty of using vigilance and energy to suppress the terrible corruption which has prevailed there and which it will be difficult to eradicate. the Naval officer & Surveyor should be equally charged on that head. they should instantly remove any officer who *accepts* more than his legal fee, and indict every individual known to offer a bribe. I sent your rough draught to mr Madison this morning and I inclose you his notes on it. Garland's commission will be made out tomorrow. affectionate salutations.

PoC (DLC). Recorded in SJL with notation "Lt. hous N. Lond. N. Orleans commns." Enclosures: (1) "An Act relating to the recording, registering and enrolling of ships or vessels in the district of Orleans," 25 Feb. 1804 (U.S. Statutes at Large, 2:259-60). (2) Dft of Gallatin to Hore Browse Trist, 27 Feb. (see Gallatin to TJ, 25 Feb., first letter). Other enclosure not found.

In a 25 Jan. 1804 letter to the commissioner of the revenue, which has not been found, Jedediah Huntington, the customs collector at NEW LONDON, recommended "several objects" for consideration by the Treasury Department. Writing Huntington on 29 Feb., Gallatin acknowledged the receipt of his letter and informed him that the president had approved an additional $25 allowance for the New London lighthouse keeper. Huntington was also authorized to erect an oil VAULT at Lynde Point and a WHARF on Falkner Island (Lb in DNA: RG 26, LL; Vol. 37:407n). CHARGE HIM MORE PARTICULARLY: in his 27 Feb. instructions to Trist, Gallatin urged the collector to take great care "in selecting Inspectors & other subordinate officers" and to pay strict attention to

their conduct. Gallatin continued: "on this subject the President of the United States has directed me to say that he expects particular vigilance & energy shall be used by the Collector, Naval Officer & Surveyor, for the purpose of eradicating the shameful and systematic corruption which has heretofore prevailed at New Orleans" (*Terr. Papers*, 9:195).

From Lafayette

MY DEAR FRIEND   La Grange 6th. Ventose febr. the 26th 1804

This Letter will be delivered By M. Petry Secretary to the french Legation—He is well known in America and will, I Hope, Be there welcome—The Sentiments He Has Expressed to me are Such as Cannot fail to be pleasing to the United States

Your friendly favor, Nov. the 4th, is the Last I Have Received—I Heartily thank you for the Regret you Express that I was not on the Spot to Be Honoured with your Choice as Governor of Louïsiana—Amidst my fervent Wishes for Every Extension of American Liberty I should Have felt particularly Happy to Cherish it on that kindred Land—But all will Combine to make these Adoptive Brethren Understand, Enjoy, and for Ever insure to themselves and posterity the Honours and Advantages of Such a Citizenship.

The Message of the 17th Oct. kindly inclosed in your Letter is a noble testimony of the Blessings to Be found in a Liberal Constitution, in an Administration Equally patriotic and Enlightened—it Chears my Heart to Hear that Language, to witness that Result—Nor am I wanting feelings for the Last word, the Signature of my friend.

to Mr Livingston's Correspondance I Refer you for the Account of a Late discovery and the publications Concerning it—While I Wonder and Grieve to find Among the impeached Names that of General Moreau, an Allusion which Needs the Support of a Legal public trial, I am Sensible of the Reality of a Counter Revolutionary plot, a Combination Against Bonaparte's Life, and a Complicity of the British Cabinet.

My friend *Tracy* Has Not Been so fortunate as His Colleague in the Safe Arrival of His Envoice to you—Both However deserved an Equal Luck as Both are impressed with the Same Veneration for your person, your principles, and your Conduct—I Have Advised Him to

Send Again His two Volumes with a Letter the Return to which will Be not Less welcome than Has been Your Answer to *Cabanis*.

I Have Already Adressed you Respecting *Beaumarchais's* Affairs not only Because it Behoves a Veteran to Remember old times But on Account of my friendship for His Heirs—the daughter's Husband Being my former Aid de Camp de La Rüe, gal dumas's Brother in Law—I am Requested to Relate to your Memory a Resolve of Congress, 1st January 1779, Expressive of their Sentiments for Services Rendered By M. Beaumarchais in the Early Exertions of the Revolutionary Contest.

to Your Kind intentions Respecting My Lands, and to Your friendly Concern in My Behalf, I Wholly, with Grateful Confidence, Refer myself—Upon you Also I depend for the Respectful Acknowledgements I did Not think Myself Authorised to Make Untill the Official Communication Had Come Either directly from the Heads of Government to me or through the Channel of Mr *Livingston*—if in this I Have Erred Be pleased to Set Me to Rights.

My Recovery from the fracture is daily Advancing and Shall in a few Months be Complete—My Wife desires to be Most Affectionately Remembered to You, and Both daughters Whom I Beg to Receive my Best Respects—We live *la famille* at La Grange, with our Children, their partners, and three Grand Children—My Son Leaves us now and then for the Inspector General to Whom He is an Aid de Camp—a Younger Son in Law is Also Entering the Military Career as a Light dragoon—M. et mde de tessé who paid us a visit in the Beggining of the winter are in Good Health.

My Best Compliments waït on our dear Madisson—Be pleased to offer to Mr Gallatin a New tender of My Grateful Sentiments— Remember me to all friends and Receive the Cordial Affection and Regard of

Your Constant friend   LAFAYETTE

RC (DLC); endorsed by TJ as received 30 Apr. 1805 and so recorded in SJL.

ACCOUNT OF A LATE DISCOVERY: several of Robert R. Livingston's February and March dispatches to Madison included details of a royalist plot against Napoleon Bonaparte that French police recently uncovered. Among the arrested conspirators were General Jean Victor Moreau, French counterrevolutionary Georges Cadoudal, and exiled general Jean Charles Pichegru. Cadoudal was executed and Pichegru was found strangled in his cell.

Moreau would be exiled (Madison, *Papers, Sec. of State Ser.*, 6:458, 459n, 472, 481, 584, 616, 617n; Jean Tulard, *Napoleon: The Myth of the Saviour*, trans. Teresa Waugh [London, 1984], 125-7).

MY FRIEND TRACY: also on 26 Feb., Lafayette addressed a letter to the president of the American Philosophical Society in Philadelphia and forwarded copies of the first two volumes of Destutt de Tracy's *Éléments d'idéologie*. The society acknowledged the gift at its 1 Nov. 1805 meeting (RC in PPAmP; APS, *Proceedings*, 22, pt. 3 [1884], 379).

YOUR ANSWER TO CABANIS: TJ to Pierre Jean Georges Cabanis, 13 July 1803 (Vol. 41:42-3).

YOUNGER SON IN LAW: Louis de Lasteyrie du Saillant, who married Lafayette's daughter Virginie in 1803 (Arnaud Chaffanjon, *La Fayette et sa Descendance* [Paris, 1976], 210, 294-5).

To Benjamin H. Latrobe

DEAR SIR   Washington Feb. 26. 04.

I think you were so good as to say you would desire mr Peale to furnish me a double penned writing box, with some particular directions which experience had pointed out to you. a drawer at each end is indispensible, or if this cannot be, it should open on the left. the principal inconvenience I find in yours, proceeds from the unequal pressure of the copying pen, which I ascribe to unevenness in the plane. mr Foxhall has undertaken to make a perfect plane of cast iron a quarter of an inch thick. I imagine the box may be finished in the usual way, and that if he succeeds I can sink it's whole thickness into the face of the box by digging into the latter a bed for it. the iron plate is to be exactly of the size of the brass plate in yours. if he does not succeed I can use the box as it comes to me. there must be no partition in either of the drawers as I had rather have them inserted here to suit my own convenience. the 7th. and 8th lines of this letter are written with glass pens, but the copying pen made a sad hand of it, so that I have recurred to the goose quill. Accept my friendly salutations.   TH: JEFFERSON

PoC (DLC); at foot of text: "Mr. Latrobe"; endorsed by TJ.

After some failed experiments with wooden joints, Charles Willson PEALE modified the polygraph, or duplicate writing machine, by screwing thick wire into a BRASS PLATE, with all movable parts riveted to the plate (Bedini, *Jefferson and His Copying Machines*, 50).

TJ had purchased 13 GLASS PENS earlier in the month (MB, 2:1119).

From Benjamin H. Latrobe

DEAR SIR,   Sunday Feby 26 1804

I have received Your note of this morning, and am very happy imperfect as it is, that the Polygraph is not useless to you. I wrote to Mr Peale two or three days ago giving him the necessary directions & particularly describing the manner of making two drawers, one on each side instead of one. If Mr. Foxall makes the plate, he should also polish or scour it. I have another idea however on this subject which will produce a much lighter machine, & which I will explain to you tomorrow morning.—I wrote to you a note enclosing my report of Aprl. 4h. 1804 yesterday evening & sent it by a Clerk. If you will be pleased to excuse the liberty I take, I will wait on you at 8 o'clock tomorrow morning, in order to obtain the advantage of a longer conversation on the public buildings with You. I am with true respect Yours faithfully   B H LATROBE

RC (DLC); endorsed by TJ as received 26 Feb. and so recorded in SJL.

Latrobe had a low opinion of the workmanship of Henry FOXALL and did not believe TJ's idea of having Foxall forge an iron plate to secure the moving parts would work, as it would only "increase the evil of *cumbrosity*" (Bedini, *Jefferson and His Copying Machines*, 61-2).

I WROTE TO YOU A NOTE: a letter from Latrobe of 25 Feb. has not been found and was not recorded in SJL. Latrobe likely enclosed a copy of his report of the previous year, as no report of that date for 1804 has been found (see Vol. 40:127-37).

From Levi Lincoln

SIR,   Washington Feby 26, 1804

The inclosed, received by the last evening's mail, from its extraordinary contents, I have felt myself constrained with reluctance to communicate. The deep confidence imposed by its nature is dispensed with, only from a belief, that it is of very great importance, you should be informed of every transaction, involving the welfare & reputation of the General Govt—the political state of Rhode Island appears to be critical. Should the inclosed communication transpire, it would probably become worse, and involve its author in great difficulty with the concerned, & me with him—I therefore have not, and shall not subject it[1] to the inspection of any person but yourself— Permit me to ask the favor of its return, after you have sufficiently weighed its contents—

I have the honor to be Sir most respectfully your most obt Sevt

LEVI LINCOLN

RC (DLC); at head of text: "Presidt of the United States"; endorsed by TJ as received 26 Feb. and so recorded in SJL. Enclosure not found.

[1] Word interlined in place of "the enclosed."

From Charles Willson Peale

Dear Sir   Museum Feby. 26. 1804.

Such Instruments as we are daily in the habit of using should be made as perfect as possible, or as human invention can make them, not only the facility of use but also their durebility must constitute a great part of their value in the economy of time, (so precious to a thinking man) that a moderate expence of first cost, will weigh light in comparison with the estimate of a constant saving.

In this point of view, Pens have been made in almost every part of the world of various metals, for years past. I have made them of Steel, silver, Gold and of Platina, but never could please myself before I saw one of Wise's Pens (of London).

Making the spring at a distance from the point gives other advantages besides making the point of a sufficient thickness to prevent it from sticking into the paper; that of letting the Ink flow more readily to the nib, thus getting over an important objection to the use of metal Pens, and the spring thus placed obtaining power on it, allows the whole instrument to be made stronger.

If artists would take pains in forming such Pens and give them a proper temper the manufacture of them might become a public benefit, in default of which I very much suspect, has been the cause we have not heard that they have superceeded the use of quills generally.

In the progress of my improvements of the Polygraph, having made a vast waste of quills, and purchasing those imported, found them not only troublesome but also an expensive article, which induced me to try metal Pens, and not being able to purchase was compeled to make them. With a hope that this sent, enclosed, will be of use to you, I beg your acceptance of it.

If the spring or nib is not perfectly to your liking, with a smooth file or a stone you can easily mend it, as the spring temper is rather of the softer than the hardest degree, yet it is of such hardness that the metal will I believe, break before it will bend. And if you rub off the Varnish, you can replace it, by taking some of the best sealing wax disolved alcohal, a simple process; breaking the wax into small pieces, and placing the vial in a gentle heat, it will disolve in the course of a night.

Viewing the uncertainty of human life, and wishing my Museum a permanent and important school of useful knowledge, I still continue to exert all my powers to put it into such a situation that those into who's hands it may fall, will have little trouble to put the encrease of articles into their proper places. Linneus's classification of Animals is framed in the Rooms. The name of each genus, the various specimens numbered, and the latten, English and French names placed over each case, so that now no visitor ought to expect any attendant to accompany them through the Rooms: This is now nearly compleated in three of the orders, and on almost every other subject is the English name. I am making a new disposition of the Minerals, and as soon as possible I will enter on the general collection of Fishes, what is now done, is only a few subjects accidently obtained, and shortly after this, I hope to put togather my observations on the most interesting subjects, as a companion to the Museum. When this is done, I may then dispose of my time in any manner that promises to promote this great object, The Museum must be great, as mediocrety will stamp no value on it.

With my Sons I am now meditating a very important appendage, which I wish at present, not to be spoken off. It is to teach the mechanical arts, by shewing the process of various branches in as clear a veiw as specimens in the detailed parts, with models, drawings and descreptions illustrative of various methods of workmanship. Manual Trades which are thought difficult to those unacquainted with them, will here be found easey, and I doubt not improvements suggested even to experienced workmen of some trades.

In this view of it I consider this undertaking of vast magnitude, as tending to promote much good to our Country.

If our Farmers were taught the process of trades, many that can be done in this mode with out serving an apprenticeship, they might employ many vacant hours especially in winter and in stormy weather, at trades that would give them profit. and by degrees we might be supplied with vast quantities of manufactured articles, without the neglect of agricultural persuits, nay they might then make many of their implements of husbandry in more useful forms. Further, that of giving sources of amusement, of which the mechanic arts are most fruitful, and certainly not the least useful would be a powerfull means to draw the Idle from vicious habits.

The want of pleasing employment is the principle cause of drinking, gambling and Horse racing being so prevalent amongst our Farmers & Planters.

I have just received a Letter from Mr. Latrobe, who desires me to send you one of my most improved Polygraphs. This shall be done with altering the Drawer as he directs, and which I beg your use off untill I can have a new construction of the form of the Desk made, which on tryal, if found better, I will send you one and the other may then be disposed off, But I suppose many Gentlemen would be glad to purchase so useful a machine, or otherwise it may be sent back by the Packet, as the season advances & this will soon become a ready conveyance.

When I have found a Packet going to Alexandria and the Polygraph put on board I will write again.

I am Dear Sir with much respect and great esteem your friend

C W PEALE

RC (DLC); at foot of text: "His Excellency Thomas Jefferson Esqr. President of the United States"; endorsed by TJ as received 29 Feb. and so recorded in SJL. PoC (Lb in PPAmP: Peale-Sellers Papers).

WISE'S PENS: Peale's son Rembrandt returned from a trip to London with a sample steel pen made by a Mr. Wise (Peale, *Papers*, 2, pt. 1:659; Bedini, *Jefferson and His Copying Machines*, 62).

From Isaac Briggs

MY DEAR FRIEND,   New Orleans 27th. of the 2nd. Mo. 1804.

I am here, with Robert Williams, on my way to the seat of Government. We expect to sail for Baltimore, within three or four days, in the Schooner Experiment, being the first vessel that offers. She is said to be a swift sailer; our hopes are therefore sanguine that we shall arrive in Washington before the end of next month.

On the 10th. instant, by the mail, I wrote to the Secretary of the Treasury, informing him that Robert Williams and myself had determined to go immediately on to the seat of Government, and stating our reasons for that measure. Permit me briefly to repeat those reasons: The business of *recording* claims, by the Register of the landoffice west of Pearl River, has but just commenced and there is no reasonable ground to believe, without a radical change of the Register's measures, that they will be recorded in twelve months. In consequence, neither the Board of Commissioners, nor myself, can act;— the public survey is at a stand, for want of sufficient compensation. Thus situated, and possessing some knowledge also respecting the Missisippi Territory and Louisiana, which is of too delicate a nature to be confided to the mail, we think it best to make an *oral* communication, previous to the rising of Congress.

We have cause to believe that the mail has, in some measure, become an uncertain channel of communication between these Southwestern Territories and the general Government—I wish there may have been no *Criminal interception* of letters.—Governor Claiborne informs me that he has not, since he left Fort Adams in the beginning of December last, received an atom of official information from the Government under which he acts; not even notice of the arrival of his letters to the department of state, although he has forwarded by every mail a full and detailed account of his proceedings, since taking possession of New Orleans.—Most of us holding offices under the United States are in a similar uncertainty. We shall bring on Governor Claiborne's duplicates.

On the 2nd. of last month, I wrote to thee from this City:—I then mentioned my friend Claiborne's wish to return to private life. The opinion I then had, remains unchanged,—an opinion which he opposed, but in which he now concurs,—that were he not to be appointed the permanent Governor of lower Louisiana, his removal could not be so managed as not to afford his enemies a triumph over him, and enable them to make it extensively believed (whether it be fact or not) that he had lost the President's confidence—which I firmly believe he values above every other thing on earth, except the consciousness of deserving it. My earnest wish for him is, that no appointment for that office, to his exclusion, may be determined on until Robert Williams and myself shall have been heard respecting his conduct.

Accept assurances of my Respect, Esteem, and affection,

ISAAC BRIGGS.

RC (DLC); at foot of text: "Thomas Jefferson, President U.S."; endorsed by TJ as received 9 Apr. and so recorded in SJL. FC (MdHi).

For Briggs's letter of 10 Feb. TO THE SECRETARY OF THE TREASURY, see Gallatin to TJ, 8 Mch. (first letter).

REGISTER OF THE LAND-OFFICE: Edward Turner.

From Christopher Ellery

Senate Chamber

SIR   27th. Feby. 1804—

I have not the confidence requisite for the frequency of applications which it seems to become my duty to make to the Executive—Indeed I address the President by letter, rather than in person, merely because I would be as little troublesome as possible—

The inclosed letters, relative to the character & qualifications of Mr. Sterry, came under cover from him to myself, accompanied by one to the Secretary of State; and it is probable that Mr. Sterry himself will visit the seat of government shortly on his way to New Orleans. Should it comport with the public interest to bestow an office upon him, Mr. Sterry, there can be no doubt of his faithfulness & ability—recommended as he is by gentlemen of the first respectability—

The other letter, respecting the Collector at New Bedford, speaks for itself—I have only to observe, in addition, that Mr. Taber has declared, in a letter to myself, that the appointment of Mr. Almy, named in Mr. Hazard's letter, would be agreeable to the republicans in Newport—With the highest respect.   CHRIST'R ELLERY

RC (DNA: RG 59, LAR); at head of text: "The President of the U. States"; endorsed by TJ as received 27 Feb. and so recorded in SJL with notation "Almy & Sterry"; also endorsed by TJ: "Almy William. to be Collector New Bedford" and "note N. Bedford is in Mass." Enclosures: (1) Asher Robbins to Ellery, Newport, 16 Dec. 1803, introducing Robert Sterry, who plans to visit Washington on his way to New Orleans "to procure letters of introduction at his destination"; he is "amiable & accomplished," has been admitted to the bar of Rhode Island, "& bids fair to distinguish himself in the profession" (RC in same; endorsed by TJ: "Sterry Robert emploimt. N.O."). (2) Arthur Fenner to TJ, 24 Dec. 1803. (3) Nathaniel Hazard to Ellery, Taunton, 9 Feb. 1804; he writes at the pressing request "of some of my, and your friends" and notes that if Edward Pope, collector at New Bedford, is removed, no man is more suitable to fill the vacancy than William Almy of Westport, "a man of respectability, of address, of prudence, of integrity, of sound judgement—very few, if any of our Republican friends, in this quarter, stand higher in point of charac-

ter," and his appointment "would give more general satisfaction, and be productive of more advantage to the party"; Hazard concludes, "whatever you can do with the President, either directly or through Mr Bishop, the Representative in Congress from this part of Massachusetts, will be very agreeable to me" (RC in DNA, RG 59, LAR; endorsed by TJ: "Almy Wm. to be Collectr New Bedford v. Pope").

For earlier calls to remove Edward Pope as COLLECTOR AT NEW BEDFORD, see Vol. 41:421-3. In a letter to Massachusetts congressman Phanuel Bishop dated Raynham, 18 Jan. 1804, Josiah Dean recommended Isaiah Weston for the post. Besides being a man of character and ability, Weston was also "steady and firm in his political Sentiments" (RC in DNA: RG 59, LAR; endorsed by TJ: "Weston Isaiah. to be Collectr. New Bedford v. Pope. Josiah Dean to mr Bishop. mr B prefers Weston to any candidate").

Constant TABER was navy agent at Newport (NDBW, 2:48; Madison, *Papers, Sec. of State Ser.*, 8:294n).

To George Jefferson

DEAR SIR   Washington Feb. 27. 04.

By last night's mail I recieved information from mr Griffin[1] that 19. hhds. of my tobo. were already at Richmond, and that the two remaining ones would go immediately. he also inclosed me the manifests of the 19. which I herein inclose to you and on the next leaf you will see a list of the numbers & weights, making in the whole 36,509. ℔. in the 21. hhds. I wish it to be sold as soon as you possibly can, so as to get it's value. according to your last advices I presume I may expect

7. Dollars for it. I could not admit well a credit of more than 60. days. perhaps you may obtain ready paiment for the amount I owe you, to wit the balance of the last account, the coal ordered and the hams. be so good as to let me know your prospects, and the actual sale as soon as it takes place as it will ease the arrangements I have to make. Accept my affectionate salutations. Th: JEFFERSON

No.	367	150.	1725 *
	878	150	1550.
	880	150	1556.
	881.	150	1689
	907.	145.	1630.*
	908.	145	1591.
	946.	150.	1793
	947	150.	1736.
	977.	140.	1878.
	1106	140.	1566.
	1107.	140.	1700.
	1108.	140.	1700.
	1109.	140.	1853.
	1165.	140.	1820
	1166.	140.	1789.
	1198.	140.	1767.
	1199	140	1928
	1200.	140.	1935
	1201.	140.	1768
	1220.	142.	1738
	1221.	142.	1797.

21. hhds		36,509
the heaviest is		1935
the lightest		1550.
the average		1738½

*these are the two which not being down the manifests are not received

PoC (MHi); at foot of first page: "Mr. George Jefferson"; endorsed by TJ. Recorded in SJL with notation "tobo. 36,509. ℔." Enclosures not found.

A letter of 17 Feb. from Burgess GRIF-FIN, recorded in SJL as received from Poplar Forest on 26 Feb., has not been found.

[1] Preposition and name interlined.

From Benjamin H. Latrobe

DEAR SIR   Washington Feby. 27h 1804.

I judged very ill in going to Thornton. In a few peremptory words, he, in fact, told me, that no difficulties existed in his plan, but such as were made by those who were too ignorant to remove them and though these were not exactly his words,—his expressions, his tone, his manner, & his absolute refusal to devote a few minutes to discuss the subject spoke his meaning even more strongly and offensively than I have expressed it.—I left him with an assurance that I should not be the person to attempt to remove them,—& had I had immediate possession of pen, ink, & paper I should have directly solicited your permission to resign my office.—

I owe however too much to you, to risk by so hasty a step, the miscarriage of any measure you may wish to promote, and I shall devote as before my utmost endeavors to excite the disposition in the Committee,—to which I am summoned tomorrow morning,—in favor of the appropriation.

In respect to the plan itself, it is impossible to convey by words or drawings to the mind of any man,—that impression of the difficulties in execution which 20 Years experience creates in the mind of a professional man.—I fear I have said already too much for the respect I owe to your opinions, though much too little for my own conviction.—The utmost praise which I can ever deserve in this work is that of la difficulté vaincue, and after receiving your ultimate directions all my exertion shall be directed to earn this degree of reputation.

My wish to avoid vexation, trouble, & enmities is weak,—compared to my desire to be placed among those whom you regard with approbation & friendship. If you therefore, *under all circumstances*, conceive that my services can still be useful, I place myself entirely at your disposal.—I am with sincere respect Your faithful hble Servt

B HENRY LATROBE

PS. In order to pass my accounts it will be necessary to produce a regular appointment from you to my office. May I beg you to give the necessary directions for this purpose. I ought to leave Washington on Wednesday morning.—

RC (DLC); addressed: "The President of the United States"; endorsed by TJ as received 27 Feb. and so recorded in SJL; also endorsed by TJ: "his appmt to commence Mar. 15. 1803."

During a conference with the president earlier in the day, Latrobe had resolved to meet with William THORNTON to discuss problems he was having with Thornton's design for the Capitol. Although TJ "had promised to see Thornton on the objectionable parts of the design," Latrobe "hoped to prepare the way for an amicable adjustment of the business by a prior meeting" (Latrobe, *Correspondence*, 1:436-7).

For the House COMMITTEE called to review Latrobe's report on the public buildings, see TJ to the Senate and the House of Representatives, 22 Feb.

LA DIFFICULTÉ VAINCUE: that is, the difficulty vanquished.

REGULAR APPOINTMENT: TJ wrote Latrobe a letter dated 15 Mch. 1803 (and on his file copy, writing "4" above the "3"), which read, "The legislature of the US. having made provision for the repairs and construction of the public buildings at Washington it becomes necessary to revive the office of Surveyor of the public buildings who was formerly charged with the immediate direction of them under the superintendance of the board of Commissioners. you are therefore hereby appointed to that office with the salary of seventeen hundred Dollars a year which was allowed to him, to commence from this day" (PoC in DLC; at foot of text: "To B. Henry Latrobe"; not recorded in SJL).

To Charles Willson Peale

DEAR SIR   Washington Feb. 27. 04.

Mr. Latrobe promised a few days ago to write to you to have me furnished with a polygraph of two pens, and that his experience would enable him to give some directions about it which would be useful. he was to desire particularly that there should be a drawer in each end, without any partitions in the drawers, because I would have them made here to suit my own convenience. I should also prefer the fountain inkpots, by which I mean those made thus their best size is of about $1\frac{3}{4}$ I. diameter or square.

Mr. Latrobe informs me you have one of Brunelle's polygraphs procured by your son Rembrandt while in London. I am afraid I shall be thought unreasonable in asking your permission to see it here. and yet I am persuaded that if packed in an external box and directed to me it would come by the stage in perfect safety, & especially if under the care of some person who should be coming here. trial alone can enable one to estimate new and curious inventions. perhaps you can also inform me what such an one costs in London should I like it well enough to send for one, and to whom I should address myself there. if you can venture yours here, it shall be returned at any date you fix and under my guarantee as to loss or injury coming & going. Accept my friendly salutations and assurances of great esteem.

TH: JEFFERSON

RC (TxU); at foot of text: "Mr. Peale." PoC (DLC); endorsed by TJ.

For Marc Isambard Brunel's (BRUNELLE'S) copying machine, see Vol. 39: 408n.

Petition from Washington Inhabitants

To the President of the United States

The petition of the Subscribers, Inhabitants of the City of Washington, respectfully represent

That great hardships and inconveniences have resulted to many of your petitioners, and a considerable check to the increase and population of the Metropolis of the United States, has arisen from the continuation of the restrictions and regulations respecting buildings and improvements in the said City—which, altho' they have measurably abated by the frequent suspensions of the first original article of the terms and conditions declared by the then President of the United States on the 17h. October 1791; and altho' many beneficial effects have arisen from such suspensions, Yet your Petitioners beg leave to represent that the Exception contained in your proclamation of the 28h December 1803, has still the power of checking Emigration; that it still impedes the Settlement in the City of many mechanics and others whose Circumstances do not admit of their erecting houses of the particular description incorporated in the said exception—and that the failure of increase of buildings, causes the holders of buildings already to ask high and exorbitant rents—Your petitioners beg leave further to state that the Expence of erecting and covering in a house of one story is as much as the expence attendant on the covering in of a house of two Stories; and further that the Space of three hundred and twenty square feet, in many instances is found inadequate to answer for buildings suitable for common purposes—

Your petitioners therefore indulge a hope that their prayer for a repeal of the said Exception, and a continuation of the suspension of the original Article, will not be deemed unreasonable, as they humbly conceive the City in general will be benefited thereby, as well as the Individuals who have already suffered in consequence of the restrictions; & Your petitioners as in duty bound will ever pray &c.

Washington February 27. 1804

RC (DLC); in Robert Ware Peacock's hand, signed by him and 23 others; endorsed by TJ: "Wooden buildings. Petns for." RC (same); in William Worthington's hand, signed by him and 48 others. RC (same); in an unidentified hand, signed by William Prout and 74 others.

SUBSCRIBERS: Robert Ware Peacock was an attorney and William Worthington and William Prout served at different times on Washington's common council (*National Intelligencer*, 8 June 1814; Vol. 37:556; Vol. 41:574n). In addition to workmen and builders in the city, most prominently George Blagden, signers included John P. Van Ness and John Breckinridge.

From William Henderson

Sumner County State of Tennessee

DEAR SIR   February 28th 1804

I congratulate you upon the Session of the Louisiana Country to the United States, we are informed that it will be divided into two Teritorial destricts, I suppose each destrict will have a Governor and am apprehensive that Andrew Jackson of this State has by some of his friends & connections been recommended to you as a proper person to fil One of those important Offices As I have some expectations of being a Citizen of that Country I feel myself somewhat interested in those appointments,

Sir from my long Acquaintance with you I have taken the liberty of droping a few hints (to you) for the good of the Public & Citizens at large respecting that Gentleman I have been Acquainted with Mr Jackson for several years and view him as a man of Violent passions, Arbitary in his disposition and frequently engaged in broils and disputes, No character escapes him, is now sued for an Assault & Battery, & in a few days will be indicted for a breach of the peace, Such a character I conceive is not a proper one to fill the Office of Governor tho he is a man of talents And were it not for those dispottic principles he might be a usefull Man—

I am Dr Sir Respectfully Your Mo: Ob. & Huml. Sevt

WILLIAM HENDERSON

RC (DNA: RG 59, LAR); endorsed by TJ as received 13 Mch. and "Jackson not to be Govr. Louisa." and so recorded in SJL.

William Henderson (1752-1807), a former officer in the Continental Army from Albemarle County, Virginia, settled in Sumner County, Tennessee, around 1790. He became postmaster of Hendersonville in 1800 (Stets, *Postmasters*, 240; Heitman, *Register*, 285; Larry L. Miller, *Tennessee Place Names* [Bloomington, Ind., 2001], 97; Walter T. Durham, *Old Sumner: A History of Sumner County, Tennessee, From 1805 to 1861* [Gallatin, Tenn., 1972], 15, 27).

John C. Henderson SUED Andrew Jackson for an assault that had taken place on 13 Feb. (Harold D. Moser and others, eds., *The Papers of Andrew Jackson*, 9 vols. [Knoxville, 1980-], 2:xxiii, 16n, 527).

To George Jefferson

DEAR SIR   Washington Feb. 28. 04.

Yours of the 23d. was recieved last night and I have this day desired mr Barnes to get a bushel and a half of clover seed for mr Craven to be forwarded to you from this place or Philadelphia without delay. although the 400. bushels of coal desired from you would last through the summer, yet I would rather recieve from you double that quantity than be obliged to buy here, where indeed it is not always to be bought. I will thank you to agree the freight with the person who brings it, & to have it delivered *here*, as every transshipment of coal is expensive crumbles and loses. Accept my affectionate salutations.

TH: JEFFERSON

PoC (MHi); at foot of text: "Mr. Jefferson"; endorsed by TJ. Recorded in SJL with notation "800. b. coal."

To Benjamin H. Latrobe

DEAR SIR   Washington Feb. 28. 04.

I am sorry the explanations attempted between Dr. Thornton & yourself on the manner of finishing the chamber of the house of representatives have not succeeded. at the original establishment of this place advertisements were published many months offering premiums for the best plans for a Capitol and President's house. many were sent in. a council was held by Genl. Washington with the board of Commissioners, and after very mature examination two were preferred and the premiums given to their authors Doctr. Thornton & Hobens, and the plans were decided on. Hobens's has been executed. on Dr. Thornton's plan of the Capitol the North wing has been executed, and the South raised one story. in order to get along with any public undertaking it is necessary that some stability of plan be observed. nothing impedes progress so much as perpetual changes of design. I yield to this principle in the present case more willingly because the plan begun for the Representative room will in my opinion be more handsome and commodious than any thing which can now be proposed on the same area. and tho the Spheroidical dome presents difficulties to the Executor, yet they are not beyond his art, and it is to overcome difficulties that we employ men of genius. while however I express my opinion that we had better go through with this wing of the Capitol on the plan which has been settled, I would not be understood to suppose there does not exist sufficient authority to controul the original plan in any of it's parts, and to accomodate it to changes of circumstances. I only mean that it is not adviseable to change that of this wing in it's present stage. tho' I have spoken of a Spheroidical roof, that will not be correctly the figure. every rib will be a portion[1] of a circle of which the radius will be determined by the span and rise of each rib. would it not be best to make the internal columns of well burnt bricks moulded in portions of circles adapted

[563]

to the diminution of the columns. Ld. Burlington in his notes on Palladio tells us that he found most of the buildings erected under Palladio's direction & described in his architecture to have their columns made of brick in this way and covered over with stucco. I know an instance of a range of 6. or 8. columns in Virginia, 20. f. high well proportioned and properly diminished, executed by a common bricklayer. the bases & Capitals would of course be of hewn stone. I suggest this for your consideration, and tender you my friendly salutations.

TH: JEFFERSON

PoC (DLC); at foot of first page: "Mr. Latrobe."

LD. BURLINGTON IN HIS NOTES ON PALLADIO: TJ was likely confusing Richard Boyle, third earl of Burlington, with English architect Inigo Jones. A 1742 edition of Andrea Palladio's four books on architecture, which TJ owned from early in his life, included notes by Jones, one of which alluded to COLUMNS MADE OF BRICK and covered with STUCCO. Burlington did sponsor an edition of Palladio's four books, which the Editors previously identified as a possible source for TJ's impression of Palladian columns, but he never published his own notes or commentary (Giacomo Leoni, *The Architecture of A. Palladio; in Four Books*, 2 vols. [London, 1742], 1:70; James Gilreath and Douglas L. Wilson, *Thomas Jefferson's Library: A Catalog with the Entries in His Own Order* [Washington, D.C., 1989], 14; DNB, s.v. "Boyle, Richard, third earl of Burlington and fourth earl of Cork"; Sowerby, Nos. 4174-5; Vol. 31:579-80).

[1] Preceding two words interlined in place of "30°."

From Benjamin H. Latrobe

DEAR SIR,   Capitol, Washington, Feby. 28th. 1804

The circumstances that attend the conflict between my wish to promote your views respecting the Capitol, and my conviction of the necessity for forming a plan different from that which is *now* said by Dr. Thornton to be the plan approved by General Washington are among the most unpleasant which I have ever had to struggle with.—It cannot in my opinion be stated that *any* plan,—that is any *practicable* plan exists, or ever existed.—I do not allude to the spheroidal dome. I will undertake to execute it under all my impressions against it,—and I have so much confidence in myself, that I hope to produce a thing not entirely displeasing.—If the house be raised to the level of the the top of the basement story, I will withdraw all further opposition to the colonade, & its eliptical form,—but it will *then* be absolutely necessary to cut off the angles, and thereby to strengthen the external Walls. Of my ideas on this subject I will in a few weeks send you compleat drawings, which I hope will perfectly satisfy your wishes, because the eliptical form, and the Colonade, the principal features of the Work will remain. But perhaps I may still be favored with an interview with you.

In a contest, similar to that in which I am engaged,—first with Mr Hallet, then with Mr. Hatfield,—Doctor Thornton was victorious.— Both these men, men of knowledge, talents, integrity and amiable manners were ruined.—Hatfield had the best expectations in England, when he was called to this country.—The Brother of Maria Cosway, & the protege of the Queen, & of Lady Chesterfield (who on her death left him a legacy of £1500) could not have failed in making a figure in his profession, had he remained at home. I knew him slightly there.—He is now starving in Washington, & Hallet was ruined some Years ago.—After seeing Dr Thornton yesterday I procured Mr. Hatfield's letter to the Commissioners in which he states his opinion of the plan.—His ideas, & almost his words are those I have often repeated. He remained Superintendant of the work for three Years. During this period the original plan disappeared.—Hatfield proposed a New Elevation rejecting the basement. ⌐⌐ The circular domed Vestibule is Hatfields, the two Libraries ⌐⌐ of this shape are his. His style is visible in many other parts of the Work.—All this has been retained while the basement, wholly incompatible with this plan, & loading it with absurdities & impracticabilities remains.—All this can be proved by the most authentic documents.—If I felt the slightest respect for the talents of the original designer *as an architect*, I should be fearless as to myself,—but placed as I am on the very spot from which Hallet & Hatfield fell,—attacked by the same weapons, & with the same activity, nothing but a very resolute defence can save me.

The Committee have just risen. Their enquiries have been most minute. I produced the plan given me by Doctor Thornton. I mean the Ground plan. Its absurdities are still more glaring than its insufficiency as a guide, by which to execute the work. I was asked whether that was the original plan? I said, no, & had I said otherwise I should have failed in my duty to myself & to truth.—I was asked for the original plan?—It is not to be found.—Whose plan was that which I exhibited?—I detailed the authors of the different parts.—Is it a good plan?—No!—What are its faults?—I confined myself to the total want of offices & accomodation of every kind.—How can they be remedied?—By raising the floor one story higher.—More questions were asked, & answered agreeably to truth,—without fear or self interest,—for it is my interest in this city, peaceably to act & speak to every body but yourself, directly contrary to my judgement.

As The result of the meeting it was understood,[1] that an appropriation of 50.000 Dollars should be recommended. I stated the necessity of removing the Earth about the public offices & the President's house. I was desired to put in writing all that I had verbally stated,— in one report, as to the Capitol,—and in a separate report, as to the removal of the Earth.—It was also asked whether I would recommend a plan,—whether the President knew the inconveniences of the present one,—& had conceived the means of remedying them?—I answered that I had stated them fully to You,—that the idea of raising the floor of the house appeared reasonable to you,—that I had however no authority to commit your opinion on the subject,—that I was persuaded that such alterations would be made by You as would produce the best accomodation possible to the house.—

In the report which I shall make tomorrow, I shall be under the necessity of speaking the truth as to the history of the plan & the causes of the defects of the building.—I am prepared for open war,— and shall suffer less by it than I have already done by that conduct that keeps greater talents than I possess out of sight.—I shall recommend *nothing*, but *generally* say that all the inconveniences & deficiencies stated, *may be easily remedied* without altering the external appearance of the building.—

I am also desired to state the probable expence of completing the work.—On this point I shall only say that in the third Year the South wing will undoubtedly be finished probably in the *second*, & that two more appropriations of 50.000 Dollars will *probably* compleat it.

The haste which, I fear is visible in the expression, as well as writing of this letter, I beg you to pardon, and to believe me with the truest respect

Your much obliged hble Servt   B Henry Latrobe.

RC (DLC); addressed: "The President of the United States"; endorsed by TJ as received 28 Feb. and so recorded in SJL.

After meeting with William Thornton and composing his letter of the previous day to TJ, Latrobe met with George Hadfield (HATFIELD) and George Blagden, who, he hoped, would help him piece together the Capitol's tortured design history. Hadfield had not, in fact, designed the CIRCULAR DOMED VESTIBULE, which was Thornton's idea, and Latrobe generally blamed Thornton for perceived flaws that might more properly be attributed to Stephen Hallet than to Thornton. Nevertheless, Latrobe's impressions, reinforced by his conference with Hadfield and Blagden, informed his testimony before the

House COMMITTEE called to look into the report TJ forwarded on 22 Feb. The committee instructed Latrobe to submit in writing the analysis of the Capitol's design that he presented to them in conference. In his report, addressed to the committee's chair, Philip R. Thompson, Latrobe offered a brief account of the evolution of the Capitol's design, which he stressed as composite in nature and not the work of a single author, and enumerated his many objections to the current plan for the south wing, chiefly that the plan left no room for OFFICES. He advised that the only eligible solution that would not deform the structure's exterior was to raise THE FLOOR OF THE HOUSE from the ground level. TJ met with Latrobe again the evening of the 28th and, persuaded of the current plan's impracticability, asked Latrobe to submit drawings of an "eligible design retaining as much as possible the features of that adopted by General Washington" (Latrobe, *Correspondence*, 1:438, 443-9; Allen, *History of the United States Capitol*, 54-6).

[1] Latrobe first began the sentence "The result of the meeting was, that" before altering the clause to read as above.

From Robert Purviance

Collrs. Office

SIR,   Baltimore Feby 28 1804

I herewith transmit a Letter receivd this day from Samuel Coleman Master of the Schooner Fame of Nantucket, accompanied with a small Bundle, which he receivd from the Captain of one of their Ships that had lately arrived from the South Seas.

I have the honor to be Sir, Most respectfully Your Obed. Servant

R PURVIANCE

RC (DLC); at foot of text: "The President of the United States"; endorsed by TJ as received 2 Mch. and so recorded in SJL. Enclosure: probably Félix Varleta to TJ, [before 2 Mch. 1804].

From William W. Woodward

DEAR SIR,   Philada. February 28th. 1804.

I have taken a liberty, which I should not have done, had I not felt confident of your approbation—In a package, which I send by this mail, you will find a Sheet and Proposal of Dr. Scotts' highly improved and admired edition of the Holy Bible—the first Volume of which will make its appearance the last of next month—and the others to be published as fast as they can be received from Europe. I have also in the press a new and much improved edition of Adams' lectures—a Sheet of it as I am now printing it, is enclosed in the package, with a proposal.—If, dear Sir, you approve of, and wish to patronize the above, I shall feel a happiness in having your name among my numerous, and respectable patrons.

I am dear Sir Your Humble Servant

W. W. WOODWARD.—

RC (CSmH); at foot of text: "His Excellency Thomas Jefferson President of the U States"; endorsed by TJ as received 3 Mch. and so recorded in SJL. Enclosure: William Woodward's proposal for printing by subscription in four volumes *The Family Bible, Containing the Old and New Testaments, with Original Notes and Practical Observations*, with commentary by the Reverend Thomas

Scott (printed copy in DLC: Printed Ephemera Collection). Other enclosure not found, but see below.

William W. Woodward (ca. 1770-1837) was a printer, stationer, and bookseller who specialized in religious, legal, and medical works from his Philadelphia shop at 52 South Second Street. Between 1804 and 1809, he produced the first American edition of Scott's Bible, based on a newly released second London edition. According to a list appended at the end of Woodward's proposal, TJ signed his name as a subscriber to one unbound copy of the Bible "in boards" (Philadelphia *Aurora*, 8 Mch. 1804; Sowerby, No. 1471; MB, 2:1195; RS, 2:321). TJ addressed a communication to Woodward at his address in Philadelphia that may have been a subscription form for Scott's Bible (MS of address sheet only, Ralph R. Weaver, Roslyn Estates, N.Y., 1960; franked; postmarked Washington, 9 Mch.; see TJ to Woodward, 21 Dec. 1806, in MoSHi: Jefferson Papers).

ADAMS' LECTURES: George Adams, Jr., a British mathematical instrument maker to King George III, was the author of *Lectures on Natural and Experimental Philosophy*, first published in London in five volumes in 1794 (DNB). In 1806, Woodward printed a revised American edition that included corrections by Robert Patterson as well as a brief outline of modern chemistry (Shaw-Shoemaker, No. 9799; Sowerby, No. 3734; Philadelphia *Aurora*, 17 Sep. 1803, 3 Apr. 1804, 7 Mch. 1805).

To Henry Dearborn

[29 Feb. 1804]

Some compliment being proper for the militia of Tennessee who went to Natchez under the command of Colo. George Dogherty may not something like the following be said on the part of the President in a letter from the Secretary at war to Colo. Dogherty or to the Governor of Tennessee?

'the President has seen with great satisfaction the willingness with which the militia under your command [or under the command of Colo. Dogherty] repaired to the standard of their country. he places it among the proofs that the body of our citizens at large are the best reliance for sudden and temporary calls, and will render unnecessary the burthening them with the maintenance of a permanent force competent to all emergences. he regrets the inconveniences and sufferings experienced in passing & repassing a desart country incapable of supplying necessaries, & so extensive as to have rendered it difficult to carry or to provide them of a sudden. these difficulties have been surmounted by zeal and energy, and have added to their titles to those thanks which the President now renders them in the name of their country.'

RC (PHi); undated, but supplied from PoC; brackets in text in TJ's hand; addressed: "The Secretary at War"; endorsed by Dearborn: "to be attended to when information is received of the return of the Tennessee Volunteers, from Natchez." PoC (DLC); date added by TJ. Recorded in SJL with notation "Tennissee militia."

From Benjamin H. Latrobe

SIR   Washington Feby. 29th 1804.—

The situation of Mr. Lenthall as Clerk of the Works at the Capitol and Presidents house, combines, the duties formerly performed by seperate persons. For instance, Mr. Williams was employed to collect materials at 800 Dollars pr. annum,—Mr. Blagden measured and superintended the Stone work at 3$. 66 Cents pr. day;—the Carpenter at 2$. 33 cts., the Sculptor or Carver at 3$,—each kept their day account. Mr. Lenthall now performs all these duties. Mr. Blagden works by contract, & Mr. Lenthall directs and measures his Work. He cannot therefore on the principle of precedent, be placed on the footing of any person formerly employed.

The advantage of employing *one* person to controul the supply and working up of materials is so evident that the regular system established in Europe, is to employ a Clerk of the Works under the Architect or Surveyor, exactly for the performance of the duties, undertaken by Mr. Lenthall. I have successfully followed the same system in America,—thereby saving to the Public, the high wages of many Agents, and avoiding their Counteraction of each other. The uncommon merit of Mr. Lenthall appears to me to entitle him at least to the wages formerly enjoyed by Mr. Blagden, while attending only to the stonework. I beg however to submit the case to your decision. His accounts have not been settled, owing to the doubt respecting the salary he merits.

I am very respectfully   B HENRY LATROBE
                                surveyor of the Public buildings.

RC (DLC); at foot of text: "The President of the United States"; endorsed by TJ as received 2 Mch. and so recorded in SJL.

MR. WILLIAMS: probably Elisha O. Williams, who in 1792 was hired by the D.C. commissioners as "general bursar of the labour in the federal City" at a rate of £250, roughly equivalent to $800, a year (DNA: RG 42, PC; William Seale, *The President's House: A History*, 2 vols. [Washington, D.C., 1986], 1:24-5).

For the resolution of Latrobe's recommendation, see TJ to Latrobe, 10 Mch. 1805.

To Samuel Miller

Feb. 29. 04

Th: Jefferson returns his thanks to the revd mr Miller for the copy of his Retrospect of the 18th. century which he has been so kind as to send him, and shall with pleasure avail himself of his first leisure to read it. he salutes him with respect & friendship.

RC (NjP: Samuel Miller Papers); addressed: "The revd. Samuel Miller New York"; franked; postmarked Washington. PrC (DLC).

TO SEND HIM: Miller to TJ, 20 Feb., received from New York on 24 Feb., is recorded in SJL but has not been found. Miller sent a copy of *A Brief Retrospect of the Eighteenth Century. Part First; in Two Volumes: Containing a Sketch of the*

Revolutions and Improvements in Science, Arts, and Literature, During that Period, which was printed by T. and J. Swords in New York in 1803 and included several references about TJ. Miller communicated with the president in June 1801 about the work, for which TJ had lent him some materials. Miller had also previously sent TJ some of his other publications (Sowerby, No. 4727; Vol. 27:26; Vol. 31:370; Vol. 34:410-12).

To the Senate and the House of Representatives

TO THE SENATE AND HOUSE OF REPRESENTATIVES OF THE UNITED STATES.

I communicate for the information of Congress a letter stating certain fraudulent practices for monopolising lands in Louisiana which may perhaps require legislative provisions.   TH: JEFFERSON
Feb. 29. 1804.

RC (DNA: RG 46, LPPM, 8th Cong., 1st sess.); endorsed by a Senate clerk. RC (DNA: RG 233, PM, 8th Cong., 1st sess.); endorsed by a House clerk. Recorded in SJL with notation "land-frauds in Louisiana." Enclosure: Captain Amos Stoddard to Henry Dearborn, dated Kaskaskia, 10 Jan. 1804; Stoddard has been informed by the attorney general of the Indiana Territory that a massive land fraud is being attempted in Louisiana; some 200,000 acres, including the best mines, have been surveyed "to various Individuals" in the last few weeks; all official papers bear the signature of "M. ——," the former Spanish lieutenant governor and current commander of a small garrison near New Orleans; Stoddard fears that he has been prevailed upon to affix his signature to a

large number of blank papers, over which antedated petitions and orders of survey have been inserted; the persons attempting the fraud probably expect that their papers will be confounded with just claims and that the United States will not be able, or even attempt, to distinguish between the just and fraudulent claims (Trs in DNA: RG 46, LPPM and DNA: RG 233, PM).

Lewis Harvie presented TJ's message and accompanying letter to the Senate and House of Representatives on 29 Feb. After reading the papers, both houses ordered them to lie for consideration (JS, 3:367-8; JHR, 4:608). For earlier reports of land fraud in Louisiana, see Isaac Briggs to TJ, 8 Sep. 1803 (Vol. 41:349-51).

Resolution on Land Titles in Louisiana

[ca. 29 Feb. to 14 Mch. 1804]

Whereas there is reason to believe that during the time which intervened between the date of the treaty of St. Ildefonso alienating the colony & province of Louisiana with all the rights & interests held by Spain in or over the same, & the transfer & delivery thereof to the US. frauds of great extent & enormity have been practised, & numerous fabrications & devices contrived,[1] by various individuals, with or without[2] the cover & semblance of legal authority, & under dates true or false,[3] for transferring to private hands great portions of those public lands, the property & interest in which were, by the said treaty of St. Ildefonso,[4] effectively alienated from the power then holding the same, in exchange for equivalents mutually satisfactory to the parties, so that no bonâ fide transfer of any part thereof could afterwards be made to the detriment or diminution of the rights & interests so alienated & exchanged:

Be it therefore ordained that all grants of lands within the said province, the title whereof, whether legal or equitable,[5] was, at the date of the said treaty, in the crown, government, or nation of Spain, & every act and proceeding, subsequent thereto, of whatsoever nature, towards the obtaining any grant, title or claim to such lands, & under whatsoever authority transacted or pretended, be, and the same are hereby declared to be, & to have been from the beginning[6] null, void, & of no effect in law or equity.

MS (DLC: TJ Papers, 137:23694); undated, entirely in TJ's hand. Dft (same, 137:26710).

The date of the above resolution is uncertain, but TJ probably composed it sometime between 29 Feb., when he forwarded Amos Stoddard's report on land fraud in upper Louisiana to Congress, and 14 Mch., when John Rhea of Tennessee offered an amendment to the bill for the government of Louisiana in the House of Representatives that very closely followed the wording of the second paragraph of TJ's resolution. The House approved Rhea's amendment on 16 Mch. by a vote of 60 to 42, and it was subsequently included in section 14 of the act for dividing Louisiana and providing for its temporary government, passed on 26 Mch. (JHR, 4:631, 657-8; *Annals*, 13:1128, 1186-7, 1196-7; U.S. Statutes at Large, 2:287-9; Bill for the Organization of Orleans Territory, [23 Nov. 1803]; TJ to the Senate and the House of Representatives, 29 Feb. 1804).

[1] In Dft TJ interlined, in two stages, the passage from "& numerous" to here.
[2] Preceding three words interlined in Dft in place of "& covered under."
[3] Phrase beginning "and under" interlined in Dft.
[4] Word interlined in Dft in place of "Domingo."
[5] Preceding four words interlined in Dft.
[6] Preceding three words interlined in Dft in place of "ab initio."

From Albert Gallatin

[February 1804]

A great anxiety prevails amongst the republicans of Ohio to have removed Z. Biggs receiv. pub. monies at Steubenville.

His office has been extremely well kept, owing, it is said to the talents of his deputy Beatty whose politics are as obnoxious as those of Biggs.   A.G.

The letters to be returned

RC (DNA: RG 59, LAR); undated, but see below. Enclosures: (1) John Sloane to Thomas Worthington, Chillicothe, 25 Jan. 1804, seeking the removal of Zaccheus Biggs as land office receiver at Steubenville; Biggs was appointed "through the influence of the leaders of the opposition to the present administration" because of his loyalty to their interests and "has constantly availed himself of the influence he possesses not only as a publick officer but as private Citizen in promoting the election to office of persons avowedly hostile to the present administration" (same). (2) Certificate signed by John Milligan, John Sloane, Samuel Dunlap, and Joseph McKee, all members of the Ohio General Assembly from Jefferson County, 26 Jan. 1804, recommending the removal of Biggs, who uniformly opposes the election of "men of known republican principles" and advocates "the election and promotion to office men avowedly hostile" to Republican measures (same; endorsed by TJ: "Biggs Zacheus. recievr of public monies in Ohio. his removal for active opposition"). (3) Milligan to Worthington, Chillicothe, 27 Jan. 1804, lamenting that previous efforts to remove Biggs have been unsuccessful; Biggs and his deputy oppose the local Republican candidates but have not directly opposed the president and vice president because the measures of the general government are so generally approved "that a direct opposition would defeat the Design"; other local Republicans have already written or will write to Worthington or the Treasury secretary soon (same). (4) Milligan to Worthington, Chillicothe, 28 Jan. 1804, enclosing a letter and certificate, perhaps Nos. 1 and 2, above, to be "at the disposal of you and your" colleagues "as you may think best"; Milligan notes that the Ohio General Assembly will not adjourn for another four weeks, giving Worthington time "to know how the Business is likely to Succeed" and inform him of it before he leaves Chillicothe (same; endorsed by TJ: "Biggs Zacheus"; for TJ's notation, see below).

Thomas Worthington probably entrusted the Treasury secretary with these letters from Jefferson County, Ohio, Republicans calling for the removal of Zaccheus BIGGS soon after he received them, and Gallatin, in turn, forwarded them to TJ with the undated note, above. After he had discussed the contents of the letters with Worthington, TJ added a notation below his endorsement on Enclosure No. 4: "Colo. Worthington recommends suspendg this. he sais he is a federalist, and has been very active in elections. but an able & very excellent man." For the Ohio senator's further assessment of Biggs, see Worthington to TJ, 17 June 1804. An Adams appointee, Biggs remained at the Steubenville land office until 1808 (JEP, 1:353, 354; 2:85; Gallatin to TJ, 7 Apr., 29 July 1808, both in DLC).

To Nicoll Fosdick

SIR   Washington Mar. 1. 04.

It is long since I recieved your favor of Nov. 12. and although business has prevented my answering it sooner, I have not been unmindful of the favor of the information it contained, and of the kindness of the communication. after the clamor which had been raised against me on account of a former letter written to the same person & published by him, I had imagined he would be more circumspect in future. but what you mention proves his discretion does not prevail at all times, and that hereafter I must exercise my own. I pray you to accept my thanks for putting me on my guard, with my salutations and best wishes for your happiness.   TH: JEFFERSON

PoC (DLC); at foot of text: "Mr. Nicholls. Fossdick."

The FORMER LETTER was likely that of 18 Mch. 1801 to Thomas Paine, in which TJ offered Paine a passage from France on a U.S. naval vessel. Paine later reported the president's offer, drawing Federalist rebukes against TJ (Malone, *Jefferson*, 4:194-5; Vol. 33:358-9).

To Charles Willson Peale

DEAR SIR   Washington Mar. 1. 04.

I recieved last night your favor of the 26th. and thank you for the pen accompanying it, which seems to perform well. I had written to you on the 27th. Ult. on the subject of the Polygraph. the reduction of the size which you propose for a future trial would certainly be a great improvement; it's present bulk being disagreeable. I observe too that after one has adjusted the pens by the gage, one of them will require to be a little moved by trial to make them write with equal strength. this being to be done by moving the pen by hand in it's sheath, it is pushed or pulled too much and is deranged. were[1] there still an interior sheath for the pen which screwed by a few threads only into the present[2] sheath which would then be the middle one a single turn or half turn would adjust it perfectly, and the pen and two screwed sheaths be still withdrawn from the outer one for mending as easily as at present. but you will probably think of a better way.   I sincerely wish you success in the new institution you now meditate as well as in every thing else you undertake. by the immense collection of treasures contained in your Museum you have deserved well of your country, and laid a foundation for their ever cherishing your memory. Accept my friendly salutations and assurances of great esteem.   TH: JEFFERSON

RC (TxU); at foot of text: "Charles W. Peale esq." PoC (DLC); endorsed by TJ.

[1] TJ here canceled "the pen."
[2] TJ here canceled "or mid."

From Félix Varleta

MI ALTO, Y PODEROSO SOR.:   [before 2 Mch. 1804]

Los positivos deseos de conocer á V.E. y de postrarme á sus Pies, me hace ser atrevido poniendo en sus poderosas manos, estas mal formadas Letras suplicandole se sirva concederme licencia; pa. pasar á sus dominios a ponerme en su Real presencia á ofrecerle á V.E. mi persona Junto con mis cortos averes; y asi mismo á exponerle mi solicitud, la qual no dudo con seguir de sus piadosas manos. Yo Señor soy un Español vecino de esta Ciudad de Coquimbo conosido de todos los Vasallos de V.E. por mis buenas Acciones como lo haré constar en todo tiempo; con este motivo me tomo la satisfacion de remitir á V.E. tres Piedras las mas particular. ql. en el dia se han hallado en este Mineral de tres Metales, Oro, Plata, y Cobre; suplicandole se sirva disimularme este atrevimto.; pues solo lo ocaciona el particular afecto ql. le profeso á V.E. a quien le deseo todas felicidades, y mientras consigo el cumplir mis deseos, quedo pidiendo á Dios gue la importante vida de V.E. dilatados años.

B. los P. de V.E. su mas humilde, y seguro servidor,

FELIS VARLETA

EDITORS' TRANSLATION

HIGH AND POWERFUL SIR: [before 2 Mch. 1804]

My positive wishes of meeting your excellency and prostrating myself at your feet, make me bold enough to put in your powerful hands these badly formed words begging you to please give me permission to pass on to your dominions and put myself in your royal presence and offer your excellency my person together with my short experiences, and in this manner I express to you my request, which I do not doubt I will obtain from your merciful hands. I, Sir, am a Spaniard, *vecino* of this city of Coquimbo known by all of your excellency's subjects for my good actions that I make known at all times; with this purpose I take satisfaction in sending you three stones, the most rare which to this day have been found in this vein of three metals, gold, silver, and copper; begging you to disregard this audacity, as it is only caused by the particular affection that I profess to your excellency; to whom I wish all happiness; and while my wishes are yet to be fulfilled, I remain asking God to preserve your excellency's important life for extensive years.

Your most humble and constant servant kisses your excellency's feet.

FELIS VARLETA

RC (MoSHi: Jefferson Papers); un-dated; addressed: "A El Exmo. Sõr. Pte. de los Estados Vnidos de la America Dn. Thomas Jefferson" and "Por la Fragta. Lio capn. José Aliti" (To His Excellency the President of the United States, Don Thomas Jefferson; by the frigate *Lio*, Captain José Aliti); endorsed by TJ, who read the signature as Felis S. Wanleja, as received from Coquimbo, Chile, on 2 Mch. and so recorded in SJL. Probably enclosed in Robert Purviance to TJ, 28 Feb.

Varleta's use of the term VECINO meant that he had the privileges and responsi-bilities of citizenship at Coquimbo (Tamar Herzog, *Defining Nations: Immigrants and Citizens in Early Modern Spain and Spanish America* [New Haven, 2003], 1-2, 6-7, 105).

From Wheeler Martin

SIR   Providence March 2d 1804

you will please to excuse me for taking the liberty to inform you that the proposed amendment to the Constitution of the US. has passed the Senate of this State Uniamous, and in the House of Rep-resentatives yesterday 5 of PM by a majority of twenty four.

You Sir will believe me to be your real friend and Humble Servant in every Sentiment of Respect   WHEELER MARTIN

RC (ViW: Tucker-Coleman Collection); at head of text: "Thos Jefferson Presi-dent of the United States"; endorsed by TJ as received 11 Mch. and so recorded in SJL.

Wheeler Martin (1765-1836) was first elected in 1791 as a justice of the court of common pleas and general sessions of the peace for Providence. Reelected to the position for many years, he also became a public notary as of 1803, and in 1819, chief justice of the court. He was an elec-tor for president and an unsuccessful can-didate for governor of Rhode Island in 1824 (Joseph Jencks Smith, comp., *Civil and Military List of Rhode Island. 1647-1800* [Providence, 1900], 488; same, *Civil and Military List of Rhode Island.*

1800-1850 [Providence, 1901], 47, 262, 335; Providence *Rhode-Island Republi-can*, 3 July 1811; *New-Bedford Mercury*, 30 July 1824; *Providence Patriot*, 12 July 1826; *Newport Mercury*, 28 May 1836; Vol. 34:702).

PROPOSED AMENDMENT: the Rhode Island General Assembly ratified the Twelfth Amendment with a unanimous vote of the senate on 29 Feb. and, after a lengthy debate on 1 Mch., a vote of 42 to 18 in the house (*Providence Phoenix*, 3 Mch. 1804; *Providence Gazette*, 3 Mch. 1804; Journal of the Rhode Island House of Representatives, Minutes of Proceed-ings, 27 Feb.-8 Mch. 1804, in William Sumner Jenkins, ed., *Records of the States of the United States of America*, microfilm ed. [Washington, D.C., 1950]).

From Alexandria Republicans

Sir   March 3d 1804

Relying with confidence on your favorable reception of every communication, which will convey to you without the trammels of form, the real sentiments of any portion of the community over whose destinies you preside, we feel authorised in offering to you our sentiments on an interesting subject—

In the exercise of your constitutional functions we are well satisfied that the Public interest has in every instance formed the basis of your public conduct—We believe however that the language of truth does not always reach you and that on one subject particularly—towit, removal from Office, the Public sentiment has been totally misrepresented—Whatever a liberal policy might at first have required towards Men hostile to our principles, time and experience have evidenced that no conciliatory measure can soften that rancorous hatred which the name Republican ever has, and ever will excite in the breast of a federalist—

It has been confidently asserted that the President of the United States has been impressed with an idea that removals are not wished but by the candidates for Office—As freemen we declare to you that but one sentiment exists with us on this subject—"to wit" that the confidence of Republicans can be with safety reposed, only in republicans. Disclaiming all idea of interference with your constitutional right of appointment, we call on you with the freedom of republicans to enquire how far our statement accords with the public sentiment— We invite your attention to the subject and rely with confidence in the opinion you will form when possessed of correct information— Apply to the new Members of Congress recently drawn from the great body of the people, and not yet infected with the official language of Washington—

If any change of Officers should take place in the District of Columbia, the removal of the Collector at Alexandria, whose conduct is obnoxious to his own party, and hateful to ours, would be gratifying to us individually, and we pronounce with confidence, to the republican party—

May your health be uniform, and durable as the public confidence— With respect we are &c—

RC (DNA: RG 59, LAR); in an unidentified hand, signed by Thomson Mason, Francis Peyton, Henry Rose, Alexander Smith, Humphrey Peake, Robert Moss, Amos Alexander, James H. Blake, William Moss, Charles Tyler, Jr., George Slacum, Presley Gunnell, Joseph Dean, John Longden, and John Cohagan; at head of text: "To the President of the United States"; endorsed by TJ as received 8 Mch. and "Alexandria Petition to remove Syms" and so recorded in SJL.

COLLECTOR AT ALEXANDRIA: Charles Simms.

From Moses Coates

West Brandywine near Downingtown
Pennsylvania 3d 3/mo 1804

RESPECTED FRIEND

It is from the Generous affability and freedom Which I Discovered in the Agreeable Plainness of thy Conversation and Deportment When in thy Company, And perceiving the scientific, and superior Machanical Powers Which thou Possess, of Course a Wellwisher to the advancement and Encouragment of the Arts in our Country, that Excuses me (altho I feel my inferiority) in attempting to Adress thee on the following Occations.—

Probably thou Mayest Recollect When I Exhibited the Model of My improvement on Saw-Mills in thy Presence at Dr. Thorntons, And having some time ago Understood thee had some mind to Erect one on My Plan, Which Will aford me a great Deal of Pleasure. And some time Last Week John Morehead a Mill-Wright from Lexington, Rockbridge County Virginia came here and said he was sent to Explore my Saw-Mill in order to construct one for thee on my Plan of improvement, he highly approved it, and took the Rights for four on his own accompt, he Apprehended he became aquainted with it so as to be Master of the Business, And Purposed to Devote himself to that business.—It is a Very Useful thing there are many of them Runing in Different Parts of the Country But I have Done nothing Yet in the Southern States I Enclose a Coppy of a Certificate from two men up the Deleware River Who has had theirs Runing a considerable time, Which no Doubt Will aford a mind like thine some satisfaction.—

I have another little Curious and Very Usefull machine for Pairing apples other fruit or Roots and allso for cuting, And there ought to be one in Every family town and Country, and I wou'd Beg leave to Suggest to thee the Idea, Whether or no there wou'd not be a Probability and Propriety for the Government of the United States Purchasing my Exclusive Right that it might Become Common to People at Large, whereby they wou'd be able to obtain them at three tenths of the cost they otherwise wou'd, As I wou'd sell to Goverment at a Reduced Price from that of Enterpriseing speculators, from Whose

[577]

Demands the People wou'd be at once Rescued, it's opperation is performed with Rapidity and neatness. One may be seen by Application to Dr. Thornton tho a Very Rough one it is true it is a little simple thing But aparenly so Universally aproved that it leaves not an enemy behind to Reprobate it, And Notwithstand the simplicity its Utility is so evidently Great that every family must wish to Enjoy them.—And where Manual Labour may be Cut off by the introduction of Machineries Particularly such as is Either Laborious or tedious it Certainly ought to meet Encouragement.—

I have other Machineries in opperation of Considerable Magnitude one for Cuting Grain and Grass with Horses which has Performed to admiration. I wou'd not wish to infringe upon thy Patience or I wou'd have given thee a Sketch of its Principles.—

If it wou'd not be Beneath thy Dignity, or interfere with thy More Momentous Concerns I wou'd Gladly Receive a line Relative to the above subjects.—

I Remain Most Cordialy thy friend and Well Wisher

MOSES COATES

RC (DLC); at foot of text: "To Thos. Jefferson President"; endorsed by TJ as received 9 Mch. and so recorded in SJL. Enclosure: Copy of a certificate, dated 12 Jan. 1804, of Mahlon Cooper and Robert Curry of Amwell Township, Hunterdon County, New Jersey, attesting to the utility of Coates's sawmill improvement; the machinery is "in no way Subject to get out of order," but will "Saw, tread Back, and Set compleatly on till the log is finished"; Cooper and Curry find the invention has both reduced their labor and increased production by one-third; Coates's machinery will provide the same advantages and satisfaction to others, and doubtful persons may see it in operation at Cooper and Curry's mills near Painter's Ferry, New Jersey (Tr in DLC; attested by Coates and entirely in his hand).

Inventor Moses Coates of Chester County, Pennsylvania, received patents for an improved sawmill in 1802, a machine for paring apples in 1803, and, with Evan Evans, an improved machine for cutting straw and hay in 1804. His inventions drew wide praise, especially his sawmill improvement that automatically returned the log upon the completion of a cut and gauged it for the next. The machinery could be attached to saws already in use. Coates printed his own pamphlet describing the invention, and sales agents included Andrew Ellicott in Lancaster, Pennsylvania, and William Thornton in Washington, D.C. James Mease included descriptions of Coates's apple paring machine, his straw cutting machine, and a horse-drawn mowing machine in his American version of the *Domestic Encyclopædia* (*List of Patents*, 27, 30, 44; *Poulson's American Daily Advertiser*, 15 June 1802; *Providence Phoenix*, 3 Aug. 1802; Moses Coates, *A New Invention and Improvement on Saw Mills* [Lancaster, Pa., 1802; Shaw-Shoemaker, No. 2042]; *Domestic Encyclopædia; or, A Dictionary of Facts, and Useful Knowledge*, 5 vols. [Philadelphia, 1803-04], 3:119-20, 4:117, 5:61).

To Henry Dearborn

TH:J. TO GENL. DEARBORNE   Mar. 3. 1804.

On the vacating of Judge Pickering's office I shall be obliged to nominate another before the rising of the Senate. J. Langdon has recommended Sherburne. a much more powerful representation is made against him and in favr. of Jonathan Steele. tho' it is probable the witnesses attending the impeachment from that state may have been prepared to give particular opinions, yet perhaps in a free and easy conversation which should not appear to look towards this question, some impartial information may be got from them. if you are on such a footing with any of them as to be able to get me any just information on the subject I shall be much obliged to you to see them & communicate what you learn. affectionate salutations

RC (PWacD: Feinstone Collection, on deposit PPAmP); addressed: "The Secretary at War"; endorsed by Dearborn. Not recorded in SJL.

RECOMMENDED SHERBURNE: see John Langdon to TJ, 20 Jan. 1803 and 13 Feb. 1804. For those in favor of Jonathan Steele, see Vol. 39:491-2; Vol. 40:261-2.

The WITNESSES in John Pickering's impeachment, all Portsmouth, New Hampshire, Republicans, included John S. Sherburne; Steele; Michael McClary, U.S. marshal; Joseph Whipple, customs collector; Richard Cutts Shannon, attorney and bankruptcy commissioner; Thomas Chadbourn, deputy marshal; Edward Hart, a deputy sheriff who knew Pickering for at least 25 years; and Ebenezer Chadwick, another deputy acquainted with Pickering for 22 years (*Annals*, 13:328, 350-9; Lynn Warren Turner, *The Ninth State: New Hampshire's Formative Years* [Chapel Hill, 1983], 214; Vol. 41:627-8). For a description of the 1803 depositions given by several of the witnesses, see Vol. 39:422-4n. TJ nominated Sherburne as U.S. district judge before Congress adjourned (TJ to the Senate, 22 Mch.).

To Mary Jefferson Eppes

Washington Mar. 3. 04.

The account of your illness my dearest Maria was known to me only this morning. nothing but impossibilities prevent my[1] instant departure to join you. but the impossibility of Congress proceeding a single step in my absence presents an insuperable bar. Mr. Eppes goes off, and I hope will find you in a convalescent state. next to the desire that it may be so, is that of being speedily informed of it and of being relieved from the terrible anxiety in which I shall be till I hear from you. god bless you my ever dear daughter and preserve you safe to be the blessing of us all.   TH: JEFFERSON

RC (DLC); addressed: "Mrs. Maria Eppes Edgehill." PoC (ViU: Edgehill-Randolph Papers); endorsed by TJ.

[1] MS: "by."

To Elbridge Gerry

DEAR SIR   Washington March 3. 04.

Altho it is long since I recieved your favor of Oct. 27. yet I have not had leisure sooner to acknolege it. in the middle & Southern states as great an union of sentiment has now taken place as is perhaps desireable. for as there will always be an opposition, I believe it had better be from avowed monarchists than republicans. New York seems to be in danger of republican division. Vermont is solidly with us. R.I. with us on anomalous grounds; N.H. on the verge of the republican shore: Connecticut advancing towards it very slowly but with steady step; your state only uncertain of making port at all. I had forgotten Delaware which will be always uncertain from the divided character of her citizens. if the amendment of the Constitution passes R.I. (and we expect to hear in a day or two) the election for the ensuing 4. years seems to present nothing formidable. I sincerely regret that the unbounded calumnies of the Federal party have obliged me to throw myself on the verdict of my country for trial, my great desire having been to retire at the end of the present term to a life of tranquility, and it was my decided purpose when I entered into office. they force my continuance. if we can keep the vessel of state as steady in her course for another 4. years, my earthly purposes will be accomplished, and I shall be free to enjoy as you are doing my family, my farm, & my books. that your enjoiments may continue as long as you shall wish them I sincerely pray, and tender you my friendly salutations and assurances of great respect & esteem.   TH: JEFFERSON

RC (KAbE); at foot of text: "Elbridge Gerry esq." PoC (DLC).

From William Lee

SIR/.   Bordeaux Mar 3: 1804

I have the honour to enclose a letter which I should have forwarded some time since had not an embargo which has existed for some weeks prevented—The bundle of books which Mr V— intended should accompany his letter I have put on board the Bordeaux Packet bound to Philadelphia and have requested the Collector of the Port to forward them to the seat of Government.—

With great respect I have the honour to remain your obdt. Servt
WILLIAM LEE

RC (MHi); endorsed by TJ as received 14 May 1804 and so recorded in SJL. Enclosures: (1) Volney to TJ, 26 Nov. 1803. (2) Probably a receipt signed by

J. Jacobs, dated Bordeaux, 23 Feb. 1804, stating that he has received on board the Bordeaux packet bound for Philadelphia a "small Bale in Linen containing Books" directed to the president, which Jacobs will deliver to the collector upon his safe arrival (MS in MHi; see TJ to J. P. G. Muhlenberg, 21 May 1804).

From William C. C. Claiborne

DEAR SIR,   New-Orleans March 4. 1804

Mr. Briggs and Mr. Williams of whose arrival in this City, I informed you in my last, have been detained longer than they had calculated on; they will however, sail on tomorrow in a Vessel bound for Philadelphia, but the Captain has promised to land them at Charleston if the wind should admit of it. I think it probable that these gentlemen will reach the seat of Government early in April.

General Wilkinson is preparing for his departure, and will probably be in readiness to set out in ten or fifteen days. Mr. Laussat has notified us of his intention to leave New-Orelans in a short time. He proposes (I understand) to proceed immediately to France. Governor Salcedo will retire in a few weeks to his retreat at the Canary Islands; and the Marquis de Casa Calvo calculates upon remaining in New Orleans for some months.

The most perfect good order continues to exist in this City, and as far as I can learn every thing is quiet in the different districts: Now and then crimes are committed, but the magistrates are vigilant, and the offenders are arrested.

I have been necessitated to pass several ordinances; I ventured reluctantly on the exercise of legislative powers, but the necessities and interests of the society have forced me to act.

I shall send you by Mr. Briggs samples of white and brown sugars manufactured in this Province; they reflect credit on the manufactories, and present a testimony of the wealth and importance of our newly acquired Territory.

I pray you to accept my best Wishes for a continuance of your private and public happiness.

I am Dear Sir, With great respect, Your faithful friend

WILLIAM C. C. CLAIBORNE

RC (DLC); in a clerk's hand, with closing and signature in Claiborne's hand; at foot of text in Claiborne's hand: "Thomas Jefferson President of the United States"; endorsed by TJ as received 9 Apr. and so recorded in SJL.

MY LAST: Claiborne to TJ, 25 Feb. 1804.

To Thomas Newton

Dear Sir   Washington Mar. 5. 1804

We have just heard of the calamitous event of Norfolk. I have not heard whether any persons are named to recieve donations for the relief of the poor sufferers, and therefore take the liberty of inclosing two hundred dollars to you, & of asking the favor of you to have it applied in the way you think best, for the relief of such description of sufferers as you shall think best. I pray not to be named in newspapers on this occasion. Accept my friendly salutations & assurances of respect.   Th: Jefferson

PrC (DLC); at foot of text: "Colo. Thos. Newton"; endorsed by TJ in ink on verso. Recorded in SJL with notation "200. D."

CALAMITOUS EVENT OF NORFOLK: on 22 Feb. a fire broke out in a store at Market Square on Maxwell's wharf, killing or injuring many people and destroying more than 260 houses, shops, and several ships. Initial estimated losses to the town exceeded one million dollars. Although the printing office of the *Norfolk Herald* was a casualty of the conflagration, news of the fire quickly spread and arrived in New York less than a week after the disaster, when a schooner from Norfolk came into port and its captain provided brief details. A fuller account from New York ran in the Philadelphia *United States Gazette* on 1 Mch. and an extract appeared in the *Washington Federalist* the following day. The most widely reprinted account, however, appeared in the Richmond *Virginia Argus* on 25 Feb., the *Alexandria Advertiser* on 3 Mch., and the *National Intelligencer* four days later (New York *Spectator*, 29 Feb.; Philadelphia *United States Gazette*, 1 Mch.; *Washington Fed-*

eralist, 2 Mch.; *National Intelligencer*, 7 Mch.; Thomas J. Wertenbaker, *Norfolk: Historic Southern Port*, 2d ed. [Durham, N.C., 1962], 128).

DONATIONS FOR THE RELIEF: the 25 Feb. account of the "deplorable" and "distressing" Norfolk fire announced a monetary fund "for the immediate relief of the *needy sufferers*," with assistance applications to be coordinated by John Nivison, a Norfolk attorney and public notary. Under 5 Mch in his financial memoranda, TJ recorded his donation in "charity for sufferers by fire Norfolk." On 19 Mch., TJ signed "An act for the relief of the sufferers by fire in the town of Norfolk" that suspended, for up to one year, the collection of bonds due to the United States by Norfolk and Portsmouth merchants who had incurred losses (Richmond *Virginia Argus*, 25 Feb.; MB, 2:1121; JS, 3:382; U.S. Statutes at Large, 6:53; *Simmons's Norfolk Directory* [Norfolk, 1801], 25, 87).

For another instance of TJ's preference NOT TO BE NAMED in the newspapers for his charitable donations, see TJ to John Langdon, 11 Jan. 1803.

From Charles Willson Peale

Dear Sir   Museum March 5th. 04.

Yours of the 27th. Ult. and 1st. Instant I have received.—A Polygraph with the alterations you desire, and also Brunelle's, which I have borrowed for your inspection, will both be sent by a Packet, said to sail on wednesday next.

The defects of the Pens in that which Mr. Latrobe lent you, I can readily account for, therefore it is easily cured. I have much to say on this subject, and doubt not of giving you pleasure in the use of this Machine, when so complete as I know I can make it. but I have not time at present to explain—I will in my next.

I am with the highest regard your friend   C W Peale

RC (DLC); at foot of text: "His Excellency Thos Jefferson Esqr."; endorsed by TJ as received 8 Mch. and so recorded in SJL. PoC (Lb in PPAmP: Peale-Sellers Papers).

Proclamation to Pardon Deserters in Louisiana

Whereas it is represented that sundry persons formerly engaged in the Military Service of the United States and having deserted from the Same, have become inhabitants of the Territory of Louisiana lately ceded to the United States, have establishments of property and families therein, and are in such habits of industry and good conduct as to give reason to believe they will be orderly and useful members of Society if a pardon for their Offence of desertion should be extended to them.[1]

I do therefore hereby in virtue of the authority vested in me by the Constitution of the United States extend & Grant to every person so having deserted from the Military service of the United States who was on the 20th. day of December 1803 an Inhabitant of the said Territory of Louisiana, a free and full pardon for his desertion aforesaid and relinquishment of the term which he was bound to serve at the time of such desertion: Provided nevertheless that no right shall be hereby revived or accrew to such person to demand or receive from the United States any arrearages of Pay or other emolument which were or might have become due had such person faithfully served through the term of their said Military engagement.[2]

In Testimony whereof I have herewith set my hand, and caused the Seal of the United States to be affixed to these presents.

Done at the City of Washington the fifth day of March in the year of Our Lord 1804 in the twenty eighth year of the Independence of the said States.   (Signed) Thos. Jefferson

FC (Lb in DNA: RG 107, LSMA, 2:193-4); in a clerk's hand; at head of text: "By the President of the United States of America—A Proclamation"; at foot of text: "By the President" and "(Signed) James Madison Secretary of State." Dft (DLC: TJ Papers, 138:23992-3); undated; in Levi Lincoln's hand, with alterations in TJ's hand (see notes below); endorsed by TJ: "Lincoln Levi. proclamn. Mar. 3. 04. deserters."

Dearborn enclosed the above proclamation in a 9 Mch. letter to William C. C. Claiborne, requesting that it be "promulgated in such manner as in your opinion will be most proper & expedient" (DNA: RG 107, LSMA). Replying to Dearborn on 14 Apr., Claiborne observed that the "humane Policy of the President in extending his Pardon to such deserters from the Army, as may have settled in Louisiana, will probably be the means of quieting the minds of some industrious members of Society, who I hope by a series of good actions, will make atonement for their former debased conduct" (Rowland, *Claiborne Letter Books*, 2:96).

[1] In Dft, Lincoln's first paragraph reads: "Whereas, there are, in the territory of Louisiana lately ceded to the U States, and, probably, in some parts of these States, and else where, persons who have deserted from the military service of the national Government, and made settlements & established themselves in families since their desertions—And whereas the reclaiming & punishing such persons thus circumstanced would distress their families, & be neither beneficial to the military service, or otherwise conducive to the public good." TJ replaced Lincoln's paragraph with one in his own hand on a separate sheet: "Whereas it is represented that sundry persons who had deserted from the military service of the US. are now established in the territory of Louisiana lately ceded to the US. with their families & property, and have so conducted themselves therein as to give reason to believe they may be orderly and useful members of society if a par-

don for their offence should be extended to them."

[2] In Dft, Lincoln's second paragraph reads: "I do therefore hereby, in virtue of the authority vested in me by the Constitution of the U States, extend and grant to each and every non commission officer, Musician, and private soldier, who may have deserted from the military service aforsd. previous to the 20th day of Decr. 1803, & who has not since joined the sd. service wheresoever he may be, a free and full pardon for his desertion aforesd. and so far as related to his subsequent absence and neglect of duty—And I do hereby dispense with such deserter's future military services under his past enlistments, provided that he shall not claim or be entitled to claim any arrearages of pay, or emoluments which may have been due to him at the time of his desertion." TJ altered the text to read: "I do therefore hereby, in virtue of the authority vested in me by the Constitution of the U States, extend and grant to every person so having deserted from the military service of the US and who was on the 20th day of Decr. 1803, an inhabitant of the said territory of Louisiana a free and full pardon for his desertion aforesd. and a relinquishment of the term which he was bound to serve at the time of his desertion Provided nevertheless that no right shall hereby be revived or accrue to demand or recieve any arrearages of pay or other emolument which were or might have become due had such person faithfully served through the term of their engagement." Lincoln concluded the Dft with a third paragraph: "And I do hereby command all and singular the Military officers of the United States, and enjoin on all the citizens and inhabitants of the said Territory to yield a due compliance herewith."

From Joseph T. Scott

SIR,   Philada. March 5th. 1804

I find that it has been asserted in Washington City, by Messrs. Duane and Leib, in the presence of several members of Congress that the *St. Patrick's society* or naturalized are going to join the third party.

As I have the honor of preciding at that society, it is a duty which I owe not only to myself; but to the society to declare to you most solemnly that the assertion is absolutely false

I do this lest a wrong impression might be made on your mind

Sir, the St. Patrick's society is composed of none but Citizens, some of whom have carried their guns, and their swords through the revolutionary war, which established the Independence of our country; and they can exhibit, at any moment, the honorable marks of their attatchment to the cause. Previous to *the declaration of Independence* we were all one people. No one can be better acquainted with this subject than you. The other members of the society consist of men generally banished from their homes, their families, and connextions, by a sanguinary government, for their attachment to republican principles. They live by their industry. They feel, they enjoy, and they rejoice at having found an asylum in this Country under your wise, pacific, and econimical administration.

To assert that men, who suffered so much, and holding such principles would instantly forsake them is a reproach to which hardly any man of Sensibility would patiently submit.

An Irishman never betrays his friend; there is no Callender among us.

I wish to god it were convenient for me to go to Washington City to give you a history of some men's politics and their veiws; although you stand upon an eminence far above all, yet perhaps you do not see every point

With Sentiments of personal respect I am yours truly

JOSEPH SCOTT

RC (CSmH); endorsed by TJ as received 7 Mch. and so recorded in SJL.

While in Washington in early 1804, William DUANE had a quarrel with the Treasury secretary. Gallatin had urged him to discontinue his support for Congressman Michael LEIB. Duane was loyal to Leib and thought Gallatin's suggestion indicated that a third party was being formed in Pennsylvania. Duane perhaps did not know that TJ had received word from several Pennsylvania congressmen in January that Leib intended to retire. They sought a patronage position for him in Philadelphia (Kim Tousley Phillips, "William Duane, Revolutionary Editor" [Ph.D. diss., University of California, Berkeley, 1968], 158-60; Joseph Clay, Jacob Richards, and Frederick Conrad to

TJ, 23 Jan. 1804). Scott, Duane, and John L. Leib, the congressman's brother, were all active in the Philadelphia ward committee meetings and were signers of the July 1803 address to TJ (Vol. 41:68-70, 75, 115, 179).

In May 1804, Duane was indicted and brought before the Mayor's Court for assaulting Scott after a ward meeting. Duane testified that Scott, as a member of the ST. PATRICK'S SOCIETY, had written "a distinguished character" to "prejudice me." Duane continued: "some think I am an enemy to the Irish—but I am attached to them, and proud of my attachment." Alexander Moore, who took an active role in ward meetings in 1803, testified that Duane charged Scott with making "free" with his character and struck him. When the court asked whether Moore

had heard of Scott's having written letters "reflecting on Mr. Duane," Moore
responded, "I believe Mr. Scott did write
to the President about him." Duane received a $12 fine. Scott did not run for
reelection as president of the St. Patrick's
Society. On 17 Mch. 1804, new officers
were elected and toasts at the celebration
included "Thos. Jefferson, the chief shepherd of the flock, learned, wise, patriotic

and virtuous.—Long life to him." In the
fall of 1804, the society was incorporated
as the St. Patrick Benevolent Society. A
few years later, Duane became the group's
president (*Aurora General Advertiser*, 14,
22 Mch. 1804; Philadelphia *United States
Gazette*, 20 June 1804; Philadelphia *Democratic Press*, 2 Apr. 1810; *The Constitution of the St. Patrick Benevolent Society*
[Philadelphia, 1804], 1, 6-8; Vol. 40:93n).

To John Barnes

DEAR SIR   Mar. 6. 04.

In my note of yesterday I forgot a sum of 41. D 10 c which I had
promised to remit to Richmond this week for the use of John Rogers,
which I must therefore pray you to enable me to do.

Your's affectionately   TH: JEFFERSON

RC (ViU); addressed: "Mr. Barnes";
receipt added to foot of text by Barnes
and signed by Joseph Dougherty for $50
received on 6 Mch.; endorsed by Barnes.

TJ's NOTE OF YESTERDAY has not been
found, nor is it recorded in SJL. For the
payment to JOHN ROGERS, see TJ to
George Jefferson, 7 Mch.

From Jean Frignet de Fermagh

PRÉSIDENT,   Alexandria ce 6th mars 1804.

Un mal'heureux Français père de famille, artiste et ayant tout perdu,
S'adresse à vous pour lui procurer de l'emploi conformément a son
état et le mettre a même d'exister.

Je suis connu dans ce quartier pour avoir operé aux nivellemens de
votre Cité, et par plusieurs Mrs. comme Carolle, Laws, Gl. Masson
&ca. mon nom est Frignet; daignez prendre des informations sur ma
conduite, mes mœurs et mes talens, et si d'après celà Vous me Jugés
capable, je reclame vos bontés.

C'est pour la deuxieme Fois, President que je perds ma fortune,
et obligé de m'expatrier et abandonner mes foyers et mes propriétés,
mais cette derniere me laisse sans ressource, et sans espoir de Jamais
rentrer en pocessions de mes biens.

Demunis des premieres nécéssités à la vie, il y a environ quatre mois,
J'allais pour vous voir et vous prier d'avoir égard à ma mal'heureuse
position; soit en m'accordant une place ou d'arpenteur, d'ingenieur,
et architecte qui est mon Etat, ici ou a la louzianne, Je n'ai pas eu le
bonheur de vous rencontrer.

Par lentremise du Général Masson, J'ai eu occasion de voir Mr. King et votre Secrétaire D'Etat, qui m'ont promis de me faire placer, et de vous en faire part. J'ignore S'ils l'ont fait je n'ai réçu aucune reponse. Mais Président, ma position devenant de jour en jour plus critique et ne pouvant même éxister d'aprés tous ce que je peux faire; L'interêt que vous prenés aux mal'heureux, me fait esperer que vous aurez égard [. . .] ma situation, et que J'ai lieu d'attendre de vous de l'occupation soit ici où a la louzianne.

Je vous le repette, Président, c'est un malheureux pere de Famille qui reclame vos bontés, comme artiste

J'ai l'honneur de vous Saluer avec des considerations President Votre obéissant serviteur   Jn. Frignet Fermagh

EDITORS' TRANSLATION

Mr. President,   Alexandria, 6 Mch. 1804
   A poor Frenchman, a father and skilled worker who has lost everything, begs your help in finding a suitable job to help him survive.
   Several people in this region, including Carroll, Law, General Mason, and others, know me from my work on surveys of your city. My name is Frignet. Please ask them about my skills, habits, and conduct. If on the basis of that information you judge me capable, I appeal to your kindness.
   This is the second time, Mister President, that I have lost my fortune and had to abandon my home, property, and country. But this time I am left with no resources and no hope of ever recovering my goods.
   About four months ago, when I was deprived of the basic necessities of life, I set out to ask if you would look favorably upon my dire situation by giving me a job, either here or in Louisiana, as a surveyor, engineer, or architect, which is my profession. I was not fortunate enough to meet you.
   Through the intermediary of General Mason, I saw Mr. King and your secretary of state, who promised to find me a job and to let you know. I do not know whether they did so and have not received a reply. But, Mister President, my situation is becoming more dire every day; despite all my training I cannot even survive. Your concern for people in need makes me hope that you will look kindly upon my plight and give me a job here or in Louisiana.
   I repeat, Mister President, it is an unfortunate father and skilled worker who begs for your favor.
   I have the honor of greeting you with respect, Mister President. Your obedient servant,   Jn. Frignet Fermagh

RC (MHi); torn; addressed: "A Mr. Jefferson President des Etats Unis D'amérique À féderale City"; endorsed by TJ as received 8 Mch. and "office" and so recorded in SJL.

In 1798, a "Mr. Frignet" residing near Georgetown attempted to secure an ap-pointment in the army, citing previous service as an engineer in France and as engineer and surveyor general at Jérémie in Saint-Domingue (Washington, *Papers, Ret. Ser.*, 2:418). From 1807 to 1810, a John Frignet advertised his services as a French language instructor and translator in Alexandria (Miller, *Alexandria Artisans,*

1:150; *Alexandria Gazette*, 27 Sep. 1808, 31 Jan. 1809, 6 Apr. 1810).

CAROLLE, LAWS, GL. MASSON: presumably Daniel Carroll of Duddington, Thomas Law, and John Mason (Washington, *Papers, Ret. Ser.*, 2:418).

To Albert Gallatin

TH:J. TO MR GALLATIN   Mar. 6. 04.

The inclosed paper got mislaid by accident so as to escape my earlier attention. I do not know how far the office of a director of the bank is compatible with mr Nourse's official duties, or the general spirit of our laws. I leave it therefore altogether to your judgment, only observing that if these admit his acceptance, I believe the bank cannot associate to themselves an honester man.

RC (NHi: Gallatin Papers); addressed: "The Secretary of the Treasury"; endorsed. Not recorded in SJL. Enclosure: probably an undated communication recorded in SJL as received from the Treasury Department on 29 Feb. 1804 with notation "Nourse bank director" but not found.

Joseph Nourse, register of the Treasury, became a DIRECTOR of the Washington branch of the Bank of the United States (*New-York Gazette & General Advertiser*, 14 Mch. 1806; *Alexandria Daily Gazette*, 16 Feb. 1809, 9 Mch. 1810; TJ to Gallatin, 13 Dec. 1803).

From George Jefferson

DEAR SIR   Richmond 6th. Mar: 1804

You will receive inclosed a bill of loading for 400 bushels of Coal. the freight you will observe is high, being as I am told 2 or 3 Cents more than is generally charged in the summer. You will of course determine whether it will not be best for you to lay in a sufficient supply in future, in that season of the year.

I have as yet done nothing with your Tobacco, 40/. being the most I have been offered. I still calculate upon 42/. at least, and hope for more. the remaining two hhds are not yet down.

I am Dear Sir Yr. Very humble servt.   GEO. JEFFERSON

RC (MHi); at foot of text: "Thos. Jefferson esqr." Recorded in SJL as received 11 Mch. Enclosure not found, but see below.

TJ acknowledged his receipt of this letter in a response of 12 Mch. (TJ to Christopher Smith, 12 Mch.). On 21 Mch., TJ issued an order on John Barnes to pay Joseph Todd $34 (MS in MHi; in TJ's hand; signed by Joseph Dougherty acknowledging payment; endorsed by Barnes). That day, Joseph Dougherty paid Todd $34.69 for the "Freight & warfage of 400 Bushels Coal" (MS in MHi; in Todd's hand; endorsed by TJ: "for frt. of Coal").

From Hore Browse Trist

Dear Sir,   New Orleans 6 March 1804

Captain Lewis by letter from Massac under date 10 November last, informed me, that he had address'd to my care at Fort Adams three Boxes, requesting two of them to be forwarded you, and the other to Mr Peale in Philadelphia. Immediately on the receipt of this letter, I wrote my Deputy at Fort Adams enjoining his strict attention to the subject, and also mentioned it particularly at Natchez to Major Claiborne. Unfortunately however the owner of the Boat in which they were sent, on his arrival at Natchez, was put in prison, and in consequence of his giving no information to any person relative to the Boxes, two of them were sunk in the river, & the third broken open, & the Contents stolen or destroyed. This to me is a most mortifying event, not only from the disappointment to Captain Lewis, but also that notwithstanding every precaution on my part for their safe conveyance, I have been prevented gratifying you with these curiosities, which in all probability would have thrown some additional light upon the natural history of our Country. Their destruction I have reason to beleive was designed, but Mr Briggs, being at the time on the spot, is better acquainted than myself, with the whole circumstances of this nefarious outrage. I have requested however that no exertions may be spared to recover them if possible.

It was my intention to have presumed upon your patience with a few observations I thought it my duty to make, relative to some particulars, as well as the general political aspect of this Country, but my friends Isaac Briggs and Robert Williams sailing tomorrow for the seat of General Government, more than precludes the necessity of such a communication, they possessing greater capacity, & being likewise able to enter more into detail verbally, than the limits of a letter would justify.

By the Ship Mars for Philadelphia I took the liberty to send you a Barrel of Paccans and by the Schooner Widow's Son for the same Port, a small Box containing a Sample of Sugar from one of our neighbouring Plantations. I hope they will be acceptable, & that ere this they have been received. With perfect esteem and respect I offer for your happiness my most sincere wishes.

Hore Browse Trist

RC (MHi); endorsed by TJ as received 20 Apr. and so recorded in SJL.

The THREE BOXES from Meriwether Lewis contained specimens from Big Bone Lick; see Vol. 41:464, 468n.

From Albert Gallatin

[7 Mch. 1804]

The within extra-account of E. Burroughs for building the light houses seems proper, being clearly work which was not contemplated by the contract. But as this is not an item of repairs, but in fact an addition to the contract for building which was approved by the President, no alteration can legally be made without his approbation. The propriety of allowing the account is respectfully submitted
by his obedt. Servt.   ALBERT GALLATIN

RC (DLC); undated; endorsed by TJ as received from the Treasury Department on 7 Mch. and "Lt. houses Smith's Pt. & O. Pt. Comft." and so recorded in SJL. Enclosure not found.

For the lighthouse contracts with Elzy BURROUGHS, see Vol. 36:506.

To George Jefferson

DEAR SIR   Washington Mar. 7. 04.

I am to pay Colo. Harvie on account of John Rogers 41. D 10. c. I now inclose you 40. D. for this purpose which I will pray you to deliver him, adding thereto the fraction which cannot be remitted in paper.   I shall shortly send from here a number of packages, to be forwarded to Monticello. they will be chiefly of groceries for my use there, as I shall make a short visit there as soon as Congress rises, which they have determined shall be on the 19th. inst. I suspect that I could get groceries in Richmond as cheap as here. if so I take a great deal of unnecessary trouble in sending them from here. you can better judge of this than I can. their delay in going hence is also a material objection. when you forward them or any earlier articles to Monticello I will thank you to send 2. doz. bottles of Syrop of punch. is it true that tobo. is rising in Richmond? affectionate salutations.

TH: JEFFERSON

PoC (MHi); at foot of text: "Mr. G. Jefferson"; endorsed by TJ. Recorded in SJL with notation "41.10. J. Harvie for Rogers."

In his financial memoranda, TJ recorded enclosing $40 "to pay 41.10 to" John

HARVIE "to the credit of John Rogers with him, acct. for whiskey." TJ recorded in SJL receiving an apparently undated letter from Rogers, who was Harvie's overseer, on 15 Feb. and sending a response on 20 Feb. Neither letter has been found (MB, 2:913, 1121).

From William J. Lewis

SIR   Campbell County, Virginia March 7h. 1804

I hope no apology is necessary for sending to you as President of the Philosophic society some articles which are either curious in themselves, maner of discovery, or as tending to elucidate phenomena perhaps hitherto veiled in obscurity.

Wraping No. 1. contains a bone found in sinking a shaft for Water, about seventy five feet below the surface of the ground, growing in a specious of quortose rock. The hill on which the shaft was sunk, is in the upper end of Buckingham County Virginia, and composes a part of the south bank of James River. It is about two hundred & eighty feet in perpendicular hight, of an oval form, and connected with the ajacent hills by a long narrow ridge forming with the River an accute angle opposed to its current. The country round this hight on both sides is hilly, and unconnected by regular chains each differing in form, hight, and direction.

On viewing this bone two questions are naturely suggested to the mind. how came it there? and what length of time has elapsed since the deposit was made? To answer the first question, we must go back to that period when the spot, in which the bone was found, formed the top of the hill. After the death of the animal to which it belonged, accident may have covered it with the soil, decomposition of that soil into stone took place around the bone, succeeding ages carried on the process of forming soil and its stony decompositions untill the hill at length arrived at its present hight, seventy five feet above the bone.

That this is a reasonable way at least of accounting for the phenomena I think may be clearly shewn—1st all lithological substances are decompositions of that part of the earth which we denominate soil, either directly, or indirectly. Quortose stones are formed directly from a decomposition of soil, such as we find them in hills, and mountains, or, by having their component parts borne along by waters untill united by affinities, or discovered in the beds of Rivers &c. Flints of every denomination, as well as, lime stone, are decompositions of clay, and clay, of soil. No. 2 is a flint formed in clay. The first visible mark of its formation was a white granulus substance adhering to the clay, and as it progressed, it became more and more compact, untill at length it assumed its present form. No. 3 is a fragment of a quortose rock, formed in a similar way but in soil. the same process attended this stone and I think that the elegant vegitable lineaments on its inner surfices prove sufficiently its origin. Thus we see in what maner the rock may have been formed above the bone, and from my own observations, corroborated by men worthy of confidence, it is a fair calculation to say that, pine land which is the most prolific of any other, will (if unburnt and uncultivated) in the space of twenty years produce a soil two inches in depth and the decomposition of this soil into stone, will generally be in the same ratio of increase. This data will give a period of 9,000 years for the formation of the above seventy five feet of rock.

That lithological bodys are thus formed from decompositions I have had satisfactory proofs for the space of three years at least not only near the surfice of the earth on plains, but under water courses; on hills and mountains to the depth of one hundred and ninety eight feet; and in every situation the same process in formation was discoverable.

In contemplating this subject, the mind will not confine itself to a single spot but stretches over the whole surface of the earth, and on viewing its inequalities asks; if those plains, those hills, and those mountains now capted with eternal snows can possibly be the effects of so simple an agent as decomposition? Yes, these mundane principles established by nature are so astonishingly perfect when combined either in one mighty whole, or a single part, that a small portion of vegetable soil suspended in space at a proper distance from the sun, and surrounded by a corrisponding atmosphere, would in time, from the simple operation of these laws alone, produce a world!

Permit me also to mention some experiments (lest accedent should prevent my compleating them) that were undertaken with a view to prove, whither the earth, at any time approximates the Sun. They were made on the North Star supposing it "to be fixed, or varyed but little." during the space of twelve months, this star was traced in an orbit of considerable magnitude from west to east. that this orbit inclined towards the earth, *that is*, the earth is not perpendicular, or, at right angles to the diameter of the Stars orbit. Not having any fit apparatus I made no attempt to measure the diameter of this orbit; it is however sufficiently large to produce and no doubt does the Vareation of the compass. Whilst the Star was making this revolution, the earth had no Visible southing, neither do I believe she has any; but, that the sun also moves in an inclined orbit like the North Star, and in her revolution is twenty three degrees and a half, nigher the earth at one period, than she is at another.

However new this theory appears to myself, yet it may be a trait well known to philosophers. My retirement for some years has rendered me ignorant of the progress of modern philosophy and if I have fallen unintentionally upon the opinions of others I have already written too much—if the contrary, the limits of a letter will not admit of a detailed development.

Should you deem those articles I send you, worthy the attention of the Philosophic society, be so good as to give them a conveyance; and after an examination, my desire is, that they be presented to Mr. Peal.

I am with great respect, your obt. St.   W J Lewis

RC (PPAmP); addressed: "Thomas Jefferson Esquire President of the Philosol. Society Washington"; endorsed by TJ as received 23 Mch. and so recorded in SJL; also endorsed for the American Philosophical Society: "donation of Bone."

Born in Augusta County, Virginia, William J. Lewis (1766-1828) purchased a plantation, which he named Mt. Athos, during the 1790s along the James River in Campbell County. In addition to farming, he operated a quarry along the James and some mills. Active in local and military affairs, he organized a regiment at the commencement of the War of 1812, represented Campbell County in the House of Delegates for four terms and also at the Staunton Convention of 1825, and served as a representative in the Fifteenth Congress (*Biog. Dir. Cong.*; Leonard, *General Assembly*, 260, 277, 281, 285; William J. Lewis to John Breckinridge, 7 Mch. 1804, in DLC: Breckinridge Family Papers; Charleston *City Gazette*, 30 Nov.

1812; *Alexandria Gazette*, 2 Aug. 1825; *Richmond Enquirer*, 11 Nov. 1828; R. H. Early, *Campbell Chronicles and Family Sketches, Embracing the History of Campbell County, Virginia, 1782-1926* [Lynchburg, Va., 1927], 455-6).

On this day, Lewis enclosed his letter to TJ in a letter to John Breckinridge, his brother-in-law, in which he explained that his note to TJ "contains only the faint outlines of a new theory that I fear will not be understood from its ambiguity of expression." He also asked Breckinridge to indicate, if the president inquired, that the theory of mountain formation did not extend to volcanic activity, which formed mountains much more rapidly. His calculations meant that the age of the earth was very old, but he would not belabor the point for "so staunch a Presbyterian" as Breckinridge (Lewis to Breckinridge, cited above; Alexander Brown, *Cabells and Their Kin: A Memorial Volume of History, Biography, and Genealogy* [Richmond, Va., 1939], 261-2).

To the Senate and the House of Representatives

To the Senate and
House of Representatives of the US.

I communicate to Congress an Extract of a letter from Governor Claiborne to the Secretary of state, with one which it covered, for their information as to the present state of the subject to which they relate.   Th: Jefferson
Mar. 7. 1804.

RC (DNA: RG 46, LPPM, 8th Cong., 1st sess.); endorsed by a Senate clerk. RC (DNA: RG 233, PM, 8th Cong., 1st sess.); endorsed by a House clerk. Re-

corded in SJL with notation "extract. Claiborne's lre on importn slaves." Enclosures: (1) Extract of a letter from William C. C. Claiborne to Madison, dated

New Orleans, 31 Jan. 1804, reporting the recent arrival of a vessel containing "fifty African Negroes for Sale"; Claiborne immediately applied to the city's former Spanish *contador*, Gilbert Leonard, for information on Spanish laws and customs regarding the African slave trade; Claiborne encloses Leonard's reply and states that Spain had permitted the importation of slaves to Louisiana; doubting his authority to forbid the sale, Claiborne has left the importer "to pursue his own wishes" (Trs in same). (2) Leonard to Claiborne, dated New Orleans, 25 Jan. 1804, replying to Claiborne's query regarding the importation of slaves to Louisiana; he states that an order by Carlos IV, dated Aranjuez, 24 Jan. 1793, expressly removed the prohibition of the slave trade, and the decree was subsequently promulgated by Don Ramón de López y Angulo, the former intendant of New Orleans, on 29 Nov. 1800; since the retrocession of Louisiana by Spain to France, "but pending the existence and the exercise of the Spanish authorities," three French vessels, carrying a total of 463 Africans, have arrived at New Orleans; all of the slaves were consigned to Jean François Merieult; Leonard adds that although the royal edict confined the trade to Spanish vessels with Spanish captains, authorities in Louisiana after the retrocession extended the privilege to the French as well; if the United States decides to alter Spanish policy regarding the slave trade, Leonard recommends that the changes "should be promulgated a reasonable time anterior to the interdiction of such commercial expeditions as may have been projected under and permitted by the Government of France or Spain" prior to the acquisition of Louisiana by the United States (RC in DNA: RG 59, TP, Orleans; Tr in DNA: RG 233, PM).

Lewis Harvie presented TJ's message, with its enclosures, to the Senate and the House of Representatives on 8 Mch. After reading them, both houses ordered the papers to lie on the table (JS, 3:371; JHR, 4:629). They were subsequently published as *Message from the President of the United States, Communicating to Congress, An Extract of a Letter from Governor Claiborne to the Secretary of State . . . 8th March, 1804* (Washington, D.C., 1804).

From Thomas Butler

Sir

City of Washington
March 8th 1804

Before entering on a subject, to the merits of which I must beg leave to solicit your Excellency's attention; it will be necessary to state, as a data, that on the 4th. inst., the Honble the Secretary of war, honored me with a conversation in his office respecting my late trial.—After his having expressed much surprise why the commanding general had so long withheld the promulgation of the proceedings, he observed, that as the general must have acted on those in my case before that period, he could not conceive that there was any impropriety in his informing me, that I stood acquitted by the court, of all the charges exhibited by the General, except the first specification, viz, Disobedience to the general order of the 30th of April 1801, regulating the uniform of the hair.—

Taking for granted, sir, that this is the case; I have reason to suppose from the decision, that the court decided on the letter of the order, without having taken in to view, whether the order itself was of such a nature, and so supported by legal authority, as to render obedience indispensable.—presuming that the court had not taken in to view the latter position; I feel myself impelled by self respect, to appeal to your Excellency, from the decision of the Court, with a hope, that you will be pleased to re-consider the merits of that specification.—

I feel sensible, Sir, how delicate this subject is, and I, with every military man must intimately feel how unfortunate it is, that any General order should render its discussion indispensable.—Yet I hope and trust, that it never will be conceded, that any citizen entering into the military service of his country, thereby puts himself out of the protection of the laws, that his honor, his conscience, his moral principles, his private and natural rights are no longer under his own guardianship, but surrendered up to whomsoever may be his military superior.—

With defference, Sir, I have at all times believed, that the power given to every officer by his commission, is the authority of the laws and constitution of his country, vested in him as the legitimate organ, the expression then of the superior officer's will, whilst confined to subjects over which the laws have given him authority, is the command of the law itself, and must be implicitly and promptly obeyed? But if directed to subjects over which the laws have given him no authority, but which on the contrary the laws and constitution of the united states, have secured as inviolable to every Citizen whether in a civil or military capacity, then I contend, please your excellency, that the order of the 30th of April 1801, being unsupported by legal authority, contains not the essence of a military command. And had the court entered in to an investigation of the legal merits of that order, they could not have held it in any higher point of view, than the expression of will from one individual to an other, which no duty requires him to respect, and no power compels him to obey.—

I would fondly hope, please your Excellency—that it will not be said, such principles as these are subversive of military subordination; for I flatter myself, that my character as an officer is so well established, as not to admit a doubt of my obedience to the orders of superiors in rank, and at all times to have paid implicit obedience to the laws of my country.—

Experience, please your Excellency, has taught me to believe, that the proper exercise of legal authority is sufficiently comprehensive for every purpose of Military duty, that the power given to superiors by Law is large enough to embrace every possible case the public service could require.—But if it were not, still the power of a general must be circumscribed by the laws, else the consequence would be, that his will alone would bound his authority, whether it directed the execution of things moral or immoral, treasonable or patriotic, honorable or base.—

I presume that I am correct, sir, in observing, that it is the indispensable duty of every officer placed over others in command, never to pass those limits, which the laws of good sense, sound policy, morality, religion and of his country must give to all delegated authority.—That the order of the 30th of April 1801, surpassed these limits, never was a question with me, because the proper and constitutional authority of the united states, had made rules and regulations for the government of the army, which I conceived were as imperative to the commanding general, as to the sentinel at his door—These acts as distinctly mark the power of the one, as the duty of the other.—The one becomes criminal if he exceeds his authority; the other when he performs his legal duty should have nothing to fear, but receive the ample protection of the laws of his country.—Has then congress by its acts, given power to any military officer, to compel an inferior in rank to any act of mutilation, to deprive himself of any private or natural right; I think, I may with safety answer no—there are no such acts; there has been no such power delegated; and when any officer, by an order, attempts to legislate on subjects not submitted to his authority, he usurps that authority which the constitution vests in congress alone.—

I hope your Excellency will pardon any expressions that may appear too strong in this address, and impute them to their true cause, namely, to the feelings of a man smarting under a load of oppression; view him, sir, as ordered by his commanding general from one of the most extreme posts of the united states, to the state of Maryland for trial, upwards of fifteen hundred miles, kept near ten months in a state of suspence, and at an expence too heavy for any officer to bear, and all this in direct violation of the 23rd article of the appendix to the rules and articles of war, as there was many intermediate posts.—Permit me to observe, sir, if a general can assume such authority as this, he has it compleatly in his power to ruin any officer in the army.—

Let me hope, Sir, that you take in to consideration the merits of the specification before alluded to, and by turning to my defence on that part of the charge, you will see my reasons for not conforming to that order, without troubling your Excellency with any further details.—

I am respectfully your Excellency's Humbl. Servt.

THOS. BUTLER
Col. 2nd. Regt. Infty

FC (LU-Ar); at head of text: "His Excellency the President of the united States"; endorsed by Butler. Recorded in SJL as received from Colonel Edward Butler on 10 Mch. with the notation "W."

Thomas Butler (1754-1805) served with distinction as an officer in the Pennsylvania Line during the American Revolution and had been twice wounded during the disastrous campaign against the northwestern Indians in 1791. Appointed a major in the U.S. Army in 1792, Butler subsequently served in a variety of western commands, in which he gained the respect and admiration of both his fellow officers and local residents. In 1802, he was promoted to colonel and placed in command of the Second Regiment of Infantry (Donald R. Hickey, "The United States Army Versus Long Hair: The Trials of Colonel Thomas Butler, 1801-1805," PMHB, 101 [1977], 466-7; Heitman, *Dictionary*, 1:270).

MY LATE TRIAL: for Butler's court-martial for refusing to comply with General James Wilkinson's order to cut his hair, see Vol. 41:155-7 and *Frederick-Town Herald*, 24 Mch. 1804, which published Butler's letter to TJ. Although the trial ended in Dec. 1803, Wilkinson did not promulgate his confirmation of the court's verdict until 1 Feb. 1804 (Hickey, "United States Army Versus Long Hair," 468-9).

APPEAL TO YOUR EXCELLENCY: Butler enclosed his letter to TJ in a brief one to Dearborn of the same date, asking the secretary to forward it "in that form, deemed by you most respectful." Butler left his letter to the president unsealed so that Dearborn could "examine the first part, to see if correctly stated" (FC in LU-Ar; *Frederick-Town Herald*, 24 Mch. 1804). Writing to Butler on 14 Mch., Dearborn stated that the president had referred Butler's letter to him for a decision. Dearborn explained that to his knowledge there was no law, custom, or usage that granted the president cognizance over appeals from the sentence of a court-martial. The president had authority to decide on court-martial proceedings in certain cases, according to the secretary of war, but did not possess "any legal Control over the sentence of any Court Martial, duly approved by the proper Officer, except by interposing the Constitutional power confided to him, in pardoning Offences" (FC in Lb in DNA: RG 107, LSMA; *Frederick-Town Herald*, 24 Mch. 1804).

From George W. Erving

RESPECTED SIR   London March 8—1804

I have deferred the gratification of acknowledgeing the rect of the letter with which you honord me on the 10th of July, only till I shou'd be able to dispatch the remainder of the books for the national library ordered from Mr. Johnson;—I am concerned to find that they coud not have been sooner collected, & even now, that there are some deficiences which you may consider important;—I can assure you however that no attention or assiduity have been wanting:—Inclosed is the Catalogue of the books now sent, the cost of which is £68.2. Stg. leaving ballance of your remittance in my hands £63.1.1 Stg.

The letters inclosed in yours for the Earl of Buchan, Sir John Sinclair, & Mr Strickland were immediately forwarded, & the rect of them duly acknowledged; by the two former gentlemen I have been desired to forward to you five letters; the other two letters of the

seven herewith inclosed I presume to be from unfortunate Seamen:—
I have thought it proper to inform Sir John Sinclair of the mistake
made in your address; this he has apologized for by referring to some
Erroneous statement lately published in an English newspaper, which
as I recollect reported a debate in the time of Washington upon the
subject of a presidential title, as tho it had taken place at the present
period.

Permit me Sir to offer you an individual tribute of congratulation
on the perfect success of the late negotiation, & on the now complete
& satisfactory acquisition of the Louisiana territory:—All rational &
honest men of the present day, & the millions who are hereafter to
succeed, must acknowledge with gratitude the immense advantages
which have been secured to our country by this measure:—Indeed its
immediate effect upon our internal affairs, besides the great & favorable impression which it has given in these countries, & the consequent security which we derive from it in such tempestuous times,
reduce the price of the Acquisition to the merest insignificance. As
far as I have had opportunities of knowing, I am persuaded that our
rights are to be respected[1] by foreign nations in proportion as we are
feared, & that by no other measure will they be Estimated:—We have
at this time happily acquired a solidity & vigor which place us without the apprehension of their direct operations, the genius of our
constitution & the manifest interests of the country will prevent our
being Embroiled by any interference in their affairs, & leave us therefore free to cultivate those advantages which nature has so abundantly given; & which must place the United States, at no very distant period, in an attitude to *command* the most exact respect from all
powers.—I have thought it useful to cause the Louisiana documents
to be republished here, omitting (to make the pamphlet more sale-
able) the greater part of the Appendix:—it is satisfactory to observe
that all the intelligent part of this community feel & confess the importance of the friendly dispositions of our government.—I forbear to
intrude upon you any remarks on the interesting scenes that are here
passing, & the awful Events which seem to hang over the European
world; the more especially as Mr Monroe will doubtless be very full
in his communications.

With the most perfect sentiments of respectful attachment I am
always Dear Sir very faithy yr obt St   GEORGE W ERVING

March 9th Another letter is inclosed received yesterday from the
Post office where it has been opened because the packet Postage has
not been paid on it by the person who put it in.

Your letter to Mr Appleton at Florence was sent Oct. 20 by a Mr Avery of Boston who was to have gone to St Sebastians, but who afterwards went to Paris, from whence he woud forward it.

RC (DLC); at foot of text above post-script: "To Thomas Jefferson"; endorsed by TJ as received 15 May and so recorded in SJL. Enclosures: (1) Earl of Buchan to TJ, 4 Feb. 1804. (2) Sir John Sinclair to TJ, 1 Jan. 1804. (3) Sylvanus Blanchard to TJ, undated (recorded in SJL as received 15 May 1804 with notation "impressd. seaman. S." but not found). (4) Francis Wood to TJ, undated (recorded in SJL as received 15 May 1804 with notation "impressd. seaman. S." but not found). (5) Probably Baron de Hanstein to TJ, 6 Feb. 1804. Other enclosures not identified.

The CATALOGUE was likely the invoice printed below. For TJ's LETTERS to the Earl of Buchan, John Sinclair, and William Strickland, see Vol. 40:637-40, 708-10. In a letter of 1 Jan., Sinclair made the MISTAKE of addressing TJ as "His Highness."

A London edition of the administration's *Account of Louisiana, Being an Abstract of Documents, in the Offices of the Departments of State, and of the Treasury* appeared in 1804. Some American editions added an APPENDIX that included a translation of Spanish-era laws and ordinances for Lousiana (Vol. 41:721n; TJ to the Senate and the House of Representatives, 29 Nov. 1803).

For TJ's message to Thomas APPLETON, see Vol. 40:657-9.

[1] MS: "to respected."

ENCLOSURE

Invoice for Books Ordered for the Library of Congress

London March 8. 1804

G W Erving Esqr.

Bought of J Johnson

1 Wards History of Laws of Nations 2 V		18.—
1 Rymers Fœdera 10 Vols	15.	15.—
1 Brokes Abridgment		14.—
1 Pickerings Statutes 43 Vols	36.	——
1 Berthelson's Danish Dicty. 2 V	3.	3.—
1 Swedish & English Dicty	3.	3.—
1 Lyes Saxon Dicty 2 V	4.	4
1 Ebers German & English Dicty 5 Vols	5.	5—
1 Abridgment of Cases in Equity 2 V	2.	16
Case 13/6 Bills Lading 4/ Primage 2/6	1.	——
Cartage & Shipping		7.6
Duty & Entry	2.	7.6
	£75.	13.0

℞ the Betsy Wm Auld for Baltimore
to the Collector
Marked S. U.S.A.
  Washington
    Discount, being for a public
    Library, & for prompt payment ten ℀ct   7. 11—
                                                         £68.   2.0

MS (DLC: TJ Papers, 139:24006); in an unidentified hand.

Erving likely acquired for the Library of Congress the second edition of the SWEDISH and English dictionary published in Sweden in 1757 (Jacob Serenius, *An English and Swedish Dictionary: Wherein the Generality of Words and Various Significations Are Rendered into Swedish and Latin* [Harg and Stenbro, Sweden, 1757]).

From Albert Gallatin

DEAR SIR   8 March 1804

I enclose a letter from Mr Briggs. I think his leaving the territory without leave of absence extremely wrong; and Mr Williams ought also to have staid. They will arrive after the adjournmt. of Congress, and there is now a bill before Congress embracing every amendment which they had suggested. That board is altogether deficient; and their decision not to take up any claims until after they had been transcribed on the record is the cause of their having done nothing. I wrote to the Register that it was wrong, and had a section introduced in the new bill to remove any doubt on the subject. I believe also that the degree of correctness contemplated by Mr Briggs could not be obtained for five times the sum allowed by law which is 4 dollars per mile—

Respectfully Your obt. Servt.   ALBERT GALLATIN

RC (DLC); endorsed by TJ as a letter of 8 Mch. received from the Treasury Department on 7 Mch. and "Briggs. Williams" and so recorded in SJL. Enclosure: Isaac Briggs to Gallatin, Washington, Mississippi Territory, 10 Feb. 1804, reporting that he has halted the business of surveying because it cannot be done "for the compensation allowed by law"; his deputies have resigned, and "without a relief, beyond what the present law enables me to give them, they are ruined"; with the business of the land commissioners proceeding very slowly, there is no prospect that Briggs will be able to commence the survey of claims for 12 months; Briggs declares: "I, myself, as Surveyor general, am here entirely idle; *here*, I am of no service to my country"; he and Robert Williams are leaving for Washington, D.C., in three or four days to "communicate some information, useful to our country, respecting the defects of the land-law of this territory—the situation of land-claims here,—and of those

likely to occur in Louisiana"; Briggs requests that Gallatin "show this letter to the President"; the surveyor general and Williams "hope to be able to make such *oral* communications, as will secure the President's and thy approbation of our attending, at this time, the seat of Government" (Gallatin, *Papers*, 9:246-7; *Terr. Papers*, 5:304-6).

EVERY AMENDMENT WHICH THEY HAD SUGGESTED: see Gallatin to TJ, 4 Jan. TJ signed the legislation on 27 Mch., the day Congress adjourned (JS, 3:403, 404).

On 25 Jan., Gallatin WROTE TO THE REGISTER, Edward Turner, that the filing of documents constituted "the legal date of the record" and the board ought to "proceed in their decisions" as soon as all the claims were filed even though the documents had not been "yet actually transcribed on the recording books of the Register" (*Terr. Papers*, 5:302-3). SECTION INTRODUCED IN THE NEW BILL: Section 2 of the act of 27 Mch. stated that nothing in the legislation on disposition of the lands "shall be construed to prevent" the commissioners from deciding any claims that had been "exhibited in the manner prescribed by law, although the evidence of the same may not, at that time, have been transcribed on the books of the register" (U.S. Statutes at Large, 2:304).

From Albert Gallatin

DEAR SIR   8 March 1804

Collectors are not supplied with seals at the public expense—Most of them have none; those of the important sea-ports generally have.

Respectfully your obedt. Servt.   ALBERT GALLATIN

RC (DLC); endorsed by TJ as a letter of 8 Mch. received from the Treasury Department on 7 Mch. and "seal for Custom H. N.O." and so recorded in SJL.

SEALS: in October 1803, Hore Browse Trist consulted with TJ on the design and execution of a seal for the custom house at New Orleans (Vol. 41:554-5).

From Michael Leib

SIR,   Thursday Morning March 8th. 1804

At the request of Mrs. Heister, I send you Gros's moral philosophy. This work was transmitted to Genl. Heister by the author, with a request, that he would deliver it to you; but death rob'd him of this pleasure. Last night he departed this life. As Mrs. Heister is preparing to depart for Hagar's town with her husband's remains, she wished this work to be immediately forwarded, & I have taken a pleasure in an immediate execution of her request.

With sentiments of affectionate respect I am Your obedient Servant

                                                  M LEIB

RC (MHi); at foot of text: "The President of the United States"; endorsed by TJ as received from Washington on 8 Mch. and so recorded in SJL. Enclosure: Johann Daniel Gros, *Natural Principles of Rectitude, for the Conduct of Man in all States and Situations of Life; Demonstrated and Explained in a Systematic Treatise on Moral Philosophy* (New York, 1795; Sowerby, No. 1255).

GENL. HEISTER: Maryland congressman Daniel Hiester, a native of Pennsylvania and brigadier general of militia during the Revolutionary War, was a cousin of fellow congressman General Joseph Hiester. His wife was the former Rosanna Hager, the daughter of the founder of Hagerstown (DAB; *Biog. Dir. Cong.*; *National Intelligencer*, 9 Mch. 1804; *Aurora*, 14 Mch. 1804; Vol. 32:46n).

From Philip Mazzei

Degmo. Carmo., e Stimsmo. Amico   Pisa, 8 Marzo, 1804.

Spero che Le sarà pervenuta per mezzo di Mr. Yeardsley, Capno. del bastimento Hannah, partito ✸ Filadelfia da Livorno sul principio del mese passato, la mia precedente cominciata il 25 8bre e terminata il 27 Gennaio. Questa venrà sul bastimento Bulah, Capn. Gardener, che è d'imminente partenza per Boston.

Sono circa 2 anni, che Le scrivo quasi continovamente sull'articolo dei Consolati degli S.U. nel Mediterraneo. Ne scrissi pure a Mr. Madison nella lettera che inclusi a Lei, e la pregai di comunicarlene il contenuto. Ultimamente ò saputo da un'Amico venuto da Napoli, che (mentre vi era il Commador Morris) il do. Commadore; quello Smith della Carolina Meridionale che è stato Membro del Congresso, ed altri aristocratici, formarono una cabala per far sì che ottenesse il Consolato di Napoli un certo Mr. Degen, oriundo tedesco, nato ed educato in Inghilterra, che non è mai stato in America, e che fece un fallimento fraudolento nell'istessa Città di Napoli. L'Amico mio mi dice, ch'egli era in società con uno che risiedeva in Inghilterra; che negò di esser tale; che fece comparire il socio come suo debitore; e in tal maniera defraudò i veri creditori. Il do. Amico non à potuto saper precisamente come fosse ordita la tela dalla sopradda. Società aristocratica, ma sa che dopo un pranzo, in mezzo al vino, fù fatto uno scritto col do. oggetto, e che fù firmato ancora da alcun Capitano di mare, i quali (suppongo io) saranno stati sedotti dall'Aristocratico Commadore. Il suo nome di famiglia mi reduce a memoria quel che Le disse all'orecchio la buona Contessa di Tessè di gamba di Legno mentre noi eramo accanto l'un dell'altro al camminetto, cio è *Il est aristocratique*, al che V.S. rispose: *s'il n'est pas Monarchique*.

Devo dirle di più, che il do. Degen è fratello di colui, che ora è in Livorno alla testa della Commissione degli S.U. per approvvisionar le flottiglie nel Mediterraneo; cosa che mi amareggia infinitamente.[1] Io ne soffro molto più che gli altri buoni Cittadini Americani che, son quà, imperocchè tutto quei del paese che simpatizzano con noi, s'indirizzano a me, come se io potessi rimediarci. Un'altra cosa mi à do. l'Amico venuto da Napoli, che pur mi amareggia non poco, cioè che là si maravigliano di non aver per anche inteso nulla dal nostro Governo, conseguentemente all'apertura fattagli per mezzo del Maggior Barnes. La cosa mi pare di grand importanza ✸ tutti i motivi che ò indicati nelle mie precedenti; Ma quando ancora Ella vedesse La cosa in diverso aspetto da quel che la vedo io, mi pare che una risposta qualunque dovrebbe darsi. Possono addursi buoni motivi per giustificar l'indugio; ma bisognerebbe che non fosse troppo lungo, specialmente a motivo delle frequenti occasioni che ci sono di bastimenti americani, che vengon d'America nel Mediterraneo.

Quanto a Mr. Appleton, ogni giorno più vedo la necessità di rimuoverlo da questo luogo. Ne parlai nella precedente quanto basta, e dopo quel tempo mi son fatto un dovere di frequentar Livorno per mettermi sempre più al fatto delle cose. Il mandarlo altrove pare a me un dovere per quel che riguarda il servizio pubblico, e si renderebbe certamente un buon servizio a lui stesso. Mi vien detto che sia vacato il Consolato di Tunis, e sia per vacare quel di Parigi. Crederei che Parigi gli convenisse più, (mentre sussista tuttavia l'idea d'avere un console in una Città Mediterranea). Ma in qualunque luogo starà meglio che qui per tutti i rapporti. Per Livorno, credo che niuno potrebb'esser meglio calcolato del Maggior Barnes. È stato conosciuto in brevissimo tempo, ed è già moltissimo stimato. Alcuni dei principali Negozianti mi ànno espresso chiaramente il lor desiderio di averlo qui. Parlando meco dell'importanza del Porto di Livorno per il commercio degli Americani, specialmente a motivo della vantaggiosa situazione. Io glie ne diedi un tocco, ma siccome non rispose, non giudicai proprio d'andar pù avanti per delicatezza, non ignorando quanto ei sia stimato in Sicilia, come pure dal Governo in Napoli. Son però persuaso, che il suo patriottismo, e la necessità ch'ei vede d'un cambiamento in Livorno, glie la farebbero accettare, se il Governo glie lo proponesse.

Non dirò altro su questo soggetto, e terminerò col pregarla di notificarmi, se à ricevuto le cose che Le mandai sul bastimento Hannah, e su i precedenti, e d'informarmi a suo tempo della riuscita che avranno fatta, ℞ mia regola, onde vedere come condurmi in futuro.

Mi conservi la sua Benevolenza, e mi creda di vero cuore usqua ad mortem. Suo &c. &c.

P.S. Il 15 Febb. dell'anno passato Le scrissi, che un'invernata senza punto freddo aveva causato dei ben fondati timori ℞ i futuri prodotti della terra; e che 8 giorni prima della data era succeduto un freddo rigidissimo, e caduta tanta neve ℞ 3 giorni continovi, che mai era seguita cosa tale a memoria d'istorie. Quest'anno la dolciura invernale à continovato fino al 20 del mese passato, cioè circa 13 giorni più dell'anno scorso, ed è stata succeduta da un'egual freddo, che tuttavia continova. È caduta della neve, ma poca. La raccolta fù l'anno passato (contro l'aspettativa) copiosissima; se campo, Le dirò a suo tempo come sarà stata in questo.

N.B. Ne ò mandata la copia ℞ il bastimento

EDITORS' TRANSLATION

WORTHY, DEAR, AND
MUCH ESTEEMED FRIEND,   Pisa, March 8, 1804.

I hope you have already received my letter begun on 25 Oct. and completed on 27 Jan., which I have sent by way of Mr. Yeardsley, captain of the *Hannah*, which set sail from Leghorn en route to Philadelphia at the start of last month. My present letter will travel on the *Beulah*, Captain Gardener, which is about to sail for Boston.

It is about two years that I have been writing almost incessantly on the issue of the U.S. consulates in the Mediterranean. I wrote to Mr. Madison as well, in the letter that I enclosed to the one I sent you, asking you to convey him its content. Most recently I have been told by a friend who came from Naples that, while Commodore Morris was there, the said commodore, that Smith from South Carolina who has been a member of Congress, and other aristocrats formed a cabal designed to have the consulate of Naples go to a certain Mr. Degen. He is of German extraction, born and raised in England; he has never been to America and he has also gone fraudulently bankrupt in the very city of Naples. My friend tells me that he partnered up with someone residing in England, who denied that he was such; he made it appear that his partner was his debtor; in this way, he defrauded the true creditors. The said friend has not been able to tell me how the fabric of that society of aristocrats was woven, but he knows that after a meal, with wine flowing, a document with that said subject was drafted and that it was signed by more than one sea captain. These—I suppose—must have been seduced by the aristocratic commodore. His family name reminds me of what the good Countess of Tessé whispered in your ear about Wooden Leg, while we were seated next to each other at the fireplace, that is, "He is an aristocrat," to which your lordship replied, "If not a monarchist."

But there is more that I have to say. The said Degen is the brother of the one who is now in Leghorn, heading the U.S. commission for provisioning the fleet in the Mediterranean, something that makes me incredibly sad. I suffer of this more than any other good American citizen who is here, since all those from this country who sympathize with us come to me as if I were in a position to remediate this situation. My friend from Naples has told me one more thing, which also makes me very sad; namely, the fact that people there marvel at not having heard anything from our government, after an opening had been made through Major Barnes. It is a matter of great importance, I think, for all the reasons I have laid out in my previous letters, and even if you were to see the matter in a different light than I, I think an answer, whatever it may be, should be given. Good reasons may be provided to justify the delay; yet such delay should not be too long, especially because there are frequent opportunities afforded by the coming of ships from America into the Mediterranean.

As for Mr. Appleton, I see every day more reasons to remove him from this place. I have spoken about this enough in my previous letter and I have since made it my duty to be present in Leghorn, to keep myself increasingly informed of the situation. I believe it is a duty to the public service to send him somewhere else; and it would be a good service for him as well. I have been told that the consulate in Tunis is vacant and the one in Paris is about to become vacant. I would think Paris a more appropriate venue for him, provided that the notion of having a consul in a city in the Mediterranean is not abandoned. In whatever place he will be, however, he will be better off than here for all relations. For Leghorn, I believe that there is nobody better suited than Major Barnes. He has made himself known in a very short time and he is already deeply appreciated. Some of the main businessmen here have clearly expressed to me their desire of having him here. While we were talking about the importance of the port of Leghorn for American commerce, especially in view of the advantageous situation, I alluded to the possibility. However, since he did not answer, I judged it inappropriate for delicacy to keep pressing the point, being not unaware of how esteemed he is in Sicily as well as by the government in Naples. I am sure, however, that his patriotism and the necessity he sees of effecting change in Leghorn will make him accept it, if the government were to propose it to him.

I will not say anything more about this topic and will close the letter by asking to please let me know whether you have received the things I sent you on the *Hannah* and on the previous vessels and to let me know, in due course, what kind of success they will have had. I will know, thus, how I will have to behave in the future.

May you continue to have goodwill toward me and believe me wholeheartedly and unceasingly yours etc., etc.

P.S. On 15 Feb. of last year I wrote you that an absolutely mild winter had caused well-founded concerns about the harvest. I also wrote that eight days before a most rigid cold had moved in, and so much snow had fallen in three days that there had been no storm so big in the annals. This year the mildness of winter has been protracted until the 20th of last month (that is, about 13 days longer than last year), and a similar cold has moved in thereafter — and it continues to this day. Snow has fallen, but not that much. Last year's harvest, against all expectations, has been really rich; if I will be alive, in due course I will tell you how it will have gone this time around.

N.B. I have sent the copy by way of the ship.

Dft (Archivio Filippo Mazzei, Pisa, Italy); part of a conjoined series of Mazzei's drafts of letters to TJ (see Margherita Marchione and Barbara B. Oberg, eds., *Philip Mazzei: The Comprehensive Microform Edition of his Papers*, 9 reels [Millwood, N.Y., 1982], 6:921-2). Recorded in SJL as received 6 June.

IL COMMADOR MORRIS: naval commander Richard Valentine Morris had been in Naples in the summer of 1803. He was a nephew of Gouverneur Morris, the loquacious diplomat with a wooden leg who defended the commodore's command in the Mediterranean during the Barbary Wars (ANB, s.v. "Morris, Gouverneur"; Cuyler Reynolds, comp., *Genealogical and Family History of Southern New York and the Hudson River Valley*, 3 vols. [New York, 1914], 3:1141-4; *Defence of the Conduct of Commodore Morris During His Command in the Mediterranean* [New York, 1804], 96; Vol. 37:161n).

QUELLO SMITH DELLA CAROLINA: Mazzei probably referred to William Loughton Smith, the former U.S. minister to Portugal who had been a Federalist congressman from South Carolina (*Biog. Dir. Cong.*; George C. Rogers, *Evolution of a Federalist: William Loughton Smith of Charleston (1758-1812)* [Columbia, S.C., 1962], 340; Vol. 41:284n).

IL CONSOLATO DI NAPOLI UN CERTO MR. DEGEN: Prussian-born Neapolitan merchant Frederick Degen was appointed to succeed John S. M. Mathieu as consul at Naples in 1805 (JEP, 2:7; Vol. 39:190, 194n). He had a familial connection to the firm of Degen, Purviance

& Co., the navy agents at Leghorn (Madison, *Papers, Sec. of State Ser.*, 4:567; Mazzei to TJ, 28 Dec. 1803).

[1] Erased and replaced with the adverb *infinitamente*: "quasi quanto mi amareggiarono l'indolenza e l'apatia che scorsi nella massima parte degli abitanti di Williamsburgo, allorchè gli Inglesi, dopo l'incendio dei bastimenti che erano nella rada di Norfolk, venivano a gran passi verso la città" (translation: "almost as much as I was embittered by the indolence and apathy I detected in the greatest part of the citizens in Williamsburg, when the English, after the ships at Norfolk had been burned, were marching speedily toward the city").

From Israel B. Parshall

Sir,   New-York 8th. March 1803 [i.e. 1804]

I would not address your Excellency if I had not hopes of Your complying with the Petition of A Poor Mechanic in Distress as I am at Present. I will Just state To Your Excellency my Situation, Viz I Began Business in New York in the Shoemaking line, about the Middle of July last, and was doing Tolerably Well, but the Epidemic Coming on the 1st of August Put everything to a Stand in this City for three Months During Which time I was one among the few that were obliged to Remain in the City During which time my Wife & self were Reduced Very low by the fever & Want of Business as we Both had it Very Severely, though not Both at one time, at the Close of the Sickness [I] Was obliged To Run in debt [for] materials To Carry on my Business and as I have had To pay off 3 months Dead Rent & 3 doctors Bills I am Reduced To almost Nothing.

What I have To ask of Your Excellency is the loan of 500 Dolls. or as much as can be Convenient To Spare for one or Two Years as Your Excellency may think Proper And if Your Excellency will be so Humane as To Oblige me I will send Your Excellency A Bill of Sale of Every thing I have or may have at the Expiration of the time if Your Excellency is Disposed So To Do To any one You wish Should Receive it at the Rate of 8 p. Cent

I should wish You To Send me an Answer as soon as Convt. To Your Excellency

By doing which You will forever Oblige Your unknown friend and Petitioner   Israel B. Parshall

Please Direct To No. 75 Nassau St. New York

RC (MHi); torn; addressed: "Thomas Jefferson Esqr. President of the U, States Washington" and "Mail"; franked and postmarked; endorsed by TJ as received 11 Mch. and so recorded in SJL.

Israel B. Parshall was registered as an insolvent debtor with the recorder for New York City on 20 Apr. 1804 and again on 16 Sep. 1819. Between those dates he appeared in New York directories as a shoemaker, once in partnership and once as a single proprietor (New York *American Citizen*, 26 May 1804; New York *National Advocate*, 22 Sep. 1819; *Longworth's American Almanac, New York Register, and City Directory, for the Thirty-Sixth Year of American Independence* [New York, 1811], 223; *Longworth's American Almanac, New York Register, and City Directory, for the Forty-Fourth Year of American Independence* [New York, 1819], 308).

To Martha Jefferson Randolph

Washington Mar. 8. 04.

Your letter of the 2d.[1] my dear Martha, which was not recieved till the last night has raised me to life again. for four days past I had gone through inexpressible anxiety. the mail which left you on the 5th. will probably be here tonight, and will I hope strengthen our hopes of Maria's continuing to recover, and mr Eppes's arrival which I presume was on the 6th. will render her spirits triumphant over her Physical debility. Congress have determined to rise on Monday sennight (the 19th.) mr Randolph will probably be with you on the 22d. and myself within 3. or 4. days after. Maria must in the mean time resolve to get strong to make us all happy. your apologies my dear for using any thing at Monticello for her, yourself, family or friends, are more than unnecessary. what is[2] there is as much for the use of you all as for myself, and you cannot do me greater pleasure than by using every thing with the same freedom I should do myself. tell my dear Maria to be of good chear, and to be ready to mount on horseback with us and continue to let us hear of her by every post. if mrs Lewis be still with you deliver her my affectionate respects and assurances of my great sensibility for her kind attentions to Maria. kiss the little ones for me, and be assured of my tenderest love to Maria & yourself.

TH: JEFFERSON

RC (NNPM); at foot of text: "Mrs. Randolph." PoC (MHi); endorsed by TJ.

Randolph's LETTER of 2 Mch., recorded in SJL as received 7 Mch., has not been found. A previous letter of 17 Feb., recorded in SJL as received 22 Feb., has also not been found.

[1] Date written on top of "1st."
[2] Preceding two words interlined in place of "every thing." TJ made the change separately on the RC and the PoC.

From Littleton W. Tazewell

Dear Sir;   Norfolk March 8h. 1804

The Assurance you give me relative to Mr. Welch's claim is perfectly satisfactory, and confident that you will bear it in mind, I shall not trouble you again upon this subject—

You ask me what is the opinion of the Mercantile Men in this quarter relative to the present order of things—I feel much difficulty in resolving such an inquiry, notwithstanding I am in the habit of much and free intercourse with them—The truth I believe is, that the American Mercantile Interest in Virginia have as yet assumed no political character, and from what I have seen, the same observation may be applied to most of the other states—Actuated by no settled principles, they are impelled altogether by the operation of accidental causes—They approve to-day, what tomorrow they will revile; and Interest seems to be the only tenet in their political faith which remains long unchanged—The reason of this probably is, that being Possessed of but small capital, with an ardent desire to enlarge it, by some of the vast schemes which are every day opening to their view, they allow themselves no leisure—Their whole attention is absorbed by calculations of pecuniary profit and loss, and reflections of any other kind are rarely permitted to disturb this chain of arithmetical reasoning—Interest makes them Insatiable in their desire of governmental advantage—And when any act is done improving their situation, the Government is extolled to the skies, but when a burden is imposed on them in common with their fellow Citizens, they murmur and complain—These Short sighted Politicians would willingly purchase the most trifling commercial advantage, at the expence of the best part of a Constitution; and complain even of the acquisition of Louisiana, because it may bring into the West India market competitors in their trade—When the advantages of Commerce shall have been enjoyed somewhat longer, we may expect that the Commercial Men here will acquire that degree of improvement and liberality which they possess in other countries, and that their views and minds becoming thus enlarged, they will here entitle themselves to the same rank in our political society, to which they are certainly entitled in England, and might formerly claim in Holland and Venice. But from the present days, little of steady support is to be expected, and little of consistent opposition is to be dreaded—They are in general opposed to your administration, not because they differ from you in principle, but for various other reasons which what I have said will at once suggest—Their opposition however which originally was violent, I think is becoming daily more faint, and I believe that the adoption of any measure now decidedly calculated for commercial benefit, would convert most of them to Republicanism—

May I be allowed to suggest that the present is a fit occasion to perform this act—That now this will be an act not only of the soundest policy, but probably is due to Justice also—Our last advices here inform us of many aggressions upon our neutral rights in the West Indies by the French Privateers, or rather of spoliations on our Commerce by French Pirates, for many of the captures are represented to have been made by unauthorized persons—The unfortunate wretches who were expelled from Saint Domingo, finding no asylum in any neighbouring ports, have many of them formed a band of lawless Buccaneers, capturing every thing they can find in the seas which encompass the Leeward Islands, including Jamaica—Our Merchants here who have much at stake are in a state of the highest consternation—Insurance on this trade can now hardly be accomplished on any terms—And it is too valuable to be relinquished, and too hazardous to be pursued—The prompt employment of a part of the Governmental force for their protection at this crisis, would force conviction upon the Mercantile Mind that Commerce was the particular care of the administration, and would bind them to its measures by the only tie by which they can be held—

I would say more, but I am fearful I have already transgressed the bounds of propriety, in thus obtruding opinions upon you, who can derive no aid from my crude remarks—Believing however, as I do, that the preservation of a free government in America depends so much on acquiring and preserving the Attachment of all classes of our Citizens to the present order of things, I felt unwilling to permit any oppy to slip by of communicating to those in power a circumstance which I thought would furnish so just a means to attain this desirable end—To this motive you will be pleased to ascribe what I have now written, and will I hope therefore pardon me—.

The last Virginia Assembly passed a law authorizing a new Bank in this state—Books are to be opened in various places and this among others for subscriptions—From what I understand there will be more subscribed in all the towns, than the number of shares allotted to them—But the late dreadful calamity has so crippled our means, that in all probability there will not be subscribed the number we are allowed—Should you feel disposed to make any investment in this institution, and under the circumstances I have stated should prefer this place for your subscription, it will give me great pleasure if you will command my services—

Accept my best wishes for your health & felicity; And believe me to be Dear Sir with much respect & esteem Your obdt. servt.

LITTON: W TAZEWELL

RC (DLC); addressed: "Thomas Jefferson esquire Washington"; franked; postmarked 10 Mch.; endorsed by TJ as received 17 Mch. and so recorded in SJL.

LAWLESS BUCCANEERS: some refugees from Saint-Domingue did go into privateering or piracy, usually targeting British trade in the Caribbean, but often neutral ships as well, and ranging as far as the Tortugas (Gabriel Debien, "The Saint-Domingue Refugees in Cuba, 1793-1815," trans. David Cheramie, in Carl A. Brasseaux and Glenn R. Conrad, eds., *The Road to Louisiana: The Saint-Domingue Refugees, 1792-1809* [Lafayette, La., 1992],

53-6; David Patrick Geggus, "Slavery, War, and Revolution in the Greater Caribbean, 1789-1815," in David Barry Gaspar and Geggus, eds., *A Turbulent Time: The French Revolution and the Greater Caribbean* [Bloomington, Ind., 1997], 23-4).

Norfolk's efforts to fill its allotment of 3,000 shares in the recently incorporated BANK of Virginia were CRIPPLED by the fire that struck the city on 22 Feb. (Samuel Shepherd, ed., *The Statutes at Large of Virginia, from October Session 1792, to December Session 1806*, 3 vols. [Richmond, 1835-36], 3:100; TJ to Thomas Newton, 5 Mch.).

From John Woodbridge

Prospect Penobscot River
[before 9 Mch. 1804]

May it Please your honor I beg your honor will Excuse me in writing to the prsedint but am under A Disseagreeable situation I have been very unfortinate For this five or six years past by losses at Different times At sea I was taking by the french once and Carred into Godalupe and lost all I had and the winter before last I was Cast Away on mount Desert Iland and like to have perrished and frose ourselves bad and lost all we had I have got a Large family and am reduce very low I have always been Inform your Honor has a tender feeling for the disstresed or I Should not have wrote to his honor I have always been A true freind to my Country and have faught and bleed For it but am reduce to the greatest Extremety and no freind To help me up I have applied to your honor for a littel assistance to put me under way once more and your honor may depend I will make good use of Every talent, and will satisfy your Honor as soon as it is in my power I live in the town of Prospect on penobscot River in the County of Hancock By your honor pleasing to write me a answer Every attension will be duly paid to it and your Humble petisoner

will Ever Pray

JOHN WOODBRIDGE

From your honor well wisher and many more good freinds your Honor on this River

RC (DLC); undated; signed: "John Wooodbridge"; endorsed by TJ as received 9 Mch. 1804 and so recorded in SJL.

From Albert Gallatin

[9 Mch. 1804]

The propriety of appointing Tucker Howland Keeper of the light house near Georgetown S. Car. is respectfully submitted—He had been recommended by Stevens the Superintendt. of light houses

A. G.

The enclosed letter to Mr Huger must, I presume, be returned.

RC (DNA: RG 59, LAR); undated, but see enclosure; written on address sheet of the enclosure; endorsed by TJ: "Howland Tucker. to be Keepr. Lt. H. Geo. T. S.C. mr Huger's lre to mr Gallatin." Enclosure: Benjamin Huger to Gallatin, at the "Capitol," 9 Mch. 1804, enclosing a letter, now missing, "from an old & very respectable Inhabitant of Georgetown," who endorses Captain Tucker Howland as a proper character to be appointed keeper of the Georgetown lighthouse (RC in same).

PROPRIETY OF APPOINTING TUCKER HOWLAND: see TJ to Gallatin, 11 Feb.

From John Wayles Eppes

DEAR SIR,   Edge-Hill March. 9. 1804.

I found Maria on my arrival here free from fever and sitting up— She has no complaint at present but weakness—Her appetite is improving daily and I have no fear but that in a short time she will be restored to health—Her child is well also from the kindness of Patsy who has nursed it with her own—Maria during her illness has lost her milk entirely, and although she expects its return I fear we shall be obliged to rely principally on feeding the child—

I had a terrible journey here—On the Evening I left Washington the high wind prevented my crossing at the Ferry—I passed at the bridge and not knowing any part of the road did not reach Wren's until late at night. I found the next days journey to Elk-run as much as I could perform being compelled to travel a great part of the way in a walk & in many places to get down and brake the Ice before my Horse could get forward—

It is not in my power by this mail to give you any information as to your affairs at Monticello as I have not been out of the enclosure here since my arrival.

Accept for your health the warm wishes of Yours with sincere affection   JNO: W: EPPES

P.S. It is a good season for sowing oats—I had intended to beg a few of you—If you could forward some by the stage to Fredericksburg I will employ the post rider to bring them, and will pay particular attention to their being well sown in good land—   JW.E.

RC (ViU: Edgehill-Randolph Papers); endorsed by TJ as received 13 Mch. and so recorded in SJL.

From Nehemiah Knight and Others

SIR   Washington City March 9th. 1804.

We take the Liberty to inclose a Letter this moment received from the Executive of our State. with the Greatest respects we are yours &c   N. KNIGHT
                              for Self & the other Delat.

RC (DLC); addressed: "President of the United States"; endorsed by TJ as received from Knight on 9 Mch. and so recorded in SJL. Enclosure not found, but see below.

EXECUTIVE OF OUR STATE: Rhode Island governor Arthur Fenner probably forwarded news of ratification of the Twelfth Amendment to the state's congressional delegation, which included Knight and Joseph Stanton in the House and Samuel J. Potter and Christopher Ellery in the Senate (Bennington *Vermont Gazette*, 20 Mch.; Madison, *Papers, Sec. of State Ser.*, 6:589, 7:218; *Biog. Dir. Cong.*).

To Charles Willson Peale

                              Washington Mar. 9. 1804

Th: Jefferson presents his salutations to mr Peale. he recieved last night his favor of the 5th. he will leave this place for Monticello a fortnight hence, and will be absent 5. or 6. weeks, which he mentions now because as the Polygraphs will arrive after his departure his acknolegement of their reception and his return of Brunelle's cannot be till his return to this place in May.

RC (TxU). PoC (DLC); endorsed by TJ.

To Joseph T. Scott

SIR   Washington Mar. 9. 04.

I have duly recieved your favor of the 5th. inst. and I hasten to assure you that neither Doctr. Leib, nor mr Duane have ever given the least hint to me that yourself or your associates of the St. Patrick's society meditated joining a third party; or schismatising in any way from the great body of Republicans. that the rudiments of such a 3d. party were formed in Pensylvania & New York has been said in the newspapers, but not proved. altho' I shall learn it with concern whenever it does happen, and think it possibly may happen that we shall divide among ourselves whenever federalism is compleatly eradicated, yet I think it the duty of every republican to make great sacrifices of opinion to put off the evil day. and that yourself and associates have as much disposition to do this as any portion of our body I have never seen reason to doubt. recommending therefore sincerely a mutual indulgence, and candor among brethren and that we be content to obtain the best measures we can get, if we cannot get all we would wish, I tender you my salutations and respects.   TH: JEFFERSON

PoC (DLC); at foot of text: "Joseph Scott esq."

To Moses Coates

SIR   Washington Mar. 10. 04.

I recieved last night your favor of the 3d. and am glad that a workman has been with you to enable himself to build a sawmill for me on the model of yours. he is employed by a person who is to rent the mill of me. I have no doubt of the excellence of the plan. I have not yet seen your paring machine but will call at the patent office for that purpose. should I like it, where nearest could I get one and what the price? you wish the public to purchase the right to the invention. the state governments alone can do that. Congress is not authorised by the Constitution to apply any money to an object of that kind. as your inventions go directly to objects of utility rather than of curiosity I wish you success in them, and tender you my salutations.

TH: JEFFERSON

PoC (DLC); at foot of text: "Mr. Moses Coates"; endorsed by TJ.

As part of his 1802 agreement with TJ, millwright James Walker was to build a SAWMILL at Shadwell in addition to the toll and manufacturing mills. Writing to Walker in September 1803, however, TJ informed him that "a person has undertaken to have the sawmill built himself & pay me rent for her." TJ did not name the individual (Vol. 38:429-30; Vol. 41:403; TJ to James Walker, 28 Jan. 1804).

To Albert Gallatin

Mar. 10. 04.

The appointment of Tucker Howland to be keeper of the Light house near Georgetown S.C. is approved   TH: JEFFERSON

RC (DNA: RG 26, MLR); addressed: "The Secretary of the Treasury"; with Gallatin's note on address sheet to John Brown, a clerk: "Please to give immediate information both to him & to the Superintt. A.G."; endorsed by a clerk. Not recorded in SJL.

On 12 Mch., Gallatin signed letters to TUCKER HOWLAND and Daniel Stevens with news of the appointment. Howland was to take up his duties by the end of the month (Lb in DNA: RG 26, LL).

From Samuel Hanson

SIR,   March 10th. 1804

Finding that there is a bill in the Senate which contemplates the creation of an additional Auditor, I beg leave, in case the bill pass into a law, respectfully to solicit the appointment.

Of my competency to the discharge of it's duties, it does not, perhaps, become myself to speak. Nor should I be induced to do it, but from the necessity of obviating an inference that may, to the prejudice of my application, be drawn from my former pursuits in life. You will permit me, therefore, to state that, though I have never hitherto been, *professionally*, employed in the adjustment of intricate accounts, nor pretend to an intimate knowledge of all the formulæ which are observed, in the construction of them, by the Clerk of a regularly-bred Merchant, yet my acquaintance with figures warrants me in saying that I am competent to the developement of any result that may be requisite in any Statement, however complex, of Dr. & Cr. The fact is that, with the power of numbers I have been, from the motive of amusement, more than usually conversant; and that I have not, as yet, met with any combination or involution of them which I could not analyze with, *at least*, the usual facility.

But, I quit this ungrateful theme; a theme on which it is extremely abhorrent from my temper to have been obliged to enter.

Should my application, made, as it is, while the act is pending, be deemed premature, you will have the goodness to excuse it, from the exigency of my case, which prompts me to be rather too early, than too late, in my efforts to provide for my large, helpless, and *suffering* family. The repeated assurances of your wish to assist them encourage me to inform you that the Post-Office of George-Town, from which I had promised myself 2 or 300$ per annm., will, in a short time, be entirely unproductive, from the circumstance of Mr Pichons removal to this City. Of the 700$ per annum, which it has lately yielded, 400$ are paid to my Deputy; the profits of Mr Pichon's Letters are estimated at 200$ per annm.—leaving a balance of 100$ in favour of the office. But, after the commencement of the next quarter, this balance must be absorbed by the expense of having a room for the office; an expense which I have not incurred for the present quarter, owing to the kindness of my friend, Mr. McLaughlin, in furnishing me with a room gratis. Under this view of the case, it will certainly be incumbent on me, immediately on Mr. Pichon's removal, to resign the office, as *responsible* though *unproductive*. My resignation, however, shall be accompanied with my acknowledgments to the Post-Master General for his well-meant, tho' unavailing, essay to serve me.

Of the little profits accruing from the business of Bankruptcy—not more than 1/6th part of which profits has been yet received—there is an entire stoppage.

Thus, for the support of a family, amounting to the number of *twelve*, I have to depend entirely on my Salary, at the War-Office, of 1000$. My economy is extreme. Scarcely an article, exclusive of the necessaries of life, in a strict acceptation of that term, enters into the composition of my expenses. yet it is not in my power to eke out my Salary to the end of the quarter. This will not appear surprizing, if it be considered how inadequate the Sum of $333\frac{1}{3}$$ would have been to the maintenance of a family of the Same number, 25 years ago: For, I think this Sum bears nearly the same ratio to my present Salary that the prices of living at that time do to those of the present.

I pray you, Sir, excuse the freedom of this address. I am prompted to it by the exigency of my case, as well as by the repeated assurances of your good-wishes, and even of your esteem. I beseech you, permit not the efforts of my Enemies, either open or concealed, to obliterate the good-opinion with which you once honoured me. Enemies, indeed, I have none, that I know of, except those of the *Bank*. Of these, not one, to my knowledge, or belief, has ever brought a charge against my integrity. The conclusion is irresistible. *They cannot.* Take it as a fact, Sir, upon the reality of which I would stake my temporal, if not my *eternal*, welfare, that, even in George-Town, the very Scene of my persecution, I number more friends, among all those not within the sphere of Bank-Influence, than the most *dignified* member of the Board of Directors. To these my promotion to office would be matter of great satisfaction, instead of discontent. To some of the best men in existence, of both parties, and in Several States, it would be a source of high gratification.

But, admitting, for the sake of the argument, that my conduct with respect to the Bank, was intemperate, contumacious, incorrect, or even *dishonourable*—though such an acknowledgment no persecution, no distress, will ever compel me to make—ought not my consequent sufferings to expiate my offence? Must the innocent suffer with the guilty? Must my unoffending wife and Children be implicated in my punishment? Must they be everlastingly exposed to the discomforts of penury, to the threatening horrors of want, for my transgression?

I conjure you, Sir, by your known love of justice, let not this be the case. On the contrary, if the boon I now ask for can be accorded, consistently with your existing engagements, cause, I implore you, the smile of joy, and the tear of gratitude, to be diffused through my *then* happy Dwelling.

with high respect, I am, Sir Your most obedt

S HANSON OF SAML

RC (DNA: RG 59, LAR); endorsed by TJ as received 10 Mch. and "to be 2d. Auditor" and so recorded in SJL.

For a previous failed attempt to introduce an ADDITIONAL AUDITOR of the Treasury, see Vol. 37:390.

YOUR WISH TO ASSIST THEM: for TJ's assurance of his efforts on behalf of Hanson and his family, see Vol. 39:67.

POST-OFFICE OF GEORGE-TOWN: Hanson filed his first returns as postmaster of Georgetown on 1 Apr. 1804 and served until early 1807 (Stets, *Postmasters*, 107; Gideon Granger to Hanson, 1 Aug. 1805, in DNA: RG 28, LPG).

MR PICHONS REMOVAL TO THIS CITY: in the spring of 1804, Louis André Pichon moved from Georgetown to Washington (David B. Mattern and Holly C. Shulman, eds., *The Selected Letters of Dolley Payne Madison* [Charlottesville, 2003], 57; Madison, *Papers, Sec. of State Ser.*, 7:322, 434).

Charles MCLAUGHLIN ran the Union Tavern in Georgetown (Vol. 37:50).

MY CONDUCT WITH RESPECT TO THE BANK: for Hanson's embittered removal as cashier of the Bank of Columbia and subsequent vendetta against the bank directors, see Vol. 35:399-400 and Vol. 39:54-6.

Preface to a Manuscript on Bacon's Rebellion

[on or before 10 Mch. 1804]

The Original Manuscript, of which the following is a copy, was communicated to me by Mr. King, our late Minister Plenipotentiary at the court of London, in a letter of Dec. 20. 1803. the transaction which it records, altho' of little extent or consequence, is yet marked in the history of Virginia as having been the only rebellion or insurrection which took place in the colony during the 168 years of it's existence preceding the American revolution; and one hundred years exactly before that event. in the contest with the house of Stuart it only accompanied the steps of the mother country. the rebellion of Bacon has been little understood, it's cause & course being imperfectly explained by any authentic materials hitherto possessed. this renders the present narrative of real value. it appears to have been written by a person intimately acquainted with it's origin, progress and conclusion, 30 years after it took place, when the passions of the day had subsided and reason might take a cool & deliberate review of the transaction. it was written too, not for the public eye but to satisfy the desire of a minister Ld. Oxford; and the candor & simplicity of the narration cannot fail to command belief. on the outside of the cover of the MS. is the No 3947 in one place, and 5781 in another. very possibly the one may indicate the place it held in Ld. Oxford's library and the other it's number in the catalogue of the bookseller, to whose hands it came afterwards; for it was at the sale of the stock of a bookseller that Mr. King purchased it.

To bring the authenticity of this copy as near to that of the original as I could, I have most carefully copied it with my own hand. the pages and lines of the copy correspond exactly with those of the original. the orthography, abbreviations, punctuation interlineations and incorrectnesses are preserved, so that it is a fac simile except as to the form of the letters. the orthography & abbreviations are evidences of the age of the writing.

The author says of himself that he was a planter (pa. 20.) that he lived in Northumberland (3.) but was elected a member of the assembly of 1676. for the county of Stafford (20) Colo. Mason being his colleague (21. 45.) of which assembly Colo. Warner was Speaker (61.) that it was the first and should be the last time of his medling with public affairs (49) and he subscribes the initials of his name T. M. whether the records of the time (if they still exist) with the aid of these circumstances, will shew what his name was, remains for further enquiry.

Tr (ViHi); undated, but see below; in Edward B. Stelle's hand.

The care with which TJ produced a personal COPY of the manuscript that Rufus King enclosed in his letter of 20 Dec. 1803 testifies to the value he placed on the first-person account. On 10 Mch., he had John March bind the copy in an octavo, calf-gilt volume, which almost certainly included the above preface. During the summer, he sent a copy, possibly his own but likely an additional one, to Richmond, where it was printed in the *Enquirer* in the issues of 1, 5, and 8 Sep. An introductory letter to the editor explained that the president had sent the "curious and interesting historical document" to George Wythe "with a permission to the bearer, to communicate its contents to the public." The author of the introduction essentially duplicated TJ's preface, altering or adding to some of the phrasing to make it a third-person rather than a first-person account and reordering some of it. Other than the reference to the copy's communication to Wythe, the only significant intervention was a new, concluding paragraph that strongly praised Nathaniel Bacon and condemned Virginia's colonial authorities. The incident offered proof, the author argued, "that insurrections proceed oftener from the misconduct of those in power, than from the factious and turbulent temper of the people." TJ retained his copy until it was included in the sale of his library to Congress. In 1816, the *National Register*, a short-lived weekly periodical published in Washington, printed the narrative along with TJ's preface from a copy "in the hand writing of Mr. Jefferson." Four years later, the Richmond-based *Virginia Evangelical and Literary Magazine* also published the narrative and preface "from a copy in the Library now belonging to Congress; but formerly the property of Mr. Jefferson." In 1821, the *National Intelligencer* reported the disappearance of the copy along with two other works from Jefferson's former collection. Apparently the copy was returned, for in 1832, Edward B. Stelle, an assistant librarian of Congress, transcribed a version from "Thomas Jefferson's *copy*" for John Tyler, then serving as a U.S. senator. Stelle explained that his version was "a literal transcript" and followed TJ's own policy for transcribing the narrative, aside from the preface, from which Stelle excluded notice of TJ's interlineations and corrections. Other than those exclusions, Stelle appears to have followed TJ's spelling, capitalization, and abbreviations. TJ's copy was lost in the 1851 Capitol fire that destroyed much of his former collection (Edward B. Stelle to John Tyler, 28 June 1832, MS in ViHi, bound with Trs of preface and narrative; *The National Register*, 1 [1816], 278; *Virginia Evangelical and Literary Magazine*, 3 [1820], 128; *Daily National Intelligencer*, 1 May 1821, 25 Dec. 1851; James Conaway, *America's Library: The Story of the Library of Congress, 1800-2000* [New Haven, 2000], 46-7; Sowerby, No. 534, 5:193; Statement of Account with John March, at 12 Mch. 1804).

ONLY REBELLION OR INSURRECTION: TJ neglected consideration of efforts in 1622 and 1644 by the Powhatan Indians to eliminate or at least constrain the spread of English settlement, both of which were featured in early histories of the colony (Frederic W. Gleach, *Powhatan's World and Colonial Virginia: A Conflict of Cultures* [Lincoln, Neb., 1993], 148-51, 156-8, 174-7; Robert Beverley, *The History & Present State of Virginia* [Chapel Hill, 2013], 39-42, 46-7).

Appendix I

E D I T O R I A L   N O T E

Jefferson kept an ongoing list of appointments and removals throughout his two terms as president, with entries extending from 5 Mch. 1801 to 23 Feb. 1809. For the first installment of this list, from 5 Mch. 1801 to 14 May 1802, see Vol. 33, Appendix I, List 4. Beginning with Volume 37, subsequent installments have appeared as Appendix I. This segment of the record includes entries for the period covered by the present volume. It begins with the president's last appointments of bankruptcy commissioners. These entries had made up a significant part of his list after the passage of the act of 29 Apr. 1802, which gave the president the authority to appoint the commissioners. Jefferson signed the repeal of the Bankruptcy Act on 19 Dec. 1803 (see Vol. 37:697-702).

It is not always clear why the president dated the appointments on his list as he did. Jefferson sent the nominations of Nicholas Fitzhugh, George Hay, and William S. Pennington to the Senate on 21 Nov., and they were confirmed on the 25th. Although all three commissions were dated 25 Nov., the State Department perhaps prepared them on different dates, and Jefferson added the names to his list as he signed the commissions. On 9 Dec., the president sent a long list of nominations to the Senate, which confirmed the appointments on 15 and 21 Dec. They appear on the list below at 29 and 31 Dec. and 4 Jan. The Senate approved the appointment of John Childress, Jr., on 15 Dec. and Thomas G. Thornton on the 21st (JEP, 1:460-1; TJ to the Senate, 9 Dec.). Jefferson nominated the remaining seven individuals on 24 Feb. See his letter to the Senate of that date for the Senate's approval of the candidates on 24, 25, and 29 Feb. An eighth nominee, Meriwether Jones, was not approved by the Senate until 9 Mch. and does not appear on the president's list until the 12th, beyond the period covered by this volume.

List of Appointments

[16 Nov. 1803-3 Mch. 1804]

16 Richard Cutts Shannon. Portsmouth. Commr. bkrptcy v. John Goddard resigned.

18. James Lyne Wm. Roberts & Wm. Hunt of Williamsboro' Comrs. bkrptcy N. Carolina

25. Nicholas Fitzhugh Assistant judge of the Circuit court of the US. for the district of Columbia. v. James Marshall resd.

30. George Hay Atty for the district of Virga v. Thos. Nelson decd.
    Wm. S. Pennington of N.J. Atty for the district of N. Jersey v.   resignd.[1]

Dec. 29. Dudley Broadstreet Hobart of Mass' Collectr & Inspector for the District & port of Bath v.

31. Samuel Derby. Mass. Collector & Inspector of Port of York.

John Cutler Maryld. do	Snowhill
Aaron Hassert. N.J. Surveyor & Inspector	New Brunswick
Erastus Granger. N.Y. Surveyor & Inspector	Buffalo creek
George Wolcott. Mass. Survr. & Inspectr.	Saybrook
Thomas J. Ferebee. N.C. do. do.	Indian town.
Peterson Gurley N.C. do. do.	Winton.

Martin Tapscott of Virginia. Collector & Inspector of port of Yeo-comico river

Francis Coffyn of Dunkirk Commercl. Agent Dunkirk

Jacob Ridgway Pensva.   do. Antwerp. in France.

Henry Wilson. Maryld.   do. Ostend in France

Lawson Alexander. Maryld. do. Rotterdam in repub. of Batavia.

John M. Forbes of N.Y. Consul of Hamburg.

William Clarke. Mass. Consul of Embden in Prussia.

John F. Brown Mass. Consul of isld. St. Thomas, allegce. of Denmark.

Isaac Prince N.Y. Consul isld. St. Bartholomews.

John Leonard N.J. Consul Barcelona. Spain

John Mitchell Pensva. V. Commercl. Agent. Havre de Grace. France.

1804.

Jan.   4. John Childress jr. of Tennessee Marshal West Tennessee
v.   removed for drunkenness
Thomas G. Thornton, Mass. Marsh. Maine v.   time expired, and active federalist.

Feb. 25. Hore Browse Trist. Missipi. Collector of the district of Missisipi.
Benjamin Morgan of N.O. Naval officer of the port of New Orleans.
Alexander Bailey of the Missipi territy. Collector of district & Inspector of revenue for the port of Natchez.

27. Wm. G. Garland Surveyor & Inspector N.O.

28. Charles Collins junr. Rhode island Collector for the district and Inspector of the revenue for the port of Bristol. R.I.

Mar.   3. John Willis Maryland Collector & Inspector for Oxford
Maryld. v.   Banning removd for irregularity in office, distant residce. & something like forgery
Charles Kilgore of Ohio. register of land office Cincinnati
v.   Ludlow decd.

MS (DLC: TJ Papers, 186:33098); entirely in TJs hand; being the continuation of a list that extends from 5 Mch. 1801 to 23 Feb. 1809; for the installment immediately preceding this one, see Vol. 41: Appendix i.

DISTRICT OF N. JERSEY: William S. Pennington replaced George Maxwell (TJ to the Senate, 21 Nov.).

PORT OF BATH: Dudley B. Hobart replaced William Webb (TJ to the Senate, 9 Dec.).

REMOVED FOR DRUNKENNESS: Robert Hays (same).

TIME EXPIRED: Isaac Parker (same).

[1] TJ next entered and canceled: "Dec. 27. Davids's poems. 1 vol. 12mo 1. D. Philad."

Appendix II

Letters Not Printed in Full

EDITORIAL NOTE

In keeping with the editorial method established for this edition, the chronological series includes "in one form or another every available letter known to have been written by or to Thomas Jefferson" (Vol. 1:xv). Most letters are printed in full. In some cases, the letter is not printed but a detailed summary appears at the document's date. Other letters have been described in annotation, which, for the period covered by this volume, are listed in this appendix. Arranged in chronological order, this list includes for each letter the correspondent, date, and location in the volumes where it is described. Examples of letters not printed include brief letters of transmittal, multiple testimonials recommending a particular candidate for office, repetitive letters from a candidate seeking a post, and official correspondence that the president saw in only a cursory way. In other instances, documents are described in annotation due to the near illegibility of the surviving text. Using the list in this appendix, the table of contents, and Appendix III (correspondence not found but recorded in Jefferson's Summary Journal of Letters), readers will be able to reconstruct Jefferson's chronological epistolary record from 16 Nov. 1803 to 10 Mch. 1804.

From Daniel Carroll Brent, 23 Nov. Noted at Petition of Jacob Hoffman and Others, 12 Nov. 1803.

From Henry Dearborn, received 28 Nov. Noted at Jared Mansfield to TJ, 5 Nov. 1803.

From Albert Gallatin, 29 Dec. Noted at TJ to Gallatin, 28 Dec. 1803.

From George Jefferson, 30 Dec. Noted at TJ to Jefferson, 27 Dec. 1803.

To Albert Gallatin, 31 Dec. Noted at Gallatin to TJ, 29 Dec. 1803.

From Daniel Carroll Brent, 6 Jan. 1804. Noted at Petition of Joseph Goodier, 4 Jan. 1804.

From Timothy Bloodworth, 17 Jan. Noted at Bloodworth to TJ, 17 Jan. 1804.

From Henry Dearborn, 17 Feb. Noted at TJ to the Senate and the House of Representatives, 16 Feb. 1804.

Appendix III

Letters Not Found

EDITORIAL NOTE

This appendix lists chronologically letters written by and to Jefferson during the period covered by this volume for which no text is known to survive. Jefferson's Summary Journal of Letters provides a record of the missing documents. For incoming letters, Jefferson typically recorded in SJL the date that the letter was sent and the date on which he received it. He sometimes included the location from which it was dispatched and an abbreviated notation indicating the government department to which it pertained: "N" for Navy, "S" for State, "T" for Treasury, and "W" for War.

From Gabriel Lilly, 17 Nov.; received 20 Nov. from Monticello.

From J. P. G. Muhlenberg, 17 Nov.; received 20 Nov. from Philadelphia; notation: "Mackey John. employmt. N.O."

From John Wayles Eppes; received 19 Nov.; notation: "Peyton Randolph to be distr. Atty. v. T. Nelson decd."

From John Gibson, 19 Nov.; received 20 Dec. from Vincennes; notation: "his son to be Captain."

From John Perry, 20 Nov.; received 27 Nov. from Shadwell.

From Mary Stewart, November; received 20 Nov. from Monticello.

To Gabriel Lilly, 21 Nov.

To James Oldham, 21 Nov.

To Mary Stewart, 21 Nov.

From John Breckinridge, 22 Nov.; received 22 Nov.; notation: "Davis Thos. T. to be Govr. Louisiana."

From Levi Lincoln, 22 Nov.; received 23 Nov.; notation: "Genl. Hull to be Govr. Louisiana. Blake emploimt. there."

From the Senate, 22 Nov.; received 22 Nov.; notation: "resoln respecting impressed seamen."

To William Stewart, 22 Nov.

From James Taylor, Jr., 22 Nov.; received 2 Dec. from Norfolk.

From John Taylor and Wilson Cary Nicholas, 22 Nov.; received 22 Nov. from Washington; notation: "John Minor to be distr. Atty."

From Robert Phillips, 23 Nov.; received 27 Nov. from Charlottesville.

From John Smith of Ohio; received 24 Nov.; notation: "Richd. Sparks to explore road."

From Richard Anderson, 24 Nov.; received 27 Nov. from Milton.

To William Davies, 25 Nov.

To Burgess Griffin, 25 Nov.

From Gabriel Lilly, 25 Nov.; received 27 Nov. from Monticello.

From Willis Alston, 26 Nov.; received 26 Nov.; notation: "Peterson Gurley Survr. Winton."

From James Oldham, 26 Nov.; received 27 Nov. from Monticello.

From John Strode; received 26 Nov.; notation: "Hedgeman Thom."

To Gabriel Lilly, 27 Nov.

To John Perry, 27 Nov.

To Robert Phillips, 27 Nov.

To Richard Anderson, 28 Nov.

From "Ogden (illegible)," 28 Nov.; received 2 Dec.; notation: "Saml. Reading to be P.M. vice Hay decd."

From Francis Wood, 28 Nov.; received 14 Mch. 1804 from "Great Nore. L'Africaine"; notation: "S."

From John Gibson, November; received 29 Nov. from Vincennes; notation: "to be contd. Secretary."

To Michael Hope, 29 Nov.; notation: "100. D."

From the Treasury Department, 29 Nov.; received 29 Nov.; notation: "nominations."

From Michael Hope, 30 Nov.; received 18 Dec. from Milton.

From Archibald Bolt, et al., 1 Dec.; received 27 Apr. 1804 from "Cambrian. Halifx"; notation: "S."

To James Taylor, Jr., 3 Dec.

From William Wardlaw, 3 Dec.; received 4 Dec. from Charlottesville.

From William Davies, 6 Dec.; received 13 Dec. from Norfolk.

From Richard Anderson, 10 Dec.; received 18 Dec. from Milton.

From Philip Mazzei, 10 Dec.; received 13 Apr. 1804 from Pisa.

From William Stewart, 10 Dec.; received 18 Dec. from Monticello.

From William Stewart, 10 Dec.; received 18 Dec. from Monticello.

To Gabriel Lilly, 12 Dec.

From Samuel W. Bridgham, 15 Dec.; received 24 Dec. from Providence.

From George Jefferson, 15 Dec.; received 20 Dec. from Richmond.

From Thomas Newton, 15 Dec.; received 20 Dec. from Richmond.

From John Perry, 15 Dec.; received 8 Jan. 1804 from Shadwell.

From Joseph Bloomfield, 17 Dec.; received 21 Dec. from Trenton; notation: "S."

From Walter Charles Davids, 17 Dec.; received 22 Dec. from Philadelphia.

From James Oldham, 17 Dec.; received 19 Dec. from Monticello.

From Thomas Mann Randolph, 17 Dec.; received 19 Dec. from Edgehill.

To Michael Hope, 19 Dec.

To Gabriel Lilly, 19 Dec.

From the Treasury Department, 19 Dec.; received 20 Dec.; notation: "Warehouses for Quarentine Baltimore."

From Edward Tiffin, 26 Dec.; received 14 Mch. 1804 from Chillicothe.

From Gabriel Lilly, 29 Dec.; received 3 Jan. 1804 from Albemarle.

From James Taylor, Jr., 29 Dec.; received 7 Jan. 1804 from Norfolk.

From Edwin Gray, 30 Dec.; received 2 Jan. 1804 from Washington; notation: "Bedinger v. Davies Collectr. Norfolk."

From Isaac Tichenor, 30 Dec.; received 15 Jan. 1804 from Bennington; notation: "S."

From Gordon Duff & Co., 31 Dec,; received 4 May 1804 from Madeira; connected by a brace with entry for letter received the same day from Hill Bissets & Co. of 31 Dec. (see Madison, *Papers, Sec. of State Ser.*, 6:248).

From Hill Bissets & Co., 31 Dec.; received 4 May 1804 from Madeira; connected by a brace with entry for letter received the same day from Gordon Duff & Co. of 31 Dec. (see Madison, *Papers, Sec. of State Ser.*, 6:248n).

From John Mackey, 3 Jan. 1804; received 6 Jan. from Philadelphia.

From David Higginbotham, 4 Jan.; received 15 Jan. from Milton; notation: "Jan. 4. (for 14.)."

From Paul Mumford, et al., 5 Jan.; received 15 Jan. from Newport; notation: "agt Nicholls' appmt."

From James Oldham, 7 Jan.; received 8 Jan. from Monticello.

From Anne Cary Randolph and Martha Jefferson Randolph, 7 Jan.; received 8 Jan. from Edgehill.

To Richard Anderson, 9 Jan.; notation: "100. D."

To Gabriel Lilly, 9 Jan.; notation: "153.27."

To John Perry, 9. Jan.; notation: "36.73."

From Aaron Vail, 10 Jan.; received 2 Aug. from Paris.

From Samuel Morse, 11 Jan.; received 3 Feb. from Savannah.

From Benjamin H. Latrobe, 12 Jan.; received 13 Jan. from Aquia; notation: "Jan. 19. for 12."

From Gabriel Lilly, 13 Jan.; received 15 Jan.

From Samuel Morse, 13 Jan.; received 3 Feb. from Savannah.

From George Jefferson, 14 Jan.; received 19 Jan. from Richmond.

From John Martin, 15 Jan.; received 30 Mch. from "Brit. brig Racoon. New Provdce."; connected by a brace with entry for letter received the same day from Henry Mayo of 13 Feb. with notation: "refd Secy. State."

To Gabriel Lilly, 16 Jan.

From John Perry, 19 Jan.; received 24 Jan. from Shadwell.

From Robert Kinnan, 20 Jan.; received 27 Jan. from Petersburg.

From John Sergeant, 20 Jan.; received 9 Feb. from New Stockbridge; notation: "W."

From James Dinsmore, 21 Jan.; received 24 Jan. from Monticello.

From Michael Hope, 21 Jan.; received 24 Jan. from Milton.

From Gabriel Lilly, 27 Jan.; received 30 Jan.

From Joseph Yznardi, Sr., 27 Jan.; received 27 Apr. from Cadiz.

To David Higginbotham, 28 Jan.

To Robert Kinnan, 28 Jan.

From DeWitt Clinton, 30 Jan.; received 3 Feb. from New York.

From Levi Lincoln, 31 Jan.; received 31 Jan.; notation: "Wm. Lyman to be Govr. upper Louisiana."

From Alexandre Baudin, 1 Feb.; received 12 Mch. from New Orleans.

From John Banthom, 3 Feb.; received 21 Feb. from Washington; notation: "W."

From Isaac Tichenor, 4 Feb.; received 19 Feb. from Windsor; notation: "ratificn."

From Christopher Ellery, 6 Feb.; received 6 Feb.; notation: "Collins to be Collector Bristol v. Russel."

To Gabriel Lilly, 6 Feb.

From Levi Lincoln, 6 Feb.; received 7 Feb. from Washington; notation: "whether negroes merchandize. T."

From Alexandre Baudin, 7 Feb.; received 26 Mch. from New Orleans; notation: "inclosd papers to Govr Claiborne, referrg to Mar. 18."

From Mathew Carey, 7 Feb.; received 13 Feb. from Philadelphia; notation: "Gamble James v. Jackson."

From William C. C. Claiborne, 7 Feb.; received 13 Mch. from New Orleans; notation: "to be Govr. Louisa. or Misipi."

To Burgess Griffin, 7 Feb.

To William Wardlaw, 7 Feb.

From Samuel Overton, 8 Feb.; received 15 Feb. from Louisa.

From "Frazer & others"; received 9 Feb.; notation: "petn for justice Navy yard."

From Meriwether Lewis, 10 Feb.; received 20 Mch. from "riv. Dubois."

To James Powell, 10 Feb.

From "Parry & others"; received 11 Feb.; notation: "petn to appt. Levi White just. peace."

To Thomas McKean, 13 Feb.

From Henry Mayo, 13 Feb.; received 30 Mch. from "Brit. brig Racoon. New Provdce."; connected by a brace with entry for letter received the same day from John Martin of 15 Jan. with notation: "refd Secy. State."

From Paul M. Mumford, 15 Feb.; received 3 Mch. from Newport; notation: "Constt Tabor Collector."

From John Rogers; received 15 Feb.

From Thomas Sumter, Sr., 15 Feb.; received 16 Feb.

From Thomas Cooper, 16 Feb.; received 14 Mch. from Northumberland; notation: "Jacob Hart. Survr. Louisa."

To Samuel Overton, 16 Feb.

From Abraham B. Venable, 16 Feb.; received 16 Feb.; notation: "Larkin Smith to be Comr. loans."

From Burgess Griffin, 17 Feb.; received 26 Feb. from Poplar Forest.

From Martha Jefferson Randolph, 17 Feb.; received 22 Feb. from Edgehill.

From James Dinsmore, 20 Feb.; received 24 Feb. from Monticello.

From Samuel Miller, 20 Feb.; received 24 Feb. from New York.

To John Rogers, 20 Feb.

From John Slocum, 21 Feb.; received 14 Mch. from Newport; connected by a brace with entries for letters received the same day from Samuel Vernon of 24 Feb. and James D'Wolf of 2 Mch. with notation: "Ellery Wm. to be Collectr. Newport."

From David Leonard Barnes, 22 Feb.; received 1 Mch. from Providence; notation: "T."

From Samuel Osgood, 22 Feb.; received 1 Mch. from New York; notation: "Kibbe Isaac. Commr. to Spain."

From John McDonald, 23 Feb.; received 29 June from "Cambrian"; notation: "S."

From Samuel Vernon, 24 Feb.; received 14 Mch. from Newport; connected by a brace with entries for letters received the same day from John Slocum of 21 Feb. and James D'Wolf of 2 Mch. with notation: "Ellery Wm. to be Collectr. Newport."

To James Dinsmore, 25 Feb.

From Meriwether Lewis, 25 Feb.; received 4 May from St. Louis.

To Gabriel Lilly, 25 Feb.

From Meriwether Lewis, 26 Feb.; received 4 May from St. Louis.

From Andrew Ellicott, 27 Feb.; received 1 Mch. from Lancaster; notation: "Walker. Gillespie. Ellicott."

From Robert Kinnan, 27 Feb.; received 2 Mch. from Petersburg.

From Henry Lee, 29 Feb.; received 3 Mch. from Alexandria.

From the Treasury Department; received 29 Feb.; notation: "Nourse bank director."

From James D'Wolf, 2 Mch.; received 14 Mch.; connected by a brace with entries for letters received the same day from John Slocum of 21 Feb. and Samuel Vernon of 24 Feb. with notation: "Ellery Wm. to be Collectr. Newport."

From Martha Jefferson Randolph, 2 Mch.; received 7 Mch. from Edgehill.

To Henry Lee, 5 Mch.

To Robert Kinnan, 6 Mch.

From Thomas Newton, 6 Mch.; received 13 Mch. from Norfolk; notation: "Thos. Newton junr. to be Collectr. Norf."

From Robert Bailey; received 7 Mch.

From Burgess Griffin, 8 Mch.; received 17 Mch. from Poplar Forest.

From James Taylor, Jr., 8 Mch.; received 17 Mch. from Norfolk; notation: "Madeira. Champ. 391.57."

From Nathaniel Anderson, 9 Mch.; received 13 Mch. from Richmond; notation: "office in Richmd."

To John Bolling, 10 Mch.

To Gabriel Lilly, 10 Mch.

To Marten Wanscher, 10 Mch.

Appendix IV

Financial Documents

E D I T O R I A L   N O T E

This appendix briefly describes, in chronological order, the orders and invoices pertaining to Jefferson's finances during the period covered by this volume that are not printed in full or accounted for elsewhere in this volume. The orders for payments to Étienne Lemaire and Joseph Dougherty pertain, for the most part, to expenses associated with running the President's House. The *Memorandum Books* are cited when they are relevant to a specific document and provide additional information.

Order on John Barnes for payment of $60.33 to Joseph Dougherty, Washington, 21 Nov. (MS in MHi; in TJ's hand and signed by him; signed by Dougherty acknowledging payment; endorsed by Barnes as paid 21 Nov.). TJ recorded this transaction at 20 Nov. as payment of Dougherty's accounts for forage, smiths, and contingencies (MB, 2:1112).

Order on John Barnes for payment of $75.76 to Étienne Lemaire, Washington, 21 Nov. (MS in MHi; in TJ's hand and signed by him; signed by Lemaire acknowledging payment; endorsed by Barnes as paid 21 Nov.). TJ recorded this transaction as payment of Lemaire's accounts from 13 to 19 Nov. for provisions and contingencies (MB, 2:1112).

Order on John Barnes for payment of $126.36 to Étienne Lemaire, Washington, 28 Nov. (MS in MHi; in TJ's hand and signed by him; signed by Lemaire acknowledging payment; endorsed by Barnes as paid 28 Nov.). TJ recorded this transaction as payment of Lemaire's accounts from 20 to 26 Nov. for provisions, wine, wood, and contingencies (MB, 2:1113).

Order on John Barnes for payment of $259.22 to Étienne Lemaire, 5 Dec. (MS in MHi; in TJ's hand and signed by him; signed by Lemaire acknowledging payment; endorsed by Barnes as paid 9 Dec.). TJ recorded this transaction as payment of Lemaire's accounts from 27 Nov. to 3 Dec. for provisions, wood, and contingencies and for payment of servants' wages to 4 Dec. (MB, 2:1113).

Order on John Barnes for payment of $15 to Wilson Bryan, [8 Dec.] (MS in ViU; undated, in TJ's hand and signed by him; signed by Bryan on 9 Dec. requesting that payment be made to "Mr. Layman"; endorsed by Barnes as paid 9 Dec.). TJ recorded this transaction in his financial memoranda at 8 Dec. as payment for a birdcage (MB, 2:1113).

Order on John Barnes for payment of $67.25 to Joseph Dougherty, 8 Dec. (MS in MHi; in TJ's hand and signed by him; signed by Dougherty acknowledging payment; endorsed by Barnes as paid 8 Dec.). TJ recorded this transaction as payment of Dougherty's accounts for smiths, forage, and contingencies (MB, 2:1113).

Order on John Barnes for payment of $28.35 to Joseph Dougherty, 19 Dec. (MS in MHi; in TJ's hand and signed by him; signed by Dougherty acknowledging payment; endorsed by Barnes as paid 19 Dec.). TJ recorded this transaction in his financial memoranda at 20 Dec. as payment of Dougherty's accounts for provender, smiths, saddlers, and contingencies (MB, 2:1114).

Order on John Barnes for payment of $139.26 to Étienne Lemaire, 19 Dec. (MS in ViU; in TJ's hand and signed by him; signed by Lemaire acknowledging payment; endorsed by Barnes as paid 19 Dec.). TJ recorded this transaction in his financial memoranda at 20 Dec. as payment of Lemaire's accounts from 11 to 17 Dec. for provisions, charcoal, servants, and contingencies (MB, 2:1114).

Order on John Barnes for payment of $15 to Amos B. Doolittle, Washington, 23 Dec. (MS in MHi; in TJ's hand and signed by him; signed by Doolittle acknowledging payment; endorsed by Barnes as paid 23 Dec.). TJ recorded this transaction as payment "for 3. profiles" (MB, 2:1114).

Order on John Barnes for payment of $91.93 to Étienne Lemaire, 26 Dec. (MS in MHi; in TJ's hand and signed by him; signed by Lemaire acknowledging payment; endorsed by Barnes as paid 26 Dec.). TJ recorded this transaction as payment of Lemaire's accounts from 18 to 24 Dec. for provisions, charcoal, and wood (MB, 2:1114).

Order on John Barnes for payment of $227.57 to Étienne Lemaire, 2 Jan. 1804 (MS in MHi; in TJ's hand and signed by him; signed by Lemaire acknowledging payment; endorsed by Barnes as paid 6 Feb.). TJ recorded this transaction as payment of Lemaire's accounts from 25 to 31 Dec. 1803 for provisions and for payment of servants' wages to 4 Jan. 1804 (MB, 2:1117).

Order on John Barnes for payment of $10 to Amos B. Doolittle, Washington, 7 Jan. (MS in ViU; in TJ's hand and signed by him; signed on verso by J. W. Jackson acknowledging payment on 12 Jan.; endorsed by Barnes as paid 12 Jan.). TJ recorded this transaction as payment "for 2. profiles" (MB, 2:1118).

Order on John Barnes for payment of $128.58 to Étienne Lemaire, 9 Jan. (MS in ViU; in TJ's hand and signed by him; signed by Lemaire acknowledging payment; endorsed by Barnes as paid 6 Feb.). TJ recorded this transaction as payment of Lemaire's accounts from 1 to 7 Jan. 1804 for provisions, President's House furniture, and contingencies (MB, 2:1118).

Order on John Barnes for payment of $26.16 to Peter Lenox, 12 Jan. (MS in CSmH; in TJ's hand and signed by him; written on invoice from Lenox to TJ, undated, for assorted packing boxes, a boot jack, a bird stand, a map frame, and a hen coop purchased from 28 May to 27 Oct. 1803; signed by Lenox acknowledging payment on 12 Jan.; MB, 2:1118).

Order on John Barnes for payment of $80.58 to Joseph Dougherty for "expences of filling the ice house," 15 Jan. (MS in ViU; in TJ's hand and signed by him; endorsed by Barnes as paid 16 Jan.; MB, 2:1118).

Order on John Barnes for payment of $83.49 to Étienne Lemaire, 16 Jan. (MS in MHi; in TJ's hand and signed by him; signed by Lemaire acknowledging payment; endorsed by Barnes as paid 6 Feb.). TJ recorded this transaction as payment of Lemaire's accounts from 7 to 13 Jan. for provisions and contingencies, including a deduction of a $4 overpayment for servants on 2 Jan.(MB, 2:1118).

Order on John Barnes for payment of $123.44 to Étienne Lemaire, 23 Jan. (MS in MHi; in TJ's hand and signed by him; signed by Lemaire acknowledging payment; endorsed by Barnes as paid 6 Feb.). TJ recorded this transaction as payment of Lemaire's accounts from 14 to 21 Jan. for provisions, cider, and portage (MB, 2:1118).

Order on John Barnes for payment of $60.75 to Étienne Lemaire, 30 Jan. (MS in MHi; in TJ's hand and signed by him; signed by Lemaire acknowledging payment; endorsed by Barnes as paid 6 Feb.). TJ recorded this transaction as payment of Lemaire's accounts from 22 to 28 Jan. for provisions, servants, and contingencies (MB, 2:1119).

Order on John Barnes for payment of $51.05½ to Joseph Dougherty, 6 Feb. (MS in MHi; in TJ's hand and signed by him; signed by Dougherty acknowledging payment; endorsed by Barnes as paid 8 Feb.).

Order on John Barnes for payment of $231.68 to Étienne Lemaire, 6 Feb. (MS in MHi; in TJ's hand and signed by him; signed by Lemaire acknowledging payment on 22 Feb.; endorsed by Barnes as paid 22 Feb.). TJ recorded this transaction as payment of Lemaire's accounts from 29 Jan. to 4 Feb. for provisions, servants' clothes, and contingencies and for payment of servants' wages to 4 Feb. (MB, 2:1119).

Order on John Barnes for payment of $10 to Amos B. Doolittle, 10 Feb. (MS in MHi; in TJ's hand and signed by him; signed by Doolittle acknowledging payment; endorsed by Barnes as paid 10 Feb.). TJ recorded this transaction as payment "for profiles" (MB, 2:1119).

Order on John Barnes for payment of $98.89 to Étienne Lemaire, Washington, 13 Feb. (MS in MHi; in TJ's hand and signed by him; signed by Lemaire acknowledging payment on 28 Feb.; endorsed by Barnes as paid 28 Feb.). TJ recorded this transaction as payment of Lemaire's accounts from 5 to 12 Feb. for provisions, wood, and contingencies (MB, 2:1120).

Order on John Barnes for payment of $102.49 to Étienne Lemaire, Washington, 20 Feb. (MS in ViU; in TJ's hand and signed by him; signed by Lemaire acknowledging payment on 3 Mch.; endorsed by Barnes as paid 3 Mch.). TJ recorded this transaction as payment of Lemaire's accounts from 12 to 18 Feb. for provisions, wood, and servants (MB, 2:1120).

Order on John Barnes for payment of $5.25 to Edward Frethy, [25 Feb.] (MS in CSmH; undated, in TJ's hand and signed by him; written on invoice from Frethy to TJ, undated, for ribbon and "one months Dressing"; signed by Frethy acknowledging payment on 25 Feb. 1804). TJ recorded this transaction in his financial memoranda at 27 Feb. (MB, 2:1120).

Order on John Barnes for payment of $86.33 to Joseph Dougherty, 27 Feb. (MS in MHi; in TJ's hand and signed by him; signed by Dougherty acknowledging payment; endorsed by Barnes as paid 27 Feb.). TJ recorded this transaction as payment of Dougherty's accounts for forage, clothing for TJ, storage, and drayage (MB, 2:1120).

Order on John Barnes for payment of $80.14 to Étienne Lemaire, 27 Feb. (MS in MHi; in TJ's hand and signed by him; signed by Lemaire acknowledging payment; endorsed by Barnes as paid 14 Mch.). TJ recorded this transaction as payment of Lemaire's accounts from 19 to 25 Feb. for provisions, wood, servants, and contingencies (MB, 2:1120).

Order on John Barnes for payment of $247.21 to Étienne Lemaire, 5 Mch. (MS in MHi; in TJ's hand and signed by him; signed by Lemaire acknowledging payment on 26 Mch.; endorsed by Barnes as paid 26 Mch.). TJ recorded this transaction as payment of Lemaire's accounts from 26 Feb. to 3 Mch. for provisions and contingencies and for payment of servants' wages to 4 Mch. (MB, 2:1121).

INDEX

English language, 242
English Press (Paris), 5n
Enquirer (Richmond), xlviii, 617n
"Enquiry concerning the Nature of Heat" (Benjamin Thompson, Count Rumford), 265n
Enquiry into the Foundation and History of the Law of Nations in Europe (Robert Ward), 599
Enterprize (U.S. schooner), 356n, 392n
Enville, Louise Elisabeth de La Rochefoucauld, Duchesse d', 353, 355
Eppes, Francis Wayles (TJ's grandson): health of, 279, 330; TJ's affection for, 330, 547
Eppes, John Wayles (TJ's son-in-law): letter from, 611-12; independent of TJ's political opinions, x, 69-70; and discontinuance of commissioners of loans, 61n, 63n, 273n; and reduction of public expenses, 63n; and transfer of Louisiana, 140, 168, 171; M. Lewis sends respects to, 194; elected to Congress, 248, 278-9, 329; and Petersburg post office, 337, 338n; slaves of, 446; return home anticipated, 547, 579, 607; and wife's health, 611-12; letter from cited, 623
Eppes, Maria Jefferson (TJ's granddaughter): birth of, xi, 547-8; health of, 611
Eppes, Mary Jefferson (Maria, Polly, Mrs. John Wayles Eppes, TJ's daughter): letters to, 47-8, 171-2, 365-6, 547-8, 579; letter from, 442-3; pregnancy, xi, 47, 48, 171, 248, 278-9, 329-30, 365, 442, 547; health of, xi-xii, 168, 442, 443n, 446, 579, 607, 611; and TJ's syllabus on doctrines of Jesus, 42, 171; TJ sends news of Washington, family matters to, 47-8, 365-6; TJ's affection for, 48, 140, 255, 330; M. Lewis sends respects to, 194; misses her husband, 278-9, 365, 442; asks TJ to sit for Saint-Mémin, 442, 443n; death, 443n; gives birth to daughter, 547-8; Lafayette sends respects to, 550
Erving, George W.: letter from, 597-9; and books for Library of Congress, 597, 599-600; and impressment of American seamen, 597-8; forwards letters for TJ, 597-9
Essai de géologie, ou Mémoires pour servir a l'histoire naturelle du globe

(Barthélemy Faujas de Saint-Fond), 246, 373
Essay, on the Means of Improving Public Education (Samuel Knox), 506-7
Essay on the Best System of Liberal Education (Samuel Knox), 506n
Essay on the Principle of Population (Thomas Robert Malthus), vii, 369, 370n, 380, 485-6, 538
Essays, Mathematical and Physical (Jared Mansfield), 367n
Essays on the Lives and Writings of Fletcher of Saltoun and the Poet Thomson (David Steuart Erskine, Earl of Buchan), 245, 250n
Eulogy on the Illustrious George Washington (Charles P. Sumner), 265
Europe: characterized as a manufacturing society, 380-1
Eustis, Jacob, 48n
Eustis, William: letter to, 68; letter from, 48; pays newspaper subscription for TJ, 48; sends fish to TJ, 68; applications to, for appointment, 96n; recommends aspirants for office, 200
Evans, Evan, 578n
Evans, John Thomas: map of Missouri River, 46, 193, 194n, 270, 325; seeks Welsh Indians, 325, 326n
Ewer, Silvanus: letter from, 122-4; claim for vessels taken by French, 122-4; identified, 124n
Examination of the Various Charges Exhibited Against Aaron Burr, Esq. (William P. Van Ness), 150-1, 214-15
Experiment (schooner), 555

Fabbroni, Giovanni, 354, 355
Falkirk, battle of, 400n
Falmouth, England, 81n
Fame (schooner), 567
Fanny (sloop), 425-8
Fantrees (Fontrees), John, 92
Faujas de Saint-Fond, Barthélemy: letter to, 373-5; *Essai de géologie,* 246, 373; TJ discusses scientific classification, western exploration with, 373-5
Fayetteville Gazette (N.C.), 88
Febvrier, Francis, 341-2, 463
Febvrier, Nicholas: letters from, 341-2, 463; seeks TJ's assistance, charity, 341-2, 463; identified, 342n
federalism, 449-50

GALLATIN, ALBERT (*cont.*)
States, ix, 104-7, 588; applications to, for appointments, 56, 186n, 241n; discontinuance of the office of supervisor, 59, 68-9; discontinuance of state loan offices, 60-1, 68-9; and revenue cutters, 72; advises on appointments, 88n, 92-3, 178-9, 203, 204, 435, 443, 451, 452, 454-5, 476-7, 511-13, 522, 523, 538-9, 572, 611, 614; and Dearborn's claim, 135-6, 185; and creation and transfer of Louisiana stock, 136, 260, 289, 303-4, 311-13, 315-16n, 328, 336-7, 400-2; and W. Bache's salary, 141-2; and lighthouses, 178-9, 203, 204, 393-4, 452, 453n, 474, 548-9, 590, 611, 614; and president's contingent expenses, 185, 216; and land fraud in Miss. Terr., 230-1; and J. Russell, 238; and the Mint, 266-7; riot at Plymouth, 336, 337, 351; and sinking fund, 401-2; and Beaumarchais heirs' claim, 415-16; calculation of state imports and exports, 452, 454-5; calendar of public debt, 452-3, 454, 455n; and delinquent accounts, 454-5; and H. Putnam's case, 456, 487-8; and R. Hartshorne's case, 456; and D. M. Randolph's account, 463-4, 474-5; commercial regulations for Louisiana, New Orleans, 475, 530, 544, 545, 548-9; establishment of Mobile customs district, 475; attends cabinet meetings, 504-6; and E. Stevens's claim, 505, 508-9, 522-3, 523-4, 529-30; and removals from office, 533-4; instructions for H. B. Trist, 544; and I. Briggs, 555, 600; and Miss. Terr. land commissioners, 600-1; custom house seals, 601. *See also* Treasury, U.S. Department of the

Gallatin, Hannah Nicholson, 154, 330n, 331
Galloway, Benjamin: letter from, 234; feud with L. Martin, 234-5
Gamble, James: letter from, 98; recommends aspirants for office, 98; seeks appointment, 225, 445, 625
Gamble, Robert, 92, 142
gambling, 554

Gardener, Capt., 602, 604
Gardiner, Robert Hallowell, 258-60
Gardiner, Sylvester, 259-60n
Garland, William G., 538-9, 541, 548, 620
Gatewood, Philemon, 454, 455n
Gayoso de Lemos, Manuel, 38-9n
Gazette of the United States (Philadelphia), 54n, 155-6, 330n, 332-3, 334n, 480
Gelston, David, 151n, 393-4
General Abridgment of Cases in Equity Argued and Adjudged in the High Court of Chancery (Robert Foley, Geoffrey Gilbert, and others), 599
General View of the Agriculture of the North Riding of Yorkshire (John Tuke), 274-5, 276n
General Washington (ship), 212
Genoa, Italy, 85, 166
geology, 246
George III, King of Great Britain, xlv
Georgetown, D.C.: newspapers, 368n; markets, 398; bridges, 461n, 533; ferry at, 611; postmaster, 615, 616n; banks, 615-16; inns, taverns, 616n
Georgetown College, 342
George Washington (U.S. ship), 386
Georgia: and slave trade, viii, 425, 466-8; and Creeks, 29-30; French commissary for, 236n; smuggling in, 367-8, 466-8. *See also* Federalists; Republicans; Savannah, Ga.
geraniums, 442
German language, 3n, 599
Germany: admiration for America in, 3; Lower Saxony, 94, 95. *See also* Hamburg, Germany; Prussia
Gerry, Mr., 480
Gerry, Elbridge: letter to, 580; TJ sends opinions on Republican increase, 580
Gerry, Samuel R., 454, 455n
Gex-Oboussier, Louis: letter from, 416-18; seeks to establish vineyard, 416-18; identified, 418n
Giannini, Anthony, 480n
Gibbons, Thomas, 367, 368n, 487-8
Gibbs, George (N.Y.), 364-5
Gibraltar, 75n, 85, 166n, 385, 390-1
Gibson, Jacob, 200
Gibson, John: reappointment as territorial secretary, 240-1, 451, 452; letters from cited, 623, 624
Gibson, William, 235

[654]

MADISON, JAMES (*cont.*)
Louisiana boundaries, 283n;
boundary convention with Great
Britain, 300n; and Eaton, 385,
391-2n, 429-30n; and Tripoli,
391n; and sinking fund, 401-2n;
Hanstein's claim, 412n; seizure
of U.S. vessel at Cuba, 480n;
attends cabinet meetings, 504-6;
E. Stevens's claim, 505, 508-9;
withdrawal of Spanish troops,
officials from Louisiana, 505n. *See
also* State, U.S. Department of

Madison, Bishop James: letter to, 539;
letter from, 366-7; and W. Prentis,
73n; and boundary dispute between
Va. and Md., 366-7; seeks professor
for college, 366-7, 539; and Powell
family's claim, 423n
Madoc, Prince, 326n
Maecenas, 20, 21
Magruder, Allan B.: letter to, 458; letter
from, 413-14; *Political, Commercial
and Moral Reflections,* 413-14, 458;
sends pamphlet to TJ, 413-14, 458;
"Character of Thomas Jefferson,"
414n; identified, 414n
Maine: boundary with Canada, 39-40,
298; York collectorship, 40-1, 92,
96, 620; Bath collectorship, 92, 93n,
96, 619, 621n; marshal for, 95, 97n,
620; land speculation in, 259, 285n;
Gardiner, 259-60; Kennebec Co.,
259-60n; Mount Desert Island, 610;
Penobscot River, 610; Prospect, 610
Malaga, Spain, 85n
Malcolm, Henry, 435-7
Malthus, Thomas Robert: *Essay on the
Principle of Population,* vii, 369, 370n,
380, 485-6, 538
mammoth: classification of, 373-4;
remains at Big Bone Lick, 508n
Manning, Owen: *Dictionarium Saxonico
et Gothico-Latinum,* 599
Mansfield, Jared, 366, 367n, 539n
*Manual of Parliamentary Practice. For
the Use of the Senate of the United
States* (Thomas Jefferson), 151, 173
manufacturing: iron, xlix, 201n, 221,
276 (illus.); boots and shoes, 101n;
candles, 124n; oil, 124n; dye, 324n;
sulfur, 324n; inferior to agriculture,
380-1; duties on manufactured goods,
482n. *See also* mills

*Map of the British and French Dominions
in North America* (John Mitchell), 8n,
281, 283n, 295, 296, 299
maps: of Missouri River region, 8n, 46,
193-4, 270-1; of U.S. coast, 145-7; as
sources of information for boundaries,
281, 283n, 295, 296, 299
March, John, 356n, 617n
Maremek River. *See* Meramec River
Markland, Edward, 512-13n
Mars (ship), 589
Marschalk, Andrew: letter from, 91;
reports transfer of Louisiana from
Spain to France, 91; identified, 91n
Marshall, James M., 23, 619
Marshall, John: *Life of George Washing-
ton,* 315, 380n; and "Curtius" letters,
372n, 379-80; as circuit judge, 477n
Marshall, William, 423-4n, 463, 464n,
474
Marshall, William (S.C.): letter to, 167;
sends map to TJ, 167
Martin, John (seaman): letter from
cited, 625
Martin, Joseph, 31n
Martin, Luther, 234-5
Martin, Wheeler: letter from, 575; and
ratification of Twelfth Amendment,
575; identified, 575n
Martin, William (Tenn.), 30-1
Martinique, W.I., 81, 82n, 209, 341,
342n
Mary (schooner), 122-4
Maryland: Snow Hill collectorship, 56,
93, 96, 620; supervisor for, 59, 68;
Anne Arundel Co., 69; Frederick,
69; legislature, 113n, 234-5, 248,
251n; Frederick Co., 113-14n; ratifies
Twelfth Amendment, 183-4; bound-
ary dispute with Va., 366, 367n; and
Chastellux claim, 376; and District
of Columbia, 423n; education in,
506n; Presbyterians in, 506n; Oxford
collectorship, 511-13, 522, 523, 524n,
538, 541, 620; Hagerstown, 601. *See
also* Baltimore, Md.; Federalists;
Republicans
Mason, David (N.J.): letter from, 124-5;
seeks removal of collector, 124-5
Mason, George (1629-86), 617
Mason, John, 235
Mason, John (Georgetown merchant),
203, 308, 586, 587, 588n
Mason, John Thomson: letter from,
501-2; and pardons, 237-8; as

Naples: U.S. relations with, 394-5, 603, 605; consul at, 602, 604, 605n

Nash, Frank: letters from, 55-6, 407; seeks passage to U.S., 55-6; sends verse to TJ, 407; death of, 407n

Natchez: land office at, 73; newspapers, 91n; and Jefferson College, 359-60; incorporation of, 361n; crime on road to, from, 494; collector at, 538, 541, 620; trade at, 544n. *See also* Mississippi Territory

Natchez Gazette, 91n

National Institute of Arts and Sciences. *See* France: National Institute of Arts and Sciences

National Intelligencer (Washington): forwarded to M. Lewis, 8; and transfer of Louisiana to U.S., 185; and Republican nominations for vice president, 547n

National Register, 618n

Natural Principles of Rectitude (Johann Daniel Gros), 601

Navy, U.S.: and the Mediterranean, 75n; navy agents, 195, 197, 198n, 364, 365n. *See also* Smith, Robert

Neagle, David, 428n

Nelms, William, 203, 204, 474n

Nelson, Mr. (Miss. Terr.), 494

Nelson, Thomas (d. 1803), 23, 619, 623

Netherlands: impressment of American seamen by, 81n

neutrality: and French right to commission privateers in U.S., 4n

neutral rights: and foreign cargoes covered by U.S. vessels, 182-3, 202-3, 208-12; and "fictitious" blockades, 209, 211, 250n; negotiations with Britain on, 247, 250-1n; in renewed war between Britain and France, 249-50; freedom of the seas, 448-9

New and Complete Dictionary of the German and English Languages (Johannes Ebers), 599

New Bourbon, 191

New Britain (Labrador), 283n, 294

Newcome, Joseph, 511n

Newfoundland, 310

New Hampshire: and Annapolis Convention, 184n. *See also* bankruptcy commissioners; Federalists; Portsmouth, N.H.; Republicans

New Harmony, Ind., 418n

New Jersey: U.S. attorney, 23, 619, 621n; lack of banks in, 60n; New

Brunswick surveyorship, 92, 93n, 96, 620; Sandy Hook lighthouse, 393-4; ratifies Twelfth Amendment, 459, 460n; Little Egg Harbor collectorship, 533, 534n; Burlington collectorship, 533-6; Burlington Co., 535n; Hunterdon Co., 578n; sawmills in, 578n. *See also* Federalists; Great Egg Harbor, N.J.; Republicans

New Jersey, College of (Princeton), 226n

New Madrid, 191, 491

New Mexico, 189, 294, 295

New Orleans: establishment of branch Bank of the United States at, ix, 104, 106; transfer of, to U.S., 7, 42-3, 89-91, 139-40, 152, 171, 177, 184, 289, 301-2, 325, 483n; marine hospital at, 12, 106-7, 141-2, 248, 435, 452; postal service, 29, 337, 365, 555-6; roads to, from, 29, 30n, 433-4; newspapers, 55n; collector at, 84, 186, 248, 326, 475, 539; naval officer at, 98, 121, 186, 475, 539, 541, 620; surveyor at, 98, 114, 121, 169, 475, 538-9, 541, 620; banks at, 104, 106; termination of right of deposit at, 133; French administration of, 140; militia, 140, 504, 505n; public buildings and fortifications in, 140, 177; commercial regulations at, 223, 475, 530, 548-9; custom house, 223, 248, 277, 475, 476-7, 530, 548-9, 601n; education in, 286; inhabitants considered decadent, extravagant, 286, 287; descriptions of, 286-7; courts, 288, 471, 472, 473n; and fur trade, 298; Spanish administration of, 339-40n, 548, 549n, 594n; views of, 359n; mayor, 437, 439, 441n; dances, balls at, 441n; discord between French and newcomers at, 441n; importation of slaves at, 473n; black militia at, 504, 505n; withdrawal of Spanish troops, officials from, 504, 505n; smuggling in, 544n; corruption in, 548, 549n; crime, 581; slave trade in, 593-4. *See also* Louisiana; Louisiana Purchase; Mississippi River

New Providence, Bahamas, 209, 425-8

newspapers: Republican, 55n, 65-7, 134, 157, 347, 368n; foreign editors of, 65-6, 67n; seek printing contracts, 131-2, 347; accused of libel, 133, 134, 368n; Federalist, 155-7, 162-3, 251n,

330, 332-3, 334n, 347, 364, 368n; maintained by advertising, not subscriptions, 333
Newton, Sir Isaac, 163
Newton, Thomas: letter to, 582; TJ orders cider, wine from, 340, 370; forwards letters, 474; health of, 520; and fire at Norfolk, 582; letters from cited, 624, 627; recommends aspirants for office, 627
Newton, Thomas, Jr., 627
New Translation of Volney's Ruins (Constantin François Chasseboeuf Volney), 46, 47
New York: gubernatorial election in, 45, 70, 408n; Burrites, 71n, 122n, 408n; Clintonians, 71n; Buffalo surveyorship, 93, 96, 620; Genesee Co., 113, 176, 206, 207, 227-8, 233-4; sulfur springs in, 113-14, 176, 206-8, 227-9, 233-4; Clifton Springs, 114n; Ontario Co., 114n, 408n; Dutchess Co., 169n; prisons, 169n; slavery in, 169n; Rome, 178n, 382; courts, 218n, 255-6n; elections in, 226n; legislature, 226n; Elmira, 254n; Newtown, 254n; Tioga Co., 254n; Columbia Co., 290n; militia, 290n; land speculation in, 408n; Hudson collectorship, 435-7; Hudson, 436-7n; Canaan, 437n; Oldenbarneveld, 493; Oneida Co., 493; Trenton, 493. *See also* bankruptcy commissioners; Federalists; Republicans
New York (U.S. frigate), 74n, 83n
New York City: booksellers, 4n; libraries, 4n; yellow fever, 22, 606; militia, 75, 76n; Democratic Society, 226n; navy agent at, 365n; merchants, 402-3, 478, 479n; collector at, 455n; shoemakers, 606-7
New-York Evening Post, 54n
New-York Herald, 155
New-York Historical Society, 226n
Nicholas, Robert C., 117, 288, 408, 475, 476
Nicholas, Wilson Cary: letter to, 420-1; letter from, 524-5; and organization of upper Louisiana, 420-1, 422n; recommends aspirants for office, 475, 476; reports on discontent in R.I., 524-5; and election of 1804, 547n; letter from cited, 623
Nichols, Walter, 625
Nicholson, John B., 315-16n

Nicholson, Joseph H.: letter from, 56; recommends aspirants for office, 56, 200, 511, 512-13n, 522; as committee member, 63n, 230n, 522n
Niles, Hezekiah, 518
Nivison, John, 582n
Norfolk, Va.: merchants, 36n, 608-9; collector at, 454, 455n, 624, 627; marine hospital at, 455n; fire at, 582, 609, 610
Norfolk Herald, 582n
Norte, Rio del. *See* Rio Grande (Rio Bravo)
North Carolina: Anson Co., 14; Fayetteville, 14, 88; Granville Co., 14n; merchants in, 14n; Williamsborough, 14n; lack of banks in, 60n; newspapers, 88, 213; Indiantown surveyorship, 93, 96, 620; Winton surveyorship, 93, 96, 620, 623; elections in, 98-9, 100n; Cape Hatteras, 135-6; lighthouses, 135-6; Shell Castle Island, 135-6; legislature, 153; ratifies Twelfth Amendment, 153; immigrants to Louisiana from, 192; Tarboro, 361, 432. *See also* bankruptcy commissioners; Federalists; Republicans; Wilmington, N.C.
North West Company, 281, 297
Northwest Ordinance of 1787, 441-2n
Norwood, Washington, 14n
Notes on the State of Virginia: and slavery, 224, 225n; praise for, 403-4; appendices to, 506-7n
Nourse, Joseph: statements of public debt, 60n; and contingent fund, 185n; and Louisiana stock, 289, 304n, 312, 313n, 315n; appointed bank director, 588, 627
Nuevitas, Cuba, 478

Oakson, Isaac, 422
oats, 612
"Observations and Experiments relating to equivocal, or spontaneous, Generation" (Joseph Priestley), 24, 25n
Ocmulgee River, 29
Ogden, Mr. (N.J.): letter from cited, 624
Ohio: Youngstown, 141; militia, 301; and transfer of Louisiana to U.S., 301; ratifies Twelfth Amendment, 311; Cincinnati land office, 443, 541, 620;

INDEX

Ohio (*cont.*)
preemption rights in, 522n; Steubenville land office, 572; Jefferson Co.,
572n; legislature, 572n. *See also*
Federalists; Republicans
Ohio River, 373
oil: for lighthouses, 178-9
Olcott, Simeon, 8n
Oldham, James: letters to, 50, 254; and
sheet iron for Monticello, 50, 254;
letters from cited, 50n, 623, 624, 625;
letter to cited, 50n, 623; payments to,
254
Olin, Gideon, 547n
Oregon, 7
Orleans Gazette (New Orleans), 55n
Orleans Territory: creation of government for, vii, 31-6, 37, 44, 103, 316,
410, 441n, 543; establishment of,
vii, 31, 316, 441n; courts, 32, 35n;
secretary, 32; legislature, 32-3, 35n;
slavery in, 33, 35n, 40; extension of
federal laws over, 35n; marshal, 169;
U.S. attorney, 177-8, 408, 494-5;
legislative council, 308; attorney
general, 373n; land claims in, 414n;
regulation of trade in, 504; governor
of, 542; calls for representative government in, 543. *See also* Louisiana;
New Orleans
Orvill, Robert, 512n
Osage River, 189
Osborne, Mary: letter from, 57-8; asks
TJ for money, 57-8; identified, 58n
Osgood, Samuel: letter from cited, 403n,
626; recommends aspirants for office,
403n, 626
Ostend, 36n, 94, 95, 620
Otis, Samuel A.: letter to, 545; as
secretary of the Senate, 131, 132n,
541n, 545
Ottawa River, 295
Otter Creek, 496
otters, 298
Otter Tail Lake, 194
Ottoman Empire, 395-6
Overton, Samuel: letter from cited, 626;
letter to cited, 626
Ovid: *Metamorphoses,* 20, 21, 224,
225n; *Remedia Amoris,* 223, 225n

Pace, Henry, 142n
Padouca River. *See* Kansas River

Page, Jesse: letter from, 69; seeks
clemency for son, 69
Page, John: letters to, 42-3, 164-5;
letters from, 11-12, 79-80, 143-4, 233;
and TJ's message to Congress, 11-12;
and removal of condemned slaves from
Va., 12, 164-5; and TJ's doctrines of
Jesus, 12, 42, 43n, 79-80, 171; and
Louisiana Purchase, 42-3, 79; and
Burk's *History of Virginia,* 73n;
recommends aspirants for office, 80;
and Twelfth Amendment, 143-4, 233;
reelected governor, 144n; and
boundary dispute with Md., 367n
Page, Margaret Lowther, 42, 80
Page, Shadrach, 69
Paine, Thomas, 334n, 492-3, 573
Painter, George, 535n
Palladio, Andrea, 564
Palmer, Sally: letter from, 371-2; asks
TJ for money, 371-2
Pamphilon, Thomas, 512n
Pani River. *See* Platte River
Panton, Leslie & Co., 130n
Pantops (Eppes estate, Albemarle Co.,
Va.), xi, 47, 366, 446
Paolina (polacre), 389, 392n
Paradise Lost (John Milton), 223,
225n
Paraguay, 374
Parallèle de Bonaparte avec Charlemagne
(Jean Chas), 245
pardons: petitions for, 125-6, 231-2,
236-8; granted by TJ, 232, 238, 525,
537, 583-4
Paris: publishing in, 5n; commercial
agent at, 543-4, 603, 604-5
Paris, Treaty of (1763), 281, 295-6,
297, 314
Parker, Isaac, 95, 621n
Parker, Thomas, 477
Parry, Mr.: letter from cited, 626
Parshall, Israel B.: letter from, 606-7;
asks TJ for loan, 606-7; identified,
606-7n
Passamaquoddy Bay, 40n
Pasteur, Thomas, 15
patents: bedsteads, 22-3; preparation
of oak bark, 310-11; dyeing, 324n;
evaporation, 324n; tanning, 324n;
sawmills, 577, 578n; apple paring
machines, 577-8, 613; straw, hay
cutting machines, 578
Paterson, John, 252, 253

A comprehensive index of Volumes 1-20 of the
First Series has been issued as Volume 21.
Each subsequent volume has its own index,
as does each volume or set of volumes
in the Second Series.

THE PAPERS OF THOMAS JEFFERSON are composed in Monticello, a font based on the "Pica No. 1" created in the early 1800s by Binny & Ronaldson, the first successful typefounding company in America. The face is considered historically appropriate for The Papers of Thomas Jefferson because it was used extensively in American printing during the last quarter-century of Jefferson's life, and because Jefferson himself expressed cordial approval of Binny & Ronaldson types. It was revived and rechristened Monticello in the late 1940s by the Mergenthaler Linotype Company, under the direction of C. H. Griffith and in close consultation with P. J. Conkwright, specifically for the publication of the Jefferson Papers. The font suffered some losses in its first translation to digital format in the 1980s to accommodate computerized typesetting. Matthew Carter's reinterpretation in 2002 restores the spirit and style of Binny & Ronaldson's original design of two centuries earlier.

✧